Mesopotamian Chronicles

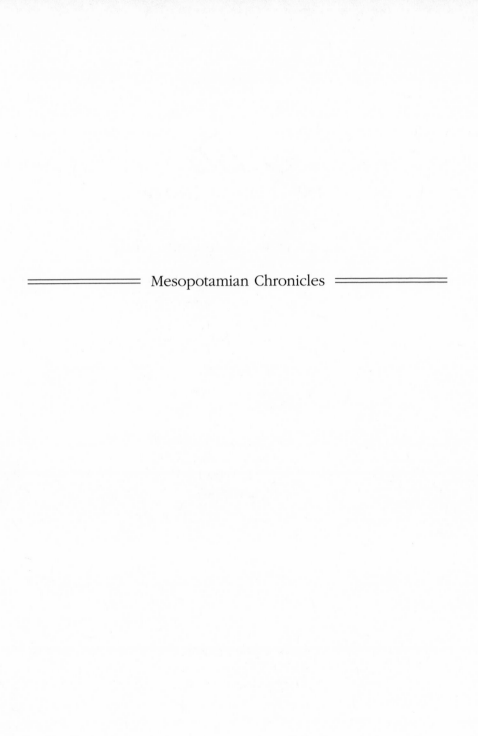

Society of Biblical Literature

Writings from the Ancient World

Theodore J. Lewis, General Editor

Associate Editors

Billie Jean Collins
Jerrold S. Cooper
Edward L. Greenstein
Jo Ann Hackett
Richard Jasnow
Ronald J. Leprohon
C. L. Seow
Niek Veldhuis

Number 19
Mesopotamian Chronicles
by Jean-Jacques Glassner
Edited by Benjamin R. Foster

MESOPOTAMIAN CHRONICLES

by
Jean-Jacques Glassner

Edited by
Benjamin R. Foster

Society of Biblical Literature
Atlanta

Original title: *Chroniques Mésopotamiennes,* presentées et traduités par Jean-Jacques Glassner, copyright © 1993 by Les Belles Lettres, Paris. English translation arranged with the approval of Les Belles Lettres from the original French edition, including additional material supplied by the author.

Library of Congress Cataloging-in-Publication Data

Glassner, Jean-Jacques.
[Mésopotamie. English]
Mesopotamian chronicles / by Jean-Jacques Glassner ; edited by Benjamin R. Foster.
p. cm. — (Writings from the ancient world ; no. 19)
Includes bibliographical references and indexes.
ISBN 1-58983-090-3 (paper binding : alk. paper)
1. Iraq—Civilization—To 634. I. Foster, Benjamin R. (Benjamin Read) II. Title. III. Series.
DS73.2.G5313 2004a
935—dc22 2004012445

12 11 10 09 08 07 06 05 04 5 4 3 2 1

Printed in the United States of America on acid-free, recycled paper conforming to ANSI/NISO Z39.48-1992 (R1997) and ISO 9706:1994 standards for paper permanence.

To Hayyim Tadmor, with respect

The past ... is a reconstruction of the societies and human beings of former times by men and for men caught up in the network of today's human realities.

— Lucien Febvre, preface to Charles Moraze, *Trois essais sur Histoire et Culture*

Concerning the flood, and Noah: it was not by chance that he took so long to build his ark. No, Noah wished to delay the flood, he dragged out the work, feeling that something of the sort would happen, that it was for a purpose that God had given him the order to build the ark. Noah was not anxious to separate himself from the world, steeped in evil, yet nonetheless familiar. He felt nostalgia for the present world, which belonged already more to the past, to a remote past that would fall into oblivion, for the waters would wash away all the roads leading there, and would carry off everything that could allow anyone to form some idea of it.... Noah suffered from nostalgia for the present, because he was alone in possessing a future.... The new world was unknown.

— Saulius T. Kondrotas, *L'Ombre du serpent*

For the supreme honor, to which the king attached the highest value, was to triumph over the gods of his enemies, whom, in spite of their gods, he had led into captivity. And when we asked them why they were kept in chains, they replied that [the king] intended, when he entered the town of Uzangué, to which he was making his way, to have them dragged in these same chains in triumph, following the victory won over them.

— F. M. Pinto, *Peregrination*

Contents

Series Editor's Foreword

Writings from the Ancient World is designed to provide up-to-date, readable English translations of writings recovered from the ancient Near East.

The series is intended to serve the interests of general readers, students, and educators who wish to explore the ancient Near Eastern roots of Western civilization or to compare these earliest written expressions of human thought and activity with writings from other parts of the world. It should also be useful to scholars in the humanities or social sciences who need clear, reliable translations of ancient Near Eastern materials for comparative purposes. Specialists in particular areas of the ancient Near East who need access to texts in the scripts and languages of other areas will also find these translations helpful. Given the wide range of materials translated in the series, different volumes will appeal to different interests. However, these translations make available to all readers of English the world's earliest traditions as well as valuable sources of information on daily life, history, religion, and the like in the preclassical world.

The translators of the various volumes in this series are specialists in the particular languages and have based their work on the original sources and the most recent research. In their translations they attempt to convey as much as possible of the original texts in fluent, current English. In the introductions, notes, glossaries, maps, and chronological tables, they aim to provide the essential information for an appreciation of these ancient documents.

The ancient Near East reached from Egypt to Iran and, for the purposes of our volumes, ranged in time from the invention of writing (by 3000 B.C.E.) to the conquests of Alexander the Great (ca. 330 B.C.E.). The cultures represented within these limits include especially Egyptian, Sumerian, Babylonian, Assyrian, Hittite, Ugaritic, Aramean, Phoenician, and Israelite. It is hoped that Writings from the Ancient World will eventually produce translations from most of the many different genres attested in these cultures: letters (official and private), myths, diplomatic documents, hymns, law collections, monumental inscriptions, tales, and administrative records, to mention but a few.

Significant funding was made available by the Society of Biblical Literature for the preparation of this volume. In addition, those involved in preparing this volume have received financial and clerical assistance from their respective institutions. Were it not for these expressions of confidence in our work, the arduous tasks of preparation, translation, editing, and publication could not have been accomplished or even undertaken. It is the hope of all who have worked with the Writings from the Ancient World series that our translations will open up new horizons and deepen the humanity of all who read these volumes.

Theodore J. Lewis
The Johns Hopkins University

Abbreviations

AA	*American Anthropologist*
AAASH	*Acta Antiqua Academiae Scientiarum Hungaricae*
AfO	*Archiv für Orientforschung*
AfOB	Archiv für Orientforschung: Beiheft
AION	*Annali dell'Istituto Orientale di Napoli*
AJ	*The Antiquaries Journal*
ALASP	Abhandlungen zur Literatur Alt-Syren-Palästinas und Mesopotamiens
AnSt	*Anatolian Studies*
AOAT	Alter Orient und Altes Testament
AoF	*Altorientalische Forschungen*
AOS	American Oriental Series
ARM	*Archives royales de Mari*
ArOr	*Archiv Orientální*
ARRIM	*Annual Review of the Royal Inscriptions of Mesopotamia Project*
AS	Assyriological Studies
ASJ	*Acta Sumerologica Japanensis*
ASOR	American Schools of Oriental Research
AuOr	*Aula orientalis*
BaM	*Baghdader Mitteilungen*
BASOR	*Bulletin of the American Schools of Oriental Research*
BBVO	Berliner Beiträge zum Vorderen Orient
BCH	*Bulletin de correspondance hellénique*
BCSMS	*Bulletin of the Canadian Society for Mesopotamian Studies*
BM	Bibliotheca Mesopotamia
BO	*Bibliotheca orientalis*
BRM	Babylonian Records, Pierpont Morgan Library

BSOAS	*Bulletin of the School of Oriental and African Studies*
CANE	*Civilizations of the Ancient Near East.* Edited by Jack Sasson. 4 vols. New York: Scribner, 1995.
CBQ	*Catholic Biblical Quarterly*
CM	Cuneiform Monographs
COS	*The Context of Scripture.* Edited by W. W. Hallo and K. L. Younger Jr. 3 vols. Leiden: Brill, 1997–2002.
CT	Cuneiform Texts from Babylonian Tablets in the British Museum
CTN	Cuneiform Texts from Nimrud
DDD	*Dictionary of Deities and Demons in the Bible.* Edited by K. van der Toorn, B. Becking, and P. W. van der Horst. Leiden: Brill, 1995.
ErIsr	*Eretz Israel*
FAOS	Freiburger Altorientalische Studien
GN	geographical name
HR	*History of Religions*
HSS	Harvard Semitic Studies
HUCA	*Hebrew Union College Annual*
IEJ	*Israel Exploration Journal*
JA	*Journal asiatique*
JAOS	*Journal of the American Oriental Society*
JCS	*Journal of Cuneiform Studies*
JEOL	*Jaarbericht van het Vooraziatisch-Egyptisch Gezelschap (Genootschap) Ex oriente lux*
JHS	*Journal of Hellenic Studies*
JNES	*Journal of Near Eastern Studies*
JSS	*Journal of Semitic Studies*
MAOG	Mitteilungen der Altorientalischen Gesellschaft
MARI	*Mari: Annales de recherches interdisciplinaires*
MDAI	Mémoires de la délégation archéologique en Iran
MJ	*The Museum Journal*
MSL	Materialien zum Sumerischen Lexikon
NABU	*Nouvelles assyriologiques brèves et utilitaires*
OBO	Orbis biblicus et orientalis
OECT	Oxford Editions of Cuneiform Texts
OIP	Oriental Institute Publications
OLA	Orientalia lovaniensia analecta
OLP	*Orientalia lovaniensia periodica*
Or	*Orientalia*
OrAnt	*Oriens antiquus*
OS	*Orientalia Suecana*
PAPS	*Proceedings of the American Philosophical Society*

PN	personal name
RA	*Revue d'assyriologie et d'archéologie orientale*
RANE	Records of the Ancient Near East
RIME	The Royal Inscriptions of Mesopotamia, Early Periods
RlA	*Reallexikon der Assyriologie*. Edited by Erich Ebeling et al. Berlin: de Gruyter, 1928–.
RS	*Revue de synthèse*
SAA	State Archives of Assyria
SAAB	*State Archives of Assyria Bulletin*
SAACT	State Archives of Assyria Cuneiform Texts
SAAS	State Archives of Assyria Studies
WAW	Society of Biblical Literature Writings from the Ancient World
S.E.	Seleucid era
SEL	*Studi epigraphici e linguistici*
SM	Sources and Monographs
StudOr	Studia orientalia
TCL	Textes cunéiformes. Musée du Louvre
TCS	Texts from Cuneiform Sources
TIM	Texts in the Iraq Museum
TUAT	*Texte aus der Umwelt des Alten Testaments*. Edited by Otto Kaiser. 3 vols. Gütersloh: Mohn 1982–2001.
UrET	Ur Excavations: Texts
UF	*Ugarit-Forschungen*
UMB	*The University Museum Bulletin*
UVB	Vorläufiger Bericht über die (. . .) in Uruk/Warka unternommenen Ausgrabungen
VAB	Vorderasiatische Bibliothek
WO	*Die Welt des Orients*
WZKM	*Wiener Zeitschrift für die Kunde des Morgenlandes*
YOS	Yale Oriental Series, Texts
ZA	*Zeitschrift für Assyriologie*

Babylonian Calendar

Nisan	March–April
Iyyar	April–May
Siwan	May–June
Dumuzi	June–July
Ab	July–August
Elul	August–September
Tešrit	September–October
Araḫsamnu	October–November
Kislev	November–December
Ṭebeth	December–January
Šebat	January–February
Addar	February–March

Explanation of Signs and Conventions

italics	Akkadian transcription is set in italics, while Sumerian is set in roman. Italics are also used to indicate an uncertain restoration or rendering in the translation.
-ra$_2$	Indices (subscript) are equivalent to sign numbers; they have no phonetic relevance.
-bu^{ki}	Determinatives (superscript) indicate semantic classes; they are not to be read.
X	A capital X represents an unidentified sign.
. . .	An ellipsis marks a gap in the text or untranslatable word(s).
KEŠ	Capitals indicate that the reading of the sign in context is unknown or uncertain.
[ ]	Brackets enclose restorations.
< >	Angle brackets enclose signs omitted by the scribe.
( )	Parentheses enclose additions in the translation.
(!)	An exclamation point indicates an unusual or aberrant form.
(?)	A question mark indicates an uncertain reading in the transcription or a doubtful rendering in the translation.
ˆ/¯	A circumflex or macron indicates a long vowel.
ḥ	The *h* with underdot represents a fricative *h* sound not found in English
ḫ	The *h* with underbreve indicates a sound like “kha.”
’	The single apostrophe represents a glottal stop.
ṣ	The *s* with an underdot indicates an emphatic *s* sound not found in English. It was pronounced like *ts* but further back in the mouth.
ś	The *s* with acute accent represents a lateral *s* sound not found in English. It was pronounced with the tongue

	held halfway between the English position for *s* and *sh*, but flattened out.
š	The *s* with hacek was pronounced like English *sh*.
ṭ	The *t* with an underdot represents an emphatic *t* sound not found in English

Preface

Intent upon delving ever deeper into the most infinitesimal detail of factual data, in order to give an ever more precise account of the peculiarities of the universe, the Mesopotamians sought to order their ideas and experiences in written form. Convinced that knowledge of the past enabled them to explain the present and to be better prepared for the future, eager to understand the swift passage and erratic flow of time, leading inexorably toward death, the Mesopotamians wrote history as well. This undertaking was not, to be sure, driven solely by disinterested thirst for knowledge. In a universe where the gods constituted the ultimate explanation, humans, ambiguous beings of clay and divine blood, played an essential role in the durability of cosmic order. They were conscious beings, informed of divine intentions; they were privileged to know the names, and thus the future, of every thing and every creature; by their piety and maintenance of the cult they enabled the processes of the universe to function. Dwelling at the center of the earth and at the heart of the cosmos, powerful in their knowledge, a king to lead them—for only the monarchical model was upheld—humans had their task to perform.

Throughout nearly two long millennia, the oldest documents dating from approximately 2200 B.C.E., the most recent from roughly 140 B.C.E., to reflect on the lessons of time gone by, men of letters wrote histories, biographies, annalistic narratives, prophecies, and chronicles: collections of facts reported in the sequence of their occurrence. The diversity of these works and the richness and variety of the information they contain make them works of reference, and the sheer bulk of their achievement inspires admiration. The Assyrian eponym chronicles, for instance, list, year after year, from the beginning of the second millennium to the middle of the first B.C.E., the accessions and deaths of kings, the names of the high officials of state as well as of their subordinates, and the annual objectives of military campaigns. They remain today a valuable guide for reconstructing the remote past of humanity, interred beneath the debris of more than two thousand years. These texts, unfortunately, as if their laconic style were not sufficient, are sometimes poorly preserved, the clay tablets that serve as their medium having, in general, resisted poorly the ravages of time. Some of them are in an advanced state of deterioration, so any attempt to read them is inevitably frustrating. But the Assyriologist, perhaps better than any other historian of antiquity, knows that he or she works with little save bits and pieces, scraps and disconnected fragments.

The chronology of Mesopotamia before the thirteenth century (except in instances indicated in the text, all dates are understood to be B.C.E.) remains provisional. This is owing primarily to different ways of interpretating astronomical events recorded by ancient scribes. In this study the so-called "middle chronology," which is most generally followed, will be employed.

This book is an English translation of a work that appeared in France in 1993, under the title *Chroniques mésopotamiennes*. Its purpose goes beyond a text edition to present a selection of more or less homogeneous documents to an interested and informed readership. Since 1993, Irving Finkel, keeper at the British Museum, has found several new chronicles or fragments. These documents are still unpublished, and because the right of publication belongs to their discoverer, they cannot take their place here.

The preliminary English translation of parts 1 and 2 was made by Nicolas Wyatt, extensively revised by Benjamin R. Foster. Part 3 was revised by Foster from my own English version. I would like to thank Bob Buller of the Society of Biblical Literature for his remarkable work in preparing the volume for publication. Finally, I wish to thank the editors of the Society of Biblical Literature for accepting this book in their series Writings of the Ancient World and Benjamin Foster for his editorial and translation work and for numerous suggestions, corrections, and updates incorporated into the text. I have taken the opportunity to update the 1993 text with the needs of an English-speaking readership in mind.

Part I
Mesopotamian Historiography

I

The Future of the Past

As its etymology indicates, the term *historiography* denotes the writing of history. This being said, the word turns out to be remarkably ambiguous, and dictionaries offer various definitions. The peoples of Sumer and Akkad had no such term, yet they produced a voluminous historical literature. We shall, therefore, so far as possible, given the tenuous evidence, examine this literature and the social status and cultural background of its authors. The writing of history has never been solely the preserve of scientific endeavor carried out in isolation. Mesopotamian historians, because they were intellectuals, and also because they normally lived close to great people in a society profoundly influenced by religion, were scarcely unaware of the ideologies they were helping to sustain, as shown by their way of writing.

Mesopotamia is a crossroads where many ethnic groups have mingled, each bringing, as so many accretions, its own traditions while unconsciously letting itself be shaped in a common mold, in a kind of ever-renewing synthesis, into which was absorbed, to a large extent, the heritage of more ancient cultures, at once assimilated and modified. Thus we may speak of Sumerian, Amorite, Babylonian, or Assyrian historiographies. Furthermore, wherever a temple or palace was built, intellectual activity flourished; schools grew up in all cities where the literate strove to cultivate their particular skills. The history of Babylonia under Assyrian control was conceived of and written about in different ways, depending on whether one was in Babylon or Uruk.[1]

History, explains Cicero, is the narration of true facts. Cicero was heir to a centuries-old tradition going back to Hecataeus of Miletus, an innovator who, rejecting myths and heroic genealogies as "ridiculous," opened the way to history. Mesopotamia had no Hecataeus, and the break between the spheres of myth and legend and history was never quite achieved. The narrators believed in the truth of their accounts, whether they were myth or history, and since they thought them true, the differences between myth and history diminished and blurred.[2] This went so far as to produce a hybrid form, myth using historical categories and history becoming "mythologized," in order to achieve exemplary significance and universal perspective. Mixture of the genres is still found in Berossus,[3] who wrote as a Hellenistic historiographer but incorporated native mythological traditions in his history of Babylonia.

Autonomous historical discourse in Mesopotamia was not achieved until very late, by the authors of certain Neo-Babylonian chronicles. This was a new departure, giving rise to a new form of discourse, a historiography deliberately avoiding tales of origins. But let us not be deceived: this new historiography was not devoid of religious beliefs, nor did it consign them to ancient fable. We can avoid the question of the origins of historical writing, since in Mesopotamia, like everywhere else, there was no mute society, without history. The constructive role of memory is a constant in all human societies.[4] As far as one can reach into the past, the very means of exchange that existed in archaic Mesopotamia already implied a certain consciousness of existing in time.[5] The innovation consisted of committing to writing remembered facts in the form of a hitherto unattested literary genre. We sense that this new interest was linked to political motivation. The monarchy of Akkade, which, without precedent, unified the entire Mesopotamian territory under a single authority, seeking to consolidate the foundations of its new power, commissioned men of letters to formulate the principles of its organization and to write its history. Two examples are sufficient to illustrate this point. First, an inscription of King Narām-Sîn, who expresses himself in these words:

> Narām-Sîn the mighty, the king of Akkade. When "the four quarters (of the earth)"[6] together rose up against him, through the love Ištar held for him, he won nine victories in a single year and captured the kings whom (the rebels) had brought (to the throne). Because in adversity he had been able to maintain the defenses of his city, its inhabitants expressed the wish to Ištar in Ayyakkum,[7] Enlil in Nippur, Dagān in Tuttul, Ninḫursag in Keš, Enki in Eridu, Sîn in Ur, Šamaš in Sippar, and Nergal in Cutha, that he should be a "divinity" of their city, and they built his dwelling in the middle of Akkade.[8]

Stylistically and semantically, this inscription is a new departure. Not content with establishing the facts in sequence, as was formerly the practice, it offered a programmatic vision of political institutions and their functioning. The royal initiative consisted of winning the consent of the assemblies of the principal cities of the land in order to bestow on the sovereign a new title, better suited to his exceptional charisma, that of "divinity," which, by metonomy, came down from the divine to enter the human sphere.[9]

The second document is a tiny scrap of a school text dating from the reign of Narām-Sîn or his successor Śar-kali-śarrī. Discovered in a private house in Tell Asmar, we owe it to an apprentice scribe, and a very clumsy one at that. In it we can still read two phrases, taken from a larger work.[10]

> [At Kiš, the population in] its [entirety] indeed brought Ipḫur-Kiš to the throne. Ipḫur-Kiš made an alliance and Lugal-ane, the king of Ur, hastened to him.
>
> ---
>
> No (?) ruler ... [...]. He established [kin]gship and the we[ll-being(?)] of his land. (...)

Too fragmentary for a fully satisfactory interpretation, this excerpt is no less a witness, because it is a school text and not a royal inscription, to the existence at this time of an otherwise lost historiographical literature. Tradition would later recall Ipḫur-Kiš and Lugal-ane. The figure of Ipḫur-Kiš, raised to royal rank by the assembled army and whose name means "He gathered Kiš" or, by one of those graphic games so dear to the ancient Mesopotamians, "He gathered the totality [of settled lands[11]]," contrasted with Narām-Sîn, grandson of Sargon, the founder of the empire, who embodied, opposite an elective form of monarchy, the practice of hereditary power. There was, therefore, in the Akkade era, a confrontation between two forms of power, two forms of legitimacy. A trial of arms would decide in favor of one of them. The historiographical literature reflects this.

As for the expression "we[ll-being(?)] of his land," *š[ulum] mātišu,* the restoration is convincing and is not insignificant. It may be seen, some centuries later, in an inscription of Śamśī-Addu I of Assyria, who declared that seven generations separated one of his own exploits from *šulum Akkade.* The Akkadian word *šulmu(m)* is ambiguous, denoting the full realization of a state or its complete ruin: scholars hesitate between the translations "apogee" and "downfall." The presence of the word in association with the concept of royalty in the present Old Akkadian school text favors the former. Later, in an omen, the word is found yet again associated with Akkade.

> If the "paths" are doubled, and the second is drawn behind the "crucible," their "mouths" to the right and left touching, it is an omen of Śar-kali-śarrī, destruction of Akkade. The enemy will sweep down on your "well-being." If it is an expedition: a leader of my army will not return.[12]

Finally, the school text is like an echo of Narām-Sîn's inscription cited above: "well-being," *šulmu(m),* is in effect opposed to "adversity," *pušqum,* the term that in the inscription referred to the disastrous situation from which the king saved his capital and his realm. This tablet fragment shows, then, that because royal authority continued to grow and scribal activity grew along with it, as its inevitable complement, people began to write variations on the official version, intended to reinforce still further the prestige of the sovereign.

History was an activity of the mind. Dipping into the ocean of events, or cutting particular swatches from the fabric of history, the learned writer made selections, manipulated facts, and constructed narratives. One need only consult the different versions of the Assyrian annals to be convinced of this. Apart from the fact that they were scarcely the place to refer to military reverses or to events unconnected with the main purpose, they were compiled at different times during kings' reigns, so that new campaigns were added and the narrative of previous campaigns often abbreviated or completely reworked. For instance, the descriptions of the first campaign of Sennacherib became, with the passage of time, increasingly brief and allusive, going so far as to omit certain important episodes, such as the flight of Marduk-apla-iddina or the enthronement of Bēl-ibni. The latter even ended up being supplanted by Aššur-nādin-šumi, his successor on the throne of Babylon, as if Assyrian power sought to erase all memory of an episode that had been a setback for it.[13] Nor were annals the only occasion for such manipulation. In another context, certain diviners had noted that Nāram-Sîn of Akkade had captured a town by the name of Apišal. Some of these diviners made an assonantal wordplay between the wording of the omen, the presence of perforations (Akkadian root *plš*) on the sheep's liver, and the toponym Apišal, in which they identified, by metathesis, the same root (*plš* < *pšl*). From this they put forward a new proposition, according to which, since the sheep's liver had perforations (*plš*), the king must have conquered the city (*pšl*) by means of making a breach (also *plš*). Reworked in this fashion, the wordplay was augmented, and the historical episode became part of a cognitive series in the art of siege warfare, for diviners, always obliged to make circumstantial responses to precise questions asked of them, could then associate different omens with different tactics: the taking of a city by assault, hand-to-hand fighting, breaches, sappers, siege engines. A king of Mari even asked, concerning the conquest of a city, "Why have you taken the omens concerning weaponry but not the capture of cities?" The new omen may even have resulted from the convergence of two series of propositions, one referring to the capture of Apišal, the other to the conquest of any fortified city by means of a breach in the fortifications. Other diviners went still further by fabricating other, similar, omens, inspired by the example of Apišal: all they had to do was to introduce a fresh nuance into the prognosis or to change the toponym in the omen.[14] Thus history distorted reality.

What this demonstrates is that articulation of the social and of the imaginary need not be reduced to a binary scheme of classification: the two sets interpenetrate to a point it is difficult to draw a line between them. To put it another way, the only historical facts are those the historian deems worth remembering. "Lest it be fogotten," proclaim certain historical texts of the first millennium, borrowing an expression belonging to the vocabulary of law or of commercial transactions, and at the same time lending a further intellectual dimension to the social function of memory.[15]

Time was the basic component of history. It was a powerful force, governing all things, that could be propitious for some activities but dangerous for others; it was even sometimes considered as a demiurge. Time past was called in Akkadian *pānānu* or *maḫru,* "formerly," that is, "before," while the future was called *warkātu,* "that which is behind." Surprisingly, the Akkadians, and the Sumerians as well (for whom e g i r, "behind," also meant "the future"), advanced backward toward the future while looking toward the past,[16] following the example of Gilgameš, who, in the Akkadian epic, advanced toward the unknown to which he turned his back: "When he had gone seven double-leagues, dense was the darkness; it would not let him see what lay behind him."

Mesopotamia did not know linear time. Two concepts of time developed simultaneously, insisting on the ideas of duration and of cycle. The first was time that flowed on, conceivable and manageable by a calendar, divisible into equal, measurable units of time that were all cyclical—years, months, and days—and referred to by the Akkadian words *dāru* and *dūru,* from the same Semitic root *dwr,* which means "to turn, to move in a circle" and denotes a time that proceeds from a point of departure but has no future limit. Mesopotamian historians[17] were concerned primarily to locate events in this first concept of time, which is also that of chronology. One curious document lists the names of the kings who reigned after the flood, of whom it is expressly stated that they are "not arranged in chronological order."[18]

Royal inscriptions are full of such indications. In Assyria, Tukultī-Ninurta I (1243–1207) considered that Ilu-šūma (the dates of whose reign are uncertain) preceded him on the throne by 720 years,[19] while Tiglath-pileser I (1114–1076) noted that Aššur-dān I (1178–1133) and Śamśī-Addu I (1808–1776) reigned respectively 60 and 641 years before him.[20] Later, Sennacherib (704–681) estimated that Tiglath-pileser I had preceded him by 418 years.[21] Nabonidus (555–539), the last king of Babylon before the Achaemenid conquest, computed the time separating him from Narām-Sîn (ca. 2202–2166) at 3,200 years and from Šagarakti-šuriaš (1245–1233) at 800 years, while Ḫammurabi (1792–1750) had reigned, also according to Nabonidus, 700 years before Burna-Buriaš II (1359–1333).[22] According to the historians of Šalmaneser I (1273–1244), 580 years separated this king from Śamśī-Addu I, while 159 years separated the latter from Ērišum I (whose regnal dates are uncertain).[23] Concerning these same intervals between these same reigns, Esarhaddon's (680–669) historians expressed very different opinions: according to them, 580 years separated his reign from that of Šalmaneser I, the latter was separated from Śamśī-Addu I by an interval of 434 years, and the last from Ērišum I by 126 years.[24] Thus the computations of ancient historians could vary. However, it did not matter much, in the final analysis, for chronology allowed things to be put in perspective and, because of the great antiquity of the examples cited, guaranteed legitimacy to the deeds of the ruling sovereign, whose reign fit into a longue durée. What Mesopotamian monarch, boasting of such remote predecessors, was not moved by a "longing for immortality" (or "eternity"), certain that his rule would endure? Several Sumerian and Akkadian expressions refer to duration and promise "eternal" life or kingship, where we have to understand "eternal" to mean so long as the life or kingship of the gods endure. One of these, u'ulli'eše, *ana ūmī ṣâti, ana ṣât ūmī* (the Akkadian versions mean "until the day of going out" or "until the going out of days"), expresses the idea of a past approaching the present to move off into the future.[25] The author of a Neo-Babylonian letter was at pains to clarify the expression "forever" in these terms: "for future days, day after day, month after month, year after year,"[26] where "day" stressed the alternation of day and night, "month" the alternation of full and new moon, "year" the alternation of seasons. All these expressions insistently recall the fact that history is the story of mortals. Gilgameš himself exclaims, regarding the plant that will give him immortality and that he names "old, man is rejuvenated": "I shall eat of it myself and shall recover my youth."[27] In other words, immortality means to recover youthfulness.

The second concept of time was the cyclical, expressed by Sumerian bala and Akkadian *palû*.[28] The latter term, denoting periods separated from one another, can also mean "change." This mode of time can be imagined by reference to the cycles of the seasons and the succession of the generations. Reckoning generations, that is, connection with ancestors, counts for more than the distance that separates them. This naturally calls to mind the genealogies given in the Sumerian epics, where a certain king is provided with an ancestor drawn from the ranks of the gods. We think too of the writing of history as practiced by the scribes of King En-mete-na of Lagaš, when they narrated the century-long war between the two rival cities of Lagaš and Umma. The accent was put not so much on the chronological progression of events as on the names of the protagonists and the genealogical connections they shared over three generations.[29] Most of all, one thinks of the Amorite royal genealogies, where the past was simply a reflection of the political and social conditions of the present time.[30]

Both notions of time were not unrelated to each other, public celebrations and familial rituals constituting so many links connecting them, but history was not exclusively a matter of events. It had another motivation, of a biographical nature, in the sense that it was concerned with the great deeds and exploits of sovereigns and with their personal lives. In a world that accepted innovation only with difficulty, always seeking examples and precedents, one invoked the past to explain the present, the arsenal of history furnishing weapons of many kinds, sometimes surprising ones. Spiritual and economic life, on the other hand, were subjects scarcely to be found, nor was there much interest in conscious, subconscious, or unconscious motives: no Mesopotamian Tacitus wrote a psychological history.

> When the land of Ibbī-Sîn rebelled against him, it looked like this.
> When the Subareans, having exchanged messages with Išbī-Erra, turned away in another direction, it looked like this.
> When the king rallied to his cause a country that had hitherto been his enemy, it looked like this.
>
> If Amurru is reduced, it will look like this.
> If an enemy plans an attack against a city and its plan is revealed, it will look like this.
> If the enemy musters with hostile intent but the prince's [army(?)], however considerable it may be, is not powerful enough, (it will look like this).[31]

Such is the testimony of some of the oldest divinatory documents known today. They appear on liver models from Mari dating from the first centuries of the second millennium. A relationship was established between an omen appearing on a liver model, reinforcing the text, and to which the formulae "it looked/will look like this" made reference, and an oracle was set forth in the text.

This evidence can be divided into two series. In the first, the verbs are in the past tense, the diviner having recorded the memory of a past observation, deducing a prognosis from an omen. Divination was a science based on experience and looked toward the past as the source of its inspiration. In the second, the diviner, surprisingly, deduces the omen from the prognosis. Furthermore, the verbs being in the present-future, the proposition consisted, implicitly, of considering a link between a social fact and a natural occurrence, a priori coincidental, as a necessary correlation, likely to recur in analogous fashion in the future. In other words, the diviner extrapolated for the future from the configurations and connections of the past. In short, this series indicates that, at the turn from the third to the second millennia, the diviner's thought was disconnected from empirical knowledge and was established as a system. At this point we may no longer speak of this as an empirical culture. A reciprocal relationship had been established between nature and culture, and the world order depended, in the final analysis, on human attitudes, since it was permissible to infer the configuration of a sheep's liver from a political or military event. Interest in the past was further validated by this development.

However, if the world was not understood using the category "progress," the sole intimation of which was self-glorification of kings that they had achieved what no king before them had done (though this may be understood as an archaic equivalent of the idea of progress, the idea of potentiality to act), it was not felt to be in a static condition. The category "change" existed, and in the juridical vocabulary of Akkadian the expression *ana dūr u pala,* "for continuity and change," meant the totality of future time. Furthermore, "rotation" did not mean simple repetition, because each repetition generated new content. The Mesopotamians did not reread ad infinitum the pages of the same book, nor were they passive spectators of the same performance repeated ad infinitum. The relationship between the past, the present, and the future was founded not on strict repetition but on similarity.[32]

In short, the study of the past fell under the rubric of analogy, history being a cyclical process, hence made up of recurrent events and peopled with avatars. According to a Sumerian tradition, Narām-Sîn of Akkade acted contrary to a decision of the gods expressed in omens that forbade him to build a temple. Similarly, Amar-Su'en, the third king of the royal dynasty of Ur, was in turn, according to another tradition and other omens, prevented from restoring a ruined temple.[33]

From an early period, dazzled by its unrivaled brilliance, Assyria set the dynasty of Akkade as a model. From the eighth century on, as attested in the historiographical compositions from the library of Aššurbanipal, the dynasty of Akkade became a paradigm for the historians of the Sargonid era, who considered that every historical cycle formed a system and that, with the passage of time from one cycle to another, allowing for variations, there existed between wording and content the same unvarying relationships.[34] Even if Esarhaddon still referred, in the manner of some of his predecessors, to former King Ušpia as though to a distant ancestor of his on the throne of Assyria, it was granted that with the dynasty of Akkade, beginning with the story of the birth of Sargon, the type of the Promethean hero who established cosmic order, with his exposure on a watercourse and the trials by which he demonstrated his legitimacy, until that other story of the irruption, like a flood, of a foreign mountain people, the Gutians or the Ummān-manda, in the reign of his grandson Narām-Sîn, a complete, exemplary cycle of history had run its course, constructed like a landscape peopled by highly individual characters.[35]

The Babylonians took little stock in these theories. For them, Sargon of Akkade was a fatherless child, in other words, a man of no antecedents, who was not of royal stock and could be seen as a usurper.[36] Playing on the writing of his name, they made him who had declared himself the "rightful king," LUGAL.GI,[37] into a "rebel king," LUGAL.IM.GI.

Who wrote history in Mesopotamia? The birth of a discipline requires a place, rules, a stylistic form, and, ultimately, humans. Beyond that, we are completely ignorant. Normally Mesopotamian writings are anonymous; at best we know the name of a copyist, and the few notable exceptions, such as Saggil-kīnam-ubbib, author of the Babylonian Theodicy, or Kabti-ilī-Marduk, author of the Myth of Erra, scarcely make up for this gap.[38] We have, indeed, an ancient list of authors, but a document that begins by citing gods or creatures of legend is hard to take seriously.[39] Access to writing implies, in any case, that authors graduated from a school where they had mastered the use of a written language different from the spoken one.

Were there, on the other hand, autonomous intellectual elites, not depending on any political class but based simply on individual qualities and intellectual aptitudes? Is not the most ancient historiographical document from the hand of an apprentice scribe working in a private house in Tell Asmar, from the last third of the third millennium? Later, there were private libraries in the Old Babylonian city of Ur, in the Middle-Assyrian city of Aššur, and in the Neo-Assyrian library of Sultantepe, which belonged to one Qurdī-Nergal, himself a priest of the god Sîn, all of them containing historical works.[40] Later still, in Babylon, men of letters collected and copied a series of historiographical works that they assembled in their libraries.[41] Finally, in Uruk, in the Seleucid period, the library of the scribe Anu-bēlšunu, son of Nidintu-Anu and a descendant of the exorcist Sîn-liqi-unninnī, the putative author of the Gilgameš Epic, contained other historiographical compositions.[42]

It is clear that throughout Mesopotamian history some families of scribes extending over several generations controlled most literary production. Some of them, in the Hellenistic period, claimed descent from a distant ancestor supposed to have lived in the Kassite period. These families played an important role, since they were responsible for the transmission of source material from the middle of the second millennium down to the Seleucid period. Did palaces and temples really play the part often credited to them in the composition, copying, and transmission of literary and historical works? Let us not misunderstand. Between the intellectual, political, and religious spheres lay no insurmountable barriers. Qurdī-Nergal was himself a priest. The temple of Šamaš at Sippar housed a rich library containing historical texts.[43] The temple could also employ men of letters, as did the assembly of the Esagila, the temple of Marduk in Babylon, which agreed to pay salaries to the astronomers charged with the making of daily observations and recording them on tablets.[44] Among the families of scribes, some were traditionally retained by kings, such as that of Arad-Ea of Babylon, while others were in the employ of temples.[45] Finally, how could we forget that in 703 a provincial notable, a member of a great family of scribes, led a revolt and ascended the throne of Babylon under the name Marduk-zākir-šumi (II)?

One tradition has it that to each reign should be assigned a sage, *apkallu,* or a learned man, *ummânu.* A list already alluded to begins with the name Adapa, contemporary of Alulu, the first antediluvian king, concluding with that of Aba-Enlil-dāri, better known by his Aramaic name Aḥiqar,[46] who is assigned to the reign of Esarhaddon. According to the same list, Kabti-ilī-Marduk lived at the end of the third millennium, at about the time of Ibbī-Sîn, an egregious error, since he composed the Myth of Erra in the second half of the ninth century, probably in the reign of Marduk-zākir-šumi. Regardless of errors and legendary features, a tradition still has it that literary production was associated with royal power. Without even mentioning Aššurbanipal, who collected a vast library in his palace at Nineveh,[47] we know that Nabû-apla-iddina, Marduk-zākir-šumi's predecessor, was directly associated with a considerable amount of editorial work.[48] Did the historian live in the shadow of power, musing on the power that he himself did not have? We cannot tell if a post of official historian existed, having office, title, and salary, solely and singly charged with writing the history of the state that retained him. The hypothesis that Ištar-šuma-ēreš, head of the palace scribes and scholar, *ummânu,* in the reigns of Aššurbanipal and Aššur-etil-ilāni, was the author of a synchronous king list[49] cannot be verified. On the other hand, we do know that in the Persian period Scylax of Caryanda made a voyage at the expense and on the instructions of Darius I, Nehemiah was the cupbearer of Artaxerxes I, Ctesias of Cnidus, the physician of Artaxerxes II, and Ezra, perhaps, a functionary in charge of Jewish affairs.

Still according to the same ancient list, to which should be added the evidence of colophons, the authors or compilers of the large literary and historical works were engaged, for the most part, in the professions of exorcist, *āšipu,* lament singer, *kalû,* or diviner, *barû.* Chance has it that archives or libraries of such specialists have been found here and there, such as the archives of the lament singer Ur-Utu at Sippar[50] or those of the diviner Asqudum at Mari[51] and above all the library of Ba'al-Mālik, "scribe of all the gods of Emar."[52] This last contained several works of a historiographical nature. Among all these people, the diviners formed a sort of corporation with its own officers. They were specialists who could carry out these functions along with others that might attach them to a temple or a palace, but without overlap. For the most part, they were in the service of the king. In the Sargonid era, the Assyrian kings normally provided to the astrologers, dispersed among various cities, houses, lands, and the staff to run them. Although we know less about the organization of exorcists and lament singers, it seems there were in fact intellectual elites, among whom the diviners, exorcists, and lament singers were prominent. These elites may be described as heterogeneous groups having complex relations with each other and among which none was the sole repository of a fully specialized knowledge.

On the fringe of historical interests, there developed during the first millennium a certain antiquarianism. We know of the taste of the Chaldean kings of the sixth century for historical research and of the religious motives and genuine historical interest that inspired them, of their attempts to reforge some of the broken links with the past to strengthen their own claims to legitimacy. Veritable museums were established in which original pieces sat side by side with copies. There was perhaps a museum in the palace in Babylon from which possibly some thirty objects have been found, among which were several statues from Mari, an inscription of Šulgi, and a stela of Darius I.[53] The Egipar at Ur, the residence of the high priestess, also housed a museum where one could admire, among other items, a foundation cone of Kudur-mabug, an inscription of Amar-Su'en of Ur, as well as a copy of it made in the seventh century "for display" (?) by the lament singer Nabû-šuma-iddina, son of Iddin-Ilabrat, when it was rediscovered by the governor of the city Sîn-balāssu-iqbi.[54] Finally, at Nippur a jar has been found in the Neo-Babylonian level containing a score of inscribed objects from all periods, notably a map of the city and its environs;[55] these may well have been items in a collection of antiquities.[56]

Private individuals took an interest in antiquities as well. The scribe Nabû-balāssu-iqbi, son of Miṣiraya, copied the "tariff" of King Sîn-kāšid of Uruk from an original preserved in the Ezida, the temple of the god Nabû at Borsippa;[57] the apprentice scribe Balāṭam, son of Baliḫu, copied the same text;[58] and another apprentice scribe, Rēmūtum, copied an inscription in Sippar of Ḫanun-Dagān, king of Mari.[59] We are more familiar with the activities of the scribe Nabû-zēr-līšir, son of Itti-Marduk-balāṭu, a descendant of Nabunnaya and author of a number of legal documents from Babylon in the reign of Nabonidus. He took an impression of a stone inscription of Śar-kali-śarrī found in the palace of Narām-Sîn at Akkade[60] and copied an inscription of Kurigalzu II engraved on a brick from the Bīt Akīti in the same city.[61] This scribe affected writing contracts for which he was commissioned using archaizing script, as favored in certain royal inscriptions of the period, particularly those of Nebuchadnezzar II, in "ancient" style. These examples are enough to show that the work of these scribes was not simply a reflection of personal quirks.[62]

There are those who, fortified with the teachings of Herodotus and Hegel, would characterize the first form of history as a narrative of things "seen." Would the first historian have been a witness? Certainly Gilgameš was one "who had seen everything," preserving for posterity the narrative of his own life. Oral memory must have played its part where one knows that custom was a practice nowhere set down and where every social activity gave rise to a public ceremony in which it was expected of the witnesses that they would later testify to what they had seen. Regarding the Assyrian annals, a mural painting in the palace at Til Barsip represents two "military" scribes watching a battle and taking note of the events; one of them is writing on a tablet in cuneiform, with a stylus, while the other is writing with a pen on a scroll, probably in Aramaic alphabetic script.[63] It is probable that scribes noted from day to day the episodes of campaigns at which they were present and that these "notes" were subsequently consulted at the time of the composition of annals.

Mesopotamian historians nevertheless privileged the written account. In Mesopotamian law, this substituted quite naturally for oral testimony, and judges accorded to the "speech" of the tablet the same value as the declaration of an eyewitness. Moreover, was not the written memory, which was not set down until what it recorded was read and scrupulously verified, an integral part of the system of apprenticeship?

Thus historians copied official texts, royal correspondence, or oracular utterances of a historical nature. They drew up chronological or genealogical lists, dynastic lists, or lists of year names. All these works could be, if not sketches for chronicles or the starting point for history, at least the beginnings of archives. And they also composed archives.[64] It has been shown, for example, that from the correspondence of the empire of Ur, only the letters dealing with the Amorite question were selected for study and copying, the task of copying them entering the curriculum of the apprentice scribes in their schools in the Old Babylonian period.

Since history was supposed to preserve a sure memory of the past, its norms of credibility had to be established. The first task of the historian consisted, therefore, in the faithful citation of the material being copied and the correct identification of sources. To be more precise, when it was a matter of the reproduction of a document or the compilation of sources, the copyist or compiler had to guard against any personal contribution or addition, however minimal. In the case of the statue of Ḫanun-Dagān, for instance, the copyist, using an original from which the royal name had been lost, avoided restoring the name and noted instead on his copy the word *ḫipi,* "(it is) broken."

However, the work of the historian did not stop there. A recently edited copy of an inscription of Narām-Sîn of Akkade offers a striking peculiarity.[65] The tablet appears to reproduce a single inscription of this king, with an initial titulatury and a closing curse formula, but the body of the text consists of a number of military adventures, the account of which is several times segmented, the scribe not copying passages he considered repetitive. In fact, preparing a new inscription that linked various events occurring separately throughout his reign, the scribe placed end to end excerpts selected from several original royal inscriptions, each of which dealt with a different campaign. Thus was reinforced the historiographical theme of the great revolt engulfing Narām-Sîn.[66] So documents that had no intrinsic connection to each other could be patched together.

At the end of the sixth century in the Greek world, Hecateus of Miletus clarified a rudimentary comparative process, intended to correct and rationalize legendary tales, consisting of consultation with outside witnesses. Herodotus's laughter at the multiplication of maps demonstrates, not long afterward, the progress made in the critical treatment of sources. Whereas scribes exercised a certain critical faculty with regard to their sources when they looked for graphic variants, which at times they were at pains to mention, no Mesopotamian historian ever compared or even mentioned different versions of the same event. Moreover, he never cited his sources. In short, history was not a science with a coherent methodology, and its most obvious weakness lay in its approach to documents.[67]

The historian also transferred a piece of information from one branch of knowledge to another, from archives to a narrative. Did not writing, then, given the fragility of the tools and methods in use, run the risk of presenting as truth a discourse that might be only a fable? Others have shown that in other geographical regions an authentic historiographical undertaking may well incorporate legend and myth.[68]

If, finally, we leave aside the work of copyist and compiler, who made books out of books, on the ground that by definition they had no style of their own, we can scarcely isolate a specific historical style. The study of historiographical works, whether prose or poetry, simply demonstrates the relative unity of style of the time.

Among historiographical works, we may distinguish copies and compilations from actual literary works.

COPIES AND COMPILATIONS

These consisted of assembling written texts and thoughts of others, or, if one likes, the composition of unified texts from various written fragments.

Copies of Royal Inscriptions

Isolated inscriptions were written on small tablets, and collections of inscriptions were arranged in uncertain chronological order on large tablets. This genre, particularly esteemed in the Old Babylonian schools of Nippur and Ur, was practiced over two whole millennia: the earliest examples known date from the end of the third millennium.[69] In every period the inscriptions of the kings of Akkade and Ur were the most prized.[70]

Comparison of the original and the copy, when possible, demonstrates the remarkable fidelity of the latter, which reproduces with great attention to detail the original document, maintaining the original grammar and layout of lines. There are, however, some exceptions. One copy shows instructive characteristics: it begins in the middle of a sentence and ends with an incomplete one; it is strewn with abbreviated words and information not in the original, representing overall an original synthesis of numerous inscription fragments, one after another. Other copies consist of only initial written signs of the original lines; their purpose was no doubt purely mnemonic.[71]

Collections of Royal Letters

The royal correspondence of the empire of Ur is partially preserved, thanks to the collections of copies made by scribal students from the Old Babylonian period, epistolary material being at that time a school subject. In contrast to the copying of royal inscriptions, the language of correspondence was modernized, since scribes used the grammar of their time.[72] Among the different letter collections, one thematic element determined the choice of material: all letters dealt with the Amorites, who lived at the time of the Ur dynasty on the northwestern and northeastern frontiers of the empire. Some scraps of the royal correspondence of Isin and Larsa were likewise preserved; they dealt in particular with problems of irrigation.[73]

Lists of Year Names

Two principal methods were used in Sumer and Babylonia to permit individual years to be identified within the flow of time: they were named by reference to an event or numbered from an arbitrary starting point. Between 2400 and 2350 the habit grew up in Uruk, Ur, and Nippur of indicating the date by reference to some noteworthy event at the beginning of the year or from the preceding year, such as "the year in which the high priestess of the god Nanna was chosen by means of the oracular lamb." This system afterward became general practice and lasted until about 1600; it only ceased finally in the course of the thirteenth century. After that, years were calculated by reigns, numbered from the completion of the first year of a king's reign.

In order to preserve a record of their chronological order, lists of year names were drawn up. These could be of various lengths, going so far as to cover 168 or 169 names, nor were they immune to mistakes: sometimes year names were interpolated.[74] The end result might suggest to us compilation serving primarily administrative or juridical purposes, but the extent of the longest lists far exceed requirements for such purposes, so we may discern in them the products of genuine chronological inquiry.

Eponym Lists

Assyria was distinctive in that it invented its own dating system, which it maintained faithfully for a millennium and a half: the "eponym" system. In this, years were named after high officers of state. Drawn at first by lot, they were later determined according to a strict hierarchical order, which, however, kings might sometimes change. Eponym lists were drawn up as chronological reference works but were no more exempt from error than Babylonian lists.[75]

King Lists

These made it possible to fix the order of succession of kings and generally went beyond the span of one dynasty. However, the mention of royal names alone was insufficient to make them useful for chronographers, and historians wishing to locate events in time and to find a way to date them added the number of years of each reign. The king lists stretched from the end of the third millennium to the Seleucid era. Among them, synchronous lists set the reigns of Assyrian and Babylonian kings in parallel.[76]

Historical Predictions

The Mesopotamians thought that the universe was permeated by a complex network of homologies, which tended to bring into relation matters that otherwise seemed remote from each other. Humanity, nature, and the cosmos existed in reciprocal relationships, each adjusting, communicating, and responding to one another. This network of sympathies was countered by groups of incompatibilities that enclosed species in their own specificity, and "evil forces" that destroyed symmetry existed. History, with its discontinuous time fragmented into numerous segments variously charged qualitatively, indefinitely repeatable yet fully dissociated one from the other, could not transcend these general laws, which divination illumined with ever-sharper focus. Thus someone could write, no doubt in the reign of Sennacherib, a "mirror for princes" setting out to offer a genuine lesson from experience that no ruler should ignore but consisting of a collection of omens that listed, in the form of oracles, unfavorable consequences of bad policy.[77]

Like so many indicators hitherto unnoticed but thereafter noteworthy, historical omens established the link between human history, the cosmos, and nature. Astrology in particular projected history into the vastness of space, the perception of which astronomy continually enhanced, tending to define cycles of history that corresponded to the motions of the stars and planets. Thus a link was established between lunar eclipses and human actions, the lunar eclipse being associated, according to the month and the year in which it occurred, with a different city or country.

Learned treatises existed that consisted of endless series of sentences, each comprising a protasis and an apodosis. The protasis set out a feature of the object in question in the form of a conditional proposition, while the apodosis stated the consequence deduced from it in the form of a main proposition. All these compositions emerged from educational methods and a mindset made possible by the development of writing. The sentences were arranged in a fixed order, in which another feature of Mesopotamian rationality may be discerned: a predilection for dualistic or triadic organization of the subject matter, using opposing or complementary pairs or triads containing a midpoint between two extremes. Following this course, diviners sought to isolate successively particular ominous patterns among all those that presented themselves simultaneously to their view and attempted to read in them what was applicable to human existence in terms of individual or collective destiny. For every pattern given prominence, a relationship with a specific event in social life was posited.[78]

Several collections of historical omens survive.[79] They are, however, generally dispersed in the body of treatises. With a few striking exceptions—legendary characters such as Gilgameš, Etana, or Queen Ku-Baba;[80] local rulers such as King Sîn-iddinam of Larsa or Dāduša of Ešnunna;[81] even Aššurbanipal,[82] who reigned in the seventh century—we see that the royal names included are primarily of those who ruled over a united Mesopotamia and that the periods explored in this genre are those of Akkade, Ur, and Isin,[83] either in the final third of the third millennium or the first two centuries of the second.

The information reported in the historical omens is deemed by some to be episodes without any real historical interest.[84] How could the purpose of history be anecdotal?[85] Anecdotes can, of course, satisfy curiosity, and, though divination was a science of the real, it could incorporate past experience in its own logical schemes. Diviners, obliged to offer a precise answer to any question that might be asked of them, since the inquirer was never satisfied with a vague reply, thought through past events according to the principles that governed all their cognitive processes and sought to establish homogeneous series made up of so many specific and virtually "repeatable" facts, which could serve as prototypes.[86]

Diaries

At the latest from the time of the reign of Nebuchadnezzar II, systematic astronomical observations were duly catalogued by professional specialists, and augmented with notes, concerning fluctuations in prices, bad weather, rises in water levels of the rivers, and occasionally historical events. These last pieces of information were admittedly rare and of unequal value. Local history was given priority, such as cultic ceremonies, but also fires and epidemics. Other events of greater political moment and consequence were also recorded, but more or less as asides.[87]

LITERARY COMPOSITIONS

There was no literary genre known as "historical literature." Nevertheless, histories, annals, pseudoautobiographies, prophecies, and chronicles were composed. Histories were written in poetic style; the other compositions were written in prose.

Historical Narratives

Historical narratives, like myths and epics, were written in verse. These works, in which no dates were required, were decked out in accordance with the best conventions of epic poetry, with a pronounced taste for narrative situation, debates between protagonists, divine assemblies, divine assistance to heroes, the leadership qualities of the victors, and the villainy of the vanquished. This writing of history relied on a theology of sin and punishment, the impious king being punished by defeat. In Babylonian texts, even at the price of certain anachronism, the supremacy of Marduk was everywhere prevalent.[88]

The oldest historical stories, including the narrative of the youth of Sargon of Akkade (the only composition in this style composed in Sumerian),[89] date from the Old Babylonian period. Later the genre was cultivated in Assyria and Babylonia.[90]

Annals

Written in the first-person singular, as if the kings themselves, always victorious, were their authors, recounting their own exploits, annals were situated on the frontier where memory was transformed into history. This kind of commemorative inscription belonged to Assyria; the Babylonians made no use of it. It appeared under Tiglath-pileser I.[91] Unlike ordinary royal inscriptions devoted to the account of a single campaign, annals collected accounts of several successive campaigns and were always arranged according to the same plan: royal titulary, account of the campaigns, account of the pious building project undertaken at the end of the final campaign. They were periodically rewritten; in each recension a new campaign was added, the scribes abridging, interpolating, recasting, and even suppressing certain current episodes before adding more up-to-date information. Often eloquently written, they constitute the best-developed genre of historical narrative.[92]

Some campaign reports were written in the form of letters to the god Aššur, their ancient name being "principal report." Custom required that the god reply, expressing his appreciation; several fragments of divine letters have survived until the present. They were really intended for the population of Aššur, the religious capital of the empire; the language is very refined, and their style of a quite exceptional literary quality.[93]

As for the large surfaces of the palace walls, as well as the metal reinforcements of the doors, they were in turn covered in "illustrated prose," bas-reliefs and paintings, illustrating or complementing the narrative of the annals and tirelessly celebrating the exploits of sovereigns.[94]

Pseudoautobiographies

These were written by kings in the first person, as though they had monopolized autobiographical narrative elevated to the status of an apologia, and were supposedly inscribed on stelae, *narê,* from which they are sometimes called *narû*. These were really pseudoautobiographies and fictitious stelae. Their genre is quite varied, ranging from a royal inscription, perhaps legendary, of Lugal-ane-mundu of Adab, known from two Old Babylonian exemplars, and inspired, it appears, by the authentic inscriptions of Narām-Sîn of Akkade, to the story of Sargon of Akkade as known from Neo-Assyrian manuscripts. The purpose of these compositions was to provide a narrative concerning an individual person, his life, or some episode within it, without treating him as one of the many actors in a historical event.[95]

Prophecies or Apocalyptic Writings

This genre consisted of a small group of texts for which it is hard to formulate a definition. In fact, there are sufficient differences among them for the very unity of this group to be called into question. The sources originate in Aššur, Nineveh, Babylon, and Uruk, the oldest dating from the eighth century and the most recent from the Hellenistic period. Formulated as if the events had not yet occurred, these documents consisted of declaratory propositions arranged in paragraphs, each paragraph opening with a formula announcing the coming of an unnamed king. The reigns thus foretold may be characterized from the double perspective of their length and their good or bad character. The unfolding of historical time was thus articulated by an alternation of qualitatively different periods.

The prediction of a favorable time went on to almost idyllic description of the effects of the reign to come. Inversely, the presentation of unfavorable reigns was no less absolute, offering a vision of despair for those accursed periods. The allusions are always sufficiently vague to allow a speculative transposition into the future. At the same time, they are not so vague as to avoid the suspicion that they were inspired by historical events.[96]

The interest the Mesopotamians felt in their own past undeniably arose from a historical way of thinking. One is struck by the remarkable effort they devoted to the copying of official texts, to the study of royal correspondence from the past, and to the compilation of chronological lists and collections of omens. We can appreciate the attempts to explain the application of the principle of causation to human events. Some historians, indeed, were not satisfied with merely narrating the facts but tried to establish connections, looking for causes and consequences. Some saw in the fall of the empire of Akkade the consequence of a foreign intervention, the invasion of the Gutians or of the Ummān-manda, two names that evoked rebellious mountain tribes or remote savage hordes, or of an indeterminate but always foreign adversary. Other commentators, on the contrary, sought a different explanation for the collapse of Akkade and believed that they had detected the beginning of its fall in palace revolutions and popular uprisings culminating in the outbreak of civil war, in which ever-bolder successors sought to make themselves heirs of the kings Narām-Sîn or Śar-kali-śarrī.

However, we should not be misled by these premises. The Mesopotamians had no profession of historian as we understand it today, nor its methods or perspective. As they saw it, the problem was not critical assessment of sources, nor was the question, fundamentally, knowing how and in what causal sequences events considered unique had occurred. The primary task was to choose, according to a definite focus of interest, among the carefully collected data from the past, certain facts that, from that point of view, had acquired universal relevance and significance.

Even as it located the historical genre in the domain of literature, historical method consisted of separating the past from the present and making the past an object of study for the edification of that same present. The past having become a source of examples and precedents, history found a special purpose: it became an educational tool for elites and governments. Consequently, the lesson of history concealed a futher one, of an ethical or political kind.

Kings themselves were credited with the desire to bequeath to posterity, in the form of inscribed stelae, *narû,* the fruit of their experiences. Narām-Sîn of Akkade left such a stela, on which he recorded the distress from which he was able to escape only in the last extremity.[97] The elderly monarch complains bitterly in it that he had not been informed of the best way to act by King Enmerkar, who had once faced a similar situation; he reproaches him for having left no stela for the edification of future kings. By an irony of fate, this reproach was addressed to Enmerkar, who was, according to a Sumerian epic, the inventor of cuneiform writing![98]

Did the lesson of Narām-Sîn have any effect? He himself advised leaving the responsibility for waging war to the gods and exhorted the future king in these terms: "you should do your task in your wife's embrace, make your walls trustworthy."[99] In another instance, when one of the final campaigns against Elam, the age-old enemy, was in course of preparation, a priest had a dream in which Aššurbanipal, king of Assyria, conversed with the goddess Ištar of Arbēla. She invited him to lead a peaceful and happy existence. "Eat your bread," she told him, "drink beer, make music, exalt my divinity," and urged him to leave to the gods the responsibility for carrying out the military campaign against the enemies.[100] Reality, it seems, was rather different from these hedonistic pastimes.

The role that jurists assigned to history remained restricted. Since the need sometimes arose to situate a disputed private legal document in its own time and in relation to the present, year names were collected and arranged in order in lists, or lists of rulers were compiled, noting the lengths of their respective reigns. In short, all that was required were some names, a few dates, and some memoranda for quick reference.

In Mesopotamia, historiography was one of those kinds of knowledge mobilized by politicians in their service. As a representation of power, it could not be divorced from the practice of politics. Rather than search for immediate causes, meditation on the fall of the empire of Akkade, for example, was raised to a higher level and fed reflection on the exercise of power. Narām-Sîn became the example of the bad king who undermined his state by acting against the judgment of the gods. Making such an example of him was not the outcome of analyzing a historical mechanism, nor was it the result of assessing influences or identifying trends. Historical mindset aside, it was a matter of grasping an analogous occurrence, of clarifying a constant element. With every historical cycle obliged to know an avatar of Narām-Sîn, the matter of history became topical. Ideally, the lesson from the past should help one to avoid repeating the same errors and their consequences. Analysis of successes and failures could provide the outlines for a science of the exercise of power.

There was, to be sure, no distinction between power and religion, theology permeating life on every level. Consequently, Mesopotamian historiography was largely, in the manner of Bossuet, a discourse on history supervised by the gods. Theology was the end, history the means to the end. This religious emphasis, far from calling into question the historical authenticity of the researches undertaken, was their very basis. It will suffice to recall, in support of this assertion, a painful episode from the history of Babylon as well as two important compositions in Mesopotamian literature: one Sumerian, the Curse of Akkade; the other Akkadian, the Myth of Erra.

On the first day of the month of Kislev in 689, Assyrian troops captured Babylon. Sennacherib, king of Assyria, intended complete destruction of the city to assuage his anger, caused, notably, by the loss of his son and the persistence of internal problems in his kingdom. Here is the description he gives of the end of the city:

> During my second campaign, bent on conquest, I marched rapidly against Babylon. I advanced swiftly, like a violent storm, and enveloped (the city) like a fog. I laid siege to it and took possession of it by means of mines and ladders. [I delivered] over to pillage its powerful [...]. Great and small, I spared no one. I filled the squares of the city with their corpses. I led away to my country, still alive, Mušēzib-Marduk, the king of Babylon, with his entire family [and] his [nobility]. I distributed to [my troops], who took possession of them, the riches of that city, the silver, the gold, the precious stones, the furniture and the property. My troops took away and smashed the gods who dwelt there, carrying off their wealth and their riches. After 418 years I took out of Babylon and returned to their sanctuaries Adad and Šala, the gods of Ekallāte, whom Marduk-nādin-aḫḫē, king of Babylon, had seized and carried off to Babylon in the time of Tukultī-Ninurta (I), king of Assyria. I destroyed, laid waste and burned the city and its houses, from the foundations to the tops of the walls. I tore (from the ground) and threw into (the waters of the) Araḫtu the interior and the exterior fortifications, the temples of the gods, the ziggurat of bricks and earth, as much as it contained. I dug canals in the middle of that city, flooded its terrain and caused even its foundations to disappear. I carried this out so that my destruction surpassed that left by the Flood. To make it impossible, in any future time, for the location of that city or the temples of the gods to be identifiable, I dissolved it in the waters and wiped it out, (leaving the place) like flooded ground.[101]

The monarch returned to the episode elsewhere:

> After I had ruined Babylon, smashed its gods, exterminated its population by the sword, so that the very soil of that city could be carried away, I took away its soil and had it thrown into the Euphrates, (thence) into the sea. Its debris drifted as far as Dilmun. The Dilmunians saw it, and fear mingled with awe inspired by the god Aššur overcame them. They

> brought their gifts.... I carried off debris from Babylon and heaped it up in (the) temple of the New Year Festival in Aššur.[102]

These accounts testify to the violence of the destruction. We see, however, that nowhere is mention made of Marduk, the sovereign deity of Babylon, the most interested party in the matter. He does figure in another inscription commemorating the fall of the city, not at the heart of his beleaguered city but rather in the procession of the god Aššur, among the protective deities of Sennacherib's kingship.[103] There is no doubt that Sennacherib carried the statue of the god off into exile: an obscure Assyrian text mentions what amounts to his imprisonment.[104] It seems indeed that Sennacherib tried throughout his reign to stress Aššur's superiority over Marduk. Marduk had formerly presided over the New Year ceremony in Assyria, but after the reign of Sargon II Aššur had taken his place,[105] and it was Aššur who replaced him, moreover, on the relief decorating the door of the temple of the New Year festival. Aššur was also endowed with the "tablet of destinies," an attribute traditionally reserved to the god of Babylon. The annalist scrupulously reflected his sovereign's intention.

Not long afterward, Esarhaddon, son and successor of Sennacherib, reported the same facts in altogether different terms.

> Formerly, in the reign of a previous king, there were evil omens in Sumer and Akkad. The people dwelling there cried out to one another (saying) "Yes!" (but meaning) "No!" Thus they lied. They neglected the cult of their gods [...] the goddesses [...] and [...]. They laid hands on the treasure of Esagila, the palace of the gods, a place into which no one may enter, and in payment (for its assistance), they gave away (its) silver, gold (and) precious stones to Elam. Filled with wrath and planning harm, Marduk, the Enlil of the gods, decided on the destruction of the country and the extinction of (its) inhabitants. The Araḫtu, an abundant watercourse, (set moving) like the deluge, released downstream an unrestrained torrent, a violent deluge, a mighty inundation. It swept over the city, its dwellings and sacred places, and reduced them to rubble. The gods and goddesses living there flew away like birds, and rose into the skies. The people living there fled to other places and sought refuge in an [unknown] land. After having inscribed [on the tablet of destinies] seventy years as the duration of its abandonment, Marduk took pity, his heart being appeased, and reversed the numerals, deciding that it should be reoccupied after eleven years.[106]

Or elsewhere:

> Before my time, the great god Marduk wroth, livid (?) and filled with anger, with rage in his heart and his spirit ablaze, flared up against Esagila and Babylon. Left uncultivated, they turned into desert. The gods and

goddesses, in fear and trembling, abandoned their shrines and rose into the skies. The people who lived there, scattered among foreign peoples, went into slavery. ... When the great god Marduk, his heart appeased and his spirit calmed, was reconciled with Esagila and Babylon which he had punished....[107]

In the space of ten years or so Sennacherib's deed of destruction had been disguised behind a theological reading of history, where human action was replaced by the violence of nature. The ideological gulf between Sennacherib and Esarhaddon was, to be sure, wide. Sennacherib had spent the better part of his reign fighting Babylon. Esarhaddon reversed his father's policy and undertook to restore the city. Once again, the annalist acted as the faithful spokesman of his master's thinking.

Strangely enough, Babylonian historians remained silent on the episode. The chronicler, in a brief cryptic allusion, barely notes that the city was captured and the king deported to Assyria.[108] Only Nabonidus, much later, broke the silence, making Sennacherib the agent of Marduk's anger.

The Curse of Akkade, a composition from the end of the third millennium and copied many times (we have over a hundred manuscripts), is one of the finest examples of Sumerian literature. It was to be found in all the great libraries of the Old Babylonian period. It enjoyed immense prestige during that period, but this was apparently short-lived, even if a chronicle followed in its wake and perpetuated its spirit down to the Hellenistic period.[109]

The philosophy of the Curse of Akkade is in no way different from those of the contemporaneous compositions, such as the Chronicle of the Single Monarchy or the history of the youth of Sargon. All three worked with the same conceptions of time and royalty, as well as with the same order of succession of the various dynasties. Having the same view of the past, they were perhaps thought up in the same climate, in the same intellectual circles. However, the author of the Curse pushed his analysis further. Raising the theme of divine anger to the status of a historical category, he explained the ruin of the empire of Akkade as the consequence of the anger of the god Enlil, supreme god of the Sumerian pantheon, which led in turn to the cursing of the city by the gods and the goddesses of Sumer. Further, he tried to establish a link between human and divine behavior, the former being the stimulus to which the latter was the response. The process lay squarely within the logic typical of Mesopotamian thought, which accepted the principle of punishment for disobedience to divine will. This mindset implicitly confirmed that it was possible to predict divine behavior, once one knew the human stimulus. So it was that Narām-Sîn provoked the breakup of his empire after offending religion and the gods. Later, interpretation of episodes of human history as if they were the outcome of divine anger, itself generated by an act of impiety on the part of a human king, would become familiar, some Babylonian and Assyrian chronicles being excellent examples of this.

The Akkadian Myth of Erra, conceived and written between 854 and 819,[110] was a no less celebrated composition, since some forty manuscripts have preserved for us a good part of its text. The manuscripts range from the eighth century to the Late Babylonian period. They were to be found in all the great cities of Assyria and Babylonia.

It is certainly a myth, since the actors are divine, and the themes developed are those of Mesopotamian mythology. The content, however, belongs to history, since it refers to events occurring between 1100 and 850. We thus see here an astonishing interaction between myth and history, the facts wrested from the time of the gods and projected directly into historical time.

The author was not interested in producing a chronicle of past centuries, of which, however, he had a profound knowledge; his aim was to make a theology of them. Nor did he wish to reconstruct a framework for the events he perceived as cataclysmic and to which he felt it was sufficient to allude. Rather, he wished to propose an explanation for them on the religious level. Wanting to know how Babylon, seat of Esagila, residence of the king of the gods and navel of the universe, could be ruined and humiliated, before regaining its primacy, and confident in all that he had learned of the system of supernatural forces acting in the world, he supposed that the city had been delivered into the hands of Erra, the god of war. Accordingly, the destruction of Babylon was in no way the result of disagreement between humans and the gods. Humanity had no blame in the affair. In the end, he justified the carnage on the level of cosmic order, the war having its place in the regular functioning of the world and the destruction of the greatest number (that is, humanity) being an indispensable part of its natural process.

No appeal is made anywhere in this document to any historiographical technique. The account of the adventures of the gods having repercussions on human affairs was sufficient explanation. We do find however, at the very heart of the narrative, a phenomenon almost unique in Mesopotamian literature,[111] beyond the allusions to punctual events, an entire sociology of war, in which we learn that there existed a class of warriors at the heart of the social hierarchy, specializing in matters of warfare. Even a psychological dimension is present, with all the consequences of war on the destiny of peoples and individuals.

A further purpose becomes clear in the final part of the composition. We discover that in order to avoid a repetition of the catastrophe, it is important to celebrate the war-god. Indeed, it is the god himself who gives details of the procedure.

In the sanctuary of the god who honors this poem, may abundance accumulate,
But let the one who neglects it never smell incense.
Let the king who extols my name rule the world,
Let the prince who discourses the praise of my valor have no rival,
Let the singer who chants (it) not die from pestilence,
But his performance be pleasing to king and prince.
The scribe who masters it shall be spared in the enemy country and honored in his own land,
In the sanctum of the learned, where they shall constantly invoke my name, I shall grant them understanding.
The house in which this tablet is placed, though Erra be angry and the Seven be murderous,
The sword of pestilence shall not approach it, safety abides upon it.[112]

Frequent recitation of the song, or its presence in a house in the form of a copy or even an extract, were pledges of divine protection and preservation. The god was indeed widely known, to judge from the number of manuscripts and, above all, among them the existence of simple extracts copied on tablets whose arrangement implies that they were to be hung up in houses as apotropaic amulets.[113] On occasion kings were not averse to citing passages from the composition in their own inscriptions.[114] The historical narrative conceived in the form of a myth had been transformed into a protective talisman!

Mesopotamian historiography moved with the history it studied and the historical context in which it developed. The courtier, the man of letters, become noblemen, the diviner or exorcist, and even the private citizen could be interested in the past. If we except the receptiveness of the Assyrian elite to Babylonian culture, however, the relationships between groups or doctrines elude us. But all agreed on one point: the gods governed the world, granting or refusing their favors to human monarchs, and a cosmic law controlled the cyclical regularity of time. The rise and fall of a dynasty were signs revealing concealed resemblances and were called forth to reproduce themselves. Being principally concerned with the fall of a state, in order to keep such recurrences to a minimum, or at least to announce the day of reckoning (for the future has something of the judicial, and one is always at liberty to influence divine judgment by adopting appropriate behavior),[115] the cause of disasters was sought in human errors, religious faults committed by kings, or the departure of the gods. Whatever the explanation, humanity, to take control of the future, had to learn from the past.

Notes

1. See Lambert 1978: 12 and n. 17. Concerning the end of Assyrian domination in Babylon, the Uruk king list (Grayson 1980a: 97) admits the presence, in one year, of two Assyrian rulers in Babylon, Sîn-šumu-līšir and Sîn-šar-iškun, while chronicle 21, dealing with the same period, speaks of an interregnum of a year. See further Na'aman 1991.

2. Myth is a story in which gods are the chief actors and that commonly deals with a creation; history, recalling past events or public figures, remains linked to concrete experience and chronology; legend, finally, clusters around places, events, or historical persons but transposes them to the realm of the supernatural.

3. The Babylonian Berossus (Greek Berossos, probably from his real name Bēl-re'ûšu, "Bēl is his shepherd") was a priest of Marduk. About 250 he wrote in Greek a history of his country in three volumes. The work is mostly lost, except for a few quotations in various authors, notably Josephus and Eusebius. See Jacoby 1958: 364–95; Burstein 1978; Verbrugghe and Wickersham 1996.

4. See Lefort 1978: 30–48.

5. Mauss 1966: 145–279. On the gift as "complete social fact" in Mesopotamia in the early third millennium, see Cassin 1987: 280–337; Glassner 1985a. For a definition of "complete social facts," see Lévi-Strauss 1960: 626.

6. That is, in the present context, the entire country, with the exception of Akkade.

7. For this reading, see Beaulieu 2002.

8. Gelb and Kienast 1990: 81–83; Frayne 1993: 113–14.

9. On this matter and the ambiguity of the choice of this title, see Glassner 1986: 14–20; 2000a: 261–66.

10. Gelb 1952: 172 ("legend"); copy: Westenholz 1977: 97, no. 7. See Frayne 1993: 108–9; Goodnick-Westenholz 1997: 223–29.

11. On this terminology, see Glassner 1984a.

12. Thompson 1904: 2:18–19.

13. For these events, see chronicle 16 below.

14. For Apišal, see Glassner 1983. On the philosophical and methodological presuppositions of such practices, see page 18.

15. *Ana lā mašê;* the expression occurs in the epilogue of chronicle 10.

16. Cassin 1969; Wilcke 1982b: 31–32; Archi 1998; NUN.EGIR, "(every) future king," can be read in the epilogue of chronicle 10. In the series *Ana ittišu* VI ii 29–38 (= Landsberger 1937: 80–81), the expression e g i r ... g u g_4 means "to examine the series of facts," that is, of the circumstances of a juridical matter, not its antecedents (Limet 1994: 199 is to be corrected).

17. Regarding perception of space, and without mentioning the journeys of merchants made up of stops and stages, if the Mesopotamians generally condensed their geography into sequences of toponyms (Reiner and Civil 1974: passim; Kraus 1955; Nemet-Nejat 1982: 5–24), they also felt the necessity of drawing up maps, admittedly another means of enumeration. Two examples are noteworthy. (1) The map of the empire of Sargon of Akkade (see most recently Grayson 1977: 56–64, pls. I and II; McEwan 1980) is presented as a long list of places enhanced with indications of distances, each province being defined on it by a plain line joining the

extreme points. We have two editions of this text, one Neo-Assyrian, which is restricted to a representation of the empire, the other Neo-Babylonian, which incorporates the representation of the empire into a more complete view of the world. (2) The Babylonian map of the world (see most recently Horowitz 1988; 1998: 20–42) is presented as a drawing and appears to be a response to a search for a model based on the qualities of circular form and on the striving for symmetry that this allows. Its layout serves to define a rational order that reduces the increasing complexity of the real world. This map, which represents a striking mastery over the forms of the universe, is not an image of the objective world but illustrates a myth or an epic.

18. Pinches 1870: 44 i 20.

19. Grayson 1972: 111.

20. Grayson 1976: 17–18.

21. Luckenbill 1924: 83:40.

22. Langdon 1912; Nabonidus 1 ii 58, iii 27; 3 ii 20–22.

23. Grayson 1972: 83.

24. Borger 1956: Ass A III 20–30.

25. See also the name of the Sumerian hero of the flood, Ziusudra: "Life of prolonged days." It was expressly said of him that he would have a long life like a god; the Akkadian name of the same hero, Ut(a)-napišti, might mean "He has found out life," but it is perhaps a hypocoristic variant of the same name, meaning "Days of life'; see Uta-napišti-rūqu, "Life of prolonged days." On the notion of prolonging days, see Brinkman 1969–70: 40:17. We encounter the expression *ana ūmē ṣâti* in the prologue of chronicle 10 as well as in chronicle 12.

26. Hunger 1992: 421:rev. 6.

27. According to the French translation of Bottéro 1992: 203. The name Gilgameš itself, Bilga-mes in Sumerian, signifies "the paternal uncle is young."

28. On the two notions of time, see Glassner 2000b; 2001a.

29. Steible 1982: Ent. 28–29; Cooper 1986: 54–57, La 5.1.

30. On the Amorite genealogies, see pages 71–72 below.

31. Rutten 1938: 36–37, nos. 7, 10, 12, 19, 22, 31.

32. Cf. Herodotus 2.82: "If the Egyptians have discovered more omens than all other men, it is because when a prodigy occurs, they make a note of the outcome, and commit it to writing. Then if something similar happens later, they infer that it will have a similar outcome."

33. Narām-Sîn: Cooper 1983: 53–55 and passim; Amar-Su'en: Michalowski 1977: 155–57; Hruška 1979.

34. On the notion of paradigm, see Berque 1974: 360–64.

35. Glassner 1986: chs. 3–4, passim; 1988: 6–8.

36. The Assyrian version of the pseudoautobiography of Sargon employs the formula "I do not know my father"; the Babylonian version is different, saying "he had no father," appearing to make of Sargon "son of a nobody," an expression denoting a man of no antecedents, not of royal stock, who seized the throne. The expression is frequently translated "usurper." However, "son of a nobody" did not necessarily have the same pejorative connotations as the English term. Did not Nabopolassar, in effect the founder of the Neo-Babylonian Empire, qualify himself as "son of a nobody" in one of his own inscriptions (Langdon 1912: no. 4:4)?

Chronicle 10 indicates that the king of Babylon Adad-apla-iddina was "son of Esagil-šadûni, son of a nobody," but historians did not agree. Chronicles 46 and 47 credit him with Itti-Marduk-balāṭu for father. Both are entirely unknown; according to our present state of knowledge, the second was perhaps a famous literary man whom certain scribal families claimed as ancestor. It appears that Adad-apla-iddina encouraged literary activity. Did the chroniclers deliberately bring these different names together? In one of his own inscriptions, Adad-apla-iddina himself claimed someone entirely different as his father. Whatever the truth of the matter, we may note that "son of a nobody" means, primarily, that the person concerned was not of royal lineage.

37. Such is the meaning usually given for this name, though there are, for Sargon II of Assyria, graphic variants reflecting several divergent scribal traditions and consequently several ancient interpretations of the royal name.

38. For more details, see Foster 1991; Glassner 2002.

39. Lambert 1957; 1962.

40. Charpin 1986, with corrections in, e.g., Glassner 2001b: 218; Pedersén 1986: passim; 1998: passim; Gurney and Finkelstein 1957; Gurney and Hulin 1964.

41. Grayson 1975b: 44.

42. See van Dijk 1962: 43–44.

43. See, e.g., Al-Jadir 1991: 194, 196.

44. Sachs and Hunger 1988–2001: 1:11–12 and notes.

45. Lambert 1957: 2 and passim.

46. See van Dijk 1962: 44–45. A Neo-Assyrian document is actually a letter of Adapa to this king; see Gurney and Hulin 1964: 176:14.

47. He did not intend to collect all the knowledge of his day but undertook to collect magical and religious texts containing remedies to prevent or cure any sickness that might affect the king. See Parpola 1983a.

48. Lambert 1957: 5 and n. 21; van Dijk 1962: 51; Bottéro 1985: 93. See also the case of Adad-apla-iddina, above n. 36.

49. On this scribe and his father Nabû-zēr-lišir, himself *ummânu* under Esarhaddon, see Parpola 1983b: 18 *sub* R.23. It is possible that the death in the same year of the kings of Babylon and Assyria, Kandalānu and Aššur-etil-ilāni, made a great impression and led to the editing of a royal synchronism list. However, the name of Ištar-šuma-ēreš is restored in the colophon of the tablet (Hunger 1968: no. 238).

50. See de Meyer 1982: 271–78; Lerberghe and Voet 1991.

51. Charpin 1985b; Durand 1988: 193–220.

52. Arnaud 1987. The tablets were not found in a temple but in his private house.

53. Unger 1931: 224–28; his assertions are to be treated with caution: the statue of Puzur-Ištar of Mari, for instance, was found along the processional way and played a part in the New Year ceremonies; it was not among the "museum" objects.

54. Woolley 1925: 383–84; Gadd, Legrain, and Smith 1928: 172.

55. Hilprecht 1903: 516–20.

56. See the remarks of Calmeyer 1995: 453–55.

57. King 1905: 13–14.

58. Unpublished text BM 33344, mentioned by Kupper and Sollberger 1971: 231, *sub* IVD 1g n. 1.

59. Durand 1985: 151.

60. Clay 1912a: 23–25; most recently, Gelb and Kienast 1990: 116–17, Shar-kali-sharri 5; Frayne 1993: 197.

61. King 1900: 3b.

62. Joannès 1988. Some scribes of the twelfth and seventh centuries copied lists of archaic written characters and put contemporary signs beside each one. See, e.g., King 1898: 7; Wiseman and Black 1996: nos. 229 and 235. See also the copy of an anonymous scribe from Borsippa in Lambert 1968.

63. Parrot 1961: 278, fig. 348. Reade (1981: 154, 162) suggests that the second person is a painter, sketching scenes afterward represented in the mural bas-reliefs of the palace. However, on the use of Aramaic in the Assyrian Empire and in Babylonia, see Parpola 1981: 123 and n. 9. Attested from 878, the use of Aramaic was so widespread in Babylonia that dignitaries and functionaries had to be dissuaded from using it (Brinkman 1984a: 14 and nn. 53–55).

64. On archives in Mesopotamia, see Veenhof 1986. On the methods of selection followed by the Babylonian armies in the archives at Mari, after the capture of a city, see the remarks in Durand 1992: 40 and n. 8.

65. Foster 1990; Wilcke 1997; Sommerfeld 2000.

66. On this theme, see Glassner 1986: 77–88; 2003.

67. We do not know the attitude of literate people toward false documents. The most celebrated example is the cruciform monument of King Man-ištusu of Akkade; it is the work of the priests of Ebabbar, the temple of Šamaš at Sippar who, in the Neo-Babylonian period, deliberately composed a forgery establishing the antiquity of certain privileges they wanted to preserve. In this case "history" helped to establish a historical claim. On this text, see Sollberger 1967–68: 50–52; Steinkeller 1982: 257 n. 80.

68. On the indisputable relation between legend and history, see Gibert 1979: 83–84.

69. For instance, the copy of an inscription of Enna'il from Kiš: Steible 1982: 2:218, Enna'il A1; Cooper 1986: 21 Ki7.

70. E.g., Charpin 1984: 65–66; Civil 1961: 79–80 n. 537; 1967; Pinches 1963: 1:2; Edzard 1960: 1–31, pls. I–IV; Gelb and Kienast 1990: passim; Goetze 1968: 57; Hirsch 1963; Kutscher 1989; Michalowski 1980b; Sjöberg 1972a; Sollberger 1965: 13 and 14; 1982, 345–48.

71. Civil 1985: 37–45.

72. Michalowski 1976: 101–32; 1980a; Ali 1964. For a late Old Babylonian catalogue of such letters from Uruk, see van Dijk 1989. The collections come from Ur, Uruk, and Nippur, while two examples come from Susa (Edzard 1974).

73. Hallo 1984: 12–19; 1991b.

74. See Ungnad 1938a.

75. Ungnad 1938b; Millard 1994; on the eponyms of the Old Assyrian period, see, e.g., Larsen 1976: passim; Veenhof 1985; 2003; for modifications to the chronological sequence, see Garelli 1974: 132–34, 231–33.

76. On these lists, see Grayson 1980b, with all the useful references. There is a list of Elamite kings from Awan and Simaški in which no lengths of reign are given. This absence, added to the fact that each of the two dynasties has the same number of rulers, renders the document suspect; see Scheil 1931: 1–8; Glassner 1996b. A fragment of an Assyrian list shows the same characteristic; see Grayson 1980b: 115.

77. Lambert 1960a: 110–15; Foster 1996: 745–47.

78. On this logic, see Glassner 1984b.

79. Starr 1986.

80. For example, Lambert 1960b: 44–46; Clay 1923: 13 (F 33); Nougayrol 1941: 83–84 (AO 7030: 21–22); 1969: 59–60 (AO 7756: 7,' 10').

81. Goetze 1947b: no 1; Hanoun 1979: 437, fig. 6; Al-Rawi 1994: 38–43.

82. Starr 1985.

83. Beyond the examples just cited, see Arnaud 1987: 6/1–2, pl. 103, 731029, 20; pl. 44, 74136a, 2; pl. 119, 731040, 14; van Dijk 1976: no. 79; Goetze 1947a; Hunger 1972; Nougayrol 1945; 1950; Oppenheim 1936; Reiner 1974; Starr 1977; Weidner 1928–29; Wilcke 1988b: 127 n. 76 and passim.

84. Güterbock 1934: 57–58; Reiner 1961: 11; 1974; see also Cooper 1980.

85. See, e.g., Glassner 1999.

86. See the opinion of Jeyes 1980: 107, 121.

87. Sachs and Hunger 1988–2001. See also Geller 1990; 1991; Bernard 1990; Slotsky 1997.

88. Assyriologists, accustomed to identifying vaguely under the same term "epic" the Myth of Erra, the Epic of Gilgameš, or the History of Tukultī-Ninurta I of Assyria, refer to this last, as though to emphasize a difference, as a "historical epic." This results in an uncritical use of terminology (a criticism already made by Van Seters 1983: 92) and posits the existence of a literary, poetic, and epic style common to several literary genres. The Sumerian epics, for example, even if a historical kernel is perhaps to be found in them, are imaginative; gods, humans, animals, plants, and objects take part in the action. Their heroes have numerous mythical aspects and are provided with fabulous genealogies, some fighting mythic beings while another is helped by a lion-headed eagle; see Krecher 1975: 27; Alster 1973; 1974.

89. Cooper and Heimpel 1984; Afanas'eva 1987; Alster 1987; Steinkeller 1987; Attinger 1994.

90. Sargon of Akkade and Narām-Sîn: Glassner 1985b; Goodnick-Westenholz 1997; Charpin 1997; the seizure of power by Zimrī-Lim of Mari: Charpin and Durand 1985: 325.

Assyria—Adad-nārāri I: Weidner 1963: 113–15, pl. V; Foster 1996: 206–7; Tukultī-Ninurta I: Machinist 1978; Foster 1996: 211–30; Tiglath-Pileser I: Hurowitz and Westenholz 1990; Foster 1996: 237–39.

Babylonia—the fall of Ur: Falkenstein 1931: 43; the siege of Uruk: Thompson 1930: pl. 59; Kurigalzu: Grayson 1975b: 47–55; Adad-šuma-uṣur: Grayson 1975b: 56–77; Nebuchadnezzar I: Foster 1996: 290–94; Nabopolassar: Grayson 1975b: 78–86; Amēl-Marduk: Grayson 1975b: 87–92; fragment: Grayson 1975b: 93–97.

91. Tadmor 1977: 209–10.

92. See Grayson 1972; 1976; Lie 1929; Luckenbill 1924; Borger 1956; Maximilian Streck 1916; Tadmor 1994.

93. Thureau-Dangin 1912; Oppenheim 1960. On the sources in general, see Borger 1971b; Grayson 1984; Ellis 1987; Sasson 1987.

94. Frankfort 1988: 156–94; Barnett 1959; Albenda 1986; Russell 1999.

95. On these texts, see Güterbock 1934: 40–41; Lewis 1980; Glassner 1988; Longman 1991; Günbattı 1997; Hecker 2001: 58–60; a list of the texts has been

drawn up by Grayson 1975b: 8 n. 11. In general on the Old Akkadian kings, see Goodnick-Westenholz 1997. We may add the pseudoautobiography of Sennacherib: Livingstone 1989: no. 33; Tadmor, Landsberger, and Parpola 1989; Glassner 1997: 108 n. 55.

96. Biggs 1967; 1985; 1987; 1992; Lambert 1978; Grayson 1975b: ch. 3; Grayson and Lambert 1964; Hallo 1966; Borger 1971a; Hunger 1976: no. 3; Wiseman and Black 1996: nos. 64, 65, and 69.

97. Foster 1996: 263–70; Goodnick-Westenholz 1997: 294–368.

98. On this narrative, see in general Glassner 2000a: ch. 1; Vanstiphout 2003. For this passage, see Vanstiphout 2003: 85. Enmerkar is also considered to be the author of various works in Sumerian.

99. Foster 1996: 257–70. See Cassin 1987: 76–77.

100. Streck 1916: 2:192, rev. 5.

101. Luckenbill 1924: 83–84, lines 43–54.

102. Ibid., 137–38, lines 36–41, 46–47.

103. Ibid., 78, line 1.

104. See Frymer-Kensky 1984; most recently Livingstone 1989: no 34.

105. In this instance the name of Aššur is written AN.ŠÁR, that is, "universal god," also the name of an ancestor of Marduk and thus superior to him in power.

106. Borger 1971a: 12–16; 1964: 143–44; 1957–58: 114. The source followed here is text A.

107. Borger 1971a: text E.

108. See chronicle 16.

109. Cooper 1983; Attinger 1984; Glassner 1986: 69–77. See chronicle 38.

110. Foster 1996: 757–89.

111. See the Epic of Zimrī-Lim: Marello 1992: 121–22; see also chronicle 52.

112. Erra v 49–58: Foster 1996: 788. See also Dalley 1991: 311–12.

113. Reiner 1960.

114. For example, Marduk-apla-iddina II: Gadd 1953: 124, line 34 = Erra v 35.

115. One could have recourse to an exorcist, *āšipu,* to "dissolve" an unfavorable omen (Bottéro 1985: 29–64). Hence one could influence the passage of time, not just of the present but of the future as well.

Part II

Analysis of the Compositions

II

Definition

Forty-eight, or perhaps fifty-three, documents have in common interest in chronology. Many more existed that remain to be discovered or are lost forever, so the present corpus is necessarily incomplete. These documents themselves are also usually incomplete, their clay medium mutilated by frustrating breaks and their text in fragments. In every case, and by definition, they are never originals, but copies, more or less perfect, more or less accurate, early or late. They come from the principal cities of Sumer, Babylonia, and Assyria and are spread out over approximately two thousand years.

Whereas histories privilege narrative and annals stress political and military affairs, chronicles concentrate on chronology, checking off, reign after reign, year in, year out, the long scheme of events deemed worthy of remembrance. Each reign or each year was normally (for there was, it seems, no hard and fast rule) separated from the others by a horizontal line drawn in the clay. These were carefully designed compositions, elaborated and molded into precise forms by historians devoted to the preservation of the memory of the distant past as well as of times closer to the present.

In the course of their discovery and decipherment, modern editors have classified them indiscriminately as "lists" or "chronicles." There has therefore been a tendency to refer to them confusingly as the Sumerian King List or the Assyrian King List but the Dynastic Chronicle. Lists and chronicles certainly belonged to the same chronographic genre, since their authors were motivated by the same concern for chronological order, so it cannot be denied that there were close ties between them. Moreover, some chronicles contain sections in list form; this suggests that the difference was not so sharply perceived in antiquity as it might be now.

Nevertheless, lists were one-dimensional; they were in general dry enumerations of signs or words classified according to graphic, semantic, or thematic criteria.[1] They were distinguished from chronicles by the absence of prose, apart from a few late examples that did not conform to this definition. King lists may be clearly distinguished from chronicles in that royal names appear alone, immediately followed or preceded by the bald mention of the number of years of the king's reign.

Three basic traits characterize chronicles. (1) They were written in prose, in the third person. This was the case even if this prose was reduced to a recurring formula and to a few more or less condensed chronological notes (e.g., Chronicle of the Single Monarchy [no. 1]), which however had the virtue of mingling synchrony and diachrony, giving the composition a multidimensional aspect. (2) Priority was given to time. The essential thing was to note the date of every event selected. There was an increasing tendency to leave no year unaccounted. (3) Brevity was the norm. Restricting themselves to the events they summarized, and running the risk of appearing brief to the point of atomization, chronicles were a kind of handbook that reduced history to a series of facts.

There seems to have been no generic term that subsumed them all into one category. Each had its own title, which, according to custom, corresponded to the first word or phrase of the opening line. The Chronicle of the Single Monarchy is called "kingship," nam.lugal, after the first word of the piece; the Babylonian Royal Chronicle (no. 3) must have been called, according to its Sumerian opening, "when Anu," u_4 an.né. Copies of two chronicles (nos. 18 and 39) have the word GIGAM.GIGAM or GIGAM.DIDLI (in both cases it is the plural of the same Akkadian word, *tēṣêtu* or *ippirū*), which occurs by itself at the end of the text or in the margin. It may be translated "battles," "conflicts," or "struggles." Did this term designate the chronicles as a literary genre? We are in no position to affirm this. Chronicle 10, cast, like the pseudoautobiographical record of Narām-Sîn, in the form of a stela, *narû,* was intended to be read by future monarchs for their benefit, while chronicle 39 takes the form of a letter sent by a king to one of his fellow-kings to give him ample good advice. From this apparent mixture of genre among chronicles, *narû,* and fictitious royal letters,[2] any ancient criteria for classification were at some remove from our own.

It was long thought that chronicles appeared only late during the Neo-Babylonian period. The recent discovery at Mari of eponym chronicles (no. 8) dating from the beginning of the eighteenth century shows that this was not true. We can now see that it is possible to go back even further in time, to the last third of the third millennium. The latest such compositions were composed or copied during the Parthian period, later than the work of Berossus.

A simple reading of the sources shows that there were several kinds of chronicles. Apart from the same concern for chronology, what do the Tummal Chronicle (no. 7), with its apparently purely local preoccupations, and the Assyrian Synchronistic Chronicle (no. 10), whose author set himself up as judge of the facts recorded, the Chronicle of the Esagila (no. 38), conceived in the form of a letter, or the Neo-Babylonian chronicles (nos. 16–37), with their restricted vocabulary and their uniform syntax, have in common with each other?

Study of various recurrent literary formulae seems to be of little help in making classification. Such an attempt has been made, but it led to lumping the great majority of sources together while leaving out a small minority.[3] Leaving literary formulae aside, another attempt might consist of treating them in purely rhetorical terms, using such Aristotelian categories as metaphor, metonymy, or irony.

Metaphor can be seen, for example, in the use of such terms as Ummān-manda, Guti, and perhaps Ḫaneans in first-millennium sources, devoid of all ethnic content, since they named peoples long disappeared. Such terms served to designate different peoples contemporary and foreign, such as Medes or Macedonians, for example, retaining only a pejorative memory of extinct peoples who had become prototypes of the barbarian invader, savage hordes without culture, whose home was far away and whom the gods had chosen as instruments of destruction.[4] Such terminology allows the possibility of a coherent classification along with such traits as backwardness, ignorance, impiety, and the like.

Metonymy occurs with the usage in the Chronicle of the Single Monarchy (no. 1) of the divine determinative dingir/*ilum* preceeding certain royal names, such as "the divine Dumuzi" or "the divine Šulgi." The determinative was a purely graphic convention, the product of a way of thinking that constructed a representation of the political and sought to bring the king into the divine sphere.[5] It was probably an allusion to certain idealized models for the transmission of power, kings supposedly being descended from gods.[6] This made it easy to delineate, at a stroke, the contours of the hierarchical totality of the social order and signaled a new, written, relationship to the world.

Irony, introducing a negative note, occurs in the Royal Chronicle of Lagaš (no. 6), which is conceived entirely in a satirical mode, like a parody of the Chronicle of the Single Monarchy. Irony is also found in remarks in the context of chronicles on the ignorance, even the stupidity, of Nabonidus, in the two sources evoking this person (nos. 26 and 53).

To these Aristotelian categories it is perhaps useful to add a further one, that of inversion. An example of this can be seen in the figure of Ku-Baba the innkeeper (nos. 1 and 38), the only woman to have acceded to kingly majesty and who, simply because she was a woman in a man's world and thus a figure of inversion, had to refound her city.

However, all these features, which occur abundantly elsewhere in Mesopotamian literature, show nothing beyond a certain unity of thought characteristic of the time. Historical traditions were preserved by a small number of literate men, scribes, priests, or diviners, and this caste of literati came to see the entire world through the metaphor of writing, every phenomenon becoming primarily, in their eyes, a graphic sign.

For a better appreciation of the range and value of the chronicles, or a classification, it would be preferable to determine and to identify the status, the place of composition, the diffusion, and the function and social position of the authors. Despite the tattered character of the sources, some slight indications do fortunately allow us, if not to complete, at least to start the inquiry in the right direction.

THE AUTHORS

A certain Nūr-Ninšubur was the author of a formal copy of the Chronicle of the Single Monarchy (no. 1, source G). Whether or not it was he who introduced the motif of the flood and the scheme of antediluvian kings into the composition, we cannot say. The fact is that the manuscript that he left to posterity is quite defective and full of errors, and he gives the impression of being a second-rate scholar, but erudition and intelligence were perhaps not necessarily essential or indispensable qualities of a chronicler. Apart from his name, we know absolutely nothing about him. As for the Tummal Chronicle (no. 7), several copies agree on attributing authorship to Lu-Inanna, the chief saddler of Enlil, in other words to a craftsman, a devotee of this god, and the holder of an official post in the temple.

Elsewhere, at Mari the colophon of a copy of the Eponym Chronicles (no. 8) specifies that the copy is the work of a certain Ḫabdu-Mālik, who wrote under the dictation of Limī-Dagān. A scribe of this name is listed as a witness in a legal document from the time of Zimrī-Lim, but this may just be another person with the same name. Later, in other places, two copies of the Assyrian Royal Chronicle (no. 5) have the names of their authors, Kandalānu and Bēl-šuma-iddin, who are thought to be not mere copyists but the actual authors of the texts. One is "scribe of the temple of Arbēla," the other "exorcist (of the city) of Aššur." The copy of the Chronicle of the Esagila (no. 38), excavated in the Ebabbar in Sippar, is signed with the name of Marduk-ēṭir-[. . .], devotee of Nabû.

Anu-balāssu-iqbi, who copied the Uruk Chronicle (no. 48) from an original belonging to a temple, wrote it for the favorable outcome of his studies and deposited the tablet, property of his father Anu-aḫa-ušabši, in the Bīt-rēši. He belonged to a large scholarly family in Uruk, a descendant of Ekur-zākir, who had been an exorcist, *šešgallû*-priest of the Bīt-rēši, an astrologer and astronomer. He counted among his kin lament singers, exorcists, astrologers, high-ranking priests, and eminent scribes. He himself left other copies in his own hand, among which are an excerpt from a myth about the god Ninurta, the celebrated "Lugale," an extract from the great astrological series *Enūma Anu Enlil,* and a description of the New Year ritual at Uruk. He lived around 250, in the reign of Antiochus II, and was thus a contemporary of Berossus. Later, in the reign of Antiochus III, another scribe from the same family copied astrological and hepatoscopic texts.

As for the copyists of chronicles 16 and 19, respectively Ea-iddin, son of Ana-bēl-ēreš, of the family of Ur-Nanna, and Nabû-kāṣir, of the family of Ea-ilūta-bāni, they were both private scribes well known from legal documents. The first, who wrote the chronicle for his father, may have worked at Babylon during the reign of Darius I; the second worked at Borsippa during the reign of Nabonidus. Links they had with temple or palace, if any, are unknown. They were not identified by any specific title.

THE FORMAT OF THE TEXTS

Let us consider the royal chronicles and the Neo-Babylonian, Persian, and Seleucid chronicles. Of the sixteen known copies of the Chronicle of the Single Monarchy (no. 1), one, possibly coming from Larsa and specifically the composition of Nūr-Ninšubur, is written on an octagonal prism. Two further copies from Susa are inscribed on perforated cylinders. Likewise, of the five copies of the Assyrian Royal Chronicle (no. 5), two are inscribed on prisms. We may suppose that all these formal copies were intended for public display. All, insofar as the state of the documents enables us to judge, were provided with colophons giving the names of their authors. Other copies are by and large library tablets.

So far as Neo-Babylonian, Persian, and Seleucid chronicles are concerned, an entirely different explanation is required. While some are inscribed on library tablets with two columns of text on each side (nos. 16, 17, 26, 27, and 41), others are written on small tablets in the format of administrative or economic documents (nos. 21, 23, 25, and 28). Documents with a colophon are rare (nos. 16, 19 and 22; in no. 18 the word "battles" appears), and the majority (nos. 21, 23, 25, 28, 30, and 32) have none. Some tablets belong to a series, such as number 16, which looks like the first tablet of a larger composition, or numbers 22–24, which all have, at the end of the text, the catchline of the following tablet. Number 26 ends with the conjunction "and," so must also form part of a series.

THE PLACE OF CHRONICLES IN LIBRARIES

Unfortunately, we do not know the principles determining the classification system of libraries. In some way or other they must have reflected requirements of teaching. In any event, historical works were scattered within them, as with an Old Babylonian library at Ur, where the surviving works, a catalogue, and an inventory have been found. Chronicles appear side by side with copies of royal inscriptions or royal correspondence, mythological compositions, hymns and prayers, debates, epics, wisdom literature, lexical texts, and even mathematical texts. The Chronicle of the Single Monarchy (no. 1) and the Babylonian Royal Chronicle (no. 3), the latter in its bilingual edition, are mentioned separately in the catalogue.[7]

THE SUCCESS OF THESE COMPOSITIONS

Of all the chronicles, the first (no. 1) had by far the greatest and most long-lasting success. We have sixteen copies, all from the Ur III and Old Babylonian periods, coming from all the great cities of Mesopotamia and its periphery, from Susa at the frontier of Elam to Šubat-Enlil in northern Syria; from Nippur, Isin, Kiš, and probably Larsa. The text history shows, furthermore, that there were at least three different manuscript traditions.[8] Its popularity went well beyond the limits of the Old Babylonian period. It inspired other royal chronicles (nos. 2–6) and, no doubt, a chronicle of ancient kings (no. 38). A drinking song in use as far afield as Emar and distant Ugarit[9] and that evokes the names of several illustrious monarchs from the past brings further proof of its wide distribution. Other royal chronicles enjoy a more restricted fame: the Babylonian Royal Chronicle (no. 3), with the exception of the Old Babylonian catalogue from Ur, is known only from Neo-Assyrian and Neo-Babylonian copies, and the Assyrian Royal Chronicle (no. 5) from five copies distributed between the tenth and eighth centuries.

If we exclude the Assyrian eponym chronicles, with five copies from Mari (no. 8) and eleven from Aššur and Sultan-Tepe (no. 9), other compositions had a more modest destiny. The undoubted fame of the Tummal Chronicle (no. 7), known in ten copies and the study of which figured in the training and education of young scribes, did not go beyond the first centuries of the second millennium nor the scriptoria of Ur and Nippur. In Assyria, the Synchronistic Chronicle (no. 10) is known from only three copies. Only one chronicle of ancient kings (no. 38) had a certain success, as attested by the seven known copies distributed between Assyria and Babylonia in the Neo-Assyrian and Neo-Babylonian periods.

The other Neo-Babylonian, Persian, and Seleucid chronicles, apart from number 16, of which we have two fragmentary copies, are known from only one manuscript, proof of mediocre success, a limited diffusion, or a brief existence. But this first remark must be qualified. If chronicles 22, 23, and 24, whose texts form a sequence, are indeed parts of a single text series, it would seem that, since each has specific and unique features (only the first possessing a colophon, and the form of the second, unlike the others, being that of an economic tablet), they actually belonged to three different editions of the same series.

Some texts are excerpts, such as manuscripts M, N, and O of the Chronicle of the Single Monarchy (no. 1), chronicle 19, which was copied from a wax tablet, or perhaps the two chronicles 25 and 28, which give an account of only one regnal year. These extracts certainly helped in one way or another the circulation of manuscripts and the diffusion of compositions.

There is nothing surprising in this textual interdependency, for it is common knowledge that success does not usually come to works of erudition but rather to those in the gray area where history, literature, and politics mingle.

STYLE

With the exception of the beginning of the Royal Chronicle of Lagaš (no. 6) and the Chronicle of the Esagila (no. 38), the typical style is sober, appropriate to a catalogue of data. A more attractive literary form would no doubt do a disservice to the aims of the authors and the wishes of readers. Some sources allow the presence of direct speech. Do the chroniclers therefore intend to record the actual words of speakers or to present their inner thoughts? We are certainly a long way from Thucydides and his use of direct speech to reflect differences in public opinion and to reconstruct the motives of political leaders. But this could simply be genre, a matter of borrowing from the literary writing of history.

One tense predominates: the preterite. In contrast, the present-future, the perfect, and the stative are rarely used.[10] In short, the chroniclers wrote in the past tense.

In conclusion, we find a whole gamut of varied compositions, ranging from official chronicles widely distributed (sometimes diplayed in places accessible to some members of the public and consulted by kings) to more modest documents of less circulation but greater erudition (e.g., items from libraries or archives). I propose the following classification for them.

Royal Chronicles

These are not ordinary works dealing with a political history but rather works intended to provide the basis for an ideological theory.

Assyrian Chronicles

These are official documents for royal consultation. The different versions of the annals of Tiglath-pileser I were dated by reference to the eponym magistrates.[11] It could be that one or another passage of the Synchronistic Chronicle (no. 10) was quoted by an Assyrian ruler.[12]

With reference to royal consultation, we know that later the Persian kings had their chronicles, for the books of Ezra and Nehemiah testify to this effect. So too Ctesias, who, according to Diodorus Siculus, claimed to have consulted them and to have found "ancient events written, as a law prescribed it." The book of Esther reports that a Persian king, suffering from insomnia, had the "Book of Memories" brought to him so that he could have someone read to him from it. The book of Ezra tells us that these royal chronicles were more commonly to guide the king's opinion and to provide a basis for his political decisions. The chronicle was a sort of "narrative metaphorization of political strategies."[13]

Local Chronicles

The Sumerian Tummal Chronicle (no. 7) might at first glance seem to be the sole survivor of sanctuary traditions that are otherwise lost, but the question has to be raised as to whether there really existed chronicles of purely local interest.

Neo-Babylonian, Persian, and Seleucid Chronicles

Preoccupied with the recent past, these are erudite compositions written in a spare style and whose existence must have been relatively precarious. They seem to have circulated more among the aristocracy than in royal courts, though this is merely an argument from silence.[14] Did they constitute a unique and homogeneous series beginning in 741 and continuing until the second century?[15] It seems rather that there were several parallel or concurrent chronological traditions, as attested, for instance, by chonicles 16, 17, and 18. Moreover, not all, if indeed any of them, intended to set forth the whole of the six or seven hundred years of history that they covered.

Neo-Babylonian Chronicles concerning Ancient Kings

In the first millennium, Mesopotamian society had a justifiable sense of a tradition of creativity and sought to recall forgotten fragments of its heritage. Wishing to fill in periods of time left blank, scholars, often the same ones (see chronicle 19, where recent events and others from earlier times are associated), made up chronicles of ancient times that ranged from the most distant beginnings, in the mists of legend, down to the eighth century and that provided food for thought.

SOURCES

The question of sources is practically insoluble. While some compositions freely mingled myth, epic, legend, and history, what is really at issue is the cultural background of the historians. We know the rudiments of their education, which was that of every scribe, but we know virtually nothing about them once they left school. Coming from scribal and educated families, they carried on the functions of diviner, exorcist, or theologian. In short, familiar with disciplines accessible to the literate, so far as the most famous were concerned, we may guess that their knowledge was encyclopedic. It was never the norm, however, to acknowledge one's sources. Moreover, invoking the threat of a divine curse on anyone who might break them,[16] colophons make frequent reference to the danger that texts or tablets might be destroyed. In a nutshell, such documents as might have shed light on sources having perhaps been deliberately destroyed in antiquity, the modern historian is very much at a loss.

Occasionally the chroniclers use formulae such as "I heard" (no. 34), "rumor has it" (no. 4), "it is said" (no. 38), or "one has said" (no. 52), all remarks that suggest that they were on the lookout for oral information that they might pick up. If we exclude chronicle 38, where the formula introduces a variant account, and chronicle 52, where the context is lost, these expressions apply to events that we suppose were contemporaneous to the writer. However, the credibility of the information given and consequently the credibility of the chronicler required that the information be derived from a recognized authority. Still, the use of the impersonal verb form in chronicle 4 tends to undermine this hypothesis. The same expressions occur, still fairly uncommonly, in the astronomical diaries, as if to show that the scribes were not themselves witnesses to the reported events, so these had perhaps been borrowed by the chroniclers just as they were.

Preference was given, in fact, to written sources over oral testimony. One should remember that in Mesopotamia written documents were compiled from others and archives consulted.[17]

The medium of the sources being clay, it was subject to breakage and gaps. One rule, taken quite seriously by chroniclers, copyists, and their readers, was that absolutely nothing could be added on one's own account to the documents consulted. They preferred to restore nothing, however justifiable it might be. In some cases, a name lost in a lacuna of an original document (nos. 1, 2, 35, and 46) was indicated as unknown or forgotten. In one instance, a scribe indicated that a certain event, which he knew about and to which he wished to allude, was not written down (no. 16). Some of the latest chronicles chose more simply to leave blank spaces (nos. 26 and 47). As a general rule, copyists were in the habit of noting the presence of a break by means of the word *ḫipi,* "break," or *ḫipi eššu,* "recent break." The chronicles teem with such remarks (no. 5, versions A and D; no. 38, version F; no. 52). Curiously, the copyist would do this when, on occasion, only a single sign on the damaged original was missing, which could easily have been restored. One of the versions of chronicle 38 offers the following sequence of signs: *ip ḫipi lis,* "*ip* BREAK *lis*." In this case it was a matter of a simple verbal form. Moreover, the three consonants of the triliteral root were already there in the text, so no grammatical sophistication was needed to restore the missing sign <*-pa*>, to provide the complete verbal form *ippalis*. Likewise, we find in document 52 the sequence TIN *ḫipi*. Given the context and the mention of the place name Borsippa in the same line, it is easy to recognize in TIN the initial sign of one of the spellings Babylon, TIN.<TIR^{ki}>, a name that the scribe evidently began to write but did not take the trouble to restore fully.[18]

However, the presence of breaks can also be the source of difficulties. The author of chronicle 6 indicates the presence in the original he was using of a break in the eighth year of the reign of Esarhaddon and another in the tenth year of the same reign. Since the ninth year is missing, one may deduce that the same break extended from the eighth to the tenth year and that there remained of this passage only a detached fragment of the tablet, which the scribe attempted with some care to insert into his own copy. The result, for modern historians, is an insoluble confusion with regard to the chronology of this period of Esarhaddon's reign.

The Assyrian chroniclers drew on royal inscriptions and official documents. The proof of this is inadvertently given by one of them (no. 10) when, concerning Šamšī-Adad V receiving tribute from the kings of Chaldea, he wrote the verbal form *amḫur,* "I received," appropriate to royal inscriptions, instead of *imḫur,* "he received," as the context required.[19] The same chronicler also used the technical jargon of treaties.

Assyrian and Babylonian chroniclers had at their disposal other historiographical writings. Information about Abī-ešuḫ's construction of a dam across the Tigris (no. 40) in all probability came from a list of year names. The account of the war between Kurigalzu and the Elamite Ḫurba-tela (no. 45) was directly inspired, as the style shows, by a history of this king's reign. The author of the Assyrian Royal Chronicle (no. 5) made no secret of the fact that beginning with the reign of Ērišum I he used eponym lists.

Sometimes authors took material from other chronicles. Some episodes in chronicle 39 were borrowed from 38. As for chronicle 10, it was indebted for some of its information to the Assyrian Royal Chronicle (no. 5) and to the Eponym Chronicle (no. 9). Beyond these isolated borrowings, however, two more important questions arise. Were astronomical diaries the preferred sources of the Babylonian chronicles? Some postulate the existence, beginning in 747 or even as early as the ninth century, of a running account of the major historical events, of which the chronicles were merely selected excerpts. This running account would be identified with the diaries.[20] All things considered, however, diaries could, at best, have been one of the potential sources of the chronicles, but certainly not the only one. The battle of Ḫirītu, for example, which took place on 27 Addar 652, was described in a chronicle (no. 19) as well as in a diary. In fact, the two documents are entirely different in their vocabulary, the chronicle being far more precise than the presumed source![21] Dependence of the chronicles on diaries is thus far from being proved. In fact, the two genres shared the same intellectual outlook, which was no longer satisfied with an approximate chronology.

Could divinatory literature, for want of any other, have been the primary source for the chronicles? The close similarity between a collection of historical omens[22] and chronicle 39, where the same royal names and the same events were repeated in practically the same order and in the same terms, tends to support the theory that there were particular links between the two historiographical genres.

Modern opinion is divided, and assessments range widely. For some, the divinatory literature should have pride of place as the source for all Mesopotamian historiographical work;[23] its greater antiquity would be the strongest argument in favor.[24] For others, this literature could have played no part beyond inspiring the minor cases of chronicles 39 and 51,[25] where the similarity is obvious. Alternatively, some think that diviners were inspired by chronicles.[26]

To some it seems unthinkable that diviners could have made up, from whole cloth, fictitious omens that were made to correlate with historical events deemed of ominous significance. To others it seems that the differences between the chronicles and the predictions are sufficient to disprove any relation between the two genres. To take one example with regard to the kings of Akkade, two diametrically opposed views emerged: the divinatory tradition expressed an entirely favorable view of these kings; the chronicles, on the contrary, emphasized the difficulties they encountered. Expressed in these terms, the problem appears insoluble. Chronographical literature was, in the first place, not so recent an invention as it at first seemed. On the other hand, the outlook of the diviners, whose method we understand better nowadays, and that of the chroniclers are not necessarily so diametrically opposed. One Old Babylonian source cites, very near to each other, two omens, of which the first evokes Narām-Sîn of Akkade, who had ruled "the totality (of the inhabited lands)," and the second links a "king of the totality" with a natural disaster personified by Nergal, precisely the god whom Narām-Sîn wanted to show himself as his henchman.[27] This shows that the view of diviners toward the extinct dynasty was not unqualifiedly favorable.

The solution to this problem cannot be found by simply toting up similarities among the fragmentary sources. In antiquity there must have been a complex textual tradition of which the merest scattered fragments remain. The guiding thread is broken, no doubt forever. We should remember that diviners and chroniclers were in fact members of the same intellectual circles and that there were close associations and family connections among them. Consider, for instance, the family of the scribe Anu-balāssu-iqbi, already cited, but there are many other examples. These people shared the same intellectual interests and the same tradition of learning. Exchanges between them were manifold and not limited to simple copying or borrowing.

Finally, there was no watertight boundary between Babylonia and Assyria. The reciprocal influences are obvious. Babylonian chroniclers took their inspiration from the Eponym Chronicle (no. 9), from which they borrowed a number of formulae, one referring to the accession of kings ("he ascended the throne" replacing the older formula of the royal chronicles "So-and-so became king"), the other referring to the participation of the ruler in the New Year festival using the formula: "(the king) took Bēl by the hand" in lieu of "(the king) took Bēl and Bēl's son by the hand." In both cases the borrowing was made keeping the tense originally used in the Assyrian chronicle, that is, the perfect instead of the preterite. The converse is no less the case, as Assyrian chroniclers sometimes used new forms in the style of Babylonian chronography.[28] Mention of the toponyms of Larak and Sarrabanu in the Eponym Chronicle (no. 9) and in the Babylonian Chronicle (no. 16) shows how close the ties were between the two chronographic traditions. Since the two chronicles give the same excerpt from a list of thirty-nine places in Bīt-Amukāni conquered by Sennacherib during his first campaign, it is very likely that one was influenced by the other.

OBJECTIVITY AND ACCURACY

Assyrian chronography has a bad reputation. Some see nothing but chauvinistic compositions intended only to glorify Assyria.[29] The Neo-Babylonian chronicles, in contrast, would be models of historical probity, since they were honest enough to mention defeats as well as victories, and no intention to persuade nor hint of propaganda can be discerned in them. With the exception of chronicles 18 and 19, considered partisan compositions, they are all seen as "objective" and "impartial" sources, exemplifying the pure intellectual pleasure of writing history.[30]

The concept of objective history certainly did flourish. Translated into the language of the historian, it represents an outmoded philosophical model, because the word "objective" is no longer in fashion today. Since the publication of Raymond Aron's studies, one can no longer be unaware that history is a social convention, that the historian reconstructs and gives status to the historical event, and that this very act of reconstruction eliminates objectivity.[31] So what of this in Mesopotamia? It would be a crass methodological error to believe that ready-made historical reality is present, in latent form, in the sources, of which it is enough that the historian gives a faithful reproduction, his own work being, in short, reduced to that of a parasite. Historical interpretation depends, in Mesopotamia as elsewhere, on an implicit philosophy based in the author's subjectivity, while he himself is imbued with the idea that he is writing "reality." Now, whether or not there was awareness of it, the paradox of the chronicles, as with other historiographical works, was that they articulated reality and discourse. Thus they are of that class of "willing witnesses"[32] whose sway over history has to be limited with the help of the "witnesses in spite of themselves" with which the historian is familiar. Some critical stance toward them must be taken.

It is not my intention to present a comprehensive historical critique of this material: one volume would be insufficient. Moreover, it is too often the case that we have no other sources than these with which to work. We may content ourselves therefore with a few examples.

(1) The chronology in the Chronicle of the Single Monarchy (no. 1) is fictitious and the computations fanciful. The numerical data for the lengths of the reigns and dynasties are frequently symbolic and cannot be taken at face value.[33] Furthermore, between any versions of the composition, the compilers may not be in agreement on the length of even the most recent reigns.

(2) Even without raising the tricky question of the text transmission of the Assyrian Royal Chronicle (no. 5), an inexhaustible wellspring of errors and omissions (the lengths of some reigns varies among the manuscripts; sometimes a name is omitted), this chronicle is strewn with erroneous genealogies of rulers: Aššur-nērārī II was the son of Aššur-rabî I, not of Enlil-nāṣir, while Aššur-rêm-nišēšu was the son of Aššur-nērārī II, not Aššur-bēl-nišēšu, and so on. The same is true of the lengths of reigns. Since the chronology was based on eponym lists, and kings at certain periods normally served as eponym only in the second or third year after their accession, the result was that some reigns were erroneously shortened by a year.[34]

(3) Chronicle 10's interest is restricted to fluctuations in the boundary separating Assyria and Babylonia, to the east of the Tigris, between the first half of the fifteenth and the beginning of the eighth century. Moreover, only Assyrian victories are reported. At the outset it commits a serious chronological error: the reigns of Kara-indaš and Aššur-bēl-nišēšu actually

followed those of Puzur-Aššur III and Burna-Buriaš I, rather than preceding them. Space does not permit me to list all the errors and omissions in this chronicle, such as Nabû-šuma-ukīn being erroneously called Nabû-šuma-iškun, where a simple comparison with chronicle 45, which deals with the same period, is informative. I merely note the deliberate falsification of the facts to which the author did not hesitate to resort. For instance, if we were to believe the chronicle, the battle of Sugaga was fought between Adad-nārārī I and Nazi-Muruttaš, and the Assyrian king defeated the Babylonian adversary. Chronicle 45 describes the same event but in entirely different terms. According to this account, Kurigalzu II, the predecessor of Nazi-Muruttaš, won the battle against his Assyrian adversary Adad-nārārī. The Babylonian chronicler is obviously open to doubt, since he made a mistake in transcribing one or other of the royal names. Since Kurigalzu II reigned before Adad-nārārī and was a contemporary of Enlil-nārārī, it appears that he confused the theophoric elements in the Assyrian king's name. Be that as it may, the geographic details mentioned by the Assyrian chronicler indicate that Assyria lost territory as a result of the battle. We may conclude that Assyria actually lost the battle.

(4) In chronicle 39 the narrator reports that, during the old age of Sargon of Akkade, he was faced by general rebellion throughout his empire and was forced to take refuge in his capital, which was besieged and from which he launched the counterattack that brought him victory. The episode of a siege followed by Sargon's victory appears, however, to have been confused with a precisely similar exploit of Narām-Sîn, his grandson, at the beginning of his reign, of which the king himself gave a full account in his own inscriptions.[35]

(5) In 720, at the battle of Dēr, Sargon II of Assyria faced a coalition made up of King Marduk-apla-iddina II of Babylon and King Ḫumban-nikaš I of Elam. According to chronicle 16, the king of Elam defeated the king of Assyria on his own, the Babylonian arriving too late to take part in the battle. The same battle was described by Sargon and Marduk-apla-iddina in their own inscriptions. There Sargon claimed to have conquered Elam, while Marduk-apla-iddina declared that he had conquered Assyria. There were therefore three protagonists and three victors! Whatever the real facts or their eventual correction, the battle inaugurated ten years of peace among the three powers. We are left mindful of the need for a close critical analysis of the chronicle.

After the death of Sargon, Sennacherib devoted practically his entire reign to the suppression of Babylonian rebellions, and, from this perspective, the chronicler presented the main facts. In doing this he passed over in silence Sennacherib's other campaigns in Media, Kurdistan and Cilicia, Phoenicia and Palestine, the last culminating in the capture of Lachish and the surrender of Hezekiah, king of Jerusalem. At Ḫalulê there was a major confrontation that, according to the chronicle, occurred in an unknown year: Ḫumban-nimena, king of Elam, at the head of the armies of Elam and Akkad, forced the Assyrians to retreat. Sennacherib's inscriptions do not allow such a reading of the events, asserting that he had taken the initiative and describing in often painstaking detail the punishments inflicted on the corpses of the vanquished enemies, as well as the booty captured and the prisoners taken, while stressing the shameful retreat of the Elamite and Babylonian kings. This hyperbolic account even leads some modern historians to take the chronicler's vision at face value, without further consideration. The date of the battle, 691, is inferred from an inscription of Sennacherib. As it was, by 690 the Assyrians were setting up a stela on the site of the battle and were laying siege to Babylon. A legal document dated 28 Ab in year 3 of the reign of Mušēzib-Marduk (that is July–August 690) shows that Babylon was under siege and that the population was already threatened by famine. The city fell fifteen months later. It seems clear, then, that the Assyrians were not stopped by a defeat at Ḫalulê but that their advance was at least slowed. Sennacherib himself, indeed, referring to operations following Ḫalulê, spoke of a "second campaign," as though at some point he had been obliged to pause and get his wind back.

After the destruction of the city, still according to the same chronicle, but also according to chronicles 18 and 20, there was an eight-year interregnum in Babylon. Ptolemy, much later, still echoes this statement. But there is no unanimity among Babylonian historians, since another historiographical document, a Babylonian king list, accords to Sennacherib the title king of Babylon.

Notes

1. On lists, see Goody 1977; Cavigneaux 1983.

2. We know of other fictitious royal letters in Akkadian. One is attributed to Gilgameš, two others to Sargon of Akkade. See Michalowski 1980a; Foster 1996: 108, 805–6; Goodnick-Westenholz 1997: 141–69. Half a dozen among them constitute a coherent group comprising teachings about history, mainly from the Kassite period: van Dijk 1986; Lambert 1998.

3. Thus Grayson 1975a: 5–7, 193–201 and passim; 1980b; note also the remarks of Brinkman 1990: 76 n. 17.

4. Malbran-Labat 1980: 18–20; Glassner 1991: 128–29. On the equivalence Ummān-manda = Medes, see Komoróczy 1977: esp. 59–61. For the Macedonians, the two terms "Macedonians" and "Haneans" were used; for their equivalence in our texts (elsewhere, "Haneans" is an equivalent for European barbarians from the north of Greece), see, for instance, Sachs and Hunger 1988–2001: 1:190.1: "Alexander, the king who (comes from) the land of the Haneans."

5. The title dingir/*ilum,* "god," pardoxically, tended to separate kings from gods, since, contrary to human kings, gods are never the dingir/*ilum* of a land or a city. They were always its "king," lugal/*šarrum*. On this see Glassner 2000a: ch. 10.

6. See Sjöberg 1972b; Narām-Sîn of Akkade was the "valiant husband" of Ištar-Annunîtum: the Akkadian *mutum* denotes at the same time "husband" and "warrior." See, however, Kienast 1990.

7. On this library, see Charpin 1986: 434–86; on the catalogue, see Kramer 1961; Charpin 1986: 455–58. The Chronicle of the Single Monarchy, under its title nam.lugal, appears in line 25, while the Babylonian Royal Chronicle under its Sumerian title u_4.an.né, followed by the Akkadian title *i-nu Anu ù* ^d*En-lîl,* appears in lines 49–50 (Glassner 2001b: 218). For other views on the identification of this last title, see Charpin 1986: 457 n. 1. On the catalogues in general, see Krecher 1980; Civil 1974: 145 n. 36.

8. See Jacobsen 1939: passim; Steinkeller 2003: passim.

9. See most recently Alster and Jeyes 1986; Alster 1990; Foster 1996: 894–95.

10. On the use of the perfect, see Weissert 1992: 277–78.

11. Grayson 1976: paragraphs 63, 75, 86, and passim.

12. Hulin 1963: 54:36; Tadmor 1977: 211 n. 30.

13. De Certeau 1975: 217.

14. According to Grayson 1975a: 24 and passim, small tablets were for private use.

15. So Grayson 1975a: 8 and passim; 1980a: 174.

16. For example, the colophon of chronicle 10.

17. On the use of written sources, see Glassner 2001a: 188–93.

18. Cf. the note in the Neo-Babylonian laws: "Its case is not complete and is not written (here)" (Roth 1997: 146).

19. For other comparisons between the chronicles and royal inscriptions or official documents, see Grayson 1975a: 54 and passim; Liverani 1990: 80 n. 4. There would of course have been reciprocal influence. See above note 12.

20. Wiseman 1956: 1–4; Grayson 1975a: 12, 13 and n. 43, 22, 29, and passim; 1980a: 174.

21. See the demonstration by Brinkman 1990: 95–96.

22. The collection is known in two editions, one Neo-Assyrian, the other Neo-Babylonian: King 1907; see new edition by Starr 1986.

23. Finkelstein 1963b: 462–63 and passim.

24. Hallo 1991a: 157.

25. Grayson 1966: 72–73; see also the reflections of Cooper 1980.

26. These points of view were expressed when the corpus of materials was still very restricted: King 1907: 1:28; Güterbock 1934: 17.

27. Goetze 1947b: no. 56: i 36–37, iii 8–9.

28. Grayson 1975: 11; and above all Weissert 1992, another reflection, perhaps, of a Babylonian influence in Assyria. Sennacherib was recognized as a descendant of Adapa (Parpola 1993: 174.8).

29. Thus, following Grayson, Van Seters 1983: 82–84.

30. Finkelstein (1963b: 470) recognized objective features in the chronicles; see above all Grayson 1965: 342; 1975a: 10–11, 23, 34, 50; the Babylonian historical running account postulated by Grayson would also have been a document of exceptional objectivity. See also Van Seters 1983: 82–84; Hallo 1988: 189.

31. See Aron 1938.

32. Bloch 1949.

33. Could a productive scheme have lain behind these numerical data? Hallo (1963: 53) sees in the first numbers in manuscript A an arithmetical progression. Steiner (1988; 1989) suggests that the length of a generation lay at the base of the system, which he estimates at forty years. The antediluvian numbers should therefore be divided by forty, with the result again to be divided by forty to obtain a plausible length of reign. After the flood, when the numbers given are greater than five hundred, it is sufficient to divide them by forty. When they are below five hundred, they are to be divided by twelve (twelve being the number of months in the year, thus one month for each year) to arrive at the same result. Other researchers have tried other explanations for the high numbers, discovering a Gaussian distribution for the durations of reigns and dynastic cycles (Lukács and Végso 1974).

34. On all these points, and with further detail, see Brinkman 1973; Weissert 1992: 274–75.

35. For a discussion of this episode, see Glassner 2003.

III

Contents

Chronology lies at the heart of the chronicler's preoccupation with establishing dates and the succession of events in time and recording the names of kings and the length of their reigns. The royal chronicles (nos. 1–5) provide the framework for a universal chronology. In Assyria, the eponym chronicles (nos. 8 and 9) were official sources that, year after year, scrupulously recorded military campaigns and were works of reference.

Conceived in this way, these writings give accounts of various events distributed throughout the period between the third millennium and the second century B.C.E. They are merely scraps of a tumultuous history, of warlike and voraciously conquering kingdoms, and of the founding and destruction of powerful empires, a history punctuated with battles, sieges of cities, usurpations, uprisings, and indeed with corpses. There also are to be found facts of the most varied kind: an epidemic striking Assyria, panic overwhelming Babylon in the days following a New Year festival, the choice of a governor, market prices for some commodities. Elsewhere a dream is mentioned; more rarely, meteorological or climatic information is given, such as the south wind rising or the bitter cold in Ḫamatu.

These writings are inspired by a double purpose: to evoke an often remote past and also to allow comparison of series of facts. A close reading allows other preoccupations to be discerned.

ROYAL CHRONICLES AND POLITICAL CHARTERS

The Chronicle of the Single Monarchy

"When kingship had come down from heaven, kingship was at Kiš": thus begins, in the oldest editions and according to manuscript C, the chronicle called the Chronicle of the Single Monarchy. The composition opens with a succinctly narrated myth with three propositions pregnant with meaning: political organization was a gift of the gods to humans; it was by nature monarchical; and this monarchy had to be manifested in one place, its first appearance being at Kiš.

All societies need to be able to appeal to an order legitimizing their existence, and this order must be manifest in a narrative for which that order by common consent is the basis. The narrative may take the form of myth, an intellectual instrument that, in a form at once symbolic and concrete, provides a framework for political and social concepts and that validates institutions, practices, and customs by its powers of naming and classification. Mesopotamian people were polytheistic; their world was an enchanted universe, teeming with a multitude of divinities, so the chronicler naturally chose to set out his solutions to the problems confronting him by means of myth and with reference to the gods.

So it was that this composition was no history of Mesopotamia but a chronicle of royal power. At the same time, since a specific tenet sustained the undertaking, it served to uphold a political doctrine affirming a principle of unitary monarchy; Mesopotamia was deemed always to have been a single monarchy with a single capital. It advanced this thesis with great skill, making out that insofar as the flow of history could be seen as a succession of royal cycles of variable duration, royal power passed from city to city, each being in turn the unique repository of an institution that had come down from heaven.

King Rīm-Sîn of Larsa, who conquered Isin in 1794, was evidently imbued with this ideology, for he counted the next thirty-one years of his reign beginning with this victory and took care to stress that Isin was "the city of kingship."

In due course, the myth was enriched to the point of conceding, still in the same chronicle, that kingship had come down from heaven on two occasions, each of which inaugurated two successive eras, one preceding a cataclysm and the other following it.

In its fully developped form, the new myth of the flood, to call the cataclysm by its name, a m a r u in Sumerian, was elaborated to include several distinct traditions. One spoke of the anger of a god against his city, which meant that he abandoned it and gave it over to destruction. This theme was relatively old and at the heart of the Sumerian literary genre of laments, and this is the metaphor evoked in the first instance by the term a m a r u.[1]

A second tradition concerned the antediluvian kings, of whom various lists give their names, and those of the cities in which they reigned and the lengths of their respective reigns. There does not seem to have been a unified tradition for these, to judge from the variation in the lists (see table 1).

TABLE 1: THE ANTEDILUVIAN KINGS

Toponyms	Name of King	Length of Reign in Years
A Ku'ara	Alulim	67,000
	[Al]al[ga]r	10,800
Bad-Tibira	Amme-lu-ana	36,000
	En-sipazi-ana	43,200
	divine Dumuzi the shepherd	36,000
Sippar	Enme(n)-dur-anki	6,000
[Šuruppak]	[Ubar]-T[u]t[u]?	[x]
	Ziusudra son of Ubar-Tutu	18,000 + [x]
B Eridu	[. . .]	[x]
Larak	Enme(n)-gal-ana	[x]
	En-sipazi-ana	[x]
Bad-Tibira	divine Dumuzi	[x]
C Eridu	[Alulim]	36,000
	[A]lalgar	72,000
Larsa	[x]kidunnu	72,000
	[x]alima	21,600
Bad-Tibira	[divine Dumu]zi the shepherd	28,800
	[Enm]e(n)-lu-ana	21,600
Larak	[En]-sipazi-ana	36,000
Sippar	Enme(n)-dur-ana	72,000
Šuruppak	Šuruppak son of Ubar-Tutu	28,800
	Ziusudra son of Šuruppak	36,000
D Eridu		
Bad-Tibira		
Larak		
Sippar		
Šuruppak		
E	Ayalu	
	Alalgar	
	Amme-lu-ana	
	Amme-gal-ana	
	Dumuzi the shepherd	
	Enme(n)-dur-anki	
F Babylon	Alôros	36,000
	Alaparos	10,800
Pautibiblon	Almelôn	46,800

	Ammelôn	43,200
	Amegaloros	64,800
	Daônos	36,000
	<Eu>edôrakos	64,800
Larak	Amempsinos	36,000
	Otiartēs	28,800
	Xisuthros or Sisuthros	64,800

A list, school exercise on the reverse of an Old Babylonian tablet from the Diyālā region; Finkelstein 1963a: 40

B list, fragment of Old Babylonian tablet from Nippur; Kraus 1952: 31

C list, Old Babylonian tablet from Sippar; Langdon 1923: pl. VIb

D the Sumerian flood story gives a list of the antediluvian cities; Civil 1969: 140–411; Bottéro and Kramer 1989: 565; Jacobsen 1987: 146–47

E list, from the Seleucid period, of the antediluvian sages (*apkallu*) and kings; van Dijk 1962: 47 and pl. 27, W.20030, 7:1–7

F list of Berossus. The last name varies according to whether the version of Abydenos or Alexander Polyhistor is used. The omission of Sippar is strange because this author states that, before embarking, the flood hero had received instructions to bury in a secure spot, in that city, all the written documents produced by humanity prior to that time. Nevertheless, according to Berossus, Sippar escaped the flood.

To these sources should be added one unpublished document, an Old Babylonian list from Tell Harmal: Finkelstein 1963a: 39 n. 1. Other fragments of lists are cited by Lambert and Millard 1969: 26–27; Borger 1974: passim.

The majority of these kings are otherwise unknown. However, Enme(n)-dur-anki was the inventor of lecanomancy and hepatoscopy; the name Enme(n)-lu-ana survives in two omens; Ziusudra was the hero of the Sumerian flood myth; Šuruppak, the only antediluvian king whose name is attested after the mid-third millennium, left to posterity a collection of maxims and aphorisms.

A final tradition centered on the theme of the interrupted sleep of the gods and the constant clamor of humanity. The Akkadian term *ḫubūru,* "noise, clamor," appears, in fact, in every text that refers to the gods resting and their inactivity. It tells in metaphorical fashion of the creative activity of an industrious humanity and of the independence of a humanity heir to the rebellious spirit of the gods and not yet submissive to divine command.[2] According to the Myth of Atraḫasis, Enlil, irritated by the clamor of humanity at work, thought up the flood as a means of silencing humanity by destroying it, thus to regain tranquillity. Moreover, the word "clamor" (*ḫubūru*) occurs in the introductory mythological narrative of the Babylonian Royal Chronicle (no. 3), a fortunate survival in the available fragments.

Much later, in the Myth of Erra, a semantic shift has occurred, introducing the idea of a humanity noisy on account of their number and thus dangerous to the gods, over whom they might gain the advantage![3]

Later yet, the myth was further enriched with a redundancy of images, and the way the cataclysm was conceived took on a certain consistency with the theme of the joining of the waters of heaven and earth. Reflecting a possibly later tradition, some first-millennium sources evoke the figures of antediluvian sages, part man, part fish, emerging from the ocean and renowned for establishing cosmic order. Since one sage was attached to each king whom he served, after a fashion, as counsellor, the distinction between king and sage seems well established. However, in the Chronicle of the Single Monarchy (no. 1) the note concerning king Mes-ki'ag-gašer, who "entered into the sea and disappeared," suggests that at least during the Isin-Larsa period there was some confusion between them. This is actually a sort of echo of the Legend of Oannes, the Uana of the Mesopotamians who, according to Berossus, was the first sage. Half-man and half-fish, he came out of the Red Sea to bring civilization to humankind, then plunged back in at sunset, going on to another life.[4] After all, were not both Mes-ki'ag-gašer and Uana solar heroes?

The image of an antediluvian humanity grew more substantial with the passage of time, people going so far as to consider that remnants of them survived. Adapa, the first of the sages, in the late period identified with Uana, would leave compositions of his own authorship to posterity. Gilgameš was credited with passing on knowledge from before the flood, and Aššurbanipal professed to have read stone inscriptions dating from before the flood, while Nebuchadnezzar I had already claimed Enme(n)-dur-anki as a remote ancestor.

Two versions of the myth of origin were thus present in the same societies at different periods: the one abbreviated, the other expanded, and the latter braided into a double strand. This introductory myth, in its modified and expanded form, allowed more weight to be given to the past and more prestige to living kings, setting out as well a scheme for historical time. One of the main functions of mythic time was to regulate, with a single comprehensive break, cycles of variable length one from another: cosmic cycles, biological recurrences, and rhythms of political and social life.

Pushing to its limits comparison between certain disastrous events and the original universal cataclysm, Mesopotamian scholars used metaphor (since it was a unique event) to integrate the flood into the pattern of historical events. Even without invoking the theory of cities ruined and abandoned by their protective deities, one is drawn to the self-evident comparison, emphasized by a Sumerian literary composition, of the irruption of the Gutians, around 2100, into Mesopotamia with the inundation of primordial times. Sennacherib used the same comparison at the conquest of Babylon, when he made sure that the effects of his destruction surpassed those caused by the flood.

The problem of the recurrence of the cataclysm was further developed and worked out by the author of the Myth of Erra, when he showed Marduk in soliloquy recalling that he once abandoned Babylon because of his anger and, in so doing, brought about the flood. The god, indeed, formulated this rule: "if I abandon my dwelling, the link [between heaven and earth] will be broken." At the same time, he envisaged his return as of equal consequence: "on my return I saw how difficult it was to put it all together again."

However, the story of the origins of kingship did not stop with its mythic enunciation. Kingship having come down from heaven, it still had to be shown forth among humans. So it is that the names of the first fourteen kings of Kiš, in their recondite fashion, tell a story of the foundation of monarchy.

The names fall into two connected lists. The first six names, only partially preserved, make up a first list and tell of humanity's first phase, before royal authority had been established. The key word, which illuminates the meaning of the entire passage, would seem to be the name Kullassina-bēl, "They are all lord," a clear allusion to a collective process of decision-making.[5] Other traditions, moreover, complete this summary description of primitive humanity, still ignorant of the institution of monarchy but having already adopted the city as place of residence and city-dwelling as a way of life.[6] This choice is explained by the fact that the city is one of the essential features that separates civilized people from uncultured populations. The idea of the city was, in Mesopotamia, one of those fixed points that avoid change and to which the notion of identity was by preference attached. This idea helps one to understand better the reasons why the author of the chronicle emphasized the geographical context of kingship.

With respect to the second list, the order of succession of the eight kings within it was never entirely fixed, it seems, since the variations from one manuscript to another are so numerous (see table 2).

TABLE 2: THE HOUSE OF ETANA

B [Kali]bu[m]	C [Kalib]um	D Mašda (!?)
[Ma]š[da]	[A]tab	Kali[bum]
Atab	Kal[ūmu]m	Atab (!?)
[Ka]lūmum	Zuqāqī[p]	Kalūmum
[Zu]qāqīp	[A]rbum son of Maška'en	Zuqāqīp
[A]rwi'um son of Mašda	[E]dana	Arwi'um son of Mašda
Etana	[Balīḫ son of Etana]	Etana
Walīḫ son of Etana	[Mašda (?)]	Balīḫ son of Etana

G	Kalibum	J	<...>
	Kalūmum		<...>
	Zuqāqīp		<...>
	Atab		<...>
	<Mašda son of> Atab		[Z]uqāqīp
	Arwi'um son of Mašda		[Ar]wi'um
	Etana		[E]dana
	Balīḫ son of Etana		Balī[ḫ] son of Etana

The letters B to J denote the various manuscripts of the Chronicle of the Single Monarchy; see the list below, in chapter 6.

One observation should be made at the outset: with the exception of Etana and his son Balīḫ (variant Walīḫ), all these kings have animal names: Kalibum, "dog"; Mašda, "male gazelle"; Kalūmum, "lamb"; Zuqāqīp, "scorpion"; and Arwi'um, "gazelle." Atab (written Á-tab) is the only name that offers any difficulty. It may be the result of contamination of two Sumerian terms, <gír>.tab, "scorpion," and ti$_8$ (graphic Á), "eagle."[7]

We should recall here the story of Etana,[8] the man who "set every land in order," as the chronicle says of him, and who was, in the imagination of the Mesopotamians, the first king of humanity. It tells of the beginnings of kingship on earth and of the ascension of the hero to heaven, holding on to the body of an eagle, in search of a mysterious "plant of birth." One version has a useful detail, making the eagle say, "You, Etana, are king over the animals." In fact, the author of the list intended to describe Etana as "king of the animals," flanked by gazelles, dogs, lambs, and scorpions. The order in which the others in the list follow him is therefore of no great importance, since Etana figures here as a king amid his court.[9]

Thus, by means of these two lists of personal names, the chronicler could evoke the first developmental stages of power, beginning at the point the institution of kingship had been lowered from heaven, but no exercise of it had yet been made, to its definitive establishment with Etana, when exercise of kingship was endowed with its specific attributes of scepter, diadem, and throne.

Other myths tell us how the demiurge created the world by dividing the universe in two. What the Sumerian mythographer of the first centuries of the second millennium was content to describe in dramatic summary, the author of The Exaltation of Marduk, at the end of the same millennium, expanded into a dense and detailed narrative.[10] The division was the first, primordial act of setting things in order, consisting of separating the antecedent unity into two opposed entities. Claude Lévi-Strauss has drawn attention to similar conceptual systems definable by "an implicit axiomatic according to which all classification proceeds by pairs of contrasts."[11] The original division ran across the social world, creating both the division of sexes and the succession of generations, as well as different opposing forms of power.[12]

Human generations, then, succeeded one another in time but were differently related to each other. Successive generations were diametrically opposed, the second generally replacing the first following a violent confrontation; for alternate generations, the third took the place of the first when it died out. In like manner, the author of the Chronicle of the Single Monarchy arranged successive dynastic sequences like human generations, creating the appearance of an opposition between two successive periods, one "conquered" or "destroyed" royal city being replaced by another, as well as a correspondence between two alternate periods, the third replacing the first when this came to an end. This correspondence is clearly expressed in the sequence Kiš–Akšak–Kiš–Uruk–Akkade–Uruk–Gutium–Uruk–Ur, where the same toponyms alternate with a striking regularity.

This recurrent presence of the same names every second generation evokes well-known facts of ethnography. In certain human groups, in fact, the heir to a role is generally chosen among the grandchildren of the deceased; he then assumes the names, titles, and roles of his predecessor.[13] In Mesopotamia, the custom is well attested from the third millennium on whereby a father gave his son the name of his own father or brother. The name was an emblem in which was concentrated the symbolic capital of a group. To give a child the name of his ancestor was to destine him to succeed that ancestor in the roles and the positions that had been his.[14]

Just as the family was not extinguished with the death of the ancestor, monarchy did not die out at the end of a dynasty but was perpetuated by its reinstitution elsewhere. In other words, after the manner of human generations experiencing birth, old age, and death, dynasties underwent foundation, deterioration, and the loss of sovereignty. This notion of deterioration was an original feature of the chronicle, according to which power did not pass directly from the first to the third generation. With loss, sovereignty passed to another, newly founded dynasty. When that was over, a third dynasty, in its turn invested with supreme authority, took the same name.

All told, no fewer than twenty dynasties were distributed among eleven different places in succession in the chronicle.

TABLE 3: ORDER OF SUCCESSION OF ROYAL CITIES

North	South		Abroad
Kiš 1	Uruk 1	Ur 1	Awan
Kiš 2			Ḫamazi

		Uruk 2/Ur 2	Ur 2/Uruk 2	Adab	Mari
Kiš 3					Akšak
Kiš 4		Uruk 3			
	Akkade	Uruk 4			Gutium
		Uruk 5	Ur 3	Isin	

Observations

1. The numbers refer to the successive dynasties of Kiš (1 to 4), Uruk (1 to 5), and Ur (1 to 3); in manuscript P, the kings of Kiš 1 to 4 are listed as the members of one single dynasty.
2. Kingship passes in turn and alternately from the north (Kiš, Akkade) to the south (Uruk, Ur).
3. In the south, a desire to have the names of Uruk and Ur consistently appear in the same order is evident among certain compilers.
4. In the south, a third city, Adab or Isin, may succeed Ur in holding kingship. However, manuscript P places Adab between Gutium and Uruk (5); there the last king of Adab, Tirigan, is elsewhere mentioned as the last of the Gutian dynasty.
5. In the north, Akkade is a second capital, its kingship joined to the last dynasty of Kiš through the person of the founder, Sargon, former cupbearer to Ur-Zababa of Kiš.
6. Awan, Ḫamazi, Mari, and Gutium were regions foreign to Mesopotamia; so far as Akšak was concerned, it was foreign to the geographical sphere envisaged by the chroniclers. Their presence and their function in the structure of the chronicle are nevertheless indispensable.

The table reveals a more complex situation than was first apparent under the simplifying effects of the linearity appropriate to writing. It emerges, in fact, that four cities—Kiš, Uruk, Ur, and Akkade—hold center stage in the chronicle, the recurring presence of three of them identifying them as the framework around which the chronicle is constructed. These four cities competed with each other to retain kingship and maintained among them relations ranging from opposition, exclusion, and emulation to complementarity. Ur and Uruk were in competition for the kingship of the south, while Akkade succeeded Kiš in the control of the north. Unfortunaltely, the laconic style of the document precludes expanding the set of oppositions and similarities.

The Sumerian language differentiates four degrees of kinship: grandfather (pabilsag); father (ab); son (dumu); and grandson (dumu.KA). These four terms mark out a vertical line of descent by which the relationships among members of family groups could be determined and located within a certain temporal range.[15] Since we know that in Mesopotamian society of the third millennium kinship relations were essential and that the kinship terms in use were the most informative, I suggest presenting the order of succession of the dynasties of Kiš, Uruk, Ur, and Akkade according to the following scheme.

TABLE 4: ORDER OF SUCCESSION OF THE DYNASTIES OF KIŠ, URUK, UR, AND AKKADE

Grandfather: pabilsag	Kiš 1	Kiš 2	Kiš 3+4	Akkade
Father: ab	Uruk 1	Uruk 2/Ur 2	Uruk 3	Uruk 4+5
Son: dumu	Ur 1	Ur 2/Uruk 2	Akkade	Ur 3
Grandson: dumu.KA	Kiš 2	Kiš 3+4		

Observations

1. Some manuscripts combine the third and fourth dynasties of Kiš into a single dynasty.
2. On the dynasty of Gutium, which separates Uruk 4 and 5, see chapter 4.
3. For the specific position of Ur in manuscript P, see below, chapter 6, note 7.

We find here the homonymy postulated between grandfather and grandson. We also discover the preeminence of the dynasty of Akkade, which both took the place of an expected dynasty of Ur and represented itself as successor and heir to the last dynasty of Kiš. Here perhaps we come up against the deep structure of the Chronicle of the Single Monarchy, which later rewritings and redactions could not entirely disguise.

Reference to family structures is only implicit in the chronicle. The Legend of Etana tells of the ascent to heaven of the hero in quest of a "plant of birth," thanks to which, it appears, his wife could present him with a son to succeed him on the throne. The presence of a son indicates that the newly founded kingship was based on the hereditary principle.

Consequently, only the vertical genealogical scheme was operative in the chronicle. Rīmuš and Man-ištūsu, the two sons of Sargon of Akkade, were the sole exception to this rule. This resulted in a certain fluidity in the genealogies, whereby Šū-Sîn, for example, was said to be the son of Amar-Su'en, although in fact he was his brother.

The author of manuscript C laid greater stress than the others on these familial structures, listing the term bala, "dynasty," to identify the familial dynasties whose longevity he notes: "1560 years, dynasty of Enme-nuna"; "1207 + [x] years <dynasty of Barsal-nuna>"; "1525 (?) years, dynasty of Enme(n)-baragesi"; "745 years, dynasty of Mes-ki'ag-gašer"; "131 (?) years, dynasty of Ku-Baba"; "157 (?) years, dynasty of Sargon." Other formulae of the same kind should perhaps be restored in the gaps in the manuscript. The duration of the dynasties varied from two to four generations.

Other sources, manuscripts D and N of the same chronicle and the Babylonian Royal Chronicle (no. 3), the oldest source for which goes back to the last years of the Isin period, called the successive periods during which one city held kingship by the same word bala. This term indicated, rather than a linear, quantitative, or homogeneous time flow, one that was seen as a structural and qualitative relationship between two points. Rather than to a duration of fixed length, it referred to a span within that duration, the specific length of which could vary from a few days to several years. It referred as well to the exercise in rotation of certain roles by quite different people, ranging from the humblest to provincial governors, kings, and even the gods themselves.[16] As shown by the presence of totals at the end of the Nippur manuscripts of the Chronicle of the Single Monarchy, time was measured by the number and the duration of the successive dynasties. In sum, its dating system was a reflection of the relationship among cycles of rule.

It has become conventional to translate bala as "dynasty," but "dynasty" denotes succession of rulers of the same bloodline.[17] Consequently, "cycle" would be preferable, allowing a distinction between family cycle and local cycle. The same local cycle may embrace several family cycles, and, conversely, family cycle and local cycle may be the same. The unfolding of history could be represented as a series of cycles, each self-contained. These cycles succeeded one another according to a definite order and lasted for their allotted time, until the cities that were home to them were "conquered," "destroyed," or "abandoned."

The transfer of kingship from one city to another, even if implicit in a divinely ordered dichotomy that set up as antagonists to one another royal dynasties originating in the same principle, was one of those moments of transition when the contrary forces constituting the universe came into conflict and when the world was vulnerable to danger. This transfer was expressed by the use of stereotypical and repeated formulae as often as required, for the transitions were points of conflict where order was threatened by transgression and only the carrying out of a socially acceptable action allowed resolution of the crisis by legitimizing the transgression. Since saying it made it so, specified formulae, reminiscent of ritualized acts such as war or implementation of divine decrees, sufficed to note normalization of the situation. Most manuscripts used the formula "city name$_1$ was defeated (or abandoned); its kingship was carried to city name$_2$." The latest sources chose another formula: "the dynasty of city name$_1$ changed; its kingship was carried to city name$_2$."

Return to a normal state of affairs thus required a process of foundation, essential for bringing about a return to order after a transition. So if we except the original foundation of kingship noted above, the chronicle contains three foundation narratives, those of Uruk 1, Kiš 3, and Akkade.

"Foundation" means marking off a space, distinguished from the rest of the world by being given a location and a name. The account of the foundation of Uruk is a good example of this, as it consists of establishing places and giving them names. The details of the chronicle speak for themselves. The first ruler of the dynasty, Mes-ki'ag-gašer, ruled over Eanna as "lord" and "king," the title "king of Uruk" appearing only with his son Enmerkar, who is said to have founded the city of this name. Moreover, knowing that Gilgameš was "lord" of Kulaba, the neighboring city to Eanna, it is easy to understand how Mes-ki'ag-gašer, "king of Eanna," conquered Kulaba, a city whose master bore the title of "lord." Enmerkar, having united the cities into one urban area, founded a new city, which he called Uruk and of which he was the ruler.

Curiously, after the foundation of universal kingship the first royal city, Kiš, had a second, later foundation, for it is said that Ku-Baba "consolidated the foundations of Kiš." Because Ku-Baba was a woman, an innkeeper, and a "king" of Kiš, she was on three counts a devotee of Inanna, patroness of inns, patron deity of the city, and goddess of sovereignty. Both were women, and this quality determined both their personalities. In a world that thought of itself in the masculine and where sovereignty was an eminently masculine quality (the word "king," lugal in Sumerian, had no feminine counterpart), the female sex was the image of inversion of the norm. It was therefore essential to refound Kiš when a woman ruled it.

The new royal city of Akkade was founded in its turn. The chronographic notice about Sargon indicates that he, a gardener's son in origin, performed the role of cupbearer to Ur-Zababa, king of Kiš, before founding the new city. In historical terms, the foundation consisted of transforming a preexisting city into a royal capital. These brief allusions prefigure the pseudoautobiography of a much later date, in which the hero, through trials and ordeals marking the stages of his achievement of power, became the archetype of the founder of a universal monarchical rule. It is noteworthy that the chronicle gave no account of the foundation of Ur.

Making use of these concise foundation narratives and chronographic notices that gave brief allusions and narrated a few spectacular actions, the chronicler created a medium by which he could record deeds of great ancestors who were subjects of legend and epic, but in only the sketchiest detail. The medium was limited on one side by myth but opened on the other into history. Myth of origins here served as prologue or as an "archaeology" introducing history. Legend portrayed a latent period that allowed history to appear. But since the chronographic notices fell within a background that did not proclaim its legendary character, and even appeared to preclude it, one sees in them a certain historiographic quality.

Enme(n)-baragesi of Kiš was certainly an epic hero, but he was also a historical person who left several original inscriptions, the oldest

Mesopotamian royal inscriptions so far known. After him, we know that Enbi-Ištar of Kiš was also a historical person and that he was defeated by En-šakuš-ana of Uruk. With this last king we enter real history and do not leave it again, even though legend and history still mingle in the person of Sargon at the beginning of the dynasty of Akkade.

Consequently, we see in the Chronicle of the Single Monarchy a theoretical construct. The linear presentation that set forth its content in a succinct manner, by simultaneously listing chronological notices and cycles, offered an economical means of giving the reader information reduced to pertinent facts and arranged according to a principle of familial order, the cycles succeeding one another in linear fashion like human generations in a genealogical tree or like kinship terms in a lexical list. The document was thus consciously and deliberately constructed, but as an inevitable result of its reduction to writing, the cyclical passage of time is no longer clearly visible. Moreover, it arranged in succession what could actually have occurred simultaneously, for an effect of writing down was to create by simplification a superficial order that was more a reflection of the physical arrangement of the text than of intellectual speculation.[18]

This is why I propose reading the Chronicle of the Single Monarchy by means of a sinusoidal diagram (table 5). This layout has the advantage

TABLE 5: THE FIRST DYNASTY OF KIŠ

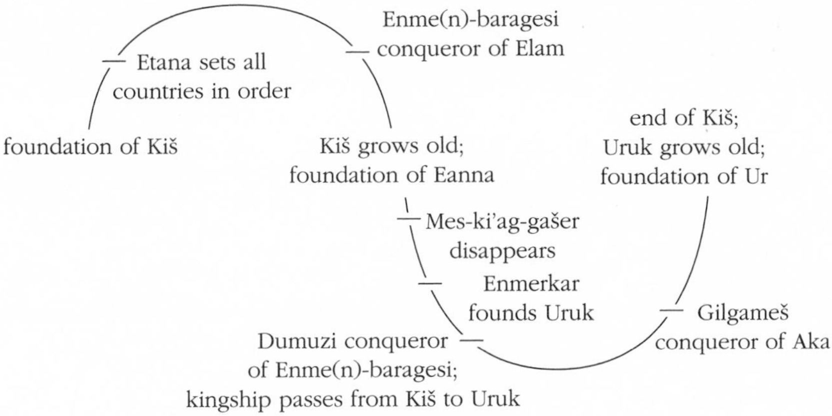

of highlighting the moments of transition and of presenting significant episodes as successive and ordered points in a linear sequence. The procedure adopted by ancient scribes, of linear deployment, simplified the author's thinking to the point of making it incomprehensible, by reducing it to a one-dimensional form, although the presence of biographical notices, however short, added a two-dimensional character. The sinusoidal diagram allows restoration of the cyclical motion that the constraints of writing had obliterated.

Let us consider, for example, version C of the chronicle. According to this, the dynasty of Uruk 1 succeeded the dynasty of Kiš 1, yet one of its kings, Dumuzi, achieved the astonishing and probably unique feat of capturing, singlehandedly, the king Enme(n)-baragesi, who had reigned 2,560 years before him! A sinusoidal reading allows the resolution of this apparent contradiction (see table 5).

The following table (table 6) includes both the linear and sinusoidal readings. We have retained the dynastic order as it appears in manuscript G, but the scheme remains true whatever the variants.

TABLE 6: HISTORY OF KINGSHIP ACCORDING TO THE CHRONICLE OF THE SINGLE MONARCHY

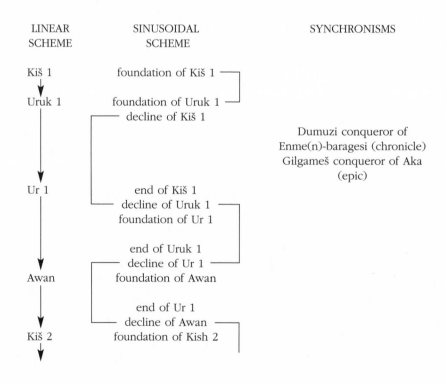

LINEAR SCHEME	SINUSOIDAL SCHEME	SYNCHRONISMS
Kiš 1	foundation of Kiš 1	
Uruk 1	foundation of Uruk 1 decline of Kiš 1	
		Dumuzi conqueror of Enme(n)-baragesi (chronicle) Gilgameš conqueror of Aka (epic)
Ur 1	end of Kiš 1 decline of Uruk 1 foundation of Ur 1	
	end of Uruk 1 decline of Ur 1	
Awan	foundation of Awan	
	end of Ur 1 decline of Awan	
Kiš 2	foundation of Kish 2	

↓	end of Awan decline of Kiš 2 foundation of Ḫamazi	
Ḫamazi ↓	end of Kiš 2 decline of Ḫamazi foundation of Uruk 2	En-šakuš-ana conqueror of Enbi-Ištar (historical inscriptions)
Uruk 2 ↓	end of Ḫamazi decline of Uruk 2 foundation of Ur 2	
Ur 2 ↓	end of Uruk 2 decline of Ur 2 foundation of Adab	
Adab ↓	end of Ur 2 decline of Adab foundation of Mari	
Mari ↓	end of Adab decline of Mari foundation of Kiš 3	
Kiš 3 ↓	end of Mari decline of Kiš 3 foundation of Akšak	
Akšak ↓	end of Kiš 3 decline of Akšak foundation of Kiš 4	the son of Ku-Baba succeeds his mother
Kiš 4 ↓	end of Akšak decline of Kiš 4 foundation of Uruk 3	
Uruk 3 ↓	end of Kiš 4 decline of Uruk 3 foundation of Akkade	Sargon cupbearer of Ur-Zababa (historiographical sources)
Akkade* ↓	end of Uruk 3 decline of Akkade foundation of Uruk 4	Sargon conqueror of Lugal-zagesi (historical inscriptions)
Uruk 4 ↓	end of Akkade decline of Uruk 4	

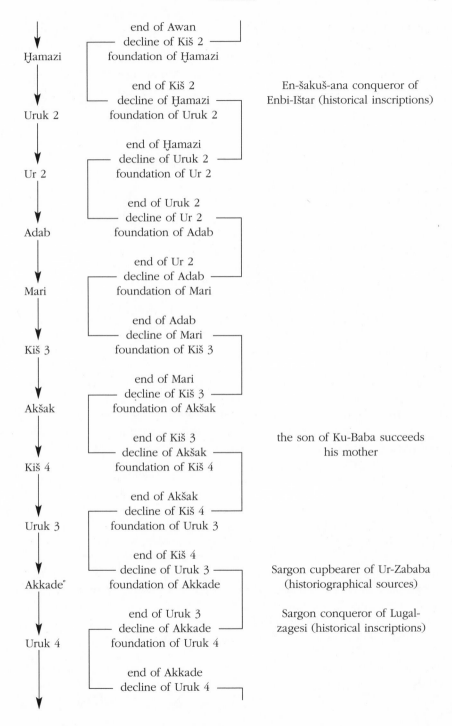

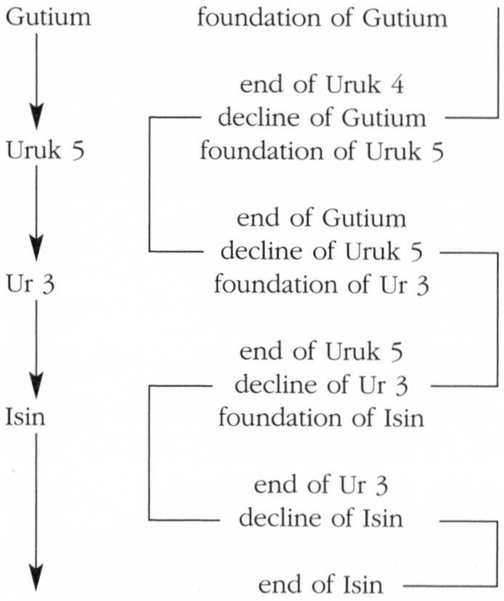

A sinusoidal reading, then, has the merit of demonstrating one aspect of the chronicler's thought that would otherwise be invisible: the affirmation of the continuity of monarchy in Mesopotamia and its discontinuity elsewhere, where in any case, if the truth be told, it had no place.

Once the formula had been found, it was merely a question of applying it. However, the linear dimension, in the course of time, appears to have eclipsed the cyclical perception. The Chronicle of the Single Monarchy was an official canon reflecting the views of its time. The indisputable quality of the work makes it a source of the first importance for the study of historical writing and political thought at the end of the third millennium.

The Babylonian and Hellenistic Royal Chronicles

The Babylonian continuations of the chronicles, with the passage of time, distanced themselves a little from their model. If the myth of origin and the foundation narratives fully retained their place in the Babylonian Royal Chronicle (no. 3), the Hellenistic Royal Chronicle (no. 4), on the other hand, ignored them completely. Similarly, the formula used to make the transition from one dynasty to another was slightly modified, henceforth expressed in these terms: "the dynasty of city $name_1$ changed; its kingship went to city $name_2$." Eventually, being already an optional usage in the Babylonian Royal Chronicle, it disappeared from the Hellenistic Royal Chronicle. This last, moreover, was open to the new fashion of writing history that began in the Neo-Babylonian period. We see that in this development the sinusoidal reading of the composition was gradually forgotten and that a more linear view of time was held, royal cycles summoned to succeed one another in time in the usual way.

The Assyrian Royal Chronicle

As with the older editions of the Chronicle of the Single Monarchy, the Assyrian Royal Chronicle (no. 5) did not know the myth of the flood and began with a list of proper names. The similarity stops there, however. While in Sumer and Akkad the cities already existed, waiting for kingship to come, the narrative of the origins of kingship began in Assyria with seventeen proper names listed under the heading "kings who dwelt in tents." A closer reading of the document leads to the subdivision of this number into two separate lists, which appear in sequence.

The first twelve names are those of Amorite tribes, of divinities, of places, or of eponymous ancestors.[19] The same names appear in a Babylonian funerary ritual, an invocation of the souls of the ancestors during a commemorative meal (*kispum*), whose purpose was to reinforce the ties binding the living and the dead by sharing the same food. This document dates from the time of Ammī-ṣaduqa of Babylon.[20]

> Aram-madara, Ṭûbti-yamuta, Yamquzzu-ḫalama, Ḫeana, Namzu, Didānu, Zummabu, Namḫû, Amnānum, Yaḫrurum, Ipti-yamuta, Buḫazum, Šū-mālika, Ašmadu, Abī-yamuta, Abī-ditāna, Mam-[. . .], Šu-[. . .]-ni-[. . .], Dādu-banaya (?), Sum[u]-abum, Sumu-lā-[El], Sabium, Apil-Sîn, Sîn-muballiṭ, Ḫammurabi, Samsu-ilūna, Abī-ēšu[ḫ], Ammī-ditā[na], the turn of the troops[21] of Amurru, the turn of the troops of Ḫana, the turn <of those> of Gutium, the turn <of all those> who are not written on this tablet and the soldiers fallen in terrible wars in the service of their rulers, sons or daughters of kings, yea, all of you, simple mortals from the rising to the setting of the sun, you who have no one to make a food-offering or to invoke your name, come, take your share of this meal and this drink, and bless Ammī-ṣaduqa, son of Ammī-ditāna, king of Babylon.

Behind the name Ṭûbti-yamuta are concealed two names, those of Ṭudiya and Adamu of the Assyrian Royal Chronicle; similarly, behind Aram-madara lie the names of Ḫarḫaru and Mandaru, while behind Yamquzzu-ḫalama lie those of Yangi and Suḫlāmu. Zummabu in one list corresponds to Zuabu in the other. Namzu corresponds to Imṣu or Ḫarṣu, and Namḫû to Nuabu. Even if the order changes, and despite the fusion of the first six names of the chronicle into three new names, it is plain that the two lists are identical. The Babylonian source added, further, the names of two Amorite tribes settled in southern Babylonia, those of Yaḫrurum and

Amnānum. We can see that all these names are Amorite, even though some of them have been transmitted to us in altered form.

A second list of personal names begins with Abazu in the Assyrian Royal Chronicle and with Ipti-yamuta in the Babylonian ritual. The Babylonian source starts this second list with a new double name formed by combining the verbal roots **yiptiḫ* and **yamwuta*. After some obscure names, one of which was perhaps Dādu-banaya, a contemporary of Ur-Ninurta of Isin, it lists in order the names of all the kings of Babylon down to Ammī-ṣaduqa, the reigning monarch and the one who commissioned the text. In other words, a theoretical list of royal ancestors was composed in this second list.

In the Assyrian chronicle, the second list is subdivided into two subgroups, distinguishable by a horizontal line marked in the clay. The final two entries in the first subgroup are identical with the last two of the second, forcefully affirming the unity of the sequence. The second subgroup, like the Babylonian ritual, gives a list of the Amorite ancestors of the reigning monarch; here Aminu is the first name on the list because the genealogy is in retrograde form.[22] As for the first subgroup, it is composed of five names of which only two, Azaraḫ and Apiašal (or, if preferred, *Aḏar-aḫ and *Api-ašal) are Amorite, a point worth emphasizing.

To understand the purport of the Assyrian chronicle better, we must attempt to reconstruct its origins. Diachronic relationship is an organizational principle of history in all archaic societies, within which ruling dynasties construct etiological genealogies embracing the birth of humanity and its division into differentiated social groups. These genealogies are works of imagination and manipulation, intended to affirm the prestige and authority of the ruling monarchs, genealogies in which the duration of time is deduced in proportion to its distance from the present and in which telescopings occur, ancestors who caused no divisions being omitted for the simple reason that they played no part in the linkages between groups.[23]

It is precisely this sort of genealogy that was set out in the Assyrian Royal Chronicle, as in the Babylonian ritual, and this is the meaning of the first list of proper names, which alluded to the most extended social groupings. It told of the origin of the Amorites. The complete identity between the two sources, Assyrian and Babylonian, is to be explained by the fact that in all probability there was only one Amorite account of their origins;[24] every name mentioned corresponded to a segmentation of the group, the person named being the ancestor-founder of a new lineage. The second list, as we have seen, offered a selective version of the respective genealogies of the two kings, Aminum on the one hand and Ammī-ṣaduqa on the other. The two sources diverge at this point. The difference can be explained by their presentation of the names of the immediate ancestors of local rulers.

Myths of origins and genealogies of dominant families are the stuff of oral memory.[25] Each list contains a dozen names. Evans-Pritchard has shown that in segmented and nonliterate societies memory never exceeds eleven or twelve generations of lineage.[26] The written Babylonian ritual exceeds these limits.

Was the founding myth of Assyrian kingship content to reproduce a purely Amorite oral tradition by reducing it to written form? It seems not. In fact, we have already noted the presence of some non-Amorite personal names mingled with the litany of the ancestors. One notes particularly Bēlū, a name meaning "They (are) lords." The term is in the plural and cannot but remind us of Kullassina-bēl, "They are all lord," used in the account of the foundation of kingship according to the Chronicle of the Single Monarchy (no. 1). So how can we fail to note the impact of this composition on the Assyrian chronicle, which in its turn was trying to evoke in its readers' minds the image of a primitive humanity unacquainted with the rule of kings?

The myth of origin, as reproduced at the beginning of the chronicle, was a result, then, of a fusion into an original synthesis of two entirely different traditions of origins: one Amorite, the other Sumero-Akkadian, the first an oral tradition, the second written. But this very process of combination must have led to alteration in the wording of both. The memory of their ancestors was henceforth lost to those wielding power, and reference to the city and city-dwelling, a way of signifying the identity of a social group, fell into disuse. The mention of the name of Bēlū in the Assyrian chronicle also conjured up an autochthonous institution, since in the Old Assyrian period *bēlum,* "lord," refered to a specific function in the assembly in the capital.[27]

In the Babylonian ritual, moreover, certain names have come down to us in an altered or intentionally distorted form. Writing allowed rearrangement, correction, and changing the meaning of certain words, as well as relocating the whole in another context and giving the entire work a new significance. There would no doubt be much to say, if the state of the sources allowed it, about the reasons that led the Babylonian scribe to alter the names of the distant ancestors of Ammī-ṣaduqa and to create from scratch names that, as their meanings show, were invented for the occasion.[28]

We may suppose that the influence of the Chronicle of the Single Monarchy was not restricted to the mythological introduction but that the author of the Assyrian chronicle likewise proposed alternation between local royal dynasties, royal power passing from city to city. Reworking of the material in the second half of the second millennium unfortunately contributed to the obscuring of this initial structure.

However, so far as we know, Aminu ruled not in Aššur but in Ekallātum, just as his father Ilā-kabkabû had and as his brother Śamśī-Addu and that king's son Išme-Dagān would after him. According to this hypothesis, at least two cities would have made up the core of the chronicle, Ekallātum and Aššur, with two royal dynasties, one running from Sulili or Sulê to Ilu-šūma[29] and another inaugurated by Ērišum I. A third city may also have appeared in the chronicle, Šeḫna, which Śamśī-Addu renamed Šubat-Enlil. He was no doubt already king of Šeḫna before renaming it. Obviously, Śamśī-Addu could not have reigned in the same place as his brother Aminu, who according to the Eponym Chronicle of Mari (no. 8) was still alive when Śamśī-Addu came to power. A dynasty of Šeḫna could have been represented, at least, by Śamśī-Addu.

We do not know who commissioned this chronicle in its first form, perhaps some king of Amorite stock who had been subject to Sumero-Akkadian culture. Śamśī-Addu seems the obvious choice. Moreover, he was certainly well acquainted with the Chronicle of the Single Monarchy, a copy of which was found in Šubat-Enlil, his capital. Another funerary ritual from Mari, a meal offered to the ancestral spirits of the ruling family, testifies as well to the mixture of cultures, Amorite and Sumero-Akkadian, during his reign: "The funerary meal (will be offered) to Sargon and Narām-Sîn, the Yaradu Ḫaneans and to those of Numḫâ and [. . .]."[30]

We find here the names of Ḫanû (the Yaradu clan is otherwise unknown) and, as Namḫû, already encountered in the Babylonian ritual, Hanû and Nuabu in the royal chronicle. They tell the same origin story, yet again, of the Amorites, but the mention of Sargon and Narām-Sîn of Akkade takes the place of the genealogy of the Amorite ruler.

Śamśī-Addu's biography recalls in many respects that of Babur, founder of the Moghul Empire, even though Śamśī-Addu's descendants did not win the same glory as that of the prince of the Ferghana. A member of the ruling family of Ekallātum, Śamśī-Addu was obliged to flee his country and found refuge in Babylonia,[31] where he was introduced to Sumero-Akkadian culture. Later, having no doubt become king of Šeḫna, he reconquered his native city before going on to conquer Aššur and Mari. He was in turn king of Ekallātum and Aššur and established himself at Šeḫna, which he made his capital under the name of Šubat-Enlil. He spent long periods in Akkade, an ostentatious demonstration of the admiration he professed for the former kings of that city in whose footsteps he wanted to follow. He adopted their titulature, became, like them, "king of Akkade," "powerful king," "king of all (civilized lands)," titles to which he added the epithet "he who bound together the lands between the Tigris and the Euphrates."[32]

The Royal Chronicle of Lagaš

In this chronicle (no. 6), the flood was parodied. One will recall that in the Myth of Atraḫasīs, humanity, created for the service of the gods, was laden with the heavy task of agricultural labor and multiplied ceaselessly; its "clamor" increased to the point of preventing the gods from enjoying their rest, and the flood was decided upon to reduce it to silence. The author from Lagaš chose to travesty these facts. The events that he described occurred, first, after the flood and not before it, and the flood was mentioned only with the laconic formula used by the author of the Chronicle of the Single Monarchy. Kingship not yet having been lowered from heaven, only "governorship" existed, an obvious satire by the author against the titulary of the kings of Lagaš who, in the mid-third millennium, had used the title "governor," ensí, in preference to the royal title lugal, no doubt to show their devotion to the gods. Furthermore, human beings, contrary to the flood myth, kept silent, for, without the right tools, they did not work but relied on the rain for sustenance. In this manner, they saw their numbers diminish, the livestock waste away, their land fall into disuse; in short, famine arrived. Worse, they did not give the gods their due respect. The gods finally decided to give them the necessary tools to allow them to begin tilling the fields. The end of the satire is unfortunately lost in a long lacuna.

In the sequel, in which the text gave details of the imaginary scheme of the kings of Lagaš, no alternation between royal dynasties is to be seen. The biographical notices told of the excavation of irrigation canals, the construction of temples, palaces, cities and their fortifications, and occasionally of the literary skills of certain rulers. These were so many allusions to the routine activities of a Mesopotamian ruler. Two notices alone strayed from this entirely normal pattern: one mentioned an as yet uncivilized humanity, while the other announced that Gudea was the son of neither his father nor his mother, obviously a reference to an inscription of this king,[33] as well as an adroit reapplication of an insignificant statement to give to Gudea the appearance of a founding hero, like Gilgameš or Sargon. Its genealogies, of course, are fictitious.

LOCAL CHRONICLES

Dionysius of Halicarnassus stated that local and priestly chronicles had preceded the historiography of Herodotus and Thucydides, and it has been established that some cities and sanctuaries in Greece had their own chronicles. Were there such chronicles in Mesopotamia? Would the Sumerian Tummal Chronicle (no. 7) be the only survival of an otherwise lost urban or local historiography?

The Tummal was a little-known sanctuary of the goddess Ninlil, the consort of Enlil, the chief god of the Sumerian pantheon. It was situated, it seems, halfway between Nippur and Šuruppak. This goddess, along with other deities including Enlil, received there at certain times of the year offerings and sacrifices. This little document, then, has all the features of a "local, unambitious legend."[34]

Local chronicles, by definition, stress the particularities of local communities, their most obvious purpose being to pay homage to the continuity and venerability of a sanctuary. This was certainly the intention of the chronicle of the Tummal, and a similar purpose is apparent in a chronicle from Uruk (no. 48). Šulgi was reproached in it, along with his associate, the blind man of letters Lu-Nanna, for having altered the rites and the cult, not of Marduk, whose treasures had already been pillaged, but of the god Anu, the ancient lord of the city whose cult, once eclipsed by that of the powerful god of Babylon, enjoyed a renaissance in the late period. Elsewhere, at Larsa, and at the cost of some manipulation of the sources, a list of antediluvian kings incorporated this city in the series of cities antedating the flood (see table 1, document C).

However, neither of these two chronicles was motivated by a single-minded purpose to restrict itself to events of local interest. It is undeniable, as the choice of royal names alone already shows, that they were attempts, separated by an interval of fifteen hundred years, to integrate local facts into the general course of history. The chronicle of Uruk recalled the figures of Ur-Namma and Šulgi, which it took care, admittedly, to link with the former king of Uruk, Utu-ḫegal. As for the chronicle of the Tummal, with the names of Enme(n)-baragesi and his son Aka, Mes-ane-pada and his son Mes-ki'ag-nuna, Gilgameš and his son Ur-lugal, Nanne and his son Mes-ki'ag-Nanna, Ur-Namma and his son Šulgi, it referred to the royal dynasties celebrated by the Chronicle of the Single Monarchy (no. 1), especially those of Kiš 1, Uruk 1, and Ur 1 to 3. The order of succession of these dynasties was the same according to all the manuscripts except one: Kiš 1, Ur 1, Uruk 1, Ur 2, and Ur 3. The last manuscript is different. It has the sequence Kiš 1, Uruk 1, Ur 1 to 3. As we shall see, it is remarkable that this order and the change of order proposed were an exact reflection of the manuscript tradition of the royal chronicle. Seeking to insert local events into the fabric of general history, it is clear that the authors of these chronicles hoped to achieve a better understanding of it.

Not the least of the merits of the Tummal Chronicle and of the Uruk Chronicle concerning the Kings of Ur was their thesis that history was always determined by the place where it happened. Numerous allusions in the Neo-Babylonian chronicles to the celebration of the New Year festival or to its interruption suggest that other sanctuary chronicles may have existed that would also have formed the basis for learned inquiry. These traditions certainly provided a reliable network of symbolic markers across the terrain of history.

THE NEO-BABYLONIAN CHRONICLES: TOWARD A SERIAL HISTORY

In the Neo-Babylonian period, intellectual life was profoundly modified, and a new passion for history emerged. The sixth-century Chaldean kings were by no means the least assiduous in this activity. The composition of the Chronicle of the Single Monarchy (no. 1) in the twenty-second century had been the product of complicity between history and power, the one serving the interests of the other. In the seventh and sixth centuries history acquired a certain autonomy. In the space of fifteen hundred years, Babylon had invented a long history for itself. A new vision of the role of history appeared, sustained by the conviction, asserted after the eighteenth century with increasing vigor, of the primacy of Babylon and of its god Marduk. This favored a political line of reasoning that no longer guided the conduct of a ruler but told him what he could or could not do. History was no longer the handmaid.

Two series of compositions began to be written that clarified each other in that the implicit philosophy of the one was revealed by the explanations of the other. Four features characterize the first series.

GREATER CONTROL OF CHRONOLOGY. This was no longer merely noted reign by reign but also year by year, noting the month and occasionally the day. Chronicle 16 marked a transitional stage in this development. In its initial stages it was highly selective, noting on average one year in three, but it became increasingly detailed, omitted years becoming the exception.

PREDILECTION FOR THE RECENT PAST OR THE CONTEMPORARY WORLD. Politics, war, and religion were the themes explored, with a wealth of events treated. The study of recent history was not restricted to Babylonia but included matters in Assyria and Elam and, later, Persia and the successors to Alexander the Great, at least insofar as they impinged on Babylonian matters.

A DESIRE TO HOLD STRICTLY TO STATEMENT OF THE FACTS. Events were simply noted one after another. The text was divided into paragraphs by horizontal lines, each paragraph covering one reign or one year, with certain exceptions (nos. 29 and 52).

A historical culture blossomed, freed from fables and supernatural interventions, and even when these interventions remained implicit, the chroniclers' silence concerning them shows that they were clearly distancing themselves from such ideas. It was for others to offer explanations. The chroniclers had no need to; the new chronicle writing was born of the rationalization of tasks. At the same time, elements constituting a new literary genre appeared, with their own style and an original narrative thrust.

The Hellenistic Royal Chronicle (no. 4), the final heir to the Chronicle of the Single Monarchy (no. 1) and the Babylonian Royal Chronicle (no. 3), seemed faithful to its models, its author even going so far as to use an archaizing form of the graphic sign AK to write the verb "to rule," as though he wished to stress this link, but departed from them in many respects. No longer considering an appeal to origins indispensable, it disengaged itself from myth and reflected the influence of the Neo-Babylonian chronicles, whose formulae and themes it adopted.

CONSTRUCTION OF SIMILAR SERIES. Taken out of the historical continuum, each event was narrated as a unique situation, but its inclusion in a chronicle also indicated that it was part of a series. The chronicler's inventory of themes focused on one particular topic according to which the reported facts were organized: war, accession and death of kings, civil disturbances, interruptions of cultic practice. Such exposition of a certain theme calls to mind the battle-history of our old schoolbooks. In any case, two chronicles have a note, "battles," in the margin.

But we should not stop here. The Neo-Babylonian chronicles were the forum in which such topics achieved their fullest development. They appear to have been compendia of suitable examples a man of letters would need to speak with authority on his chosen subject. Choice of topic obviously served to provide multiple instances.

It would be pointless to dwell on war, with its long lists of battles (at times indecisive), of sieges, of numbers of dead or prisoners, with here a king slipping away from his adversary and there the enemy taking flight. Three isolated events suffice: the exploit of taking assault towers across the Euphrates (no. 22), the capture of Babylon at night by Nabopolassar's troops (no. 21), and the decapitation of the kings of Sidon, Kundu, and Sissû, whose heads were sent to Assyria (nos. 16 and 18). The report of decapitation was a brief allusion to Assyrian custom that Aššurbanipal recalled as fullfilling an ancient oracle: "you shall cut off the heads of your enemies, and you shall pour out a libation of wine over them."[35] The justification for this had a long history, since Gilgameš himself did it when he cut off Ḫuwawa's head. A bas-relief from an Assyrian palace shows a prisoner carrying a severed head hung around his neck, and royal annals were prolix on the subject. The most famous example is that of the king of Elam, Tepti-Ḫumban-Inšušinak, beheaded along with his son when attempting to flee the battlefield. A son-in-law or brother-in-law of the king is shown wounded on another bas-relief, beseeching an Assyrian soldier to cut his head off and to carry it to his master to win him fame. Dunanu, the sheikh of the Gambūlu and an ally of Elam, was forced to parade through the streets of Arbēla with the king's head hanging from his neck. His brother Samgunu and the royal herald Ḫumban-kiden were displayed in their turn with the head of another Elamite, Šutur-Naḫḫunte, governor of Ḫîdalu. The king's head ultimately hung from a tree in the gardens of the royal palace. On a final bas-relief we glimpse a bucolic scene in which Aššurbanipal and the queen sip drinks under a trellis, the king stretched out on a couch, the queen seated, and accompanied by musicians.[36] (See also no. 53: Nabonidus cutting off the heads of the population of Ammanānum.)

An important motif of warfare narrations in the chronicles was deportation of gods. Chronicles 16, 17, and 19 tell of the deportation of the gods of Šapazza, Dēr, and Uruk to Assyria. Chronicle 19 and others tell of Nergal carried off to Babylon. Curiously, chronicle 16 remains silent on the exile of Marduk.[37]

Mesopotamian gods were localized and visible, made manifest in their statues. Those whose statues were carried off into exile, removed from their territory and deprived of their daily cult, were thus powerless. Along with the deportation of populations, the desecration of shrines, the violation of tombs by removing bones (some of the vanquished even being forced to crush the bones of their own ancestors), and the carrying off of a symbolic piece of conquered soil (for such was the terrible ritual elaborated by the Assyrians), the exile of the gods completed the physical and cultural reduction of the defeated country to the point of nonexistence and bestowed incomparable luster on a now irreversible royal victory.[38]

We do not know the fate reserved for divine statues following their exile, but they were never destroyed,[39] since they could always be returned to their original shrines if peace was reestablished or if victory went to the other side later. We see the return of gods to Susa (no. 21), to Akkade (nos. 16 and 18), to Dēr (nos. 16 and 18), to Uruk (no. 16), and to Sippar (no. 18). The statue of Marduk, exiled in 689, returned with great ceremony to Babylon only in 668, some twenty years later, with the accession of Šamaš-šuma-ukīn. The new king escorted it with an army, and the gods Šamaš, Nergal, and Nabû gathered to welcome it (nos. 18 and 20).

The theme of accession in the Neo-Babylonian chronicles, for which four types may be observed, was perhaps a borrowing from Assyrian historiography. In one type, the king succeeded his father (nos. 16, 21, and 24). In the case of Aššurbanipal and Šamaš-šuma-ukīn, who both succeeded their father Esarhaddon, the former ascended the Assyrian throne at the end of 669, while the latter ascended that of Babylon at the beginning of 668. A disparity of a year was thus contrived, which the official chronology took into account in giving precedence to the king of Assyria. So, too, it was handled in chronicle 18, but chronicle 16 refers to simultaneous accession of the two kings.

In another type, the king was put on the throne by a foreign ruler. In chronicle 16, Sennacherib chose successively a Babylonian nobleman brought up at the Assyrian court and then his own son to rule over Babylon. Another type was the successful individual, as in chronicle 21, with the case of Nabopolassar, whose seizure of power in Babylon was described briefly, taking a certain liberty with chronology, as well as the war in which he drove out the Assyrian occupier. A last type was a rebel who seized power (no. 16).

Beyond the specific instances, the chronicles sometimes show they knew how institutions were supposed to work. For instance, chronicle 16 notes that Ḫumban-nikaš of Elam was succeeded by his sister's son, an evident allusion to the ancient custom of succession in Elamite royal families. The remark was relevant beyond pure erudition, for an Elamite princess, sister of king Tammaritu, had married a member of the Babylonian family of Gaḫal, to which belonged Nergal-ušēzib, whom another king of Elam had set on the throne of Babylon. A certain Šuma, of the same family of Gaḫal, who was certainly a son of this union, as a Babylonian letter asserts, was therefore entitled to call himself "son of the sister of the king of Elam" and so was in fact in a position to make a legitimate claim to the Elamite throne.[40]

Another example of this kind of interest is offered by chronicles 39 and 40, when presenting king Erra-imittī of Isin offering the throne to a substitute king, the gardener Enlil-bāni. But on that occasion, the legitimate king died and the substitute king took the throne. One can see here the attempt of the Babylonian chroniclers to criticize the Assyrian institution of a substitute king (during the reign of the substitute king, the rightful one was designated with the title "the gardener") by showing its inefficacy.[41]

The theme of the death of kings also allows a typology: natural death (nos. 16, 17, and 18), death as a result of illness (nos. 16, 17, and 18; also in no. 26, mention of the illness of Nabonidus, from which, however, he recovered); assassination (no. 16; Berossus adds two further examples, those of Amēl-Marduk and Labāši-Marduk); death in war (no. 17, Šamaš-šuma-ukīn died in the burning of his palace, defeated by his brother Aššurbanipal; curiously, Ctesias creates Sardanapalus from this, a corruption of the name Aššurbanipal) or in captivity (nos. 16 and 17). The death of queens was not systematically recorded; the only instances are those of the principal wife of Esarhaddon (no. 18; the allusion is too vague to allow identification of the dead woman, but perhaps it was Ešarra-ḫamat) and the mother of Nabonidus, whose influence on her son is well known (no. 26).

The kings of Elam were particularly subject to disease. Ḫumban-nimena, paralyzed and no longer able to speak, lived on eleven months before dying. Ḫumban-ḫaltaš I, falling ill at noon, died the same evening.[42] Visibly impressed by this sequence of events, the chronicler drew attention to the fact that Ḫumban-ḫaltaš II died in his palace although he was not sick.

Among assassinations, that of Sennacherib roused considerable interest. Two different historiographical traditions emerged. According to one, reproduced by the Babylonian chronicler and Berossus, a single son killed the king. Berossus names him as Ardumuzan (A. Polyhistor) or Adramelos

(Abydenos). According to the other, several sons plotted against the monarch. This was the version officially favored by Esarhaddon in his own inscriptions. A Babylonian prophecy also evoked the figures of two sons standing by their father while Esarhaddon suffered exile. The Bible reproduced this second tradition, identifying the two murderers by name, Adrammelech and Šareṣer, and stating that, the infamous deed done, they fled to Urarṭu. Much later, Nicolas of Damascus related the story of two sons of queen Semiramis plotting against their mother in order not to let her third son, Ninyas, be her successor on the throne. Today, thanks to the evidence of a letter from the time of Esarhaddon, we know that Sennacherib's assassin was his eldest son, Arda-Mulišši.[43]

The death of Sargon II in combat, perhaps near Tabal in Anatolia, taken by surprise in his camp, vanquished and deprived of a royal burial, caused some disquiet.[44] The pseudoautobiography of Sennacherib[45] tells of his quest to find the reasons for such a death.

Aššur-nādin-šumi, Sennacherib's son, died in captivity in Elam. However, the chronicle stopped short of saying that he was handed over to his enemy by his own subjects in Babylon. Another chronicle remains equally silent regarding the end of Nabonidus. According to Xenophon, he was perhaps put to death (but the unnamed king might be Bēlšazzar). According to Berossus, Cyrus spared his life, making him governor of Carmania. A Babylonian historiographical text, the "dynastic prophecy," gives some credence to this second version.

Revolts and insurrections punctuated the history of government, with their procession of individual or collective executions (nos. 18, 19, 20, 24, 29, 30, and 36), in connection with revolts of cities (no. 21), of populations (nos. 16, 17, 18, and 22), of civil war among the Diadochi (no. 30), of Astyages' army, which handed the king over to Cyrus (no. 26), or the Assyrian army that submitted to a usurper (no. 21).

Šamaš-šuma-ukīn was a client king with no autonomy in military, diplomatic, or even internal affairs. His rebellion and that of Babylon against Aššurbanipal shook Assyrian power and was one of the great events of his time. He obtained support from Elam, the Arabs, and perhaps Manasseh of Judah. The uprising began on 19 Ṭebet 652 (no. 20). On 8 Šebat 652 the king of Babylon slipped away from confrontation with the enemy (nos. 20 and 21). Nevertheless, two important battles were fought: one at Ḫirītu, in the province of Sippar, on 27 Adar 652, at which the Babylonians were defeated (no. 21); the other at Mankisu, near Baghdad, where the Elamites were repulsed.[46] For all this the fighting spirit of the Babylonians was not diminished. They continued to wage war and even to have some successes (no. 20). However, on 11 Dumuzi 650 (no. 21) Babylon was besieged, falling in 648. In the interim, an uprising in Assyria may have delayed the progress of operations (nos. 20 and 21).

Kings were obliged to take care of the well-being of the gods and the maintenance of temples (nos. 30, 31, and 32). This activity was duly noted by the chroniclers, who mentioned the return of divine statues to their shrines, the celebration of festivals, the presentation of offerings and sacrifices, or the investiture of a high priestess (no. 53, concerning Nabonidus's daughter). Particular attention was paid, whenever the sources came from Babylon, to the celebration there of the New Year or Akītu-festival, according to its Babylonian name, or to its interruption. It was in the course of this festival that the gods set down in writing on the "tablet of destinies" the destiny of the king and the country for the following year. The Babylonians and the Assyrians, and later the Persians and the Macedonians, were scrupulous in their observance of it with the necessary pomp and solemnity. The festival was still being celebrated in 204.[47] The celebration was recorded using two expressions that referred to two crucial moments in the proceedings: the gesture of the king in which he took the god's hand ("he seized the hand of Bēl," variant "he seized the hand of Bēl and the son of Bēl"), or the arrival of Nabû from Borsippa to take part in the procession of Marduk (nos. 17, 24, 26, 27, 35, etc.).

The chroniclers, in fact, devoted more attention to interruptions than to observances of the festival, so also chronicle 16, which notes the interruption of the cult of Šamaš at the time of the Elamite raid. Thus chronicles 16, 17, 18, 19, 20, and 26 observe that "Bēl did not go out, and Nabû did not come," while chronicles 19 and 20 stress that this interruption lasted twenty years. This interruption was pregnant with meaning, since it put in danger the stability of the world. The relationship uniting humans and gods was seriously threatened, while the gods, moreover, were unable to determine destinies. Chronicles 19 and 20, through selection of events that they recounted, established an implicit relation between the noncelebration of the festival and the ruin of Babylon.

Concerning respect for the gods and the cults, chronicle 26 adds a final detail that sounds a warning. Indeed, it declares, Cyrus had grown old in the faithful performance of every religious ceremony from the time of his arrival in Babylon, but his son Cambyses had committed a grave error in seeking to enter the Ezida wearing an Elamite garment. It is clear that there were appropriate clothes to wear when one came before the gods.[48]

Does this set of themes have antecedents before the Neo-Babylonian period? The notes of the Chronicle of the Single Monarchy (no. 1), which are often regarded as anecdotal, like historical omens, mentioned mostly foundation myths and heroic exploits, such as the setting of the world in order by Etana and his ascent to heaven, the victory of Enme(n)-baragesi over Elam, the foundation of Uruk by Enmerkar, the capture of Enme(n)-baragesi by Dumuzi, the refounding of Kiš by Ku-Baba, or the founding of Akkade by Sargon. Only the allusion to the weakening of Sumer at the time of the collapse of the empire of Ur was not in this repertory. As we shall see, it reveals new preoccupations of the historians of the period of Isin, for whom even the most illustrious royal dynasties were destined to perish. The hard facts are somewhat sparse, and their underlying similarities tell the same story. With these notes we are dealing with an archetypal view of history, a way of thinking that saw in events the "repetition" of exemplary types.

With the Neo-Babylonian chronicles everything was changed. A considerable, and cumulative, development in powers of observation had taken place. The chroniclers acquired a more precise knowledge of events, and their powers of analysis were more subtle. One aspect of this enrichment is that now more questions could be asked of these same events than had been possible in the past.

We encounter the same ponderous style, the same tedious repetitions, the deliberate strategy of saying the same things in exactly the same words and a desire to note the same developments by means of the same expressions (always written with the same graphic signs) and the same word order, such as concerning the extent or significance of pillages ("pillage," "despoil," "devastate," "loot," "lay waste and put to sack," "despoil, extort, and hand over to pillage," etc.) or the scope of defeats ("defeat," "inflict a crushing defeat," "inflict defeat and let no one escape," "defeat and exterminate to the point of complete annihilation," etc.). Such clichés greatly ease the reading of the texts and assist the reader in understanding them. At the same time, they are incipient typologies. With regard to vocabulary dealing with revolts, for example, authors play incessantly with the terms "uprising," "insurrection," "rebellion," and "troubles." No doubt they discerned in such usage significant nuances no longer meaningful to us.

This proceeding nourished original reflection on history, which sought to draw attention to the role of conflict and specific facts in the evolution of society. Loath to catalogue every fact coming to their knowledge, the chroniclers gave special attention to those events that were filled with potential for change, all events, ultimately, that concerned the person and the attitude of the king and that became effectively historical categories. Wars, internal conflicts, the accession and death of kings, and the interruptions of the cult were, in effect, those factors that typically led to upheavals. Even if in Assyria, to avoid a defeat or endangering the king, there was preparatory ritual designed to make a war victorious, there was a risk for the sovereign, since the battles determined victors. The ritual consisted of a fictitious conflict in which the enemy was represented by a figurine with the head turned backward as a sign of flight and defeat. In the ritual the king, the actual commander-in-chief, was replaced by one of his superior officers, bearing his name and wearing his breastplate, for battle was supernaturally dangerous.

In short, the Neo-Babylonian chroniclers offer a dry account, hardly more than a word list, of threats of subversion against the cosmic order. The underlying intention was to add up the innumerable tiny clues that hinted at these threats in order to show their significance and to warn against them. The totality of selected facts brought together in this way constituted a data bank from which a serial history could be constructed. These allowed a conservative reading of history, and if they did not preclude immediate utility, they nevertheless looked toward a future that would take into account lessons of the recent past. One remembers the conclusion of an astrological report sent to the king by Bayâ, an astrologer who lived in the time of king Esarhaddon of Assyria, which said, "Have no fear, Esarhaddon! Like a skilled pilot I will steer the ship into a good harbour. The future will be like the past!"[49] On an entirely different level, none of this prevented them from being diverted to more immediate and down-to-earth interests, such as those of the clergy of Babylon, directly affected by the vicissitudes of the fortunes of their god Marduk.

Study of the remote past and of its changes could of course contribute to an understanding of the present, by clarifying causes and predicting consequences that similar developments might occasion in the contemporary world. What was proposed, after a fashion, was an understanding of present history as portentous for the future because of a very long past.

Research was thus begun to explore the upheavals of past history, and a second series of chronicles was born. It was the work of the same historians as the preceding group, as may be deduced from chronicle 19, whose content was divided between the study of the recent and the earlier past. It was characterized by several features.

APPROXIMATE CHRONOLOGY. Research undertaken in the remote past had, first, a practical importance: the establishment of a chronology, even if ancient authors were content to date events by reigns, dating by years being the exception.

STUDY OF THE EARLIER PAST. Narration of events ran from remote times until the end of the eighth century.

CHOICE OF TOPIC. This was the same as that of chronicles of the recent past. (1) War was a central interest, with the victories of Sargon of Akkade against Kazallu or Subartu (the erection of stelae testified to his universal triumph), those of Narām-Sîn against Apišal or Magan, and later that of Ḫammurabi against Larsa; or elsewhere, the victorious wars of Kurigalzu against Elam and Assyria, without omitting the capture of Babylon by the Hittites, and the eviction of king Enlil-nādin-šumi by the Elamites (nos. 39 and 45). The theme of the removal or capture of hostile gods had a prominent place (nos. 38 and 45);

(2) The accession of kings, especially the seizure of power by parvenus and usurpers, was the subject of sustained attention; the placing of

Kurigalzu on the throne of Babylon by the Assyrians is also mentioned (nos. 41, 45, 46, and 47).

(3) The death of kings appears to be a preoccupation shared by historians and diviners (nos. 38, 39, 40, 44, and 45).[50] All the deaths recorded were extraordinary: the body of Utu-ḫegal was swept away by a river; that of Šulgi was eaten; Amar-Su'en died of a "bite" of a shoe or was gored to death; Erra-imittī died while eating a stew. The unusual and exceptional deaths of former kings were so many prototypes serving to complete the range of possible variations.

(4) Civil disturbances, such as the revolt of the whole world against the aging Sargon of Akkade, the uprising of the Kassite population against Kadašman-Ḫarbe I, the rebellion of the Assyrian nobility, or, finally, a revolt fomented by Adad-šuma-uṣur himself against a usurper (nos. 38, 39, 45, and 46) also received attention.

(5) The interruption or alteration of the cult was also the subject of interest (nos. 38 and 40). Sometimes there was reference to its normal performance, such as the celebration of the New Year festival in the reign of Erība-Marduk (no. 47) or to its restoration (no. 46).

The need for explanation. Not satisfied with simply mentioning numerous facts, some reduced in scale to memorable images, the chroniclers wanted to explain events. However varied, all explanations took up the same thesis, that vagaries of human fortune came about through the retributive will of Marduk. Enlil is virtually absent from these chronicles, the authors of which were not afraid of anachronisms: Marduk's star did not rise until the eighteenth century. It was Marduk who recompensed pious kings by bringing prosperity to their realms but punished others.

In other words, the chronicles exemplify an attempted interpretation of events of human history, according to which they were the consequences of divine anger aroused by some impious deed of a human ruler. Since by far the greater number of chronicles were written in Babylon, they were all naturally preoccupied, even exclusively concerned, with the glory of Marduk, whose cult was to be celebrated with splendor. Every change in reign was legitimized by relating it to the king's inadequate attention to Marduk's cult.

The need to explain was all the more imperative insofar as the vicissitudes of power were a lesson for future ages. So the questions raised by chronicles of former kings were really questions pertinent to the present. Four examples will suffice to make the point.

The great revolt against Sargon of Akkade. At the end of his reign, the elderly monarch was forced to confront a general insurrection throughout his territories, he himself being condemned to restlessness (nos. 38 and 39). This uprising echoed, in reality, events that occurred in Sumer and Akkad at the beginning of the reign of Narām-Sîn, and we have already seen how some Old Babylonian scribe manipulated the sources to give this a universal character.[51] It was a sort of anticipation of the great rebellion of Šamaš-šuma-ukīn and Babylon against Aššurbanipal.

THE RITE OF THE SUBSTITUTE KING. At Isin, at the beginning of the second millennium, a subsitute king by name Enlil-bāni was brought to power but stayed on, the rightful king having died (nos. 39 and 40). We have every reason to doubt the authenticity of this event, since the custom of having a substitute king is attested, so far as known, only in first-millennium Assyria under Adad-nērārī III and Esarhaddon. This practice was intended to save the life of the king when he was supernaturally condemned, his life being found in danger through divination, for example, when an eclipse occurred. It consisted of finding a subsitute for him, who was placed on the throne. When the danger was past, the substitute was put to death. At the end of the reign of Esarhaddon at least, the rite was revived. One of the substitutes was a high-ranking Babylonian, whose execution provoked serious troubles in Babylon. The example of Enlil-bāni turns out to be a counter-example, since in his case it was the legitimate king who died, not the substitute. We have already seen here an implicit criticism of an Assyrian institution by a Babylonian chronicler.[52]

THE DEATH OF TUKULTĪ -NINURTA I. The narrative explicitly made use of a causal connection, positing a direct link between the death of this king, assassinated by his son, and the sack of Babylon he had perpetrated (no. 45). Since Sennacherib suffered the same fate, one can scarcely doubt that in the mind of the chronicler his demise was provoked by the same cause (no. 16). Aššurbanipal was therefore taking a considerable risk when in his turn he besieged the city. The same could be said, after him, of Xerxes and of Antigonus.

The chronicler's choice was all the more specific in relation to the New Year festival. Every year, at the time of its celebration in Babylon, the *šešgallû*-priest removed from the king the accoutrements of his office, slapped him, then, pulling him by the ears, brought him before Marduk and made him kneel. The king then addressed the god in these terms:

> [I have commit]ted no sin, O King of all lands, I have not been negligent with regard to your divinity. [I have not des]troyed Babylon, I have not commanded its scattering. I have not [profaned] Esagila. I have not forgotten its rites. ... [I watch] over Babylon, I have not destroyed its walls.

Next, having answered the king and restored to him his royal dignity, the same *šešgallû*-priest would slap him again; a favorable or unfavorable prediction was inferred from the king's reaction: "If his tears flow, Marduk is well disposed; if his tears do not flow, it is because Marduk is angry; enemies will rise up and bring about his downfall."[53]

We understand, by reversing the facts, that the king who distinguished himself as not having destroyed Babylon nor profaned Esagila would enjoy a prosperous reign, exercised under the protection of the gods; in contrast, every other king would be deposed by these same gods. We can compile a long list of those who had restored Esagila: Tiglath-pileser III, Sargon II, Esarhaddon (to whom a prophecy had announced, even before he took power, that he would "reconstruct Babylon and rebuild Esagila" and that veiled his father's crime behind antique Babylonian rhetoric), Aššurbanipal, Nebuchadnezzer II, Cyrus, Alexander, Seleucus I, and Antiochus I and IV. This series contrasted with that of the destroyers of the city: Tukultī-Ninurta I, Sennacherib, Aššurbanipal, Xerxes, and Antigonus. Among these latter, Aššurbanipal, apparently aware of these speculations, made a point of proclaiming his devotion to the gods and temples[54] after storming the city.

So a rule may be formulated: the god's anger against the city signified its destruction; reconciliation between the god and his city went hand in hand with its reconstruction.

THE REPLICA OF BABYLON. Two chronicles explained the tragic end of Sargon of Akkade by reference to a sacrilege he had committed by removing soil from Babylon and constructing a replica of the city elsewhere (nos. 38 and 39; see also the enigmatic founding of a city in no. 46). Should we see here an allusion to the Assyrian practice of transporting soil from conquered territories to be trampled daily under the feet of its conquerors? This seems dubious. Rather, comparison with Nabonidus seems more likely, as he was reproached for wanting to construct at Tayma, in the north of the Arabian peninsula, a replica of the palace in Babylon.[55] The notables of Babylon, especially the clergy of Marduk, seeing their power crumbling away in proportion to their distance from the king, made desperate efforts to prevent new foundations. We know through Appian that the foundation of Seleucia displeased them and that they tried every means to oppose it.[56]

What is evident from all this is great concern for the interpretation backed up by the narrative, for the chronicles were narratives, and the explanations of the chroniclers were nothing if not a form of special pleading. To reach this level of expression, appropriate concepts had to be worked out and new ones formulated. Lengthening the list of events, strict thematic choices, and greater precision in chronology show this broadened conceptualization of the scope of history. Perspective was refined, this being the price for the historian's autonomy.

Two chroniclers made in three exceptional instances a judgment on an event. One of them, with respect to the capture of Aššur by the Medes, exclaimed, "they inflicted a terrible defeat on a great people"; a few lines later, describing the fall of Nineveh under the combined blows of the Medes and the Babylonians, he repeated, "they inflicted a crushing defeat on a [gr]eat [people]" (no. 22). Another chronicler (or perhaps it was the same one) made the same judgment concerning the destructions brought about in Babylonia by the king of Elam, Kiden-Ḫutran: "[he inflicted] a terrible defeat on a very great people" (no. 45).

Is not the historian supposed to restrain his own feelings? This exclamation of horror or admiration (we cannot tell which) in connection with such major events as the conquests of the two capitals of the Assyrian Empire, certainly has, to use Paul Ricoeur's expression, "a specific function of individuation."[57] In the view of Mesopotamian historians, such events were quite exceptional and so by definition unrepeatable. Thus the real purpose of the chronicler's judgments was to isolate them by declaring them unique.

ASSYRIAN CHRONICLES AND ASSYRIAN "NATIONALISM"

The scraps of some Assyrian chronicles are what remain of chronographic activity carried on during the last four centuries of the second millennium. It was in this period that the Assyrian Royal Chronicle (no. 5) was thoroughly reworked. After Śamšī-Addu, Assyrian historiography experienced major reexamination.

A fragment of a dissident king list[58] mentions, in sequence, royal names distributed among three dynasties. The first concludes with Ērišum I; the second has Śamšī-Addu I for founder and includes Išme-Dagān I, [Mūl]t-Aškur,[59] and Rēmū . . . [. . .]. The end of the last name is lost in a lacuna. The third dynasty was founded by Šū-Ninua. Comparison of this document with the royal chronicle highlights several distinctive traits in the dissident document: the successors of Śamšī-Addu were more numerous, and the sequence of kings from Aššur-dugul to Lullāya was left out.

Next, a royal inscription of a certain Puzur-Sîn complicates matters. He calls himself "vice-regent of Aššur" and claims that he drove out Asīnum, grandson of Śamšī-Addu, both being qualified as "of foreign extraction," "of non-Assyrian stock."[60]

After the disappearance of Śamšī-Addu, the balance among the great powers was profoundly altered. Šeḫna/Šubat-Enlil was occupied by the Elamites, who remained for some months. It then fell into the hands of Atamrum, king of Andarig. Išme-Dagān himself lost control of Assyria, which broke away, and, after several conflicts, he was obliged to take refuge with Ḫammurabi of Babylon. We know nothing of his successors, of whom a sketchy tradition preserves only the names.

The only certain thing is that the text of the royal chronicle was reworked and modified to present a new perspective. An element of censorship was applied, the grandsons of Śamšī-Addu being omitted. More importantly, Śamšī-Addu himself, after having been apparently contested, was rehabilitated, and this king even became the central character in the composition. He was considered, if we accept the quite unparalleled biographical notice dedicated to him, to be the real founder of the Assyrian monarchy. The revision consisted of adding several new royal names between Išme-Dagān and Šū-Ninua. Most prominent among these were seven parvenus, whom the chronicle presents as "sons of nobodies," who probably struggled for power. The last among them, Adasi, was the founder of a new and extensive royal lineage.

At a time when Assyrian power, once feeble, became a reality again, this revision was based on Assyrian "nationalism." Only the point of view of Aššur was henceforth to be taken into account, the names of other capitals being simply obliterated. Privileged links even appear to have been initiated between the city and the chronicle. Of the five known copies, two were discovered there, a third was copied in antiquity from an original from the same provenience, and a fourth belonged to an exorcist of the city.

The long chronographic note devoted to Śamśī-Addu demonstrates that the Assyrian ruler who sponsored the revision of the chronicle wished himself to be seen as the perpetuator of the former's achievement.

Śamśī-Addu had introduced the use of the royal title *šarrum*[61] to Assyria. This title, so far as known from the sources, reappeared in Aššur under Erība-Adad and his son Aššur-uballiṭ I, from whose reign on it became standard. This same Aššur-uballiṭ chose, moreover, in his own inscriptions, to set out the list of his ancestors in reverse of their chronological order, the same procedure used in the royal chronicle with the genealogy of Aminu. It is probably to him or one of his near successors that we may attribute the rewriting of the chronicle. In any event, the new composition cannot be dated later than the reign of Tukultī-Ninurta I.[62]

In its final form, the royal chronicle set out, from the origins of the world, an unbroken sequence of just the Assyrian kings, individuals who came from different families but who belonged to one continuous lineage in power from their beginnings down to the eighth century, the date of the last known edition of the composition. The perspective imposed on it was that the monarchy never left Aššur, the only royal city ever to have existed.

Whether the royal chronicle or the eponym chronicles (nos. 5, 8, and 9), which, year after year, told of the political and military history of Assyria, with remarkable continuity from the beginning of the second to the middle of the first millennium, Assyrian chronographic writing presented the official history. Such was the destiny, in fact, of the whole of the Assyrian historiographical corpus, so flagrant was the dependence of history in this land on the political sphere.

The Epic of Tukultī-Ninurta I[63] has been shown to be a major effort on the part of Assyrian scribes to carry on a competition with Babylon, for even when the conflict was won on the ground, it continued on the level of culture and ideology. The conquest of Babylon, the sack of the palace and the temples, and the deportation of its gods were viewed by some as sacrilegious acts, so the poem sought to show, on the contrary, that the king of Assyria was valiant while the Kassites were treacherous and impious. The demonstration of this depended on three points: the Kassite king showed himself to be unqualified to rule by committing a sin against Assyria and Šamaš, the god who oversaw an earlier treaty between the two countries; the gods of Babylon had abandoned the city, and this abandonment justified destruction and deportation; and, finally, the Assyrian king claimed to have emerged unscathed from a trial by ordeal, thus reversing the responsibilities in the affair. In short, the aggressor was innocent of the crimes of the object of his aggression.

Such, without doubt, was the theme developed in the contemporary Assyrian chronicles (nos. 11–15); they were practically all concerned with warfare between Assyria and Babylonia but are too fragmentary to be of much use.

The Synchronistic Chronicle (no. 10), which is, on the other hand, better preserved, sought to justify Assyrian claims on territory disputed by Babylon. Its author made no secret of this fact, concluding his work with a forthright condemnation of Babylonia, accusing it of lies and treachery.

At this time Assyrian imperialism, fortified by its universalist ideology, had equated warfare with a struggle against the forces of evil. Conceived of as a trial by ordeal, war became a basic element of the cosmic order. It saved civilization, the king being the instrument of divine justice and the god Aššur becoming a warrior god. We see, progressively, the elaboration of a warrior ritual and a veritable orgy of massacres and mutilations where what is described was no combat but a slaughter. Everything that was not Assyrian was equated with barbarism; anything was acceptable to destroy it. The enemy's status as hostile and the opposite of all civilized values meant that the destruction and devastation took on a positive character. The Assyrian king was always good and just, while the foe was mendacious, evil, and impure. The Assyrian historians, zealous servants of the king, echoed this official ideology.

Babylon, however, held a particular place in this ideology. Its high level of culture fascinated the Assyrian elite, and Assyria could maintain a boundary with it.[64] Was the Synchronistic Chronicle, which tells the story of this boundary, composed, as is sometimes thought, at a time Assyria was enfeebled, following the reign of Adad-nērārī III?[65] We cannot be sure. If this were the case, its purpose would have been to tell a tale of Assyrians triumphant to Assyrians dispossessed. The past, whatever happens, is a guaranteed source of perpetuity, and the Mesopotamian conceptualization of the domain of history surely implied the obligation to relive it forever, even if only in the mind.

Notes

1. On this term, see below pages 109.
2. See Machinist 1983; Moran 1987: 252–54; Michalowski 1990: 385–89.
3. Erra I 81–82; see Foster 1996: 761.
4. The list of the sages varies: see Wilcke 1988b: 127–30; Reiner 1961; Borger 1974: 190–91. The Akkadian term designating them is ***kulullu,*** "fish+man." Representations of such creatures are found: Parrot 1961: fig. 82. On Oannes, see Komoróczy 1973: 142–43. The name Uana may well have derived from the Babylonian Royal Chronicle, whose first words in Sumerian are u_4 an-né, "When Anu." See Wilcke 1988b: 140. The name Oannes may be discerned in Duwänäy in Nabatean agronomic texts. See El Faïz 1995: 29 n. 18.
5. Manuscript P reads x-x-*la-na-bi-ir.*e, possibly Ila-nawir. Steinkeller (2003: 277) suggests that *-na-be-el* might be a misreading of *-na-bi-ir,* which is difficult to assume. In fact, the two names attest two different traditions.
6. "The Dispute between the Date-Palm and the Tamarisk," in which it is recalled that the gods had "built cities for the distant humanity" (see most recently Foster 1996: 891–93); "The Legend of Etana," whose ancient title was "the gods drew the plan of the city" (see Kinnier-Wilson 1985; Foster 1996: 437–57; Haul 2000; Novotny 2001).
7. I broadly follow the exegesis of Wilcke 1988b: 134–35.
8. See above n. 6. We do not know if the name Etana, "he who went up to heaven," was drawn from the legend or the legend was constructed around the name. There is reason to think that the story is very old; the ascent to heaven of someone mounted on the back of an eagle was already a figurative motif well known in Old Akkadian glyptic art. It was probably a matter of an old folklore motif, which survives a long time in Persian and Arab legend, passing by way of the ascent of Alexander. Note also the Sumerian expression an.šè ... e_{11}, "ascend to heaven," and the ascent of Šulgi and Išbī-Erra (Yoshikawa 1989; Wilcke 1988a; Steinkeller 1992). The last antediluvian sage, Utu-abzu, whose name means "born of the ocean of sweet water," is also reputed to have gone up to heaven. In his case the an.šè ... e_{11} indicates a myth of ascent.
9. A certain compiler (manuscript C) introduced the names of Arbum son of Maška'en in the places occupied by Arwi'um son of Mašda. In doing so he made a distinction between Mašda, who must surely be restored after Balīḫ, and Maška'en. The noun maška'en, borrowed from the Akkadian *muškēnum,* denoted a person of modest circumstances who sells his services to make a living (the French *mesquin*—also rarely in English, "mesquin" [*OED*]—derives from it, by way of Akkadian *muškēnum* and Arabic *miskīn*). In the third and the very beginning of the second millennium, it was frequently written maš.ka_{15} instead of the later form maš.$EN+KA_{15}$. In cuneiform, the sign DÙ can be read either dà or ka_{15}, so we can choose, for the same graphic sign, the values dà and ka_{15}, to write two different names, maš.dà or maš.ka_{15}. Furthermore, the same scribe, in writing Arbum rather than Armum or Arwi'um, perhaps altered the sense of this other noun: there were two terms *arbum* in Akkadian; one meant "grasshopper"; the other, rarer and less known, it seems, before the middle of the second millennium, meant "a person with no family." Did the copyist replace the pair "Female gazelle

son of male gazelle" with "Without family son of Mesquin"? On maš.ka$_{15}$.en, see Stol 1997: 492.

10. "The Invention of the Hoe" (see Farber 1997); "The Exaltation of Marduk" (see Foster 1996: 350–401).

11. Lévi-Strauss 1966: 217.

12. On the conceptualization of binary and tertiary opposing structures and contradictions in Mesopotamian thought, see Glassner 1984b: 24–25; 1995b.

13. Among many others, see Cunnison 1957.

14. Eckhard 1937; for Mesopotamia, see Glassner 1996a: 103–5; Wilcke 1987a. For a comprehensive theory, see Bourdieu 1980: 285–86.

15. Compare the reflections of Evans-Pritchard 1940: 139–47.

16. On bala, see above page 8.

17. Cf., however, Polybius 6.50.6 and 15.9.5, for whom all known parts of the inhabited world passed under the *dynasteia* of Rome.

18. On these phenomena, see Goody 1977: passim.

19. Kraus 1965; Finkelstein 1966; Röllig 1969: 269–73.

20. Finkelstein 1966: passim.

21. ERÍN denotes any person obliged to perform a civil or military task during a set period (Krecher 1974: 260 n. 22); in the present text it designates the whole range of royal service.

22. The list of royal ancestors is not that of Śamśī-Addu, as is generally believed, but that of Aminu; it is, after all, his name that heads the series! Śamśī-Addu himself appears only much later. If the name Aminu has not been sufficiently noticed it is because, since he is scarcely known, he has scarcely had any historical reality until recently. He is mentioned in only one or two texts from Mari. We have, notably, a seal of one of his retainers (in general, see Birot 1985: 221). He is better known today thanks to the information contained in the Eponym Chronicle from Mari (no. 8).

23. See, for example, Vansina 1965: passim.

24. Compare, later, the Ugarit king list with, mainly, the mention of Didānu (see, e.g., Kitchen 1977). Compare also the genealogy of David and the position of Judah in the list of the tribes. Could one discover, in a split form, in 1 Chr 2:1–15 and Ruth 4:18–22, the narrative of the origins and dispersion of the tribes and that of the genealogy of David? See also the fragments of genealogy in 1 Sam 9:1; 14:50–51 and Saul's genealogy in 1 Chr 8:25–9:35.

25. See, for example, Ballandier 1985: 221–22; Le Goff 1988: 111–15.

26. Evans-Pritchard 1940: 245; Ballandier 1982: 109, fourteen generations.

27. Larsen 1976: 147–48.

28. These were double names constructed from two originally distinct components. It is not within the scope of the present study to explain the amalgamations by means of which polyglot scribes, juggling the Sumerian and the Babylonian syllabic values of the graphic signs and skillfully playing on words in Sumerian, Akkadian, and Amorite, constructed new and appropriate names for use in the funerary meal; see Kraus 1965; Finkelstein 1966; Charpin and Durand 1986: 159–60. The first double name, Aram-madara, means "The lover (?) is in tears," the second, Ṭûbti-yamuta, "My happiness has died," and the third, Yamquzzu-halama, "Ruin befell him."

29. Sulili/Sulê son of Aminu: this filiation is generally taken to be a late addition; see, for example, Kupper 1957: 210 and n. 3. Larsen (1976: 38–39) identifies him with Silulu son of Dakiki. The name Ilu-šūma appears in chronicle 39; according to Larsen, he was a contemporary of Iddin-Dagān or Išme-Dagān of Isin.

30. Birot 1980.

31. An irony of fate: his own son Išme-Dagān later had the same misadventure as he (Lafont 1988: 469 and n. 39).

32. It is difficult to agree with the view of Durand (Charpin and Durand 1997a: 372 n. 36; Durand: 1998–2000: 2:108) that Śamśī-Addu was originally from Akkade; these sources merely tell of his admiration for these ancient kings but do not suffice to establish historical facts. The importance of ideological propaganda is evident in the invocation of royal names in the funerary ritual.

33. Thureau-Dangin 1925: A iii 6–7; Edzard 1997: 70.

34. So Civil 1980: 230.

35. Weidner 1932–33: 180, no. 4.

36. On this episode, see Cogan 1991: 124–25. More generally, like vanquished monsters in mythological narratives, which served as protective spirits of doors and passages, severed heads obtained an apotropaic use; see Wiggerman 1992: 146. Severed heads appear as early as the documentation from Ebla. For other examples, see Charpin 1994: no. 59; see also Russell 1999: 156–205.

37. There were occasionally other motives for the removal of gods. When, according to chronicle 21, Šamaš and the gods of Sippar went to Babylon, it was to avoid their capture by the Assyrians.

38. See Cassin 1987: 249–53. To avoid the dissolution of his kinship group, Marduk-apla-iddina, when fleeing to Elam, took with him the bones of his ancestors and the gods of every part of his kingdom (Luckenbill 1924: 85.8–9).

39. On the imprisonment of Marduk, see Livingstone 1989: 82–86. When Sennacherib claimed to have "smashed" the gods of Babylon, we should consider a metaphorical use of the verb *šebēru/šubburu,* "smash a person." Similarly, when Aššurbanipal stated that he had reduced the gods of Susa to nothing more than a "puff of wind," he stressed the nonexistence of gods driven out of their sanctuaries (following Cassin 1987: 250 n. 43).

40. A recurrent question in Babylonian historiography: van Dijk 1986; Lambert 1998; the situation in Elam: Glassner 1994.

41. Glassner 1999.

42. The first of these illnesses was identifed and treated with Babylonian medicine: Labat 1960: 171 rev. 5 and passim; on the second, see Labat 1949.

43. On this question, see Parpola 1980; Frame 1992: 64 and n. 1. Arda-Mulišši (this is the name we find in corrupted form as Ardumuzan, Adramelos, or Adrammelech) was the only one among Sennacherib's sons who bore the title "crown prince." It is sometimes asserted, though without proof, that Esarhaddon himself was the assassin. Aššurbanipal (Streck 1916: 38, iv 70–71) stated that the murder took place in front of a bull-colossus, the guardian of a temple gateway, while the Bible (2 Kgs 19:37 = Isa 37:38) states that it took place in the temple of Nisroch (perhaps Ninurta?) See Black and Green 1992: 14; Uehlinger 1995; Zawadzki 1990a.

44. On this event, see Frahm 1999.

45. For references, see ch. 1 n. 95.

46. There may have been only one battle: Brinkman 1984a: 97; Frame 1992: 289–92.

47. Sachs and Hunger 1988–2001: 2:202.14–19. On this festival, see Marzahn 1981; Black 1981; Bidmead 2002.

48. On the garment worn by the king when he took Marduk's hand, see Waetzoldt 1980: 27.

49. Parpola 1997: 14, 2.2.

50. On this motif, see Hallo 1991a: 148–49; Glassner 1997; 1999.

51. See above, pages 14–15.

52. Glassner 1999.

53. Thureau-Dangin 1921: 144–45, lines 423–28, 450–52.

54. On this issue, see J. Z. Smith 1976: 4–5; Machinist 1976; Brinkman 1984b; Michalowski 1990: 392–93.

55. S. Smith 1924: 27–28, ii 28–29.

56. On the foundation of Seleucia, see Bouché-Leclerq 1913: 1:38; Will 1979–82: 2:60–61.

57. Ricoeur 1985: 339–40.

58. Grayson 1980b: 115.

59. This person is known as a son of Išme-Dagān and thus grandson of Śamśī-Addu. He bears an Amorite name; see Durand 1991.

60. Grayson 1985: 12.

61. The Assyrian kings from before his time bore the titles *iššiʾakkum, rubāʾum,* or *waklum*. On the use of *šrr* at Aššur in the same period for denoting the finest garments, see Veenhof 1972: 192–94.

62. Lambert 1976.

63. Machinist 1978; Foster 1996: 211–30.

64. See Liverani 1990: passim.

65. Grayson 1975a: 53.

IV

Genesis

We are not certain of the date of origin of the earliest chronicles. For the earliest of all, the Chronicle of the Single Monarchy (no. 1), opinions waver among the reigns of Utu-ḫegal of Uruk, Ur-Namma of Ur, and Ur-Ninurta of Isin,[1] even if recent assessements are less certain and support for the possibility of several successive editions is gaining ground.

Was the Chronicle of the Single Monarchy thought up in the circles of Old Akkadian political power? Perhaps the phrase, which is, to be sure, partly restored in a royal inscription, "Akkade having received the kingship, [so and so ruled],"[2] evokes the existence of the first draft of a similar document. The argument from language, Sumerian and not Akkadian, which might allow this view to be questioned, is of little weight, since Mesopotamian culture at this time was characterized by bilingualism.

There are several further pieces of evidence corroborating that the chronicle was first composed during the Old Akkadian period, presumably under the reign of Narām-Sîn.[3] (1) Mesopotamia was then unified for the first time in its history. (2) As already noted,[4] the city of Akkade took a central and exceptional place in the chronicle and appeared in the place of Kiš and Uruk in the order of succession of the dynasties. (3) The three cities of Kiš, Uruk, and Ur were those that elected the three rebel kings who confronted Narām-Sîn: Ipḫur-Kiš, Amar-girid, and Lugal-ane. This particular historical background might explain the decision of the chronicler deliberately to ignore any other Mesopotamian kingdom. (4) One principle found in the chronicle was that kingship was hereditary, a position developed in Narām-Sîn's own inscriptions as well as in the historiographical work about this king; the chronicle did not consider election a legitimation of kingship. (5) A second principle in the chronicle was that victory was also a principle of legitimation of the king. This too was an important topic in Narām-Sîn's inscriptions as well as in the historiographic work about him. (6) If the chronicle was a creation of the Old

Akkadian period, one understands better why Kiš was chosen as the first capital city.

The underlying scheme of the work was, of course, in principle, imaginable for any period when control of these three cities and the concurrent use of the two titles "lord," en, and "king," lugal, implied sovereignty over the whole of Mesopotamia and when these were claimed by one and the same person.

A quick review of Mesopotamian royal titles highlights the antiquity of these terms. They appear toward the end of the fourth millennium in Uruk. In this early period, however, public affairs may have been managed by an assembly of notables. Later, throughout the third millennium, lugal was not applied exclusively to persons of royal blood but to anyone invested, alone or collegially, with the highest authority within a kinship group. As for en, a royal title belonging to Uruk, it more commonly denoted either the high priest or high priestess of a deity or of deceased ancestors who were objects of a cult. While lugal referred usually to a ruler's relationship with people, in the Sumerian epic tradition of the kings of Uruk, en referred to the relationship that ruler maintained with ancestors.[5]

As far as we may judge, given the condition of our sources, a first attempt at the unification of Mesopotamia under the authority of one king took place about 2400, when En-šakuš-ana of Uruk, already invested with the titles of "lord of Kenger" and "king of Kalama," Kenger denoting the country of Uruk[6] and Kalama that of Ur, destroyed Kiš and captured its king. His successor, Lugal-kiniš(e)-dudu, was "king of Kiš," "king of Ur," and "lord of Uruk." Later another king of Uruk, Lugal-zagesi, tried again to unify Mesopotamia, but his attempt was cut off in its prime by Sargon of Akkade.[7]

A textual argument, finally, supports a rewriting of the chronicle in Uruk. Manuscript C does not in fact use the usual formula "its kingship was carried to Uruk," when the second and third dynasties of Uruk were founded, but another expression, "kingship returned for the second/third time to Uruk."

Bearing in mind the exceptional place of Akkade in the work, we should look for its sponsor among one of the kings of Uruk, who succeeded its dynasty and who, filled with admiration for it, represented himself as continuing it. Among these the name of Utu-ḫegal stands out.

With the collapse of Old Akkadian power, it took great audacity on the part of this brilliant successor to lay claim to its imperial heritage, to venture into its extinct culture so far as to return with the aura of a universal ruler. We know little about him. He acted as mediator in the territorial dispute between Ur and Lagaš, and, appropriating part of the titulary of Narām-Sîn, he claimed to have triumphed over the Gutians and restored the kingship of Sumer, which they had carried off abroad.[8]

A double motivation led him and his followers to explore the past. In the first place, other new monarchies were contesting the prestigious heritage of the dynasty of Akkade, which had promoted kingship far beyond every other institution, elevating it to the point of contact between the divine and human spheres. Henceforth, by the authority and wealth emanating from his person, the king alone occupied the first place. He was the king at the center of military and economic activity; he was the pinnacle of the social hierarchy, the friend of the gods. But to prevail over his peers and to confirm his position as the worthy successor to the royal crown, victory and battlefield were insufficient. Utu-ḫegal also had to show that monarchy was not something to be shared and that he himself was the unique repository of an ancient legitimacy.

In the second place, the irruption of turbulent neighbors, the Gutians and the Elamites, into Mesopotamian affairs and the arrival of new elements in the population, the Amorites, made it ever more imperative to specify the terms of communal identity.

The Gutians in particular were a mountain-dwelling people from the Zagros, located either in the region of Kermānšāh or in the basin of the Lower Zāb. They were herdsmen who normally enjoyed peaceful and friendly relations with the Mesopotamian states, even if periodic crises might arise whose causes are difficult to grasp. Thus, taking advantage of the fragmentation of Old Akkadian power, several Gutian kings ruled over various Sumerian cities, even though we cannot be sure whether their power was effective or nominal. We know several of their names: Yarlagan, Si'u, Lā-'arābum, Erridu-pizir, and Tirigan. There is no reason to doubt the victory of Utu-ḫegal over Tirigan, the outcome of some minor conflict somewhere in the territory of the city of Umma.

However, the ancient Mesopotamians have accustomed us to seeing in the Gutians subnormal beings, not conforming to the customs and laws of civilization. A picture of the earth and its inhabitants had been sketched out as early as the end of the third millennium, according to which there was a highly civilized center, contrasting with a surrounding zone populated by barbarians characterized by negative criteria. They lived in noncivilized areas. They had the intelligence of dogs and the appearance of monkeys. Their languages were confused babble. They were ignorant of agriculture, of cooked foods, of fermented drinks, and of table manners. They knew nothing of houses and cities. They did not bury their dead, and, having no scruples, they knew nothing of prohibitions or how to keep their word. They showed no respect for the gods. The Gutians and the Amorites, at the transition from the third to the second millennium, were the very models of barbarism.

Utu-ḫegal, ahead of anyone else, agreed with the rewriter of the Chronicle of the Single Monarchy; he was the first to call these same

Gutians "snakes" and "scorpions" of the mountains, while the chronicler gave their kings with derisive names, such as Ingišū, "They went astray," Ikūkum-lā-qabā, "Oil of an unspeakable stench," I''ar-lā-qabā, "He goes off without a word." These epithets and nicknames[9] are the product of an attempt at classification, which tried to give a comprehensive account of the other. They were so many derogatory designations, contrasting them to the civilized world. Perhaps proper names even more than epithets could mark a veritable frontier of nomenclature with foreign parts.

With clearly political motives, Utu-ḫegal chose to transform his modest victory into an event of universal significance, turning the Gutians into a destructive scourge that had mercilessly ravaged the land of Sumer. Bringing violence and evil, they had carried the monarchy off abroad, a scourge the horror of which was emphasized the more forcibly so the achievement of overcoming them might enhance even more the image of their conqueror. In one move the king of Uruk brought back kingship from abroad and reestablished the values of civilization.

This was also the precise intention of the chronicler. In addition, as though in his turn to give more significance to the event, he made up entirely an important dynasty of Gutium. This dynasty was a fiction. It suffices to recall the nicknames attached to some of its kings, the schematic length of their reigns, always varying between either three and six years, not to mention the complete disorder of the manuscript tradition from one account to another. All surviving manuscripts are in total disagreement concerning the length of the dynasty, the number, and the identities of its kings. Tirigan himself, the last Gutian king, is presented in the oldest known manuscript as a king of the city of Adab.

In so doing, and wishing to define Mesopotamian identity in opposition to the other, the rewriter of the chronicle, as though desirous of stressing the essence of what separated it from and opposed it to foreign lands, characterized Mesopotamia by the presence of the institution of kingship and made sure to add (for the attention of competitors) that this kingship was one and indivisible. So the chronicle was rewritten in intellectual circles gravitating around a king of Uruk who busied himself in consolidating his own power while struggling to preserve a political ideal in the face of a host of rivals. He focused attention on external dangers as a threat to order and presented kingship as the cornerstone of Mesopotamian identity.

To conclude, the Old Akkadian kings had recourse to the skills of professional scribes, to whom they entrusted the task of exploring the past and of manipulating memory in order to construct an ideological basis for their energetic but fragile power.

Although the Chronicle of the Single Monarchy was the monument of a new-fledged power, still in formation but already writing its own history, a historiographical approach certainly governed its composition, because this was from the outset a rewriting. The chronicle offered the new monarchy (which would prove to be short-lived) a long past, which once formulated, that monarchy need only restore.

Notes

1. Jacobsen 1939: 135–41; Rowton 1960; Kraus 1952: 46–49; Michalowski 1984.

2. Glassner 1995a: 23.

3. For more details, see Glassner 2003; forthcoming. The same hypothesis is formulated independently on the basis of other arguments by Steinkeller 2003.

4. See above, page 64 and table 4.

5. A third royal title, e n s í, emphasized the relation linking the king with the gods. In brief, in relation to contact between humans, the ancestors, the land, and the gods, kingship was the guarantee of the perpetuity of the social order; see Glassner 1993; 2000a: ch. 10; 2000c; Michalowski 2003: 202–6.

6. On the use of Kenger to denote the territory of Uruk, see Krebernik 1984: 280; Visicato 1995: 66.

7. According to the Curse of Akkade (Cooper 1983: line 6), which dates at the latest from the time of Ur, Enlil confers on Sargon, "king of Kiš," the "quality of lord," n a m . e n, and the "quality of king," n a m . l u g a l.

8. The inscriptions of Utu-ḫegal have recently been reedited by Steible 1991: 2:324–32; Frayne 1993: 280–96. The authenticity of the inscription concerning the victory over the Gutians (Römer 1985), known only from three Old Babylonian copies, is sometimes doubted. Steible quite rightly omits it. However, we should remember that the inscriptions of Narām-Sîn, also transmitted in Old Babylonian copies, were long supposed by specialists to be late fictions. The discovery of originals allows us to correct this judgment today. Now, it seems that this inscription of Utu-ḫegal falls into the lineage of those of Narām-Sîn, showing the same taste for setting the scene, the same narrative style, and the same discourse.

9. Compare these with the name of a genuine Gutian king, Lā-'arābum, "Without adversary."

V

Diachrony

Utu-ḫegal's good fortune lasted only a little while. Dissension among princes pretending to the succession of the Old Akkadian monarchy meant that before long royal authority was called into question. The collapse of the last Akkadian principality, under the assaults, it appears, of the Elamite Kutik-Inšušinak, took place as the foundations of the empire of Ur were already being laid.

Ur-Namma and Šulgi reacted firmly to this situation, basing their power on a bureaucracy so imposing that historians regard it as the essential hallmark of their state. The new empire of Ur set ever more precise boundaries: political, fiscal, and military. Within these boundaries, the kings imposed their justice, their administration, their fiscal policies, their standard weights and measures—in short, their centralized order. They could do this thanks to an ever-increasing number of functionaries employed and controlled by arms of government that were constantly being further diversified.

Ur cuts a poor figure in the Chronicle of the Single Monarchy (no. 1). No foundation narrative recalls its origins, and no historiographic note evokes the exploits of its kings. Indeed, apart from the chronicle, no epic or historical literature celebrates its past. Curiously, the modern historian seems better equipped to know the history of the city than was the ancient chronicler. Today we know the names of several of its kings who reigned during the third millennium: Ur-pabilsag, A-kalam-du, Mes-kalam-du, his son Mes-ane-pada and grandson A-ane-pada, and, finally, Elili and probably Mes-ki'ag-nuna, though the beginning of his name, lost in a lacuna, is restored. Corruption of sources is insufficient to explain the presence in the chronicle of names such Elulu and Balulu, "esoteric" names that occur frequently in oriental antiquity, which are "stateless" and of which linguistic analysis can make nothing, but which nevertheless spring up and proliferate according to rules of their own.[1] It really seems as if any memory of the kings of Ur from the beginning of the third millennium had become completely blurred, despite their having been solemnly buried, with astonishing pomp, amid cohorts of their servants.[2] The chronicler was therefore obliged to resort to invention to fill the gaps. So, the second dynasty of Ur, whatever the written variants, simply duplicates the first one!

Several features, notably the existence of one manuscript (manuscript P), give us reason to think that, in spite of all, there was at least one edition, and probably more, of the Chronicle of the Single Monarchy composed at Ur during the time of the dynasty founded by Ur-Namma. First, the scribes censored the notice recording the capture of Enme(n)-baragesi by Dumuzi (a notice featuring in only one manuscript probably from Uruk) in order to harmonize historical knowledge with the lesson taught by the royal hymns, according to which it was Gilgameš and not Dumuzi who brought kingship from Kiš to Uruk. Second, there was some revision in the order of succession of certain royal dynasties. This was in fact invariably the same, with the major exception of the sequence Ur 2–Uruk 2, which sometimes appears in reverse order, Uruk 2–Ur 2. This inversion led to the repetition, still in the same order, of the same sequence of Kiš–Uruk–Ur in every place these cities occurred, throughout the work. Thus, on every occasion Ur could find itself in the last position in the royal cycle, as heir of its predecessors.

TABLE 7: VARIANTS IN THE ORDER OF SUCCESSION OF ROYAL CYCLES

(a)	Ur 2	(b)	Uruk 2	(c)	Ur 2	(d)	Uruk 2
	Uruk 2		Ur 2		Uruk 2		Ur 2
	Adab		Adab		Adab		Adab
	Mari		Mari		Mari		Akšak
	Kiš 3		Kiš 3		Kiš 3+4		Mari
	Akšak		Akšak		Akšak		Kiš 3+4
	Kiš 4		Kiš 4		<Uruk 3>		Uruk 3
	Uruk 3		Uruk 3				

Variant a is represented by sources A and L and also probably B.
Variant b is represented by source G.
Variant c is represented by source F, which is erroneous by omitting <Uruk 3>.
Source O (an extract) is to be placed either with a or with c.
Variant d is represented by sources C and K.
Sources I and N are without doubt to be placed with group d.
For variant P, see page 106 below.

Third, the first kings of Ur never stopped emphasizing their kinship with the family of Gilgameš. Šulgi flaunted himself as his "brother" and extolled him for having brought kingship from Kiš to Uruk, after conquering

Enme(n)-baragesi. This was because in their view association by kinship was the determining factor in the gaining of royal power.

With kingship passing at the same time from Uruk to Ur and from one brother to the other, it was still necessary to show that a connection by lineage linked Gilgameš to Enme(n)-baragesi and his son Aka. So it is that in one of the Sumerian epics concerning Gilgameš, Gilgameš and the Cedar Forest, we learn that Enme(n)-baragesi was none other than a sister of the king of Uruk.[3]

Gathering the bits of information concerning the imaginary genealogy of the kings of Ur allows us to draw a mythic genealogical table that is quite impressive, since it goes back, in direct line, to the primordial pair.[4]

TABLE 8: THE MYTHICAL GENEALOGY OF THE KINGS OF UR

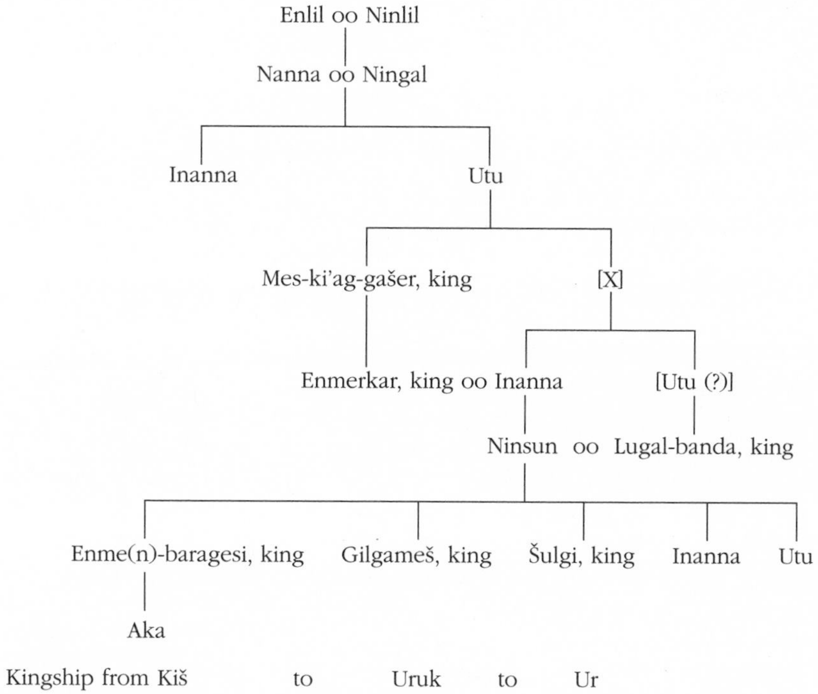

Note the recurrent presence, every second generation, of the names Inanna and Utu. The sources and identifications are as follows: (1) The Chronicle of the Single Monarchy (no. 1): Aka is a son of Enme(n)-baragesi; Mes-ki'ag-gašer is a son of Utu, the sun-god; Enmerkar is a son of Mes-ki'ag-gašer; Gilgameš is the son of an "invisible being," líl; (2) mythological sources: the god Utu, son of Nanna and Ningal, is a brother of Inanna, Nanna himself being the son of Enlil and Ninlil, the primordial couple; (3) Sumerian epics: Enmerkar is son of the god Utu; Inanna is

the sister or cousin (the Sumerian family being of Hawaiian type, "sister" also means "cousin": Civil 1974: 142) of Enmerkar; Lugal-banda marries the goddess Ninsun, whom he finds in the mountains confined with her family, and brings her back to Uruk, where he becomes king of the city; Inanna declares herself to be his mother-in-law (?); Gilgameš is the son of Lugal-banda and Ninsun; Enme(n)-baragesi is a sister of Gilgameš; Gilgameš is the conqueror of Aka of Kiš, whose life he strangely spares; Gilgameš is the brother of Inanna and Utu; (4) royal hymns: Ur-Namma and Šulgi claim to be brothers of Gilgameš and children of Ninsun and Lugal-banda; (5) Aelian, *De Natura animalium* 12.21: King Euechoros (= Enmerkar) of Babylon, on learning that his daughter was going to give birth to a child who would drive him from his throne, ordered her to be closely guarded. Despite the precautions taken, the girl became pregnant through the agency of an "invisible being," *'aphanēs,* and bore a child whom the guards hastened to throw from the top of the citadel. An eagle saved the child and carried it away on its back; he was later adopted by a gardener who taught him his profession. The child was named Gilgameš, and he became king of Babylon.
The oldest document dates from 2600 B.C.E., the most recent from the beginning of the third century C.E.

Thus, just as Gilgameš had brought the kingship previously in the possession of his sister Enme(n)-baragesi from Kiš to Uruk, so Šulgi brought to Ur the kingship of Uruk exercised by his brother Gilgameš. However, this exegesis would have no meaning were it not possible to compare its results with the facts of events in Mesopotamia in the third millennium.

There are good grounds, first, for the hypothesis that Ur-Namma of Ur was a brother of Utu-ḫegal of Uruk (but see no. 48). One votive inscription was even dedicated to the goddess Ningal by a military governor of Ur for the life of his brother King Utu-ḫegal. Even though the governor's name is partly lost, due to a lacuna in the text from which the theophoric element is missing, it is a reasonable possibility that it was Ur-[Namma].[5]

Second, the question arises of the capacity of a woman to transmit property and titles in ancient Mesopotamia. Sumerian juridical documents of the third millennium tend to show that such indeed was the case, even though they do not allow us to appreciate with the precision we would like the exact position the woman occupied in this transmission.[6]

Finally, thanks to two royal inscriptions we know the genealogy of a king of Umma who was a contemporary of Lugal-kiniš(e)-dudu, one Giššakidu, who married his cousin Bara-irnun. The first source[7] explains that Bara-irnun was the daughter of Ur-Lumma, king of Umma. She was the granddaughter or niece of En-a-kale, another king of Umma, and married Gišša-kidu, he being king of Umma, and by this marriage became the daughter-in-law, é.gi$_4$.a, of Ila, also king of Umma. The second source[8] indicates that Ila was the son of E-anda-mu, who had no royal title, and grandson or nephew of En-a-kale. The presence of the term é.gi$_4$.a, which commonly designates a woman who, on marrying, leaves the parental home to enter the house of her in-laws,[9] sufficiently demonstrates that royal marriages conformed to the exogamous principles of Sumerian society. We may thus reasonably conjecture that Bara-irnun was born of the marriage of Ur-Lumma to a sister of Ila. We end up with the following genealogical table.

TABLE 9: THE GENEALOGY OF THE KINGS OF UMMA

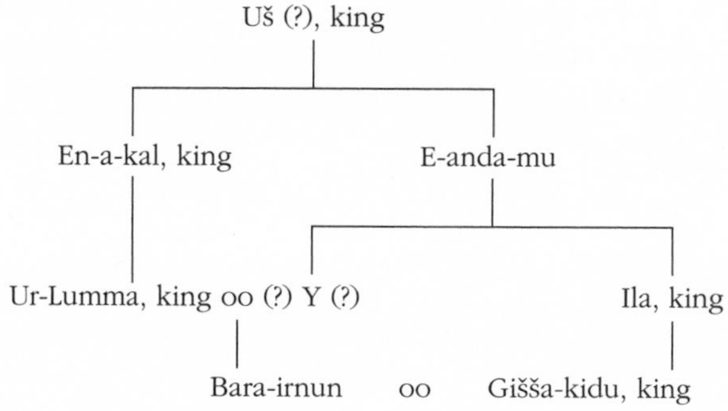

In the part they have in common, the two genealogies of Ur and Umma are strictly identical. Lugal-banda and Gišša-kidu each married a cousin, Ur-Lumma and Enmerkar having both perhaps, in the preceding generation, married a patrilineal first cousin. The two genealogical diagrams, while based on very dissimilar sources, both reproduce official representations of familial structures, and their similarity makes them significant. But the essential point lies elsewhere, in the fact that at this moment the rule passed from one branch of the royal family to another. Only the context changes. Gilgameš was presented as a living threat to the power of his grandfather Enmerkar, and the narrative develops a theme around this, that of succeeding at trials of his legitimacy. It goes without saying that the royal inscriptions of Umma know nothing of this, being obliged to draw a veil over a palace revolution following a military defeat. An inscription of En-mete-na of Lagaš actually records that, following a disastrous expedition against his neighbor, Ur-Lumma was overthrown by Ila, who belonged to a cadet branch of the royal family.[10]

The Chronicle of the Single Monarchy may thus have been revised and rewritten during the period of Ur, most probably during or at the end of the reign of Šulgi.[11] At this time its significance was fundamentally altered.

The rewriting consisted of laying stress on the importance of kinship connections: horizontal links when it was a matter of connecting one royal dynasty with another, vertical links within the same dynasty.

The only manuscript of the chronicle from the period of Ur that we know is manuscript P. It was written during the reign of King Šulgi and differs greatly from the preceding exegesis. It represents in great probability a previous conceptualization of the text for which there is no longer any other evidence, but one might also suggest that several traditions circulated simultaneously during the period of Ur.

As already noted, the dynasties of Kiš 1 to 4 are not separated from one another in this document. Moreover, one discovers the unusual presence of two kings of Ur between Kiš and Uruk; they are more precisely connected to the list of the kings of Kiš, as if they were their direct continuators. In reality, with the help of a subtle play of writing, the author of this variant of the chronicle finished off the list of the names of the kings of Kiš with those of Nanne and his son Mes-nune, two abbreviated forms of the names of Mes-ane-pada and of his son Mes-ki'ag-nuna, two kings of Ur who held, in their own inscriptions, the title "king of Kiš"! To achieve this, the procedure used by the author was obvious and simple: having reached the name of Nanniya in the list of the kings of Kiš, he chose to abbreviate the writing of this last name and to write Nanne (with simple omission of the graphic sign -ia at the end of the name), transforming Nanniya into Nanne and introducing the name of a king of Ur in the sequence of those of Kiš. In this way, the monarchy of Ur acquired a greater legitimacy by being presented as the direct heir to that of Kiš.

On the basis of the assertions of the historians of Isin, we can guess, as will be seen, that the kings of Ur and the intellectuals in their entourage, motivated by a secret "longing for eternity," developed a thesis according to which the monarchy of Ur, the legitimate successor to the monarchies of Kiš and Uruk, was called upon to last forever, or if we wish to paraphrase A. Dupront, that the mark of eternity was on the city. Although scarcely begun, the course of history would already have reached its goal!

The historians of Isin reacted vigorously against this theory. With them the idea of the mortality of historical dynasties grew in importance. Royal power was certainly exercised absolutely, but every dynasty was mortal. We meet this idea in the lament over the destruction of Sumer and Ur,[12] where it is conceded that the word uttered by An and Enlil cannot be revoked and that, so far as Ur was concerned, while kingship had certainly been given to it, an "everlasting dynasty" had, however, not been granted. Furthermore, says the text, no one has ever seen a dynasty that lasted forever. Even if the dynasty of Ur had enjoyed a great longevity, it was decreed in the order of things that it would one day come to an end.

Until the recent discovery of manuscript P, the oldest known manuscripts of the Chronicle of the Single Monarchy dated from the Isin period; consequently, many specialists have proposed dating its composition to that time. According to them, its underlying purpose could only have been conceived when Mesopotamia had broken up into numerous small rival states. Its function would have been, ultimately, "the legitimization of the territorial claim of the weak dynasty of Isin."[13]

Certainly one question that the collapse of Ur added was ever more pressing: the legitimacy of political power. It is true that the kings of Isin effectively presented themselves as the legitimate successors of the kings of Ur; the first three of them assumed their titulary. One list gives the supposed succession of its kings and their total lengths of reign from Ur-Namma to Damiq-ilišu. Certain rituals, as well, give the names of their kings in sequence. But it is also true, and I adhere to this view, that a text could easily have been reedited several times, each edition opening up new possibilities of reading and interpretation.

In the period of Isin it is clear that there were several successive editions for which there are several possible explanations. Version F was perhaps written during the reign of Išme-Dagān, the last ruler mentioned, whose reign was assigned only eighteen years, instead of the expected nineteen (the end of the text, which no doubt gave the totals, as with all other editions from Nippur, is unfortunately lost). Versions A, B, and perhaps I were edited under Ur-Ninurta. Version I ends in the twenty-first year of this reign, which was a total of twenty-eight years in length. As for A and B, we read the following wish concerning this king: "son of Iškur, year of the flood; a good reign: may he have a life of happiness."

Manuscript B, however, while having signs of originally being composed under Ur-Ninurta, is dated to the eleventh king and from the 159th year of the dynasty, that is, the reign of Enlil-bāni. However, there is a difficulty. According to the list of the kings of Ur and Isin, the 159th year does indeed coincide with the reign of Enlil-bāni, but the eleventh king is Zambiya, his successor. This is also the reading of manuscript G of the chronicle. In fact, manuscripts C and D, unlike the other sources, introduce in the tenth position in the dynasty a newcomer, a certain Ikūn-pî-Ištar, who reigned six months (C) or one year (D). This person, whose name, barely legible, is still present only in version D of the chronicle, occurs elsewhere, in a ritual, among the rulers of Isin. He must have appeared in the gap of manuscript B as well.

Versions D and G conclude respectively with mention of Sîn-māgir (G) and his son Damiq-ilišu (D). Each being credited with his full length of reign, we may suppose that the two versions were written after their respective deaths, the second in all probability during the reign of Rīm-Sîn of Larsa. In fact, Damiq-ilišu, the last king of Isin, was defeated first by Sîn-muballiṭ of Babylon, who took control of Isin for a while, then by Rīm-Sîn.

Each edition has a different intention and meaning. Under Išme-Dagān, the monarchy at Isin underwent a period of change, and a new spirit appeared. This king abandoned the former titulary, a legacy of the empire of Ur, and introduced the title "king of Isin," not previously used. As for Ur-Ninurta, the qualification "son of the god Iškur" leads us to suspect that he was perhaps not the son of his predecessor but a usurper needing legitimacy.

With Enlil-bāni, a further change appears. Isin, from which Ur had already broken free some time previously, now lost control of Nippur to Larsa. Although the city was recaptured several times, the king could not hold on to it. Furthermore, Uruk became independent as well. In short, his power was crumbling, and for this very reason it was important for him to see his name associated with a redaction of the chronicle.

Two Neo-Babylonian chronicles (nos. 39 and 40) present him as a gardener chosen to play the role of a substitute king who assumed real power on the death of the titular king. We have already seen what is to be made of the supposed existence, in this early period, of the ritual of the substitute king. Perhaps the adventure of the gardener elevated to royal dignity recalls the figure of Sargon of Akkade, himself a gardener, or the story told by Agathias about Beletaras, the chief gardener of the royal palaces who, following the extinction of the royal line of Semiramis under Beleus, succeeded to the throne. We cannot entirely dismiss the possibility that there was basis in historical reality for these speculations and imaginary tales, having to do with the seizure of power by Enlil-bāni. The presence of a rival in the person of Ikūn-pî-Ištar[14] suggests that the affair did not go without a hitch (see further no. 41).

Under Damiq-ilišu, Larsa was finally victorious over Isin. It was at this point, at the very end of the nineteenth or at the beginning of the eighteenth century, that the myth of the flood suddenly entered the chronicle, as though to reinforce on the ideological level the picture of a power enfeebled politically and militarily at its last gasp. Only two or three manuscripts of the chronicle actually contain the long version of the myth of origin: D, G, and J. The oldest of the three, G, which cannot predate 1816, is the only one preserved. In J, the myth appeared perhaps in abbreviated form. The large number of errors committed by the scribe of G in the antediluvian part of the composition shows that the incorporation of the passage within the chronicle could have taken place only a little before his own copy was made. Perhaps he himself was its author.

There is no doubt that the borrowing was made from a flood story in which Enlil was the chief protagonist. To our present state of knowledge, the oldest witness to such a story is found in the Babylonian Myth of

Atraḫasīs,[15] whose composition can scarcely go back beyond the eighteenth century, of which the similar Sumerian myth, known from a single manuscript from about 1600, is only an adaptation.[16]

Indeed, the theme of the flood was not an ancient narrative motif. In origin the Sumerian word we translate as "flood," a m a r u, indicates a meteorological phenomenon or a fearful weapon in the hands of the war-goddess Inanna.[17] In the sense of "flood," it appears in a hymn glorifying Išme-Dagān of Isin. Here it refers to the abandonment of a city by its god and to the destruction that follows. The same hymn continues with the elevation of Išme-Dagān to royal office "after the flood had leveled everything."[18] The hymn uses the same formula as the chronicle, a point worth emphasizing.

It was thus at the very end of the twentieth century and at the beginning of the nineteenth century that theologians and mythographers of Isin agreed to locate in mythic time, that is, at the beginning, the phenomenon referred to as a m a r u, at the same time giving it a universal reference. The horizon of myth is always within the same temporal perspective. No mythological event can precede another, because myth, which is a narrative "with no location within historical events, being outside history and opening onto history" (D. Anzieu) is invariably "in the beginning." So we are not surprised to find the author of another hymn, this time glorifying Ur-Ninurta, noting carefully that the flood, a m a r u, was indeed situated "in the beginning."[19]

About a century later, at the transition from the nineteenth to the eighteenth century, historians in turn introduced the flood into the fabric of history. The long and detailed introduction of the Babylonian Royal Chronicle (no. 3) shows that this was definitively achieved by the end of the Old Babylonian period.[20]

The overwhelming arrival of the Amorites, at the end of the third and the beginning of the second millennium, was accompanied almost everywhere by their assumption of power. It provoked a real crisis, the coexistence of two systems of values inevitably leading to conflict. At the same time, shaken by foreign domination, society began to change. If the Akkadians perhaps accepted certain elements of Amorite culture, the new arrivals also undoubtedly adopted certain features of the dominant autochthonous one. Important elements of the former social organization persisted, but the traditional representation of power was difficult to sustain.

Following the collapse of Ur, the royal family of Isin, of Amorite origin, remained attached to the prestige of the defunct dynasty. Later, when the Amorites had freed themselves from the cultural overburden of the Sumero-Akkadian world and gave up, for example, "babylonizing" (P. Celan) their names, they abandoned the old style of legitimation. Now they appealed to their own family lineages, in reality to the single Amorite narrative of royal genealogy of which the Assyrian Royal Chronicle (no. 5) and a Babylonian funerary ritual give the fullest list.[21]

After Zabāya and Gungunum of Larsa, the Amorites began to feel that their legitimacy stemmed from these genealogies, so they no longer made use of the established Sumero-Akkadian tradition. Zabāya and Gungunum called themselves "son of Samium" and appear to have been satisfied with this declaration. A list of year names from Larsa, on the other hand, the work of more demanding intellectuals, began with a longer enumeration of the names of Gungunum's predecessors.[22] Later, in Uruk, Sîn-kāšid and Sîn-gāmil proclaimed themselves "king of Amnānum," after the name of the Amorite tribe settled in the environs of the city. Elsewhere Sîn-gāmil of Diniktum took the title "chief of the Amorites" and "son of Sîn-šēmi." On the other hand, Anam, an Amorite in the service of Sîn-gāmil who ascended the throne of Uruk, claimed no relationship to any Amorite lineage or tribe. But he was perhaps not himself of royal stock.[23]

Notwithstanding these examples, Śamśī-Addu of Assyria and Ḫammurabi of Babylon still seem to hesitate—the former in the Assyrian Royal Chronicle (no. 5), the latter in the prologue to his law code—between the one form of legitimation and the other. In Babylon, we have to wait until the time of Ḫammurabi's successors for a final decision on this to be made.

Deep down, the intellectual elites showed a fierce loyalty to the old Sumero-Akkadian tradition and responded to the foreign intrusion with only limited acculturation. The Chronicle of the Single Monarchy (no. 1) continued to be copied throughout the Old Babylonian period (versions F, H, I, J, M, and O), until the end of the dynasty of Ḫammurabi (version N). The manuscripts come from such diverse sites as Isin, Kiš, Sippar, Šubat-Enlil, and Susa, a list to which Ur should be added. This alone illustrates how much favor it continued to enjoy.

However, there seem to be no new editions that brought it up to date. It persisted but as the historiographical component of the political project for which it had been worked up and continued to develop only within a scribal intellectual tradition.

Some scribes were inspired by its example and wrote new chronicles, such as the Old Babylonian manuscript from Nippur (no. 2) or the Babylonian Royal Chronicle (no. 3). However, its influence did not stop there. Leaving aside from more distant continuations such as the Assyrian Royal Chronicle (no. 5) or the parody from Lagaš (no. 6), we see the tradition perpetuated down to the Parthian period with the Hellenistic Royal Chronicle (no. 4).

Other compositions were inspired by it, of which traces remain, a certain chronicle (no. 38), a drinking song in which the spirits of great kings from the past were invoked,[24] or a short fragment listing the names of the kings of Ḫammurabi's dynasty.[25] In the twelth century, Nebuchadnezzar I tried to provide himself a venerable ancestor in the person of Enme(n)-duranki, from among the antediluvian kings of the chronicle.[26]

During the first millennium, intellectual life was marked by the development of a new branch of historical research. The Neo-Babylonian chronicles, by their greater chronological precision, their style, and their choice of subject, contrast with previous historiography.

Berossus of Cos, cited by Syncellus, informs us that it was from the time of Nabonassar's reign that the custom was established of noting the movements of the stars and their duration. He adds that Nabonassar gathered together and destroyed all the evidence concerning his predecessors, thus making the history of the Chaldean kings begin with his own reign.[27] As though echoing this statement, Alexander Polyhistor indicates that Berossus's second book ended with the mention of Nabonassar's name and that the facts reported by Berossus concerning the king's predecessors were anecdotal. Ptolemy is even more precise. According to him, the astronomical observations with which he was familiar went back as far as the reign of Nabonassar, who had founded a historical era that began on 26 February 747 at midday. His *canon basileōn* begins with him in 746 B.C.E., ending with Antoninus in 137 C.E.[28] Later, al-Bīrūnī still remembered an era of Nabonassar in his "chronology of ancient nations."

There is no a priori reason to doubt the assertions of Berossus or Ptolemy,[29] so we must ask if the Babylonian sources confirm the information given by the Greek-speaking authors. In other words, did history begin in Mesopotamia with Nabonassar, and did renewed interest in chronology go hand in hand with the growth of astronomical studies?

Did Nabonassar destroy the written sources from before his own reign? The fashion for antiquities in the following centuries disproves or at any rate severely qualifies this claim. If there was an attempt at destruction, it was doomed to failure.

So we must return to Berossus. We find that the author plays two characters off against each other, Ziusudra and Nabonassar. One appears at the beginning of the second book of his work, the other at the end of the same book, two characters who form a pair of contrasting figures: the first saved from the flood the writings of antediluvian humanity; the second, on the contrary, destroyed all historical writings existing before his reign, so the significance and scope of his testimony are to be modified accordingly.

This need not have prevented a new historiography from beginning in the reign of Nabonassar or under his impetus. It was characterized by a greater demand for accuracy in matters of dating and chronology.

Overall, it is difficult to see any truth in this proposition. The dates 748 (the year of Nabonassar's accession) or 747 (that of his first full year of reign) do not appear to be a decisive break. Chronicle 16 begins in the third year of the reign, with the accession to the throne not of the king of Babylon but of the king of Assyria, Tiglath-pileser III, and Assyrian military intervention in Babylon. Chronicle 17, which lacks some fifteen lines at the beginning, may have gone back to the preceding reign. The Babylonian Royal Chronicle (no. 3) in its present condition ends with Nabonassar, but an entire column of text is lost. As for a certain Chronicle of Former Kings (no. 47), it continues in its present condition to the accession of the Assyrian king Šalmaneser V, at the end of the eighth century, but its end is also missing. Among the other chronographic sources one (no. 52) ends in the tenth century. No other known document, including the "dynastic prophecy" and the Uruk king list, ends or begins in 748 or 747.

Hence, there is no certainty that this year was a pivotal date in the development of Mesopotamian historiography and chronography. The Babylonian sources are hardly more explicit as regards the existence of an era of Nabonassar.[30]

The Babylonian year was a lunar one of twelve months, so there was a discrepancy of just over eleven days between it and the solar year. The addition of an intercalary month to harmonize the lunar and the solar years was an obligatory and long-standing practice in Mesopotamia. From the third millennium, rulers decided, in an arbitrary and erratic manner, to duplicate a month wholly or in part when the need became apparent. Only twelfth-century Assyria was an exception, having no intercalations.

With respect to the conception of an era, it would be necessary to have a regular method of intercalating a supplementary month and astronomical computations of great precision. The Babylonians discovered two methods enabling them to calculate and plan for the regular intercalation of a month into the calendar. One was based on the cycle falsely called the "Saros," which equaled 223 lunations and defined a period of eighteen years.[31] The second was based on the metonic cycle, which lasts 235 lunar months and defines a period of nineteen years.[32]

Certainly astronomy enjoyed a significant revival in the second half of the eighth century. A spectacular conjunction of the moon and the planets was observed in 747. In the same year (although this may be a chance discovery) began an undertaking of considerable scale, systematically recording lunar eclipses. Some reports had already listed these in series of eighteen years.[33] Two later tablets set out lists of specific years of different kings of Babylon, one at intervals of eighteen years, the other of nineteen years. The first went back in time from 99 B.C.E. (a remarkable year in which two particularly long lunar eclipses were observed, on 11 April and 5 October) to 747; the second stopped in 732. The oldest entries were, however, calculated a posteriori, and in some cases incorrectly.[34]

However, all specialists agree that the development of mathematical astronomy could not, in the middle of the eighth century, have computed automatic intercalation of months. At that time there were still several ways of establishing the need for the introduction of a supplementary month, such as the calculation of the relative length of day and night in a day of twelve double-hours, a calculation attested by one source from the middle of the seventh century,[35] or the observation of the conjunction of the moon and the Pleiades, about which Babylonian scientists held conflicting theories.[36] Royal correspondence under Nabonidus, and the correspondence of high officials under Cyrus and Cambyses, still attest to decrees determining the intercalation of a month.[37]

In reality, progress came only later. According to our present state of knowledge, the drawing up of procedures began after 652, the year in which the great rebellion of Šamaš-šuma-ukīn broke out, and regular intercalation began only with the application of the metonic cycle, named after the Athenian astronomer Meton, immortalized by Aristophanes, in the Achaemenid period. This was implemented from 498, 481, or 360. Opinion is divided on the matter.[38]

As for Nabonassar himself, we know very little about him. He appears to have been weak, with his authority contested, and lost territories to the advantage of Assyria. Be that as it may, he was able, after a reign of fourteen years, to leave his throne to his son, Nabû-nādin-zēri, who reigned for two years; we know nothing about him. The documents from their time give no indication of any kind of era.

We are still at liberty, however, to propose the hypothesis that the existence of an era was imagined, retrospectively, well after the death of Nabonassar, at a time when mathematical astronomy made it possible.[39]

Notes

1. Limet 1968: 99–112; Laroche 1966: 240.
2. The practice of the ritual killing of servants is not otherwise known in Mesopotamia, unless it is attested in a Sumerian epic describing the funeral obsequies of Gilgameš (Cavigneaux and Al-Rawi 2000; for English translations, see George 1999: 195–208; Foster 2001: 143–54; see also Veldhuis 2001). This document cannot have been unknown to the intellectuals of the period of Ur.
3. Shaffer 1984. See also Michalowski 2003.
4. Wilcke (1989b: 562–63) has independently proposed a similar exegesis, with a significantly different result.
5. On this text, see Wilcke 1974: 193; the restoration "b[rother]" is fairly certain.
6. Glassner 1989: 84–85.
7. Thureau-Dangin 1937.
8. Stephens 1937: 6.

9. Kraus 1973: 246–51; Wilcke 1987a: 239–40.

10. On this text, see above 8 n. 30. Ila, who had at first been successful against Lagaš, was himself conquered in turn.

11. According to Wilcke, there were at least two editions of the chronicle from the period of Ur: one under Ur-Namma, the other under Šulgi.

12. Michalowski 1989: 364–69.

13. Civil 1980: 230; see also the views of, e.g., Kraus 1952: 46–49; Rowton 1960; Steiner 1979: 134 and passim; Michalowski 1984: 240–43.

14. See Sigrist 1984: 43.

15. Lambert and Millard 1969; Foster 1996: 160–203; Shehata 2001.

16. Civil 1969; Bottéro and Kramer 1989: 564–67, with all the useful references.

17. Eichler 1993; Glassner 1992.

18. Römer 1965: 46.119–20.

19. See Civil 1972: 88–89, sub C.

20. The Neo-Babylonian manuscripts are derived from Old Babylonian originals: Finkel 1980: 71; the title of this chronicle appears in a catalogue from this period: see 52 n. 7 above. Note, however, the reservations of Finkel (1980: 71–72) on such an early date for this introductory formula.

21. See pages 71–72 above. On this question, see Lambert 1974b; Michalowski 1984.

22. Thureau-Dangin 1918.

23. The same hypothesis has been advanced by Michalowski (1984) concerning Išbi-Erra of Isin.

24. See Foster 1996: 894–95.

25. Arnaud 1985: 407, no. 74159ac.

26. Lambert 1974b: passim.

27. According to Jacoby 1958: 395, it was Pseudo-Berossus; according to Burstein 1978: 5–6, it was Berossus himself.

28. Toomer 1984: 10–11.

29. Thus Hallo 1988; Lambert 1990: 27–28.

30. Its existence is allowed by some authors: Grayson 1975a: 13–14; 1980a: 174, 178, 193; Hallo 1988.

31. Kugler 1924: 17, 64, 163–64; Sachs 1948: 282–83; Neugebauer 1975: 1:549–50; 1957: 151, 179; Rochberg-Halton 1988: 41.

32. Neugebauer 1948: 209–10; 1957: 24–25, 177; Sachs 1952: 105–6.

33. On the various problems, see Kugler 1924: 368, 371; Pinches and Sachs 1955: nos. 1414–19, 1422–29.

34. BM 34476: Strassmaier 1892: 198–201; 1893; BM 33809: Frame 1992: 18.

35. Pingree and Reiner 1974: 50–55.

36. Schaumberger 1935: 340–41; Hunger and Reiner 1975.

37. Hallo 1988: 187 n. 101.

38. Seven supplementary months were introduced into the calendar in the third, sixth, eighth, eleventh, fourteenth, seventeenth, and nineteenth years; six times it was the twelth month, once the sixth. Opinions vary on the date: Hallo 1988: 187 n. 103; Wacholder and Weisberg 1971: 240; Sachs 1952: 110; Neugebauer 1957: 177.

39. See, for example, the suggestions of Beaulieu 1997.

Part III

The Documents

VI

The Royal Chronicles

1. CHRONICLE OF THE SINGLE MONARCHY

Sources: Sixteen copies are known that originated between the twenty-first and seventeenth centuries in the principal Mesopotamian sites and the surrounding area.

Bibliography:

A Jacobsen 1939: manuscript L_1; Kramer 1952: 19: Ni 9712a, b, and c. Tablet fragments. Provenience: Nippur. Date: copy from the time of Isin-Larsa or from the beginning of the Ḫammurabi dynasty.

B Jacobsen 1939: manuscripts L_2+P_2; Civil 1961: 80: N 3368. Tablet fragments belonging, perhaps, to two different editions. Provenience: Nippur. Date: copy from the Isin-Larsa period.

C Jacobsen 1939: manuscripts P_3 and P_4; Hallo 1963: 54, CBS 13484; BT 14, unpublished: Klein 1991: 123–29. Fragments of a two-tablet edition of the text. Provenience: Nippur. Date: copy from the Isin-Larsa period.

D Jacobsen 1939: manuscript P_5. Tablet fragment. Provenience: Nippur. Date: second half of the Ḫammurabi dynasty.

E Michalowski 1984: 247, UM 29-15-199. Tablet fragment. Provenience: Nippur. Date: copy from the Isin-Larsa period.

F Wilcke 1987b: pls. 35–36, IB 1564+1565. Tablet fragments. Provenience: Isin. Date: copy from the reign of Ḫammurabi or Samsu-ilūna of Babylon.

G Jacobsen 1939: manuscript WB 444. Octagonal prism. Some breaks. Provenience uncertain, perhaps Larsa. Date: copy from the Isin-Larsa period. I wish to express my gratitude to W. W. Hallo for his generosity in providing me with his collations of the text.

H Jacobsen 1939: manuscript G. Tablet fragment. Provenience: Kiš. Date: second half of the Ḫammurabi dynasty.

I Jacobsen 1939: manuscript Su$_1$. Fragment of a perforated cylinder. Provenience: Susa. Date: middle of the Ḫammurabi dynasty.

J Jacobsen 1939: manuscript Su$_2$. Fragment of a perforated cylinder. Provenience: Susa. Date: middle of the Ḫammurabi dynasty.

K Jacobsen 1939, manuscript Su$_3$+$_4$. Fragments of a perforated cylinder. Provenience: Susa. Date: middle of the Ḫammurabi dynasty.

L Vincente 1990; 1995. Tablet fragments. Provenience: Tell Leilān/Šubat-Enlil. Date: middle or third quarter of the eighteenth century (Eidem 1991: 117).

M Jacobsen 1939: manuscript J. Tablet fragment. Excerpt. Provenience unknown. Date: middle of the Ḫammurabi dynasty.

N Jacobsen 1939: manuscript S. Tablet almost complete. Excerpt. Provenience: Sippar. Date: second half of the Ḫammurabi dynasty.

O van Dijk 1976: 36. Fragment of a school tablet. Excerpt. Provenience unknown. Date: copy from the Old Babylonian period.

P Steinkeller 2003. Provenience unknown. Date: copy from the Ur III period, end of King Šulgi's reign.

Language: The language is Sumerian, but some manuscripts, which were prepared by scribes more familiar with Akkadian, show signs of Akkadian grammar and expression.

Date: Although the copies are all more recent, the work was most probably composed during the reign of Narām-Sîn of Akkade and rewritten under Utu-ḫegal of Uruk.

Contents: history of the monarchy from its origins to the end of the first dynasty of Isin at the beginning of the eighteenth century. I have chosen to present the manuscript G, the most complete one. The Nippur sources usually give numerical totals; the most complete manuscript with these is B.

MANUSCRIPT G

(i)[1][nam].lugal an.ta.e$_{11}$.dè.a.ba [2][Eri]du[ki] nam.lugal.la [3]Eridu[ki] Á.lu.lim lugal<.àm> [4]mu 28,800 ì.ak [5]Á.làl.gar mu 36,000 ì.ak [6]2 lugal [7]mu<.bi> 64,800 íb.ak [8]Eridu[ki] ba.šub [9]nam.lugal.bi Bàd.tibira[ki].šè ba.de$_6$

[10]Bàd.tibira[ki] En.me.en.lú.an.na <lugal.àm> [11]mu 43,200 ì.ak [12]En.me.en.gal.an.na [13]mu 28,800 ì.ak [14][d]Dumu.zi sipa mu 36,000 ì.ak [15]3 lugal [16]mu.bi 108,000 íb.ak [17]Bàd.tibira[ki] ba.šub.bé.en[sic] [18]nam.lugal.bi La.ra.ak[ki]<.šè> ba.de$_6$

[19]La.ra.ak[ki] En!.sipa.zi.an.na <lugal.àm> [20]mu 28,800 ì.ak [21]1 lugal [22]mu.bi 28,800 íb.ak [23]La.ra.ak[ki] ba.šub.bé.en[sic] [24]nam.lugal.bi Zimbir[<ki>].šè ba.de$_6$

When kingsh[ip] had come down from heaven, kingship (was) at [Eri]du. At Eridu, Alulim <was> king; he reigned 28,800 years; Alalgar reigned 36,000 years; two kings reigned 64,800 years. Eridu was abandoned; its kingship was taken to Bad-tibira.[1]

At Bad-tibira, Enme(n)-lu-ana reigned 43,200 years; Enme(n)-gal-ana reigned 28,800 years; the divine[2] Dumuzi, the shepherd, reigned 36,000 years; three kings reigned 108,000 years. I abandon[sic][3] Bad-tibira; its kingship was taken <to> Larak.

At Larak, En(!)-sipazi-ana reigned 28,800 years; one king reigned 28,800 years. I abandon[sic] Larak; its kingship was taken to Sippar.

^{25}Zimbir^{ki} En.me.en.dúr.an.na ^{26}lugal.àm mu 21,000 ì.ak ^{27}1 lugal ^{28}mu.bi 21,000 íb.ak ^{29}Zimbir^{ki} ba.šub.bé.en^{sic} ^{30}nam.lugal.bi Šurup-pak^{ki}<.šè> ba.de$_{6}$

^{31}Šuruppak^{ki} [Ubu]r.tù.tù ^{32}lugal.àm mu 18,600 ì.ak ^{33}[1] lugal ^{34}mu.bi 18,600 íb.ak

^{35}5 uru.ki.meš ^{36}8 lugal ^{37}mu<.bi> 385,200^{sic} íb.ak ^{38}a.ma.ru ba.ùr <<ra ta>> ^{39}egir a.ma.ru ba.ùr.ra.ta ^{40}nam.lugal an.ta.e$_{11}$.dè.a.ba ^{41}Kiši^{ki} nam.lugal.la

^{42}Kiši^{ki} Giš.ùr ^{43}lugal.àm ^{44}mu 1,200 ì.ak ^{45}*Kúl-la-śí-*<<an>>*-na-b*[*e*]*-el* ^{46}mu 900 (?) ì.ak (ii)^{1}[Na.an.GIŠ.li.iš.ma ^{2}mu ... ì.ak ^{3}En.dàra.an.na ^{4}mu ... iti 3 u$_{4}$ 3½ ì.ak] ^{5}*Ba-b*[*u-um* mu ... ì.ak] ^{6}*Pu-an-*[*na-um*] mu [8]40 ì.ak ^{7}*Kà-li-bu-um* ^{8}mu 900 ì.ak ^{9}*Qà-lu-mu* mu 840 ì.ak ^{10}*Zú-qá-qi$_{4}$-ip* ^{11}mu 900 ì.ak ^{12}Á.tab mu 600 ì.ak ^{13}<Maš.dà dumu> Á.tab.ba mu 840 ì.ak ^{14}*Ar-wi-ú-um* dumu Maš.dà.ke$_{4}$ ^{15}mu 720 ì.ak ^{16}E.ta.na sipa lú.an.šè ^{17}ba.e$_{11}$.dè ^{18}lú kur.kur.ra mu.un.gi.na ^{19}lugal.àm mu 1,500 ì.ak ^{20}*Ba-li-iḫ* ^{21}dumu E.ta.na.ke$_{4}$ ^{22}mu 400 ì.ak ^{23}En.me.nun.na mu 660 ì.ak ^{24}Me.lám.Kiši^{ki} dumu En.me.nun.na ^{25}mu 900 ì.ak ^{26}Bar.sal.nun.na dumu En.me.nun.na ^{27}mu 1,200 ì.ak ^{28}Súmug$^{sà\text{-}mug}$ dumu Bar.sal.nun.na ^{29}mu 140 ì.ak ^{30}*Ti-iz-kàr* dumu Súmug$^{sà\text{-}mug}$ ^{31}mu 305 ì.ak ^{32}*Il-ku-ú* mu 900 ì.ak ^{33}*Il-ta-śa-du-um* ^{34}mu 1,200 ì.ak ^{35}En.me.en.bára.ge.si! ^{36}lú ma.da.Elam^{ki}.ma ^{37} ^{giš}tukul.bi íb.ta.an.gúr ^{38}lugal.àm mu 900 ì.ak ^{39}Ak.kà ^{40}dumu En.me.en.bára.ge.si!.ke$_{4}$ ^{41}mu 625 ì.ak ^{42}23 lugal ^{43}mu.bi 23,310 iti 3 u$_{4}$ 3 u$_{4}$ ½ íb.ak ^{44}Kiši^{ki} ^{giš}tukul ba.an.sàg ^{45}nam.lugal.bi É.an.na.šè ba.de$_{6}$

^{46}É.a[n.n]a.k[a (iii)^{1}Mes.ki].ág.ga.[še.er ^{2}dumu] ^{d}Utu e[n.àm ^{3}lugal].àm mu 32[4] ì.ak [Mes].ki.ág.ga.[še.er] ^{5}ab.ba ba.an.ku$_{4}$ ^{6}ḫur.sag.šè ba.e$_{11}$ ^{7}En.me.kár(!) dumu Mes.ki.á[g.ga.še.er] ^{8}lugal Unu^{ki}.ga lú U[nu^{ki}] ^{9}mu.un.dù.a ^{10}lugal.àm ^{11}mu 420 ì.ak ^{12} ^{d}Lugal.bàn.da sipa ^{13}mu 1,200 ì.ak ^{14} ^{d}Dumu.zi šuku$_{x}$ ^{15}uru.ki.ni Ku'ara^{ki} ^{16}mu 100 ì.ak ^{17} ^{d}Bìl.ga.mes ^{18}ab.ba.ni líl.lá ^{19}en Kul.ab.ba.ke$_{4}$ ^{20}mu 126 ì.ak ^{21}Ur.^{d}Nun.gal ^{22}dumu ^{d}Bìl.ga.mes ^{23}mu 30 ì.ak ^{24}U.dùl.kalam.ma ^{25}dumu Ur.^{d}Nun.gal.ke$_{4}$ ^{26}mu 15 ì.ak ^{27}*La-ba-še-er* ^{28}mu 9 ì.ak ^{29}En.nun.dàra!.an.na ^{30}mu 7 ì.ak ^{31}Mes.ḫé simug mu 36 ì.ak ^{32}Me.lám.an.na ^{33}mu 6 ì.ak ^{34}Lugal.ki(!).GIN(!) mu 36 ì.ak ^{35}12 lugal ^{36}mu.bi 2,310 íb.ak ^{37}Unu^{ki} ^{giš}tukul ba.an.sàg ^{38}nam.lugal.bi Urí^{ki}.šè ba.de$_{6}$

^{39}Urí^{ki}.ma ^{40}Mes.an.né.pà.da ^{41}lugal.àm mu 80 ì.ak ^{42}Mes.ki.ág.^{d}Nanna^{sic} ^{43}dumu Mes.an.né.pà.da ^{44}lugal.àm ^{45}mu 36 ì.ak (iv)^{1}[E-lu-lu mu 25 ì.ak ^{2}Ba-lu-lu mu 36 ì.ak ^{3}4 lugal ^{4}mu.bi 177 íb.ak ^{5}Urí^{ki} ^{giš}tukul ba.an.sàg ^{6}nam.lugal.bi *A-wa-an*^{ki}.šè ba.de$_{6}$

^{7}*A-wa-an*^{ki}.na ^{8}... lugal.àm ^{9}mu ... ì.ak ^{10}... lú(?)] ^{11}mu [... ì.ak] ^{12}*Ku-ul-*[...] ^{13}mu 36 [ì.ak] ^{14}3 [lugal] ^{15}mu.bi 356 [íb.ak] ^{16}*A-wa-an*^{ki} ^{giš}[tukul ba.an.sàg] ^{17}nam.l[ugal.bi] ^{18}Kiši^{ki}.šè [ba.de$_{6}$]

At Sippar, Enme(n)-dur-ana was king; he reigned 21,000 years; one king reigned 21,000 years. I abandon[sic] Sippar; its kingship was taken <to> Šuruppak.

At Šuruppak, U[bar]-Tutu was king; he reigned 18,600 years; [one] king reigned 18,600 years.

Five cities; eight kings ruled 385,200[sic] years.[4] The flood swept over. After the flood had swept over, when kingship had come down from heaven, kingship (was) at Kiš.

At Kiš, Gišur was king; he reigned 1,200 years; Kullassina-bēl reigned 900 (?) years; [Nan-GI(Š)-lišma reigned 1,200 (?) years; En-dara-ana reigned 420 years, 3 months, (and) 3½ days]; Bāb[um reigned 300 years;] Pū'an[num] reigned 840 (?) years; Kalibum reigned 900 years; Kalūmum reigned 840 years; Zuqāqīp reigned 900 years; Atab reigned 600 years; <Mašda, son of> Atab, reigned 840 years; Arwi'um, son of Mašda, reigned 720 years; Etana the shepherd, the one who went up to heaven, who put all countries in order, was king; he reigned 1,500 years; Balīḫ, son of Etana, reigned 400 years; Enme-nuna reigned 660 years; Melam-Kiš, son of Enme-nuna, reigned 900 years; Barsal-nuna, son of Enme-nuna, reigned 1,200 years; Samug, son of Barsal-nuna, reigned 140 years; Tizkar, son of Samug, reigned 305 years; Ilku'u reigned 900 years; Ilta-śadûm reigned 1,200 years; Enme(n)-baragesi, the one who destroyed Elam's weapons, was king; he reigned 900 years; Aka, son of Enme(n)-baragesi, reigned 625 years. Twenty-three kings reigned 23,310 years, 3 months, (and) 3½ days.[5] Kiš was defeated; its kingship was taken to Eanna.

In Ea[nn]a, [Mes-ki']ag-ga[šer, son] of Utu, was lo[rd (and) was king]; he reigned 32[4] years; [Mes-]ki'ag-ga[šer] entered into the sea and disappeared; Enmekar, son of Mes-ki'a[g-gašer], the king of Uruk, the one who founded Ur[uk], was king; he reigned 420 years; the divine Lugal-banda, the shepherd, reigned 1,200 years; the divine Dumuzi, the fisherman, whose city was Ku'ara, reigned 100 years; the divine Gilgameš—his father was an invisible being—the lord of Kulaba, reigned 126 years; Ur-Nungal, son of the divine Gilgameš, reigned 30 years; Udul-kalama, son of Ur-Nungal, reigned 15 years; Lā-bašer reigned 9 years; Ennun-dara-ana reigned 7 years; Mesḫe, the metalworker, reigned 36 years; Melam-ana reigned 6 years; Lugal-ki-GIN reigned 36 years; twelve kings reigned 2,310 years.[6] Uruk was defeated; its kingship was taken to Ur.

At Ur, Mes-ane-pada was king; he reigned 80 years; Mes-ki'ag-nuna(!), son of Mes-ane-pada, was king; he reigned 36 years; [Elulu reigned 25 years; Balulu reigned 36 years; four kings reigned 177 years.[7] Ur was defeated; its kingship was taken to Awan.

At Awan, ... was king; he reigned ... years; ... Lu (?) reigned ... years]; Kul[... reigned] 36 years; three [kings reigned] 356 years.[8] Awan was defea[ted]; its kin[gship was taken] to Kiš.

^{19}Kiši^{ki} S[u$_8$.sùd.da ^{lú}túg] ^{20}lugal.à[m] ^{21}mu 200+[... ì.ak] ^{22}Da.da.se$_{11}$ mu [... ì.ak] ^{23}Má.má.gal.la [má.laḫ$_4$] ^{24}mu 360 (?)[+... ì.ak] ^{25}*Ka-al-bu-*[*um*] ^{26}dumu Má.gal.gal.la.[ke$_4$] ^{27}mu 195 ì.[ak] ^{28}TÚG.e mu 360 ì.ak ^{29}Men.nun.na mu 180 ì.ak ^{30}*I-bi*(erased)-[*Iš$_8$-tár*] <<...>> ^{31}mu 290 (?) ì.ak ^{32}Lugal.gu$_{10}$ mu 360 ì.ak ^{33}8 lugal ^{34}mu.bi 3,195 í[b.ak] ^{35}Kiši^{ki} ^{giš}tukul ba.an.sàg ^{36}nam.lugal.bi ^{37}*Ḫa-ma-zí*^{ki}.šè ba.de$_6$

^{38}*Ḫa-ma-zí Ḫa-tá-ni-iš* ^{39}<lugal.àm> ^{40}mu 360 ì.ak ^{41}1 lugal ^{42}mu.bi 360 íb.ak ^{43}*Ḫa-ma-zí*^{ki} ^{giš}tukul ba.an.sàg ^{44}nam.lugal.bi Unu^{ki}.šè ba.de$_6$

^{45}Unu^{ki}.ga En.UG(?).ša$_4$.an.na ^{46}lugal.àm mu 60 ì.ak ^{47}<Lugal.ur.e mu 120 ì.ak ^{48}Ar.ga.an.dé.a mu 7 ì.ak> (v)^{1}[3 lugal ^{2}mu.bi 187 íb.ak ^{3}Unu^{ki} ^{giš}tukul ba.an.sàg ^{4}lugal.bi Urí^{ki}.šè ba.de$_6$

^{5}Urí^{ki}.ma Na.an.né ^{6}lugal.àm ^{7}mu 54+... ì.ak ^{8}Mes.ki.ág.^{d}Nanna ^{9}dumu Na.an.né.ke$_4$ ^{10}mu 48 (?) ì.ak ^{11}... ^{12}dumu Mes.ki.ág.^{d}Nanna].ke$_4$ ^{13}[mu 2 ì.ak ^{14}3] lugal ^{15}mu.bi [...] íb.ak ^{16}[Urí^{ki} ^{giš}tukul ba.an.sàg ^{17}nam.lugal.bi Adab^{ki}.šè ba.de$_6$

^{18}Adab^{ki}.a Lugal.an.né.mu.un.dù ^{19}lugal.àm mu 90 ì.ak ^{20}1] lugal ^{21}[mu.bi 9]0 íb^{sic}.ak ^{22}[Adab^{ki}] ^{giš}tukul ba.an.sàg ^{23}[nam.lugal.b]i *Ma-rí*^{ki}.šè ba.de$_6$

^{24}[*Ma-rí*^{ki}].šè^{sic} *Anu-bu* ^{25}[lugal.àm] mu 30 ì.ak ^{26}[An.ba] dumu *Anu-bu*.ke$_4$ ^{27}[mu 17] ì.ak ^{28}[*Ba-zi* lú].ašgab mu 30 ì.ak ^{29}[*Zi-zi*] lú.túg mu 20 ì.ak ^{30}[*Li?-im-e*]*r* gudu$_4$ mu 30 ì.ak ^{31}[Lug]al-[*i-ti*]*-ir* mu 9 ì.ak ^{32}6 lugal ^{33}[mu.bi] 136 ì^{sic}.ak ^{34}[*Ma-rí*^{ki} ^{giš}tukul] ba.an.sàg ^{35}[nam.lugal].bi ^{36}[Kiši^{ki}.šè] ba.de$_6$

^{37}[Kiši^{ki}.a Kù.^{d}]Ba.ba$_6$ ^{38}[^{munus}lú.kurun].na ^{39}[suḫuš Kiši]^{ki} mu.un.gi.na ^{40}[lugal].àm mu 100 ì.ak ^{41}1 lugal ^{42}mu.bi 100 ì.ak ^{43}Kiši^{ki} ^{giš}tukul ba.an.sàg ^{44}nam.lugal.bi Akšak^{ki}<.šè> ba.de$_6$

^{45}Akšak^{ki}.šè^{sic} Un.zi ^{46}lugal.àm mu 3[0 ì.ak] ^{47}Un.da.lu.lu mu 6 ì.ak ^{48}Ur.ur mu 6 ì.ak (vi)^{1}[*Puzur$_4$*-^{d}Niraḫ mu 20 ì.ak ^{2}*I-šu-il* mu 24 ì.ak ^{3}*Šu*-^{d}EN.ZU dumu *I-šu-il* mu 7 ì.ak ^{4}6 lugal ^{5}mu.bi 93 íb.ak] ^{6}Akšak^{ki} ^{giš}tukul [ba.an.sàg ^{7}nam].lugal.bi ^{8}Kiši^{ki}.šè ba.de$_6$

^{9}Kiši^{ki} *Puzur$_4$*-^{d}EN.ZU ^{10}dumu Kù.^{d}Ba.ba$_6$.ke$_4$ ^{11}lugal.àm mu 25 ì.ak ^{12}[U]r.^{d}Za.ba$_4$.ba$_4$ ^{13}[dumu] *Puzur$_4$*-^{d}EN.ZU.ke$_4$ ^{14}[m]u 400 ì.ak ^{15}[*Sí-m*]*u-dar-ra* mu 30 ì.ak ^{16}[*Ú*]*-ṣí-wa-tár* mu 7 ì.ak ^{17}*Iš$_8$-tár-mu-ti* mu 11 ì.ak ^{18}*Iš-me-*^{d}UTU mu 11 ì.ak ^{19}*Na-an-ni-ia* zadim mu 7 ì.ak ^{20}7 lugal ^{21}mu.bi 491 íb.ak ^{22}Kiši^{ki} ^{giš}tukul ba.an.sàg ^{23}nam.lugal.bi Unu^{ki}.šè ba.de$_6$

^{24}Unu^{ki}.ga lugal.zà.ge.si ^{25}lugal.àm mu 25 ì.ak ^{26}1 lugal ^{27}mu<.bi> 25 ì.ak ^{28}Unu^{ki} ^{giš}tukul ba.an.sàg ^{29}nam.lugal.bi ^{30}*A-kà-dè*^{ki}.šè ba.de$_6$

^{31}*A-kà-dè*$^{<ki>}$ *Śar-ru-ki-in* ^{32}ab!.ba.ni nu.kiri$_6$ ^{33}sagi Ur.^{d}Za.ba$_4$.ba$_4$ ^{34}lugal *A-<kà>-dè*^{ki} lú *A-kà-dè*^{ki} ^{35}mu.un.dù.a ^{36}lugal.àm mu 56 ì.ak ^{37}*Rí-mu-uš* dumu *Śar-ru-ki-in* ^{38}mu 9 ì.ak ^{39}*Ma-ni-iš-ti-iš-šu* ^{40}šeš.gal *Rí-mu-uš* <<uš>> ^{41}dumu *Śar-ru-ki-in* ^{42}mu 15 [ì.ak] ^{43}*Na-ra-am-*^{d}[EN.ZU] ^{44}dumu *Ma-*[*ni-iš-ti-iš-šu*] ^{45}mu [37? ì.ak] ^{46}*Ś*[*ar-kà-lí-śar-rí* ^{47}dumu *Na-ra-am-*^{d}EN.ZU mu 25 ì.ak (vii)^{1}a.ba.àm lu]gal a.ba.àm nu lugal ^{2}[*Ì-gi$_4$*]*-gi$_4$* lugal

At Kiš, S[u-suda, the fuller,] was king; he [reigned] 200 + ... years; Dadase reigned [...] years; Mamagal, [the boatman,] reigned 240 (?) + ... years; Kalbum, son of Magalgal, [reigned] 195 years; TUG reigned 360 years; Men-nuna reigned 180 years; Enbi-[Ištar] reigned 290 (?) years; Lugalgu reigned 360 years; eight kings [reigned] 3,195[sic] years.[9] Kiš was defeated; its kingship was taken to Ḫamazi.

At Ḫamazi, Ḫataniš <was king>; he reigned 360 years; one king reigned 360[10] years. Ḫamazi was defeated; its kingship was taken to Uruk.

At Uruk, En-šakuš-ana was king; he reigned 60 years; <Lugal-ure reigned 120 years; Argandea reigned 7 years>; [three kings reigned 187 years.[11] Uruk was defeated; its kingship was taken to Ur.

At Ur, Nanne was king; he reigned 54 + ... years; Mes-ki'ag-Nanna, son of Nanne, reigned 48 (?) years; ..., son of Mes-ki'ag-Nanna (?) reigned 2 years]; [three] kings reigned ... years.[12] [Ur was defeated; its kingship was taken to Adab.

At Adab, Lugal-ane-mundu was king; he reigned 90 years; one] king reigned [9]0 years.[13] [Adab] was defeated; its [kingship] was taken to Mari.

[At Mari], Anubu[14] [was king]; he reigned 30 years; [Anba], son of Anubu, reigned [17] years; [Bazi], the leather worker, reigned 30 years; [Zizi], the fuller (!), reigned 20 years; [Lim-e]r, the *pašīšu*-priest, reigned 30 years; [Šarr]um-[īt]er reigned 9 years; six kings reigned 136 [years.[15] Mari] was defea[ted; its kingship] was taken [to Kiš.

At Kiš, Ku]-Baba, [the innkeeper], the one who strengthened [the foundations of Kiš], was [king]; she reigned 100 years; one king reigned 100 years. Kiš was defeated; its kingship was taken <to> Akšak.

<At> Akšak, Unzi was king; [he reigned] 3[0] years; Undalulu reigned 6 years; Urur reigned 6 years; [Puzur-Niraḫ reigned 20 years; Išu-Il reigned 24 years; Šū-Sîn, son of Išu-Il, reigned 7 years; six kings reigned 93 years.][16] Akšak [was defea]ted; its kingsh[ip] was taken to Kiš.

At Kiš, Puzur-Sîn, son of Ku-Baba, was king; he reigned 25 years; [U]r-Zababa, [son] of Puzur-Sîn, reigned 400 years; [Sim]udara reigned 30 years; [U]ṣi-watar reigned 7 years; Ištar-mūti reigned 11 years; Išme-Šamaš reigned 11 years; Nanniya, the stonecutter, reigned 7 years; seven kings reigned 491 years.[17] Kiš was defeated; its kingship was taken to Uruk.

At Uruk, Lugal-zagesi was king; he reigned 25 years; one king reigned 25 years.[18] Uruk was defeated; its kingship was taken to Akkade.

At Akkade, Sargon—his father was a gardener—the cupbearer of Ur-Zababa, the king of A<kka>de, the one who founded Akkade, was king; he reigned 56 years; Rīmuš, son of Sargon, reigned 9 years; Man-ištūsu, elder brother of Rīmuš, son of Sargon, [reigned] 15 years; Narām-[Sîn], son of Ma[n-ištūsu, reigned 37 (?)] years; Ś[ar-kali-śarrī, son of Narām-Sîn, reigned 25 years. Who was k]ing? Who was not king? [Irgi]gi (was) king,

^{3}[*Na-nu-um*] lugal ^{4}[*I-mi*] lugal ^{5}[*E-lu-lu*] lugal ^{6}[4.bi] lugal ^{7}[mu 3] ìb.ak ^{8}[*Du-du* m]u 21 ì.ak ^{9}[*Šu-dur-ùl*] dumu *Du-du*.ke$_{4}$ ^{10}[mu] 15 ì.ak ^{11}11 lugal ^{12}mu.bi 181 ìb.ak ^{13}*A-kà-dè*^{ki} ^{giš}tukul ba.an.sàg ^{14}nam.lugal.bi Unu^{ki}.šè ba.de$_{6}$

^{15}Unu^{ki}.šè^{sic} Ur.nigìn lugal.àm ^{16}mu 7 ì.ak ^{17}Ur.^{giš}gigir dumu Ur.nigìn.ke$_{4}$ ^{18}mu 6 ì.ak ^{19}Ku$_{5}$.da mu 6 ì.ak ^{20}*Puzur$_{4}$-ì-lí* mu 5 ì.ak ^{21}Ur.^{d}Utu mu 6 ì.ak ^{22}5 lugal ^{23}mu.bi 30 ìb.ak ^{24}Unu^{ki} ^{giš}tukul ba.an.sàg ^{25}nam.lugal.bi ^{26}ugni<m> *Gu-tu-um*<^{ki}.šè> ba.de$_{6}$

^{27}ugni<m> *Gu-tu-um*^{ki} ^{28}lugal mu nu.tuk ^{29}Ní.bi.a lugal.àm mu 3 ì.ak ^{30}*In-ki-šu$_{4}$* mu 6 ì.ak ^{31}Ì.ḪAB-*lagab*$^{la\text{-}gab}$ mu 6 ì.ak ^{32}*Šul-me-e* mu 6 ì.ak ^{33}*Si-lu-lu-meš* mu 6 ì.ak ^{34}*I-ni-ma-ba-ke-eš* mu 5 ì.ak ^{35}*I-ge$_{4}$-a-uš* mu 6 ì.ak ^{36}*Ia-ar-la-gab* mu 5 ì.ak ^{37}*I-ba-te* mu 3 ì.ak ^{38}*Ia-ar-la* mu 3 ì.ak ^{39}*Ku-ru-um* mu 1 ì.ak ^{40}[*A*]-*pil-ki-in* mu 3 ì-ak ^{41}[*La-'à*]-*ra-bu-um* mu 2 ì.ak ^{42}*I-ra-ru-um* mu 2 ì.ak ^{43}*Ib-ra-nu-um* mu 1 ì.ak ^{44}*Ḫa-ab-lum* mu 2 ì.ak ^{45}*Puzur$_{4}$*-^{d}EN.ZU dumu *Ḫa-ab-lum* ^{46}mu 7 ì.ak ^{47}[*Ià*]-*ar-la-ga-an-da* mu 7 ì.ak ^{48}[*Si*]-*u$_{4}$* mu 7 ì.ak ^{49}[*Ti-ri-g*]*a* u$_{4}$ 40 ì.ak ^{50}21 lugal ^{51}[mu.bi 91] u$_{4}$ 40 ìb.ak (viii)^{1}ugnim *G*[*u-tu-um*^{ki}] <^{giš}tukul ba.an.sàg> ^{2}nam.lugal.bi Unu^{ki}.šè [ba.de$_{6}$]

^{3}Unu^{ki}.ga ^{d}Utu.ḫé.g[ál lugal.àm] ^{4}mu 420 7 u$_{4}$ [ì.ak] ^{5}1 [lugal] ^{6}mu.bi 420 6^{sic} u$_{4}$ [ì.ak] ^{7}Unu^{ki} ^{giš}tukul ba.an.sàg ^{8}nam.lugal.bi Ur[í^{ki}.šè] ba.de$_{6}$

^{9}Urí^{ki}.ma Ur.[^{d}Namma] lugal<.àm> ^{10}mu 18 [ì].ak ^{11} ^{d}Šul.gi dumu ^{d}Ur.^{d}Namma.ke$_{4}$ ^{12}mu 46 ì.ak ^{13} ^{d}Amar.^{d}EN.ZU dumu ^{d}Šul.gi.ke$_{4}$ ^{14}mu 9 ì.ak ^{15}*Šu*-^{d}EN.ZU dumu ^{d}Amar.^{d}EN.ZU ^{16}mu 9 ì.ak ^{17}*I-bí*-^{d}EN.ZU dumu *Šu*-^{d}EN.ZU.ke$_{4}$ ^{18}mu 24 ì.ak ^{19}4^{sic} lugal ^{20}mu.bi 108^{sic} ìb.ak ^{21}Urí^{ki}.ma ^{giš}tukul ba.an.sàg ^{22}nam.lugal.bi Ì.si.in^{ki}.šè ba.de$_{6}$

^{23}Ì.si.in^{ki}.na *Iš-bi-Èr-ra* lugal<.àm> ^{24}mu 33 ì.ak ^{25} ^{d}*Šu-ì-lí-šu* dumu *Iš-bi-Èr-ra*.ke$_{4}$ ^{26}mu 20 ì.ak ^{27}*I-din*-^{d}*Da-gan* dumu *Šu-ì-lí-šu* ^{28}mu 21 [ì.ak] ^{29}*Iš-me*-^{d}*Da-g*[*an* dumu *I-din*-^{d}*Da-gan*.ke$_{4}$] ^{30}mu [20 ì.ak] ^{31} ^{d}*L*[*i-pí-it-Iš$_{8}$-tár* dumu *Iš-me*-^{d}*Da-gan*.ke$_{4}$] ^{32}mu [11 ì.ak] ^{33} ^{d}Ur.[^{d}Nin.urta mu 28 ì].ak ^{34} ^{d}*Bur*-^{d}EN.[ZU dumu ^{d}Ur.^{d}Nin.urt]a.ke$_{4}$ ^{35}mu 21 ì.ak ^{36} ^{d}*Li-pí*-[*it*-^{d}E]n.líl ^{37}dumu *Bur*-^{d}EN.ZU.ke$_{4}$ mu 5 ì.ak ^{38} ^{d}*Èr-ra-i-mi-ti* mu 8 ì.ak ^{39} ^{d}En.líl-*ba-ni* mu 24 ì.ak ^{40} ^{d}*Za-am-bi-ia* mu 3 ì.ak ^{41} ^{d}*I-te-er-pi$_{4}$-ša* mu 4 ì.ak ^{42} ^{d}Ur.du$_{6}$.kù.ga mu 4 ì.ak ^{43} ^{d}EN.ZU-*ma-gir* mu 11 ì.ak ^{44}13^{sic} lugal ^{45}mu.bi 213 ìb.ak

---

šu *Nu-úr*-^{d}Nin.šubur

Totals of B

(xi)^{1}šu.nigín 40 lá [1 lugal] ^{2}mu.bi 14,400[+. . . +]9 mu [3 iti 3 u$_{4}$] ìb.a[k] ^{3}a.rá 4 [kam] ^{4}šà Kiši[^{ki}] ^{5}šu.nigín 22 lu[gal] ^{6}mu.bi 2610[+. . . mu] 6 iti 14+. . .

[Nanum] (was) king, [Imi] (was) king, [Elulu] (was) king; [those four] kings reigned [3 years; Dudu] reigned 21 years; [Šū-Durul], son of Dudu, reigned 15 years; eleven kings reigned 181 years.[19] Akkade was defeated; its kingship was taken to Uruk.

<At> Uruk, Ur-nigin was king; he reigned 7 years; Ur-gigir, son of Ur-nigin, reigned 6 years; Kuda reigned 6 years; Puzur-ili reigned 5 years; Ur-Utu reigned 6 years; five kings reigned 30 years.[20] Uruk was defeated; its kingship was taken <to> the army of Gutium.

The army of Gutium: a king whose name is unknown; Nibia was king; he reigned 3 years; Ingišū reigned 6 years; Ikūkum-lā-qabā reigned 6 years; Šulme reigned 6 years; Silulumeš reigned 6 years; Inimabakeš reigned 5 years; I(g)ge'a'uš reigned 6 years; I''ar-lā-qabā reigned 5 years; Ibate reigned 3 years; Yarla reigned 3 years; Kur(r)um reigned 1 year; Apil-kīn reigned 3 years; [Lā-'a]rābum reigned 2 years; Irarum reigned 2 years; Ibranum reigned 1 year; Ḫablum reigned 2 years; Puzur-Sîn, son of Ḫablum, reigned 7 years; [Y]arlaganda reigned 7 years; [Si]'u reigned 7 years; [Tirig]a reigned 40 days; twenty-one kings reigned [91 years] and 40 days.[21] The army of G[utium] <was defeated>; its kingship [was taken] to Uruk.[22]

At Uruk, Utu-ḫega[l was king; he reigned] 420 years and 7 days; one [king reigned] 420 years and 6[sic] days.[23] Uruk was defeated; its kingship was taken [to] Ur.

At Ur, Ur-[Namma] <was> king; he reigned 18 years; the divine Šulgi, son of the divine Ur-Namma, reigned 46 years; the divine Amar-Su'en, son of the divine Šulgi, reigned 9 years; Šū-Sîn, son of the divine Amar-Su'en, reigned 9 years; Ibbi-Sîn, son of Šū-Sîn, reigned 24 years; four[sic] kings reigned 108[sic] years.[24] Ur was defeated; its kingship was taken to Isin.

At Isin, Išbi-Erra <was> king; he reigned 33 years; the divine Šū-ilišu, son of Išbi-Erra, reigned 20 years; Iddin-Dagān, son of Šū-ilišu, [reigned] 21 years; Išme-Dag[ān, son of Iddin-Dagān, reigned 20] years; the divine L[ipit-Ištar, son of Išme-Dagān, reigned 11] years; the divine Ur-[Ninurta] reigned [28 years;] the divine Būr-Sî[n, son of Ur-Ninurt]a, reigned 21 years; the divine Lipi[t-E]nlil, son of Būr-Sîn, reigned 5 years; the divine (?) Erra-imittī reigned 8 years; the divine (?) Enlil-bāni reigned 24 years; the divine Zambiya reigned 3 years; the divine Iter-pîša reigned 4 years; the divine Ur-dukuga reigned 4 years; the divine (?) Sîn-māgir reigned 11 years; thirteen[sic] kings reigned 213 years.[25]

Hand of Nūr-Ninšubur.[26]

Total: thirty-nine [kings] reigned 14,409 + . . . years, [3 months, (and) 3 days]; four times at Kiš. Total: twenty-two ki[ngs reigned] 2,610 + . . . years,

u$_4$ íb.[ak] ^{7}a.rá 5 kam ^{8}šà Unu^{ki}.ga ^{9}šu.nigín 12? lugal ^{10}mu.bi 396 mu íb.ak ^{11}[a].rá 3 kam ^{12}[šà] Urí^{ki}.ka ^{13}[šu.ni]gín 3 lugal ^{14}mu.bi 356 mu íb.ak ^{15}a.rá 1 kam ^{16}šà *A-wa-an*^{ki} ^{17}[šu].nigín 1 lugal ^{18}mu.bi 420 mu [íb.ak] ^{19}a.rá 1 [kam] ^{20}šà *Ḫ[a-ma-zi]* (...) (xii)$^{1'}$[šu.nigín 11] lugal $^{2'}$[mu.bi 1]97 [mu] íb.ak $^{3'}$[a.rá] 1 kam $^{4'}$[šà *A*]-*kà-dè*^{ki} $^{5'}$šu.nigín 21 lugal $^{6'}$mu.bi 125 mu 40u$_4$ íb.ak $^{7'}$a.rá 1 kam $^{8'}$[šà] ugnim *Gu-ti-um*^{ki} $^{9'}$[šu.nigín] 11 lugal $^{10'}$[mu.b]i 159 mu íb.ak $^{11'}$[šà I.si.i]n^{ki}.na

---

$^{12'}$11 $^{13'}$[uru.ki] nam.lugal.la $^{14'}$[nì.Š]I[D].AK.bi $^{15'}$[šu].nigín 134 lugal $^{16'}$[šu].nigín mu.bi 28,800+[...]+76 $^{17'}$ [...] ... [...] (...)

2. CONTINUATORS: AN OLD BABYLONIAN FRAGMENT FROM NIPPUR

Source: fragments of tablet.
Bibliography: Jacobsen 1939: P$_6$; Civil 1961: 80, N 1610.
Language: Sumerian.
Date: copy from the Old Babylonian period.
Place: Nippur.
Contents: king list or history of the monarchy; the document is too fragmentary to specify times and places.

(...) (i')$^{1'}$4[+... mu ì.ak] $^{2'}$ ^{d}I[r...] $^{3'}$Ur.[...] $^{4'}$dumu nu.mu.[un.tuk] $^{5'}$8 mu ì.[ak] $^{6'}$*Su-mu-a-bu-[um]* $^{7'}$iti 8 mu ì.ak $^{8'}$[*I-k*]*u-un-pi*$_4$*-Iš*$_8$*-tár* l[ugal(?).àm(?)] $^{9'}$[... mu ì].ak (...) (ii')$^{1'}$[šu.nigín ... luga]l $^{2'}$[... mu].bi 125 [+...] íb.ak $^{3'}$[a.r]á 6 kam $^{4'}$[šà ...]^{ki}.a $^{5'}$[šu.nigín ... luga]l (...)

3. CONTINUATORS: THE BABYLONIAN ROYAL CHRONICLE

Sources: fragmentary tablets; four known copies.
Bibliography: Johns 1898: 888; King 1907: 117, 143, and 145; Lambert 1973: 271–75; 1974a; Grayson 1975a: no. 18; Finkel 1980: 65–72.
Language: Babylonian; the Neo-Babylonian versions are bilingual, Babylonian and Sumerian.
Date: two copies are Neo-Assyrian, the other two Neo-Babylonian. The presence of its title in an Old Babylonian catalogue indicates that it was composed much earlier than the extant manuscripts.
Place: Nineveh, library of Aššurbanipal; Babylonia, precise origin unknown.
Contents: history of the Babylonian monarchy from its beginnings to the middle of the first millennium. Unfortunately, the end of the document is lost. The antediluvian section and the flood story were most probably inspired by the so-called "Eridu Genesis" (Jacobsen 1987: 145–50).

6 months, (and) 14½ days; five times at Uruk. Total: twelve (?) kings reigned 396 years; three times at Ur. [To]tal: three kings reigned 356 years; once at Awan. Total: one king [reigned] 420 years; once at Ḫ[amazi. Total: one king reigned 90 (?) years; once at Adab. Total: six (?) kings reigned 136 (?) years; once at Mari. Total: six (?) kings reigned 99 (?) years; once at Akšak. Total: eleven] kings reigned [1]97 [years]; once at Akkade. Total: twenty-one kings reigned 125 years (and) 40 days; once [in] the army of Gutium. [Total]: eleven kings reigned 159 years; [once at Is]in.

Eleven royal cities. Their [count]: total: 134[27] kings. Total: 28,876 + ... years, [... months, (and) ... days.]

(...) [... reigned] 4 + [...] years; I[r-...]; Ur-[...], son of: his name is not [known], reigned 8 years; Sumu-abu[m] reigned 8 months; [Ik]ūn-pî-Ištar w[as king]; he reigned (...)

[Total: ... king]s reigned 125 + [...] years; six dynasties [of ...]a.[28] [Total: ... king]s (...)

(i) 1 [u$_4$ An ^{d}En.líl ^{d}En.ki giš.ḫur.ḫur an.ki.ke$_4$ mu.un.gi.na.eš.a.ba]
[u$_4$ ^{d}*A-nu*]*m* ^{d}En.líl ^{d}[*É-a uṣ-ṣu-rat* an^e ki^{tim} *uk-tin-nu*]
2 [An] ^{d}En.líl.bi.da ^{d}En.ki m[u.un...]
[^{d}*A-nu*]*m* ^{d}En.líl *u* ^{d}*É-a* [...]
3 [n]am.lugal.la kalam.ma.šè m[u.un...]
[*š*]*ar-ru-ti ina ma-a-ti ú-*[...]
4 [l]ugal.e nam.sipa kalam.ma.šè mu.un.[gar.(re.)eš]
šar-ru a-na re-é-ut ma-a-ti iš-[*ku-nu*]
5 un nam.sipa.e.ne mu.un.sum.mu.[(uš)]
ni-ši a-na re-é-<*ú*>*-ti id-di-nu-*[*šum*]
6 nigin sag.gig.ga gìr.a.ni.šè mu.un.gúr.[(ru.uš)]
nap-[*ḫa*]*r ṣal-mat qaq-qa-di a-na še-pi-šú ú-kan-ni-š*[*u*]
7 a[n].ub.da.límmu.ba nam.en.bi pa.è aka.e.dè.eš
[*ina kib-rat ár-b*]*a-'-i be-lu-ut-su ú-šá-pu-ú*
8 [nam.lug]al.la an.ta e$_{11}$.dè.eš.[a.ba]
[*iš-tú šar-ru-t*]*ú iš-tu* an^e *ú-še-ri-da*
9 [nam.lu]gal.la an.ta e$_{11}$.dè.eš.[a.ba]
[*iš-tú šar-r*]*u-tú iš-tu* an^e *ur-da*
10 [Eridu^{ki}.ga] nam.lugal.la
[*i-na Eri$_4$-du$_{10}$*] *šar-ru-tu*
11 [A.lu.lim lugal.e] mu 36,000 in.ak
12 [A.lal.gar] mu 43,200 in.ak
13 [2-àm lugal.e.ne bala Eridu^{ki}.ga] mu 79,200 in.ak
14 [Eridu^{ki}.ga bala.bi ba.kúr nam.lu]gal.bi Bàd.tibira^{ki}.šè ba.nigin
[*Eri$_4$-du$_{10}$* bala-*šú* kúr *šar-ru*]*-ut-su a-na* min *is-sa-ḫar*
15 [En.me.lu.an.na lu]gal.e mu 43,200 in.ak
16 [En.m]e.gal.an.na 46,800 [(+ ...?) in.ak]
17 [Dum]u.zi sipa [mu ... in.ak]
18 [3-à]m lugal.e.ne [bala Bàd.tibira^{ki} mu ... in.ak]
19 [Bàd.ti]bira^{ki} bala.bi ba.kúr nam.lugal.bi Z[imbir^{ki}.šè ba.nigin]
20 [Zimbir]^{ki} En.me.dur.an.ki lugal.e mu 54,[600 in.ak]
21 1 luga[l.e b]ala Zimbir^{ki} mu 54,60[0 in.ak]
22 Zimbir^{ki} b[ala].bi ba.kúr nam.lugal.bi La$_7$.rà.ak^{ki}.šè ba.nigin
23 La$_7$.rà.ak.a^{ki} E[n.sip]a.zi.an.na lugal.e mu 37,200 [(+ ...?) in.a]k
24 1 lugal.e bala L[a$_7$.rà.ak^{k}]^{i} mu 37,200 [(+ ...?) in.ak]
25 La$_7$.rà.ak.a^{ki} bala.b[i ba.kúr na]m.lugal.bi Šuruppak^{k}[^{i}.šè ba.nigin]
26 Šuruppak^{ki} Ubar.^{d}[Tu.tu lu]gal.e m[u ... in.ak]
27 Zi.u$_4$.sud.ra dumu U[bar.^{d}Tu.tu mu ... in.ak]
28 2-àm lugal.e.ne bal[a Šuruppak^{ki} mu ... in.ak]
29 5 uru.didli 9 lugal.e.[ne mu ... in.ak]
30 ^{d}En.líl.le na[m ...]
^{d}En.líl *u* [*š*-...]
31 mu$_7$.mu$_7$ íb.[...]

[When A]nu, Enlil, and [Ea had fixed the plans of heaven and earth, Anu,] Enlil, and Ea [ordained the destinies (?). They established (?)] kingship in the land. [They set up] a king to be shepherd of the land. They gave the people [to him] as shepherd. They made all the black-headed people[29] bow down at his feet. They made his sovereignty resplendent in the "four quarters."[30] After they lowered kingship from heaven, after kingship had come down from heaven, kingship (was) [at Eridu.]

[Alulim, the king,] reigned 36,000 years; [Alalgar] reigned 43,200 years; [two kings, the dynastic cycle of Eridu;] they reigned 79,200 years. [The dynastic cycle of Eridu changed;] its [kin]gship went to Bad-tibira.

[Enme(n)-lu-ana], the king, reigned 43,200 years; [Enm]e(n)-gal-ana [reigned] 46,800 + [. . .] years; [Dum]uzi, the shepherd, [reigned . . . years; three] kings, [the dynastic cycle of Bad-tibira; they reigned . . . years.] The dynastic cycle of [Bad-ti]bira changed; its kingship [went to Sippar.]

[At Sippar,] Enme(n)-dur-anki, the king, [reigned] 54,600 years; one king, the dynastic cycle of Sippar; [he reigned] 54,600 years. The dynastic c[ycle] of Sippar changed; its kingship went to Larak.

At Larak, E[n-sip]azi-ana, the king, reigned 37,200 + [. . .] years; one king, the dynastic cycle of Larak; [he reigned 37,200 + . . .] years. The dynastic cycle of Larak [changed]; its kingship [went to] Šuruppak.

At Šuruppak, Ubar-[Tutu, the ki]ng, [reigned . . .] years; Ziusudra, son of U[bar-Tutu, reigned . . . years]; two kings, the dynastic cycle of [Šuruppak; they reigned . . . years.]

Five cities; nine kings [reigned . . . years.]

Enlil t[ook an aversion to humankind (?)].

ḫu-bur ... [...]
^{32}gul.g[ul.e.dè ...]
a-ba-[*tu* ...]
^{33}ub.d[a ...]
kib-r[*at* ...]
^{34}nì.dím.d[ím.ma ...]
bu-u[*n-na-né-e* ...]
^{35d}En(?).ki [...]
[^{d}*É-a*(?) ...]
(...)
(ii) $^{2'}$[...] šu íb.[ta.an.gar(?)]
[...]-*me-e* šu *iš-ta-*[*kan*]
$^{3'}$[... kalam.m]a dagal.la mi.ni.íb.< >.eš.a.[ba]
[...] *i-na ma*(?)-*a-*[*ti*(?)] *ur-tap-piš*
$^{4'}$[... kalam.m]a ba.ni.íb.gál.la.eš.a.ba
[...]-bu *i-na ma-a-ti uš-tab-ši*
$^{5'}$[...] sila.dagal.la.ke$_4$ in.dub.e.ne
[...]-*im la-bi-ru ina re-ba-a-ti ú-tab-ba-ka*
$^{6'}$[...] kú.kú.e
[...] *ik-ka-la*
$^{7'}$[...] numun.bi ba.sal.sal
[...] *ze-ra-ši-na ir-ta-pi-iš*
$^{8'}$[... nam.lú].u$_{18}$.lu gá.la ba(!).an.dag
[... *i-na n*]*i-ši it-ta-par-ku*
$^{9'}$[...] an.na ba.da.tùm
[...] *a-na* an^{e} *uš-te-eš-še-er*
$^{10'}$[nam.lugal.la] an.ta e$_{11}$.dè.eš.[a.ba]
[*iš-tú šar-ru-tú*] *iš-tu* an^{e} [*ú*]-*še*[*ri-da*]
$^{11'}$[nam.lugal.la] an.ta e$_{11}$.[dè.eš.a.ba]
[*iš-tú šar-ru-tú iš-tu* an^{e} *ur-da*]
(...)

$^{2''I}$An.illat dumu kimin [mu ... in.ak] $^{3''}$ ^{I}En.men.nun.na [mu ... in.ak] $^{4''}$ ^{I}*Me$_5$-lám-Kiš-šú* dumu [En.men.nun.na mu ... in.ak]

(...)

(iv)$^{1'}$Tin.tir[^{ki} ^{I}*Su-mu-a-bu-um* lugal.e mu 14 in.ak] $^{2'}$ ^{I}*Su-mu-* [*la-Él* mu 36 in.ak] $^{3'}$ ^{I}*Sà-bu-ú* [mu 14 in.ak] $^{4'}$ ^{I}*A-pil-*^{d}[30 mu 18 in.ak] $^{5'}$ ^{Id}30-*m*[*u-bal-liṭ* mu 20 in.ak $^{6'I}$*Ḫa-am-mu-ra-bí* mu 43 in.ak $^{7'I}$*Sa-am-su-i-lu-na* mu 38 in.ak $^{8'I}$*A-bí-e-šu-uḫ* mu 28 in.ak] $^{9'}$ ^{I}*Am-me-*[*ṣa-du-qá* mu 21 in.ak] $^{10'}$ ^{I}*Am-mé-e-d*[*i-ta-na* mu 37 in.ak] $^{11'}$ ^{I}*Sa-am-su-d*[*i-ta-na* mu 31 in.ak]

$^{12'}$11 lugal.e.ne bal[a Tin.tir^{ki} mu 300 in.ak.meš] $^{13'}$Tin.tir^{ki} bala.bi b[a.kúr nam.lugal.bi kur a.ab.ba.šè ba.nigin]

The uproar of [… kept him awake]. In order to destroy [...]. The "four quarters" [...]. The form [...]. Ea [...] (...) [...] held [...]. After he had made [...] spread over the land, after he had produced [...] in the land, [...] old [...] were dumped into the streets. [Humans] ate [...], their seed became widespread [...]. Within humanity, [the famine (?)] ceased. [...] prospered for heaven. [After they had] made [kingship] com[e down] from heaven, [after kingship] had come down from heaven,

(...)

Balīḫ, son of ditto (= Etana), [reigned … years;] Enme-nuna [reigned … years]; Melam-Kiš, son of [Enme-nuna, reigned … years;]

(...)

[At] Babylon, [Sumu-abum, the king, reigned 14 years]; Sumu-lā-El [reigned 36 years]; Sabium [reigned 14 years]; Apil-[Sîn reigned 18 years]; Sîn-muballiṭ [reigned 20 years; Ḫammurabi reigned 43 years; Samsu-ilūna reigned 38 years; Abī-ēšuḫ reigned 28 years]; Ammī-[ṣaduqa reigned 21 years]; Ammī-d[itāna reigned 37 years];[31] Samsu-d[itāna reigned 31 years.]

Eleven kings, the dynastic cycle [of Babylon; they reigned 300 years]. The dynastic cycle of Babylon [changed; its kingship went to the Sealand.]

$^{14'}$É.uru.kù.ga^{ki} [^{I}*Ili-ma*-AN lugal.e mu 60 (?) in.ak] $^{15'}$ ^{I}Ki.an-*ni-bu* [mu 56 (?) in.ak] $^{16'}$ ^{I}*Dam-qí-ì-lí-šu* [mu 36 (?) in.ak $^{17'}$ ^{I}*I*]*š-ki-bal* [mu 15 (?) in.ak $^{18'}$ ^{I}*Šu*]*-uš-ši* [mu 24 (?) in.ak]

(. . .)

(v)$^{1'}$[Ì.si.in^{ki} bala.bi ba.kúr nam.lugal.bi] kur a.ab.ba.šè(?) ba.nigin

---

$^{2'}$aga.ús lú.tuš.a kur.a.ab.ba.ke$_4$ ^{I}*Sim-bar-ši-pak* dumu ^{I}*Eri-ba*-^{d}30 $^{3'}$erín bala Sig$_5$.dingir-*šú* ^{giš}tukul.ta ba.an.sìg.gi.in mu 17 in.ak $^{4'}$*ina* é.gal Lugal.gi.na *qí-bir* $^{5'}$ ^{Id}*É-a-mu-kin*-numun lugal im.gi dumu ^{I}*Ḫaš-mar* iti 3 in.ak $^{6'}$*ina raq-qa-ti šá* É-^{I}*Ḫaš-mar qí-bir* $^{7'}$ ^{Id}*Kaš-šú-ú*-sum.šeš dumu ^{I}*SAP-pa-a-a* mu 3 in.ak *ina* é.gal <. . . *qí-bir* >

$^{8'}$3 lugal.e.ne bala kur.a.ab.ba mu 23 in.ak.meš

$^{9'}$[^{I}*É*]*-ul-maš*-gar.mu dumu ^{I}*Ba-zi* mu 14 in.ak *ina* é.gal *Kar*-^{d}Amar.utu [*qí-bir* $^{10'}$ ^{Id}Bar.nì].du.šeš dumu ^{I}*Ba-zi* mu 2 [in].ak $^{11'}$[^{I}*Ši-rik-ti*]-^{d}*Šu-qa-mu-na* kimin 3 iti in.ak *ina* é.gal . . . [. . .] lib

---

$^{12'}$[3 lugal.e.n]e bala É-^{I}*Ba-zi* mu 20 iti 3 [in].ak.meš

$^{13'}$[^{Id}Dumu.é.ibila.ùr]i šà.bal.bal libir.[ra(?)] Elam.ma^{ki} mu 6 in.ak $^{14'}$*ina* é.gal Lugal.gi.na *qí-bir*

$^{15'}$[1 lugal.e] bala [Elam.m]a^{ki} mu 6 in.ak

(. . .)

$^{1''}$kur [. . . ^{Id}Amar.utu.en.numun(?) . . .] $^{2''}$ ^{lú}aga.[ús . . .]

$^{3''}$ ^{Id}Amar.utu.a.ùri [mu . . . in.ak]

$^{4''}$1 lugal.e bala nu.[zu(?) mu . . . in.ak]

$^{5''}$ ^{kur}*Kal-di* bala.bi ba.kúr na[m.lugal.bi kur a.ab.ba.šè ba.nigin]

$^{6''}$kur a.ab.ba ^{I}*Eri-ba*-^{d}[Amar.utu mu . . . in.ak]

$^{7''}$1 lugal.e ba[la kur a.ab.ba mu . . . in.ak] $^{8''}$kur a.ab.ba [bala.bi ba.kúr nam.lugal.bi ^{kur}*kal-di*.šè ba.nigin]

At E'urukuga, [Ili-ma-AN, the king, reigned 60 (?) years]; Itti-ili-nībī [reigned 56 (?) years]; Damiq-ilišu [reigned 36 (?) years]; Iškibal [reigned 15 (?) years; Šu]šši [reigned 24 (?) years];

(. . .)[32]

[The dynastic cycle of Isin changed; its kingship] went to the Sealand.

Simbar-Šipak, a soldier, a resident of the Land of the Sea, a descendant of Erība-Sîn, a soldier who died in combat during the reign of Damiq-ilišu, reigned 17 years; he was buried in Sargon's palace. Ea-mukīn-zēri, a usurper, a son of Ḫašmar, reigned 3 months; he was buried in the marshland of the Bīt-Ḫašmar. Kaššû-nādin-aḫḫē, son of SAPpaya, reigned 3 years; <he was buried> in the palace of <. . .>.

Three kings, the Sealand dynastic cycle; they reigned 23 years.

[E]ulmaš-šākin-šumi, a son of Bazi, reigned 14 years; [he was buried] in the palace of Kār-Marduk. [Ninurta-kud]urrī-uṣur (I), a son of Bazi, [rei]gned 2 years. [Širikti]-Šuqamuna, ditto (= a son of Bazi), reigned 3 months; he was [buried] in the palace of [. . .]

[Three king]s, the Bīt-Bazi dynastic cycle; they [rei]gned 20 years and 3 months.

[Mār-bīti-apla-uṣu]r, a distant descendant of Elam, reigned 6 years; he was buried in Sargon's palace.

[One king], the [Ela]m dynastic cycle; he reigned 6 years.

(. . .)

[Marduk-bēl-zēri (?) . . .] a soldier [. . .]

Marduk-apla-uṣur [reigned . . . years.]

---

1 king, an unk[nown (?)] dynastic cycle; [he reigned . . . years.]

The dynastic cycle of Chaldea changed; [its] ki[ngship went to the Sealand.]

In the Sealand, Erība-[Marduk reigned . . . years.]

One king, the [Sealand] dynastic cyc[le; he reigned . . . years.]

[The dynastic cycle of] Sealand [changed; its kingship went to Chaldea.]

$^{\text{9''}}$ ^{kur}*Kal-di* [^{Id}Nà.mu.gar mu 13 (?) in.ak]

$^{\text{10''}}$1 lu[gal.e bala ^{kur}*Kal-di* mu 13 (?) in.ak] $^{\text{11''}}$ ^{kur}[*Kal-di* bala.bi ba.kúr nam.lugal.bi . . . šè ba.nigin]

$^{\text{12''}}$[^{Id}Nà.kúr(?) . . .]
(. . .)

4. CONTINUATORS: THE HELLENISTIC ROYAL CHRONICLE

Sources: tablet; only one copy known.
Bibliography: Grayson 1980b: 98–100.
Language: Babylonian.
Date: after 145 B.C.E.
Place: Babylon (?).
Contents: king list or history of kingship from Alexander the Great to King Arsaces of the Parthians or one of his immediate successors, and the last Seleucids.

$^{\text{1}}$[. . .^{I}]*A-lik-sa-an-dar* [mu] 7 [in.ak] $^{\text{2}}$ $^{\text{[I]}}$*Pi-lip-su* šeš-*šú šá* ^{I}*A-lik-sa-a*[*n*]-*dar* m[u 8 $^{\text{3}}$3+]1 mu lugal *ina* kur nu tuk ^{I}*An-ti-gu-nu-us* $^{\text{4[l]ú}}$gal.érin^{meš} kur *ú-ma-'i-ir* $^{\text{5}}$ ^{I}*A-lik-sa-an-dar* a *šá* ^{I}*A-lik* m[u] 6 $^{\text{6}}$mu 7.kám *šá ši-i* mu 1.kám ^{I}*Si-lu-ku* lugal $^{\text{7}}$mu 25 in.ak $^{\text{8}}$mu 31.kám Kin ^{I}*Si* LUGAL *ina* kur *Ḫa-ni-i* ga[z $^{\text{9}}$m]u 32.kám ^{I}*An* a *šá* ^{I}*Si* lugal mu 20 in.ak $^{\text{10}}$[m]u 51.kám Gu_4 16 ^{I}*An* lugal gal^{ú} nam^{meš} $^{\text{11}}$[m]u 52.kám ^{I}*An* a *šá* ^{I}*An* lugal 15(!) mu(!) [in.ak $^{\text{12}}$m]u 1š^{u} +6.kám Ne *ina* E^{ki} *i*[*t*]-*te-e*[*š-me*] $^{\text{13}}$um-ma ^{I}*An* lugal gal[^{ú} . . .] . . . [(nam^{meš}?) $^{\text{14}}$mu] 1š^{u} +7.kám ^{I}*Si* [a *šá* ^{I}*An* lugal $^{\text{15}}$mu 20 in.ak (.?.) $^{\text{16}}$mu 8]7.kám ^{I}*Si* [lugal mu 3 in.ak $^{\text{17}}$mu] 90.kám ^{I}*An* lugal *ina* aš.[te] t[uš^{ab} $^{\text{18}}$mu] 35 in.ak $^{\text{19}}$[ta] 1-me 2.kám en 1-me 19 ^{I}*An* [. . . $^{\text{20}}$. . .] *u* ^{I}*An* a^{meš} lugal $^{\text{21}}$mu 1-me 25.kám Sig *ina* E^{ki} *it-te-eš-me* $^{\text{22}}$*um-ma* u_4 25.kám ^{I}*An* lugal *ina* ^{kur}E-lam^{ki} gaz $^{\text{23}}$mu.bi ^{I}*Si* a-*šú ina* aš.te tuš^{ab} mu 12 in.ak $^{\text{24}}$mu 1-me 37.kám Kin u_4 10.kám ^{I}*Si* lugal nam^{meš} <<diš ši>> $^{\text{25}}$iti.bi ^{I}*An* a-*šú ina* aš.te tuš^{ab} mu 11 in.ak $^{\text{26}}$[mu.b]i ^{iti}Apin ^{I}*An u* ^{I}*An* a-*šú* lugal^{meš} $^{\text{27}}$[mu 1-me] 42.kám Ne *ina a-mat* ^{I}*An* lugal ^{I}*An* lugal a-*šú di-ik-ku* $^{\text{28}}$[mu 1-me.4]3.kám ^{I}*An* lugal $^{\text{29}}$[mu 1-me 48.kám] Gan *it-te-eš-me šá* ^{I}*An* l[ugal nam^{meš} $^{\text{30}}$. . .] . . . [. . . $^{\text{31}}$(.?.) $^{\text{32}}$. . .] a . . . [. . . $^{\text{32}}$. . .] iti [. . . $^{\text{33}}$. . .] ^{I}*Di* a *šá* ^{I}*Di* [. . . $^{\text{34}}$. . .] ^{I}*Ar*(?) lugal [. . .].

In Chaldea, [Nabû-šuma-iškun reigned 13 (?) years.]

One kin[g, the dynastic cycle of Chaldea; he reigned 13 (?) years.]
[The dynastic cycle of] Ch[aldea changed; its kingship went to . . .]

[Nabonassar (?) . . .]
(. . .)[33]

[. . .] Alexander (III) (the Great) [reigned] 7 [years]. Philip (III) (Arrhidaeus), Alexander's brother: [8 ye]ars. For [4] years there was no king in the country. Antigonus (Cyclopus), the general, was regent [. . .]. Alexander (IV), son of Alex<ander> (III) (the Great), (was acknowledged king?) in year 6 (of the Seleucid era). Year 7 (S.E.), which was the first year (of his reign), Seleucus (I) was king; he reigned 25 years. Year 31, in the month of Elul, Se<leucus>, the king, was murdered in the land of the Ḫaneans. Year 32, An<tiochus> (I), son of Se<leucus>, was king; he reigned 20 years. Year 51, the 16th of the month of Ayyar, An<tiochus>, the great king, died. Year 52, An<tiochus> (II), son of An<tiochus>, was king; he reigned 15 years. Year 66, in the month of Ab, it was rumored in Babylon that "An<tiochus>, the great king, [died]." Year 67, Se<leucus> (II), [son of An<tiochus>, was king; he reigned 20 years. (.?.). Year 8]7, Se<leucus> (III) [was king; he reigned 3 years. Year] 90, An<tiochus> (III), the king, [ascen]ded the throne; he reigned 35 [years. From] the year 102 until the year 119, An<tiochus> and An<tiochus>, his son (!), were kings (!). Year 125, in the month of Siwan, it was rumored in Babylon that "the 25th day An<tiochus>, the king, was killed in Elam." That same year, Se<leucus> (IV), his son, ascended the throne; he reigned 12 years. Year 137, in the month of Elul, the 10th day, Se<leucus>, the king, died. That same month, An<tiochus> (IV), his son, ascended the throne; he reigned 11 years. That sa[me year], in the month of Araḫsamnu, An<tiochus> and An<tiochus>, his son, were kings. [Year 1]42, in the month of Ab, on the order of An<tiochus>, the king, An<tiochus>, the king, his son, was put to death. [Year 14]3, An<tiochus>,

5. CONTINUATORS: THE ASSYRIAN ROYAL CHRONICLE

Sources: tablets, two of which are amulet-shaped; five copies known.
Bibliography: Grayson 1980b: 101–15; Yamada 1994: 11–37.
Language: Assyrian.
Date: copies range from the eleventh to the eighth century, but the work is earlier; composed during the reign of Śamśī-Addu I, it was later rewritten.
Place: Assyria, specifically Aššur, the city with which this document was closely linked.
Contents: history of Assyrian kingship from its beginnings to Šalmaneser V, at least in its most recent edition.

(B i)^{1} ^{I}*Ṭu-di-ia*[34] ^{2} ^{I}*A-da-mu* ^{I}*Ia-an-gi* ^{3} ^{I}*Suḫ*$_{4}$*-la-a-mu* ^{I}*Ḫar-ḫa-ru* ^{4} ^{I}*Man-da-ru* ^{I}*Im-ṣu*[35] 5 ^{I}*Ḫar-ṣu* ^{I}*Di-da-a-nu* 6 ^{I}*Ḫa-nu-ú* ^{I}*Zu-a-bu*[36] ^{7} ^{I}*Nu-a-bu* ^{I}*A-ba-zu* ^{8} ^{I}*Be-lu-ú* ^{I}*A-za-ra-aḫ* ^{9} ^{I}*Uš-pi-a* ^{I}*A-pi-a-šal*

---

^{10}pap 17 lugal^{meš} $^{\textit{a-ni}}$ *a-ši-bu-tu kúl-ta-ri*

---

^{11} ^{I}*A-mi-nu* dumu ^{I}*Ila-kab-ba-bi* ^{12} ^{I}*Ila-kab-ka-bi* dumu ^{I}*Ia-az-kur-Èl* ^{13} ^{I}*Ia-az-kur-Èl* dumu ^{I}*Ia-ak-me-ni* ^{14} ^{I}*Ia-ak-me-ni* dumu ^{I}*Ia-ak-me-si* ^{15} ^{I}*Ia-ak-me-si* dumu ^{I}*Ilu-Me-er* ^{16} ^{I}*Ilu-Me-er* dumu ^{I}*Ḫa-ia-a-ni* ^{17} ^{I}*Ḫa-ia-a-ni* dumu ^{I}*Sa-ma-a-ni* ^{18} ^{I}*Sa-ma-nu* dumu ^{I}*Ḫa-le-e* ^{19} ^{I}*Ḫa-le-e* dumu ^{I}*A-pi-a-šal* ^{20} ^{I}*A-pi-a-šal* dumu ^{I}*Uš-pi-a*

---

^{21}pap 10 lugal^{meš} $^{\textit{ni}}$ *ša* ad^{meš}-*šú-nu-ni*

---

^{22} $^{[I]}$*Su-li-li*[37] dumu ^{I}*A-mi-ni* ^{23}[^{I}*Ki-i*]*k-ki-a* ^{I}*A-ki-a* ^{24}[^{I}*Pu-zu*]*r-Aš-šur* ^{24} ^{I}*Šal-lim*-pap^{meš} ^{25}[^{I}*Ilu-š*]*um-ma* pap 6 lugal^{meš} $^{\textit{ni}}$ ^{26}[. . .] sig$_{4}$ *šá li-ma-ni-šú-nu la-ú-ṭu-ni*

---

^{27}[^{I}*E-r*]*i-šu* dumu ^{I}*Ilu-šum-ma* ^{28}[*šá li-ma-ni*]-*šu-ni* 40 mu^{meš} lugal$^{\textit{ta}}$ dù$^{\textit{uš}}$

---

^{29}[^{I}*I-ku-n*]*u* dumu ^{I}*E-ri-šu* ^{30}[. . . mu^{meš}] lugal$^{\textit{ta}}$ dù$^{\textit{uš}}$

---

^{31}[^{I}Lugal-*ki-in*] dumu ^{I}*I-ku-nu* ^{32}[. . . mu^{meš} lugal$^{\textit{ta}]}$ dù$^{\textit{uš}}$

---

^{33}[^{I}*Pu-zur*]-*Aš-šur* dumu ^{I}Lugal-*ki-in* ^{34}[. . .] mu^{meš} lugal$^{\textit{ta}}$ dù$^{\textit{uš}}$

---

was (sole) king. [Year 148], in the month of Kislev, it was rumored that "An<tiochus>, the king, [was dead"...] son [...] month [...] De<metrius> (II), son of De<metrius> (I), [...] Ar<saces> (?), the king, [...]

Ṭudiya, Adamu, Yangi, Suḫlāmu, Ḫarḫaru, Mandaru, Imṣu,[38] Ḫarṣu, Didānu, Ḫanû, Zuabu,[39] Nuabu, Abazu, Bēlū, Azaraḫ, Ušpia, Apiašal.

Total: seventeen kings who dwelt in tents.

Aminu, son of Ilā-kabkabû, Ilā-kabkabû, son of Yazkur-El, Yazkur-El, son of Yakmeni, Yakmeni, son of Yakmesi, Yakmesi, son of Ilu-Mer, Ilu-Mer, son of Ḫayāni, Ḫayāni, son of Samāni, Samāni, son of Ḫalê, Ḫalê, son of Apiašal, Apiašal, son of Ušpia.

Total: ten kings who were ancestors.[40]

Sulili,[41] son of Aminu, Kikkiya, Akiya, Puzur-Aššur (I), Šalim-aḫum, Ilu-šūma.

Total: six kings [whose names were written on (?)] bricks (but) whose eponyms are not known (?)[42]

Ērišum (I), son of Ilu-šūma, [whose eponyms] are numbered 40,[43] reigned.

Ikūnum, son of Ērišum, reigned [... years.]

Sargon (I), son of Ikūnum, reigned [... years.]

Puzur-Aššur (II), son of Sargon, reigned [...] years.

---

^{35}[^{I}*Na*]-*ram*-^{d}30 dumu ^{I}*Pu-zur-Aš-šur* ^{36}[...+] 4 mu^{meš} lugal^{ta} dù^{uš}[44]

---

^{37} $^{[I]}$*E-ri-šu* dumu ^{I}*Na-ram*-^{d}30 ^{44}[...] mu^{meš} lugal^{ta} dù^{uš}

---

^{39}[^{Id}*Šam*]-*ši*-^{d}Iškur dumu ^{I}*Ila-kab-ka-bi* ^{40}[*i-na t*]*ar-ṣi* ^{I}*Na-ram*-^{d}30 ^{41}[*a-na* ^{kur}*Kar-du-ni*]-*áš* gin^{ik} *ina lim-me* ^{I}*Ib-ni*-^{d}Iškur ^{42}[^{Id}*Šam-ši*-^{d}]Iškur ta ^{kur}*Kar-du-ni-áš* ^{43}[*e-la-a* ^{uru}É.gal]^{meš} *iṣ-bat* ^{44}3 mu^{meš} *ina* ^{uru}É.gal^{meš} *lu ú-ši-ib* ^{45}[*ina lim-me* ^{I}*A-ta-mar*-^{d}15] ^{Id}*Šam-ši*-^{d}Iškur ^{46}[ta ^{uru}É.gal^{meš} *l*]*u e-la-a* ^{47}[^{I}*E-ri-šu* dumu ^{I}*Na-ram*-^{d}30 *ina* ^{gi}]^{š}gu.za *lu-šat-bi* (ii)^{1} ^{giš}gu.za *iṣ-bat* 33 mu^{meš} lugal^{ta} dù^{uš}

---

^{2} ^{I}*Iš-me*-^{d}*Da-gan* dumu ^{Id}*Šam-ši*-^{d}Iškur ^{3}40 mu^{meš} lugal^{ta} dù^{uš}

---

^{4} ^{I}*Aš-šur-du-gul* dumu *la ma-ma-na* ^{5}*la* en ^{giš}gu.za 6 mu^{meš} lugal^{ta} dù^{uš}

---

^{6}*ina tar-ṣi* ^{I}*Aš-šur-du-gul-ma* dumu *la ma-ma-na* ^{7} ^{I}*Aš-šur*-ibila-*i-di* ^{I}Pap^{ir}-^{d}30 ^{8} ^{Id}30-*na-mir* ^{I}*Ip-qi*-^{d}15 ^{9} ^{Id}Iškur-*ṣa-lu-lu* ^{I}*A-da-si* ^{10}6 lugal^{meš} ^{ni} dumu *la ma-ma-na* ^{11}ká *ṭup-pi-šú* lugal^{ta} dù^{uš}

---

^{12} ^{I}En-*ba-ni* dumu ^{I}*A-da-si* ^{13}10 mu^{meš} lugal^{ta} dù^{uš}

---

^{14} ^{I}*Li-ba-a-a* dumu ^{I}En-*ba-ni* ^{15}17 mu^{meš} lugal^{ta} dù^{uš}

---

^{16} ^{I}*Šar-ma*-^{d}Iškur dumu ^{I}*Li-ba-a-a* ^{17}12 mu^{meš} lugal^{ta} dù^{uš}

---

^{18} ^{I}*Ip-tar*-^{d}30 dumu ^{I}*Šar-ma*-^{d}Iškur ^{19}12 mu^{meš} lugal^{ta} dù^{uš}

---

^{20} ^{I}*Ba-za-a-a* dumu ^{I}En-*ba-ni* ^{21}28 mu^{meš} lugal^{ta} dù^{uš}

---

^{22} ^{I}*Lu-ul-la-a-a* dumu *la ma-ma-na* ^{23}6 mu^{meš} lugal^{ta} dù^{uš}

---

^{24} ^{I}*Šú*-^{uru}Ninua dumu ^{I}*Ba-za-a-a* ^{25}14 mu^{meš} dù^{uš}

---

^{26} ^{I}*Šar-ma*-^{d}Iškur dumu ^{I}*Šú*-^{uru}Ninua ^{27}3 mu^{meš} lugal^{ta} dù^{uš}

---

^{28} ^{I}*E-ri-šu* dumu ^{I}*Šú*-^{uru}Ninua ^{29}13 mu^{meš} lugal^{ta} dù^{uš}

---

^{30} ^{Id}*Šam-ši*-^{d}Iškur dumu ^{I}*E-ri-ši* ^{31}6 mu^{meš} lugal^{ta} dù^{uš}

---

^{32} ^{I}*Iš-me*-^{d}*Da-gan* dumu ^{Id}*Šam-ši*-^{d}Iškur ^{33}16 mu^{meš} lugal^{ta} dù^{uš}

Narām-Sîn, son of Puzur-Aššur, reigned [... +] 4 years.

Ērišum (II), son of Narām-Sîn, reigned [...] years.

Śamśī-Addu (I), son of Ilā-kabkabû, went to Karduniaš [in the t]ime of Narām-Sîn. During the eponymy of Ibni-Addu, [Śamśī]-Addu [went up] from Karduniaš. He took [Ekallātum]. For three years he resided at Ekallātum. During the eponymy of Ātamar-Ištar, Śamśī-Addu went up [from Ekallātum]. He drove [Ērišum (II), son of Narām-Sîn,] from the throne. He took the throne. He reigned 33 years.

Išme-Dagān (I), son of Śamśī-Addu, reigned 40 years.

Aššur-dugul, son of a nobody, who had no right to the throne, reigned 6 years.

In the time of Aššur-dugul, a son of a nobody, Aššur-apla-idi, Nāṣir-Sîn, Sîn-nāmir, Ipqi-Ištar, Adad-ṣalūlu, Adasi, six kings, sons of nobodies, ruled at the beginning of his brief reign.

Bēl-bāni, son of Adasi, reigned 10 years.

Libāya, son of Bēl-bāni, reigned 17 years.

Šarma-Adad (I), son of Libāya, reigned 12 years.

Iptar-Sîn, son of Šarma-Adad, reigned 12 years.

Bazāya, son of Bēl-bāni, reigned 28 years.

Lullāya, son of a nobody, reigned 6 years.

Šū-Ninua, son of Bazāya, reigned 14 years.

Šarma-Adad (II), son of Šū-Ninua, reigned 3 years.

Ērišum (III), son of Šū-Ninua, reigned 13 years.

Šamšī-Adad (II), son of Ērišum, reigned 6 years

Išme-Dagān (II), son of Šamšī-Adad, reigned 16 years

---

34 ^{I}*Šam-ši*-^{d}Iškur dumu ^{I}*Iš-me*-^{d}*Da-gan* [šeš-*šú*] *ša* ^{I}*Šar-ma*-^{d}Iškur 35 [dumu] ^{I}*Šú*-^{uru}Ninua 16 mu[^{meš} lugal^{ta} dù^{uš}]

---

36 ^{I}*Aš-šur*-érin.[táḫ dumu ^{I}*Iš-me*-^{d}*D*]*a-gan* 37 26 mu[^{meš} lugal^{ta} dù^{uš}]

---

38 ^{I}*Pu-zur-Aš-šur* dumu ^{I}*Aš-šur*-érin.táḫ 14[45] [mu^{meš}] kimin

---

39 ^{Id}Be.pap^{ir} dum[u ^{I}*Pu-z*]*ur-Aš-šur* 13 mu^{meš} 40 lugal^{ta} dù^{uš}

---

41 ^{I}Zalag-*ili* dumu ^{Id}Be.pap^{ir} 42 12 mu^{meš} lugal^{t}[^{a} dù^{uš}]

---

43 ^{I}*Aš-šur*-kur$^{ú-ni}$ dumu [^{I}Zalag-*ili*] 44 1 iti u_4^{meš} ^{te} lugal^{ta} dù^{uš}

---

45 ^{I}*Aš-šur*-gal^{bi} dumu ^{Id}Be.pap^{ir} [^{I}*Aš-šur*-kur$^{ú-ni}$ *ina* ^{giš}gu.za(?)] 46 *ú-šat-bi* ^{giš}gu.za *iṣ-bat* [... mu^{meš} lugal^{ta} dù^{uš}]

---

47 ^{I}*Aš-šur*-sum.pap^{meš} dumu ^{I}*Aš-š*[*ur*-gal^{bi} ... mu^{meš} kimin]

(iii)1 ^{Id}Be.pap^{ir} šeš-*šú* *ina* ^{giš}gu.za *ú*-[*šat-bi*(-*šú*) 2 6 mu^{meš} lugal^{ta} [dù^{uš}]

---

3 ^{I}*Aš-šur*-érin.táḫ dumu ^{Id}Be.pap^{ir} 4 7 mu^{meš} lugal^{ta} dù^{uš}

---

5 ^{I}*Aš-šur*-en.un^{meš}-*šú* dumu ^{I}*Aš-šur*-érin.táḫ 6 9 mu^{meš} lugal^{ta} dù^{uš}

---

7 ^{I}*Aš-šur*-ág.un^{meš}-*šu* dumu ^{I}*Aš-šur*-en.un^{meš}-*šú* 8 8 mu^{meš} lugal^{ta} dù^{uš}

---

9 ^{I}*Aš-šur*-sum.pa[p^{meš} dumu] ^{I}*Aš-šur*-ág.[u]n^{meš}-*šu* 10 10 m[u^{meš} lugal]^{ta} [dù]^{uš}

---

11 ^{I}Su.^{d}[Iškur dumu ^{I}*Aš*]-*šur*-en.u[n^{meš}]-*šú* 12 27 m[u^{meš} lugal]^{ta} [dù^{u}]^{š}

---

13 ^{I}*Aš-šur*-ti.[la dumu] ^{I}Su.[^{d}I]škur 14 36 mu[^{meš} lugal]^{ta} dù^{uš}

---

15 ^{Id}Be.érin.táḫ dumu ^{I}*Aš-šur*-ti.la 10 mu^{meš} kimin

---

16 ^{I}Gíd.di-*ili* dumu ^{Id}Be.érin.táḫ 12 mu^{meš} kimin

---

17 ^{Id}Iškur.érin.táḫ šeš-*šú* *ša*[46] ^{I}Gíd.di-*ili* 18 32 mu^{meš} lugal^{ta} dù^{uš}

---

19 ^{Id}*Šùl-ma-nu*-bar dumu ^{Id}Iškur.érin.táḫ 30 mu^{meš} kimin

---

20 ^{Igiš}*Tukul-ti*-^{d}Maš dumu ^{Id}*Šùl-ma-nu*-bar 37 mu^{meš} kimin

---

Šamšī-Adad (III), son of Išme-Dagān (himself the) [brother] of Šarma-Adad, son of Šū-Ninua, [reigned] 16 years.

Aššur-nēr[ārī (I), son of Išme-D]agān, [reigned] 26 years.

Puzur-Aššur (III), son of Aššur-nērārī, ditto 14[47] years.

Enlil-nāṣir (I), so[n of Puz]ur-Aššur, reigned 13 years.

Nūr-ili, son of Enlil-nāṣir, reig[ned] 12 years.

Aššur-šadûni, son of [Nūr-ili], reigned 1 month.

Aššur-rabî (I), son of Enlil-nāṣir, drove [Aššur-šadûni from the throne (?)]. He took the throne. [He reigned . . . years.]

Aššur-nādin-aḫḫē (I), son of Aššur-rabî, [ditto . . . years.]

Enlil-nāṣir (II) [drove] his brother from the throne. He [reig]ned 6 years.

Aššur-nērārī (II), son of Enlil-nāṣir, reigned 7 years.

Aššur-bēl-nišēšu, son of Aššur-nērārī, reigned 9 years.

Aššur-rēm-nišēšu, son of Aššur-bēl-nišēšu, reigned 8 years.

Aššur-nādin-aḫḫē (II), [son] of Aššur-rēm-nišēšu, [reigned] 10 years.

Erība-[Adad (I), son of Aš]šur-rēm-nišēšu, [reigned] 27 years.

Aššur-uball[iṭ (I), son] of Erība-[Adad, rei]gned 36 years.

Enlil-nārārī, son of Aššur-uballiṭ, ditto 10 years.

Arik-dēn-ili, son of Enlil-nārārī, ditto 12 years.

Adad-nārārī (I), brother[48] of Arik-dēn-ili, reigned 32 years.

Šalmaneser (I), son of Adad-nārārī, ditto 30 years.

Tukultī-Ninurta (I), son of Šalmaneser, reigned 37 years.

---

21 ^{Igiš}*Tukul-ti-*^{d}Maš *da-a-ri* ^{I}*Aš-šur*-sum.ibila dumu-*šú* ^{22} ^{giš}gu.za *iṣ-bat* 3[49] mu^{meš} lugal^{ta} dù^{uš}

---

23 ^{I}*Aš-šur*-érin.táḫ dumu ^{I}*Aš-šur*-pap.a[50] ^{24}6 mu^{meš} lugal^{ta} dù^{uš}

---

25 ^{Id}Be-*ku-dúr*-pap dumu ^{I}*Tuk*[*ul-ti*]-^{d}Maš ^{26}5 mu^{meš} lugal^{ta} dù^{uš}

---

27 ^{Id}Maš.ibila.É.kur dumu ^{I}*Ili^{i}-ḫad-da* ^{28}*lìb-lìb-bi ša* ^{I}Su.^{d}Iškur *ana* ^{kur}*Kar-du-ni-áš i*[*l-lik*] ^{29}ta ^{kur}*Kar-du-ni-áš e-la-a* ^{giš}gu.za *iṣ-bat* ^{30}3[51] mu^{meš} lugal^{ta} dù^{uš}

---

31 ^{I}*Aš-šur-dan^{an}* dumu ^{Id}Maš.a.É.kur 46 mu^{meš} kimin

---

32 ^{Id}Maš-*tukul-ti-Aš-šur* dumu ^{I}*Aš-šur-dan^{an}* ^{33}*ṭup-pi-šú* lugal^{ta} dù^{uš}

---

34 ^{I}*Mu-tak-kil-*^{d}*Nuska* šeš-*šú* ki-*šú i-duk* ^{35}*a-na* ^{kur}*Kar-du-ni-áš e-bu-uk-šú* ^{36}*ṭup-pi-šú* ^{I}*Mu-tak-kil-*^{d}*Nuska* ^{giš}gu.za *uk-ta-il* kur^{a} *e-mid*

---

37 ^{I}*Aš-šur*-sag-*i-ši* dumu ^{I}*Mu-tak-kil-*^{d}*Nuska* ^{38}18 mu^{meš} lugal^{ta} dù^{uš}

---

39 ^{Igiš}*Tukul-ti*-a-*É-šár-ra* dumu ^{I}*Aš-šur*-sag-*i-ši* ^{40}39 mu^{meš} lugal^{ta} dù^{uš}

---

41 ^{I}*A-šá-rid*-a.É.kur dumu ^{Igiš}*Tukul-ti*-a.É.šár.ra ^{42}2 mu^{meš} lugal^{ta} dù^{uš}

---

43 ^{I}*Aš-šur*-en-*ka-la* dumu ^{Igiš}*Tukul-ti*-a.É.šár.ra ^{44}18 mu^{meš} lugal^{ta} dù^{uš}

---

45 ^{I}Su.^{d}Iškur dumu ^{I}*Aš-šur*-en-*ka-la* 2 mu^{meš} kimin

---

(iv)^{1}[^{Id}*Šam-ši-*^{d}Iškur dumu ^{Igiš}*Tukul-ti*]-a.É.šár.ra ^{2}[ta ^{kur}*Kar-du-n*]*i-áš e-la-a* ^{I}Su.^{d}Iškur ^{3}[dumu ^{I}*Aš-šur*-en-*ka*]-*la*(!?)[52] *ina* ^{giš}gu.za *ú-šat-bi* ^{4}[^{giš}gu.za] *iṣ-bat* 4 mu^{meš} kimin

---

^{5}[^{I}*Aš-šur*-pap.a dumu] ^{Id}*Šam-ši-*^{d}Iškur 19 mu^{meš} kimin

---

6 $^{\text{[Id]}}$*Šùl-ma-nu*-bar dumu ^{I}*Aš-šur*-pap.a ^{7}[. . .]+2 mu^{meš} lugal^{ta} dù^{uš}

---

8 ^{I}*Aš-šur*-érin.táḫ dumu ^{Id}*Šùl-ma-nu*-bar 6 mu^{meš} kimin

---

9 ^{I}*Aš-šur*-gal^{bi} dumu ^{I}*Aš-šur*-pap.a 41 mu^{meš} kimin

---

10 ^{I}*Aš-šur*-sag-*i-ši* dumu ^{I}*Aš-šur*-gal^{bi} ^{11}5 mu^{meš} lugal^{ta} dù^{uš}

---

12 ^{Igiš}*Tukul-ti*-a.É.šár.ra dumu ^{I}*Aš-šur*-sag-*i-ši* ^{13}32 mu^{meš} lugal^{ta} dù^{uš}

During the lifetime of Tukultī-Ninurta, Aššur-nādin-apli,[53] his son, took the throne. He reigned 3[54] years.

Aššur-nērārī (III), son of Aššur-nāṣir-apli,[55] reigned 6 years.

Enlil-kudurrī-uṣur, son of Tuk[ultī]-Ninurta, reigned 5 years.

Ninurta-apil-Ekur, son of Ili-ḫadda, descendant of Erība-Adad, w[ent] to Karduniaš. He went up from Karduniaš (and) took the throne. He reigned 3[56] years.

Aššur-dān (I), son of Ninurta-apil-Ekur, ditto 46 years.

Ninurta-tukultī-Aššur, son of Aššur-dān, reigned for a short period.

Mutakkil-Nuska, his brother, fought him. He exiled him to Karduniaš. Mutakkil-Nuska held the throne for a brief period. He departed this life.[57]

Aššur-rēša-iši (I), son of Mutakkil-Nuska, reigned 18 years.

Tiglath-pileser (I), son of Aššur-rēša-iši, reigned 39 years.

Ašarēd-apil-Ekur, son of Tiglath-pileser, reigned 2 years.

Aššur-bēl-kala, son of Tiglath-pileser, reigned 18 years.

Erība-Adad (II), son of Aššur-bēl-kala, ditto 2 years.

[Šamšī-Adad (IV), son of Tiglath]-pileser, went up [from Kardun]iaš. He drove Erība-Adad, [son of Aššur-bēl-ka]la, from the throne. He took [the throne]. ditto 4 years.

[Aššurnaṣirpal (I), son of] Šamšī-Adad, ditto 19 years.

Šalmaneser (II), son of Aššurnaṣirpal, reigned [... +] 2 years.

Aššur-nērārī (IV), son of Šalmaneser, reigned 6 years.

Aššur-rabî (II), son of Aššurnaṣirpal, reigned 41 years.

Aššur-rēša-iši (II), son of Aššur-rabî, reigned 5 years.

Tiglath-pileser (II), son of Aššur-rēša-iši, reigned 32 years.

---

^{14} ^{I}*Aš-šur-dan*^{an} dumu ^{Igiš}*Tukul-ti*-a.É.šár.ra ^{15}[23] mu^{meš} lugal^{ta} dù^{uš}

---

^{16} ^{Id}Iškur.érin.táḫ dumu ^{I}*Aš-šur-dan*^{an} ^{17}21 mu^{meš} lugal^{ta} dù^{uš}

---

^{18} ^{Igiš}*Tukul-ti*-^{d}Maš dumu ^{Id}Iškur.érin.táḫ 7 mu^{meš} kimin

---

^{19} ^{I}*Aš-šur*-pap.ibila dumu ^{Igiš}*Tukul-ti*-^{d}Maš ^{20}25 mu^{meš} lugal^{ta} dù^{uš}

---

^{21} ^{Id}*Šùl-ma-nu*-bar dumu ^{I}*Aš-šur*-pap.ibila ^{22}35 mu^{meš} lugal^{ta} dù^{uš}

---

^{23} ^{Id}*Šam-ši*-^{d}Iškur dumu ^{Id}*Šùl-ma-nu*-bar ^{24}13 mu^{meš} lugal^{ta} dù^{uš}

---

^{25} ^{Id}Iškur.érin.táḫ dumu ^{Id}*Šam-ši*-^{d}Iškur ^{26}28 mu^{meš} lugal^{ta} dù^{uš}

---

^{27} ^{Id}*Šùl-ma-nu*-bar dumu ^{I}U.érin.táḫ ^{28}10 mu^{meš} lugal^{ta} dù^{uš}

---

^{29} ^{I}*Aš-šur-dan*^{an} šeš-*šú ša* ^{Id}*Šùl-ma-nu*-bar ^{30}18 mu^{meš} lugal^{ta} dù^{uš}

---

^{31} ^{I}*Aš-šur*-érin.táḫ dumu ^{I}U.érin.táḫ ^{32}10 mu^{meš} lugal^{ta} dù^{uš}

(C iv)^{24}*Tukul-ti*-a.É.šár.ra dumu ^{I}*Aš-šur*-érin.táḫ ^{25}18 mu^{meš} man^{ta} dù^{uš}

---

^{26} ^{Id}*Šùl-ma-nu*-bar dumu ^{Igiš}*Tukul-ti*-a.É.šár.ra ^{27}5 mu^{meš} man^{ta} dù^{uš}

COLOPHON (VERSION B)

^{33}gaba.ri ^{uru}*Bal-til*^{ki} ^{34}šu ^{I}*Kan-dàl-a-nu* ^{lú}dub.sar é dingir ^{35}*ša qí-rib* ^{uru}*Arba-ìl*^{ki} ^{36} ^{iti}*Lu-lu-bé-e* u_4 20.kam ^{37}*li-mu* ^{Id}Iškur.en.gin ^{38} ^{lú}gar.kur ^{uru}Šà.uru ^{39}*ina* 2e *lim-me-šú*

COLOPHON (VERSION C)

^{28}gin$_7$ libir.ra-*šu šà-ṭir ba-rì* ^{29}*ṭup-pi* ^{I}En.mu.aš ^{lú}maš.maš ^{uru}*Bal-til*^{ki} *u* ^{30}[*ša*] *i-tab-bal-lu* ^{d}*Šá-maš lit-bal-šu*

6. A PARODY: THE ROYAL CHRONICLE OF LAGAŠ

Sources: tablet; only one copy known.
Bibliography: Sollberger 1967: 279–91.
Language: Sumerian.

Aššur-dān (II), son of Tiglath-pileser, reigned [23] years.

Adad-nērārī (II), son of Aššur-dān, reigned 21 years.

Tukultī-Ninurta (II), son of Adad-nērārī, reigned 7 years.

Aššurnaṣirpal (II), son of Tukultī-Ninurta, reigned 25 years.

Šalmaneser (III), son of Aššurnaṣirpal, reigned 35 years.

Šamšī-Adad (V), son of Šalmaneser, reigned 13 years.

Adad-nērārī (III), son of Šamšī-Adad, reigned 28 years.

Šalmaneser (IV), son of Adad-nērārī, reigned 10 years.

Aššur-dān (III), brother of Šalmaneser, reigned 18 years.

Aššur-nērārī (V), son of Adad-nērārī, reigned 10 years.[58]

Tiglath-pileser (III), son of Aššur-nērārī, reigned 18 years.

Šalmaneser (V), son of Tiglath-pileser, reigned 5 years.

COLOPHON (VERSION B):

Aššur copy. Hand of Kandalānu, scribe of the temple of Arbēla. Month of Lulubû, 20th day, eponymy of Adad-bēla-ka''in, governor of Aššur. During his second eponymy.

COLOPHON (VERSION C):

Written and checked with the original. Tablet of Bēl-šuma-iddin, Aššur's exorcist. [Whoever] carries (this tablet) away, may Šamaš take him.

Date: copy from the middle of the Old Babylonian period. The work, which is based on an imitation of the flood narrative, cannot be earlier than the eighteenth century.
Place: probably Lagaš.
Contents: history of the kings of Lagaš from the beginning of the world to Gudea. The city of Lagaš, as well as other cities, was ignored by chronicle 1. This text, in the form of a humorous parody, fills the gap. Should it also be seen as a critique of a prevailing ideology?

^{1}[egir a.m]a.ru ba.ùr.ra.ta ^{2}[ù gi]l.le.èm kur.ra.ke$_{4}$ ba.an.gar.ra.ta ^{3}n[am].l[ú].lu$_{8}$ da.re.eš i.ak.a.ba ^{4}numun nam.lú.lu$_{8}$ im.mi.in.tag$_{4}$.a.ba ^{5}un sag gi$_{6}$.ga im.bi.a im.mi.in.íl.la.a.ba ^{6}u$_{4}$ an.né ^{d}En.líl.le ^{7}nam.lú.lu$_{8}$ mu.bi sa$_{4}$.a.ta ^{8}ù nam.énsi in.g[ar.r]a.ta ^{9}nam.lugal aga ur[u.à]m ^{10}an.t[a nu].ub.ta.an.è.[a.ba] ^{11} ^{d}[ni]n.[gí]r.su ^{giš}al ^{giš}[mar] ^{12} ^{gi}dusu ^{giš}apin.e zi.šà.gál kalam.[ma] ^{13}un sì.ga šár.a nu.gar.re.eš.a.ba ^{14}u$_{4}$.ba lú tur dàn.dàn.na.ka ^{15}mu 100 ì.ak ^{16}nam.bùlug.gá.ni.ta mu 100 bí.in.ak ^{17}kin.gi$_{4}$.a li.bí.íb.ge$_{4}$.ge$_{4}$ ^{18}ì.tur ì.tur.tur ì.gál ama.a.ni ^{19}udu(?).a.ni tùr.re im.ma.an.d[e$_{5}$.d]e$_{5}$ ^{20}u$_{4}$.ba a Lagaša^{ki} dù.[ù.uš.a] ^{21}Gír.su^{ki} šà.gar [ì.gál.àm] ^{22}i$_{7}$ nu.un.dun.[na.àm] ^{23}e.pa$_{5}$.re šu.lu[ḫ] nu.ak.[àm] ^{24}a.gàr gal.gal.e ^{g}[^{iš}sún].na nu.un.[nag] ^{25}gá[n].né gána zi.d[è a ḫ]é.gál.la [nu.un.dé] ^{26}nam.lú.lu$_{8}$ igi.bi im.šèg.šèg.[gá in.bar] ^{27} ^{d}Ašnan še gu.nu nu.ub.ta.[an.mú] ^{28}ab.sín.na [ka.bi nu.un.du$_{8}$.ḫa.àm] ^{29}gú nu.mu.u[n.gùr] ^{30}an.edin.na [nu.un.úru.àm] ^{31}gú nu.mu.u[n.gùr] ^{32}kur.kur un lu.a dingir.[re.ne.er] $^{33[ká]š}$ ^{ú}ulušin^{i}$_{7}$ ^{káš}kúru[n ...] $^{34[ká]š}$kúrun du$_{10}$ ... [... ^{35}nu].mu.u[n.ne.éb.bal.bal] ^{36}a.[š]à gal ^{gi}[^{š}apin.ta ^{37}nu.mu.u]n.n[e].e[b.úru] (...) ^{48}i$_{7}$ [...] ^{49}a.šà.b[i ...] ^{50}i$_{7}$ dun.n[e.dè] ^{51}e.pa$_{5}$.re š[u(!).luḫ ak.dè] ^{52}a.gàr gal.gal.e ^{g}[^{iš}sú.na nag.e.dè] ^{53}gán.né gána zi.d[è a ḫé.gál.la] im.[ta.an.dé.dè] ^{54giš}al ^{giš}mar ^{g}[^{i}dusu ^{giš}apin.e] ^{55}zi.šà.gál k[alam.ma] ^{56}un.šè im.ta.an.[gar.re.eš] ^{57}u$_{4}$.bi.a še e$_{11}$.d[è.da] $^{58[géš].túg}$geštu.ga.a.ni na.a[n.gub] ^{59}[ki.s]ikil.šè igi.ni.šè ba.š[i].in.gub.ba.a[š] ^{60}u$_{4}$ gi$_{6}$.bi.ta k[i] ulušin.b[i.šè] ^{61}sag.ba ba.š[i].i[n.íl] ^{62} ^{d}Ašnan še numun.bi mu.[m]ú.a ^{63}ki.a bí.in.za.za.aš im.m[i.n]i.in.e$_{11}$.[dè.eš] ^{64} ^{d}[Ašnan še] gu.nu mu.[mú].a ^{65}[...] ku [...] eš ^{66}[... i]n.[íl] ^{67}[... d]u (...) ^{99}mu [... ì.ak] ^{100}Igi.ḫuš ... [...] ^{101}i$_{7}$ BUM m[u.un.dun] ^{102}mu 2,760 ì.[ak] ^{103}En.á.ki.gal.la.[gub.ba] ^{104}dingir.ra.ni ^{d}... [...] ^{105}i$_{7}$ Sirara^{ki} giš.tug.àm [mu.un.dun] ^{106}mu 1,200 ì.a[k] ^{107}u$_{4}$.ba m[u s]ar nu.me.a ... [...] ^{108}i$_{7}$ nu.un.dun ^{gi}dusu [nu.un.íl] ^{109}u$_{4}$.bi.a á úr lugal.[la.šè] ^{110}un giš.tag.ga guškin si.sá.a ^{111}e$_{11}$.ne.ra ḫuša.na ḫuš.a ^{112}ba.ni.in.gar ^{113}...tag.ga utul$_{9}$ zi.[dè] ^{114}un.šè im.ta.an.è ^{115}a suḫur ab.ba abrig ùr.ra ^{116}sag.šè mu.ni.rig$_{7}$ ^{117}En.^{d}Nin.gír.su.ki.ág ^{118}dumu En.á.ki.gal.la.gub.ba ^{119}mu 1,320 ì.ak ^{120}En.^{d}En.líl.le.ki.ág ^{121}dumu En.^{d}Nin.gír.su.ki.ág ^{122}mu 1,800 ì.ak ^{123}Ur.^{d}Ba.ba$_{6}$ dumu En.^{d}en.líl.l[e.k]i.ág ^{124}mu 900 ì.ak ^{125}Á.gal dingir.ra.ni ^{d}Ig.alim ^{126}mu 660 ì.ak ^{127}KU.e dumu Á.gal.la.ke$_{4}$ ^{128}mu 1,200 ì.ak ^{129}Ama.alim dum[u K]U.[e ...] ^{130}mu 600 ì.[ak ^{131}*D*]*a-an-*... [... ^{132}mu ... ì.ak] ^{133}... [...] ^{134}m[u ... ì.ak] ^{135}A... [...]

After the flood had swept over and caused the destruction of the earth, when the permanence of humanity had been assured and its descendants preserved, when the black-headed people had risen up again from their clay, and when, humanity's name having been given and government having been established, An and Enlil had not yet caused kingship, crown of the cities, to come down from heaven, (and) by (?) Ningirsu, they had not yet put in place the spade, the hoe, the basket, nor the plow that turns the soil, for the countless throng of silent people,[59] at that time the human race in its carefree infancy had a hundred years. Coming into an advanced age, it had (another) hundred years. (But) without the ability to carry out the required work, its numbers decreased, decreased greatly. In the sheepfolds, its sheep and goats died out. At this time, water was short at Lagaš, there was famine at Girsu. Canals were not dug, irrigation ditches were not dredged, vast lands were not irrigated by a shadoof,[60] abundant water was not used to dampen meadows and fields, (because) humanity counted on rainwater. Ašnan did not bring forth dappled barley, no furrow was plowed nor bore fruit! No land was worked nor bore fruit! No country or people made libations of beer or wine, [. . .] sweet wine [. . .], to the gods. No one used the plow to work the vast lands.

(. . .)

[. . .] The canals [. . .]. Their fields [. . .]. In order to dig the canals, in order to dredge the irrigation ditches, in order to irrigate the vast lands by a shadoof, in order to utilize abundant water so that the meadows and fields were moistened, (An and Enlil-) [put] a spade, a hoe, a basket, a plow, the life of the l[and], at the disposal of the people. After this time (human beings) gave all their attention to making the barley grow. Before the Young Lady, in front of her they stood upright (ready to work). Day and night, whenever necessary, they were attentive. They bowed down before Ašnan who produces the barley seed and began to work. Before Ašnan who produces the late barley, they [. . .]

(. . .)

[. . . reigned . . .] years. Igi-ḫuš[. . .] dug the canal [". . ."]; he [reigned] 2,760 years. En-a-kigala-guba, whose god was [. . .], dug the canal "He [bends] an ear to Sirara"; he reigned 1,200 years. At that time there was still

^{136}m[u … ì.ak] ^{137}*'À*-[…] ^{138}… [… ^{139}mu … ì.ak ^{140}…] ^{141}i$_7$ [… mu.un.dun] ^{142}mu [… ì.ak ^{143}… ^{144}…] ^{145}i$_7$ M[aḫ i$_7$ …] ^{146}i$_7$ Pirig.[g]e$_{18}$.gin [i$_7$ …] ^{147}i$_7$ Pirig ka i$_7$ L[ugal.ka] ^{148}i$_7$ Gána.[ḫ]i.li.an.na i$_7$ T[e…] ^{149}i$_7$ ^{d}Nanše.pà.da mu.un.[dun] ^{150}a.gàr gal.gal aš.e èn.bi tar.[re.dè] ^{151}pa$_5$ a.du$_{11}$.ga AMAR.TI.AN [mu.un.dun] ^{152}mu 2,220 ì.ak ^{153}Ur.^{d}Nanše du[mu] … ma ke$_4$ ^{154}É.sìrara é šà.ḫúl.la.ni ^{155}Sirara^{ki} uru ki.ág.gá.ni mu.dù.a ^{156}mu 1,080 ì.ak ^{157}An.né.túm dumu Ur.^{d}Nanše.ke$_4$ ^{158}ki alim.ma.na dingir.re.e.ne ^{159}mu.un.gub.ba sag.du(?) ^{d}En.líl gal… ^{160}dingir.ra.ni ^{d}Šul.utul ^{161}mu 690 ì.ak ^{162}[…gi]bil dumu An.né.túm ^{163}mu […+]360 ì.ak ^{164}[En].èn.tar.zi dingir.ra.ni ^{d}Mes.an.DU ^{165}n[um]un u$_4$ ri.a uru.da mú.a ^{166}mu 990 ì.ak ^{167}[…e]n.da.in.si dumu En.èn.tar.zi ^{168}[i$_7$ Ur.ma]ḫ.bàn.da i$_7$ tab.ta(?).gú(!?).gál ^{169}[mu.un.dun] dingir.ra.ni ^{d}Mes.an.DU ^{170}[lugal.a.ni] ^{d}Nin.gír.su ^{171}[é.a.ni dù.dè] mu.un.na.du$_{11}$ ^{172}mu 960 ì.ak ^{173}[E]n.[^{d}En.líl.l]e.su mu 600 ì.ak ^{174}E[n…] du[mu En.^{d}En.líl.l]e.su ^{175}[dingir.ra].ni ^{d}Ni[n.a].sú mu 660 ì.ak ^{176}[…d]u$_8$ mu 1,110 ì.ak ^{177}[*Puzur$_4$*-^{d}Nin.líl]l m[u … šu].ši 1 ì.ak ^{178}[En.^{d}Mes.an.DU dumu *Puz*]*ur$_4$*-^{d}Nin.líl.lá ^{179}[dingir.ra.ni ^{d}… mu] 2 šu.ši ì.ak ^{180}[*D*]*a-du* dumu En.^{d}Mes.an.DU mu 160 ì.ak ^{181}TÚG.GUR dumu *Da-du* mu 160 ì.ak ^{182}*La*-… mu 120 ì.ak ^{183}*Puzur$_4$*-^{d}Ma.ma dub.sar [^{d}N]in.k[i] ^{184}dingir.ra.ni ^{d}Za.za.ru mu […] ì.ak^{185}LAM.KU.nì.gi.na šà.tam *Puzur$_4$*-^{d}Ma.ma ^{186}lú bàd Gír.su^{ki} é.[a].ni ^{187}é.gal T[i].ra.áš [k]i Lagaša^{ki} mu.dù.a ^{188}mu 280 ì.ak ^{189}[Ḫé.en].gál dumu LAM.KU.nì.gi.na ^{190}[dingir.ra.ni] ^{d}…bil.sag mu 140 <ì.ak> ^{191}[…] dumu Ḫé.en.gál mu 144 <ì.ak> ^{192}[Ur].^{d}Nin.MAR.KI.ka dub.sar um.mi.a ^{193}[…u]su.sag.dúr.ra [din]gir.ra.ni ^{d}Ḫa.ià ^{d}Nisaba ^{194}[mu …+]20 ì.ak ^{195}[Ur.^{d}]Nin.gír.su dumu Ur.^{d}N[in.MAR.KI.ka mu … š]u.ši <ì.ak> ^{196}[Ur.^{d}]Ba.ba$_6$ dub.sar Ur.^{d}[Nin.gír.su.ka l]ú ^{197}… unken.na [… mu …+]30 <ì.ak> ^{198}Gù.dé.a šeš bàn.da Ur.^{d}Ba.ba$_6$.k[a …] ^{199}dumu ama.na dumu ad.da nu.me.a [mu … ì.ak] ^{200}é.dub.ba sar.ra ^{d}Nisaba z[à.mí]

no writing [. . .], no canals were dug, no baskets were carried. At that time, in the manner of a royal [. . .], humanity presented offerings of polished gold, red . . . The faithful shepherd brought forth [. . .] to the . . . people, the steward[61] offered him fish. . . . En-Ningirsu-ki'ag, son of En-a-kigala-guba, reigned 1,320 years. En-Enlile-ki'ag, son of En-Ningirsu-ki'ag, reigned 1,800 years. Ur-Baba, son of En-Enlile-ki'ag, reigned 900 years. Agal, whose god was Igalim, reigned 660 years. KUe, son of Agal, reigned 1,200 years. Ama-alim, son of KUe, [reigned] 600 years. Dan[. . .] reigned [. . .] years. [. . . reigned . . .] years. A[. . . reigned . . .] years. 'A[. . ., son of . . ., reigned . . . years. . . . dug] canal [". . ."; he reigned . . .] years. [. . . , son of (?) . . .] dug the "Eminent" canal, [the ". . ." canal], canal "Which moves like a lion," [the ". . ." canal], the "Lion" canal at the mouth of canal "Royal," the canal "Field, heaven's delight," the [". . ."] canal, canal "Choice of Nanše." To take care, alone, of the vast watered areas, he [dug] irrigation ditches . . . [. . .]; he reigned 2,220 years. Ur-Nanše, son of [. . .]ma, who built E-sirara, the residence that was his heart's joy, (and) Sirara, his beloved city, reigned 1,080 years. Ane-tum, son of Ur-Nanše, on the . . . on which the gods stood upright, the . . . of Enlil [. . .], whose god was Šulutula, reigned 690 years. [. . . gi]bil, son of Ane-tum, reigned [. . .] + 360 years. [En]-entar-zi, whose god was Mes-an-DU, seed of days of old who grew up with the city, reigned 990 years. [. . .]enda-insi, son of En-entar-zi, [dug] the "Ferocious lion" canal and canal ". . . is canal inspector"; his god was Mes-an-DU. [His king] Ningirsu enjoined [him to build his temple]; he reigned 960 years. En-[Enlil]e-su reigned 600 years. En[. . .], so[n of En-Enlil]e-su, whose [god] was Ni[na]su, reigned 660 years. [. . . d]u reigned 1,110 years. [Puzur-Ninl]il reigned [. . .] x 60 + 1 years. [En-Mes-an-DU, son of Puz]ur-Ninlil, [whose god was . . .], reigned 120 [years]. Dādu, son of En-Mes-an-DU, reigned 160 years. TUG-GUR, son of Dādu, reigned 160 years. La[. . .] reigned 120 years. Puzur-Mama, [N]ink[i]'s scribe, whose goddess was Zazaru, reigned [. . .] years. LAM-KU-nigina, Puzur-Mama's administrator, the one who constructed the wall of Girsu, his residence, (and) the T[i]raš palace in Lagaš, reigned 280 years. [Ḫen]gal, son of LAM-KU-nigina, whose god was . . . (?)-bilsag, <reigned> 140 years. [. . .], son of Ḫengal, reigned 144 years. [Ur]-Nin.MAR.KI, scribe and expert, [. . .] . . . , whose gods were Ḫaya and Nisaba, reigned [. . .] + 20 years. [Ur]-Ningirsu, son of Ur-Ni[n.MAR.KI,] <reigned> [. . .] x 60 years. [Ur]-Baba, scribe of Ur-[Ningirsu], the one who [. . .] in the assembly, <reigned> [. . .] + 30 years. Gudea, younger brother of Ur-Baba, [. . .], who was not the son of either his mother or father, [reigned . . . years].

Written in the Academy. Pr[aise] to Nisaba.

Notes

1. The wording used to indicate the change of cycles varies, see page 65 above; most manuscripts—A, B, C, E, G, I, K, M, O—adopt GN_1 ^{giš}tukul ba(.an).sàg nam.lugal.bi GN_2.šè ba.de$_6$, "GN_1 was defeated; its kingship was carried to GN_2"; manuscript J opts for the phrase GN_1 ba.gul etc., "GN_1 was destroyed; . . . ," L using alternately the two formulae; in the antediluvian part of G and once of E, another formula is used: GN_1 ba.šub etc., "GN_1 was abandoned; . . ."; in D and N, the formula chosen is GN_1 bala.bi ba(.an).kúr etc., "the reign of GN_1 was alienated. . ."; finally, in C, about Uruk, we find one last formula: nam.lugal a.rá n kam.ma.šè Unu^{ki}.šè ba?.e?.gur, "the kingship for the nth time returned to Uruk"; about this last formula, see the comments on page 96 above.

In several manuscripts, the order of succession of certain dynastic cycles varies: see the commentary on page 102, table 7.

In source I iv we find a unique dynastic cycle composed of five royal names: [lugal].àm, [. . .] mu ì.na, [. . .]x x, [dumu . . .].ke$_4$?, [. . . , . . . mu] ì.na, [. . .]né, [. . . mu] ì.na, [. . .]gi$_4$, [. . .] mu ì.na, [. . .]^{d}Utu, [dumu . . .].x.gi$_4$.ke$_4$, [. . .] mu ì.na [5] lugal.

2. Sometimes the names of kings were preceded by a written sign, a divine determinative that seems to put them into a category of gods; for this metonymic use, see the comments on page 39 above.

3. On the numerous scribal errors in the antediluvian introduction, see the commentary on pages 57–58 above, table 1.

4. Other lists of kings from before the flood exist; none is clearly tied to the chronicle. On these lists, see the commentary on page 58 above.

5. First dynasty of Kiš:

Restorations are taken from manuscript B; I omits several names; the sequence of kings who succeed to Pū'annum varies: see pages 60–61 above and table 2.

Main graphic variants: Gá(?).DAGAL(?).ùr(?) for Giš.ùr in C; as Berossus offers the name of Eueksios, possible corruption for Euekoros (Jacoby 1958: 384 and n. to line 4), for the first postdiluvian king, Wilcke 1989b: 570, proposes a reading [En?].^{giš}[ig?(.šu)].ùr; a reading Giš.ùr, possible equivalent of the royal name Gušur mentioned in a historical omen (Frayne and George 1990), is now established by manuscript P, a confirmation of the collation of manuscript G by W. W. Hallo. *Ku-la-śí-na-be-el* for *Kúl-la-śí*!-<<AN>>*-na-be-el* in B, C, and D; P offers a different name: x-x-*la-na-bi-ir*-e, possibly ^{d}*Ì-la-na-bi-ir*-e for *Ila-nawir;* Berossus recalls the name of Kosmabelos, whom he assumes to be the son of Eueksios. ŠÀ(?).TAG.TAG.TAR-ku-um-e instead of Nan-GI(Š)-lišma in P. In P, in the gap between Pū'annum and Enme-nuna, there is space for only six or seven names. Me-en-nun-na-ke$_4$ in P for Enme-nuna. *Maš-ka*$_{15}$*-en* for Maš.dà in C; *Ar-bu-um* for *Ar-wi-ú-um* in C; concerning these two names and their possible interpretation, see above, page 91 note 9. E.da.na for E.ta.na in C and I. *Wa-li-iḫ* for *Ba-li-iḫ* in B. [Su/Sa-mu]-úg for Samug in L; Melam-Kiš, Su/amug and Tizkar are omitted in P. P offers the name *Il-qí-śa-dú* instead of Ilku'u and Ilta-śadûm. Ak for Ak.ka in C and P.

Length of reigns: Gišur: 2,160 years in P; x-x-la-nawir: 960 years in P; ŠÀ(?).TAG.TAG.TAR-ku-um: 1,770 years in P; En-dara-ana: [. . .] years, 3 months and 2½ days in J; Kalūmum: 900 years in C; Zuqāqīp: 840 years in C; Etana: 725

years in B; Balīḫ: 410 years in B; Enme-nuna: 611 years in B, 1,200 in P; Melam-Kiš: 75 years in B; Barsal-nuna: 900 years in P; Ilqi-śadû: 300 years in P; Enme(n)-baragesi: 600 years in P; Aka: 1,500 years in P; total: 14,400 + [. . .] years, 3 months, and 3½ days in C, 20,970 years, 3 months, and 2½ days in J, 18,000 + [. . .] years in L.

Others: Su/amug is son of Barsal-nuna in B. In C, descendants of Enme-nuna end with Barsal-nuna. About the bala of Enme-nuna and Enme(n)-baragesi, see page 64 above.

6. First dynasty of Eanna/Uruk:

Main graphic variants: Mes.ki.in.ga.še.er for Mes.ki.á.ga.še.er in A and B, Mes.ki.in.ág.še.er in C. En.me.er.kár for En.me.kár in A and B; possibly in Aelian, *De natura animalium* 12.21, the name of Seuechoros, which is perhaps to be corrected to Euechoros, is a reminiscence of Enmekar. Ur.lugal for Ur.^{d}Nun.gal in J. In C, the names of Lugal.bàn.da and Dumu.zi are not preceded by the divine determinative, nor in J and L that of Lugal.banda.

Length of reigns: Mes-ki'ag-gašer: 325 years in B; Enmerkar: [. . .] + 900 years in L; Dumuzi: 110 years in L; Melam-ana: 75 years in K; Lugal-ki-GIN: 7 years in K; total: 3,588 years in K.

The phrase ḫur.sag.šè . . . e_{11}, "to climb the mountain," is a euphemism for "to disappear," "to die"; compare the Akkadian *šadâ rakābu,* which has the same literal sense and same usage. This occurrence brings to mind the story as told by Berossus. Are they not both solar heroes? Compare this to another euphemism, *šadâ(šu) emēdu,* "to go up (his) mountain" or "to pass away," the word "mountain" meaning the world of the dead. The place of the sentence added after the mention of the length of the reign shows that the intent is no longer to celebrate a feat of that king. See also the comments of Vincente 1995: 249–50, *sub* i 24'.

Others: about the bala of Mes-ki'ag-gašer in C, see page 64 above. Between Enmerkar and Lugal-banda, manuscript L adds another king: Lugal.si.nam.SAR; this is obviously a scribe's error: see Vincente 1995: 251 *sub* i 28'. Manuscript C adds this biographical note to illustrate Dumuzi's reign: šu.aš En.me.bára.ge_4.e.si nam.ra ì.ak, "singlehandedly, he captured Enme(n).baragesi."

The names of the kings of Uruk (I to III) are lost in the gap of cols. iii and iv in P. There is space for no more than nine or ten names before Lugalzagesi to be restored.

7. First dynasty of Ur:

Restorations are taken from manuscript B.

Main graphic variants: Mes.ki.ág.nun.na for Mes.ki.ág.^{d}Nanna in B and F (restored in A): G's copyist mistook the name for Mes.ki'ag.Nanna from the second dynasty of Ur.

Length of reigns: Mes-ki'ag-nuna: 30 years in B; total: 171 years in B and, probably, in A.

In manuscript P, the king of Ur Nanne (length of reign: 40 years) and his son Mes-nune are linked to the theory of the kings of Kiš. Perhaps a further name is to be restored in the following gap.

8. Dynasty of Awan: restorations are taken from manuscript F, itself defective.

9. Second dynasty of Kiš:

Restorations are taken from manuscript O.

Main graphic variants: I-bí-[. . .] in A, I-bi-. . . [. . .] in L, for En-bi-Iš$_8$-tár.

Others: Men-nuna is said to be son of TUG in A; the last two kings are listed in reverse order in A and L; manuscript P lists *Kiši-iš$_x$-qí-šú* as first king, Da.da.se$_{11}$-LUM.e and Má.má.gal.e as second and third; in the following gap, there is space for, at least, five names, possibly Kalbum, TUG, Men-nuna, Enbi-Eštar, and Lugalgu, before Kù-Baba is to be restored.

Length of reigns: Kiš-išqišu: 420 years in P; DadaseLUM: 1,500 years in P; Magalgal: 420 years in A; Kalbum: 132 years in A; Lugalgu: 420 years in A; total: 3,792 years in A.

10. Variant: 420 years in B.

11. Second dynasty of Uruk:

Restorations: text G is corrupt; restorations are taken from manuscript A.

Main graphic variants: [En].UG.šà.an.na for En.UG(?).ša$_4$.an.na in L, En.š[à. . .] in A.

Source K makes no mention of the second king of the dynasty; source C replaces Lugal-ure by Lugal.ki.ni.šè.[du.du].

12. Second dynasty of Ur:

Restorations are taken from manuscripts F, L, and O.

Length of reigns: total: 582 years in F, 578 in L.

13. Restorations are taken from manuscripts A and L, but manuscript P adds a dynasty of Adab between Gutium and Uruk; see note 22 below.

14. The name syllabically written (*A-nu-bù*), appears in the letter from Enna-Dagān of Mari to the king of Ebla: Pettinato 1980: 238: ii 1; Edzard 1981: 89-97. See also Bonechi 1990: no. 124.

15. Dynasty of Mari:

Restorations are taken from manuscript L.

Main graphic variants: Ná?/Zi?-ší/zi for An.ba in A; Lugal-i-ter for [Lug]al-[i-ti]-ir in L; gú.du for gudu$_4$ in L.

Length of reigns: Anubu: 90 years in L; Anba: 7 years in L; Šarrum-īter: 7 years in L; total: 184 years in L.

Several readings were proposed for the reading of the name AN.BU: *Ilum-pû*, *Ilšu*, *Ili-īšer*. On that dynasty, see the comments of Vincente 1995: 257–60.

16. Dynasty of Akšak:

Restorations are taken from manuscript N.

Length of reigns: Undalulu: 12 years in A, L, and N; total: 99 years in L and N, 5 kings and 87 years in F, 7 kings and 96 + [. . .] years in A.

F omits Undalulu; A mentions seven kings, though the names of the first two are lost.

17. Third and fourth dynasties of Kiš:

Main graphic variants: Kù.^{d}Bu.[ú] for Kù.^{d}Ba.ba$_6$ in L; *Na-ni-ia* for *Na-an-ni-ia* in N, *Be-lí-*[. . .] in F, where the text should probably be emended to read *N*<*a*>*-ni-*[*ia*], the second half of the sign NA having been omitted by the scribe.

Length of reigns: Puzur-Sîn: 4 years in P; Ur-Zababa: . . . + 20 years in A, 6 years in N and P; Simudara: 30 + . . . years in F, 7 years in I, 20 years in P; Uṣi-watar: 6 years in N; Imi-Šamaš: 6 years in P; Nanniya: 3 years in N; total: probably 487 years in L; in manuscripts I, K, and N, in which the two dynasties of Kiš 3 and 4 are regrouped, the totals are, respectively: 7 kings and 485 years,

[5] kings and ... years (this manuscript omits the last three royal names), 8 kings and 190 years.

Others: Uṣi-watar is omitted in P; Simudara is replaced by Zi.gu_{10}.ì.ak.e in L (for that name, see Vincente 1995: 261–62, *sub* iii 12); Ištar-mūti by *Il*!-*mu-ti* in N; Išme-Šamaš by *I-mu-*^{d}UTU in N, by *I-mi-*^{d}UTU in P; also in N, Uṣi-watar is the son of Simudara; in L, he is the son of Zigu-iake; in manuscript I, only the last three royal names are kept: Išme-Šamaš, Šu-ilišu, and Simudara; about the bala of Ku-Baba, see page 64 above.

In manuscript P, the last king of the dynasty, Nanniya, is replaced by Nanne of Ur and his son Mes-nune.

18. Third dynasty of Uruk:

Variant: ... in.si for Lugal.zà.ge.si in L.

F omits this dynasty.

19. Dynasty of Akkade:

Restorations are taken from manuscripts A and C.

Main graphic variants: Śar-ru-gin$_{7}$-né in P; *Ma-ni-iš-ti-šu* in L; *Ma-ni-iš-te-šu* in A; *Ma-an-iš-ti*(?)*-šu* in F; *Ma-an-iš-ti-su* in P; *ma-nu-um* lugal *ma-nu-um la* lugal in A and C, *ma-an-nu śar-ru-um ma-an-nu la śar-ru-um* in P; *Ir-ki-ki* in A; *Ir-gi*$_{4}$*-gi*$_{4}$ in K and N; *Ìr-gi*$_{4}$*-gi*$_{4}$ in P; *Na-ni* in C; *Na-an-né* in F; *Na-núm* in P; *I-mi-*[...]*-a* in F; *I-lu-lu* in F and K.

Length of reigns: Sargon: 55 years in A, 54 years in L, 40 years in P; Rīmuš: 15 years in A, B, and C, 8 years in P, 7 years in F and N; Man-ištūsu: 7 years in A; Narām-Sîn: 56 years in A, 54 years and 6 months in P; Śar-kali-śarrī: 24 years in C; total: 177 years in K, 12^{sic} kings and 197 years in N; it is possible that in some manuscripts there was a confusion between the lengths of Sargon's and Narām-Sîn's reigns.

Others: Man-ištūsu before Rīmuš in P; Narām-Sîn is omitted in K; the names of Irgigi, Imi, Nanum, and Ilulu are not always in the same order; K does not mention the last two kings of the dynasty; in F, *Ir-gi*$_{4}$<*-gi*$_{4}$> is son of *Na*<*-ra-am-*^{d}EN.ZU>, but in P he is said to be arad *śar-ru-um*, "either servant or king"; for the bala of Sargon in C, see the observations on page 64 above.

In manuscript P, after Nanum and Elulu, restore the name Imi and the expression [4 lugal.e.ne mu x ì.na.ke_{4}.éš], "four kings, they reigned x years." There is no space for another name.

20. Fourth dynasty of Uruk:

Length of reigns: Ur-nigin: 3 years in F and N, 30 years in I, 15 years in K; Ur-gigir: 7 years in F and K, 15 years in I; Puzur-ili: 20 years in F; Ur-Utu: 25 years in K; total: 26 years in N, 43^{sic} years in F, 3 kings and 47 years in F.

Others: Ur-Utu is a son of Ur-gigir in K; source I inserts the name of Lugal.me.lám, son of Ur-gigir, assigning him a reign of 7 years.

21. Dynasty of Gutium:

Main graphic variants: Gu-ti-um^{ki} in A, B, C, E, M, N; Gu-du-um^{ki} in K; P mentions only *um-ma-núm*^{ki}.

Each source presents a different list: A: lugal nu.ub.tuk, Ní.bi.a, *In-gi*$_{4}$*-šú, Zà*^{ar}*-la-ga-ba, Ia-ar-la-ga-aš,* [..., ..., ..., ..., *Ia-ar-la*]*-gáb,* [*I-b*]*a-ti,* [*Ia-ar*]*-la-an-gab,* [...]-bi, (...) [*Ti-ri-ga*], total: 12 kings 124 years and 40 days; B: 21 kings, 125 years and 40 days; C: the list begins with Ní.bi.a, *In-ki-*[*šu*$_{4}$, ... *l*]*a-gab,* (...), total: 23

kings, 99 years; E: (...), *Si-lu-lu*.e, Du_{10}.ga, *I-lu*-dingir, *Ia-ar-la-ga-ab*, [*Ku-r*]*u-um*, [...]-x-*um*, (...); F: (...), [..., *Ti-ri-ga*] u_4 40 ì.ak, (...); H: (...), [lugal mu] nu.tuk, [..., ...], [..., ..., ..., I-ni-ma-ba-ke-e]š, [...], (...); K: only the ends of the names of the first two kings are preserved: [...]an-dé, [...]-ba; P: lugal nu.tuk, Ní.bi.šè, *Šul-me*-DAG.e, *E-ṭam-kis-ki-sú*, ^{d}UTU-*ka-bar*.e, *I-gi₄-gi₄*, *Ar-an-da-gaba*, *Si₄-lu-lu* [...].

Length of reigns: the lengths of the reigns vary and are always very short.

Concerning the beginning of the dynasty, some manuscripts are corrupt; we read: "a king whose name is unknown." We should perhaps consider the formula of manuscript A "the army of Gutium had no king; together it reigned 5 years," the first king being, then, Ingišū.

22. P adds a dynasty of Adab between Gutium and Uruk. Four kings belong to it, [x], *Puzur₄-zu-zu*, Sad.du-KI+ÀŠ/Ašgi, and *Ti-rí-ga-a-an*. The last one is otherwise known to be the last Gutian king; both of them reigned 40 days. For his possible links with the city of Adab, see Steinkeller 2003: 283.

23. Variants: H: 26 years, ... months, and 15 days; L: 7 years, 6 months, and 7 days; M: 7 years, 6 months, and 7 days; P: 7 years. 420 being written "7 šu.ši," i.e., "7 x 60"; a scribe could add or omit the element šu.ši to change the length of the reign.

24. Third dynasty of Ur:

In K, the name of Šulgi alone is preceded by the divine determinative; in I, all the names seem to have been preceded by the determinative; in D and L, on the contrary, the determinative is absent.

Length of reigns: Šulgi: 48 years in K and L, 58 years in D; Amar-Su'en: 25 years in K; Šū-Sîn: 7 years in D, 20 + ... years in I, 16 years in K; Ibbi-Sîn: 25 years in D and I, 15 years in K, 23 (?) years in L; total: 5 kings and 117 years in D, 5 kings and 120 + ... years in I, 5 kings and 123 years in K, 5 kings and ... years in M.

Source K ends with the fall of Ur, adding: Urí.ma^{ki} ^{giš}tukul ba.sìg suḫuš Ki!.en.[gi.ra] mu.un.[sír.sír] ... [...] ... [...] (...), "Ur was defeated, the foundation of Su[mer?] was [weakened/brought to an end(?)]." Source P ends during the reign of Šulgi, of whom it says: lugal.gu_{10} u_4 sud.šè ḫa.ti.il, "my king, may he live until distant days."

25. Dynasty of Isin:

The divine determinative precedes all the royal names in E and I but is absent in D.

Length of reigns: Išbi-Erra: 32 years in D; Šū-ilišu: 10 years in D and E, 15 in I; Iddin-Dagān: 25 years in I; Išme-Dagān: 8 years in E; Ur-Ninurta: 21 (?) years in I; Erra-imittī: 7 years in D; total: 11 kings and 159 years in B; 16 kings and 226 years in C; [16] kings and 225 years and 6 months in D.

Others: E ends after the reign of Išme-Dagān; I seems to end after that of Ur-Ninurta; D adds, between the reigns of Erra-imittī and Enlil-bāni, that of *I-k*[*u-un*]*-pi-Iš₈-tár*, to which it assigns a length of 6 months; the same source adds, at the end, the name of *Da-mi-iq-ì-lí-šu*, son of Sîn-māgir, whose reign lasted 23 years; source C must have been identical with D; A and B add, concerning Ur-Ninurta, dumu ^{d}Iškur.ke_4 mu.ḫé.gál.la bala $ša_6$.ga ti nì.du_{10}.ga u_4 ḫa.ba.zal.[zal], "son of Iškur, year of abundance, a good reign, may he enjoy a happy life."

26. Another colophon was preserved in N: ^{iti}sig_4.a u_4 30.kam, "month of Siwan, 30th day."

27. Variant: 139.

28. In chronicle 1, only the city of Uruk had a succession of five dynastic cycles. Could this be a sixth dynasty of Uruk? This is highly improbable, given the place-name ending in -a, lost in the lacuna.

29. As the Sumerians described themselves.

30. The whole world.

31. Ammī-ditāna was actually the predecessor of Ammī-ṣaduqa.

32. Missing are the last kings of the Sealand, the Kassite kings, and those of the second Isin dynasty, a total of fifty-three kings.

33. It is impossible to know if the document ended with the mention of this king. If so, one column was left empty in the Nineveh copy.

34. For minor variants, see Grayson 1980b: passim.

35. Variant: ^{I}*Aḫ*(?)-*ḫe-ṣu.*

36. Variant: $^{\mathrm{[I]}}$*Su-m*[*a*(?)-*a*(?)-*b*]*u.*

37. Variant: ^{I}*Su-le-e.*

38. Variant: Aḫḫēṣu.

39. Variant: Summabu.

40. A translation "my predecessors" is also possible, with Garelli 1985: 94.

41. Variante: Sulê.

42. On this passage, see Landsberger 1954: 108 nn. 198 and 200; Freydank 1975: 173–75.

43. Variant: [. . . +] 30.

44. Concerning this reign and its chronology, see Veenhof 2003: passim.

45. Variant: 24.

46. Variant: dumu.

47. Variant: 24.

48. Variant: "son of."

49. Variant: 4.

50. Variant: ^{I}*Aš-šur*-sum.ibila.

51. Variant: 13.

52. Restoration from manuscripts A and C; text B has [. . .]-. . .-*bi.*

53. Variant: Aššur-nāṣir-apli.

54. Variant: 4.

55. Variant: Aššur-nādin-apli.

56. Variant: 13.

57. *šadâ*(*šu*) *emēdu*: "to go up his mountain," a euphemism meaning "to depart this life," found also in other Assyrian chronicles, nos. 10 and 15.

58. End of one of the versions of the chronicle.

59. The writing sì-ga is asked for instead of si-ga. On this graphic shift, see Römer 1965: 194. The expression means humanity destroyed by the flood (on si-ga, see Berlin 1979: 83 and commentary on line 198); the scribe resorted to a metaphor in order to refer to postdiluvian humanity.

60. A device to raise water for irrigation, made of a pole turning on a pivot, with a bucket on one end of the pole and a weight on the other.

61. Royal title.

VII

Sumerian Chronography

7. THE TUMMAL CHRONICLE

Sources: tablets; ten copies known.
Bibliography: Sollberger 1962: 40–47; Ali 1964: 99–104; Oelsner 2003: 209–24.
Language: Sumerian.
Date: copies are from the Old Babylonian period.
Place: Ur and Nippur.
Contents: history of the Tummal sanctuary near Nippur, residence of the goddess Ninlil, integrated into the general history of Mesopotamia. The influence of the Chronicle of the Single Monarchy (no. 1) is obvious.

[1]En.me.bára.ge$_4$.si lugal.e iri.na.nam [1a]é.^{d}En.líl.lá in.dù [2]Ak.kà dumu En.me.bára.ge$_4$.e.si.ke$_4$ [3]Tum.ma.al^{ki}.e pa bí.è [4] ^{d}Nin.líl Tum.ma.al^{ki}.šè in.túm

[5]a.rá.1.kam.a Tum.ma.al^{ki} ba.šub [6]Més.an.né.pà.da lugal.e Bur.šú.šú.a^{ki} [6a]é.^{d}en.líl.lá in.dù [7]Mes.ki.ág.nun.na dumu Mes.an.né.pà.da.ke$_4$ [8]Tum.ma.al^{ki}.e pa bí.è [9]^{d}Nin.líl Tum.ma.al^{ki}.šè in.túm

[10]a.rá.2.kam Tum.ma.al^{ki} ba.šub [11] ^{d}Bil$_4$.ga.mes Du$_6$.^{u}númun.bur.ra [11a]bára.^{d}En.líl.lá in.dù [12] ^{d}Ur.lugal dumu ^{d}Bil$_4$.ga.mes.ke$_4$ [13]Tum.ma.al^{ki}.e pa bí.è [14] ^{d}Nin.líl Tum.ma.al^{ki}.šè in.túm

[15]a.rá.3.kam Tum.ma.al^{ki} ba.šub [16]Na.an.né ^{giš}kiri$_6$.maḫ.àm [16a]é.^{d}En.líl.lá in.dù [17]Mes.ki.ág.^{d}Nanna dumu Na.an.né.ke$_4$ [18]Tum.ma.al^{ki}.e pa bí.è [19] ^{d}Nin.líl Tum.ma.al^{ki}.šè in.túm

[20]a.rá.4.kam Tum.ma.al^{ki} ba.šub [21]Ur.^{d}Namma É.kur.ra in.dù [22] ^{d}Šul.gi dumu Ur.^{d}Namma.ke$_4$ [23]Tum.ma.al^{ki}.e pa bí.è [24] ^{d}Nin.líl Tum.ma.al^{ki}.šè in.túm

[25]a.rá.5.kam Tum.ma.al^{ki} ba.šub [26]mu Amar.^{d}EN.ZU.ka.ta [26a]en.na mu ^{d}*I-bí*-^{d}EN.ZU lugal.e [27]En.am.gal.an.na en ^{d}Inanna Unu^{ki}.ga [27a]máš.e

In his city (of Nippur), Enme(n)-baragesi, the king, built Enlil's temple; Aka, Enme(n)-baragesi's son, made the Tummal splendid (and) introduced Ninlil there.

For the first time the Tummal fell into ruin. Mes-ane-pada, the king, built the Buršušua of Enlil's temple; Mes-ki'ag-nuna, the son of Mes-ane-pada, made the Tummal splendid (and) introduced Ninlil there.

For the second time the Tummal fell into ruin. Gilgameš built the Dunumunbura, Enlil's dais; Ur-lugal, the son of Gilgameš, made the Tummal splendid (and) introduced Ninlil there.[1]

For the third time the Tummal fell into ruin. Nanne designed the ornamental garden of Enlil's temple; Mes-ki'ag-Nanna, Nanne's son, made the Tummal splendid (and) introduced Ninlil there.

For the fourth time the Tummal fell into ruin. Ur-Namma built the Ekur; Šulgi, Ur-Namma's son, made the Tummal splendid (and) introduced Ninlil there.

For the fifth time the Tummal fell into ruin. From the year Amar-Su'en <became king> until the year of Ibbi-Sîn, the king, during which

in.pà.dè [28] ^{d}Nin.líl Tum.ma.al^{ki}.šè ì.gin

[29]ka Lú.^{d}Inanna ašgab.gal ^{d}En.líl.lá.aš sar.ra
[30] ^{d}*Iš-bi-Èr-ra* É.kur.ra.igi.gál.la [31]É.gi.na.ab.du ^{d}En.líl.lá in.dù[2]

En-amgal-ana,[3] the en-priest of Inanna of Uruk, was chosen by the oracular lamb,[4] Ninlil went (several times) to the Tummal.

Written according to the word of Lu-Inana, Enlil's head saddler.

Išbi-Erra built the Ešutum of Enlil's Ekura'igigala.[5]

Notes

1. A manuscript from Ur reverses the order of the second and third kings, placing Gilgameš before Mes-ane-pada; see above, page 151 note 6.

2. For all the scribal variants, see Oelsner 2003.

3. The latest manuscript has the name of Enme(n)-gal-ana instead of En-amgal-ana; this is obviously a scribal error, since Enme(n)-gal-ana was a priestess of Nanna during the reign of Abī-sarē.

4. That is, from the first year of the reign of Amar-Su'en to the second year of reign of Ibbi-Sîn.

5. This name of an Enlil temple is also found in chronicle 47.

VIII

Assyrian Chronicles

EPONYM CHRONICLES

8. EPONYM CHRONICLE (SECOND MILLENNIUM)

Sources: five fragments of at least two different editions of the text, one more recent than the other.
Bibliography: Birot 1985; Yuhong 1994: passim; van Koppen 1997: 426 n. 33; Durand and Guichard 1997: 43; Veenhof 2003; Charpin and Ziegler 2003.
Language: Babylonian (with some local idioms).
Date: beginning of the eighteenth century.
Place: Mari.
Contents: history of northern Mesopotamia from the accession of Narām-Sîn of Aššur to the last years of Śamśī-Addu I.

(M.7481 obv. and dupl.)^{1}*iš-tu re-eš* ^{giš}gu.[za lugal^{ut}(?) *Na-ra-am-*^{d}EN.ZU … *m*]*i*(?)*-im* 1 *iš-tu li-mu* [. . .] ^{2} ^{I}*Š*[*u*-^{d}EN.ZU (?)] ^{3} ^{I}[^{d}*A-šur-ma-lik* (?) ^{4} ^{Id}*A-šur-i-mi-ti* (?) ^{5} ^{I}*En-na-*^{d}EN.ZU (?)] ^{6}*i-na* [^{I}*A-ku-tim* . . .]^{ki} [. . . *iṣ-ba*]*-at* ^{7} ^{I}*Ma-ṣí-a-am-*DIN[GIR (?)] ^{8} ^{I}*I-dí-a-ḫu-um* [(?)] ^{9}*i-na Sa-*[*m*]*a-nim A-mi-nu-um Ša-du-pé-em iṣ-ba-at* ^{10}*i-na Ì-lí-en-nam* ^{d}EN.ZU*-a-bu-um ma-a-at Ṣi-it*^{ki} *iṣ-ba-at* ^{11}*i-na En-na-*[*ma-nu-um* . . .] ^{12}*i-na En-nam-*^{d}*A-šur* ^{13} ^{I}[*I-p*]*í-i*[*q*]-^{d}Iškur *a-na* é^{1} *a-bi-šu i-ru-ub* $^{13'}$*i-na En-na-*^{d}EN.ZU [. . .] ^{14}*i-na Ḫa-na-*^{d}*Na-ri-im A-mi-nu-um da-aw-da-a-am ša I-pí-iq-*^{d}Iškur *i-du-uk* ^{15}*i-na Da-di-ia* [. . .] ^{16}*i-na Ka-pa-ti-ia I-pí-iq-*^{d}Iškur *da-aw-da-a-am ša A-mi-nim i-du-uk* ^{17}*i-na Iš-me-*^{d}*A-šur I-pí-iq-*^{d}Iškur *Zi-qú-ra-tam iṣ-ba-at* ^{18}*i-na* ^{d}A*-šur-mu-tab-bi-il I-*[*pí-ip-*^{d}Iškur(?) … ^{19}*i-na*] *Šu-*^{d}Niraḫ [… ^{20}*i-na*] *I-d*[*í*]*-a-bu-um* ^{d}EN.Z[U*-a-bu-um*(?) … ^{21}*i-na*] *Ì-l*[*í*]*-da-an* [. . .] (A.1288 i)$^{21'}$[^{I}]^{d}*A-šur-i-mi-ti* $^{22'}$[^{I}*B*]*u-za-a-ia* $^{23'}$[*i-na*] *I*(!)*-na*(!)*-ia*(!) lugal

[ca. 1876/75] From the beginning of the rei[gn of Narām-Sîn, . . .]. . . , from the eponymy [of . . .].

Šū[-Sîn (?). Aššur-mālik (?). Aššur-imittī (?). Ennam-Sîn (?)]. In (the eponymy of) [Akūtum, . . . too]k (?) [. . .]. Maṣiam-ilī. Idi-aḫum. In (the eponymy of) Samānum, Aminum took Šaduppûm. In (the eponymy of) Iliennam, Sîn-abum took the land of Ṣit. In (the eponymy of)Ennam-Anum, [. . .]. In (the eponymy of) Ennam-Aššur, [Ip]i[q]-Adad entered the house of his father. In (the eponymy of) Ennam-Sîn [. . .]. In (the eponymy of) Ḫannanārum, Aminum defeated Ipiq-Adad. In (the eponymy of) Dādiya, [. . .]. In (the eponymy of) Kapatiya, Ipi[q]-Adad defeated Aminum. In (the eponymy of) Išme-Aššur, Ipiq-Adad took Ziqquratum. In (the eponymy of) Aššur-muttabbil, I[piq-Adad (?) . . . In] (the eponymy of) Šū-Niraḫ, [. . . In] (the eponymy of) Idi-abum, Sî[n-abum . . . In] (the eponymy of) Ili-dān [. . .].

dUtu*ši*-dIškur 24'*wa-li-id* 25'[*i-na* ... *n*]*a-aḫ-du-ur* dUtu 26'[*ib-ba-ši-ma m*]*u*(!)-*ut*(!) *A-mi-nim* 27'[...]...-dIškur 28'[... *iṣ-ba-a*]*t*? (...)

(S.115.26 and dupl.)1' Id*A-šur-ma-lik* 2'*i-na Da-ni-ia ṣa-ba-at Ḫu-up-ši-im*k[i] 3'*i-na En-nam*-dEN.ZU *mi-lum ša ma-a-tim ru-uq-ti*[*m*] 4' Id*A-šur-ba-la-ṭì* 5' I*En-nam*-d*A-šur* 6' I*I-túr*-d*A-šur* 7'*i-na Šu-be-li I-la-kab-ka-bu-ú* 8'*Ṣú-up-ra-a-am iṣ-ba-at* 9'*i-na* Lugal-dIškur *da-aw-da-a-am* 10'*ša I-pí-iq*-dIškur lúElam *i-du-uk* 11'*ù* lugal dUtu*ši*-dIškur *a-na* é *a-bi-šu* 12'*i-ru-bu*sic 13' I*Šu-La-ba-an* 14'*i-na* d*A-šur-i-mi-ti* 15'*Lu-ul-lu-um da-aw-da-a-am ša* lugal 16'*i-na La-za-pa-tim i-du-uk* 17'*i-na Da-da-a-ia Mu-ut-Ab*(!)-*bi-iḫ* [...] 18'*i-na Da-da-a-ia* mìn *I-pí*-[*iq*-dIškur] 19'*Ar-ra-ap-ḫa-am*ki *iṣ-ba*-[*at*] (A.1288 ii and dupl.)14'*i-na A-ḫi-ša-lim ṣa-ba-at Ga-s*[*ú-ri-im*ki(?)] 15' I*Ú-ṣúr-ša-Iš*8-*tár* 16' I*Ka-ta-a-i*[*a*(?)] 17'*i-na Šu*-dEN.[ZU ...] 18'*i-na A-bu-ša-lim ṣa-ba-at* dE[N.ZU-*a-bu-šu*?] 19'*ša Né-ri-ib-ti*[*m*] 20' I*Šu-Da-a*-[*ia*?] 21'*i-na Šu-Da-di-im ṣa-ba-at Ne*-...[...] 22'*i-na* d*A-šur-tu-kúl-ti da-aw*-[*da-a-am*] 23'*ša Ú-ni-ne-a-i*[*m* dUtu*ši*-dIškur(?) 24'*i-du-uk ù*] 25'*da-aw-da-a*-[*am ša*] 26' I*Mu-ut-ia*-...[... *i-du-uk*] (S.24.1 obv.)7'*i-na Puzur*4-*Iš*8-*tár* dUtu*ši*-dIškur [...] 8'*i-na A-ta-na*-[*aḫ*] *I-pí-iq*-dIškur *da-a*[*w-da-a-am ša* .. *i-du-uk*] 9'*ù ma*-[*a-at* ... *iṣ-ba-at*(?)] 10'*i-na E-ri-ši-im* dUtu*ši*-dIškur *da-aw*-[*da-a-am ša* ...] 11'*i-na* Bàd.[... *i-du-uk*] 12' Id*A-šur-en-nam-ša-lim* 13'*i-na I-ni-i*[*b-Iš*8-*t*]*ár I-pí-iq*-dIškur [...] 14' Id*A-šur-ma-al-ki*-[*i*] 15'*i-na Be*?-[...] *ki-ir-ba-na-a* [...] 16'*i-na* [...] dUtu*ši*-dIškur [...] 17'*i-na* [...] dUtu*ši*-dIškur [... 18'*i-na Šu-ì-l*]*í-šu* 19' dUtu*ši*-dI[škur ...] *š*[*a* ... 20'*i-na Ib-ni*-dIškur ... 21'... 22'... 23'... 24'*i-na A-ta-mar-Iš*8-*tár* ...] (...)

(S.24.3 obv.)1'[... 2'...] ka [... 3'*i-na Id-na*(?)]-d*A-šu*[*r*] dUtu*ši*-d[Iškur ... 4'*i-na*] *A*(?)-*ta-nim* dUtu*ši*-d[Iškur *da-aw-da-a-am ša*] 5'12 lugalmeš *i*-[*du-uk-ma* ...] 6' I*Ia-aḫ-du-un*-[*Li-im* lugal *Ma-rí*ki ...] 7'lugalmeš-*šu-nu ut-t*[*e*(-*er*)-*ru* ... 8'*i-n*]*a* d*A-šur-ták-la-ku* dUtu*ši*-d[Iškur *da-aw-da-a-am ša*] 9' I...[... *i-du-uk* 10'*i-na* ... 11'*i-na Ḫa-ià-ma-lik* ... 12'*i-na Ša-lim*-d*A-šur* ... 13'*i-na Ša-lim*-d*A-šur* ...] (S.24.2 rev.)1'[*i-na En-n*]*am*(?)-[d]*A-šur* <<...>> dUtu*ši*-dIškur *ma*-[*a-at* ... *iṣ-ba-at* 2'*i-na* dE]N.ZU-*mu-ba-al-li-iṭ* dUtu*ši*-dIškur *ma-a*-[*at* ... *iṣ-ba-at* 3'*i-na R*]*i-iš*-dUtu *Iš-me*-d*Da-gan da-aw-da-a-a*[*m ša* ... *i-du-uk* 4'*i-na I*]*b-ni*-dIškur dUtu*ši*-dIškur *ma-a-at* [... *iṣ-ba-at* 5'*i-na* d*A*]-*šur-i-mi-ti* dUtu*ši*-dIškur *da-aw*-[*da-a-am ša* ... *i-du-uk-ma a-na* šu-*šu*

Aššur-imittī. [B]uzāya. [In (the eponymy of)] Inaia (!), King Śamśī-Addu was born. [In (the eponymy of) . . .] a solar eclipse [happened; dea]th(!) of Aminum. [. . .]-Addu, [. . .].

[Lacuna of about ten years.]

Aššur-mālik.

[1840/39] In (the eponymy of) Daniya, taking of Ḫupšum.

In (the eponymy of) Ennam-Sîn, a flood in a "remote land." Aššur-balāṭi. Ennam-Aššur. Itūr-Aššur.

[1835/34] In (the eponymy of) Šū-bēli, Ilā-kabkabû took Ṣuprum (?).

In (the eponymy of) Šarrum-Adad, the man of Elam defeated Ipiq-Adad, and King Śamśī-Addu entered the house of his father. Šū-Laban. In (the eponymy of) Aššur-imittī, the Lullû defeated the king in Lazapatum. In (the eponymy of) Dādāya, Mūt-Abbiḫ [. . .].

[1830/29] In (the eponymy of) Dādāya, *ditto*, Ipiq-Adad too[k] Arrapḫa.

In (the eponymy of) Aḫī-šālim, the taking of Gas[ur(?)]. Uṣur-ša-Iš[tar]. I[n] (the eponymy of) Katāy[a, . . .]. In (the eponymy of) Šū-Sîn, [. . .].

[1825/24] In (the eponymy of) Abu-šālim, the taking of Sîn-[abušu(?)] of Nērebt[um].

In (the eponymy of) Šū-Da[ya(?)]. In (the eponymy of) Šū-Dādim, the taking of Ne[. . .]. In (the eponymy of) Aššur-tukultī, [Śamśī-Addu (?)] de[feated] the man of Unnina, and (?) Mūt-Ia[. . .] def[eated . . .]. In (the eponymy of) Puzur-Iš[tar], Śamśī-Addu [. . .].

[1820/19] In (the eponymy of) Ātanaḫ, Ipiq-Adad de[feated . . .] and [took (?)] the la[nd (?) of . . .].

In (the eponymy of) Ērišum, Śamśī-Addu de[feated . . .] in Dūr-[. . .]. Aššur-ennam-šalim. In (the eponymy of) Ini[b-Iš]tar, Ipiq-Adad [(*died*?)]. Aššur-bēl-malki.

[1815/14] In (the eponymy of) Be(?)[. . ., . . .] Kirbanâ (?) [. . .].

In (the eponymy of) [. . ., . . .] Śamśī-Addu [. . . . In (the eponymy of) . . ., . . .] Śamśī-Addu [. . . In (the eponymy of) Šū-il]išu (?), Śamśī-Addu [. . . In (the eponymy of) Ibni-Addu, (*Śamśī-Addu went back from Babylon*) . . .].

[1808/7] [In (the eponymy of) Ātamar-Ištar, (*Śamśī-Addu took Aššur*)[2]. (. . .)

[In (the eponymy of) . . ., . . . In (the eponymy of) Idna(?)]-Aššur, Śamśī-Addu [. . . In] (the eponymy of) Atānum (?), Śamśī-Addu [defeated] twelve kings; Yaḫdun-[Lim, king of Mari, . . .], these kings retur[ned (?). . . . I]n (the eponymy of) Aššur-taklāku, Śamśī-Addu [defeated . . .].

[1795/94] [In (the eponymy of) . . ., . . .

In (the eponymy of) Ḫaya-mālik, (*Śamśī-Addu took Mari*).[3] In (the eponymy of) Šalim-Aššur, . . . In (the eponymy of) Šalim-Aššur,[4] . . . In (the eponymy of) Enna]m-Aššur, [. . .] Śamśī-Addu [took (?)] the land of [. . .].

[1790/89] [In] (the eponymy of) Sîn-muballiṭ, Śamśī-Addu [took (?)] the land of [. . .].

ma-a-tam] $^{6'}$*ša-a-tu ú-te-er ma-a-at* [... *ma-a-at*] $^{7'}$*Me-Tu-ra-an*^{ki} *ma-a-at* [...] $^{8'}$ ^{I}*Da-du-š*[*a* ... *iṣ-ba-at*] $^{9'}$*i-na Ì-l*[*í*-i]llat^{t}[^{i} ...] $^{10'}$*i-na Ri-ig-m*[*a-ni*]*m Mu-n*[*a* ...] $^{11'}$*i-na I-ku-u*[*n-pí*]*-ia Mu-na-*[...] $^{12'}$*da-aw-da-a-a*[*m ša* ... *i-du-uk*] $^{13'}$*ù* ^{d}Utu^{ši}-^{d}[Iškur ...] $^{14'}$*Me-Tu-ra-an*^{ki} [...] $^{15'}$*a-na Da-du-ša* [...] $^{16'}$*i-na* [*As-qú-di-i*]*m* ^{d}Utu^{ši}-^{d}Iškur [*Qa-ab-ra*^{ki} *iṣ-ba-at*] $^{17'}$*i-na* [^{d}*A-šur*]*-ma-lik Iš-me-*^{d}*Da-gan da-aw-da-a-*[*am ša A-ḫa-zi-im i-du-uk*] $^{18'}$*ù* ^{d}Utu^{ši}-^{d}Iškur *Nu-ur-*[*ru-ga-am*^{ki} *iṣ-ba-at-ma*] $^{19'}$ ^{I}*Ki-ib-ra-am* lugal [...] $^{20'}$ ^{I}*Ia-šu-ub-*^{d}Iškur lugal [*A-ḫa-zi-im* ...] $^{21'}$ ^{I}*Ia-šu-ub-Li-im* lugal [...] $^{22'}$9(!) lugal^{meš} *an-nu-tim ik-š*[*u-ud ki-ma*(?) *ša-al-la-tim*(?)] $^{23'}$*a-*[*n*]*a Da-d*[*u-ša id-di-in* $^{24'}$*i-na* ... *-i*]*a*(!?) *Tu-ru-u*[*k-ku-ú ik-ki-ru* ^{d}Utu^{ši}-^{d}Iškur *ù*] $^{25'}$ ^{I}[*Iš-me-*^{d}*Da-gan* ...] (A.1614a)$^{1'}$[*i-na Bu-ru-ul*(?)]*-la-an da-aw-da-am* <*ša*> *Tu-ru-u*[*k-ki-i*^{ki} $^{2'}$*ù* ...]^{ki} *i-du-ku* ^{I}*Ia-ás-ma-aḫ-*^{d}[Iškur $^{3'}$*da-aw*]*-da-am ša* Dumu^{meš} *Ia-mi-na* [*i-du-uk-ma* $^{4'}$*ù a-aḫ* ^{i}]$_{7}$Buranun *ú-ga-me-*[*er* ... $^{5'}$...]*-a*^{ki} *m*[*a*(?)-... $^{6'}$...]*-a ša* [...] (?)

(M.7481 rev.)$^{1'}$[*i-na* ...]*-ia Mu-*[*tu-bi-si-ir*(?) $^{2'}$... $^{3'}$...] $^{4'}$*a-*[...] $^{5'}$4 [...] $^{6'}$*da-*[*aw-da-am ša* ... *i-na* ká *Sa-ag-ga-ra-tim*^{ki} *i-du-uk*]

colophon of one edition:

$^{7'}$šu.nígin 60+[10+... *ša-na*]*-tum a-di da-aw-de-e-em ša* ká *Sa-ag-ga-r*[*a-tim*^{ki}] $^{8'}$šu *Ḫa-ab-du-ma-lik mu-uš-ta-as-sú-ú Li-mi-*^{d}*Da-gan*

9. EPONYM CHRONICLE (FIRST MILLENNIUM)

Sources: fragmentary tablets; in total, ten different sources.
Bibliography: Millard 1994; Deller 1994; Finkel and Reade 1995; 1998; Frahm 1998.
Language: Assyrian.
Date: Neo-Assyrian copies.
Place: Aššur, Nineveh, and Sultan-Tepe.
Contents: the names of the eponyms and the objectives of annual military campaigns from 858 to 699, with a few gaps. The horizontal lines note either changes of reign or a king's eponymy.

(...) (B5) ^{1}[bala(?)] *ša* ^{Id}*Šùl-ma-nu-*bar dumu ^{I}*Aš-šur-*pap^{ir}.a *š*[*àr* ^{kur}*Aš-šur*^{ki}]

---

^{2}[*ina l*]*i-me* ^{I}Lugal.téš.un^{meš} *a-*[*na* ... $^{3;5}$] ^{Id}*Šùl-ma-nu-*bar *šàr* ^{kur}*Aš-šur*^{ki} *a-*[*na* ... $^{4;}$] ^{I}*Aš-šur-*en.gin^{in} ^{lú}*tur-ta-nu a-*[*na* ... $^{5;}$] ^{I}*Aš-šur-*dù*-a-a-*pap ^{lú}gal.kaš.lul *a-*[*na* ... $^{6;}$] ^{I}Ad-*ina-*é.gal*-lil-bur* ^{lú}nimgir.é.gal [... $^{7;}$] ^{I}Di.ku$_{5}$-

[In] (the eponymy of) Rīš-Šamaš, Išme-Dagān de[feated ... In] (the eponymy of) Ibni-Addu, Śamśī-Addu [took] the land of [...[6]. In] (the eponymy of) Aššur-imittī, Śamśī-Addu de[feated ... and] took it; Dāduša [took (?)] the land of [..., the land] of Mê-Turan, [the land of ...]. In (the eponymy of) Il[i-e]llāti, [...].

[1785/84] In (the eponymy of) Rigm[ānu]m, Mun[a...].

In (the eponymy of) Ikūn-[pî]ya, Muna[...] def[eated ...] and Śamśī-[Addu ...] Mê-Turan [...] for Dāduša [...]. In [(the eponymy of) Asqud]um, Śamśī-Addu [took Qabra]. In [(the eponymy of) Aššur]-mālik, Išme-Dagān def[eated Aḫazum] and Śamśī-Addu [took (?)] Nur[rugum and] captured these nine (!) kings: Kibrum, king of [...; ..., king of ...; ..., king of ...]; Yašub-Addu, king of [Aḫazum; ..., king of ...; ..., king of ...]; Yašub-Lim, king of [...; ..., king of ...; ..., king of ...; he gave them as booty (?)] to Dāduša. [In (the eponymy of) Aḫiyaya/Awiliy]a (?), the Turuk[keans opened hostilities. Śamśī-Addu and Išme-Dagān] defeated the Turukkeans and the [... in Burul]lan (?); Yasmaḫ-[Addu def]eated the Yaminites and unifi[ed the banks] of the Euphrates [...].[7]

(.?.)

[In (the eponymy of) Aḫiyaya/Awili]ya, Mu[tu-Bisir (?) ...] d[efeated (?)... at the gate of Saggarātum].

colophon of one edition:

Total: seven[ty + ... yea]rs, until the victory of the gate of Saggar[ātum]. Hand of Ḫabdu-Mālik; Limī-Dagān, the one who dictated.

(...) [reign (?)] of Šalmaneser (III), son of Aššurnaṣirpal (II), k[ing of Assyria].

---

[858] [During the e]ponymy of Šarru-balti-nišī, (campaign) agai[nst ...].

[*ditto*] Šalmaneser, the king of Assyria, (campaign) aga[inst ... *ditto*] Aššur-bēla-ka''in, the commander in chief, (campaign) aga[inst ...].

Aš-šur ^{lú}*tur-ta-nu* [... ^{8}:] ^{Id}Utu.ad-*u-a* ^{lú}*šá-kìn* ^{uru}*Na-ṣibi-na* [... ^{9}:] ^{Id}Utu.en.pap *ša* ^{uru}*Kal-ḫa* [... ^{10}:] ^{I}En.dù-*a-a* ^{lú}nimgir.é.gal [... ^{11}:] ^{I}*Ḫa-di-i-li-pu-šú ša* ^{uru}*N*]*a*(?)-*'i*(?)-*r*[*i*(?) ... ^{12}:] ^{Id}Maš.maš.gin.igi *ša* [... ^{13}:] ^{I}*B*[*i*]*r*-^{d}[*Ra*]-*ma-n*[*a ša* ... ^{14}: ^{Id}Maš.gin.un^{meš} *ša* ... ^{15}: ^{Id}Maš.sum.mu *ša* ... ^{16}: ^{I}*Aš-šur*-dù-*a-a ša* ... ^{17}: ^{I}Du$_{10}$.^{d}Maš *ša* ... ^{18}: ^{I}*Tàk-lak-a-na*-lugal *ša* ^{uru}*Né-med*-^{d}15 ... (B4 and duplicates) $^{1'}$... ^{Id}Iškur-*rém-a-ni ša* ^{uru}*Gu-za-na*(?) ... $^{2'}$... ^{Id}Utu/En.ad-*u-a ša* ^{uru}*Ra-ṣa-pa a-na* kur ^{giš}er]in $^{3'}$[... ^{I}*Šùl-mu*-en-*la-mur ša* ^{uru}*A-ḫi*-^{i}$_{7}$*Z*]*u-ḫi-na a*-[*na*] ^{uru}*Qu-u-e* $^{4'}$[... ^{Id}Maš-*kib-si*-pap *ša* ^{uru}*R*]*a-ṣap-pa a-na* ^{kur}[*Ma*]-*la-ḫi* $^{5'}$[... ^{Id}Maš-*ila-a-a ša* ^{uru}*A-ḫi*]-^{i}$_{7}$*Zu-ḫi-na a-na* ^{kur}*Da-na-bi* $^{6'}$[... ^{I}*Qur-di-Aš-šur ša* ^{uru}]*Raq-mat a-na* ^{kur}*Ta-ba-li* $^{7'}$[... ^{I}Gìr$_{\text{ii}}$.man *ša* ^{uru}*Ḫ*]*ab-ru-ri a-na* ^{kur}*Me-li-di* $^{8'}$[... ^{Id}Maš.maš-*mu-dam-miq ša* ^{uru}*N*]*i-nu-a a-na* ^{kur}*Nam-ri* $^{9'}$[... ^{I}*Ia-ḫa-lu*] ^{lú}a-grig *a-na* ^{kur}*Qu-e* $^{10'}$[...] ^{I} ^{i}[^{ti}Ki]n-*a*-[*a ša* ^{uru}*Kà*]*l-zi a-na* ^{kur}*Qu-e* $^{11'}$[... ^{I}Man]-*ḫat-t*[*i*]-*be*-[*li ša* ... *a*]-*na* ^{kur}*Qu-e* An gal ta ^{uru}*De-ri it-tal-ka* $^{12'}$[...] ^{Id}Nè.iri$_{11}$.gal-*ila-a*-[*a ša* ^{uru}*I-s*]*a-na a-na* ^{kur}*Ur-ar-ṭi* $^{13'}$[... ^{I}*Ḫu-ba-a-a ša* ^{uru}...]-*ḫi a-na* ^{kur}*Un-qi* $^{14'}$[... ^{I}*I*]*lu*-gi[n.pap *ša* ...-*ḫ*]*a a-na* ^{kur}*Ul-lu-ba*

$^{15'}$[*ina li-me* ^{I}]^{d}*Šùl-ma-n*[*u*-bar] *šar*$_{4}$ $^{\text{<kur>}}$*Aš-šur* [*a-na* ^{kur}*Man-n*]*a-a-a* $^{16'}$[: ^{I}]Di.ku$_{5}$-[*Aš-šur* ^{lú}*tur-ta-nu*] *si-ḫu* $^{17'}$[: ^{Id}*A*]*š-šur*-dù-*a-a*-[pap ^{lú}gal.kaš.lul] *si-ḫu* $^{18'}$[: ^{I}*A*]-*a-ḫa-a*-[*lu* ^{lú}*tur-ta-n*]*u si-ḫu* $^{19'}$[: ^{I}]En.dù-*a*-[*a* ^{lú}nimgir.é.gal] *si-ḫu*

(B10) ^{20}[35 m]u^{meš} ^{Id}*Šù*[*l-ma-nu*-bar] *šar*$_{4}$ ^{kur}*Aš-šur*

(B4 and duplicates) $^{20'}$[*ina li-me* ^{I}]*Šam-ši*-^{d}10 *šar*$_{4}$ [^{kur}*Aš-šur*] *si-ḫu* $^{21'}$[: ^{I}*Ia-ḫ*]*a-lu* ^{lú}[*tur-ta-nu s*]*i-ḫu* $^{22'}$[: ^{I}En]-*dan*^{an} ^{lú}[nimgir.é.gal *si-ḫu-um d*]*a-ri-is*[8] $^{23'}$[: ^{Id}Maš]-*ub-lam* ^{lú}[*šá-kìn* ^{uru}... *a-na* ^{k}]^{ur}*Man-na-a-a* $^{24'}$[: ^{Id}Utu]-*ila-a-a* ^{lú}[*šá-kìn*] ^{u}[^{ru}... *a-na* ...]-*šum-me*[9] $^{25'}$[: ^{Id}Maš.maš-*il*]*a-a-a* ^{lú}*šá-k*[*ìn* ^{uru}*I-sa-na*(?) *a-na* ^{ku}]^{r}*T*[*i*]*l*-[*l*]*e-e* $^{26'}$[: ^{I}*Aš-šur*-dù]-*a-a*-pap ^{lú}gal.[kaš.lul] *a-na* ^{kur}*Til-l*[*e*]-*e* $^{27'}$[: ^{I}Lugal-*ḫat-ti-i*]-*be-el* ^{lú}*šá-kìn* ^{uru}[*N*]*a-ṣi-bi-na a-na* ^{kur}*Za-ra-a-te* (B1 and duplicates) $^{4'}$[: ^{I}En-*lu-ba-la*]*ṭ* ^{lú}*t*[*ur-ta-n*]*u a-na* ^{uru}*De-ri* An gal

[855] [*ditto*] Aššur-būnāya-uṣur, the chief butler, (campaign) aga[inst . . .].

[*ditto*] Abī-ina-ēkalli-lilbur, the palace herald, [. . . *ditto*] Dayān-Aššur, the commander in chief, [. . . *ditto*] Šamaš-abūa, governor of Naṣibīna, [. . . *ditto*] Šamaš-bēla-uṣur, (governor) of Kalḫu, [. . .].

[850] [*ditto*] Bēl-būnāya, the palace herald, [. . .].

[*ditto*] Ḫadi-lipūšu, (governor) of Na'iri (?), [. . . *ditto*] Nergal-ālik-pāni, (governor) of [. . . *ditto*] B[ū]r-[Ra]mmān, [(governor) of . . . *ditto* Inūrta-mukīn-nišī, (governor) of . . .].

[845] [*ditto* Inūrta-nādin-šumi, (governor) of . . .].

[*ditto* Aššur-būnāya, (governor) of . . . *ditto* Ṭāb-Inūrta, (governor) of . . . *ditto* Taklāk-ana-šarri, (governor) of Nēmed-Ištar, . . . Adad-rēmanni, (governor) of Gūzāna (?) , . . .].

[840] [. . . Šamaš-abūa, (governor) of Raṣappa, (campaign) against the] cedar [mountain].

[. . . Šulma-bēli-lāmur, (governor) of Aḫiz]ūḫina, (campaign) against Qu'e. [. . . Inūrta-kibsī-uṣur, (governor) of R]aṣappa[sic],[10] (campaign) against [Ma]laḫi. [. . . Inūrta-ilāya, (governor) of Aḫi]zūḫina[sic],[11] (campaign) against Danabu. [. . . Qurdī-Aššur, (governor) of] Raqmat, (campaign) against Tabal.

[835] [. . . Šēp-šarri, (governor) of Ḫ]abrūri, (campaign) against Milīdu.

[. . . Nergal-mudammiq, (governor) of N]ineveh, (campaign) against Namri. [. . . Yaḫalu,] the chamberlain, (campaign) against Qu'e. [. . .] Ulūlāy[u, (governor) of Ka]līzi, (campaign) against Qu'e. [. . . Šarru]-ḫat[ta]-ipē[l, (governor) of . . .], (campaign against) Qu'e; Anu the Great left Dēr.[12]

[830] [. . .] Nergal-ilāy[a, (governor) of Is]āna, (campaign) against Urarṭu.

[. . . Ḫubāyu, (governor) of . . .]ḫi, (campaign) against Unqu. [. . . I]lu-mu[kīn-aḫi, (governor) of . . . ḫ]a, (campaign) against Ulluba.

[During the eponymy] of Šalman[eser (III)], the king of Assyria, [(campaign) against Mann]ea. [*ditto*] Dayān-[Aššur, the commander in chief], revolt.

[825] [*ditto* Aš]šur-būnāya-[uṣur, the great butler], revolt.

[*ditto* Y]aḫa[lu, the commander in chief], revolt. [*ditto*] Bēl-būnāy[a, the palace herald], revolt.

[Thirty-five ye]ars, Ša[lmaneser], king of Assyria

[During the eponymy of] Šamšī-Adad (V), the king [of Assyria], revolt. [*ditto* Yaḫ]alu, [the commander in chief, r]evolt.

[820] [*ditto* Bēl]-dān, [the palace herald, the insurrection was s]uppressed.[13]

[*ditto* Inūrta]-ubla, [governor (?) of . . . , (campaign) against] Mannea. [*ditto* Šamaš]-ilāya, [governor of . . . , (campaign) against . . .]šumme. [*ditto* Nergal-il]āya, govern[or of Isāna (?), (campaign) against] Ti[ll]ê. [*ditto* Aššur-būn]āya-uṣur, the chief [butler], (campaign) against Tillê.

a-na ^{uru}*De-ri it-ta-lak* $^{5'}$[: ^{I}*Mu-še-e*]*k-niš* ^{lú}[*šá*]-*kì*[*n* ^{uru}*Ḫ*]*ab-ru-ri a-na* ^{kur}*Aḫ-sa-na* $^{6'}$[: ^{Id}Maš].bar ^{lú}*šá-kìn* [^{uru}*R*]*aq-mat a-na* ^{kur}*Kal-di* $^{7'}$[: ^{Id}Utu-*k*]*u-mu-u-a* ^{lú}*š*[*á-kìn* ^{uru}*Ar*]*rap-ḫa ana* Ká.dingir.ra^{ki} $^{8'}$[: ^{I}*Be-e*]*l-ka-ṣa-bat* ^{l}[^{ú}*šá-kìn* ^{uru}*M*]*a-za-mu-a i-na* kur

---

(B10) ^{35}[13 mu]^{meš} [^{Id}*Šam-ši*-^{d}Iškur *šar*$_4$ ^{kur}*Aš-šur*]

(B1 and duplicates) $^{9'}$[*ina li-me* ^{Id}Iškur.érin].táḫ [*šar*$_4$ ^{kur}]*Aš-šur*^{ki} *a-na Mad-a-a* $^{10'}$[:] ^{I}Maš.maš-*ila-a-a* [^{lú}*tur-t*]*a-nu a-na* ^{uru}*Gu-za-na* $^{11'}$[:] ^{I}En-*dan*^{an} [^{lú}nimgir].é.gal *a-na* ^{kur}*Man-na-a-a* $^{12'}$: ^{I}*Ṣi-il*-en ^{lú}[gal].kaš.lul *a-na* ^{kur}*Man-na-a-a* $^{13'}$: ^{I}*Aš-šur-tak-lak* ^{lú}agrig *a-na* ^{kur}*Ar-pad-da* $^{14'}$: ^{I}*Ilu*-ta-*ia* ^{lú}gar.kur *a-na* ^{uru}*Ḫa-za-zi* $^{15'}$: ^{Id}Igi.du.uru$_4$^{eš} [*ša* ^{uru}*R*]*a-ṣap-pa a-na* ^{uru}*Ba-a'-li* $^{16'}$: ^{I}*Aš-šur*-téš.É.[kur *ša* ^{uru}]*Arrap-ḫa a-na* ugu *tam-tì mu-ta-nu* $^{17'}$: ^{Id}Maš-*ila-a-a ša* ^{uru}*A-ḫi-i*$_7$*Zu-ḫi-na a-na* ^{uru}*Ḫu-bu-uš-ki-a* $^{18'}$: ^{I}Gìr$_{\text{ii}}$.^{d}15 *ša* ^{uru}*Na-ṣib-i-na a-na Mad-a-a*[14] $^{19'}$: ^{Id}Mes.ḫal-*a-ni ša* ^{uru}*A-me-di a-na Mad-a-a*[15] $^{20'}$: ^{I}*Mu-tak-kil*-^{d}Mes ^{lú}gal.sag^{meš} *a-na* ^{uru}*Lu-u-ši-a* $^{21'}$: ^{I}En.lá^{iṣ}-*ilu-ma ša* ^{uru}*Kal-ḫi*[16] *a-na* ^{kur}*Nam-ri* $^{22'}$: ^{I}*Aš-šur*-en.pap *ša* ^{kur}*Ḫab-ru-ri a-na Man-ṣu-a-te* $^{23'}$: ^{Id}Amar.utu.kur^{u-ni} *ša* ^{uru}*Raq-mat a-na* ^{uru}*De-e-ri* $^{24'}$: ^{I}Gin.ad-*u-a ša* ^{uru}*Tuš-ḫa-an a-na* ^{uru}*De-e-ri* $^{25'}$: ^{I}*Man-nu-ki-i-Aš-šur ša* ^{uru}*Gu-za-na a-na Mad-a-a*[17] $^{26'}$: ^{I}*Mu-šal-lim*-^{d}Maš *ša* ^{uru}*Til-le-e a-na Mad-a-a* $^{27'}$: ^{I}En.ba^{šá}-*a-ni ša* ^{uru}*Šib-ḫi-niš a-na* ^{kur}*Ḫu-bu-uš-ki-a* $^{28'}$[:] ^{I}Gìr$_{\text{ii}}$.^{d}Utu *ša* ^{uru}*I-sa-na a-na* ^{kur}*I-tu-u'-a* $^{29'}$: ^{Id}Maš.gin.pap *ša* ^{uru}*Ni-nu-a a-na Mad-a-a* $^{30'}$: ^{Id}Iškur-*mu-šam-mer ša* ^{uru}*Kàl-zi a-na Mad-a-a* $^{31'}$uš$_8$ *ša* é ^{d}Nà *ša* Ninua^{ki} *kar-ru* $^{32'}$: ^{I}*Ṣi-il*-en ^{d}15 *ša* ^{uru}*Arba-ìl a-na Mad-a-a* ^{d}Nà *a-na* é gibil *e-ta-rab* $^{33'}$: ^{Id}Nà.man.pap *ša* ^{uru}*Tal-mu-si a-na* ^{kur}*Ki-is-ki* $^{34'}$: ^{Id}Iškur-*ú-bal-liṭ ša* ^{uru}*Ta*[*m*]-*nun-na a-na* ^{kur}*Ḫu-bu-uš-ki-a* An gal *a-na* ^{uru}*De-e-ri it-ta-lak* $^{35'}$: ^{Id}Mes.man.pap[18] *ša* ^{ur}[^{u}*Ar-b*]*a-ìl a-na* ^{kur}*Ḫu-bu-uš-ki-a* $^{36'}$: ^{Id}Maš.pap^{ir} *ša* [^{uru}*Z*]*a-mu-a a-na* ^{kur}*I-tu-'a* $^{37'}$: ^{I}*Ilu-ma*-zu *ša* [^{uru}*Na-ṣ*]*i-bi-na a-na* ^{kur}*I-tu-'a*

[815] [*ditto* Šarru-ḫattu-i]pēl, governor of [N]aṣibīna, (campaign) against Zarātu.

[*ditto* Bēl-lū-bal]āṭ, the co[mmander in chie]f, (campaign) against Dēr; Anu the Great went to Dēr.[19] [*ditto* Muše]kniš, [go]verno[r of Ḫ]abrūri, (campaign) against Aḫsana. [*ditto* Inūrta]-ašarēd, governor of [R]aqmat, (campaign) against Chaldea. [*ditto* Šamaš-kū]mūa, go[vernor of Ar]rapḫa, (campaign) against Babylon.

[810] [*ditto* Bē]l-qātē-ṣabat, g[overnor of M]āzamua, (the king stayed) in the land.

[Thirteen year]s [Šamšī-Adad, king of Assyria].

[During the eponymy of Adad-nēr]ārī (III), [the king] of Assyria, (campaign) against Media. [*ditto*] Nergal-ilāya, [the command]er in chief, (campaign) against Gūzāna. [*ditto*] Bēl-dān, [the] palace [herald], (campaign) against Mannea. *ditto* Ṣil-bēli, [the chief] butler, (campaign) against Mannea.

[805] *ditto* Aššur-taklāk, the chamberlain, (campaign) against Arpad.

ditto Ilu-issīya, the governor of Aššur, (campaign) against Ḫazāzu. *ditto* Nergal-ēreš, [(governor) of R]aṣappa, (campaign) against Ba'alu. *ditto* Aššur-bālti-ekur[ri, (governor) of] Arrapḫa, (campaign) against the Sea(land); plague. *ditto* Inūrta-ilāya, (governor) of Aḫizūḫina, (campaign) against Ḫubuškia.

[800] *ditto* Šēp-Ištar, (governor) of Naṣibīna, (campaign) against Media.[20]

ditto Marduk-išmânni, (governor) of Āmedi, (campaign) against Media.[21] *ditto* Mutakkil-Marduk, the chief eunuch, (campaign) against Lūšia. *ditto* Bēl-tarṣi-iluma, (governor) of Kalḫu,[22] (campaign) against Namri. *ditto* Aššur-bēla-uṣur, (governor) of Ḫabrūri, (campaign) against Manṣuāte.

[795] *ditto* Marduk-šadûni, (governor) of Raqmat, (campaign) against Dēr.

ditto Kīnu-abūa, (governor) of Tušḫan, (campaign) against Dēr. *ditto* Mannu-kī-Aššur, (governor) of Gūzāna, (campaign) against Media.[23] *ditto* Mušallim-Inūrta, (governor) of Tillê, (campaign) against Media. *ditto* Bēl-iqīšanni, (governor) of Šibḫiniš, (campaign) against Ḫubuškia.

[790] [*ditto*] Šēp-Šamaš, (governor) of Isāna, (campaign) against Itu'a.

ditto Inūrta-mukīn-aḫi, (governor) of Nineveh, (campaign) against Media. *ditto* Adad-mušammer, (governor) of Kalīzi, (campaign) against Media; foundations of Nabû temple in Nineveh laid. *ditto* Ṣil-Ištar, (governor) of Arbēla, (campaign) against Media; Nabû entered the new temple. *ditto* Nabû-šarra-uṣur,[24] (governor) of Talmūsu, (campaign) against Kisku.

[785] *ditto* Adad-uballiṭ, (governor) of Ta[m]nuna, (campaign) against Ḫubuškia; Anu the Great went to Dēr.

(B10) 25[2]8 mu^{meš} ^{I}[^{d}Iškur.érin.táḫ] *šar*$_4$ ^{kur}*Aš-šur*

38' *ina li-me* ^{Id}*Šùl-ma-nu*-bar [*šar*$_4$ ^{kur}*Aš-š*]*ur*^{ki} *a-na* ^{kur}*Ur-ar-ṭi* 39': ^{I}*Šam-ši-ilu* [^{lú}*t*]*ur-ta-nu a-na* ^{kur}*Ur-ar-ṭi* 40': ^{Id}Amar.utu-*rém-a-ni* [^{lú}]gal.kaš.lul *a-na* ^{kur}*Ur-ar-ṭi* 41': ^{I}En.si.sá [^{lú}]nimgir.é.gal *a-na* ^{kur}*Ur-ar-ṭi* 42': ^{Id}Nà.suḫuš-*ia*-gin^{in} [^{lú}]agrig *a-na* ^{kur}*I-tu-u'-e* 43'[:] ^{I}Igi-*Aš-šur*-igi [^{lú}]gar.kur *a-na* ^{kur}*Ur-ar-ṭi* 44'[:] ^{Id}Igi.du-uru$_4$^{eš} [^{lú}]*šá-kìn* ^{uru}*Ra-ṣa-pa a-na* ^{kur}*E-re-ni* 45'[:] ^{Id}15.bàd [^{lú}]*šá-kìn* ^{uru}*Na-ṣib-bi-na a-na* ^{kur}*Ur-ar-ṭi* ^{kur}*Nam-ri* 46'[:] ^{I}*Man-nu-ki*-^{d}Iškur [^{lú}*šá*]-*kìn* ^{uru}*Ra-aq-ma-at a-na* ^{uru}*Di-maš-qa* 47': ^{I}*Aš-šur*-en.pap [^{lú}*šá*]-*kìn* ^{uru}*Kal-ḫi a-na* ^{uru}*Ḫa-ta-ri-ka*

(B10) 36[10] mu^{meš} [^{Id}]*Šùl-ma-nu*-bar *šar*$_4$ ^{kur}*Aš-šur*^{ki}

(B1 and duplicates) 48' *ina li-me* ^{I}*Aš-šur-dan*^{an} *šàr* ^{kur}*Aš-šur*^{ki} *a-na* ^{uru}*Ga-na-na-a-ti* 49': ^{I}*Šam-ši-ilu* ^{lú}*tur-ta-nu a-na* ^{uru}*Ma-ra-ad* 50': ^{I}En-*ila-a-a ša* ^{uru}*Arrap-ḫa a-na* ^{kur}*I-tu-'a* 51': ^{I}Ibila-*a-a ša* ^{uru}[*Ma*]-*za-mu-a i-na* kur 52': ^{I}*Qur-di-Aš-šur ša* ^{uru}[*A-ḫi*]-^{i}$_7$*Zu-ḫi-na a-na* ^{kur}*Gán-na-na-ti* 53': ^{I} ^{mu}Silim.^{d}Maš *ša* ^{uru}*Til-e a-na Mad-a-a* 54': ^{Id}Maš.gin.un^{meš} *ša* ^{kur}*Ḫab-ru-ri a-na* ^{kur}*Ḫa-ta-ri-ka mu-ta-nu* 55': ^{I}*Ṣi-id-qi-ilu ša* ^{kur}*Tuš-ḫa-an i-na* kur

---

56' *ina li-me* ^{I}*Bur*-^{d}*Sa-gal-e* [*š*]*a* ^{uru}*Gu-za-na si-ḫu ina* ^{uru}Šà.uru *i-na* ^{iti}Sig$_4$ ^{d}Utu an.mi gar^{an} 57': ^{I}Du$_{10}$.ga.en [*š*]*a* ^{uru}*A-me-di si-ḫu ina* ^{uru}Šà.uru 58': ^{Id}Nà.gin.p[ap *š*]*a* ^{uru}*Ni-nu-a si-ḫu ina* ^{uru}*Arrap-ḫa* 59': ^{I}*La-qi-*[*pu ša*] ^{uru}*Kàl-zi si-ḫu ina* ^{uru}*Arrap-ḫa* 60': ^{I}Igi-^{d}*Aš-šur-la-*[*mur ša*] ^{uru}*Arba-ìl si-ḫu ina* ^{uru}*Gu-za-na mu-ta-nu* 61': ^{I}*A-na*-en-*tàk-*[*l*]*a*[*k ša* ^{ur}]^{u}*I-sa-na a-na* ^{uru}*Gu-za-na šùl-mu ina* kur 62': ^{Id}Maš.a[š *ša* ^{ur}]^{u}*Kur-ba-ìl ina* kur 63': ^{I}En.kur^{u}-*a* [*ša* ^{u}]^{ru}*Tam-nun-na ina* kur 64': ^{I}*I-q*[*i*]-*s*[*u ša* ^{uru}]*Šib-ḫi-ni-iš a-na* ^{kur}*Ḫa-ta-ri-ka*

ditto Marduk-šarra-uṣur,[25] (governor) of [Ar]bēla, (campaign) against Ḫubuškia. *ditto* Inūrta-nāṣir, (governor) of [Māz]amua, (campaign) against Itu'a. *ditto* Iluma-lē'i, (governor) of [Naṣ]ibīna, (campaign) against Itu'a.

[Twenty-]eight years, [Adad-nērārī], king of Assyria.

During the eponymy of Šalmaneser (IV), [the king of Assyria,] (campaign) against Urarṭu.

[780] *ditto* Šamšī-ilu, [the c]ommander in chief, (campaign) against Urarṭu.

ditto Marduk-rēmanni, the chief butler, (campaign) against Urarṭu. *ditto* Bēl-lēšer, the palace herald, (campaign) against Urarṭu. *ditto* Nabû-iš-dēya-ka''in, the chamberlain, (campaign) against Itu'a. [*ditto*] Pān-Aššur-lāmur, the governor of Aššur, (campaign) against Urarṭu.

[775] [*ditto*] Nergal-ēreš, governor of Raṣappa, (campaign) against the cedar mountain.

[*ditto*] Ištar-dūri, governor of Naṣibīna, (campaign) against Urarṭu and Namri. [*ditto*] Mannu-kī-Adad, [gov]ernor of Raqmat, (campaign) against Damascus. [*ditto*] Aššur-bēla-uṣur, [gov]ernor of Kalḫu, (campaign) against Ḫatarikka.

[Ten] years, Šalmaneser, king of Assyria.

During the eponymy of Aššur-dān (III), the king of Assyria, (campaign) against Gananāti.

[770] *ditto* Šamšī-ilu, the commander in chief, (campaign) against Marad.

ditto Bēl-ilāya, (governor) of Arrapḫa, (campaign) against Itu'a. *ditto* Aplāya, (governor) of [Mā]zamua, (the king stayed) in the land. *ditto* Qurdī-Aššur, (governor) of [Aḫi]zūḫina, (campaign) against Gananāti. *ditto* Mušallim-Inūrta, (governor) of Tillê, (campaign) against Media.

[765] *ditto* Inūrta-mukīn-nišī, (governor) of Ḫabrūri, (campaign) against Ḫatarikka; plague.

ditto Ṣidqi-ilu, (governor) of Tušḫan, (the king stayed) in the land.

During the eponymy of Būr-Saggilê, (governor) [o]f Gūzāna, revolt in Libbi-āli; in Siwan, eclipse of the sun. *ditto* Ṭāb-bēlu, (governor) of Āmedi, revolt in Libbi-āli. *ditto* Nabû-mukīn-a[ḫi], (governor) [o]f Nineveh, revolt in Arrapḫa.

[760] *ditto* Lā-qī[pu, (governor) of] Kalīzi, revolt in Arrapḫa.

ditto Pān-Aššur-lā[mur, (governor) of] Arbēla, revolt in Gūzāna; plague. *ditto* Ana-bēli-taklā[k, (governor)] of Isāna, (campaign) against

$^{65'}$: ^{Id}Maš-*še*-[*zib-a-ni ša* $^{ur]u}$*Tal-mu-si a-na* ^{kur}*Ar-pad-da* $^{66'}$ta ^{uru}*Aš-šur ta-a-a-ar-tú*

$^{67'}$*ina li-me* ^{I}*Aš-šur*-[érin.táḫ *šar*$_4$ $^{kur]}$*Aš-šur*^{ki} *i-na* kur $^{68'}$: ^{I}*Šam*-[*ši-ilu* ^{lú}*tu*]*r-ta-nu i-na* kur $^{69'}$: ^{Id}M[es-*šal-lim-an-ni* ^{lú}nim]gir.é.gal *i-na* kur $^{70'}$: ^{I}En-*dan*^{an} [^{lú}ga]l.kaš.lul *i-na* kur $^{71'}$[:] ^{Id}U[tu.gin-*du-gul* ^{lú}ag]rig *a-na* ^{kur}*Nam-ri* $^{72'}$[:] ^{Id}Is[kur.en.gin ^{lú}]gar.kur *a-na* ^{kur}*Nam-ri* $^{73'}$[:] ^{Id}3[0-*šal-lim-a-ni ša* ^{kur}]*Ra-ṣap-pa i-na* kur $^{74'}$[:] ^{I}N[è.iri$_{11}$.gal.pap^{ir} *ša* $^{ur]u}$*Na-ṣi-bi-na si-ḫu ina* ^{uru}*Kal-ḫi*

$^{75'}$[*ina li-me* ^{Id}Muati.en.pap *ša* $^{ur]u}$*Arrap-ḫa ina* ^{iti}Gu$_4$ u$_4$ 13.kám $^{76'}$[^{I}*Tukul*]-*ti*-ibila.É.šár.ra *ina* ^{giš}gu.za *it-tu-šib* $^{77'}$[*ina* ^{iti}D]u$_6$ *a-na bi-rit* i$_7$ *it-ta-lak* $^{78'}$[: ^{I}En-*dan*^{an} *š*]*a* ^{uru}*Kal-ḫi a-na* ^{kur}*Nam-ri* $^{79'}$[: ^{I}*Tukul-ti*-ibila.É.šár.ra *šà*]*r* ^{kur}*Aš-šur*^{ki} *ina* ^{uru}*Ar-pad-da* $^{80'}$[*d*]*i-ik-tú ša* ^{kur}*Ur-ar-ṭi di-kat* $^{81'}$[: ^{Id}Muati.kal^{in}-*an-ni*] ^{lú}*tur-ta-nu a-na* ^{uru}*Ar-pad-da* $^{82'}$[: ^{I}En.Kaskal.en.pap $^{l]ú}$nimgir.é.gal *a-na* ^{uru}: *a-na* 3 mu^{meš} *ka-šid* $^{83'}$[: ^{Id}Muati.kar-*an-ni* $^{l]ú}$gal.kaš.lul *a-na* ^{uru}*Ar-pad-da* $^{84'}$[: ^{Id}30-*tak-lak* $^{l]ú}$agrig *a-na* ^{kur}*Ul-lu-ba* ^{uru}*Bir-tu ṣab-ta-at* $^{85'}$[: ^{Id}Iškur.en.gin] ^{lú}gar.kur ^{uru}*Kul-la-ni-i ka-šid* $^{86'}$[: ^{I}En.igi.lá-*an-ni*] *ša* ^{kur}*Ra-ṣap-pa a-na Mad-a-a* $^{87'}$[: ^{Id}Maš-*ila-a-a*] *ša* ^{uru}*Na-ṣi-bi-na a-na* gìr$_{ii}^{me}$ ^{kur}*Na-al* $^{88'}$[: ^{I}*Aš-šur-šal-lim-an-ni*] *ša* ^{kur}*Arrap-ḫa a-na* ^{kur}*Ur-ar-ṭi* $^{89'}$[: ^{I}En-*dan*^{an}] *ša* ^{uru}*Kal-ḫa a-na Pi-liš-ta* $^{90'}$[*ina li-me* ^{I}*Aš-šur*-kal^{in}-*an-ni*] *ša* ^{uru}*Ma-za-mu-a a-na* ^{kur}*Di-maš-qa* $^{91'}$[: ^{Id}Muati.en.pa]p *ša* ^{uru}*Si-i'-me-e a-na* ^{kur}*Di-maš-qa* $^{92'}$[: ^{Id}Nè.iri$_{11}$.gal-*ú-bal-li*]*ṭ ša* ^{uru}*A-ḫi*-i$_7$*Zu-ḫi-na a-na* ^{uru}*Šá-pi-ia* $^{93'}$[: ^{I}En-*lu-da-r*]*i ša* ^{uru}*Til-e i-na* kur $^{94'}$[: ^{I}*Líp-ḫur-il*]*u ša* ^{kur}*Ḫab-ru-ri* lugal šu$_{ii}$ ^{d}En dib^{bat} $^{95'}$[: ^{I}Bàd-*Aš-šu*]*r ša* ^{uru}*Tu*[*š-ḫ*]*a-an* lugal šu$_{ii}$ ^{d}En dib^{bat} ^{uru}*Ḫ*[*i-*... *ka-šid*(?)]

Gūzāna; peace in the land. *ditto* Inūrta-id[din, (governor) of] Kurba'il, (the king stayed) in the land. *ditto* Bēl-šadûa, [(governor) of] Tamnuna, (the king stayed) in the land.

[755] *ditto* Iq[ī]s[u, (governor) of] Šibḫiniš, (campaign) against Ḫatarikka.

ditto Inūrta-šē[zibanni, (governor) of] Talmūsu, (campaign) against Arpad; return from Aššur.

During the eponymy of Aššur-[nērārī (V), the king of] Assyria, (the king stayed) in the land. *ditto* Šam[šī-ilu, the com]mander in chief, (the king stayed) in the country. *ditto* Mar[duk-šallimanni, the] palace [herald], (the king stayed) in the land.

[750] *ditto* Bēl-dān, [the chi]ef butler, (the king stayed) in the land.

[*ditto*] Ša[maš-kēnu-dugul, the chamber]lain, (campaign) against Namri. [*ditto*] Ad[ad-bēla-ka''in], governor of Aššur, (campaign) against Namri. [*ditto*] S[în-šallimanni, (governor) of] Raṣappa, (the king stayed) in the land. [*ditto*] Ne[rgal-nāṣir, (governor) of] Naṣibina, revolt in Kalḫu.

---

[745] [During the eponymy of Nabû-bēla-uṣur, (governor) of] Arrapḫa, in Ayyar, the thirteenth, [Tigla]th-pileser (III) ascended the throne; [in Te]šrit, he marched on Mesopotamia.[26]

[*ditto* Bēl-dān, (governor) o]f Kalḫu, (campaign) against Namri. [*ditto* Tiglath-pileser, the kin]g of Assyria, there was a massacre among the Urarṭeans in Arpad.

[*ditto* Nabû-da''inanni], the commander in chief, (campaign) against Arpad. [*ditto* Bēl-Ḫarrān-bēla-uṣur], the palace herald, (campaign) against *ditto*; (the city) was taken after three years.

[740] [*ditto* Nabû-ēṭiranni], the chief butler, (campaign) against Arpad.

[*ditto* Sîn-taklāk], the chamberlain, (campaign) against Ulluba; Bīrtu was captured. [*ditto* Adad-bēla-ka''in], the governor of Aššur, Kullanīa was captured. [*ditto* Bēl-ēmuranni], (governor) of Raṣappa, (campaign) against Media. [*ditto* Inūrta-ilāya], (governor) of Naṣibīna, (campaign) at the foot of Mount Nal.

[735] [*ditto* Aššur-šallimanni], (governor) of Arrapḫa, (campaign) against Urarṭu.

[*ditto* Bēl-dān], (governor) of Kalḫu, (campaign) against Philistia.

[During the eponymy of Aššur-da''inanni], (governor) of Māzamua, (campaign) against Damascus. [*ditto* Nabû-bēla-uṣu]r, (governor) of Si'immê, (campaign) against Damascus. [*ditto* Nergal-uballi]ṭ, (governor) of Aḫizuḫina, (campaign) against Šapiya.

[730] [*ditto* Bēl-lū-dār]i, (governor) of Tillê, (the king stayed) in the land.

[*ditto* Lipḫur-il]u, (governor) of Ḫabrūri, the king took the hand of Bēl. [*ditto* Dūr-Ašš]ur, (governor) of Tu[šḫ]an, the king took the hand of Bēl; the

---

(B3 and duplicates) $^{6'}$[*ina li-me* ^{I}En.Kaskal.en.pap] *ša* [^{uru}*Gu-z*]*a-na a-na* $^{ur[u}$... $^{7'}$ ^{I}*Šùl-ma-n*]*u*-bar *ina* $^{gi[š}$gu.za *it-tu-šib* $^{8'}$: ^{Id}Mes.en.pap *ša* ^{uru}*A-me*]-*di i*-[*na* kur $^{9'}$: ^{I}*Maḫ-de-e ša* ^{uru}]Ninua *a-n*[*a* ... $^{10'}$: ^{I}*Aš-šur*-ḫal-*a-ni ša* ^{uru}*Kàl*]-*zi a-n*[*a* ... $^{11'}$: ^{Id}*Šùl-ma-nu*-bar *šàr* ^{kur}*Aš-šur*]^{ki} *a*-[*na* ... $^{12'}$: ^{Id}*Maš-ila-a-a tur-t*]*an*(?) (B4 rev. and duplicates) $^{1'}$: ^{Id}Muati.lal^{iṣ} ... *a-na* ...-*t*]*i* $^{2'}$[: ^{I}*Aš-šur*-giš-*ka*-kal^{in} ...]-*ru* $^{3'}$[: ^{I}Man.gin *šar*$_4$ ^{kur}*Aš-šur*^{ki} ... *e*]-*ta-rab* $^{4'}$[: ^{I}Numun.d]ù *šá-kìn Ra*-[*ṣap-pa a-na* ^{kur}*Ta*]-*ba-la* $^{5'}$[: ^{I}Du$_{10}$-*šar*$_5$-*Aš-šur* ^{lú}agrig ^{uru}Bàd.Man].gin *kar-ru* $^{6'}$[: ^{I}Du$_{10}$-*ṣil-é-šár-ra šá-kìn* Šà.uru *a-na* $^{ur]u}$*Man-na-a-a* $^{7'}$[: ^{I}*Tak-lak-ana*-en *ša* ^{uru}*Na-ṣib-i-na* $^{lú]}$nam^{meš} *šak-nu* $^{8'}$[: ^{Id}15.bàd *ša* ^{uru}*Arrap-ḫa a-na* ^{kur}*Ur-a*]*r-ṭi* ^{uru}*Mu-ṣa-ṣir Ḫal-di-a* <*i-ta-bak*(?)> $^{9'}$[: ^{I}*Aš-šur-ba-ni ša* ^{uru}*Kal-ḫa* ^{lú}g]al^{meš} *ina* ^{kur}*El-li-pa* $^{10'}$[...] é gibil *e-ta-rab* $^{11'}$[*a*]-*na* ^{uru}*Mu-ṣa-ṣir* $^{12'}$[: ^{I}Man.igi.lá-*an-na ša* ^{kur}*Za-mu-a*] *i-na* kur $^{13'}$[: ^{Id}Maš.gin.igi *ša* ^{uru}*Si-i'-me-e*] *a-na* ^{uru}*Mar-qa-sa* $^{14'}$[: ^{Id}Utu.en.pap *ša Ar*-$^{i}_{7}$*Zu-ḫi-na*] *a-na* ^{uru}É.^{I}Numun^{i} lugal *ina Kiši*^{ki} *bi-e-di* $^{15'}$[: ^{I}*Man-nu-ki-Aš-šur*-zu *ša Til*]-*e* ^{I}Man.gin šu$_{ii}$ ^{d}En *iṣ-ṣa-bat* $^{16'}$[: ^{Id}Utu-*ú*]-*pa*-[*ḫír ša* ^{kur}*Ḫab-ru*]-*ri* ^{uru}*Ku-mu-ḫa ka-šid* ^{lú}nam *šá-kìn*[27] (B6 rev. and duplicates) ^{3}*ina lim-me* ^{I}*Šá-Aš-šur-du-ub-bu* ^{lú}*šá-kìn* ^{uru}*Tuš-ḫa-an* lugal ta Ká.dingir.ra^{ki} ^{4}*is-suḫ-ra* sukkal(!) ^{lú}gal^{meš} *šal-lu-tú ša* ^{uru}Bàd-*Ia-kin*$_7$ *na-ṣa* ^{5}[...] ur ^{uru}Bàd-*Ia-kin*$_7$ *na-píl* ^{iti}Du$_6$ u$_4$ 22.kám dingir^{meš} *ša* ^{uru}Bàd.^{I}Man.gin *a-na* é^{meš}-*šú-nu e-tar-bu* ^{6}*ina lim-me* ^{I}*Mu-tak-kíl-Aš-šur* ^{lú}*šá-kìn* ^{uru}*Gu-za-na* man *ina* kur ^{lú}g[al^{m}]^{eš} *ina* ^{kur}*Kar-al-li* ^{7}*ina* ^{iti}Gu4 u$_4$ 6.kám ^{uru}Bàd.Man.gin *šar-ru na*-[...] *maḫ-ra*

---

^{8}*ina lim-me* ^{I}Nigin.en ^{lú}*šá-kìn* ^{uru}*A-me-di* lu[gal ...] ^{9}*ina* ugu ^{I}*Qúr*(!)-*di-i* ^{lú}*Ku-lum-ma-a-a da*-[...] ^{10}lugal gaz *ma-dak-tú ša šàr* ^{kur}*Aš-šur*^{ki} *lu*-[...] ^{11}*ina* ^{iti}Ne u$_4$ 12.kám ^{Id}30.pap^{meš}.su l[ugal(?) ...] ^{12}*ina lim-me* ^{Id}Muati-*de-ni*-dù^{uš} ^{lú}*šá-kìn* ^{uru}Ninua *a*-[*na* ...] ^{13} ^{uru}*La-rak* ^{uru}*Sa-rab-a-nu* [...] ^{14}é.gal *ša* ^{uru}*Kàl-zi e-pe-eš ka-nu ina* [...] ^{15} ^{lú}gal^{meš} *ina* ugu ^{lú}*Ku-lum-ma-a-a* [... ^{16}*ina l*]*i*[*m*]-*me* ^{I}Ḫé.nun-*a-a* [*ša* ^{uru}*Kàl-zi* ... ^{17}*ina lim-me* ^{Id}Muati.zu *ša* ^{uru}*Arba-ìl* ... (B 7) $^{1'}$:(?) ^{I}*Ḫ*]*a-n*[*a-nu* ^{lú}*šá-kìn* ^{uru}*Til-bàr-sip* ... $^{2'}$... t]a ^{kur}*Ḫal-zi* a lal [... $^{3'}$:(?)] ^{I}*Mi-tu-nu* ^{lú}*šá-k*[*ìn* ^{uru}*I-sa-na* $^{4'}$^{I}*Aš*]-*šur*-sum.mu dumu [^{Id}30.pap^{meš}.su $^{5'}$...] *ša* é.gal múru ^{uru}[... $^{6'}$...] ^{giš}[ù]r *ere-ni*

city of Ḫi[... was captured (?)].

[During the eponymy of Bēl-Ḫarrān-bēla-uṣur], (governor) of [Gūz]āna, (campaign) against [...; Šalman]eser (V) [asc]ended the thro[ne. *ditto* Marduk-bēla-uṣur, (governor) of Āme]di, (the king stayed) i[n the land].

[725] [*ditto* Maḫdê, (governor) of] Nineveh, (campaign) against [...].

[*ditto* Aššur-išmânni, (governor) of Kalī]zi, (campaign) against [...]. [*ditto* Šalmaneser, the king of Assyr]ia, (campaign) ag[ainst ... *ditto* Inūrta-ilāya, the commander in chi]ef (?). *ditto* Nabû-tāriṣ, ... t]i.

[720] [*ditto* Aššur-nīrka-da''in ...]ru.[28]

[*ditto* Sargon (II), the king of Assyria] entered[29] [... *ditto* Zēru-ibn]i,[30] governor of Ra[ṣappa, (campaign) against Ta]bal. [*ditto* Ṭāb-šār-Aššur, the chamberlain, Dūr-Šarru]kēn was founded. [*ditto* Ṭāb-ṣil-Ešarra, governor of Libbi-āli, (campaign) against] Mannea.

[715] [*ditto* Taklāk-ana-bēli, (governor) of Naṣibīna, gov]ernors were appointed.

[*ditto* Ištar-dūrī, (governor) of Arrapḫa, (campaign) against Urar]ṭu (and) Muṣaṣir; Ḫaldiya <was deported (?)>. [*ditto* Aššur-bāni, (governor) of Kalḫu, the no]bles (*fought*) at Ellipi; [the god ...] entered his new temple, to Muṣaṣir. [*ditto* Šarru-ēmuranni, (governor) of Māzamua], (the king stayed) in the land. [*ditto* Inūrta-ālik-pāni, (governor) of Si'immê], (campaign) against Mar'aš.

[710] [*ditto* Šamaš-bēla-uṣur, (governor) of Aḫizūḫina], (campaign) against Bīt-zērî; the king stayed in Kiš.

[*ditto* Mannu-kī-Aššur-lē'i, (governor) of Till]ê, Sargon took the hand of Bēl. [*ditto* Šamaš-u]pa[ḫḫir, (governor) of Ḫabrū]ri, Kummuḫu was captured; a governor was appointed.[31] During the eponymy of Ša-Aššur-dubbu, governor of Tušḫan, the king returned from Babylon; the chief vizier, the nobles, the booty of Dūr-Yakīn was carried off; [...] Dūr-Yakīn was destroyed; in Tešrit, the twenty-second, the gods of Dūr-Šarrukēn entered their temples. During the eponymy of Mutakkil-Aššur, governor of Gūzāna, the king (stayed) in the land; the no[ble]s (were) in Karalla; in Ayyar, the sixth, Dūr-Šarrukēn was completed; [...] received.

---

[705] During the eponymy of Nasḫur-bēl, governor of Āmedi, the ki[ng marched on Tabal (?)]; against Gurdī, the Kulummaean, [...] the king was killed; the camp of the king of Assyria [...] In Ab, the twelfth, Sennacherib, the k[ing (?) ...].

During the eponymy of Nabû-dēnī-ēpuš, governor of Nineveh, t[o ...] Larak and Sarrabanu; the palace of Kalīzi was restored, in [...] the nobles against the Kulummaean [... During the e]po[ny]my of Nuḫšāya, [(governor) of Kalīzi, ... During the eponymy of Nabû-lē'i, (governor) of Arbela, ... *ditto* (?) Ḫ]an[ānu, governor of Til-Barsip, ...] from Ḫalzi ...[32] [...].

gal[meš ... 7'...] na$_4$giš.nu$_{11}$.gal *ina* šà k[ur*Am-ma-na-na*(?) 8'...] *ina* šà Uru.še-*da-ar-gi-l*[*i*(?) 9'...] ... -*ú a-na* ma(?) [... 10'...] *ša* lu[gal] ... e [... 11':(?) I]E[n-*šar$_4$-an-ni* lú*šá-kìn* uru*Kur-ba-ìl* ...] (...)

B. OTHER CHRONICLES

10. SYNCHRONISTIC CHRONICLE

Sources: fragmentary tablets; three copies of the work are known.
Bibliography: Grayson 1975a: no. 21.
Language: Babylonian, with a few Assyrian idioms.
Date: the copies are from the seventh century.
Place: Nineveh, Aššurbanipal's library.
Contents: concise history of the relations between Assyria and Babylonia from Puzur-Aššur III to Adad-nērārī III. Attention was mainly on the marking of the boundary east of the Tigris that separated the two states. With errors and gaps, and some Babylonian victories omitted, the chronicle was written on a stela for the edification of future generations. Its pro-Assyrian stance was forcefully stated.

Although subject to the authority of the Mitanni for a long time, Assyria seems to have enjoyed a great degree of autonomy. Puzur-Aššur III was able to negotiate with Babylonia and constructed the fortification of Aššur, an act usually considered usurpation, and Aššur-nādin-aḫḫē II entered into diplomatic relations with Egypt. Having shaken off the Mitannian yoke, Aššur-uballiṭ I was the architect of Assyrian resurgence. With him a political expansion began, with Babylonia the primary victim.

Having a prologue and an epilogue makes the chronicle unique.

(i)(B)1[... *a*]-*na Aš-šur* 2[... *zi*]-*kir-šu* 3[... *d*]*a-ad-me* 4[... *Me*(?)-*li*(?)-*š*]*i*(?)-*pak* 5[...] *u$_4$-me* <<a>> *ṣa-a-ti* 6[...] *ú-šá-pa zík-ra* 7[... *t*]*a-na-ti li-ta* 8[...] *ki i-pe-lu gim-ri* 9[... *ša*]*r*(?)-*ri maḫ-ru-ti* 10[...] *iṣ-ṣab-tu* 11[...] šub*at*

(...)

(A)1' I*Ka-ra-in-da-áš šar$_4$* [kur]*Kar-d*[*u-ni-áš*] 2'*ù* I*Aš-šur*-en.unmeš-*šú šar$_4$* kur*Aš-šur rík-sa-a-ni* 3'*ina bi-rit-šú-nu a-na a-ḫa-meš ú-ra-ki-su* 4'*ù ma-mi-tu ina* ugu *mi-iṣ-ri an-na-ma a-na a-ḫa-meš id-di-nu*

5' I*Pu-zur-Aš-šur šar$_4$* kur*Aš-šur ù* I*Bur-na-bur-ia-áš* 6'*šar$_4$* kur*Kar-du-ni-áš it-mu-ma mi-iṣ-ri* 7'*ta-ḫu-mu an-na-ma ú-ki-nu*

[700) [*ditto* (?)] Metūnu, governo[r of Isāna, Aš]šur-nādin-šumi, the son of [Sennacherib ...] of the palace, in the city [...], great cedar logs [...] alabaster in [Ammanānum [...] in Kapri-Dargil[i ...] for [...] the king [...].

[*ditto* (?)] Bē[l-šarrāni, governor of Kurba'il, ...].

(...)

[...] for Aššur [...] his word [...] settlements [... Meli-Ši]pak (?) [...] forever [...] he made famous the name [...] praise of the vigor [...] when he governed all [...] of the earlier kings [...] he was taken [...] fall [...]

(...)

King Kara-indaš of Kard[uniaš] and King Aššur-bēl-nišēšu of Assyria concluded a mutual accord and reciprocally took an oath, specifically on the matter of this boundary.

King Puzur-Aššur (III) of Assyria and King Burna-Buriaš (I) of Karduniaš took an oath concerning the border and fixed this same boundary line.

$^{8'}$*ina tar-ṣi* ^{I}*Aš-šur-*^{ú}ti.la *šar*$_4$ ^{kur}*Aš-šur* ^{I}*Ka-ra-ḫar-da-áš* $^{9'}$*šar*$_4$ ^{kur}*Kar-du-ni-áš* dumu ^{munus}*Mu-bal-li-ta-at-*^{d}*Še-ru-ú-a* $^{10'}$dumu.munus ^{I}*Aš-šur-*^{ú}ti.la érin^{meš} *Kaš-ši-e* $^{11'}$*ib-bal-ki-tu-ma* gaz-*šu* ^{I}*Na-zi-bu-ga-áš* $^{12'}$[^{kur}*Kaš-šá*]*-a-a* dumu *la ma-ma-na* lugal$^{ú-te}$ *a-na* ugu-*šú-nu iš-šú-ú*

$^{13'}$[^{I}*Aš-šur-*^{ú}ti.l]a [*a-na tu-u*]*r-ri gi-mil-li* $^{14'}$[*šá* ^{I}*Ka-r*]*a-in-da-áš* dumu [dumu.munus-*šú*(?)] *a-na* ^{kur}*Kar-du-ni-áš il-lik* $^{15'}$[^{I}*Na-z*]*i-bu-ga-áš šar*$_4$ ^{kur}*Kar-du-ni-áš i-duk* $^{16'}$[^{I}*Ku-r*]*i-gal-zu ṣe-eḫ-ru* dumu ^{I}*Bur-na-bur-ia-áš* $^{17'}$[*a*]*-na* lugal$^{ú-ti}$ *iš-kun ina* ^{giš}gu.za ad-[*šu*] *ú-*[*še-šib*]

$^{18'}$*ina tar-ṣi* ^{Id}Be.érin.táḫ *šar*$_4$ <^{kur}>*Aš-šur* ^{I}*Ku-ri-gal-zu ṣe-eḫ-ru* [*šar*$_4$ ^{kur}*Kar-du-ni-áš*] $^{19'}$ ^{Id}Be.érin.táḫ *šar*$_4$ ^{kur}*Aš-šur i-na* ^{uru}*Su-ga-gi ša* ugu ^{i_7}[*Ì-diq-la*]*t* $^{20'}$*it-ti-šú i-duk a-bi-ik-*<*ta*>*-šu iš-kun* érin^{meš}-*šú* [*i*]*-duk* $^{21'}$*uš-ma-nu-šú e-bu-uk ul-tú Ša-si-li* ^{kur}*Šu-ba-ri* $^{22'}$[*a-na*] ^{kur}*Kar-du-ni-áš* a.šà^{meš} *ú-šam-ši-lu-ma i-zu-zu* $^{23'}$*mi-iṣ-ru ta-ḫu-mu iš-kun-nu*

$^{24'}$ ^{Id}Iškur.érin.táḫ *šar*$_4$ ^{kur}*Aš-šur* ^{I}*Na-zi-múru-taš šar*$_4$ ^{kur}*Kar-du-ni-áš* $^{25'}$*it-ti a-ḫa-meš ina* ^{uru}Kar.^{d}15 *ana* A.gàr-*sa-al-lu i-duk* $^{26'}$ ^{Id}Iškur.érin.táḫ *a-bi-ik-tú šá* ^{I}*Na-zi-múru-taš iš-kun* $^{27'}$ŠI.ŠI-*šú im-ḫa-aṣ* karaš-*su* ^{d}ùri.gal^{meš}-*šú i-pu-ga-šú* $^{28'}$*i-na* ugu *mi-iṣ-ri ta-ḫu-mu an-ni-me* $^{29'}$*mi-ṣir-re-šu-nu iš-tu tar-ṣi* ^{kur}*Pi-la-as-qi* $^{30'}$*ša* gìr$_{ii}$ *am-ma*<<ma>>*-te ša* ^{i_7}Ḫal.ḫal ^{uru}*Ar-ma-an* A.gàr-*sa-li* $^{31'}$*a-di Lu-lu-me-e iš-ku-nu-ma i-zu-zu*

(ii)(C)^{1}[^{I}*Tukul-ti-*^{d}Maš *šar*$_4$ ^{kur}*Aš-šur*] ^{I}*Kaš-*[*til*]*-a-šú šar*$_4$ ^{kur}*Kar-du-ni-*[*áš*] ^{2}[. . .] . . . *i-na qí-rib tam-ḫa-z*[*i*] ^{3}[. . .] . . . [. . .]

(. . .)

(B)$^{1'}$ ^{lú}ìr^{meš}-*šú e-pu-uš* [. . .] $^{2'}$*a-di* ^{uru}*Kúl-la-ar* . . . [. . .]

$^{3'}$ ^{Id}Be-*ku-dúr*-pap *šar*$_4$ ^{kur}*Aš-šur* ^{Id}[Iškur.mu.pap(?) *šar*$_4$ ^{kur}*Kar-du-ni-áš it-ti a-ḫa-meš*] $^{4'}$*i-du-ku* ^{Id}Be-*ku-dúr*-pap ^{Id}Isk[ur.mu.pap (.?.)] $^{5'}$*ina* múru *ti-du-ku-ma* ^{Id}Maš.a.É.[kur . . .] $^{6'}$*a-na* kur-*šu* gur érin$^{ḫi\ meš}$-*šú ma-*[*'-du-ti id-ka-ma*] $^{7'}$*a-na* ^{uru}Šà.uru *a-na ka-šá-di il-l*[*i-kam* . . .] $^{8'}$*ina qí-rib-šú im-ḫaṣ/qut is-ḫur-ma* [*a-na* kur-*šú* gur]

$^{9'}$*ina tar-ṣi* ^{Id}*Za-ba*$_4$*-ba*$_4$-mu.aš *šar*$_4$ ^{kur}[*Kar-du-ni-áš*] $^{10'}$ ^{I}*Aš-šur-dan*^{an} *šar*$_4$ ^{kur}*Aš-šur a-na* ^{kur}*Kar-du-ni-*[*áš ú-rid*] $^{11'}$ $^{[uru]}$*Za-ban* ^{uru}*Ir-ri-ia* ^{uru}A.gàr-*sa-al-*[*lu* . . .] $^{12'}$[*ik-šud šal-l*]*a-su-nu ma-'a-tu a-na* ^{kur}*Aš-*[*šur il-qa-a*]

(. . .)

(A)$^{1''}$[. . .]*-ti-iš ṭu-ub-ta su-*[*lu-um-ma-a ga-am-ra it-ti a-ḫa-meš iš-ku-nu*] $^{2''}$ma nu ma *a-na* kur-*šú* gur *ar-ki-šu* ^{Id}Mu[ati-*ku-dúr*-pap] $^{3''}$*ni-pí-še-šu*

In the time of King Aššur-uballiṭ (I) of Assyria, Kassite troops rebelled against King Karaḫardaš of Karduniaš, son of Muballiṭat-Šerūa, the daughter of Aššur-uballiṭ, and killed him. They put Nazi-Bugaš, [a Kas]site, son of a nobody, as king over them.

[Aššur-uball]iṭ (I) marched on Karduniaš [in order to ave]nge [Kar]a-indaš[sic], son of [his daughter]. He killed [Naz]i-Bugaš, king of Karduniaš, made [Kur]igalzu (II) the Younger, son of Burna-Buriaš, king and made him as[cend] the throne of [his] father.

In the time of King Enlil-nārārī of Assyria, Kurigalzu (II) the Younger [(was) king of Karduniaš]. King Enlil-nārārī of Assyria fought him at Sugaga, which is on the [Tigr]is, and inflicted a total defeat on him. [He m]assacred his troops and swept away his camp. From Šasili in Subartu [up to] Karduniaš, they divided the land into (two) equal parts (and) fixed the boundary line.

King Adad-nārārī (I) of Assyria and King Nazi-Muruttaš of Karduniaš fought at Kār-Ištar of Ugarsallu. Adad-nārārī inflicted a total defeat on Nazi-Muruttaš; he crushed him, swept away his camp, and seized his standards by force. Concerning this frontier line, specifically, they fixed it and shared the boundaries from Pilasqu, on the other side of the Tigris, (and) Arman of Ugarsallu as far as Lullumē.

[King Tukultī-Ninurta (I) of Assyria] (and) King Kaš[til]iaš (IV) of Karduniaš, [. . .] in open battle [. . .]

(. . .)

[. . .] he made [. . .] his servants. [. . .] up to Kullar [. . .].

King Enlil-kudurrī-uṣur of Assyria (and) [King Adad-šuma-uṣur (?) of Karduniaš fou]ght. As Enlil-kudurrī-uṣur and Adad-[šuma-uṣur (.?.)] were engaged in conflict, Ninurta-apil-E[kur . . .] returned to his country. [He assembled] his numer[ous] troops and marched on Libbi-āli (= Aššur) in order to take it. [But (?) . . .] arrived unexpectedly. He retreated and went back to his country].

In the time of King Zababa-šuma-iddina of [Karduniaš], King Aššur-dān (I) of Assyria [went down] toward Karduniaš; [he took] Zabban, Irriya, Ugarsal[lu, . . . , (and) carried away] their massive booty to Assyria.

(. . .)

[. . . they concluded] a mutual agreement [and a total peace], . . . he returned to his country. Later Ne[buchadnezzar (I)] brought up his siege

iš-šá-a a-na Za-an-qi bir-ti ša ^{kur}[*Aš-šur*] $^{4"}$*a-na ka-šá-di il-li-ka* ^{I}*Aš-šur*-sag-*i-ši šar*$_4$ ^{kur}*Aš-šur* $^{5"}$ ^{giš}gigir^{meš}-*šu id-ka-a a-na* ugu-*šu a-na a-la-ki* $^{6"}$ ^{Id}Muati-*ku-dúr*-pap *áš-šu ni-pí-še la-a pu-a-gi-šú ina* izi *iš-ru-up* $^{7"}$*is-ḫur-ma a-na* kur-*šu i-tur* $^{8"}$ ^{Id}Muati-*ku-dúr*-pap-*ma* ^{giš}gigir $^{<meš>}$ *ù zu-ki a-na I-di bir-ti* $^{9"}$*ša* ^{kur}*Aš-šur a-na ka-šá-di il-li-ka* ^{I}*Aš-šur*-sag-*i-ši* $^{10"}$ ^{giš}gigir^{meš} *zu-ki a-na ni-ra-ru-te iš-pu-ur* $^{11"}$*it-ti-šú i-duk a-bi-ik-tú-šu iš-kun* érin^{ḫi} ^{meš}-*šú i-duk* $^{12"}$*uš-ma-an-šú e-bu-uk* 40 ^{giš}gigir^{meš}-*šú ḫal-lu-up-tum ú-te-ru-ni* $^{13"}$ ^{I}*Karaš-tu a-lik pa-an* érin^{ḫi}-*šú iṣ-ba-tu-ni*

$^{14"}$ ^{giš}*Tukul-ti*-a<<é>>.pap *šar*$_4$ ^{kur}*Aš-šur* ^{Id}Amar.utu.sum.pap^{meš} *šar*$_4$ ^{kur}*Kar-du-ni-áš* $^{15"}$2-*šú si-dir-tu ša* ^{giš}gigir^{meš} *ma-la ina* ugu ^{i}$_7$$^{(!33)}$*Za-ban* $^{16"}$*šu-pá-le-e ina tar-ṣi* ^{uru}*Ar-zu-ḫi-na iš-kun* $^{17"}$*ina* 2-*te* mu.an.na *ina Gur-mar-ri-ti šá e-liš* ^{kur}Uri^{ki} *i-duk* $^{18"}$ ^{uru}Bàd-*Ku-ri-gal-zu* ^{uru}*Si-ip-par šá* ^{d}*Šá-maš* $^{19"}$ ^{uru}*Si-ip-par šá* ^{d}*A-nu-ni-tu*$_4$ $^{20"}$Ká.dingir.ra^{ki} ^{uru}*Ú-pe-e ma-ḫa-zi* gal$^{[meš]}$ $^{21"}$*a-di ḫal-ṣi-šú-nu ik-šu-*[*ud*] $^{22"}$*i-na u*$_4$*-me-šú* ^{uru}A.gàr-*sa-a*[*l-lu*] $^{23"}$*a-di* ^{uru}*Lu-ub-di iḫ-*[*bu-ut*] $^{24"}$ ^{kur}*Su-ḫi a-di* ^{uru}*Ra-pi-qi a-na* zag *gim-ri* [*i-pe-el*]

$^{25"}$*ina tar-ṣi* ^{I}*Aš-šur*-en-*ka-la šar*$_4$ [^{kur}*Aš-šur*] $^{26"}$ ^{Id}Amar.utu-*šá-pi-ik*-numun <<kur>> *šar*$_4$ ^{kur}*Kar-du-*[*ni-áš*] $^{27"}$*ṭu-ub-ta su-lu-um-ma-a ga-am-*[*ra*] $^{28"}$*it-ti a-ḫa-meš iš-ku-*[*nu*] $^{29"}$*ina tar-ṣi* ^{I}*Aš-šur*-e[n]-*ka-la šar*$_4$ ^{kur}[*Aš-šur*] $^{30"}$ ^{Id}Amar.utu-*šá-pi-ik*-numun *šar*$_4$ ^{kur}*Kar-du-ni-áš* kur-*šú e-*[*mid*] $^{31"}$ ^{Id}Iškur.a.sum^{na} a ^{I}É.sag.gíl.kur$^{ú-ni}$ a *la ma-ma-na* $^{32"}$*a-na* lugal$^{ú-te}$ *ina* ugu-*šú-nu iš-kun* $^{33"}$ ^{I}*Aš-šur*-en-*ka-la šar*$_4$ ^{kur}*Aš-šur* $^{34"}$dumu.munus ^{Id}Iškur.a.sum^{na} *šar*$_4$ ^{kur}*Kar-du-ni-áš e-ḫu-zu* $^{35"}$*iš-tu nu-du-ni-šá ma-'-di a-na* ^{kur}*Aš-šur il-qa-*[*a*] $^{36"}$un^{meš} ^{kur}*Aš-šur* ^{kur}*Kar-du-ni-áš* $^{37"}$*it-ti a-ḫa-meš ib-ba-*[*lu*]

(iii)(A)^{1}*ina tar-ṣi* ^{Id}Iškur.érin.táḫ *šar*$_4$ ^{kur}*Aš-š*[*ur*] ^{2} ^{Id}Utu.^{mu}sig$_5$ *šar*$_4$ ^{kur}*Kar-du-ni-áš* ^{3}*i-na* gìr ^{kur}*Ia-al-man si-dir-tu lu iš-kun-*[*ma*] ^{4} ^{Id}Iškur.érin.táḫ *šar*$_4$ ^{kur}*Aš-šur a-bi-ik-tù ša* ^{Id}Utu.^{mu}sig$_5$ ^{5}*šar*$_4$ ^{kur}*Kar-du-ni-áš iš-kun* ^{6}ŠI.ŠI-*šú im-ḫa-aṣ* ^{giš}gigir^{meš}-[*šu* anše.kur.ra^{meš} lá]^{ad} ^{7}*ni-ri-šú* [*il*(?)]-*q*[*í*(?)] ^{8} ^{Id}Utu-^{mu}sig$_5$ *šar*$_4$ ^{kur}[*Kar-du-ni-áš* kur-*šú*] *e-mid* ^{9} ^{Id}Muati.mu.gar^{un} dumu [... *ina* ^{giš}gu.za dúr^{ab}(?)] ^{10} ^{Id}Iškur.érin.táḫ *šar*$_4$ [^{kur}*Aš-šur it-ti*] ^{Id}Muati.mu.gar^{un} ^{11}*šar*$_4$ ^{kur}*Kar-*[*du-ni-áš im-t*]*a-ḫi-iṣ* ŠI.ŠI-*šú iš-kun* ^{12}[^{uru}...]-*ban-ba-la* ^{uru}*Ḫu-da-*[... ^{13}...] uru^{meš} ^{ni} *ma-'-du-*[*ti* ^{14}*ik-šu-ud*] *šal-la-su-nu ma-'a-*[*tu* ^{15}*a-na* ^{kur}*Aš-šur*] *il-qa-*[*a* ^{16}...] ... ni ma ti kur-*šú lu e-sir-*[*šú*(?) ^{17}...] ḫur šu dumu.munus$^{<meš>}$-*šu-nu a-na a-ḫa-meš id-*[*di-nu*] ^{18}[*ṭu-ub-ta s*]*u-lu-um-ma-a ga-ma-ra it-ti a-ḫa-meš* [*iš-ku-nu*] ^{19}un^{meš} [^{kur}*Aš*]-*šur* ^{kur}Uri^{ki} *it-ti a-ḫa-meš ib-ba-*[*al-lu*] ^{20}*iš-tu* ^{uru}Du$_6$.É-*ba-ri šá el-la-an* ^{i}$_7$$^{(sic)}$*Za-*[*ban*] ^{21}*a-di* Du$_6$-*šá*-^{I}*Ba-ta-a-ni ù* <Du$_6$>-*šá*-^{uru}*Zab-da-ni ku-dúr ú-kí*[*n-nu*]

---

machines and marched on Zanqi, a fortress [of Assyria], in order to take it. King Aššur-rēša-iši of Assyria mobilized his chariots to march on him. Nebuchadnezzar burned (his own) siege machines in order to avoid their capture, retreated, and went back to his country. Nebuchadnezzar marched on Īdu, a fortress of Assyria, with his chariots and his infantry in order to take it. Aššur-rēša-iši sent chariots and infantry to the rescue, engaged battle, inflicted him a total defeat, massacred his soldiers, (and) carried away his camp and forty of his chariots with (their) equipment. His general, Karaštu (?), was taken prisoner.

King Tiglath-pileser (I) of Assyria twice drew up chariots, as many as there were, on the Lower Zāb, facing Aḫizūḫina, in line of battle (against) King Marduk-nādin-aḫḫē of Karduniaš. The second year, he defeated (him) at Gurmarritu, which is up-river from Akkad. He too[k] Dūr-Kurigalzu, Sippar of Šamaš, Sippar of Annunītu, Babylon, and Upû, the grea[t] holy cities, with their citadels. At that time, he pi[llaged] Ugarsa[llu] as far as Lubda. [He governed] Suḫu in its entirety as far as Rāpiqu.

In the time of King Aššur-bēl-kala [of Assyria], Marduk-šāpik-zēri (was) king of Kardu[niaš]. They conclud[ed] a mutual agreement and a tota[l] peace. In the time of King Aššur-bē[l]-kala [of Assyria], Marduk-šāpik-zēri, king of Karduniaš, die[d]. He imposed (on the Babylonians) Adad-apla-iddina, son of Esagil-šadûni, son of a nobody, as king. King Aššur-bēl-kala of Assyria married a daughter of King Adad-apla-iddina of Karduniaš and to[ok] her to Assyria with her massive dowry. The peoples of Assyria and Karduniaš were brought together.

In the time of King Adad-nērārī (II) of Assy[ria], King Šamaš-mudammiq of Karduniaš set up a line of battle at the foot of Mount Yalman [and] King Adad-nērārī of Assyria inflicted a total defeat on King Šamaš-mudammiq of Karduniaš, crushed him, [took] his chariots [and] his teams of draft-[horses]. King Šamaš-mudammiq of [Karduniaš die]d. Nabû-šuma-iškun, son of [..., ascended the throne]. King Adad-nērārī of [Assyria engag]ed [battle with] King Nabû-šuma-iškun of Kar[dunaiš]. He defeated him, [took ...]banbala, Ḫuda[...], numerous towns, [(and)] carr[ied] away their massive booty [into Assyria ...]. He encircled (?) [...] his country. [... he rec]eived from him (?) [...]. They mutually gav[e] their daughters for wives. They concluded a mutual agreement and a total peace. The peoples of Assyria and Akkad were brought together. They establi[shed] a permanent boundary line from Til-bīt-Bāri, which is up-river on the Zā[b] as far as Til-ša-Ab/ptāni and <Til>-ša-Zabdāni.

---

^{22}[*ina tar*]-*ṣi* ^{Id}*Šùl-ma-nu*-maš *šar*$_4$ ^{kur}[*Aš-šur* ^{23} ^{Id}Muati.ib]ila.sum^{na} *šar*$_4$ ^{kur}*Kar-du-ni-*[*áš* ^{24}*ṭu*]-*ub-ta su-lu-um-ma ga-am-*[*ra* ^{25}*it-t*]*i a-ḫa-meš iš-ku-nu ina tar-ṣi* ^{Id}*Šùl-ma-nu*-maš šar$_4$ [^{kur}*Aš-šur* ^{26} ^{Id}Muati].ibila.sum^{na} *šar*$_4$ ^{kur}*Kar-du-ni-áš* kur-*šu e-*[*mid* ^{27} ^{Id}]Mes.mu.mu *ina* ^{giš}gu.za ad-*šú ú-*[*šib* ^{28} ^{Id}Am]ar.utu.en-*ú-sa-a-te* šeš-*šú* ki-*šú ib-bal-*[*kit* ^{29} ^{uru}]*Da-ban lu iṣ-bat* ^{kur}*Ak-ka-di-*[*i*] ^{30}*ma*[*l-m*]*a-liš i-zu-zu* ^{Id}*Šùl-ma-nu*-maš *šar*$_4$ ^{kur}*Aš-*[*šur*] ^{31}*a-na ni-ra-ru-ti ša* ^{Id}Amar.utu.mu.[mu] ^{32}*šar*$_4$ ^{kur}*Kar-du-ni-áš il-l*[*ik*] ^{33} ^{Id}Amar.utu.en-*ú-sa-a-te* lugal im.gi ^{34}[*a-d*]*i* érin^{meš} en *ḫi-ṭi šá it-ti-šú i-duk* ^{35}[... ^{uru}Gú].du$_8$.a^{ki} Ká.dingir.ra$^{\text{k[i]}}$

(...)

(C)$^{1'}$[...] um(?) $^{2'}$[*ṭu-ub-ta su-lu-um-ma-a ga-ma-ra it-ti a-ḫa-meš iš-ku*]-*nu* $^{3'}$[un^{meš} ^{kur}*Aš-šur* ^{kur}*Kar-du-ni-áš*/Uri^{ki} *it-ti a-ḫa-meš ib*]-*bal-lu* $^{4'}$[...] ... meš $^{5'}$[*mi-iṣ-ru ta-ḫu-mu an-na-ma ú*]-*kín-nu*

$^{6'}$[^{Id}Utu.^{d}Iškur *šar*$_4$ ^{kur}*Aš-šur* ^{Id}Amar.utu.ti.la-*su-iq-b*]*i šar*$_4$ ^{kur}*Kar-du-ni-áš* $^{7'}$[... ^{Id}Utu].^{d}Iškur *šar*$_4$ ^{kur}*Aš-šur* $^{8'}$[ŠI.ŠI *šá* ^{Id}Amar.utu.ti.la-*s*]*u-iq-bi iš-kun* $^{9'}$[... ad$_6^{\text{meš}}$ *qu-ra*]-*di-šú ú-ma-li* edin

(...)

(iv)(A)^{1}*lu e-sir-šú* uru *šu-ú ik-šud* ^{Id}*Ba-ba*$_6$-pap.aš ^{2}*a-di* nì.ga-*šú ni-ṣir-ti* é.gal-*šú a-na* ^{kur}*Aš-šur il-qa-a* ^{3} ^{uru}Bàd.an^{ki} ^{uru}*La-ḫi-ru* ^{uru}*Ga-na-na-a-te* ^{4}Bàd <<šú>> .^{d}Pap.sukkal É-*re-du-ti* ^{uru}A^{meš}-*Tùr-an* ^{5}uru$^{\text{meš}\text{-}ni}$ *ma-'-du-te šá* ^{kur}*Kar-du-ni-áš* ^{6}*a-di* ^{uru}*ḫal-ṣi-šú-nu* dingir^{meš}-*šú-nu šal-la-su-nu i*[*ṣ-bat*] ^{7}An gal ^{d}*Ḫum-ḫum-ia*$_5$ ^{d}Gašan-Bàd.an^{ki} ^{d}Gašan.Uri^{ki} ^{8} ^{d}*Ši-ma-li-ia* ^{d}Igi.du ^{d}*A-nu-ni-tú* ^{d}Dumu.é ^{9}*šá* ^{uru}*Ma-li-ki ub-la ana* ^{uru}Gú.du$_8$.a ^{uru}Ká.dingir.ra^{ki} ^{10}*Bar-sip*^{ki} *e-li* udu.suskur^{meš} kù^{meš} *lu e-pu-uš* ^{11}*a-na Kal-di ú-rid ma-da-at-tú šá* lugal$^{\text{meš}\text{-}ni}$ ^{12}*ša* ^{kur}*Kal-di am*^{sic}-*ḫur* ^{lú}[...] nu^{meš}-*šú* ^{13}*igi-šá* ^{kur}*Kar-du-ni-áš i*[*m*(?)-*ḫ*]*u*(?)-*r*[*u*(?) ...] ^{14}*e-pu-uš mi-ṣir ta-ḫu-ma* [*an-na-ma ú-kín-nu*]

---

^{15} ^{Id}Iškur.érin.táḫ *šar*$_4$ ^{kur}*Aš-šur* ^{Id}...[... *šar*$_4$ ^{kur}*Kar-du-ni-áš*] ^{16}*ik-nu-uš*(?) [...] ... tu ma du ... [...] ^{17}*i-na* ... [...] ... [...] ^{18}... [...] *um-ma-ni-šú*(?) dingir^{meš} [...] ^{19}un^{meš} *šal-lu-te a-na áš-ri-šú ú-t*[*e-er*(*-ma*)] ^{20}*iš-qu gi-na-a* še.pad^{meš} *ú-kín-šú-nu-ti* ^{21}un^{meš} ^{kur}*Aš-šur* ^{kur}*Kar-du-ni-áš it-ti a-ḫa-meš ib-bal-lu* ^{22}*mi-iṣ-ru ta-ḫu-mu* 1^{niš} *ú-kín-*[*nu*] ^{23}nun egir^{ú} *šá ina* ^{kur}*Ak-ka-di-*[*i*] ^{24}*ú-šá-*<*áš*>*-ka-nu šu-ma šá li-ti ki-šit-ti-*[*šú*] ^{25}*lil-ṭu-ur-ma a-na* $^{\text{na}_4}$na.rú.a *an-n*[*i-ma* ...] ^{26}*ka-a-a-ma-nu-ma a-na la ma-še-e* lid [...] ^{27}*um-ma-a-nu e-ḫa-zu liš-me ma-la šá* ḫi ... [...] ^{28}*ta-na-ti* ^{kur}*Aš-šur lid-lu-lu a-na u*$_4$*-me* [*ṣa-a-ti*] ^{29}*šá* ^{kur}*Šu-me-ri* ^{kur}*Ak-ka-di-i ṣi-lip-t*[*a-ši-na*] ^{30}*li-pa-še-ra ana ka-liš kib-ra-a-*[*ti*]

---

^{31}[é.gal ^{Id}*Aš-šur*-dù.a *šàr kiš-šá-ti*] *šàr* ^{kur}*Aš-šur*^{ki} [...]

[In the tim]e of King Šalmaneser (III) [of Assyria, Nabû-ap]la-iddina (was) king of Karduniaš. They concluded a mutual agreement and a tota[l] peace. In the time of King Šalmaneser [of Assyria, Nabû]-apla-iddina, king of Karduniaš, die[d]. Marduk-zākir-šumi (I) as[cended] the throne of his father. [Mar]duk-bēl-usāte, his brother, rebel[led] against him (and) seized Daban. They apportioned Akkad equally. King Šalmaneser of As[syria] wen[t] to the aid of King Marduk-zākir-[šumi] of Karduniaš (and) defeated Marduk-bēl-usāte, the usurper, as well as the rebel troops that were with him. [... C]utha, Babylon, [...].

(...)

[... They conclu]ded [a mutual agreement and a total peace. The peoples of Assyria and Akkad were br]ought [together. ... Together they establi]shed [a permanent boundary line].

[King Šamšī-Adad (V) of Assyria (and) Marduk-balāṭsu-iqb]i, king of Karduniaš, [.... Šamšī]-Adad, king of Assyria, [de]feated [Marduk-balāṭs]u-iqbi. He filled the plain [with the corpses of] his [soldi]ers.

(...)

He encircled the city, and he himself took it. He took Baba-aḫa-iddina with his wealth and palace treasures to Assyria. He t[ook] the gods and the booty of Dēr, Laḫiru, Gananāti, Dūr-Papsukkal, Bīt-ridūti, Mê-Turan, numerous cities of Karduniaš with their surroundings. He took away Anu the Great, Ḫumḫumia, Šarrat-Dēri, Bēlet-Akkadī, Šimalyia, Palil, Annunītu, Mār-bīti of Māliku. He went up to Cutha, Babylon, (and) Borsippa (and) performed the pure sacrifices. He went down to Chaldea. In Chaldea, he (!) received[34] the tribute of its kings. His officers (?) collected gifts from Karduniaš. He did [.... Together they established] a permanent boundary line.

King Adad-nērārī (III) of Assyria [..., king of Karduniaš], bowed down (?) [...] ... [...] in [...] his troops (?), the gods [...]. He made the deported civilians [return] home [and] granted them income, privileges, and food rations. The people of Assyria and Karduniaš were brought together. Together they established a permanent boundary line.

May (any) future prince who wants to make a name in Akkad be able to record the courage of [his] important achievements. [May he] constantly [turn (?)] to this stela [and reflect (?) upon it] lest it be forgotten! May the expert (?) adviser hear everything that [is engraved (?)] there (and) may it ever be proclaimed to the glory of Assyria! May the treachery of Sumer and Akkad be made known in all parts of the land.

[Palace of Aššurbanipal, king of all lands], king of Assyria, [etc.].

11. CHRONICLE OF ENLIL-NĀRĀRĪ (1327–1318)

Sources: fragment on the reverse of a tablet; perhaps the same tablet as chronicle 15.
Bibliography: Grayson 1975a: 184–85.
Language: Assyrian.
Date: Middle Assyrian Period.
Place: Aššur.
Contents: history of relations between Assyria and Babylonia.

(. . .) ^{1}[. . .]-*a-ti* ^{Id}*En-líl*-[érin.táḫ . . .] ^{2} [. . . ^{m}]^{eš} ^{kur}*Ki-li-zi ú*-[. . .]

---

^{3}[*i-na li-me*] ^{I}Mí^{lí}-^{d}Iškur ^{Id}*En-líl*-érin.táḫ man ^{kur}*Aš-šu*[*r* . . . ^{4}. . .] *ik-šu-ud šal-la-a-su* . . . [. . . ^{5}. . .] ^{I}*Ku-ri-gal-zu* man ^{kur}*Kar-du-ni-áš* [. . . ^{6}. . .] *a-na* ^{kur}*Ki-li-zi pa-ni-šu iš-ku-u*[*n* . . . ^{7}. . .] *iš-me-ma a-na* ^{kur}*Ki-li-zi a-na* [. . . ^{8}. . .] ^{I}*Ku-ri-gal-zu* man ^{kur}[*Kar-du-ni-áš* . . . ^{9}. . .] *iš-me-ma ki-i a* [. . .^{10}. . .] . . . [. . .] . . . [. . .] (. . .)

12. CHRONICLE OF ARIK-DĒN-ILI (1317–1306)

Sources: fragment of the obverse of a tablet.
Bibliography: Grayson 1975a: 185–87; Postgate 1982: 188.
Language: Assyrian.
Date: Middle Assyrian period.
Place: Aššur.
Contents: history of the wars of Arik-dēn-ili. His adversary is uncertain; perhaps allusion to a civil war.

(. . .) ^{1}[. . .] ki [. . . ^{2}. . .] ni(?) . . . uru(?) . . . ke e *a-di* . . . [. . . ^{3}. . .] 100 *ṣe-ni-šu-nu* 100 gu$_4$^{meš}-*šu-nu* [. . . ^{4}. . .] *a-na* ^{uru} ^{d}*A-šur ub-la i-na u*$_4$*-mi-šu-ma* [. . . ^{5}. . .] . . . te 7,000 pisan *i-na* ka-*ši-na a-na* igi *ša* [. . . ^{6}. . .] . . . *ia-šu-ba* gal-*ma e-pu-uš* ^{I}gíd.di.dingir [. . . ^{7}. . .] . . .-*na* nì.ba-*šu a-na* ^{d}Ešdar [. . . ^{8}. . .] . . . -*ṭi-šu i-qiš* [. . .]

---

^{9}[. . .] *gap-šu* ^{I}gíd.di-*ili* buru$_{14}$ *ša* ^{I}*E-si-ni* [. . . ^{10}. . . *e*(?)]-*ki-ma* ^{I}*E-si-ni* 33 ^{giš}gigir^{meš} *ša* . . . [. . . ^{11}. . .] . . . *i-na ši-di-te i-duk* ^{I}gíd.di-*ili i-na* [. . . ^{12}. . .] . . . ru te *ša* ^{giš}gigir^{meš}-*šu ir-di* ^{giš}gigir[^{meš} . . . ^{13}. . . ^{uru}*Ar*]-*nu-na ša* ^{kur}*Ni-gim-ḫi* bàd kur *iš*-[. . . ^{14}. . . ^{I}*E-si*]-*ni i-na* ^{uru}*Ar-nu-ni e-si-ir* . . . [. . . ^{15}. . .] . . .-*šu* ká.gal-*šu ú-sa-ri-iḫ* . . . [. . . ^{16}. . .] . . . ^{I}gíd.di-*ili ú-sà-pu-uḫ* . . . [. . . ^{17}. . .] *gab-be ma-me-ta a-na* ^{I}gíd.di-*ili* . . . [. . .]

(...)

[...] Enlil-[nārārī ...] the [...] of Kilīzi [...].

[During the eponymy of] Ṣillī-Adad, Enlil-nārārī, king of Assyr[ia], conquered [...], plu[ndered] it [...]. Kurigalzu (II), king of Karduniaš, [...]. He set out to Kilīzi [...] he heard and [...] on Kilīzi, in order to [...]. Kurigalzu, king of [Karduniaš ...] he heard and when [...].

(...)

(...)

[... from(?)] ... the city of [...] to [...], a hundred head of their sheep and goats and a hundred head of their cattle [...] he brought to Aššur. At this time [...] seven thousand baskets, by their order, before [...]. He made a large battering ram. Arik-dēn-ili, [...] his gift to Ištar [...] he offered [...].

[...] proud, Arik-dēn-ili [...] the crop of Esini [... he carr]ied away (?) and Esini [...] thirty-three chariots of [...] he killed with (*a weapon*). Arik-dēn-ili [...] in [...] he loaded on his chariots. The chariot[s ...] he [... Ar]nuna of Nigimḫi, the fortress of the country of [...]. He surrounded [Esi]ni in Arnuna [...] he destroyed its gateway [...]. Arik-dēn-ili scattered (?) [...] all [... he took an] oath before Arik-dēn-ili [...].

---

^{18}[...] ... 1 ma.na$^{ta.àm}$ še *iš-ši-kín* ^{I}gí[d.di-*ili* ... ^{19}...] ... *-tu-ri-ḫa* ^{uru}*Ḫa-ba-ru-ḫa ša a-na* [... ^{20}... u]^{ru}*Ku-ti-la* érin^{meš}*-šu-nu is-su-ḫ*[*a* ... ^{21}... u]^{ru}*Tar-bi-ṣi* ^{uru}*Ku-di-na ú-*[... ^{22}...]*-ta id-di-na-šu-nu* ^{uru}*Ku-ti-la* [... ^{23}...]*-pe-lu i-na* u_4*-šu-ma i-na* 90 ^{giš}gigir^{meš}*-šu* [... ^{24}... *š*]*ap-li-a-te e-bir* 600 lú^{meš} ^{uru}*Ḫi-*[... ^{25}...] ... *i-na ši-di-te i-duk* ^{I}*Re-ma-ku* [... ^{26}...] ... *a-na ár-ni* ^{uru}*Na-gab-bil-ḫi i-duk* [...]

---

^{27}[...] i da mí.kal.ga 2 ma.na$^{ta.àm}$ še *i-ši-kí*[*n* ... ^{28}...] ...*-e iš-tu* ^{kur}*Ḫa-la-ḫi a-di* <u_4*-mi*> *ṣa-ti* ... [... ^{29}...] ... *íḫ-bu-ta* 254,000 lú[^{meš} ... ^{30}...] *i-duk dáb-da-šu-nu iš-ku-un šal-l*[*u-su-nu* ... ^{31}... *a-na*] ^{uru} ^{d}*A-šur ub-la i-na* u_4*-mi-šu-ma* 100(?) [... ^{32}... *it*]*-ta-bal-kat* ^{I}*A-si-ni a-di* ... [... ^{33}...] ... a giš ... su a ... [... ^{34}...] ... [...] (...)

13. CHRONICLE OF TUKULTĪ-NINURTA I (1243–1207)

Sources: tablet fragment.
Bibliography: Grayson 1975a: 280, 288–89.
Language: Assyrian.
Date: Middle Assyrian period. Use of a Babylonian month name (Elul) has to be later than the reign of Tiglath-pileser I.
Place: Aššur.
Contents: history of a war between Tukultī-Ninurta and Kaštiliaš that came to an end with the taking of Babylon.

(...) $^{1'}$[...] bi iš [... $^{2'}$...] *Tukul-ti-*^{d}Maš [man kiši man *dan-nu* man ^{kur}*Aš-šur* (.?.) $^{3'}$nun e]n *gim-ri* ša gál [... $^{4'}$...] ^{kur}*Kar-du-ni-áš iṣ-bat-an-*[...] $^{5'}$*ub-la-an-ni i-na* ^{uru}šà.uru [...] $^{6'}$*ú-ša-am-ši ú-šu-ni-iš* [...] $^{7'}$*ša* ^{kur}*Kar-du-ni-áš a-na* [...] $^{8'}$*a-na* ḫul ^{I}*Kaš-til-a-šu* [...]

---

^{iti}kin ud 16 kám *ša-mu-*[...]

14. CHRONICLE OF AŠŠUR-RĒŠA-IŠI I (1132–1115)

Sources: tablet fragment in four columns.
Bibliography: Grayson 1975a: 184, 187–88.
Language: Assyrian.
Date: Middle Assyrian period.
Place: Aššur.
Contents: history of a war between Assyria and Babylonia.

[. . .] the price of grain was fixed at one mina (of copper), Ari[k-dēn-ili . . .]turiḫa, Ḫabaruḫa, which [. . .] for [. . .] Kutila, he turned away their troops [. . .] he [. . .] of Tarbiṣu, Kudina [. . .] gave them up. Kutila [. . .]. At this time, with ninety of his chariots [. . .] he crossed the lower [. . .]. He killed six hundred men of Ḫi[. . .] with (*a weapon*). Rēmāku [. . .] he killed as punishment against Nagabbilḫi [. . .].

[. . .] famine; the price of grain was fixed at two minas (of copper) . . . [. . .] of Ḫalaḫḫu, forever (?) [. . .] he plundered. He killed 254,000 me[n . . .]. He inflicted a defeat on them. [He led away (?) their shackled] prison[ers and] brought [them to] Aššur. At this time, one hundred (?) [. . .] he [ro]se up. Asini [. . .] to [. . .].

(. . .)

(. . .)

[. . .] Tukultī-Ninurta (I), [king of all (the civilized lands), powerful king, king of Assyria (.?.), prince, lor]d of all . . . [. . .] took Karduniaš. [. . .] brought into Libbi-āli [. . . Kaštiliaš (IV), king] of Karduniaš [marched] on [. . .] for evil. Kaštiliaš [. . .].

In the month of Elul, the sixteenth day . . . [. . .].

(i)(. . .) 1'[. . .] *ana* ugu-*šu-nu* [. . . 2'. . . -*t*]*i-šu-nu* [. . . 3'. . .] *ri*(?)-*ik-sa* [. . . 4'. . .] dam.gàrmeš [. . . 5'. . .] . . . -*ú-ri ú-da-*.. 7'[*dab*(?)-*da*(?)-*š*]*u*(?)-*nu iš-ku-u*[*n*]

8'[. . .] . . . *ki-ši-it-ti* 9'[I*Aš-šur*-sag-*i*]-*ši* man kur*Aš-šur* 10'[. . .] . . . *i-na* šà bàd *šu-a-te* 11'[. . .] . . .-*ta šu-bat Aš-šur* en-*šu* 12'[. . .] . . . [*i*]*k ša* zabar 13'[. . .] . . . urudidli.meš-ni 14'[. . .] *le-'-ut Aš-šur* 15'[. . . *li*(?)-*i*]*t qur-di-šu* 16'[. . .] *ù* kur.kurmeš 17'[. . .] *ša* kur*Aš-šur* 18'[. . .]*de-e* 19'[. . . *ki*]-*ib-ra-te* 20'[. . .]-*ni* 21'[. . .] . . .

(. . .)

(iv?) 1[. . .] . . . 2[. . .]-. . .-*du-ni* 3[. . .] kur.kurmeš(?) 4[. . .] *am-ma-te* 5[. . .] *i-duk* 6[. . .] . . .-*ri-ib-te* 7*i-d*[*uk*] *i-na* mu-*ma ši-a-*[*ti*] 8 I*Aš-šur*-sag-*i-ši* man kur[*Aš-šur*] 9*ḫu-ra-su*meš gišgigirmeš-*šu* 10[*il*]-*q*[*í-ma a-n*]*a* uru*Arba-ili* 11*il-li-ka* I[d*Nin-u*]*rta*-sum.mumeš 12man kur*Kar-du-ni-*[*ia*]-*áš* 13*a-l*[*ak* I*Aš-šur*-s]ag-*i-*[*ši* man] k[ur*Aš-šur*] 14*iš-me-ma* é[rin]meš-*šu* 15*e-mu-qe-šu ù* [. . .] . . . 16. . . kur*Kar-du-ni-*[*ia-áš*] 17*in-na-bi-du* .. [. . .] 18*il-te-šu-ma iš-*[. . .] 19*iṭ-ru-da* [. . .] 20*i-na* ugu *a-ni-*[. . . 21. . .] . . . [. . .] (. . .)

15. CHRONICLE OF TIGLATH-PILESER I (1114–1076)

Sources: tablet fragment; perhaps the same tablet as chronicle 11.
Bibliography: Grayson: 1975a: 184, 189; Na'aman 1994: 33–35.
Language: Assyrian.
Date: Middle Assyrian period.
Place: Aššur.
Contents: history of a war between Assyria and Babylonia. A second theme concerned a matter of survival and search for the living.

(. . .)
1'[. . .] . . . dU.gur [. . .]

2'[*ina li-me* . . . *bu-bu-tu* gál*ši* unme]š uzumeš *a-ḫa-iš e-ku-l*[*u a-na ba-la-ṭí* 3'*ki-ma a-ge-e me-e ez*]-*zu-ti* émeš kur*Ar-ma-a-ia*me[š 4'*im-'i-du* buru14 kur*Aš-šur i*]*ḫ-tab-bu-tu ḫu-la-a-ni*meš *iṣ-bu-tu* 5'[*ḫal-ṣi ma-'-du-tu* k]ur*Aš-šur ik-šu-du il-qi-ú* 6'[unmeš *a-n*]*a* kurmeš-*ni* kur*Ḫab-ri-ú-ri a-na ba-la-ṭí* 7'[záḫmeš guškin]-*šu-nu* kù.babbar-*šu-nu* nì.šu-*šu-nu il-qi-ú* 8'[IdAmar.utu.sum.šešmeš man kur]*Kar-du-ni-aš* kur*a e-mid* IdAmar.utu.[dub]*ik*.numun 9'[*ina* gišgu.za ad-*š*]*u* ku4*ub* 18 balameš IdAmar.utu.sum.šešmeš

10'[*ina li-me* . . .] buru14 kur d*A-šur ka-li-š*[*u ma*(?)-*ḫi*]-*iṣ* 11'[émeš kur*Ar-ma-a-ia*meš] *im-'i-du iṣ-*[*bu*]-*tu ši*[*d*]-*d*[*i* í7]Idi[igna] 12'[. . .] *I-di ḫal-ṣi*

(...)

[...] against them [...] their [...] an alliance (?) [...] the merchants [...] he inflicted [a defeat (?)] on them.

[...] conquest. [Aššur-rēša-i]ši (I), king of Assyria, [...] in this fortress [...] the residence of Aššur, his lord, [...] of bronze [...] the towns [...] the majesty of Aššur [...] of his bravery [...] and the lands [...] of Assyria [... the s]ides [...].

(...)

[...] the lands [...] the other [side (?) ...] he killed. [... the d]esert (?) [...] he k[illed]. That year, Aššur-rēša-iši, king of [Assyria], to[ok] his soldiers and his chariots [and] marched [o]n Arbēla. [Ninu]rta-nādin-šumi, king of Karduniaš, heard of the ma[rch of Aššur-r]ēša-iši, king of [Assyria]. He [...] his [troops]. His forces and [...] Karduniaš [...] fled [...] with him [...] he sent [...] against [...]

(...)

(...)

[...]... -Nergal [...]

[In the eponymy of ..., the peop]le ate one another's flesh [to save (their) lives (?). Like a flood's (?) ra]ging [water (?)] the Aramean "houses" [increased], plundered [the crops (?) of Assyria], conquered and took [many fortified cities of] Assyria. [People fled to]ward the mountains of Ḫabrūri to (save their) lives. They (= the Arameans) took their [gold], their silver, (and) their possessions. [Marduk-nādin-aḫḫē, king of] Karduniaš, died. Marduk-[šāpik]-zēri entered upon hi[s father's throne]. Eighteen years (of reign) of Marduk-[nādin-aḫ]ḫē.

[In the eponymy of ...], all the harvest of Assyria was [ruin]ed. [The Aramean tribes] increased and seized the b[ank] of the Ti[gris. They

^{uru}*Ninua* ^{kur}*Ki-li-*[*zi iḫ-bu-tu*] $^{13'}$[*i-na* mu-*ma ši-a-ti* ^{I}*Tukul-ti*-a-*é*]-*šár-ra* man ^{kur}*Aš-šur a-na* ^{kur}*Kat-mu-ḫi* [*il-lik*]

(. . .)

plundered . . .], Īdu, the district of Nineveh, Kilī[zi. In that year, Tiglath-pil]eser (I), king of Assyria, [marched] to Katmuḫu.

(. . .)

Notes

1. Variant: *a-na* <<^{giš}gu.za>> é.

2. Compare the biographical notice on Śamśī-Addu in the Assyrian Royal Chronicle (no. 5).

3. This is the year in which one expects to place the conquest of the city by Śamśī-Addu, an event that D. Charpin places during the eponymy of Ḫaya-mālik (Charpin 1985a: 249.

4. These are two homonymous dignitaries: Charpin 1985a: 257. Restorations follow the proposals of Anbar 1991: 36.

5. The colon indicates the cuneiform sign marking repetition.

6. With Durand 1990: 274–75, one can recognize in A.1288 iv a variant of this passage: $^{2'}$[*i-na Ib-ni-*^{d}]Iškur *ma-a-at* $^{3'}$[*Ma-ar-da-m*]*a-nim Še-er-wu-nim*$^{k[i]}$ *ù Ḫa-bu-ra-tim* lugal *iṣ-ba-a*[*t*] $^{4'}$Bàd.^{d}[Iškur] $^{5'}$*ù* Bàd.^{d}Utu$^{\check{s}i}$-^{d}[Iškur^{ki} lugal] $^{6'}$*i-na da-ad-mi ib-*[*ni-ma*] $^{7'}$*da-aw-da-a-am š*[*a Su-mu-e-pu-uḫ?*] $^{8'}$*i-na ta-ri-š*[*u i-du-uk*] $^{9'}$*Ra-pí-qa-*[*am*^{ki} ^{d}*Íd*$^{ki?}$] $^{10'}$*ù I*[*a?-ab-li-ia*$^{ki?}$ lugal *iṣ-ba-at*]: "[in (the eponymy of) Ibni]-Addu, [the king took the land [of Mardam]ān, of Šerwūnum, and of Ḫābūrātum. Hav[ing built] Dūr-[Addu (?)] and Dūr-Śamśī-Addu in the kingdom of Aleppo, on the road back, he de[feated Sumu-epuḫ. The king (?) took] Rāpiqum, [Id, and] Y[abliya]."

7. Fragments S.24-1+ and M.7481+ are not part of the same tablet; collation shows a slight difference in the writing of the signs.

8. Variant: *si-ḫi.*

9. Variant: [. . .] . . . *si*(?)-*mat.*

10. Mistake due to a copyist: see Finkel and Reade 1998: 249; he was governor of Na'iri.

11. Mistake due to a copyist: see n. 10: dittography: governor of [. . .].

12. Scribe's mistake: see Finkel and Reade 1998: 249.

13. Variant: insurrection.

14. Variant: *ina* ^{kur}*Man-n*[*a-a*]-*a.*

15. Variant: ^{kur}*Man-na-a-a.*

16. Variant: [*Kil*]*i*([LAGA]B?)-*zi.*

17. Variant: ^{uru}*D*[*e-e-ri*].

18. Variant: ^{I}10-*mu-šá-mer*(!) ^{lú}*šá-kì*[*n*] $^{ur[u}$. . .].

19. See Finkel and Reade 1998: 250.

20. Variant: against the Mann[ea]ns.

21. Variant: against the Manneans.

22. Variant: [Ka]līzi.

23. Variant: against D[ēr].

24. This name was omitted in one of the versions and replaced by his successor. This displacement and a series of errors had repercussions on the following three

lines. For Balāṭu [^{lú}*šá-kìn* $^{\text{u]ru}}$ *Ši-ba-ni-ba* between Ṣil-Ištar and Nabû-šarra-uṣur, see Finkel and Reade 1998: 250.

25. Variant: Adad-mušammer, governor of [. . .].
26. This campaign against Babylonia is described in chronicle 16.
27. Variant: ^{lú}gal^{meš} *a-na* ^{uru}*Kúm-muḫ-ḫi* . . . [. . .].
28. Perhaps foundation of a new temple; see Finkel and Reade 1998: 252.
29. For a conjectural restoration, see ibid.
30. For the eponym of 718, see ibid.
31. Variant: the officers [*fought* (?)] against Kummuḫu.
32. For a conjectural restitution, see Finkel and Reade 1998: 252.
33. Text: uru.
34. The text reads "I have received."

IX

Chronicles from the Neo-Babylonian, Persian, and Seleucid Periods

16. FROM NABONASSAR TO ŠAMAŠ-ŠUMA-UKĪN (745–668)

Sources: tablet and duplicating fragment. The only Neo-Babylonian chronicle known in more than one copy. They were library tablets in four columns; one of them, according to the colophon, was the first tablet of a series otherwise lost.
Bibliography: Grayson 1975a: nos. 1A, C; Brinkman 1990: 73–104.
Language: Babylonian.
Date: one of the copies perhaps dated to the twenty-second year of the reign of Darius I, or 499, but the royal name is not clearly legible.
Place: Babylon.
Contents: in 745, Nabonassar had reigned for three years. Babylonia was coming out of a long period of trouble and economic and social decline, but without recovering politically. The hereditary principle of the monarchy, obsolete since 812, remained so until 605, with the sole exception of Nabû-nādin-zēri, who succeeded his father Nabonassar. The Arameans and the Chaldeans were established in the land, where they controlled large amounts of territory. The dominant structure was the family, from which the most influential governed the political and religious life of the cities. Borsippa was in open revolt, while some leading citizens at Uruk usurped the royal privilege of building a temple. For eighty-five years, during the 120 years between 747 and 626, Babylonian kingship was in the power of Assyria.

The chronicler was interested in the parallel histories of Babylonia, Assyria, and Elam, for the main concern at the time was the resistance of Babylonia, with the support of Elam, against Assyrian imperialism.

(i) ^{1}[mu 3 ^{d}Nà.kúr] *šàr* Tin.tir^{ki} ^{2}[*Tukul-ti*-a-*é-šár-ra*] *ina* $^{ku[r]}$*Aš-šur ina* aš.te dúr ^{3}mu.bi [*šàr* ^{kur}*Aš-šur*] *ana* ^{kur}Uri^{ki} *ur-dam-ma* ^{4} ^{uru}*Rab-bi-lu u* ^{uru}*Ḫa-am-ra-nu iḫ-ta-bat* ^{5}*u* dingir^{meš} *šá* ^{uru}*Šá-pa-az-za i-ta-bak*

---

^{6}*a-na tar-ṣi* ^{d}Nà.kúr *Bar-sip*^{ki} ^{7}ki Tin.tir^{ki} *it-te-kìr ṣal-tu*$_{4}$ *šá* ^{d}Nà.kúr ^{8}*a-na* šà *Bar-sip*^{ki} *i-pu-šú ul šá-ṭir*

---

^{9}mu 5 ^{d}Nà.kúr *Um-ma-ni-ga-áš* ^{10}*ina* ^{kur}Elam *ina* aš.te dúr^{ab}

---

^{11}mu 14 ^{d}Nà.kúr gig-*ma ina* é.gal-*šú* nam^{meš} ^{12}14 mu^{meš} ^{d}Nà.kúr lugal^{ut} Tin.tir^{ki} dù^{uš} ^{13} ^{I}*Na-di-nu* dumu-*šú ina* Tin.tir^{ki} *ina* aš.te dúr^{ab}

---

^{14}mu 2 *Na-di-nu ina si-ḫi* gaz ^{15}2 mu^{meš} *Na-din* lugal^{ut} Tin.tir^{ki} dù^{uš} ^{16} ^{I}Mu.gi.na en nam en *si-ḫi ina* aš.te dúr^{ab} ^{17}iti 2 u$_{4}$[$^{meš(?)}$ M]u.gin lugal^{ut} Tin.tir^{ki} dù^{uš} ^{18} ^{I}Gin.numun [dum]u *A-mu-ka-na ina* aš.te zi-*šú-ma* aš.te *iṣ-bat*

---

^{19}mu 3 Gin.numun *Tukul-ti*-ibila-*é-šár-ra* ^{20}*ana* ^{kur}Uri^{ki} *ki-i ú-ri-dam* ^{21}É-*A-mu-ka-nu iḫ-ta-pi u* Gin.numun *ik-ta-šad* ^{22}3 mu^{meš} Gin.numun lugal^{ut} Tin.tir^{ki} dù^{uš} ^{23} ^{I}*Tukul-ti*-ibila-<<aš>>-*é-šár-ra ina* Tin.tir^{ki} *ina* aš.te dúr^{ab}

---

^{24}mu 2 *Tukul-ti*-ibila-*é-šár-ra ina* ^{iti}Ab nam^{meš} ^{25}<18> mu^{meš} *Tukul-ti*-ibila-*é-šár-ra* lugal^{ut} ^{kur}Uri^{ki} ^{26}*u* ^{kur}*Aš-šur* dù^{uš} 2 mu^{meš} *ina* šà *ina* ^{kur}Uri^{ki} dù^{uš} ^{27} ^{iti}Ab u$_{4}$ 25 *Šul-man-a-šá-red ina* ^{kur}*Aš-šur* ^{28}<*u* Uri>^{ki} *ina* aš.te dúr^{ab} ^{uru}*Šá-ma-ra-'-in iḫ-te-pi*

---

^{29}mu 5 *Šul-man-a-šá-red ina* ^{iti}Ab nam^{meš} ^{30}5 mu^{meš} *Šul-man-a-šá-red* lugal^{ut} ^{kur}Uri^{ki} *u* ^{kur}*Aš-šur* dù^{uš} ^{31}^{iti}Ab u$_{4}$ 12.kám Lugal.gin *ina* ^{kur}*Aš-šur ina* aš.te dúr^{ab} ^{32}*ina* bár ^{Id}Amar.utu.a.mu *ina* Tin.tir^{ki} *ina* aš.te dúr^{ab}

---

^{33}mu 2 ^{d}Amar.utu.a.mu *Um-ma-ni-ga-áš šàr* Elam ^{34}*ina* nam Bàd.an^{ki} *ṣal-tu*$_{4}$ *ana* šà Lugal.gin *šàr* ^{kur}*Aš-šur* dù-*ma* ^{35}bala ^{kur}*Aš-šur* gar^{an} ŠI.ŠI-*šú-nu ma-'-diš* gar^{an} ^{36}^{Id}Amar.utu.ibila.mu *u um-ma-ni-šú šá a-na re-ṣu-tu*$_{4}$ ^{37}*šàr* Elam.ma^{ki} gin^{ku} *ṣal-tu*$_{4}$ *ul ik-šu-ud ana* egir-*šú* lá^{sa}

[In the third year (of the reign) of Nabonassar], king of Babylon, [Tiglath-pileser (III)] ascended the throne of Assyria. The same year, [the king of Assyria] went down into Akkad, pillaged Rabbilu and Ḫamrāna, and deported the gods of Šapazza.

In the time of Nabonassar, Borsippa revolted against Babylon, (but) the battle that Nabonassar had with Borsippa was not written down.

The fifth year (of the reign) of Nabonassar, Ḫumban-nikaš (I) ascended the throne of Elam.

The fourteenth year, Nabonassar became ill and went to his destiny[1] in his palace. Nabonassar reigned fourteen years over Babylon. His son (Nabû)-nādin-(zēri) ascended the throne of Babylon.

The second year, (Nabû)-nādin-(zēri) was killed during an insurrection. (Nabû)-nādin-(zēri) reigned two years over Babylon. (Nabû)-šuma-ukīn (II), a governor, leader of the insurrection, ascended the throne.

(Nabû)-šuma-ukīn reigned one month and two (?) days over Babylon. (Nabû)-mukīn-zēri, the Amuka[nit]e, dethroned him and took the throne.

The third year (of the reign) of (Nabû)-mukīn-zēri, Tiglath-pileser having gone down into Akkad, he ravaged the Bīt-Amukāni and captured (Nabû)-mukīn-zēri. (Nabû)-mukīn-zēri reigned three years over Babylon.[2] Tiglath-pileser ascended the throne of Babylon.

The second year, in the month of Ṭebeth, Tiglath-pileser went to his destiny. Tiglath-pileser reigned <eighteen> years[3] over Akkad and Assyria. Of those (eighteen years), two years he reigned over Akkad. In the month of Ṭebeth, the twenty-fif<th> day, Šalmaneser (V) ascended the throne of Assyria and <Akkad>. He ravaged Samaria.

The fifth year, in the month of Ṭebeth, Šalmaneser went to his destiny. Šalmaneser reigned five years over Akkad and Assyria. In the month of Ṭebeth, the twelfth day, Sargon (II) ascended the throne of Assyria. In the month of Nisan,[4] Merodach-baladan (II) ascended the throne of Babylon.

The second year (of the reign) of Merodach-baladan, King Ḫumban-nikaš of Elam joined battle with King Sargon of Assyria in the district of Dēr; he brought about Assyria's withdrawal and inflicted a crushing defeat on it. Merodach-baladan, who had gone with his army to the aid of the king of Elam, did not join the battle in time and withdrew.

---

^{38}mu 5 ^{d}Amar.utu.a.mu *Um-ma-ni-ga-áš* lugal Elam nam^{meš} ^{39}[26] mu^{meš} *Um-ma-ni-ga-áš* lugal^{ut} ^{kur}Elam dù^{uš} ^{40}[*Iš-tar-ḫu-u*]*n-du* dumu *a-ḫa-ti-šú ina* ^{kur}Elam *ina* aš.te dúr^{ab} ^{41}[ta sag lugal^{ut}] ^{d}Amar.utu.ibila.mu *a-di* mu 10.kám ^{42}[^{kur}*Aš-šur i*]*t-ti* [^{d}Amar.utu.a.]mu *na-kìr*

---

^{43}[mu 10 ^{d}Amar.utu.a.m]u [É ...]*-ri* ^{44}[*iḫ-te-pi ḫu-bu-ut-s*]*u* [*iḫ-ta-ba*]*t* (ii) ^{1}mu [12 ^{d}Amar.utu.a.mu Lugal.gin *ana* ^{kur}Uri^{ki} *ur-dam-ma*] ^{2}*ṣal-tu*$_4$ [*ana* šà ^{Id}Amar.utu.a.mu dù^{uš}*-ma*] ^{3} ^{d}Amar.u[tu.a.mu *ina* igi-*šú* bala^{it} *ana* ^{kur}Elam.ma záḫ] ^{4}12 m[u^{meš} ^{d}Amar.utu.a.mu lugal^{ut} Tin.tir^{ki} dù^{uš}] ^{5}Lugal.gin [*ina* Tin.tir^{ki} *ina* aš.te dúr^{ab}]

$^{6-9}$[mu 1.kám ^{d}30.šeš^{meš}.su ...] ^{10} ^{d}[Amar.utu.a.mu ... ^{11}...] ^{12}mu 2.ká[m(?) ^{d}30.šeš^{meš}.su *ana* ^{kur}Uri^{ki} ^{13}*u*[*r-dam-ma ṣal-tu*$_4$ *ana* šà ^{d}Amar.utu.a.mu ^{14}*ina* ugu *Kiši*^{ki} dù*-ma* ^{d}Amar.utu.a.mu *ina* igi-*šú* bala^{it} ^{15}*ana* ^{uru}*Gu-zu-um-ma-ni*(?) záḫ *ina* Tin.tir^{ki} ^{d}30.šeš^{meš}.su *ana* é.gal] ^{16} ^{d}Amar.[utu.a.mu *i-te-ru-ub-ma ni-ṣir-ti*(?) lugal^{ti}*-šu*(?) ...] ^{17}*it-ta-*[... *iš-lul*(?)*-ma*] ^{18}lú Tin.tir$^{ki.meš}$ *ul* bir *mi-iṣ-ri* [...^{d}Amar.utu.a.mu ...] ... ^{19}*ir-dip-ma* ^{d}Amar.utu.a.mu *u-*[*ul in-na-mir*(?)] ^{20}*ḫu-bu-ut* kur-*šú iḫ-ta-bat* ... [...] ... ^{21} ^{uru}*La-rak u* ^{uru}*Sar-ra-ba-*[*nu* ...] ... ^{22}*ki-i* lá^{su} ^{Id}En-*ib-ni ina* Tin.tir^{ki} *ina* aš.te *ul-te-šib*

---

^{23}mu 1.kám ^{d}En-*ib-ni* ^{d}30.šeš^{meš}.su ^{24} ^{uru}*Ḫi-ri-im-ma u* ^{uru}*Ḫa-ra-ra-tu*$_4$ *iḫ-te-pi*

---

^{25}mu 3.kám ^{Id}En-*ib-ni* ^{d}30.šeš^{meš}.su *ana* ^{kur}Uri^{ki} ^{26}*ur-dam-ma ḫu-bu-ut* ^{kur}Uri^{ki} *iḫ-ta-bat* ^{27} ^{Id}En-*ib-ni u* ^{lú}GAL^{meš}*-šú ana* ^{kur}*Aš-šur ul-te-eg-lu* ^{28}3 mu^{meš} ^{d}En-*ib-ni* lugal^{ut} Tin.tir^{ki} dù^{uš} ^{29} ^{d}30.šeš^{meš}.su An.šár.mu.mu dumu-*šú* ^{30}*ina* Tin.tir^{ki} *ina* aš.te *ul-te-šib*

---

^{31}mu 1.kám An.šár.mu.mu *Iš-tar-ḫu-un-du šàr* Elam ^{32}*Ḫal-lu-šú* šeš-*šú iṣ-bat-su-ma* ká *ina* igi-*šú ip-ḫi* ^{33}18 mu^{meš} *Iš-tar-ḫu-un-du* lugal^{ut} ^{kur}Elam dù^{uš} ^{34}*Ḫal-lu-šú* šeš-*šú ina* ^{kur}Elam *ina* aš.te dúr^{ab}

---

^{35}mu 6.kám An.šár-*na-din*-mu ^{d}30.šeš^{meš}.su ^{36}*ana* ^{kur}Elam *ú-rid-ma* ^{uru}*Na-gi-tu*$_4$ ^{uru}*Ḫi-il-mi* ^{37} ^{uru}*Pi-il-la-tu*$_4$ *u* ^{uru}*Ḫu-pa-pa-nu iḫ-t*[*e-p*]*i* ^{38}*ḫu-bu-us-su-nu iḫ-ta-bat* egir *Ḫal-lu-šú šàr* Elam ^{39}*ana* ^{kur}Uri^{ki} gin^{kám}*-ma ina* til <iti>Du$_6$ *ana* Zimbir^{ki} ku$_4$ ^{40}un^{meš} gaz ^{d}Utu ta *É-babbar-ra* nu è ^{41} ^{I}An.šár-*na-din*-mu dib-*ma ana* ^{kur}Elam *a-bi-ik* ^{42}6 mu^{meš} An.šár.mu.mu lugal^{ut} Tin.tir^{ki} dù^{uš} ^{43}*šàr* Elam ^{d}U.gur-*ú-še-zib ina* Tin.tir^{ki} ^{44}*ina* aš.te *ul-te-šib*

The fifth year (of the reign) of Merodach-baladan, King Ḫumban-nikaš of Elam went to his destiny. Ḫumban-nikaš reigned [twenty-six] years over Elam. [Šutur-Naḫḫ]unte, son of his sister, took the throne of Elam. [From the year of the accession] of Merodach-baladan until the tenth year, [Assyria] was at war [ag]ainst [Merodach-bal]adan.

[The tenth year, Merodach-balad]an [wrecked] and [sa]cked the [Bīt-. . .]ri.

The [twelfth] year [(of the reign) of Merodach-baladan, Sargon went down into Akkad and joined] battle [with Merodach-baladan. Before him], Mero[dach-baladan beat a retreat and fled into Elam. Merodach-baladan reigned] twelve year[s over Babylon]. Sargon [ascended the throne of Babylon].

(. . .)

[The first year (of the reign) of Sennacherib, . . .], M[erodach-baladan . . .].

The second year [(of the reign) of Sennacherib, he went down into Akkad. Before Kiš, he joined battle with Merodach-baladan. Before him, Merodach-baladan beat a retreat and fled to Guzummanu. In Babylon, Sennacherib entered into the palace of Merodach-baladan and *the royal treasury* . . .] . . . [. . . *he plundered* . . . but] he did not disperse the inhabitants of Babylon. He pursued [Merodach-baladan (?) . . .] the territory [. . .], but Merodach-baladan [remained undiscoverable]. He sacked his land,[5] [. . . and took] Larak and Sarrabanu. On his return he made Bēl-ibni ascend the throne of Babylon.[6]

The first year (of the reign) of Bēl-ibni, Sennacherib ravaged Ḫirimmu and Ḫararātum.[7]

The third year (of the reign) of Bēl-ibni, Sennacherib went down into Akkad and sacked Akkad. He took Bēl-ibni and his nobles into exile in Assyria. Bēl-ibni reigned three years over Babylon. Sennacherib made his son Aššur-nādin-šumi ascend the throne of Babylon.

The first year (of the reign) of Aššur-nādin-šumi, Ḫallušu-(Inšušinak I) captured King Šutur-Naḫḫunte of Elam, his brother, and locked him up. Šutur-Naḫḫunte reigned eighteen years over Elam. Ḫallušu-(Inšušinak), his brother, ascended the throne of Elam.

The sixth year (of the reign) of Aššur-nādin-šumi, Sennacherib went down to Elam, ra[va]ged and sacked Nagītum, Ḫilmu, Pillatum, Ḫuppapānu. Later, King Ḫallušu-(Inšušinak) of Elam went to Akkad; at the end <of the month> of Tešrit, he entered Sippar (and) massacred the inhabitants. Šamaš did not leave the Ebabbar. Aššur-nādin-šumi was captured and deported to Elam. Aššur-nādin-šumi reigned six years over Babylon. The

k[i.]b[ala^{u}]^{t} ^{kur}*Aš-šur* gar^{an}

---

^{45}mu 1.kám ^{Id}U.gur-*ú-še-*[*zib*] ^{iti}Šu u$_4$ 16.kám ^{46} ^{d}U.gur-*ú-še-zib* Nib[ru]^{ki} dib^{bat} sar sar ir ir^{lal} ^{47} ^{iti}Du$_6$ u$_4$ 1.kám erín [^{kur}]*Aš-šur ana* Unu^{ki} ku$_4$^{meš} (iii) ^{1}dingir^{meš} *ša* Unu^{ki} *u* un^{meš}-*šú iḫ-tab-tu* ^{2} ^{d}U.gur-*ú-še-zib* egir lú.Elam gin-*ma* dingir^{meš} *ša* Unu^{ki} ^{3}*u* un^{meš}-*šú i-te-*[*e*]*k-mu* ^{iti}Du$_6$ u$_4$ 7.kám *ina pi-ḫat* Nibru^{ki} ^{4}*ṣal-tu$_4$ ana* šà erín ^{kur}*Aš-šur* dù^{uš}-*ma ina* mè edin *ṣa-bit-ma* ^{5}*ana* ^{kur}*Aš-šur a-bi-ik* mu 1 6 iti[^{meš} ^{d}]U.gur-*ú-še-zib* ^{6}lugal^{ut} Tin.tir^{ki} dù^{uš} [^{iti}Du$_6$] u$_4$ 26.kám ^{7}*Ḫal-lu-šú šàr* Elam un^{meš}-*šú is-ḫu-*[*šú* k]á *ina* igi-*šú* <<šú>> ^{8}*ip-ḫu-ú* gaz-*šú* 6 mu^{meš} *Ḫ*[*al-lu-šú* <lugal^{ut}>] ^{kur}Elam dù^{uš} ^{9}Nì.du *ina* ^{kur}Elam *ina* aš.te dúr^{ab} egi[r ^{d}30.še]š^{meš}.su ^{10}*ana* ^{kur}Elam *ú-rid-ma* ta ^{kur}*Ra-a-*[*ši*] *a-di* ^{11}*É-Bur-na-ki iḫ-te-pi ḫu-bu-ut-su iḫ-ta-bat* ^{12}*Mu-še-zib-*^{d}Amar.utu *ina* Tin.tir^{ki} *ina* aš.te dúr^{ab}

---

^{13}mu 1.kám *Mu-še-zib-*^{d}Amar.utu ^{iti}Ne u$_4$ 17.kám ^{14}Nì.du *šàr* ^{kur}Elam *ina si-ḫi ṣa-bit-ma* gaz 10 iti ^{15}Nì.du lugal^{ut} ^{kur}Elam dù^{uš} *Me-na-nu ina* ^{kur}Elam ^{16}*ina* aš.te dúr^{ab} mu nu zu ^{I}*Me-na-nu* erín ^{kur}Elam ^{kur}Uri^{ki} ^{17}*id-ke-e-ma ina* ^{uru}*Ḫa-lu-le-e ṣal-tu$_4$ ana* šà ^{kur}*Aš-šur* ^{18}dù^{uš}-*ma* bala$^{tu}_{4}$ ^{kur}*Aš-šur* gar^{an} ^{19}mu 4 *Mu-še-zib-*^{d}Amar.utu ^{iti}Bár u$_4$ 15.kám ^{20}*Me-na-nu šàr* ^{kur}Elam *mi-šit-tu$_4$ i-mi-šid-su-ma* ^{21}ka-*šú ṣa-bit-ma at-ma-a la le-'i* ^{22}*ina* ^{iti}Gan u$_4$ 1.kám uru *ṣa-bit Mu-še-zib-*^{d}Amar.utu ^{23}*ṣa-bit-ma ana* ^{kur}*Aš-šur a-bi-ik* ^{24}4 mu^{meš} *Mu-še-zib-*^{d}Amar.utu lugal^{ut} Tin.tir^{ki} dù^{uš} ^{25}*ina* ^{iti}Še u$_4$ 7.kám *Me-na-nu šàr* ^{kur}Elam nam^{meš} ^{26}4 mu^{meš} *Me-na-nu* lugal^{ut} ^{kur}El[am] d[ù^{uš}] ^{27}*Ḫum-ba-ḫal-da-šú ina* ^{kur}Elam *ina* aš.te dúr^{ab}

---

^{28}mu 8.kám lugal *ina* Tin.tir^{ki} nu tuk ^{iti}Šu u$_4$ 3.kám ^{29}dingir^{meš} *ša* Unu^{ki} ta [El]am^{ki}[8] *ana* Unu^{ki} ku$_4$^{meš} ^{30}*ina* ^{iti}Du$_6$ u$_4$ 23.kám *Ḫum-ba-*[*ḫal*]*-da-šú šàr* Elam *ina* an.izi ^{31}*ma-ḫi-iṣ-ma ina* šú^{e} ^{d}[utu u]g$_7$^{ut} 8 mu^{meš} *Ḫum-ba-ḫal*(!)-*da-šú* ^{32}lugal^{ut} ^{kur}Elam dù^{uš} ^{33}*Ḫum-ba-ḫal-da-šú* 2^{ú} [dumu]-*šú ina* aš.te dúr^{ab} ^{34} ^{iti}Ab u$_4$ 20.kám ^{d}30.[še]š^{meš}.su *šàr* ^{kur}*Aš-šur* ^{35}dumu-*šú ina si-ḫi* gaz-*šú* [24(?)] mu^{meš} ^{d}30.šeš^{meš}.su ^{36}lugal^{ut} ^{kur}*Aš-šur* dù^{uš} t[a] u$_4$ 20.kám *šá* ^{iti}Ab *a-di* ^{37}u$_4$ 2.k[ám š]*á* ^{iti}e *si-ḫi ina* ^{kur}*Aš-šur sa-dir* ^{38} ^{iti}Še u$_4$ [2]8(?).kám An.šár.šeš.mu dumu-*šú ina* ^{kur}*Aš-šur ina* aš.te dúr^{ab}

king of Elam made Nergal-ušēzib ascend the throne of Babylon. He brought about the re[trea]t of Assyria.

The first year (of the reign) of Nergal-ušēzib, in the month of Dumuzi, the sixteenth day, Nergal-ušēzib took Nip[pur], sacked and plundered it. In the month of Tešrit, the first day, the Assyrian army entered Uruk. It held the gods and the inhabitants of Uruk for ransom. After the arrival of the Elamites and the rounding-up of the gods and the inhabitants of Uruk (by the Assyrians), in the month of Tešrit, the seventh day, Nergal-ušēzib joined battle with the Assyrian army in the district of Nippur; he was captured on the battlefield and deported to Assyria. Nergal-ušēzib reigned one year—(precisely) six months—over Babylon. In the month of [Tešrit], the twenty-sixth day, the subjects of King Ḫallušu-(Inšušinak) of Elam revolted [against him], locked him up, (and) killed him. Ḫ[allušu-(Inšušinak)] reig<ned> six years over Elam. Kudur-(Naḫḫunte) ascended the throne of Elam. Lat[er, Sennach]erib went down to Elam, ravaged and sacked (the country) from Rāši to Bīt-Purnaki. Mušēzib-Marduk ascended the throne of Babylon.

In the first year (of the reign) of Mušēzib-Marduk, in the month of Ab, the seventeenth day, King Kudur-(Naḫḫunte) of Elam was taken and killed during an insurrection. Kudur-(Naḫḫunte) reigned ten months over Elam. Ḫumban-nimena ascended the throne of Elam.

In an unknown year, Ḫumban-nimena mustered the army of Elam and Akkad; he joined battle with Assyria at Ḫalulê and caused the withdrawal of Assyria.

The fourth year (of the reign) of Mušēzib-Marduk, in the month of Nisan, the fifteenth day, King Ḫumban-nimena of Elam was seized by a paralytic stroke, and his mouth was held fast so that it was impossible for him to speak. In the month of Kislev, the first day, the city (= Babylon) was taken. Mušēzib-Marduk was captured and deported to Assyria. Mušēzib-Marduk reigned four years over Babylon. In the month of Adar, the seventh day, King Ḫumban-nimena of Elam went to his destiny. Ḫumban-nimena [rei]gned four years over El[am]. Ḫumban-ḫaltaš (I) ascended the throne of Elam.

The eighth year when there was no king in Babylon, in the month of Dumuzi, the third day, the gods of Uruk returned from [Assy]ria (!) to Uruk. In the month of Tešrit, at noon, the twenty-third day, King Ḫumban-ḫaltaš of Elam fell ill. He [di]ed at sun[set]. Ḫumban-ḫaltaš reigned eight years over Elam. Ḫumban-ḫaltaš (II), his [son], ascended the throne. In the month of Ṭebeth, the twentieth day, during an insurrection, the son of King Sennacherib of Assyria killed his (father). Sennacherib reigned [twenty-four] years over Assyria. In Assyria, the insurrection lasted from the month of Ṭebeth, the

---

^{39}mu 1.kám An.šár.šeš.mu ^{I}Numun.gin.si.sá gar Kur *Tam-tì* ^{40}*ki-i iš-qa-a ina* ugu Urí^{ki} *it-ta-di* uru *u*[*l* dib] ^{41}*ina* igi ^{lú}gal^{meš} *šá* ^{kur}*Aš-šur* záḫ-*ma ana* ^{kur}Elam *i*-[*te-ru-ub*] ^{42}*ina* ^{kur}Elam *šàr* ^{kur}Elam *iṣ-bat-su-ma ina* ^{giš}tukul g[az-*šú*] ^{43}iti nu zu *ina* Nibru^{ki} ^{lú}gú.[en.na ...] ^{44}*ina* ^{iti}Kin ^{d}Ka.di *u* dingir^{meš} [*šá* Bàd.an^{ki} ta ...] ^{45}*ana* Bàd.an^{ki} gin^{meš} ... [...] ^{46}*ana* Bàd.Lugal.gin gin^{meš} [...] ^{47} ^{iti}Še ta/uš ši šá ud [...]

---

^{48}[mu 2].kám ^{lú}gal.é [*ina* ^{kur}Urí^{ki} *bi-ḫir-tu$_4$ ib-te-ḫir* ^{49}... ^{50}...]

(iv) ^{1}[mu 3.kám ^{Id}...še]š^{meš}-*šul-lim* ^{lú}gú.en.na ^{2}[^{Id}Utu-*ib-ni* dumu ^{I}*Da-k*]*u-ri ana* ^{kur}*Aš-šur ab-ku-ma ina* ^{kur}*Aš-šur* gaz^{meš}

---

^{3}[mu 4.kám ^{ur}]^{u}*Ṣi-du-nu ṣa-bit šal-lat-su šal-lat* ^{4}[mu.b]i ^{lú}gal.é *ina* ^{kur}Urí^{ki} *bi-ḫir-tu$_4$ ib-te-ḫir*

---

^{5}mu 5.kám ^{iti}Du$_6$ u$_4$ 2.kám erín ^{kur}*Aš-šur Ba-az-za* ^{6}*iṣ-ṣab-tu ina* ^{iti}Du$_6$ sag.du *šá* lugal *šá* ^{uru}*Ṣi-du-nu* ^{7}ku$_5$^{is}-*ma ana* ^{kur}*Aš-šur na-ši ina* ^{iti}Še sag.du *šá* lugal ^{8}*šá* ^{kur}*Kun-du u* ^{kur}*Si-su-ú* ku$_5$^{is}-*ma ana* ^{kur}*Aš-šur na-ši*

---

^{9}mu 6.kám *šàr* Elam *ana* Zimbir^{ki} ku$_4$ gaz gaz ^{d}Utu *ul-tu* ^{10}*É-babbar-ra* nu è <erín> ^{kur}*Aš-šur ana* ^{kur}*Mi-li-du* <gin>^{me} $^{\langle iti\rangle}$Kin 7 ^{11}*Ḫum-ba-ḫal-da-šú šàr* ^{kur}Elam nu gig *ina* é.gal-*šú* ug$_7$ ^{12}5 mu^{meš} *Ḫum-ba-ḫal-da-šú* lugal^{ut} ^{kur}Elam dù^{uš} ^{13}*Ur-ta-gu* šeš-*šú ina* ^{kur}Elam *ina* aš.te dúr^{ab} ^{14}iti nu zu ^{I}Mu.mu ^{lú}gú.en.na ^{15}*u* ^{I}Nì.du dumu ^{I}*Da-ku-ri ana* ^{kur}*Aš-šur ab-ku*<-*ma ina* ^{kur}*Aš-šur* gaz^{meš}(?)>

---

^{16}mu 7.kám ^{iti}Še u$_4$ 5.kám érin ^{kur}*Aš-šur ina* ^{kur}*Mi-ṣir* gaz^{meš} ^{17}*ina* ^{iti}Še ^{d}Inanna *A-kà-dè*^{ki} *u* dingir^{meš} *šá A-kà-dè*^{ki} ^{18}ta ^{kur}Elam gin^{meš} ^{nim}-*ma ina* ^{iti}Še u$_4$ 10.kám *ana A-kà-dè*^{ki} ku$_4$^{meš}

---

^{19}mu 8.kám An.šár.šeš.mu ^{iti}Ab u$_4$ *ḫe-pí* ^{20} ^{kur}*Šub-ri*-<<za>>-*a-a ṣa-bit šal-lat-su šal-lat* ^{21}*ina* ^{iti}Gan *šal-lat-su ana* Unu^{ki} *i-ter-bi* ^{22} ^{iti}Še u$_4$ 5.kám dam lugal ug$_7$^{at}

---

^{23}mu 10.kám ^{iti}Bár érin ^{kur}*Aš-šur ana* $^{\langle kur\rangle}$*Mi-ṣir* gin *ḫe-pí* ^{24} ^{iti}Šu u$_4$ 3.kám u$_4$ 16.kám u$_4$ 18.kám ^{25}3-*šú di-ik-tu$_4$ ina* ^{kur}*Mi-ṣir di-kât* ^{26}u$_4$ 22.kám

twentieth day, to the month of Adar, the second day. In the month of Adar, the [twenty-]eighth (?) day, Esarhaddon, his son, ascended the throne of Assyria.

The first year (of the reign) of Esarhaddon, (Nabû)-zēr-kitti-līšir,[9] governor of the Sealand, having gone upstream, set up camp before Ur but did no[t take] the city. He fled before the leaders of Assyria and re[ached] Elam. In Elam, the king of Elam captured him and cau[sed him] to be executed. In an unknown month, at Nippur, the go[vernor . . .]. In the month of Elul, Ištarān and the gods [of Dēr] went from [. . .] to Dēr. [. . .] went to Dūr-Šarrukīn [. . .]. In the month of Adar [. . .].

[The second ye]ar, the majordomo [carried out a selection[10] in Akkad . . .].

[The third year, *Divine name*]-aḫḫē-šullim, governor of Nippur, [(and) Šamaš-ibni, the Dakku]rean,[11] were deported to Assyria and executed.

[The fourth year], Sidon was taken and plundered. [The sa]me year, the majordomo carried out a selection in Akkad.[12]

The fifth year, in the month of Tešrit, the second day, the army of Assyria took Bāza. In the month of Tešrit, the head of the king of Sidon was cut off and carried to Assyria. In the month of Adar, the head of the king of Kundu and Sissû was cut off and carried to Assyria.[13]

The sixth year, the king of Elam entered Sippar. There was a massacre. Šamaš did not leave the Ebabbar.[14] The <army> of Assyria <marched> on Milīdu. In the <month> of Elul, the seven<th day>, King Ḫumban-ḫaltaš of Elam, without being ill, died in his palace. Ḫumban-ḫaltaš reigned five[15] years over Elam. Urtak, his brother, ascended the throne of Elam. In an unknown month, Governor Šuma-iddina of Nippur and Kudurru, the Dakkurean,[16] were deported to Assyria <and executed (?)>.

The seventh year, the fifth day of Adar, the army of Assyria was decimated in Miṣir. In the month of Adar, Ištar of Akkade and the gods of Akkade came from Elam; they entered Akkade in the month of Adar, the tenth day.

The eighth year (of the reign) of Esarhaddon, in the month of Ṭebeth, the BREAK day, the land of Šubria was taken and plundered. In the month of Kislev, its booty entered Uruk. In the month of Adar, the fifth day, the queen died.[17]

The tenth year, in the month of Nisan, the army of Assyria marched on Miṣir. BREAK. In the month of Dumuzi, the third, the sixteenth, and the

Me-em-pí u[ru lugal^{tú} *ṣ*]*a-bit* ^{27}lugal-*šú ul-te-zib* dumu^{meš}-*šú u* š[eš-*šú ina* šu$_{ii}$ *ṣa-a*]*b-tu* ^{28}*šal-lat-su šal-lat* un^{meš}-*šú ḫab-ta* nì.šu-*šú* [*iš-tal*]-*lu-ni*

---

^{29}mu 11.kám lugal *ina* ^{kur}*Aš-šur* ^{lú}gal^{meš}-*šú* [*ma-du-tú ina* ^{giš}tukul] *id-du-uk*

---

^{30}mu 12.kám lugal ^{kur}*Aš-šur* [*ana* ^{kur}*Mi-ṣir* gin^{a}]^{k} ^{31}*ina* kaskal gig-*ma ina* ^{iti}Ap[in u]$_{4}$ 10.kám nam^{meš} ^{32}12 mu^{meš}An.šár.šeš.mu lugal^{ut} ^{kur}*Aš-šur* dù^{uš} ^{33} ^{d}Giš.šir.mu.gi.na *ina* E^{ki} ^{I}An.šár.dù.a *ina* ^{kur}*Aš-šur* 2 dumu^{me}-*šú ina* aš.te dúr^{me}

---

^{34}mu sag ^{Id}Giš.šir.mu.gi.na *ina* ^{iti}Gu$_{4}$ ^{35} ^{d}En *u* dingir^{meš} *šá* ^{kur}Uri^{ki} *ul-tu* ^{uru}Šà.uru ^{36}*ú-ṣu-nim-ma ina* ^{iti}Gu$_{4}$ u$_{4}$ 1[4/24.kám] *ana* Tin.tir^{ki} ku$_{4}$^{meš}-*ni* ^{37}mu.bi ^{uru}*Kir-bi-tu*$_{4}$ *ṣ*[*a-bit*] lugal-*šú ka-šid* ^{38} ^{iti}Ab u$_{4}$ 20.kám ^{Id}En.kar^{ir} di.ku$_{5}$ Tin.tir^{ki} *ṣa-bit-ma* gaz

---

^{39}*pir-su reš-tu-ú ki-ma* sumun-*šú* sar-*ma ba-ru ù up-pu-uš* ^{40}*ṭup-pi* ^{I}*A-na*-^{d}En.kám a-*šú šá* ^{I}*Li-ib-lu-ṭu* ^{41}dumu ^{I}Ur.^{d}Nanna *qa-at* ^{Id}*É-a*-mu a-*šú šá* ^{42} ^{I}*A-na*-^{d}En.kám dumu ^{I}Ur.^{d}Nanna Tin.tir^{ki} ^{43} ^{iti}[... u$_{4}$ 2]6(?).kám mu 22.kám ^{I}*Da-ri-*[*ia-muš*] *šàr* E^{ki} [lug]al kur.kur

17. FROM NABONASSAR TO ESARHADDON (748/747–669)

Source: fragment of a library tablet in four columns.
Bibliography: Grayson 1975a: no. 1B; Brinkman 1990: 73–104.
Language: Babylonian.
Date: late Babylonian period.
Place: Babylon.
Contents: this chronicle covered the same period as the preceding one. However, some differences are observable between the two sources. This second chronicle, of which the beginning is lost, perhaps began before Nabonassar's accession.

(i)$^{1'}$[mu ... ^{d}Nà.kúr ^{d}E]n(?) nu [UD]+DU

$^{2'}$[mu 3 ^{d}Nà.kúr *šà*]*r* Tin.tir^{ki} *Tukul-ti*-a-*é-šár-ra* $^{3'}$[*ina* ^{kur}*Aš-šur ina* aš.te dú]r^{ab} mu.bi $^{4'}$[*šàr* ^{kur}*Aš-šur ana* ^{kur}Uri^{ki} *ur-da*]*m-ma* ^{uru}*Rab-bi-lu* $^{5'}$[^{uru}*Ḫa-am-ra-nu*] *iḫ-ta-bat* $^{6'}$[*u* dingir^{meš} *šá* ^{uru}*Šá-pa*]-*az-zu i-ta-bak*

eighteenth days, three times, there were massacres in Miṣir. The twenty-second day, Memphis, the [royal] res[idence, wa]s taken, abandoned by its king, (whose) children and br[other were tak]en. (The city) was plundered, its inhabitants held for ransom, their property [loo]ted.[18]

The eleventh year, in Assyria, the king caused [a large number] of his nobles [to be executed].

The twelfth year, the king of Assyria [marched on Miṣir]. On the way he fell ill and, in the month of Araḫ[samnu], the tenth [da]y, he went to his destiny. Esarhaddon reigned twelve years over Assyria. His two sons ascended the throne, Šamaš-šuma-ukīn in Babylon, Aššurbanipal in Assyria.[19]

The year of the accession of Šamaš-šuma-ukīn, in the month of Iyyar, Bēl and the gods of Akkad left Aššur; they entered Babylon in the month of Iyyar, the [four]teen/twenty-[four]th (?) day. The same year, Kirbītum wa[s taken], its king captured. In the month of Ṭebeth, the twentieth day, Bēl-ēṭir, the judge of Babylon,[20] was arrested and executed.

First section, copied, reread, and checked according to its ancient model, tablet of Ana-Bēl-ēreš, son of Liblutu, descendant of Ur-Nanna. Babylon, month of [..., ... +] sixth day, the twenty-second year (of the reign) of Dar[ius (I?)], king of Babylon, [king] of all lands.

(...)

[The ... year (of the reign] of Nabonassar, ... B]ēl did not [lea]ve.

[The third year (of the reign) of Nabonassar, k]ing of Babylon, Tiglath-pileser (III) [as]cended [the throne of Assyria]. The same year, [the king of Assyria we]nt down [to Akkad], pillaged Rabbilu [and Ḫamrāna and] deported [the gods of Šap]azza.

$^{7'}$[mu 5 ^{d}Nà.kúr *Um-m*]*a-ni-ga-áš* lugal $^{8'}$[*ina* ^{kur}Elam *ina* aš].te dúr^{ab}

$^{9'}$[mu ... *Tukul-t*]*i*-a-*é-šár-ra* $^{10'}$[... *ik-ta*]-*šad*

$^{11'}$[...] ... kur *ur-ra-du*

$^{12'}$[...] ad lu

$^{13'}$[...] nam šá

$^{14'}$[...] ki

(...)

(ii) $^{1'}$lugal^{ut} [^{kur}Elam dù^{uš} *Iš-tar-ḫu-un-du*] $^{2'}$dumu nin-[*šú ina* ^{kur}Elam *ina* aš.te dúr^{ab}]

$^{3'}$mu 6 ^{kur}*Aš-šu*[*r* ...] $^{4'}$ta sag lu[gal^{ut} ^{d}Amar.utu.ibila.mu] $^{5'}$*a-di* mu 10.[kám ^{kur}*Aš-šur*] $^{6'}$*it-ti* ^{d}Amar.[utu.a.mu *na-kìr*]

$^{7'}$mu 10 ^{d}Amar.utu.a.mu É ... [...-*r*]*i* $^{8'}$*iḫ-te-pi ḫu-bu-ut-su iḫ*-[*ta*]-*bat*

$^{9'}$mu 1[2] ^{d}Amar.utu.a.mu Lugal.gin [*ana* ^{kur}Uri]^{ki} $^{10'}$*ur-dam-ma ṣal-tu*$_{4}$ *ana* ŠÀ ^{Id}[Amar.utu.a].mu $^{11'}$dù^{uš}-*ma* ^{d}Amar.utu.a.mu *ina* igi-[*šú* bala^{i}]^{t} $^{12'}$*ana* ^{kur}Elam.ma záḫ 12 mu^{meš} ^{d}[Amar.utu.a.m]u $^{13'}$lugal^{ut} Tin.tir^{ki} d[ù^{u}]^{š} $^{14'}$Lugal.gin *ina* Tin.tir^{ki} *ina* aš.te dú[r^{ab}]

$^{15'}$mu 13 Lugal.gin šu ^{d}En *iṣ-ṣa*-[*bat*] $^{16'}$Bàd-*Ia-a-ki-nu ik-ta-š*[*ad*]

$^{17'}$mu 14 lugal *ina* [kur]

$^{18'}$[mu] 15 ^{iti}Du$_{6}$ u$_{4}$ 22.kám dingir^{meš} *šá* Kur *Tam-t*[*im* $^{19'}$*ana*(?)] ki-*šú-nu* gur^{meš} bad^{meš} *ina* ^{kur}*Aš-šur* gar$^{[nu(?)]}$

$^{20'}$[mu 17(?) Lugal.gi]n *ana* ^{kur}*Ta-ba-lu* [... $^{21'}$...]

(...)

(iii) $^{1'}$[(^{Id}U.gur-*ú-še-zib*) ... ^{iti}Du$_{6}$ u$_{4}$ 7.kám *ina pi-ḫat* Nibru]^{ki} *ṣal-tu*$_{4}$ *ana* šà [érin ^{kur}*Aš-šur*] $^{2'}$dù^{uš}-*ma ina* mè edin *ṣa-bit*-[*ma ana* ^{kur}*Aš-šur*] $^{3'}$*a-bi-ik* ^{iti}Du$_{6}$ u$_{4}$ 26.kám *Ḫal*-[*lu-šú*] $^{4'}$*šàr* ^{kur}Elam un^{meš}-*šú is-ḫu-šú-ma* [(?)] $^{5'}$gaz^{meš}-*šú* 6 mu^{meš} *Ḫal-lu-šú* lugal^{ut} ^{k}[^{ur}Elam] $^{6'}$dù^{uš} Nì.du *ina* ^{kur}Elam *ina*

[The fifth year (of the reign) of Nabonassar, Ḫumb]an-nikaš (I), the king, ascended [the thr]one [of Elam].

[The ...th year ...], Tiglath-pileser [too]k [...].

[...] they went down (?).

[...]

[...]

(...)

[Ḫumban-nikaš reig]ned [twenty-six years] over [Elam. Šutur-Naḫḫunte], son of [his] sister, [ascended the throne of Elam].

The sixth year, Assyria [...]. From the year of the acces[sion of Merodach-baladan (II) to the tenth year, [Assyria was at war] against Mero[dach-baladan].

The tenth year, Merodach-baladan ravaged and sa[cke]d the Bīt-[...]ri.

The twelfth year (of the reign) of Merodach-baladan, Sargon (II) went down [into Akkad] and joined battle with [Merodach-bal]adan. Before him, Merodach-baladan beat a retreat and fled into Elam. Merodach-baladan reigned twelve years over Babylon. Sargon a[scended] the throne of Babylon.

The thirteenth year,[21] Sargon grasp[ed] the hand of Bēl. He conquer[ed] Dūr-Yakīn.

The fourteenth year, the king (remained) in [his country].

The fifteenth [year], in the month of Tešrit, the twenty-ninth day, the gods of the Se[a]land returned [to] their sanctuaries. Epidemics raged in Assyria.

[The seventeen(?)th year, Sarg]on [marched] on Tabal.[22]

(...)

[Nergal-ušēzib ...] joined battle with [the army of Assyria in the month of Tešrit, the seventh day, in the district of Nippu]r; he was captured on the battlefield and deported [to Assyria]. In the month of Tešrit, the twenty-sixth day, the subjects of King Ḫallušu-(Inšušinak I) of Elam revolted against him,

aš.te dúr^{ab} $^{7'}$egir ^{d}30.šeš^{meš}.su *ana* ^{kur}Elam *ú-rid-ma* $^{8'}$ta ^{kur}*Ra-a-ši* en É-*Bu-na-ak-ku* $^{9'}$*iḫ-te-pi ḫu-bu-ut-su iḫ-ta-bat* $^{10'}$ ^{I}*Mu-še-zib*-^{d}Amar.utu *ina* Tin.tir^{ki} *ina* aš.te dúr^{ab}

$^{11'}$mu 1.kám *Mu-še-zib*-^{d}Amar.utu ^{iti}Ne u$_4$ 8.kám $^{12'}$N[ì.du *šàr*] ^{kur}Elam *ina si-ḫi ṣa-bit-ma* gaz $^{13'}$10 [iti]^{meš} Nì.du lugal^{ut} ^{kur}Elam dù^{uš} $^{14'}$*Me-na-nu ina* ^{kur}Elam *ina* aš.te dúr^{ab} $^{15'}$mu nu zu *Me-na-nu* érin ^{kur}Elam *u* ^{kur}Uri^{ki} $^{16'}$*id-ke-e-ma ina* ^{uru}*Ḫa-lu-le-e* $^{17'}$*ṣal-tu*$_4$ *ana* šà érin ^{kur}*Aš-šur* dù^{uš}-*m*[*a*] $^{18'}$bala^{ti} ^{kur}*Aš-šur* gar$^{[an]}$

$^{19'}$mu 4.kám *Mu-še-zib*-^{d}Amar.utu ^{iti}Bár u$_4$ 1[5.kám] $^{20'}$*Me-na-nu šàr* Elam *mi-šit-tu*$_4$ [*i-mi-šid-su-ma*] $^{21'}$ka-*šú* [*ṣa-bit-ma at-ma-a la le-'i*] $^{22'}$[*ina*] ^{iti}G[an u$_4$ 1.kám uru *ṣa-bit Mu-še-zib*-^{d}Amar.utu $^{23'}$*ṣa*]-*b*[*it-ma ana* ^{kur}*Aš-šur a-bi-ik*]

(. . .)

(iv) $^{1'}$[mu 3.kám ^{Id}. . .šeš^{meš}-*šul-lim* ^{lú}gú.e]n.na $^{2'}$[^{Id}Utu-*ib-ni* dumu ^{I}*Da-ku-ri ana*] ^{kur}*Aš-šur* $^{3'}$[*ab-ku-ma ina* ^{kur}*Aš-šur di*]-*i-ku*

$^{4'}$[mu 4.kám ^{uru}*Ṣi-du-nu ṣa-bit šal-lat-su*] *šal-lat* $^{5'}$[mu.bi ^{lú}gal.é *ina* ^{kur}Uri^{ki} *bi-ḫir-tu4 ib-t*]*e-ḫir*

$^{6'}$[mu 5.kám ^{iti}Du$_6$ u$_4$ 2.kám érin ^{kur}*Aš-šur Ba-az-z*]*a*

(. . .)

18. ESARHADDON'S CHRONICLE; BEGINNING OF THE REIGN OF ŠAMAŠ-ŠUMA-UKĪN (680–668)

Sources: tablet in one column.
Bibliography: Grayson 1975a: no. 14.
Language: Babylonian.
Date: copy from the Neo-Babylonian period.
Place: unknown.
Contents: another version of the history of the reign of Esarhaddon and the accession of Šamaš-šuma-ukīn.[23]

^{1}[mu 1.kám ^{I}An.šár.šeš.sum^{na} ^{I}Numun.gin.si.sá gar Kur *Tam-tì* ^{2}*ki-i iš-qa-a ina* ugu Urí^{ki} *it-ta-di* uru *ul* dib ^{3}*ina* igi ^{lú}gal^{meš} *šá* ^{kur}*Aš-šur* záḫ-*ma ana* ^{kur}Elam *i-te-ru-ub* ^{4}*ina* ^{kur}Elam] *šàr* ^{kur}Elam [*iṣ-bat-su-ma ina* ^{giš}tukul

lock[ed] him up and killed him. Ḫallušu-(Inšušinak) reigned six years over [Elam]. Kudur-(Naḫḫunte) ascended the throne of Elam. Later, Sennacherib went down to Elam, ravaged and sacked (the country) from Rāši to Bīt-Bunakku. Mušēzib-Marduk ascended the throne of Babylon.

The first year (of the reign) of Mušēzib-Marduk, in the month of Ab, the eighth day, King Kudur-(Naḫḫunte) of Elam was taken and killed during an insurrection. Kudur-(Naḫḫunte) reigned ten [months] over Elam. Ḫumban-nimena ascended the throne of Elam. In a year not known, Ḫumban-nimena mustered the army of Elam and Akkad; he joined battle with Assyria at Ḫalulê and caused the withdrawal of Assyria.

The fourth year (of the reign) of Mušēzib-Marduk, in the month of Nisan, the fif[teenth] day, King Ḫumban-nimena of Elam [was seized by] a paralytic stroke, and his mouth [was held fast so that it was impossible for him to speak. In the month of] Kis[lev, the first day, the city (= Babylon) was taken. Mušēzib-Marduk was t]ak[en and deported to Assyria].

(...)

[The third year, *Divine name*-aḫḫē-šullim, govern]or of Nippur, [and Šamaš-ibni, the Dakkurean, were deported] to Assyria [and] executed.

[The fourth year, Sidon was taken and plun]dered. [The same year, the majordomo] carried out a selection [in Akkad].[24]

[The fifth year, in the month of Tešrit, the second day, the army of Assyria took Bā]za.

(...)

[The first year (of the reign) of Esarhaddon, (Nabû-zēr-kitti-līšir, governor of the Sealand, having gone upstream, set up camp before Ur but did not take the city. He fled before the officers of Assyria and reached Elam.

ug$_7$-*šú* ^{5} (.?.) ^{I}An].šár.šeš.sum^{na} *Na-i-*[*id*-^{d}Amar.utu šeš-*šú* gar Kur *Tam-tì* gar] ^{6}*ina* ^{iti}Kin An gal *u* dingir^{me} *ša* Bàd.[an^{ki} *ina* Bàd.an^{ki} ku$_4$^{meš}] ^{7} ^{d}*Ḫum-ḫum-ia u* ^{d}*Ši-ma-li-*[*ia ina* Zimbir^{ki} ku$_4$^{meš}] ^{8}*ina* ^{iti}Du$_6$ kisal(?) ku šu ur ru *ina* ^{iti}[. . .] ^{9}mu 2.kám ^{lú}gal.é *ina* ^{kur}Uri^{ki} *b*[*i-ḫir-tú ib-te-ḫir*] ^{10}mu.bi ^{uru}*Ar-za-*[*a*]*-a ṣa-bit* [*šal*]*-lat-su š*[*al-lat*] ^{11}[un]^{meš} *ḫab-tu* lugal *u* dumu-[*šú ina*] *qa-ti ṣab-tu* ^{12}*di-ik-tú ina* ^{kur}*Bu-uš-šu-ú-a u* ^{kur}*Gi-*[*mi*]*r-ra-a ina* ^{kur}*Šu-bu*(?)*-uḫ-nu di-k*[*át*] ^{13}mu 3.kám ^{Id}. . .-šeš^{me}-*šul-lim* ^{lú}gú.[en.n]a ^{Id}Utu-*ib-ni* a ^{I}*Da-ku-ru* ^{14}*a-na* ^{kur}*Aš-šur ab-ku ina* ^{kur}*Aš-šur di-i-ku* ^{15}mu 4.kám ^{uru}*Ṣi-da-nu ṣa-bit šal-lat-su šal-*[*lat*] mu.bi ^{lú}gal.é *ina* ^{kur}Uri^{ki} *bi-ḫir-tú ib-te-ḫir* ^{16}mu 5.kám ^{iti}Du$_6$ u$_4$ 2.kám érin$^{ni\text{-meš}}$ ^{kur}*Aš-šur* ^{uru}*Ba-az-za iṣ-ṣab-tu* ^{17}*ina* ^{iti}Du$_6$ sag.du *šá* lugal *šá* ^{kur}*Ṣa-'-i-du-nu na-kis-ma ana* ^{kur}*Aš-šur na-ši* ^{18}mu 6.kám érin^{me} ^{kur}*Aš-šur ana* ^{kur}*Mi-li-du* gin^{meš} *ina* ugu <uru>*Mu-gal-lu* šub^{meš} ^{19} ^{iti}Kin u$_4$ 5.kám ^{d}*Ḫum-ba-ḫal-da-šú š*[*àr* ^{kur}El]am.ma^{ki} nu gig ti-*su ina* é.gal-*šú* ug$_7$ ^{20}6 mu^{meš} ^{d}*Ḫum-ba-ḫal-da-šú* l[ugal^{u}]^{t} ^{kur}Elam.ma^{ki} dù^{uš} ^{21} ^{I}*Ur-ta-gu* šeš-*šú ina* ^{kur}Elam.ma^{ki} *ina* ^{giš}gu.za *it-t*[*a-š*]*ab* ^{22} ^{I}Mu.mu ^{lú}gú.en.na *u* ^{I}Nì.du dumu ^{I}*Da-ku-ru* g[az^{m}]^{e} ^{23}mu 7(!).kám ^{iti}Še u$_4$ 8.kám érin^{meš} ^{kur}*Aš-šur a-na* ^{uru}*Šá-*lú^{meš} [gin^{me}]^{š} ^{ku} ^{24}mu.bi ^{d}Inanna *A-kà-dè*^{ki} *u* dingir^{meš} *ša A-kà-dè*^{ki} ta ^{k}[^{ur}Elam.ma^{k}]^{i} gin^{meš} ^{25}*ina* ^{iti}Še u$_4$ 10.kám a-na *A-kà-dè*^{ki} [ku$_4$^{meš}] ^{26}mu 8(!).kám ^{iti}Še u$_4$ 6.kám dam lugal *mi-t*[*a-at*] ^{27} ^{iti}Še u$_4$ 18.kám érin^{meš} ^{kur}*Aš-šur* ^{kur}*Šub-r*[*i-a-a iṣ-ṣab-tu*] ^{28}*šal-lat-su iš-tal-lu* mu 10.kám ^{iti}Bár érin^{me} ^{kur}*Aš-šur* [*ana Mi-ṣir* gin^{meš}] ^{29} ^{iti}Du$_6$ u$_4$ 3.kám *di-ik-tú ina* ^{kur}*Mi-ṣir d*[*i-kát*] ^{30}mu 11.kám lugal [*ina* ^{kur}]*Aš-šur* ^{lú}gal^{me}-*šú ma-du-tu ina* [^{giš}tukul ga]z ^{31}mu 12.kám *šàr* ^{kur}*Aš-šur ana* ^{kur}*Mi-ṣir it-*[*ta*]*-lak* ^{32}*ina* kaskal$_{\text{ii}}$ gig-*ma* ^{iti}Apin u$_4$ [10].kám ug$_7$ ^{33}12 mu^{meš} ^{I}An.šár.šeš.mu lugal$^{ú\text{-}tu}$ ^{kur}*Aš-šur* dù^{uš}

---

^{34}8 mu^{meš} ^{Id}30.šeš^{meš}-*eri$_4$-ba* 12 mu^{meš} ^{I}An.šár.šeš.sum^{na} ^{35}20 mu^{meš} ^{d}En [*ina* B]al.til^{ki} *a-šib-ma i-sin-nu a-ki-tú ba-ṭi-il* ^{36} ^{d}Nà ta *Bár-sipa*^{ki} *a-na* è^{e} ^{d}En *u-ul* gin^{ku} ^{37}*ina* ^{iti}Gan ^{I}An.šár.dù.ibila du[mu-*šú*] *ina* ^{kur}*Aš-šur ina* ^{giš}gu.za dúr^{ab} ^{38}mu.sag ^{Id}Giš.šir.mu.g[i.n]a *ina* ^{iti}Gu$_4$ ^{d}En *u* dingir^{me} *š*[*a*

In Elam,] the king of Elam [captured him and executed him.... E]sarhaddon [named his brother] Nā'i[d-Marduk governor of the Sealand].[25] In the month of Elul, Anu the Great and the gods of Dē[r entered Dēr]; Ḫumḫumia and Šimali[ya entered Sippar]. In the month of Tešrit, the court (?) .... In the month of [...].

The second year, the majordomo carri[ed out a selection] in Akkad.[26] The same year, Arzā was taken and [pl]under[ed], the [inhabit]ants ransomed; the king and [his] son were taken. There w[as] a massacre in Buššua, and casualties were inflicted on the Cim[me]rians in Šubuḫnu (?).

The third year, *Divine name*-aḫḫē-šullim, go[vern]or of Nippur, and Šamaš-ibni, the Dakkurean, were deported to Assyria and executed.

The fourth year, Sidon was taken and plun[dered]. The same year, the majordomo carried out a selection in Akkad.[27]

The fifth year, in the month of Tešrit, the second day, the troops of Assyria took Bāza. In the month of Tešrit, the head of the king of Sidon was cut off and carried to Assyria.

The sixth year, the troops of Assyria marched on Milīdu and set camp facing Mugallu. In the month of Elul, the fifth day, K[ing] Ḫumban-ḫaltaš (II) [of El]am, having (no) illness, died in full health in his palace. Ḫumban-ḫaltaš rei[gn]ed six years over Elam. Urtak, his brother, as[cende]d the throne of Elam. Šuma-iddina, the governor of Nippur, and Kudurru, the Dakkurean, we[re execu]ted.

The seventh (!)[28] year, in the month of Adar, the eighth day, the troops of Assyria [march]ed on Šamēlē.[29] The same year, Ištar of Akkade and the gods of Akkade came from [Elam] and, in the month of Adar, the tenth day, [they entered] Akkade.

The eighth (!)[30] year, in the month of Adar, the sixth day, the queen di[ed]. In the month of Adar, the eighteenth day, the troops of Assyria [took] Šub[ria] and plundered it.

The tenth year, in the month of Nisan, the troops of Assyria [marched on Miṣir]. In the month of Tešrit, the third day, there [was] a massacre in Miṣir.

The eleventh year, [in] Assyria, the king [execut]ed a large number of his nobles.

The twelfth year, the king of Assyria m[ar]ched on Miṣir. On the way he fell ill, and he died in the month of Araḫsamnu, the [tenth] day.

For twelve years Esarhaddon reigned over Assyria.

For eight years under Sennacherib, for twelve years under Esarhaddon, that is to say, for twenty years, Bēl stayed [at B]altil, and the New Year's festival was not celebrated. Nabû did not go from Borsippa to Bēl's procession.

^{kur}Uri]^{ki} ^{39}ta Bal.til^{ki} *ú-ṣ*[*u-n*]*im-ma* ^{iti}Gu$_4$ u$_4$ 25.kám *ana* Tin.tir[^{ki} ku$_4$^{meš} *n*]*u* ^{40} ^{d}Nà *u* dingir^{meš} *ša Bár-sipa*^{ki} *a-na* Tin.tir^{ki} *i*[*t-tal-ku-ni*] ^{41}mu.bi ^{uru}*Kir-bi-ti ṣa-bit* lugal-*šú k*[*a-šid*] ^{42} ^{iti}Ab u$_4$ 20.kám <^{Id}En.kar^{ir}> ^{lú}di.ku$_5$ Tin.tir^{ki} *ṣa-*[*bit-ma* gaz]

---

^{43}mu 1.kám ^{Id}Giš.šir.mu.gi.na ... [...] ^{44}*a-na* [...] ^{45} ^{I}*Tar-qu-ú šàr* ^{kur}*M*[*i-ṣir* ...] ^{46} ^{kur}*Mi-*[*ṣir* ...] ^{47} ^{I}*Ni-ik-ku-ú* [*šàr*] ^{kur}*Mi-*[*ṣir* ...]

---

^{48}mu 2.kám [...] (...)
(left edge) gigam.gigam

19. FROM THE END OF AŠŠUR-NĀDIN-ŠUMI TO THE REVOLT OF ŠAMAŠ-ŠUMA-UKĪN (694–652) AND A FEW EARLIER REIGNS

Sources: small damaged tablet.
Bibliography: Grayson 1975a: no. 15.
Language: Babylonian.
Date: reign of Nabonidus.
Place: Borsippa (?).
Contents: excerpts, occasionally faulty (Širiqti-Šuqamuna was not the brother of Nebuchadnezzar I but of Ninurta-kudurrī-uṣur I), but the motives for the selection are obscure. Concerning the Neo-Babylonian part, it seems that the chronicler was concerned about the interruption of the New Year's festival at Babylon, which he apparently connected with the end of Aššur-nādin-šumi, son of Sennacherib, handed over to the Elamites by the Babylonians (694), and of Šamaš-šuma-ukīn, son of Esarhaddon, besieged by the troops of his brother Aššurbanipal (652).

^{1}mu 6 An.šár-*na-din*-mu ^{iti}Zíz u$_4$ 1 An gal ta Bàd.an^{ki} *ana* ^{kur}*Aš-šur* gin ^{2}mu 4.kám ^{d}Giš.šir.mu.gi.na ^{iti}Du$_6$ u$_4$ 12.kám ^{3}dumu lugal *šá* ^{kur}Elam.ma^{ki} [*ana* ^{kur}]*Aš-šur* záḫ

---

^{4}mu 14 ^{giš}ná *šá* ^{d}En *pa-ni-tú* t[a *Bal-til*^{k}]^{i} *ana* Tin.tir^{ki} gin^{kám}

---

^{5}mu 15 ^{giš}gigir *šá* ^{d}En gibil^{tú} ^{I}...[...] *ana* Tin.tir^{ki} *u-še-bi-lam*

---

^{6}mu 16 Zíz 8 lugal *l*[*a-pan* ^{lú}kúr *an*]*a* Tin.tir^{ki} ku$_4$^{ba}

In the month of Kislev, Aššurbanipal, [his s]on, ascended the throne of Assyria.

The year of the accession of Šamaš-šuma-u[kī]n, in the month of Iyyar, Bēl and the gods of [Akka]d le[f]t Baltil, and, in the month of Iyyar, the twenty-fifth day, they [enter]ed Babylon. Nabû and the gods of Borsippa c[ame] to Babylon. Kirbītum was taken the same year, its king ca[ptured]. In the month of Ṭebeth, the twentieth day, <Bēl-ēṭir>, the judge of Babylon, was ar[rested and executed].

The first year (of the reign) of Šamaš-šuma-ukīn, [. . .] toward [. . .]. Taḥarqa, the pharaoh, [. . .] M[iṣir . . .] Necho, the p[harao]h [. . .].

——— (. . .)

Battles (?).

The sixth year (of the reign) of Aššur-nādin-šumi, in the month of Šebat, the first day, Anu the Great went from Dēr to Assyria.

The fourth year (of the reign) of Šamaš-šuma-ukīn, in the month of Tešrit, the twelfth day, the son of the king of Elam fled [into] Assyria.

The fourteenth year, Bēl's ancient bed came from [Baltil] to Babylon.

The fifteenth year, [. . .] sent Bēl's new chariot to Babylon.

The sixteenth year, in the month of Šebat, the eigh<th day>, the king, sl[ipping away from his enemy], returned [t]o Babylon.

---

^{7}mu 17 Kin 2.kám u$_4$ 9 ^{d}Giš.šir.mu.gi.[na ...]^{ki} érin^{me}-*šú id-ke-e-ma* ^{8}*ana* Gú.du$_8$.a^{ki} gin^{ik}-[*ma* uru *i*]*ṣ-ṣa-bat* ^{9}*di-ik-tam ina* šà érin ^{kur}*Aš-šur u* G[ú.du$_8$.a$^{ki\ me}$ *i-d*]*uk* ^{10}[alan] ^{d}U.gur *iṣ-bat-am-ma ana* T[in.tir^{ki} *i-b*]*u-kám* ^{11}[^{iti}...] u$_4$ 27.kám ^{lú}gal^{me} *šá* ^{kur}*A*[*š-šur is-ḫu* ^{12}...] *ra-kib* anše.kur.ra *a*[*na* ^{uru}*Šá-pi-i-*^{d}]En(?) gin-*ma* ^{13}[^{Id}Nà.e]n.mu^{meš} ^{lú}*šá-kìn* [Kur *Tam-tì* ^{14}...]-*li-šú-nu-ti-ma ki-i* [... k]i(?) ^{15}[...] e *ki-šú ú-še-rib-šú* ... [...] u$_4$ ^{16}[ŠI.ŠI -*š*]*ú-nu iš-kun-ma la i-zi-ba ma-na-ma* ^{17}[*a-lik* igi *šá* ér]in ^{kur}*Aš-šur iṣ-bat-am-ma* ^{18}*ki is-ḫúp-pu a-na šàr* Tin.tir^{ki} *il-qa-a*

---

^{19}[mu] 18 ^{iti}Šu u$_4$ 11.kám ^{lú}kúr *ana* Tin.tir^{ki} *is-sa-an-qa*

---

^{20}3 iti^{meš} ^{I}*Ši-rik-ti-*^{d}*Šu-qa-mu-nu* ^{21}šeš ^{d}Nà.nì.du.ùri lugal^{ut} Tin.tir^{ki} *i-pu-uš*

---

^{22}mu 5 mu 6 ^{d}Nà.mu.gar^{un} ^{d}Nà *ana* è ^{d}En nu gin^{ku}

---

^{23}mu.mu nu ur.a^{me} ta ugu ^{giš}da *ana taš-lim-da* zi^{me}-*ni* ^{24} ^{im}*gì-ṭi* ^{Id}Nà-*ka-ṣi-ir* a ^{I}40-*ilu-ta*-dù

20. CHRONICLE OF THE NEW YEAR'S FESTIVAL (689–626)

Sources: tablet in a good state of preservation except for the upper right corner.
Bibliography: Grayson 1975a: no. 16.
Language: Babylonian.
Place: unknown.
Contents: another narrative of Šamaš-šuma-ukīn's revolt in connection with the interruption of the New Year's festival. There is no doubt that the chronicle, which records events from 689 (Babylon's destruction by Sennacherib) to 626 (independence of Babylonia under Nabopolassar), while passing over 648 (the twentieth year of Šamaš-šuma-ukīn's reign; enthroned in 668) and the taking of Babylon by Aššurbanipal, sought to establish implicit relations among all those events. By Nabonidus's account, Sennacherib brought blame on himself and condemned Assyria to ruin by destroying Babylon.

^{1}[8] mu^{meš} *ina* ^{Id}3[0.šeš.su] ^{2}12 mu^{meš} ^{I}An.šár.[šeš.sum] ^{3}20 mu^{meš} ^{d}En *ina Bal-til*^{ki} *a-*[*šib-ma*] ^{4}*i-sin-nu a-ki-tú ba-ṭi-*[*il*] ^{5}mu.sag ^{Id}Giš.šir.mu.gi.na *ina* ^{iti}Gu$_4$ [^{d}En] ^{6}*u* dingir^{meš} *ša* ^{kur}Uri^{ki} ta *Bal-til*^{ki} *ú-ṣ*[*u-nim-ma*] ^{7}*ina* ^{iti}Gu$_4$

The seventeenth year, in the supplementary month of Elul, the ninth day, Šamaš-šuma-uk[īn] mustered his troops [at ...], marched on Cutha, [and] took [the city]. He [inflict]ed losses on the Assyrian army and on the Cu[theans]. He took [the statue] of Nergal and [ca]rried it away to B[abylon. In the month of ...], the twenty-seventh day, the Assyrian officers [revolted (?) ...]. He went on horseback to [Ša-pî]-Bēl (?). [Nabû-b]ēl-šumāti, governor [of the Sealand, ...] them and like [...] he made him enter with him [...]. He inflicted [a defeat] on them and let no one escape. [...]. He took [the general (?)] of the Assyrian army and, having won, led [him] to the king of Babylon.

The eighteenth year, in the month of Dumuzi, the eleventh day, the enemy besieged Babylon.

Širikti-Šuqamuna, the brother of Nebuchadnezzar, reigned three months over Babylon.

The fifth and sixth years (of the reign) of Nabû-šuma-ukīn, Nabû did not go to Bēl's procession.

Nonintegral entries, extracted from a wax tablet for the sake of completeness. Tablet in one column by Nabû-kāṣir, descendant of Ea-ilūta-bāni.

For [eight] years under Sennacherib, for twelve years under Esarhaddon, that is to say, for twenty years, Bēl sta[yed] at Baltil, [and] the New Year's festival was not celebr[ated].

u$_4$ 24.kám *a-na* Tin.tir^{ki} ku$_4^{meš-[ni]}$ ^{8} ^{d}Nà *u* dingir^{meš} *ša Bár-sipa*^{ki} *ana* Tin.tir^{ki} *it-tal-ku-ni*

---

^{9}mu 16.kám ^{d}Giš.šir.mu.gi.na ta ^{iti}Gu$_4$ en ^{iti}Ab ^{10} ^{lú}gal.é *ina* ^{kur}Uri^{ki} *bi-ḫir-ti ib-te-ḫir* ^{11} ^{iti}Ab u$_4$ 19.kám ^{kur}*Aš-šur u* ^{kur}Uri^{ki} kúr^{meš} ^{12}lugal *la-pan* ^{lú}kúr *a-na* Tin.tir^{ki} *i-ter-ba* ^{13}Še 27 érin^{ni} ^{kur}*Aš-šur u* érin ^{kur}Uri^{ki} ^{14}*ṣal-tu*$_4$ *ina Ḫi-rit* dù^{meš}-*ma* érin ^{kur}Uri^{ki} ^{15}*ina* mè edin bala^{me}-*ma* ŠI.ŠI-*šú-nu ma-a-diš* gar^{in} ^{16} ^{mí}kúr gar^{at} *ṣal-tu*$_4$ *sad-rat*

---

^{17}mu 17.kám [*saḫ-m*]*a-šá-a-tú ina* ^{kur}*Aš-šur u* ^{kur}Uri^{ki} gar[^{me}-*ma*] ^{18} ^{d}Nà ta [Bár-sipa^{k}]^{i} *ana* è ^{d}En nu gin^{ku} ^{19} ^{d}En nu è^{a}

---

^{20}mu 18.kám ^{d}Nà ta *Bár-sipa*^{ki} *ana* è ^{d}En nu gin^{ku} ^{21} ^{d}En nu è^{a}

---

^{22}mu 19 ^{d}Nà nu gin ^{d}En nu è^{a}

---

^{23}mu 20 ^{d}Nà nu gin ^{d}En nu è^{a}

---

^{24}egir ^{I}*Kan-da-la-nu ina* mu.sag ^{d}Nà.ibila.ùri ^{25}*saḫ-ma-šá-a-ti ina* ^{kur}[*Aš*]-*šur u* ^{kur}Uri^{ki} gar^{me}-*ma* ^{26}*nu-kúr-tú* gar^{at} *ṣal-tú sad-rat* ^{27}[^{d}N]à nu gin^{ku} ^{d}En nu è$^{[a]}$

---

21. CHRONICLE OF THE FIRST YEARS OF NABOPOLASSAR (626–623)

Sources: tablet in the format of an administrative text; the upper left corner is missing.
Bibliography: Grayson 1975a: no. 2; Na'aman 1991: 243–67; Gerber 1998: 72–93.
Language: Babylonian.
Date: Neo-Babylonian period.
Place: Babylon.
Contents: Šamaš-šuma-ukīn's great revolt shook the Assyrian Empire by revealing its weaknesses. The demise of Aššurbanipal tolled its death knell. Through the efforts of Nabopolassar, perhaps a Babylonian of a family originally from Uruk, Babylonia gained its independence with difficulty, variously alternating between success and failure. With the cooperation of

The year of the accession of Šamaš-šuma-ukīn, in the month of Iyyar, Bēl and the gods of Akkad le[ft] Baltil, [and], in the month of Iyyar, the twenty-fourth day, they enter[ed] Babylon. Nabû and the gods of Borsippa came to Babylon.

The sixteenth year (of the reign) of Šamaš-šuma-ukīn, from the month of Iyyar to that of Ṭebeth, the majordomo carried out a selection in Akkad.[31] In the month of Ṭebeth, the nineteenth day, Assyria and Akkad went to war. Slipping away from the enemy, the king returned to Babylon. In the month of Adar, the twenty-seventh day, the army of Assyria and the army of Akkad joined battle at Ḫirītu. The army of Akkad stopped fighting, and a crushing defeat was inflicted on it. A state of war was prolonged;[32] there was a succession of battles.

The seventeenth year, [tro]ubles took pla[ce] in Assyria and Akkad. Nabû did not go from [Borsippa] to Bēl's procession. Bēl did not go out.

The eighteenth year, Nabû did not go from Borsippa to Bēl's procession. Bēl did not go out.

The nineteenth year, Nabû did not go nor Bēl go out.

The twentieth year, Nabû did not go nor Bēl go out.

After Kandalānu,[33] the year of Nabopolassar's accession, troubles took place in Assyria and Akkad; a state of war was prolonged; there was a succession of battles. [Na]bû did not go nor Bēl go out.

---

the Medes, Babylon finally attacked an Assyria with back against the wall but still capable of aggressive resistance. This accomplished, Nabopolassar founded the Neo-Babylonian Empire, which lasted nearly a century.

^{1}[ina ^{iti}... ^{Id}Nà.ibila.ùri érin^{meš}] *ana* Tin.tir^{ki} *ki-i iš-pu-ru ina* ge$_6$ ^{2}[*ina* šà uru ku$_4$^{meš}] *ù*(?) *kal u*$_4$*-mu ṣal-tu*$_2$ *ina* šà uru dù^{meš} ^{3}[ŠI.ŠI gar^{meš} ^{lú}*šu-lu*]-*tu šá* ^{Id}30-šàr-gar^{un} *ana* ^{kur}*Aš-šur* záḫ^{me} ^{4}[... š]à(?) uru *ip-ta-qid ina* ^{iti}Kin u$_4$ 12.kám érin ^{kur}*Aš-šur* ^{5}[*it-tar-du-nu*] ^{uru}*Šá-az-na-ku* ku$_4$^{meš} izi *ana* é.kur šub^{me} ^{6}[nì.ga è^{me}] *ù ina* ^{iti}du$_6$ dingir^{me} *šá Kiši*^{ki} *ana* Tin.tir^{ki} gin^{me} ^{7}[*ina* u$_4$ ...kám érin^{me}]^{š} ^{kur}*Aš-šur ana* Nibru^{ki} gin^{me}-*nim-ma* ^{Id}Nà.ibila.ùri *ina* igi-*šú-nu* bala-*ma* ^{8}[érin^{meš} ^{kur}*Aš-š*]*ur u* Nibru^{ki-me} en šà Unu^{ki} egir-*šú it-tal-ku* ^{9}*ina* Unu^{ki} *ṣal-tú ana* šà ^{Id}Nà.eduru.ùri dù^{meš}-*ma ina* igi ^{Id}Nà.eduru.ùri bala^{meš} ^{10}*ina* ^{iti}Gu$_4$ érin ^{kur}*Aš-šur ana* ^{kur}Uri^{ki} *it-tar-du-nu ina* ^{iti}Du$_6$ u$_4$ 12.kám érin ^{kur}*Aš-šur* ^{11}*ana* ugu Tin.tir^{ki} *ki-i il-lik-ú-nu ina* u$_4$.bi ^{lú}Tin.tir^{ki-me} ^{12}ta Tin.tir^{ki} *ki-i ú-ṣu-ú ṣal-tú ana* šà érin ^{kur}*Aš-šur* dù^{meš}-*ma* ^{13}ŠI.ŠI érin ^{kur}*Aš-šur ma-a-diš* gar^{meš} *ḫu-bu-ut-su-nu iḫ-tab-tu* ^{14}1^{et} mu.an.na lugal *ina* kur nu gál ^{iti}Apin u$_4$ 26.kám ^{Id}Nà.ibila.ùri ^{15}*ina* Tin.tir^{ki} *ina* aš.te dúr^{ab} sag lugal^{tú} *šá* ^{Id}Nà.ibila.ùri *ina* ^{iti}Še ^{16}dingir^{me} *šá* ^{kur}*Šu-šá-an šá* ^{kur}*Aš-šur i-bu-ku-nim-ma ina* Unu^{ki} *ú-še-ši-bu* ^{17}dingir^{me}-*šu-nu* ^{Id}Nà.eduru.ùri *ana* ^{uru}*Šu-šá-an ul-taḫ-ḫi-is*

---

^{18}mu 1.kám ^{Id}Nà.eduru.ùri ^{iti}Bár u$_4$ 17.kám *ḫat-ti ana* uru šub^{ut} ^{19} ^{d}Utu *u* dingir^{me} *šá* ^{uru}*Šá-pa-az-zu a-na* Tin.tir^{ki} *it-tal-ku-ni* ^{20} ^{iti}Gu$_4$ u$_4$ 21.kám érin^{me} ^{kur}*Aš-šur a-na* ^{uru}*Raq-*[*mat i-t*]*er-bu* nì.ga è^{me} ^{21}<^{iti}Sig$_4$/Šu(?)> u$_4$ 20.kám dingir^{me} *šá* Zimbir^{ki} *ana* Tin.tir^{ki} *it-tal-*[*ku-nim-ma*] ^{22} ^{iti}Ne u$_4$ 9.kám ^{Id}Nà.ibila.ùri *u* érin^{me}-*šú ana* ^{uru}*Raq-m*[*at* gin^{nim}]-*ma* ^{23}*ṣal-tú ana* ^{uru}*Raq-mat* dù-*ma* uru *ul iṣ-bat* érin^{me} ^{kur}*Aš-šur ik-šu-du-nim-ma* ^{24}*ina* igi-*šú-nu* bala-*ma ana* egir-*šú* lá^{is}

---

^{25}[mu 2.ká]m ^{Id}Nà.eduru.ùri sag ^{iti}Kin érin^{meš} ^{kur}*Aš-šur* ^{26}[*ana* ^{kur}Uri^{ki}] *ú-ri-du-nim-ma ina* ugu i$_7$ ^{d}*Ba-ni-tú* šub^{me} ^{27}[*ṣal-tú ana* šà ^{Id}N]à.ibila.ùri dù^{meš}-*ma mim-ma ul il-qu-u* ^{28}[érin^{meš} ^{kur}*Aš-šur*...]-*suḫ-ma ana* egir-*šú-nu iḫ-ḫi-su*

---

^{29}[mu 3.kám ^{iti}... u]$_4$ 8 Bàd.an^{ki} ki ^{kur}*Aš-šur it-te-kìr* ^{iti}Du$_6$ u$_4$ 15 ^{30}[^{I}*I-ti*-dingir *ṣal-tú ana* Nibru^{ki} dù mu].bi lugal ^{kur}*Aš-šur u* érin^{me}-*šú ana* ^{kur}Uri^{ki} *ur-dam-ma* ^{31}[Bàd.an^{ki}(?) *iṣ*(?)-*bat*(?) nì.ga è]-*ma ana* Nibru^{ki} *ul-te-rib* egir ^{I}*I-ti*-dingir ^{32}[gin Unu^{ki} *iḫ-te*]-*pe-e-ma* ^{lú}*šu-lu-tu ana* Nibru^{ki} *ul-te-li* ^{33}[*ina*

[In the month of . . . , Nabopolassar] having sent [troops] to Babylon, [they entered the city] by night, and for a whole day they joined battle in the city. [They inflicted a defeat on Assyria. The garri]son of Sîn-šar-iškun fled into Assyria. The city was entrusted to [. . .]. In the month of Elul, the twelfth day, the Assyrian army [went down <to Akkad>], entered Šasanaku, set fire to the temple, [*and plundered it*]. In the month of Tešrit, the gods of Kiš went to Babylon.[34] [The . . . th day, the troo]ps of Assyria reached Nippur; Nabopolassar beat a retreat before them. [The troops of Assy]ria and the inhabitants of Nippur pursued him as far as Uruk. In Uruk they joined battle with Nabopolassar but beat a retreat before Nabopolassar. In the month of Iyyar the Assyrian army went down to Akkad. In the month of Tešrit, the twelfth day, the Assyrian army having marched on Babylon, that very day the Babylonians left Babylon, joined battle with the Assyrian army, inflicting a crushing defeat on them and taking prisoners. For one year[35] there was no king in the country. In the month of Araḫsamnu, the twenty-sixth day, Nabopolassar ascended the throne of Babylon.

The year of Nabopolassar's accession, in the month of Adar, Nabopolassar returned to Susa the gods of Susa that Assyria had deported and assigned to a residence in Uruk.[36]

The first year (of the reign) of Nabopolassar, in the month of Nisan, the seventeenth day, panic reigned in the city (= Babylon). Šamaš and the gods of Šapazza came to Babylon. In the month of Iyyar, the twenty-first day, the Assyrian troops [en]tered Raq[mat]; they took away its treasures. In the month <of Siwan/Dumuzi (?)>, the twentieth day, the gods of Sippar ca[me] to Babylon,[37] and in the month of Ab, the ninth day, Nabopolassar [came] to Raqm[at] with his troops and joined battle for Raqmat but did not take the city. The Assyrian troops arrived; he retreated before them and withdrew.

[The seco]nd [year] (of the reign] of Nabopolassar, at the beginning of the month of Elul, the Assyrian troops went down [to Akkad] and maintained their quarters near the canal Banītu. They joined [battle with Na]bopolassar without any result. [The Assyrian troops broke up ca]mp(?) and made their way back.

[The third year, in the month of . . .], the eighth da[y], Dēr rebelled against Assyria. In the month of Tešrit, the fifteenth day, [Itti-ili (?)[38] joined battle with Nippur (?). The sam]e year, the king of Assyria went down to Akkad with his troops and [took possession of Dēr; he took out [its

^{iti}... ^{I}... ta] *e-bir* i_7 *iš-qa-am-ma ina* ugu ^{34}[^{kur}*Aš-šur* gin-*ma* ^{uru}...]-*nu iḫ-te-pi u ana* ugu Ninua^{ki} igi-*šú iš-ta-kan* ^{35}[érin^{meš} *šá* ^{Id}30-*šàr*-gar^{un} *šàr* ^{kur}*Aš*]-*šur šá ana ṣal-tú ana pa-ni-šú* gin^{ku} ^{36}[... *ki*]-*i i-mur-uš ana pa-ni-šú in-daq-tu* ^{37}[...] šeš ^{38}lugal im.gi^{u} [...] ^{39}1-me u_4*-me* [... ^{40}...] ... *ki-i* be [... ^{41}lugal] im.gi [...]

22. NABOPOLASSAR AND THE FALL OF THE ASSYRIAN EMPIRE (616–609)

Sources: tablet; lacuna in the middle of the document. Same series as chronicles 23 and 24.
Bibliography: Grayson 1975a: no. 3; Zawadzki 1988.
Language: Babylonian.
Date: Neo-Babylonian period.
Place: unknown.
Contents: narrative of the fall of Assyria. Curiously, from the middle of the text on, the Medes, allies of the Babylonians in the war against Assyria, are no more called by name but Ummān-manda, a term whose pejorative tone is well known. One may associate this with Nabonidus, who condemned the Medes for attacking Ḫarrān and the Eḫulḫul, Sîn's temple in that city, he himself posing as the avenger of the city and its temple.

^{1}mu 10.kám ^{Id}Nà.eduru.ùri *ina* ^{iti}Gu$_4$ érin ^{kur}Uri^{ki} *id-ke-e-ma* gú ^{i_7}Bura-nun gin-*ma* ^{2} ^{kur}*Su-ḫa-a-a* ^{kur}*Ḫi-in-da-na-a-a ṣal-tú ana* šà-*šú ul* dù^{šu} *man-da-at-ta-šú-nu a-na* igi-*šú iš-ku-nu* ^{3} ^{iti}Ne érin ^{kur}*Aš-šur ina* ^{uru}*Gab-li-ni ik-ṣur-ú-ma* ^{Id}Nà.eduru.ùri *ana muḫ-ḫi-šú-nu iš-qí-ma* ^{4} ^{iti}Ne u$_4$ 12.kám *ṣal-tú a-na* šà érin ^{kur}*Aš-šur* dù-*ma* érin ^{kur}*Aš-šur ina* igi-*šú* bala^{me}-*ma* ŠI.ŠI ^{kur}*Aš-šur ma-a-diš* gar^{an} ^{5}*ḫu-bu-ut-su-nu ma-a-diš iḫ-tab-tu* ^{kur}*Man-na-a-a šá ana re-ṣu-ti-šú-nu* gin^{me}-*ni u* ^{lú}gal^{me} *šá* ^{kur}*Aš-šur* ^{6}*uṣ-ṣab-bi-tu ina* u_4*-mu šá-a-šú* ^{uru}*Gab-li-ni iṣ-ṣa-bat ina* ^{iti}Ne-*ma šàr* Uri^{ki} érin^{ni} ^{meš}-*šú* ^{7}*ana* ^{uru}*Ma-né-e* ^{uru}*Sa-ḫi-ri u* ^{uru}*Ba-li-ḫu iš*-[*qí-m*]*a ḫu-bu-ut-su-nu iḫ-tab-tu-nu* ^{8}*šil-lat-su-nu ma-at-tú iš-tal-lu-nu* dingir^{me}-*šú-nu i-tab-ku-nu ina* ^{iti}Kin *šàr* Uri^{ki} *u* érin^{me}-*šú* ^{9}*ana* egir-*šú* gur-*am-ma ina* kaskal-*šú* ^{uru}*Ḫi-in-da-nu u* dingir^{me}-*šú ana* Tin.tir^{ki} *il-te-qa-a* ^{10}*ina* ^{iti}Du$_6$ érin^{ni} ^{kur}*Mi-ṣir u* érin^{ni} ^{kur}*Aš-šur* egir *šàr* Uri^{ki} en ^{uru}*Gab-li-ni* gin^{me}-^{nim}-*ma* ^{11}*šàr* Uri^{ki} *la ik-šu-du a-na* egir-*šú-nu iḫ-ḫi-su ina* ^{iti}Še érin ^{kur}*Aš-šur u* érin ^{kur}Uri^{ki} ^{12}*i-na* ^{uru}*Ma-da-nu šá* ^{uru}*A-rap-ḫu ṣal-tú ana* šà *a-ḫa-meš* dù^{me}-*ma* érin ^{kur}*Aš-šur* ^{13}*ina* igi érin ^{kur}Uri^{ki} bala^{me}-*ma* ŠI.ŠI-*šú-nu ma-a-diš* gar^{meš} *a-na* ^{i_7}*Za-ban it-ta-du-šú-nu-tú* ^{14} ^{gi}[^{š}gigir^{me}-*š*]*ú-nu u* anše.kur.ra^{me}-*šú-nu uṣ-ṣab-bi-tu-nu ḫu-bu-ut-su-nu ma-a-diš iḫ-tab-tu-nu* ^{15}[...]-*šú ma-du-tu ki-šú-nu* ^{i_7}*Ì-diq-lat ú-še-bi-ru-nim-ma ana* Tin.tir^{ki} ku$_4$^{me}-*ni*

treasures] and had (them) sent to Nippur. [He pursued] Itti-ili, ravaged [Uruk (?)], and set up a garrison at Nippur. [In the month of . . . , . . .] went up [from] beyond the Euphrates and set out toward [Assyria]. He plundered [. . .]nu and set out toward Nineveh. [Whe]n [the troops of King Sîn-šar-iškun of Assy]ria, which had moved for engagement [. . .], saw him, they threw themselves on the ground before him in a sign of submission. [. . .]. A usurper [. . .] one hundred days [. . .] when [. . .]. The usurper [. . .].

The tenth year (of the reign) of Nabopolassar, in the month of Iyyar, he mustered the army of Akkad and moved along the bank of the Euphrates. The Suḫeans and the Ḫindaneans did not join battle but laid down their tributes before him. In the month of Ab, Assyria's army placed itself in combat formation at Gablīni. Nabopolassar went up toward it, and, in the month of Ab, the twelfth day, he joined battle with Assyria's army; the Assyrian army beat a retreat before him, and he inflicted a crushing defeat on Assyria. He took many prisoners among them; he captured the Manneans who had come to (their) aid and the Assyrian officers. The same day, he took Gablīni. Still in the month of Ab, the king of Akkad and his troops went up toward Manê, Saḫiri, and Balīḫu, sacked them, took a large amount of booty, and deported their gods. In the month of Elul, the king of Akkad made his way back with his troops, and on the way he took Ḫindānu and its gods to Babylon. In the month of Tešrit, the army of Miṣir and the army of Assyria pursued the king of Akkad as far as Gablīni but did not catch the king of Akkad. They withdrew. In the month of Adar, the army of Assyria and the army of Akkad came face to face in a pitched battle at Madanu, on Arrapḫa's (territory); the Assyrian army beat a retreat before the army of Akkad, (which) inflicted a crushing defeat on it and

---

^{16}[mu 11.kám *šàr*] Uri^{ki} érin^{meš}-*šú id-ke-e-ma* gú $^{i}{}_{7}$Idigna gin-*ma ina* ^{iti}Gu$_4$ *ina* šà *Bal-til*^{ki} šub^{di} ^{17}[*ina* u$_4$ ...k]ám *šá* ^{iti}Sig$_4$ *ṣal-tú ana* šà uru dù-*ma* uru *ul iṣ-bat šàr* ^{kur}*Aš-šur* érin^{me}-*šú id-kám-ma* ^{18}*šàr* Uri^{ki} ta *Bal-til*^{ki} *is-kip-ma* en ^{uru}*Tak-ri-i-ta-in* [uru] *šá* gú *Ì-diq-lat* egir-*šú* gin^{ik} ^{19}*šàr* Uri^{ki} érin^{me}-*šú ana bir-tú* šá ^{uru}*Tak-ri-i-ta-in ul-te-li šàr* ^{kur}*Aš-šur u* érin^{ni}-*šú* ^{20}*ina* ugu érin^{ni} *šàr* Uri^{ki} *šá ana* ^{uru}*Tak-ri-i-ta-in šu-lu-ú id-di-ma* ^{21}10 *u*$_4$-*me ṣal-tú ana lìb-bi-šú-nu* dù^{uš}-*ma* uru *ul iṣ-bat* érin^{ni} *šàr* Uri^{ki} *šá ana bir-tú šu-lu-ú* ^{22}ŠI.ŠI ^{kur}*Aš-šur ma-a-diš* gar^{an} *šàr* ^{kur}*Aš-šur u* érin^{me}-*š*[*ú is-ki-pu*]-*ma a-na* kur-*šú i-tur*

^{23}*ina* ^{iti}Apin ^{kur}*Ma-da-a-a ana* ^{kur}*A-rap-ḫu ur-dam-ma* [...]

---

^{24}mu 12.kám *ina* ^{iti}Ne ^{kur}*Ma-da-a-a ana* ugu Ninua^{ki} *ki-i* [igi-*šú iš-ta-kan šàr* ^{kur}*Aš-šur u* érin-*šú* ^{25}*ana ri-ṣu-ut-su*] *i-ḫi-šam-ma* ^{uru}*Tar-bi-ṣu* uru *šá pi-ḫat* Ninua^{ki} *iṣ-ṣab-tu* [... ^{26} $^{i}{}_{7}$*Ì-d*]*iq-lat* uš-*ma ina* ugu *Bal-til*^{ki} *it-ta-di ṣal-tú ana* šà uru dù-*ma* [... ^{27}...] *it-ta-qar* ŠI.ŠI un^{me} gal^{me} *lim-niš* gar^{an} *ḫu-bu-ut-su iḫ-tab-bat šil-*[*lat-su iš-ta-lal* ^{28}*šàr*] Uri^{ki} *u* érin^{me}-*šú šá ana re-ṣu-ut* ^{kur}*Ma-da-a-a* gin^{ku} *ṣal-tú* nu kur^{du} uru [*ki-i iṣ-ṣab-tu* ^{29}*šàr* Uri^{ki} *u*] ^{I}*Ú-*[*ma-ki*]*š-tar ina* ugu uru *a-ḫa-meš* igi^{meš} du$_{10}$^{tú} *u su-lum-mu-u* ki *a-ḫa-meš* gar^{meš} ^{30}[egir-*šú*(?) ^{I}*Ú-ma-ki-i*]*š-tar u* érin^{me}-*šú ana* kur-*šú it-tur šàr* Uri^{ki} *u* érin^{me}-*šú ana* kur-*šú* gur^{ru}

---

^{31}[mu 13.kám *ina* ^{iti}G]u$_4$ ^{kur}*Su-ḫa-a-a šàr* Uri^{ki} bala^{me}-*ma* ^{mí}kúr *i-te-ép-šu* ^{32}[*šàr* Uri^{ki} ér]in^{meš}-*šú id-ke-e-ma ana* ^{kur}*Su-ú-ḫu il-lik ina* ^{iti}Sig$_4$ u$_4$ 4.kám ^{33}[*ṣal-tú ana* šà ^{u}]^{ru}*Ra-ḫi-i-lu* uru šá múru^{tú} *Pu-rat-tú* dù-*ma ina* u$_4$-*šú-ma* uru *iṣ-ṣa-bat* ^{34}[...]-*šú ib-ni* lú^{ut} *šá* gú $^{i}{}_{7}$*Pu-rat-tú a-na* igi-*šú it-tar-du-ni* ^{35}[... *ina* ugu] ^{uru}*A-na-ti it-ta-di ṣa-pi-t*[*ú* ta] bal.ri ^{d}Utu.šú.a ^{36}[...]-*kir ṣa-pi-tú ana* bàd *uq-tar-rib ṣal-tú ana* šà [uru] dù-*ma* u[ru(?) *ul iṣ-bat*(?) ^{37}... *šàr* ^{kur}]*Aš-šur u* érin^{me}-*šú ur-dam-ma šàr* Uri^{ki} *u* érin^{me}-*šú* [*is-ki-pu*]

---

^{38}[mu 14.kám] *šàr* Uri^{ki} *u* érin^{me}-*šú id-ke-*[*e-ma ana* ^{kur}*Aš-šur* gin^{i}]^{k} *šàr* Érin-*man-da ana tar-ṣi* šàr Uri$^{[ki]}$ ^{39}[gin-*ma šàr* Uri^{ki} *u* ^{I}*Ú-ma-kiš-tar ina*

pushed it back as far as the Zāb. It captured it[s chariots] and horses and increased the number of prisoners. With many [. . .] it made cross the Tigris with it and made (them) enter Babylon.

[The eleventh year, the king] of Akkad mustered his troops; he moved along the bank of the Tigris, and, in the month of Iyyar, he set up camp before Baltil. [The . . . th day] of Siwan, he joined battle in the city but did not take it. The king of Assyria mustered his troops, pushed back the king of Akkad in front of Baltil and chased him as far as Takrita'in, [a city] situated on the bank of the Tigris. The king of Akkad garrisoned his troops in the fortress of Takrita'in. The king of Assyria and his army set up camp facing the army of the king of Akkad that was stationed in Takrita'in; for ten days they joined in battle but did not take the city. The army of the king of Akkad who was stationed in the city inflicted a crushing defeat on Assyria. The king of Assyria and his army [withdrew (?)] and returned to their own country. In the month of Araḫsamnu, the Medes went down to Arrapḫa and [. . .].

The twelfth year, in the month of Ab, the Medes [being en route] to Nineveh, [the king of Assyria] pushed forward [with the help of his army]. They took possession of Tarbiṣu, a town in the district of Nineveh, [. . .]. They went along the [Ti]gris and set up camp before Baltil. They joined battle in the city and [. . .] they demolished [. . .]. They inflicted a formidable defeat on a great people, pillaged and plun[dered] them, and rob[bed] them. [The king] of Akkad and his troops, who had gone to the aid of the Medes, did not arrive in time for the battle. The town [was taken. The king of Akkad and] C[ya]xares met outside the city and concluded a mutual accord and a total peace. [*Later* (?), Cya]xares and his troops returned to their own country. The king of Akkad and his troops returned to their own country.

[The thirteenth year, in the month of I]yyar, the Suḫeans rebelled against the king of Akkad and began hostilities. [The king of Akkad] mustered his [troo]ps and marched on Suḫu. In the month of Siwan, the fourth day, he joined [battle at] Raḫi-ilu, a town situated in the midst of the Euphrates, and at this time he took the town. He built his [. . .]. The inhabitants on the banks of the Euphrates came to him [. . .]. He set up camp [facing] Ānati, and [he made] assault towers [cross (?) from] the west bank, [. . .], he brought assault towers up to the wall, joined battle in the town but [did not take it (?), ... The king of] Assyria went down with his troops, and the king of Akkad [withdrew (?)] with his troops.

[The fourteenth year], the king of Akkad mustered his troops [and marched on Assyria]. The king of the Ummān-manda [went] into the

^{uru}...]-*ú a-ḫa-meš i-ta-am-ru* ^{40}*šàr* Uri^{ki} [u érin^{me}-šú ^{i_7}*Ì-diq-lat* bala-*ma*] ^{I}*Ú-m*[*a-kiš-tar* ^{i_7}*Ra-da*]-*a-ni ú-še-bir-ma* ^{41}gú ^{i_7}*Ì-diq-lat* gin^{me}-*ma* [*ina* ^{iti}Sig$_4$ u$_4$ ...kám *i*]*na* ugu Ninua[^{ki} šub]^{meš} ^{42}ta ^{iti}Sig$_4$ en ^{iti}Ne 3 ta.àm [...] ú ^{43}*ṣal-tú dan-na-tú ana* šà uru dù^{šu} ^{iti}Ne [u$_4$ ...kám ŠI.ŠI un^{me} g]al^{me} *ma-a-diš* gar^{an} ^{44}*ina u*$_4$*-mi-šú-ma* ^{Id}30-*šàr*-gar^{un} *šàr* ^{kur}*Aš-š*[*ur* ug$_7$.(?).] ^{45}*šil-lat* uru *u* é.kur dugud^{tú} *iš-tal-lu* uru *ana* du$_6$ *u ka*[*r-me* gur ...] ^{46}šá ^{kur}*Aš-šur la-pan* ^{lú}kúr *iš-ḫi-ṭam-ma* gìr$_{ii}$ *šàr* Uri^{ki} *ana* din^{ti} *i*[*ṣ-bat*] ^{47} ^{iti}Kin u$_4$ 20.kám ^{I}*Ú-ma-kiš-tar u* érin^{me}-*šú ana* kur-*šú it-tur* egir-*šú šàr* Uri[^{ki} *u* érin^{me}-*šú*] ^{48}*a-di* ^{uru}*Na-ṣi-bi-ni il-li-ku ḫu-ub-ti u ga-lu-tu ka*-[...] ^{49}*u* ^{kur}*Ru-ṣa-pu ana pa-ni šàr* Uri^{ki} *ana* Ninua^{ki} *ú-bil-lu-ni ina* ^{iti}[... u$_4$ ...kám ^{I}An.šár-*ú-bal-liṭ*] ^{50}*ina* ^{uru}*Ḫar-ra-nu ana* lugal^{ut} ^{kur}*Aš-šur* <dù> *ina* aš.te dúr^{ab} en ^{iti}[...u$_4$ ...kám ...] ^{51}*ina* Ninua^{ki} [... t]a u$_4$ 20.kám *šá* ^{iti}[...] *šàr* [Uri^{ki}(?) ...] ^{52}*is-suḫ-ma ina* ^{uru}[...]

---

^{53}mu 15.kám *ina* ^{iti}Šu [*šà*]*r* Uri^{ki} [érin^{me}-*šú id-ke-e-ma*] ^{54}*ana* ^{kur}*Aš-šur* gin-[*ma ina* ^{kur}*Aš-šur*] *šal-ṭa-niš* [gin^{me}] šá ^{kur}[...] ^{55}*u* ^{kur}*Šu*-[...]-*a ik-šu-ud ḫu-b*[*u-ut-su-nu*] *iḫ-tab-tu šil-lat-su-nu* du[gud *iš-tal-lu*] ^{56}*ina* ^{iti}[Api]n *šàr* Uri^{ki} *pa-ni* érin^{me}-*šú i*[*ṣ-bat-ma ina*] ugu ^{uru}*Ru-ug-gu*-[*lí-ti* gin-*ma*] ^{57}*ṣal-tú ana* šà uru dù-*ma* ^{iti}Apin u$_4$ 28<.kám> uru dib [...] *e-du* lú *ul e*-[*zib* .(?). *ana* kur-*šú*] gur^{ra}

---

^{58}mu 16.kám *ina* ^{iti}Gu$_4$ *šàr* Uri^{ki} érin^{me}-*šú id-ke-e-ma ana* ^{kur}*Aš-šur* gin^{ik} t[a ^{iti}...] en ^{iti}Apin ^{59}*ina* ^{kur}*Aš-šur šal-ṭa-niš* gin^{me} *ina* ^{iti}Apin ^{kur}Érin-*man-da* [*ana*] *re-ṣu-ut šàr* Uri^{ki} gin^{me} ^{nim}-*ma* ^{60}érin^{me}-*šú-nu ana* šà *a-ḫa-meš is-mu-ḫu-ma ana* ^{uru}*Ḫar-ra-nu* [*ana* ugl]u ^{Id}[*Aš-šur*-din]^{iṭ} *šá ina* ^{kur}*Aš-šur ina* aš.te *ú-ši-bi* ^{61}gin^{me}-*ma* ^{I}An.šár-*ú-bal-liṭ u* érin ^{kur}*Mi*-[*ṣir šá ana re-ṣu-ti-šú*] gin^{me} ^{ni} ^{62}*ḫat-tú* ^{lú}kúr *im-qut-su-nu-ti-ma* uru *ú-maš-š*[*i-ru-ma* ^{i_7}Buranun(?)] *i-bi-ru* ^{63}*šàr* Uri^{ki} *a-na* ^{uru}*Ḫar-ra-ni ik-šu-dam-ma* [*ṣal-tú ana* šà-*šú* dù-*ma*] uru *iṣ-ṣa-bat* ^{64}*šil-lat* uru *u* é.kur dugud^{tú} *iš-ta-lal ina* ^{iti}Še *šàr* Uri^{ki} [érin^{me}-*šú u* karaš]-*šú-nu ú-maš-šìr-ma* ^{65}*šu-ú ana* kur-*šú* gur^{ra} *u* Érin-*man-da šá ana re-ṣu-ut šàr* Uri^{ki} gi[n^{me} *ana* egir-*šú-nu i*]*t-te-eḫ-su*

---

^{66}<mu 17.kám> *ina* ^{iti}Šu ^{I}An.šár.din^{iṭ} *šàr* ^{kur}*Aš-šur* érin ^{kur}*Mi-ṣir ma-at-tú* [...] ^{67}i$_7$ bala-*ma ana* ugu ^{uru}*Ḫar-ra-nu ana ka-šá*-[*di*] gin[^{me} ...

presence of the king of Akkad, [and the king of Akkad and Cyaxares] met at [. . .]u. The king of Akkad and his army [crossed the Tigris, Cy]axares had to cross the [Rad]ānu, and they moved along the bank of the Tigris; in the [month of Siwan, the . . . th day, they set up camp] before Nineveh. From the month of Siwan to the month of Ab, for three months, [they (?) . . . (and)] they joined a hard battle in the city. In the month of Ab, [the . . . th day], they inflicted a crushing [defeat] on a [gr]eat [people]. At this time King Sîn-šar-iškun of Assy[ria died. .(?).]. They took a great amount of plunder in the city and in the temple and [reduced] the city to a heap of ru[bble. The . . .] of Assyria escaped from the enemy and, for his life, [seized] the feet of the king of Akkad. In the month of Elul, the twentieth day, Cyaxares and his troops returned to their own country. After their departure, the king of Akkad [and his troops] moved as far as Naṣibina. Pillage and banishment [. . .] and the Rusapeans were brought to Nineveh before the king of Akkad. In the month [of . . . , the . . . th day, Aššur-uballiṭ (II)] ascended the throne at Ḫarrān to <reig>n over Assyria. Until the [month of . . . , the . . . th day], in Nineveh [. . .]. On the twentieth day of the month of [. . .], the king of [Akkad (?)] went off and in [. . .].

The fifteenth year, in the month of Dumuzi, [the king] of Akkad mustered his troops [and] marched on Assyria, [traveled through Assyria] victoriously, took possession of [. . .] and of Šu[. . .]a, sa[cked] and [took] a great amount of booty. In the month of [Araḫsam]nu, the king of Akkad [took] leadership of his troops, [marched] on Ruggu[litu], joined battle in the town, and took it in the month of Araḫsamnu, the twenty-eighth day. He lef[t] no one (alive) [.(?).]. He returned [to his own country].

The sixteenth year, in the month of Iyyar, the king of Akkad mustered his troops and marched on Assyria. Fro[m the month of Siwan (?)] to the month of Araḫsamnu, he traveled through Assyria victoriously. In the month of Araḫsamnu, the Ummān-manda came [to the ai]d of the king of Akkad, uniting their troops (with those of Akkad) and marched on Ḫarrān [again]st [Aššur-uball]iṭ, who had ascended the throne of Assyria. (As for) Aššur-uballiṭ and the army of Mi[ṣir, which had] come [to his aid], they were seized with fear of the enemy; they abandoned the city and crossed [the Euphrates (?)]. The king of Akkad reached Ḫarrān, [joined battle], and took the city. He took a great amount of plunder in the city and in the temple. In the month of Adar, the king of Akkad left [his troops and] their [camp]; he returned to his own country, and the Ummān-manda who [had com]e to the aid of the king of Akkad withdrew.

<The seventeenth year>, in the month of Dumuzi, Aššur-uballiṭ, king of Assyria, and a large Egyptian army [. . .] crossed the river (= the Euphrates)

iṣ]-*ṣab-tu* [68]*šu-lu-tu šá šàr* Uri^{ki} *ana lìb-bi ú-še-lu-ú id-du-k*[*u k*]*i-i* [ga]z^{ku} *ina* ugu ^{uru}*Ḫar-ra-nu it-ta-*[*du*] [69]en ^{iti}Kin *ṣal-tú ana* šà uru dù^{uš} *mim-ma ul il-*[*qi-ma ana* egir-*šú-nu*] nu lá^{su} [70]*šàr* Uri^{ki} *ana re-ṣu-ut* érin^{me}-*šú* gin-*ma ṣal-tú* [*ul* dù^{uš} *ana* ^{kur}*I*]-*za-al-la i-li-ma* [71]uru^{me} *šá* kur^{me} *ma-a-du-tú* [. . .]-*šú-nu ina* izi *iš-ru-up* [72]*ina* u_4-*mi-šú-ma* érin^{me} [*šá* . . .] en *pi-ḫat* ^{uru}*Ú-ra-áš-ṭu* [73][gi]n *ina* kur(?) [. . .]^{me}-*šú-nu iḫ-tab-tu* [74]*šu-lu-tu šá* lugal [. . . *ina* šà-*šú ú-še-lu is-su*]-*ḫu-nim-ma* [75]*ana* ^{uru}[. . .] *i-lu-ú* [. . .] *šàr* Uri^{ki} *ana* kur-*šú* gur^{ra}

---

[76]*ina* mu [18.kám *ina* ^{iti}Ki]n *šàr* Uri^{ki} érin^{me}-*šú id-ke-e-ma*
(erased or blank line)
[77][*šá* ^{d}N]à *u* ^{d}Amar.utu *i-ra-a*[*m-m*]*u li-iṣ-ṣu-ur ana* $šu_{ii}$ nu è

23. CHRONICLE OF NABOPOLASSAR (608–606)

Sources: tablet in the same format as an administrative text; continuation of the preceding chronicle.
Bibliography: Grayson 1975a: no. 4.
Language: Babylonian.
Date: Neo-Babylonian period.
Place: unknown.
Contents: continues the history of Nabopolassar's reign.

[1]mu 18.kám ^{d}Ak.ibila.ùri *ina* ^{iti}Kin lugal Uri^{ki} érin^{me}-*šú id-ke-e-ma* [2]gú $^{i}_{7}$Idigna uš-*ma ana* kur^{i} *šá* É-^{I}*Ḫa-nu-ni-ia* [3]*pi-ḫat* ^{kur}*Ú-ra-áš-ṭu i-li-ma* URU^{me} *ina* izi *iš-ru-up* [4]*ḫu-bu-ut-su-nu ma-diš iḫ-tab-ta ina* ^{iti}Ab lugal Uri^{ki} *ana* kur-*šú* gur^{ra}

---

[5]mu 19.kám *ina* ^{iti}Sig$_4$ lugal Uri^{ki} érin^{me}-*šú id-ke-e-ma* [6] ^{Id}Ak.nì.du-*ú-ṣu-ur* dumu-*šú* gal^{ú} dumu lugal šá É *re-e-du-tú* [7]érin^{me}-*šú id-ke-e-ma a-na* kur^{meš} *šá* ^{kur}*Za-*.. [gin^{ku}]-*ma* [8]lugal Uri^{ki} dumu lugal *u* érin^{me}-*šú ina* kur *ú-maš-šìr u šu-*[*ú*] *ina* ^{iti}Šu *ana* Tin.tir^{ki} gur^{ra} [9]egir-*šú* ^{d}Ak.nì.du.ùri *a-na* ^{uru}[*Bi-ra-na-a-t*]*ú šá* kur^{me} *ṣal-tú* dù-*ma* [10]^{uru}*Bi-ra-na-a-tú iṣ-bat ina* [izi *iš-ru-u*]*p ḫu-bu-ut* kur^{i} [11]*ma-a-diš iḫ-*[*tab*]-*ta* en *pi-ḫat* ^{kur}[*Ú-ra-áš-tú*(?) *gi-mi*]*r* kur^{me} *ik-šu-ud* [12][*ina* ^{it}]^{i}Kin dumu lugal *ana* Tin.tir^{ki} gur-*am-ma ina* ^{iti}Du$_6$ lugal Uri^{ki} érin-*šú id-ke-ma* [13][*ana* ^{ur}]^{u}*Ki-mu-ḫu šá* gú $^{i}_{7}$Buranun *il-lik* [14][i$_7$] *i-bir-ma ṣal-tú ana* šà uru dù-*ma ina* ^{iti}Gan uru *iṣ-ṣa-bat* [15][*šil-lat-s*]*u iš-ta-lal* ^{lú}*šu-lu-ti-šú ana* šà *ul-te-li ina* ^{iti}Zíz *ana* kur-*šú* gur

and marched on Ḫarrān in order to take posses[sion] of it. [They to]ok (?) [. . .]. They massacred the garrison that the king of Akkad had set up there. Once victors, they set up camp facing Ḫarrān. Until the month of Elul they joined battle in the city without ce[asing], but it ca[me] to nothing. The king of Akkad came to the aid of his troops but [*did not join battle* (?)]. He went up to [I]zalla and set fire to the [. . .] in many mountain localities. At this time the troops [of (?) . . . m]oved as far as the region of Uraštu. In [. . .] they pillaged their [. . . They dro]ve out the garrison that the king [of . . . had set up there] and went up to [. . .]. The king of Akkad returned to his own country.

In the [eighteenth year, in the month of El]ul, the king of Akkad mustered his troops and. . .

[May the one who] lo[v]es [Na]bû and Marduk watch (over this tablet) and not let it fall into (other) hands.

The eighteenth year (of the reign) of Nabopolassar, in the month of Elul, the king of Akkad mustered his troops, moved along the bank of the Tigris, climbed the mountain of Bīt-Ḫanūniya, a region of Uraštu, burned and pillaged towns. In the month of Ṭebeth, the king of Akkad returned to his own country.

The nineteenth year, in the month of Siwan, the king of Akkad mustered his troops, and Nebuchadnezzar, his eldest son, the crown prince, mustered his troops. [They marched] on the Za. . . mountains, and in the month of Dumuzi the king of Akkad left the prince and his troops in the country while he returned to Babylon. After his departure, Nebuchadnezzar joined battle at [Bīrānāt]i situated in the mountains; he took Bīrānāti and [burned it] down. He took many prisoners in the mountains. He conquered [al]l of the mountains as far as the region of [Uraštu (?). In the mo]nth of Elul, the prince returned to Babylon, and, in the month of Teš rit, the king of Akkad mustered his army, marched [on] Kimuḫu on the bank of the Euphrates. He crossed [the river], joined battle in the town,

---

^{16}mu 20.kám érin^{ni} ^{kur}*Mi-ṣir ana* ^{uru}*Ki-mu-ḫu ana* ugu *šu-lu-tú* ^{17}*šá* lugal Uri^{ki} *a-na lìb-bi ú-še-lu-ú* gin^{me} ^{nim}-*ma* 4 iti^{me} ^{18}*ṣal-tú ana* šà uru dù^{me}-*ma* uru *iṣ-ṣab-tú šu-lu-tú šá* lugal Uri^{ki} *id-du-ku* ^{19}*ina* ^{iti}Du$_{6}$ lugal Uri^{ki} érin^{me}-*šú id-ke-e-ma* gú *Pu-rat-tú* gin-*ma* ^{20}*ina* ^{uru}*Qu-ra-ba-ti šá* gú *Pu-rat-tú* karaš *id-di* ^{21}érin^{me}-*šú Pu-rat-tú ú-še-bir-ma* ^{uru}*Šu-na-di-ri* ^{uru}*E-lam-mu* ^{22}*u* ^{uru}*Da-ḫa-am-mu* uru^{me} *šá* ^{kur}*E-bir*-i$_{7}$ *iṣ-ṣab-tu* ^{23}*ḫu-bu-ut-su-nu* sar^{me}-*ni ina* ^{iti}Zíz lugal Uri^{ki} *ana* kur-*šú* gur^{ra} ^{24}érin ^{kur}*Mi-ṣir šá* ^{uru}*Gal-ga-meš Pu-rat-tú i-bi-ru-nim-ma* ^{25}*ana* ugu érin ^{kur}Uri^{ki} šá *ina* ^{uru}*Qu-ra-ba-ti na-du-u* ^{26}gin^{me} ^{nim}-*ma* érin ^{kur}Uri^{ki} *is-ki-pu u ana* egir-*šú-nu i-tu-ru*

---

^{27}mu 21.kám lugal Uri^{ki} *ina* kur-*šú* ^{Id}Ak.nì.du.ùri dumu-*šú* gal^{ú} ^{28}dumu lugal šá É uš$^{ú-tu}$ érin ^{kur}Uri^{ki} *id-ke-e-ma*

24. THE DEATH OF NABOPOLASSAR AND THE FIRST YEARS OF NEBUCHADNEZZAR II (605–595)

Sources: very poorly preserved tablet; the text is a continuation of the preceding chronicle.
Bibliography: Grayson 1975a: no. 5; Tyborowski 1996.
Language: Babylonian.
Date: Neo-Babylonian period.
Contents: the chronicle began with an account of the battle of Carchemiš, whose outcome was crucial in the invasion of Syria. The Egyptians had made the city the cornerstone of their defense system. Once this was lost, all Syria and Palestine fell, almost without resistance, into the hands of the Babylonians.

(Obv.)^{1}[mu 21.ká]m lugal Uri^{ki} *ina* kur-*šú* ^{Id}Ak.nì.du.ùri dumu-*šú* gal^{ú} [dumu] lugal *šá* é *re-e-du-tú* ^{2}[érin ^{kur}Uri^{ki} *i*]*d-ke-e-ma pa-ni* érin^{me}-*šú iṣ-bat-ma ana* ^{uru}*Gal*-[*ga*]-*meš šá* gú *Pu-rat-tú* gin-*ma* ^{3}[*ana* ugu érin ^{kur}*Mi*]-*ṣir šá ina* ^{uru}*Gal-ga-meš na-du-ú* i$_{7}$ *i-bir-ma* ^{4}[*ṣal-tú ana* šà-*šú* dù-*ma a*]-*ḫa-meš im-ḫa-ṣu-ma* érin ^{kur}*Mi-ṣir ina* igi-*šú* bala-*ma* ^{5}[ŠI.ŠI]-*šú-nu iš-kun* en *la ba-še-e i*[*g-mu*]*r-šú-nu-tú šit-ta-a-tú* érin ^{kur}*M*[*i-ṣir* ^{6}*šá ina*] ŠI.ŠI *iš-ḫu-ṭu-ma* ^{giš}tukul *la ik-šu-du-šú-nu-tú ina pi-ḫat* ^{kur}*Ḫa-ma-a-t*[*ú*] ^{7}érin^{me} ^{kur}Uri^{ki} *ik-šu-du-šú-nu-ti-ma* [ŠI].ŠI-*šú-nu iš-ku-nu e-du* lú *ana* kur-*šú* [*ul* gur] ^{8}*ina u*$_{4}$-*mi-šu-ma* ^{Id}Ak.nì.du.ùri ^{kur}*Ḫa*-[*ma-a*]-*tú a-na paṭ*

and, in the month of Kislev, took the town, [pi]laged it, (and) set up his garrison there. In the month of Šebat, he returned to his own country.

The twentieth year, the army of Miṣir marched on Kimuḫu, against the garrison that the king of Akkad had set up there; for four months it joined battle in the town, and it took the town. It massacred the garrison of the king of Akkad. In the month of Tešrit, the king of Akkad mustered his troops; he moved along the bank of the Euphrates and set up camp at Qurabati on the bank of the Euphrates. He made his troops cross the Euphrates, and they took Šunadiri, Elammu, and Daḫammu, towns beyond the Euphrates. They pillaged them. In the month of Šebat the king of Akkad returned to his own country. The army of Miṣir, which was in Carchemiš, crossed the Euphrates and marched on the army of Akkad that was encamped at Qurabati; it pushed back the army of Akkad and made its way back.

The twenty-first year, the king of Akkad (remained) in his country. Nebuchadnezzar, his eldest son, the crown prince, mustered his army and…

[The twenty-fir]st [year], the king of Akkad (remained) in his country. Nebuchadnezzar, his eldest son, the crown [pri]nce, [mu]stered [the army of Akkad], took the leadership of his troops, marched on Car[che]miš on the bank of the Euphrates, crossed the river [to meet the army of Miṣir], which had its quarters in Carchemiš, and [*joined battle with it*]. They fought, and the army of Miṣir beat a retreat before him; he [de]feated and destroyed it until it was completely annihilated. The Akkadian troops overtook the survivors of the army of Mi[ṣir who] had escaped the defeat and whom the weapons had not reached and [deci]mated them in the district of

gim-ri-šú ik-šu-ud ^{9}21 mu.an.na^{meš} ^{Id}Ak.ibila.ùri lugal^{ut} Tin.tir^{ki} dù^{uš} ^{10}*ina* ^{iti}Ne u$_4$ 8.kám nam^{meš} *ina* ^{iti}Kin ^{Id}Ak.nì.du.ùri *ana* Tin.tir^{ki} gur*-am-ma* ^{11}*ina* ^{iti}Kin u$_4$ 1.kám *ina* Tin.tir^{ki} *ina* aš.te lugal$^{ú-tú}$ *ú-ši-ib*

---

^{12}*ina* mu.sag ^{Id}Nà.nì.du-*ú-ṣu-ur ana* ^{kur}*Ḫat-tú ana* egir-*šú* gur-*ma* en ^{iti}Zíz *ina* ^{kur}*Ḫat-ti* ^{13}*šal-ṭa-niš* gin^{me} *ina* ^{iti}Zíz gú.un ^{kur}*Ḫat-tú* dugud^{tú} *ana* Tin.tir^{ki} *il-qa-a* ^{14}*ina* ^{iti}Bár šu$_{ii}$ ^{d}En u dumu ^{d}En *iṣ-bat* ezen *a-ki-tú i-pu-uš*

---

^{15}mu 1.kám ^{Id}Nà.nì.du-*ú-ṣu-ur ina* ^{iti}Sig$_4$ érin$^{ni\ meš}$-*šú id-ke-e-ma* ^{16}*a-na* ^{kur}*Ḫat-tú* gin-*ma* en ^{iti}Gan *ina* ^{kur}*Ḫat-ti šal-ṭa-niš* gin^{me} ^{17}lugal^{meš} *šá* ^{kur}*Ḫat-tú ka-li-šú-nu a-na* igi-*šú* gin^{me} ^{nim}*-ma bi-lat-su-nu* dugud^{tú} *im-ḫur* ^{18}*a-na* ^{uru}*Iš-ki-il-lu-nu* gin-*ma ina* ^{iti}Gan *iṣ-ṣa-bat-su* ^{19}lugal-*šú ik-ta-šad ḫu-bu-ut-su iḫ-tab-ta šil-lat-sa* [*iš-ta-lal-ma*] ^{20}uru *ana* du$_6$ u *kar-me ut-tir ina* ^{iti}Zíz gin-*ma ana* Tin.t[ir^{ki} gur^{ra}]

---

^{21}[mu 2.]kám ^{iti}Gu$_4$ *šàr* Uri^{ki} érin-*šú* dugud^{tú} *ik-ṣur-ma* [*ana* ^{kur}*Ḫat-tú* gin] ^{22}[. . .] *id-di ṣa-pa-a-ti* gal^{meš} *uš-bal-k*[*it* . . . ^{23} . . . ta ^{iti}]Gu$_4$ en ^{i}[^{ti}. . . *ina* ^{kur}*Ḫat-tú šal-ṭa-niš* gin^{me} (. . .) (Rev.)$^{1'}$. . . *ú*(?)*-maš*(?)*-š*]*ìr-ma* [*ana*(?) Tin.tir^{ki}(?) gur^{ra}(?)]

$^{2'}$[mu 3.kám *ina* iti. . . u$_4$] 13.kám ^{Id}Nà.mu.si.sá [. . . $^{3'}$*ina* ^{iti}. . . *šàr* Ur]i^{ki} érin^{me}-*šú id-ke-e-ma a-na* ^{kur}*Ḫat-tú* [gin^{ik} . . . $^{4'}$ . . . *u*(?) *šil-la-tú*(?)] *ma-a-du-tú šá* ^{kur}*Ḫat-tú*^{ki} *ul-te-ri-i*[*b*]

$^{5'}$[m]u 4.kám *šàr* Uri^{ki} érin^{me}-*šú id-ke-e-ma ana* ^{kur}*Ḫat-tú* gin^{ik} *ina* ^{kur}*Ḫat-tú šal-ṭ*[*a-niš* gin^{me}] $^{6'}$*ina* ^{iti}Gan *pa-ni* érin^{me}-*šú iṣ-bat-ma ana* ^{kur}*Mi-ṣir* gin^{ik} *šàr* ^{kur}*Mi-ṣir iš-me-e-ma* érin^{me}-*šú id-ke-*[*e-ma*] $^{7'}$*ina* mè.edin.gaba *a-ḫa-meš im-ḫa-ṣu-ma* ŠI.ŠI *a-ḫa-meš ma-a-diš* gar^{meš} *šàr* Uri^{ki} *u* érin^{me}-*šú* gur^{am}*-ma ana* Tin.tir^{ki} [gur^{ra}]

$^{8'}$mu 5.kám *šàr* Uri^{ki} *ina* kur-*šú* ^{giš}gigir^{meš} *u* anše.kur.ra-*šú ma-a-du-tú ik-ta-ṣar*

Ḫamath. Not one man [returned] to his country. At this time, Nebuchadnezzar conquered the entire country of Ḫa[ma]th. Nabopolassar reigned twenty-one years over Babylon. In the month of Ab, the eighth day, he went to his destiny. In the month of Elul, Nebuchadnezzar returned to Babylon, and in the month of Elul, the first day, he ascended the royal throne of Babylon.[39]

In the year of his accession, Nebuchadnezzar returned to Ḫatti. Until the month of Šebat he traveled through Ḫatti victoriously. In the month of Šebat, he carried Ḫatti's massive tribute to Babylon. In the month of Nisan,[40] he took the hand of Bēl and of the son of Bēl and celebrated the New Year's festival.

The first year (of the reign) of Nebuchadnezzar, in the month of Siwan, he mustered his troops and marched on Ḫatti. Until the month of Kislev he traveled through Ḫatti victoriously. All the kings of Ḫatti came into his presence, and he received their massive tribute. He marched on Aškelôn; he took it in the month of Kislev, seized its king, pillaged and [plu]ndered it. He reduced the city to a heap of rubble. In the month of Šebat, he set forth and [went back] to Bab[ylon].

[The seco]nd [year], in the month of Iyyar, the king of Akkad strengthened his powerful army and [marched on Ḫatti]. He set up his quarters at [...]. He made cross [...] large siege towers. [... from the month of] Iyyar to the month of [..., he traveled through Ḫatti victoriously].

(...)

[... he lef]t (?) and [returned to Babylon (?)].

[The third year, in the month of ..., the] thirteenth day, Nabû-šumalīšir[41] [... In the month of ..., the king of Akk]ad mustered his troops and [marched] on Ḫatti. He caused [the] vast [... and booty (?)] from Ḫatti to be br[o]ug[ht] to Akkad.

The fourth [ye]ar, the king of Akkad mustered his troops and marched on Ḫatti. [He traveled] through Ḫatti victor[iously]. In the month of Kislev, he took leadership of his troops and marched on Miṣir. Having learned of it, the king of Miṣir muster[ed] his troops, [and] they joined in a pitched battle. They both inflicted heavy losses. The king of Akkad turned back with his troops and [went back] to Babylon.

The fifth year, the king of Akkad (remained) in his country. He strengthened his numerous chariotry and cavalry.

9'mu 6.kám ^{iti}Gan *šàr* Uri^{ki} érin^{me}-*šú id-ke-ma ana* ^{kur}*Ḫat-tú* gin^{ik} ta ^{kur}*Ḫat-tú* érin^{me}-*šú iš-pur-ma* 10'*mad-ba-ri* uš-*ma* ^{kur}*A-ra-bi ma-du-tu* nì-*šú-nu bu-li-šú-nu u* dingir^{me}-*šú-nu ma-diš iḫ-tab-tu-nu ina* ^{iti}Še lugal *ana* kur-*šú* gur

---

11'mu 7.kám ^{iti}Gan *šàr* Uri^{ki} érin^{me}-*šú id-ke-ma a-na* ^{kur}*Ḫat-tú* gin-*ma* 12'*ina* ugu ^{uru}*Ia-a-ḫu-du* šub-*ma ina* ^{iti}Še u$_4$ 2.kám uru *iṣ-ṣa-bat* lugal *ik-ta-šad* 13'lugal *šá* šà-*šú ina lìb-bi ip-te-qid bi-lat-sa* dugud^{tú} *il-*[*qa-am-m*]*a ana* Tin.tir^{ki} ku$_4$^{ib}

14'mu [8.kám ^{it}]^{i}Ab *šàr* Uri^{ki} *a-na* ^{kur}*Ḫat-tú* en ^{uru}*Gal-ga-meš* [gin^{ik}] 15'*ul* [. . .] *ina* ^{iti}Zíz [lugal *ana*] kur-*šú* g[ur^{ra}]

16'mu 9.kám [^{iti}. . . *šàr* Ur]i^{ki} *u* érin^{me}-[*šú* g]ú *Ì-diq-la*[*t* gin-*ma*] 17'*šàr* ^{kur}El[am(?).ma(?)^{ki} . . .] . . . mu ú [. . .] 18' *šàr* Uri^{ki} . . . [. . .] 19'*šá* gú *Ì-diq-lat* karaš-*su id-di ma-lak* u$_4$ 1.kám *ina bi-ri-šú-*[*nu* gál^{ši}] 20'*šàr* ^{kur}Elam.ma^{ki} *ip-làḫ-ma ḫat-tú šub-su-ma ana* kur-*šú i-t*[*ur*]

21'[mu] 10.[kám *šàr* U]ri^{ki} *ina* kur-*šú* ta ^{iti}Gan en ^{iti}Ab *bar-tu ina* ^{kur}Uri^{ki} [gál(?) 22'. . . érin]^{me}-*šú ma-du-tú ina* ^{giš}tukul *id-duk a-a-bi-šú* šu$_{ii}$-*su* kur^{ud} (Lower edge)23'[egir *ana* ^{ku}]^{r}*Ḫat-tú* gin-*ma* lugal^{me} *šá* ^{kur}[*Ḫat-tú ka-li-šu-nu a-n*]*a* 24'[igi-*šú* gin]^{me} ^{nim}-*ma bi-lat-su-nu* dugud^{tú} [*im-ḫur-ma an*]*a* Ti[n.tir^{ki}] gur^{ra}

25'[mu 11].kám *ina* ^{iti}Gan *šàr* Uri^{ki} érin^{me}-[*šu id-ke-e-ma* 26'*ana* ^{kur}*Ḫ*]*at-tú* gin^{ik}

25. CHRONICLE OF THE THIRD YEAR OF NERIGLISSAR (557)

Sources: tablet in the same format as an administrative text.
Bibliography: Grayson 1975a: no. 6.
Language: Babylonian.
Date: Neo-Babylonian period.
Place: unknown.
Contents: apparently an excerpt from a longer chronicle.[42] The abundance of details and the style stand apart from other chronicles. Neriglissar, an officer of high rank and wealthy landowner, seized power from the family of Nabopolassar.

The sixth year, in the month of Kislev, the king of Akkad mustered his troops and marched on Ḫatti. From Ḫatti, he dispatched his troops, and they went in the direction of the desert. They carried away astonishing riches, cattle and the gods of the many Arabs. In the month of Adar the king returned to his country.

The seventh year, in the month of Kislev, the king of Akkad mustered his troops, marched on Ḫatti, and set up his quarters facing the city of Yeḫud.[43] In the month of Adar, the second day, he took the city and captured the king. He installed there a king of his choice. He colle[cted] its massive tribute and went back to Babylon.

[The eighth] year, [in the mon]th of Ṭebeth, the king of Akkad [marched] on Ḫatti as far as Carchemiš. [. . .] he [. . .] not [. . .]. In the month of Šebat, [the king] we[nt back to] his own country.

The ninth year, [in the month of . . . , the king of Akk]ad and [his] troops [moved] along the bank of the Tigris. The king of E[lam (?) . . .]. The king of Akkad [. . .]. He set up his camp [at . . .] on the bank of the Tigris. [It was] a day's journey between them. The king of Elam became frightened, and, fear having gripped him, he w[ent back] to his own country.

[The] ten[th year, the king of Akk]ad (remained) in his country. From the month of Kislev to the month of Ṭebeth [there was] an uprising in Akkad [. . .]. He executed many of his [troops], captured his adversary. [Later], he marched on Ḫatti; [all] the kings of (!) [Ḫatti cam]e [int]o [his presence, (and) he received] their massive tribute [and] went back [to] Ba[bylon].

[The eleven]th [year], in the month of Kislev, the king of Akkad [mustered his] troops and marched [on] Ḫatti.

^{1}mu 3.k[ám ^{iti}... u$_4$ ...kám] ^{I}*Ap-pu-ú-a-šú* lugal *šá Pi-rin-du* ^{2}*um-ma-ni-š*[*u ma-du-tú id*]*-kám-ma a-na ḫa-ba-tu*$_4$ *u šá-l*[*a-lu*] ^{3}[*a-n*]*a e-bir* i$_7$ [igi-*šú iš*]*-ta-kan* ^{Id}U.gur.lugal.ùri ^{4}érin$^{\text{ni-meš}}$-*šú id-*[*ke-e-ma*] *ana* ^{uru}*Ḫu-me-e ana muḫ-ḫi-šú il-l*[*i-ik*] ^{5}*la-mi-šú* ^{I}*Ap-pu-*[*ú*]*-a-šú* (erased) ^{6}érin^{me} *u kal-li-i šá* anše.kur.ra^{me} *šá ik-ṣu-ru* ^{7}*ina na-aḫ-la šá* kur^{meš} *a-na šu-šu-ba-a-tú ú-še-šib-ma* ^{8} ^{Id}U.gur.lugal.ùri *ik-šu-ud-su-nu-ti-ma iš-kun* ŠI.ŠI-*šú-*[*nu*] ^{9}érin^{ni} *ma-a-du-tú i-duk* érin^{ni}-*šú u* anše.kur.ra-*šú* ^{10}*ma-a-du-tú uṣ-ṣab-bi-ta ar-ki* ^{I}*Ap-pu-ú-a-šú* ^{11}15 danna *qaq-qar* kur^{ú} *mar-ṣu šá* lú *ár-ki* lú *il-la-ku* ^{12}*a-di* ^{uru}*Ú-ra-'* uru lugal$^{\text{ú-ti}}$-*šú ir-dip-ma* ^{13}[šu$_{ii}$ *l*]*a ik-šu-ud-su* ^{uru}*Ú-ra-' iṣ-ṣa-bat šil-lat iš-ta-lal* ^{14}(erased) ^{15}*ul-tu* ^{uru}*Ú-ra-' a-di* ^{uru}*Ki-ir-ši* ^{16}uru lugal$^{\text{ú-tú}}$ *šá* ad^{meš}-*šú* 6 danna *qaq-qar* kur^{ú} *dan-nu* ^{17}*ni-ri-bi mar-ṣu ki-i il-li-ku* ^{18} ^{uru}*Ki-ir-ši* uru *dan-nu* uru lugal$^{\text{ú-ti}}$-*šú iṣ-ṣa-bat* ^{19}bàd-*šú* é.gal-*šú u* un^{me}-*šú ina i-šá-tú iq-ta-li* ^{20} ^{uru}*Pi-tu-su* kur^{ú} *šá ina* murub$_4$^{tú} i$_7$*Mar-rat* ^{21}*ù* 6 lim érin^{ni} *e-piš ṣal-tú šá ana* šà *i-lu-ú* ^{22}*ina* ^{giš}*sa-pi-na-a-tú iṣ-ṣa-bat* uru-*šú it-tab-lu* ^{23}*u* un^{me}-*šú uṣ-ṣab-bi-ta* mu.bi *ul-tu ni-ri-*[*bi*] ^{24}*šá* ^{uru}*Sa-al-lu-né-e a-di* ugu *mi-ṣir* ^{25}*šá* ^{uru}*Lu-ú-du ina i-šá-tú iš-ta-rap* ^{I}*Ap-pu-ú-a-š*[*ú*] ^{26}*iḫ-liq-ma* šu$_{ii}$ *la* [*ik-š*]*u-ud-su ina* ^{iti}Še *šár* Uri^{ki} ^{27}*a-n*[*a* kur-*š*]*ú i-tu-ra*

---

26. CHRONICLE OF NABONIDUS (556–539)

Sources: library tablet with two columns on each face, but very damaged.
Bibliography: Grayson 1975a: no. 7.
Language: Babylonian.
Date: Seleucid period.
Place: Babylon.
Contents: the reign of Nabonidus was marked by two major events. He opposed the absolute power of the priests of Marduk by proclaiming his devotion to the cult of Sîn at Ḫarrān. He went to reside in the northern Arabian peninsula at the oasis of Tayma, a crossroads of primary importance, leaving to his son Bēl-šar-uṣur, the Bēlšazzar of the Bible, responsibility for directing the affairs of state from Babylon.

There were two diametrically opposed historiographical traditions concerning Nabonidus. One was favorable to him, represented by a Babylonian document in the Aramaic language by a priest who presented him as a just king. The other was hostile, gleaning its information from Persian writings of the time of Cyrus that sought to discredit him. This is represented by a poetic narrative from the Persian period and a historical

The thi[rd] year, [the month of . . . , the . . . th day], King Appuašu of Pirindu [mus]tered h[is numerous] troops and [set out on the] road [tow]ard beyond the Euphrates to pillage and plun[der]. Neriglissar mus[tered] his troops and march[ed] on Ḫumê to meet him. Before his (arrival), App[u]ašu posted the troops and mounted couriers that he had brought together in an ambush in a pass. Neriglissar overtook them and defeated th[em]. He decimated the large army, captured its many troops and horses. He chased Appuašu over a distance of fifteen double hours, across difficult mountains where the men had to march one behind the other, as far as Ura', his royal residence; he did [n]ot capt[ure] him, (but) he took Ura' (and) plundered (it). After a march over a distance of six double hours, in a very mountainous region, through difficult passes, from Ura' to Kirši, the royal residence of his ancestors, he took Kirši, the mighty city, the home of its kingship. He burned its surrounding wall, its palace, and its inhabitants with fire. With the aid of boats, he took Pitusu, a land in the middle of the Ocean, and the six thousand soldiers, fighters stationed in the town. He destoyed the town and took its inhabitants prisoners. The same year, he set fire (to the country) from the Sallunê crossi[ng] to the border of Lydia. Appuaš[u] fled, and he could not capture him. In the month of Adar, the king of Akkad returned t[o h]is own [country].

---

document preserved by a copy from the Parthian period (no. 53). The present chronicle belonged to the latter tradition.[44]

(i) ^{1}[mu 1(?).kám ^{Id}Pa.i lugal . . . ^{2}. . .]-*šú iš-ši* lugal (erased) ^{3}[. . .] *ma-ti-šú-nu ana* E^{ki} *ú-bil-lu* ^{4}[. . .]-*ti* ^{5}[. . .] *is-ḫu-ḫu-ma ul iš-ši* ^{6}[. . .] im.ri.a-*su-nu ma-la* gál^{ú} ^{7}[. . .] lugal érin-*šú id-ke-ma ana Ḫu-me-e* ^{8}[. . .] kit

---

^{9}[mu 2(?).kám . . .] *ina* ^{iti}Ab *ina* ^{kur}*Ḫa-ma-a-tú* šed$_7$ ^{10}[. . .]

---

^{11}[mu 3(?).kám . . .^{it}]^{i}Ne *ana* ^{kur}*Am-ma-na-nu šá-di-i* ^{12}[*il-lik-ma* . . .] ^{giš}*ṣip-pa-a-tú* gurun *ma-la ba-šu-ú* ^{13}[. . .] *ina lìb-bi-ši-na ana qí-rib* E^{ki} ^{14}[*ú*(?)-*bil*(?) (.?.) lugal gi]g-*ma* tin$^{ut!}$ *ina* ^{iti}Gan lugal érin-*šú* ^{15}[*id-ke-ma* . . .]-*tì u ana* ^{d}Nà-*tat*(!)-*tan*-ùri ^{16}[. . .]-*mu šá* ^{kur}Mar.dú *a-na* ^{17}[. . . *ina* ugu ^{uru}*Ú*]-*du-um-mu it-ta-du-ú* ^{18}[. . .]-*ma* érin^{meš} *ma-du-tu* ^{19}[. . . k]á.gal ^{uru}*Šin-ṭi-ni* ^{20}[. . .] gaz-*šú* ^{21}[. . .] qu ^{22}[. . . ér]in^{meš}
(. . .)

$^{1'}$[mu 6.kám . . .^{I}*Iš-tu-me-gu* érin-*šú* (ii) ^{1}*id*]-*ke-e-ma ana* ugu ^{I}*Ku-raš* lugal *An-šá-an ana ka-š*[*á-di i*]*l-lik-ma* [. . .] ^{2} ^{I}*Iš-tu-me-gu* érin-*šú* bala-*su-ma ina* šu$_{\text{ii}}$ *ṣa-bít a-na* ^{I}*Ku-raš id-d*[*in*] ^{3} ^{I}*Ku-raš a-na* ^{kur}*A-gam-ta-nu* uru lugal$^{ú\text{-}tu}$ <*il-lik-ma*> kù.babbar guškin nì.šu nì.ga [. . .] ^{4}*šá* ^{kur}*A-gam-ta-nu iš-lul-ú-ma a-na* ^{kur}*An-šá-an il-qí* nì.šu nì.ga *šá* érin$^{\text{me[š}}$ . . .]

---

^{5}mu 7.kám lugal *ina* ^{uru}*Te-ma-a* dumu lugal ^{lú}gal^{meš}-*šú* érin^{meš}-*šú ina* ^{kur}Uri^{ki} [lugal *ana* ^{iti}Bár] ^{6}*a-na* E^{ki} nu gin^{ku} ^{d}Nà *ana* Ká.dingir.ra^{ki} nu gin^{ku} ^{d}En nu è ez[en *a-ki-tú ba-ṭil*] ^{7}sískur *ina É-sag-gíl u É-zi-da* dingir^{meš} *ša* Tin.tir^{ki} *u Bár-sipa*^{ki} *k*[*i šal-mu*] ^{8}sum^{nu} šeš.gal *is-ruq-ma* é *ip-qid*

---

^{9}mu 8.kám

---

^{10}mu 9.kám ^{Id}Pa.i lugal <*ina*> ^{uru}*Te-ma-a* dumu lugal ^{lú}gal^{meš} *u* érin^{ni} *ina* ^{kur}Uri^{ki} lugal *ana* ^{iti}Bár *ana* Tin.tir^{ki} ^{11}nu gin^{ku} ^{d}Nà *ana* Ká.dingir.ra^{ki} nu gin^{ku} ^{d}En nu è *i-sin-nu a-ki-tú ba-ṭil* ^{12}sískur^{meš} *ina É-sag-gíl u É-zi-da* dingir^{meš} *ša* <Tin.tir^{ki}> *u Bar-sip*^{ki} *ki šal-mu* sum^{na} ^{13} ^{iti}Bár u$_4$ 5.kám ama lugal *ina* Bàd-*ka-ra-šú šá* gú $^{\text{i}}{}_7$Buranun *e-la-nu Sip-par*^{ki} ^{14}*im-tu-ut* dumu

[The first (?) year, Nabonidus, the king, ...] lifted [...]. The king [...] of their country [whom] he brought to Babylon. [...] they trembled, and he did not lift [........] their family, as many as there were [...]. The king mustered his army and [marched] on Ḫumê [...].

[The second (?) year], in the month of Ṭebeth, it was cold at Ḫamath. [...].

[The third (?) year, in the] month of Ab, [he marched] on the Ammanānum [and ...] the orchards, fruits as many as there were, [...] among them, [he brought] into Babylon. [. ?. . The king be]came ill but recovered. In the month of Kislev, the king [mustered] his army [...] and to Nabû-tattan-uṣur [...] of Amurru to [...] they set up their quarters [facing E]dom [...] and the numerous troops [... ga]teway of Šinṭīni [...] he killed him [... the tr]oops [...].

(...)

[The sixth year, ... Astyages] mustered [his troops] and, with con[quest] in view, [m]arched on King Cyrus of Anšan in order to seize him and [...]. The army of Astyages revolted against him, captured him, and deliv[ered] him to Cyrus. Cyrus <marched> on Agamtanu (= Ecbatana), the royal residence, and took to Anšan the silver, gold, goods, valuables, [and ...] that he had taken as plunder (in) Agamtanu. The goods and valuables that the troops [...].

The seventh year, the king stayed in Tayma. The prince, his officers, and his troops stayed in Akkad. [In the month of Nisan, the king] did not go to Babylon. Nabû did not go to Babylon. Bēl did not go out. The fes[tival of the New Year was not celebrated]. The sacrifices to the gods of Babylon and Borsippa were offered in the Esagila and the Ezida a[s in normal times]. The *šešgallû*-priest made a libation and inspected the temple.

The eighth year,

The ninth year, Nabonidus, the king, stayed <in> Tayma. The prince, the officers, and the army were in Akkad. In the month of Nisan, the king did not go to Babylon. Nabû did not go to Babylon. Bēl did not go out. The New Year's festival was not celebrated. The sacrifices to the gods of Babylon and Borsippa were offered in the Esagila and the Ezida as in

lugal *u* érin^{meš}-*šú* 3 *u*$_4$-*mu šu-du-ru* ér gar^{at} *ina* ^{iti}Sig$_4$ *ina* ^{kur}Uri^{ki} ^{15}*bi-ki-tú ina* ugu ama lugal gar^{at} *ina* ^{iti}Bár ^{I}*Ku-raš šàr* ^{kur}*Par-su* érin-*šú id-ke-e-ma* ^{16}*šap-la-an* ^{uru}*Ar-ba-'-il* $^{i}_{7}$Idigna *i-bir-ma ina* ^{iti}Gu$_4$ *ana* $^{<kur>}$*Lú-ú-*[*di il-li*]*k* ^{17}lugal-*šú* gaz *bu-šá-a-šú il-qí šu-lit šá ram-ni-šú* <<aš>> *lu ú-še-li-*[*iš*] ^{18}egir *šu-lit-su ù šar-ri ina* šà gál^{ši}

---

^{19}mu 10.kám lugal *ina* ^{uru}*Te-ma* dumu lugal ^{lú}gal^{meš} *u* érin^{ni}-*šú ina* ^{kur}Uri^{ki} lugal *ana* [^{iti}Bár *ana* Tin.tir^{ki} nu gin^{ku}] ^{20} ^{d}Nà *ana* E^{ki} nu gin^{ku} ^{d}En nu è^{a} ezen *a-ki-tú ba-ṭil* sískur *ina É-*[*sag-gíl u É-zi-da*] ^{21}dingir^{meš} *ša* Tin.tir^{ki} u *Bar-sip*^{ki} *ki šal-m*[*u* s]um^{na} *ina* ^{iti}Sig$_4$ u$_4$ 21.ká[m...] ^{22}*šá* ^{kur}*E-lam-mi-ia ina* ^{kur}Uri^{ki} [...] ^{lú}gar.kur *ina* Unu^{k}[^{i} ...]

---

^{23}mu 11.kám lugal *ina* ^{uru}*Te-ma-a* dumu lugal ^{lú}gal^{meš} *u* érin-*šú ina* ^{kur}Ur[i^{ki} lugal *ana* ^{iti}Bár *ana* Tin.tir^{ki} nu gin^{ku} ^{24} ^{d}Nà *ana*] E^{ki} nu gin^{ku} ^{d}En nu è^{a} ezen *a-ki-tú ba-ṭil* sí[skur *ina É-sag-gíl u É-zi-da* ^{25}dingir^{meš} *ša* Tin].tir^{ki} *u* [*Bar-sip*^{ki} *ki šal-mu*] sum^{na} [...]

(...)

(iii) $^{1'}$[...] gaz $^{i}_{7}$Idi[gna(?) ... $^{2'}$...$^{iti(?)}$]Še ^{d}Inanna Unu^{ki} [... $^{3'}$...érin]^{meš} *šá* ^{kur}*Pa*[*r-su* ... $^{4'}$... érin]^{meš} ^{ni} [...]

$^{5'}$[mu 17(?).kám *ina* ^{iti}Bár ^{d}]Nà ta *Bar-sip*^{ki} *ana* è^{e} [^{d}En gin^{ku} ^{d}En è^{a} $^{6'}$*ina* ^{iti}]Ab lugal *ana É-tùr-kalam-ma* ku$_4$ *ina* é [... $^{7'}$...]-*ut-tì* bala$^{tu}_{4}$ geštin bal-a^{qí} *tum* ... [... $^{8'}$ ... ^{d}E]n è^{a} ezen *a-ki-tú ki šal-mu* dù^{šú} *ina* ^{iti}[... $^{9'}$dingir]^{meš} *šá Marad-da*^{ki} ^{d}*Za-ba*$_4$*-ba*$_4$ *u* dingir^{meš} *šá Kiši*^{ki} ^{d}*Nin-líl* [*u* dingir^{meš} $^{10'}$*šá*] *Ḫur-sag-kalam-ma ana* Tin.tir^{ki} ku$_4^{meš}$ ^{ni} en til ^{iti}Kin dingir^{meš} *šá* ^{kur}Uri^{ki} [...] $^{11'}$*šá* ugu IM *u* ki.ta IM *ana* E^{ki} ku$_4^{meš}$ ^{ni} dingir^{meš} *šá Bar-sip*^{ki} Gú.du$_8$.a[^{ki}] $^{12'}$*u Sip-par*^{ki} nu ku$_4^{meš}$ ^{ni} *ina* ^{iti}Du$_6$ ^{I}*Ku-raš ṣal-tu*$_4$ *ina* Ud.kús-ˇu^{ki} *ina* ugu [gú] $^{13'}$ $^{i}_{7}$*Ì-diq-lat ana* šà érin^{ni} ^{kur}Uri^{ki} *ki* dù^{šú} un^{meš} ^{kur}Uri^{ki} $^{14'}$bala.ki sar sar un^{meš} gaz u$_4$ 14 Zimbir^{ki} *ba-la ṣal-tu*$_4$ *ṣa-bit* $^{15'}$ ^{Id}Nà.i záḫ u$_4$ 16 ^{I}*Ug-ba-ru* ^{lú}nam ^{kur}*Gu-ti-um u* érin^{meš} ^{I}*Ku-raš ba-la ṣal-tu*$_4$ $^{16'}$*ana* E^{ki} ku$_4$ egir ^{d}Nà.i *ki* lá^{sa} *ina* E^{ki} *ṣa-bit* en til iti ^{kuš}tuk-šu^{me} $^{17'}$*šá* ^{kur}*Gu-ti-um* ká^{meš} *šá É-sag-gíl* nigin *baṭ-la šá mim-ma ina É-sag-gíl u* é.kur^{meš} <<diš>> $^{18'}$*ul iš-šá-kin ù si-ma-nu ul* dib^{iq} ^{iti}Apin u$_4$ 3.kám ^{I}*Ku-raš ana* E^{ki} ku$_4$ $^{19'}$*ḫa-ri-né-e ina* igi-*šú* diri^{meš} *šu-lum ana* uru *šá-kin* ^{I}*Ku-raš šu-lum ana* Tin.tir^{ki} $^{20'}$*gab-bi-šú iq-bi* ^{I}*Gu-ba-ru* ^{lú}nam-*šú* ^{lú}nam^{meš} ina E^{ki} *ip-te-qid* $^{21'}$ta ^{iti}Gan en

normal times. In the month of Nisan, the fifth day, the king's mother died at Dūr-karašu on the bank of the Euphrates, upstream from Sippar. The prince and his troops mourned for three days, and there was weeping. In the month of Siwan, a lamentation was set up in Akkad for the king's mother.[45] In the month of Nisan, King Cyrus of Persia mustered his army and crossed the Tigris downstream from Arbēla and, in the month of Iyyar, [march]ed on Ly[dia].[46] He put its king to death, seized its possessions, [and] set up his own garrison [there]. After that, the king and his garrison resided there.

The tenth year, the king stayed in Tayma. The prince, the officers, and his army were in Akkad. In the [month of Nisan], the king [did not go to Babylon]. Nabû did not go to Babylon. Bēl did not go out. The New Year's festival was not celebrated. The sacrifices to the gods of Babylon and Borsippa were [of]fered in the Esagila and the Ezida as in norm[al] times. In the month of Siwan, the twenty-first day, [. . .] of Elammiya, in Akkad [. . .], governor (of the Sealand?), in Uruk [. . .].

The eleventh year, the king stayed in Tayma. The prince, the officers, and his army were in Akk[ad. In the month of Nisan, the king did not go to Babylon. Nabû] did not go [to] Babylon. Bēl did not go out. The New Year's festival was not celebrated. The sa[crifices to the gods of Baby]lon and [Borsippa] were offered [in the Esagila and the Ezida as in normal times].

(. . .)

[. . .] was killed. The Tig[ris . . . (?). In the month of] Adar (?), Ištar of Uruk [. . .] the [troops] of Per[sia . . ., the troop]s [. . .].

[The seventeenth year, in the month of Nisan], Nabû [went] from Borsippa to the procession of [Bēl. Bēl went out. In the] month of Ṭebeth, the king entered the Etur-kalama. In the temple (?) [. . .] he offered a wine libation [. . .]. Bēl went out. The New Year's festival was celebrated as in normal times. In the month of [. . ., Lugal-Marada and the god]s of Marad, Zababa and the gods of Kiš, Ninlil [and the gods of] Ḫursag-kalama entered Babylon. Until the end of the month of Elul, the gods of Akkad [. . .], upstream and downstream from Isin (?), entered Babylon. The gods of Borsippa, Cutha, and Sippar did not enter. In the month of Tešrit, Cyrus having joined battle with the army of Akkad at Upû on the [bank] of the Tigris, the people of Akkad fell back. He pillaged and massacred the population. The fourteenth, Sippar was taken without a struggle. Nabonidus fled. The sixteenth, Governor Ugbaru of Gutium and the army of Cyrus made their entrance into Babylon without fighting. Later, having returned, Nabonidus was taken in Babylon. Until the end of the month, the shield-(carriers) of

^{iti}Še dingir^{meš} *šá* ^{kur}Uri^{ki} *šá* ^{Id}Nà.i *ana* E^{ki} *ú-še-ri-du-*[*ni*] $^{22'}$*a-na ma-ḫa-zi-šú-nu* gur^{me} ^{iti}Apin gi$_6$ u$_4$ 11.kám ^{I}*Ug-ba-ru* ug$_7$ *ina* ^{it}[^{i}... $^{23'}$dam] lugal ug$_{7}^{at}$ ta 27 *šá* ^{iti}Še en u$_4$ 3 *šá* ^{iti}Bar *bi-ki-tu*$_4$ *ina* Uri[^{ki} gar^{at}] $^{24'}$un^{meš} *gab-bi* sag.du-*su-nu* du$_8^{meš}$ u$_4$ 4.kám ^{I}*Kám-bu-zi-ia* dumu *šá* ^{I}*K*[*u-raš*] $^{25'}$*a-na É-*^{nì}*gidri-kalam-sum-mu ki* gin lú *É-gidri* ^{d}Nà *šá* pa [... $^{26'}$*ki*] gin^{ku} *aš-šu lu-bu-uš-bi* Elam.ma^{ki} šu$_{ii}$ ^{d}Nà [*ul ú-šá-aṣ-bi-it-su* $^{27'giš}$*as-m*]*a-re-e u* ^{kuš}*iš-pat*^{meš} ta [...du]mu lugal *ana du*[*l-li*(?) ... $^{28'}$...] ^{d}Nà *ana É-sag-gíl* nigin ... ki ... *ina* igi ^{d}En *u* dumu ^{d}E[n ...]

(...)

(iv) $^{1'}$[...] en $^{2'}$[...] E^{ki} a^{meš} $^{3'}$[...]^{meš} *iq-ta-tur* $^{4'}$[...] ka gan iti ká *na-pi-il* $^{5'}$[...] *É-an-na šá* EZENxKAS^{ki} $^{6'}$[...é] *mu-um-mu* è $^{7'}$[...] zi $^{8'}$[...] *ina* E^{ki} ... ḫi $^{9'}$[...] Tin.tir^{ki} *iṣ-rim-ma*

27. FRAGMENT OF A NEO-BABYLONIAN CHRONICLE

Sources: small fragment of the obverse of a library tablet in two columns.
Bibliography: Grayson 1975a: 280.
Language: Babylonian.
Date: Neo-Babylonian period.
Place: probably Babylon.
Contents: only some beginnings of lines are still legible.

(...) (Obv.) (i)$^{1'}$[...] ... 1.kám $^{2'}$[...]... $^{3'}$[...]... $^{4'}$[...]... (...) (ii)$^{1'}$šú ... la ... [...] $^{2'}$*su-un-qa* ... 17 [...] $^{3'}$... ig [...]

$^{4'}$mu 8.kám *ina* ^{iti}Bar u$_4$ [...k]ám ... [...] $^{5'}$ ^{d}[...] $^{6'}$diri [...]

$^{7'}$mu 10.kám *ina* ^{iti}B[ar ...] $^{8'}$[...]

$^{9'}$mu 11.kám *ina* ^{iti}B[ár(?) ...] (...)

Gutium encircled the gates of the Esagila, but there was no interruption (of rites) of any kind in the Esagila or in any other temple and no (festival) date was missed. In the month of Araḫsamnu, the third day, Cyrus entered Babylon. (Drinking) straws (?) were filled up before him. Peace reigned in the city; Cyrus decreed peace for all Babylon. He installed Gubaru as governor of (all) the governors in Babylon. From Kislev to Adar, the gods of Akkad that Nabonidus had sent to Babylon returned to their sanctuaries. In the month of Araḫsamnu, the night of the eleventh day, Ugbaru died. In the month of [..., the que]en died. From the twenty-seventh day of Adar to the third day of Nisan [there was] mourning in Akkad. All the inhabitants covered their heads. The fourth day, as Cambyses, son of C[yrus], went to the Egidri-kalama-sumu, [on his] arrival, the one in charge of the Egidri of Nabû who [...] the scepter, [did not let him take (?)] the hand of Nabû because of his Elamite dress. [Sp]ears and sheaths [...]. For the cor[vée (?), the p]rince [...] Nabû to the Esagila [...] before Bēl and the son of B[ēl ...].[47]

(...)

[...] Babylon, the waters [...] darkened. [...] the gate was demolished. [...] the Eanna of EZENxKAS [...] he left the [*b*]*īt mummi.* [...] in Babylon [...] he planned [...] Babylon and...

(...)

The eighth year, in the month of Iyyar, the [...]th day , [...].

The tenth year, in the month of Iyy[ar, ...].

The eleventh year, in the month of Nisan, the [...]th day, [...].

(...)

28. CHRONICLE OF THE FOURTEENTH YEAR OF ARTAXERXES III (345/344)

Sources: tablet in the same format as an administrative text; only one side inscribed.
Bibliography: Grayson 1975a: no. 9.
Language: Babylonian.
Date: Late Babylonian period.
Place: Babylon.
Contents: the year 539 was not a historical break, even though Babylon lost all vestige of supremacy. The historian's work was pursued as before.

The document, dealing with only one year, was probably an excerpt.[48] It dealt with the fate of the prisoners of Sidon.

^{1}[mu] 14.kám ^{I}*Ú-ma-su šá* ^{I}*Ar-tak-šat-su* ^{2}[mu-*šú*] sa$_{4}$^{ú} ^{iti}Du$_{6}$ ^{lú}sar^{tú} *šá* lugal ^{3}[*ina*(?) ^{kur}]*Ṣi-da-nu* sar^{tú} *ana* E^{ki} *u* ^{uru}*Šu-šá-an* ^{4}[...i]ti.bi u$_{4}$ 13.kám ^{lú}érin *i-ṣu-tu* ^{5}[ta *l*]*ìb-bi-šú-nu ana* E^{ki} ku$_{4}$^{meš}-*ni* ^{6}u$_{4}$ 16.kám munus^{meš} gál^{meš} sar^{tú} *šá* ^{kur}*Ṣi-da-nu* ^{7}*šá* lugal *ana* E^{ki} *iš-puru* u$_{4}$.bi ^{8}*ana* é.gal lugal ku$_{4}$^{meš}

29. CHRONICLE CONCERNING DARIUS III (335–331) AND ALEXANDER (330–323)

Sources: upper right portion of a tablet.
Bibliography: Grayson 1975a: no. 8; van der Spek 2003 (not accessible to me), with new readings that could not be considered here.
Language: Babylonian.
Date: Seleucid period.
Place: Babylon.
Contents: a double allusion to the Ḫaneans, which usually designates populations of the north of Greece, including the Macedonians, and to a King Darius recalls an episode of the war that Alexander the Great conducted against Darius III. The names of Kidinnu, Nabû-bulli-..., or Merodach-baladan (?) are too common to give us any exact information. Perhaps it was also concerned with the celebration of the New Year's festival.

(Obv.) (...)

$^{3'}$[... *ina* ^{giš}g]u.za-*šú id*(?)-*di-ku-šú* ^{I}*Bi-š*[*ú*(?) *šá*(?) $^{4'}$*Ar-tak-šat*-su mu-*šú* mu-' x x ^{I}*A-lik-sa u* $^{\langle\text{lú}\rangle}$érin [^{meš}-*šú* ... $^{5'}$... ^{lú}érin]^{meš}-*šú i-ṣu-tu* ta ^{lú}érin$^{\text{me[š'}}$... $^{6'}$...] '... *id-duk* ^{lú}érin *Ḫa-né-e* ^{lú}érin^{meš}-*šú š*[*á* '... $^{7'}$... Ká].din-gir.ra^{ki} ^{I}*Da*(?)-*ri-ia*(?)-*a-muš* lugal lug[al^{meš}]

The fourteenth [year] (of the reign) of Umasu, who [was cal]led Artaxerxes (III), in the month of Tešrit, the prisoners whom the king had taken [at] Sidon [were led] to Babylon and Susa. [In the month of . . .], that month, the thirteenth day, a small number [of] them entered Babylon. The sixteenth day, the women remaining (among) the prisoners of Sidon whom the king had sent to Babylon entered that day into the palace of the king.

(. . .)

[. . .] they [dep]osed him. Bes[sus who] was called [Artaxerxes] . . . Alexa(nder) and [his] troops [. . . his] few [troop]s since the troops [. . .] he defeated. The army of the Hanaeans, his own troops that [. . . Ba]bylon, Darius, king of ki[ngs].

$^{8'}$[mu ....kám *ina* ^{iti}... u]$_4$ 15 ^{I}*Ki-di-nu ina* ^{giš}tukul gaz kin u$_4$ [....kám ...]

$^{9'}$[mu ...kám *ina* ^{iti}...] kur si ^{uru}*Ia-a-nu* uru *šá* ^{kur}*Gu-ti-i* [... $^{10'}$...]

$^{11'}$[... é].gal E^{ki} *ul-te-ṣu šá*(?) ... [... $^{12'}$...] *e*(?)*-pe-šú šá* ez[en *a-ki-ti*(?) ... $^{13'}$ ...] *ana e-pe-šú šá* ezen *šá* ^{d}En *ana Bár*(?)-[*sipa*^{ki}(?) ...]

$^{14'}$[...] ^{d}En-... *mu-ma-'-ir* [... $^{15'}$ ... $^{16'}$ ...]

$^{17'}$[...] ... ar ... [...]
(...)
(Rev.) (...)

$^{2'}$[...]... *ina* ^{giš}tukul g[az(?) ... $^{3'}$...] *ip-qid* iti.bi [... $^{4'}$...]-...*-pi-ta-nu* ^{lú}érin[^{meš} ... $^{5'}$... ^{i}$_7$]Buranun a^{meš}-*šú a-na* [...]

$^{6'}$[...]

$^{7'}$[...] nì.šu^{meš} *u mim-ma ana aš-ri* ^{d}[... $^{8'}$...] *na-din* [...]

$^{9'}$[... érin(?) maḫ^{tum} *ina* ka ^{Id}Nà-*bu-ul-li*-[... $^{10'}$... ^{Id}Amar.u]tu (?).eduru.sum-a' u$_4$ 10.kám ... [...]

$^{11'}$[... *ina*] ka lugal tar sag [...]

$^{12'}$[...] *ú-mar-ri ma-dak-ta-šú di-k*[*i-at* ...]

$^{13'}$[...] ... ka du ... [...]
(...)

30. CHRONICLE OF THE DIADOCHI (321/320–309/308)

Sources: two contiguous tablet fragments.
Bibliography: Grayson 1975a: no. 10; Funck 1971; Oelsner 1974; Geller 1990; Stolper 1990; van der Spek 1992: 245–49.
Language: Babylonian.
Date: Seleucid period.
Place: Babylon.
Contents: history of the Diadochi from the death of Perdiccas and the partition of Triparadeisos, when Babylonia fell to Seleucus, to the failure of the

---

[The . . . th year (?), in the month of . . .], the fifteenth day, he executed Kidinnu. The month of Elul, [the . . . th] day, [. . .].

[The . . . th year (?), in the month of . . .], Yanu, a town of Gutium, [. . .].

[. . .] they made go out of the [pa]lace of Babylon [. . .] the celebration of the festival [of the New Year (?), . . .] for the celebration of the feast of Bēl, toward Bor[sippa . . .].

[. . .] Bēl-. . . , the satrap of [. . .].

(. . .)

[. . . he execu]ted [. . .] he placed [. . .] in charge. The same month, [. . .] the troop[s . . .] the Euphrates, its waters to [. . .].

[. . .].

[. . .] the goods and everything given for the sacred space of the god [. . .].

[. . . a] large [army (?)] on orders of Nabû-bulli-. . . [. . . Meroda]ch-baladan. The tenth day [. . .].

[. . . on] the king's order [. . .].

[. . .] there w[as a massacre (?)] in its camp [. . .].

(. . .)

Babylonian policy of Antigonus; from the third year of the reign of Philip III to the ninth of the reign of Alexander IV.[49] It was especially concerned with the war that pitted Seleucus against Antigonus for control of Babylonia and the difficulties encountered by Seleucus eliminating his rival.

(Obv.) (…) [mu 4(?).kám ^{I}*Pi-líp-i-si* … 2'ding]ir^{meš}-*ma šá* … […] sipa(?) […] 3'*a-na* ^{lú}gal.unkin$^{\textit{ú-tu}}$ ^{kur}U[ri^{ki}(?) …] 4' ^{iti}Gu$_4$ lugal *ṣal-tu*$_4$ ki ^{lú}gal.unkin ^{kur}*Mi-ṣir* dù-*ma* ^{I}*P*[*i-ir-di-ka*(?)*-su* gaz] 5' ^{lú}érin lugal ^{lú}érin^{meš} lugal *ina* ^{giš}tukul gaz^{meš} ^{iti}Apin u$_4$ 10[+…kám ^{I}*Si-luk-ku*] 6' ^{lú}gal.unkin ^{kur}Uri^{ki} *ana* E^{ki} ku$_4$ mu.bi saḫar^{ḫá} [*šá É-sag-íl id-di-ku-ú*]

7'mu 5.kám ^{I}*Pi-líp-i-si* iti nu zu lugal ^{I}*An-ti-gu-n*[*u-su* …] 8'*a-na* ^{kur}*Ma-ak-du-nu i-bir-ma ana* egir-*šú* nu gur *ub*-[…] 9'egir *ḫe-pu-ú* izi kú-*šú* ^{I}*Si-lu-uk-ku* ^{lú}gal.unkin ^{k}[^{ur}Uri^{ki}…] 10'mu 6.kám ^{I}*Pi<-lip-i-si>* ^{iti}Kin ^{lú}gal.unkin ^{kur}Uri^{ki} ^{ú}AŠ kù.babbar *šá* kù.babba[r …] 11'*u* ^{lú}érin ^{kur}Uri^{ki} *gab-bi* gar$^{\textit{an}}$ kù.babbar *ina* bar *a-a*-RID-… […] 12'^{kur}Uri^{ki} ^{giš}ig^{meš} *šá* Du$_{10}$.ga.amaš-*šú* bàd *Bár*-[*sipa*^{ki} …] 13'mu.bi ^{I}*Pi-líp-i-si ina* ^{kur}*Ma-ak-ka-du-nu* […]

14'mu 7.kám ^{I}*Pi-il-i-si* ^{iti}Du$_6$ ^{lú}érin^{meš} lugal *šá ana Du*-[…] 15'… *tu*$_4$ é.gal E^{ki} *i-kim-šú-nu-ti-ma* ^{lú}[érin^{meš}(?) …] 16'$^{\text{[lú]}}$gal<.unkin> ^{kur}Uri^{ki} *ḫu-uṣ-ṣu šá* gi *ir*-[…] 17'$^{\text{[lú]}}$*Ḫa-ni-i šá* lugal *ana du-nun* en.nun *ina bi-rit* [… *ú-še-lu* 18'…] ^{I}*An-ti-gu-nu-su* ^{lú}gal.unkin [^{lú}gal.^{lú}érin^{meš} gar(?)]

19'[mu 8.kám ^{I}*Pi*]*-líp-i-si* ^{iti}Šu ^{I}*An-ti-g*[*u-nu-su* ^{lú}gal.^{lú}érin^{meš} … 20'…] *šá ina* é.gal lugal *šá* [… 21'…]^{meš} un^{meš} […]

(…)

(Rev.) 2'[bal.ri.^{d}Utu.è].a *u* bal.ri.^{d}Utu.šú [… 3'…] ku *iq-bi um-ma* mu 7.kám ^{I}*An-ti-g*[*u-nu-su ana* mu 6.kám ^{I}*A-lik-sa-an-dar* lugal a-*šú šá* 4' ^{I}kimin *u*] ^{I}*Si-lu-uk-ku* ^{lú}gal.^{lú}érin^{meš} šid *ina* ^{iti}[Sig$_4$/Šu(?) ki] 5' ^{I}*Si-lu-uk-ku* ^{lú}šà.tam *É-mes-lam it-ta*-[*bal-kit-šum-ma* …] 6'é.gal šu$_{\text{ii}}$-*su* nu kur iti.bi 40(?) gú.un kù.babbar *šá* […] 7' ^{iti}Ne ^{I}*Si-lu-uk-ku áš-šú ṣa-bat* é.gal E^{ki} […] 8'*iṣ-bu-ub-ma* $^{\text{i}}_{7}$Buranun nu *is-kir* … […šu$_{\text{ii}}$-*su* nu kur] 9'*ina lìb-bi* lu … ^{I}*Si-lu-uk-ku* ta E^{ki} *ana* […] 10'*šá ina muḫ-ḫi* $^{\text{i}}_{7}$Idigna …^{meš} è … pa ar […] 11' ^{iti}Apin *ṭab-ti ù* … […] 12' ^{lú}érin ^{kur}*Gu-ti-i ù* ^{lú}érin^{meš} […] 13'mu.bi saḫar^{ḫá} *šá É-s*[*ag*]*-í*[*l id-di-ku-ú*]

(. . .)

[The fourth[50] year (of the reign) of Philip (III), . . . the go]ds and [. . .] for the office of satrap of Ak[kad (?) . . .]. In the month of Iyyar, the king joined battle with the satrap of Miṣir, but Pe[rdiccas was killed]; the royal army executed royal troops. In the month of Araḫsamnu, the ten [+. . . th (?)] day, [Seleucus], the satrap of Akkad, entered Babylon. The same year, the rubble [of Esagila was cleared away].

The fifth year (of the reign) of Philip, in an unknown month, the king [. . .] Antigo[nus. Antipater] went into Macedonia and did not return. [. . .]. Once broken down, fire consumed it. Seleucus, the satrap of Ak[kad . . .].

The sixth year (of the reign of Phi<lip>, in the month of Elul, the satrap of Akkad [. . .] the AŠ plant, silver coming from the sil[ver . . .], and he put the army in position throughout entire Akkad. Silver in half-shekel (?) pieces [. . .] Akkad, the gates of Ṭāb-supuršu, the wall of Borsi[ppa . . .]. The same year, Philip [. . .] into Macedonia.

The seventh year (of the reign) of Philip, in the month of Tešrit, the king's troops who [. . .] against Du[. . .]. From them, he (= Antigonus) took the palace of Babylon by force and the tr[oops (?) . . .]. The sat<rap> of Akkad [. . .] of the reed huts. The Ḫaneans whom the king [had installed] to reinforce the guard between [. . .]; Antigonus, the satrap [was promoted (?) strategos of the royal forces].[51]

[The eighth year (of the reign) of Phi]lip, in the month of Dumuzi, Antig[onus, strategos of the royal forces, . . .] who [. . .] in the king's palace [. . .] the [. . .] of the people [. . .].

(. . .)

[. . . in the Eas]t and in the West [. . .], called the seventh year (of the reign) of Antig[onus, but] which is counted (as) the sixth year (of the reign) of Alexander (IV), the king, son of *ditto* (= Alexander (III), and] Seleucus, strategos of the royal forces, in the month of [Siwan/Dumuzi (?)], the administrator of the Emeslam, rev[olted with] Seleucus [and . . .]. He did not take possession of the palace. The same month, forty (?) talents of silver, which [. . .]. In the month of Ab, in order to take the palace of Babylon, Seleucus [. . .] carried out a movement to turn around (?) but did not set up a barrage over the Euphrates; [. . . he could not take possession of . . .]. In [. . .] Seleucus, from Babylon to [. . .] that is on the Tigris [. . .] left [. . .]. In the

---

$^{14'}$mu 7.kám ^{I}*A-lik-sa-an-dar* lugal a-*šú šá* ^{I}kimin *u* ^{I}[*Si-lu-uk-ku* lúgal.^{lú}érin^{meš}] $^{15'}$ ^{I}*An-ti-gu-nu-su ṣal-tu*$_4$ ki ^{lú}érin^{meš} ^{I}*Si*-[*lu-uk-ku* dù ... $^{16'}$ta] ^{iti}Ne en ^{iti}Ab [... $^{17'}$*ṣal*]-*tu*$_4$ ki *a-ḫa-a-m*[*eš* dù^{meš} ... $^{18'}$... ^{I}*An-t*]*i-gu-nu-su* bala-*ma* [... $^{19'}$...] *bi-rit É-sag-íl u É*-[... $^{20'}$... ^{I}*An-t*]*i-gu-nu-su it-ti* ^{lú}érin maḫ^{t}[$^{u}{}_4$ ... $^{21'}$... *i*]*t-ti-šú* ku$_4{}^{ub}$ ta u$_4$ 8.kám *šá* ^{iti}Bár(?) [en u$_4$ ...kám *šá* ^{iti}...] $^{22'}$... si É *Ḫa-re-e* šu$_{\text{ii}}$-*su* nu kur ^{iti}Zíz u$_4$ [...kám ...] $^{23'}$*bi-kit u si-ip-du ina* kur gar^{an} ^{d}im.gàl.lu [...] $^{24'}$ta E^{ki} è sar^{ut} uru *u* edin sar nì.šu [...] $^{25'}$u$_4$ 2.kám *ana* Gu.du$_8$.a^{ki} e$_{11}$-*ma* sar^{ut} [uru *u* edin sar] $^{26'}$un^{meš} bala.ki izi *ana* é nì.ga *šá* ^{d}U.gur [šub (.?.)] $^{27'}$*A-ri-is-ki-la-mu a-na* ^{lú}gal.unkin$^{\text{ú-tu}}$ [^{kur}Uri^{ki} gar(?) $^{28'}$*ina li*]-*be* E^{ki} ki-*šú ip-qid* mu.bi še 0,0.1.0 zú.lu[m.ma ... $^{29'}$...] ti meš mu.bi é^{meš} maḫ^{meš} *ina* ki$^{ti}{}_3$ [... $^{30'}$ta(?)] E^{ki} *ana ki-di* è^{meš} saḫar^{ḫá} *šá É*-[*sag-íl id-di-ku-ú*]

$^{31'}$[mu 8.ká]m ^{I}*A-lik-sa-an-dar* lugal a-*šú šá* kimin *u* ^{I}*Si-lu*-[*uk-ku* ^{lú}gal.^{lú}érin^{meš} $^{32'}$ ^{lú}gal.unkin ^{kur}U]ri^{ki} *ana Bára-sipa*^{ki} gin-*ma* še bar [... $^{33'}$...] *šá li-be Bára-sipa*^{ki} *u qí-rib* [... $^{34'}$...] *É-sag-gíl ip-te-qid* u$_4$ 12 13 1[4(?)... $^{35'}$...] nigin^{ru} ^{lú}dumu E^{ki} a an [... $^{36'}$...] ...^{meš} *bi-kit u sip-du ina* kur gar[^{an} ... $^{37'}$...]-*ma* sar^{ut} uru *u* edin sar [... $^{38'}$...] ^{lú}dumu E^{ki} ḫu [... $^{39'}$...] la *šá ina* mu 1.kám ^{I}*A*-[*lik-sa-an-dar* ... $^{40'}$...] lugal *ana* ^{lú}dumu [E^{ki}(?) ... $^{41'}$mu 9.kám ^{I}*A-lik-sa-an-dar* lugal a-*šú šá* kimin *u* ^{I}*Si-lu-uk-ku* ^{lú}gal.^{lú}érin^{meš} ^{I}*A-r*]*i-is-ki-la-mu*(!) *u* ^{lú}érin^{meš} ^{I}*An-ti-gu-nu-su a-n*[*a* ... $^{42'}$...] ^{iti}Ne u$_4$ 25/26(?).[kám ...] ku *ṣal-tu*$_4$ *ina* igi ^{lú}érin^{meš} ^{I}*Si-lu-uk-ku* [dù^{meš} ...]

31. MENTIONS OF ARSES (337–336) AND OF ALEXANDER THE GREAT (330–323)

Sources: fragment of a tablet.
Bibliography: Sachs 1977: 144–47.
Language: Babylonian.
Date: Seleucid period.
Place: Babylon (?).
Contents: allusion to the decision of Alexander the Great to restore the Esagila. It is known from various sources that some work was undertaken there in 330, 324, 322, 320, 309, 308, 305–292, 273.

month of Araḫsamnu, an alliance [. . .]. The army of Gutium and the troops [. . .]. The same year, the rubble of Esagi[la was cleared away].

The seventh year (of the reign) of Alexander, the king, son of *ditto*, [and Seleucus, strategos of the royal forces], Antigonus [joined] battle with the troops of Se[leucus. From the] month of Ab to the month of Ṭebeth [. . . plunged] into battle against each other [. . .]. Antigonus crossed [. . .] and [. . .], entered the Esagila and the E[. . . Ant]igonus and (his) large army [. . .] entered with him. From the eighth day of the month of Nisan (?) [to the . . . th day of the month of . . .], he could not take possession of the [. . .] of the Bīt-Ḫarê. In the month of Šebat, the [. . .th] day, [. . .] there was weeping and mourning in the country. The south wind [. . .]. He came out of Babylon, pillaged town and field. Goods [. . .]. The second day, he reached Cutha and plun[dered town and field]. The inhabitants escaped. He [set] fire to Nergal's storehouse. [He named A]rchesilas for the office of satrap [of Akkad] and put him in charge of Babylon. The same year, barley and a *sûtu* of dates were taken [illegally]. The same year, many temples [. . .] on the ground. They went out [of] Babylon to the country. The rubble of E[sagila was cleared away].

[The eigh]th [year] (of the reign) of Alexander, the king, son of *ditto*, and Sele[ucus, strategos of the royal forces, the satrap (?) of Ak]kad went to Borsippa and the barley [. . .] of Borsippa and in [. . .] he took the Esagila in charge. The twelfth, thirteenth, (and) fourteenth days, they regrouped [. . .]. The inhabitants of Babylon [. . .] there was weeping and mourning in the country [. . .], and he plundered town and field. [. . .] the inhabitant of Babylon [. . .] who, in the first year (of the reign) of A[lexander (IV?) . . .] the king [. . .] to the inhabitant [of Babylon . . .].

[The ninth year (of the reign) of Alexander, the king, son of *ditto*, and Seleucus, strategos of the royal forces, Ar]chesilas and the troops of Antigonus [marched] on [. . .]. In the month of Ab, the twenty-fifth/twenty-sixth (?) day, [they joined] battle with the troops of Seleucus [. . .].

(. . .) $^{2'}$[. . .] *ina* izi [šub(?) . . . $^{3'}$. . .]-*ú u* ^{lú}érin^{meš} [. . . $^{4'}$. . .] *šá* šu$_{ii}$-*šú* saḫar^{ḫá} ta [*É-sag-gil* $^{5'}$. . .] *id-de-ku-ú u*$_{4}$*-mu* [*šá-a-šú*(?) . . . $^{6'}$mu . . .].kám ^{I}*Ár-šú* a *šá* ^{I}*Ú-me-šu šá* ^{I}*Ár-tak-šat-s*[*u* gar. . . $^{7'}$. . .] ku$_{4}$^{ú} *ù* é ^{d}*A-nu-ni-tu*$_{4}$ *lìb-bi* ^{ur}[^{u}. . . $^{8'}$ ^{I}*A-lik-sa-an*]-*dar-ri-is* lugal gal^{u} dù$^{u'}$ *at-tu-nu* dumu^{meš} E[^{ki} . . . $^{9'}$. . .^{m}]^{eš} *u* é^{meš} *ana* nì.ga *É-sag-gil u* dumu^{meš} E^{ki} gur[. . . $^{10'}$ . . .] *É-sag-gil* dù$^{uš-u'}$ *ú-qu* [. . . $^{11'}$. . . er]ín^{meš} *i-ṣu-tu* [. . .] (. . .)

32. CHRONICLE FROM THE TIME OF ANTIOCHUS I, CROWN PRINCE (294/293–281/280)

Sources: fragments of a large tablet.
Bibliography: Grayson 1975a: no. 11; unpublished fragments in the British Museum.
Language: Babylonian.
Date: Seleucid period.
Place: Babylon.
Contents: Antiochus was designated royal co-regent in 294 or 293, so the events reported were after this date. There is allusion to the policy of the Seleucids vis-à-vis Babylonian cults and the role of the crown prince.[52]

(Obv.) ^{1}[mu . . .kám ^{iti}. . .] iti.bi ^{I}*A*[*n-ti-'-uk-su* dumu lugal . . .] ^{2}*ina* ^{uru}Ku/Ma ši an ta ^{uru}[. . .] ^{3} ^{iti}Šu iti.bi [. . . ^{4}. . . ^{5}. . .] ku$_{4}$^{ut} mu.bi saḫar^{ḫá} *šá É-sag-gí*[*l id-di-ku-ú*]

---

^{6}[mu . . .kám ^{iti}. . .] iti.bi u$_{4}$ 20.kám ^{I}*An-ti-'-uk-su* dumu lugal [. . . ^{7}u$_{4}$] 7[+. . .(?)].kám *a-na bar*(?)*-tu*$_{4}$ *ú-ma*(?)*-mu ana* bal.ri.^{d}Ut[u.è/šú.a ^{8}. . . u$_{4}$ . . .k]ám dumu lugal *šá* é.uš^{tu}$_{4}$ *ina qí-bi šá* 1^{en} ^{lú}dumu [E^{ki}(?) . . . ^{9}. . .] *gi-nu-ú šá* 30 *É-giš-nu*$_{x}$*-gal-u* 30 en [. . . ^{10} ^{I}*An-ti-'-uk-s*]*u* dumu lugal *ina* é ^{d}30 *É-giš-nu*$_{x}$*-gal-u* [. . .] ^{11}lú [. . .] *uš-kin-nu* dumu lugal 1^{en} udu.nitá *ana nin-*[*da-be-e* . . .] ^{12}. . .[. . .] *É-giš-nu*$_{x}$*-gal-u* é ^{d}30 en [. . . ^{13}. . .] . . . *ina* E^{ki} *ana* ^{uru}*É-gu-ra-'* è ^{iti}[. . . iti.bi u$_{4}$ . . .kám ^{I}*An-ti-'-uk-su* dumu lugal] ^{14}*šá* [é].uš^{tu}$_{4}$ $^{[u]ru}$*Si-l*[*u*]*-ku-a* ^{lú}érin^{meš}*-šú* [. . . ^{15}. . .] mud lugal [. . .] ku . . . [. . . ^{16}. . .] guškin [. . .]

(. . .)

(Rev.) $^{1'}$[^{iti}. . . iti.bi] u$_{4}$ 18.kám a^{meš} *ana lìb-b*[*i* . . .] $^{2'}$u$_{4}$ 28 ^{I}[. . .]-uṭ-ṭu-da-a ^{lú}*E-man-na-a*[(*-a*). . .] $^{3'}$ ^{iti}Zíz iti.bi [u$_{4}$ . . .+]8 ^{I}*An-ti-'-uk-su* dumu lugal [*šá* é uš^{tu4}] $^{4'}$. . . [. . .] *ana* ^{uru}*É-gu-r*[*a-'* . . . $^{5'}$*ina* . . . [. . . $^{6'}$. . .] ^{I}*An-ti-'-uk-su* dumu l[ugal *šá* é.uš^{tu}$_{4}$. . . $^{7'}$. . .]-*da-na-a-a-ku-su šá ina* E^{ki} [. . . $^{8'}$. . .] tu . . . ta E^{ki} [. . .]

(. . .)

[. . . he set (?)] fire [. . .] and the troops [. . .] of his hands. The rubble o[f Esagila] was cleared away. [The same] day [. . .. The . . .]th [year of] Arses, son of Umašu who [was called] Artaxerxe[s (III), and . . .] entered [. . .] and the temple of Annunītu at [. . .. " . . . that Alexan]der, the great king, built, you, Babylonians, [. . .]." The [. . .] and the temples again became the possession of the Esagila and the Babylonians. [. . .] built [. . .] of the Esagila [. . .]. The army [. . .] of the few [troops . . .].

(. . .)

[The . . . th year, in the month of . . .], that very month, A[ntiochus, the prince, . . .] into . . . from [. . .]. In the month of Dumuzi, that very month, [. . .]. The same year, the debris of the Esagi[la was carried away].

[The . . . th year, in the month of . . .], that very month, the twentieth day, Antiochus, the prince, [. . .]. On the evening (?) [of the] seventh [day, . . .] the cattle (?) [. . .] toward the Ea[st]/We[st] (?). [The . . . th [day], the prince, the crown prince, on the advice of an inhabitant of [Babylon (?), . . . , instituted (?)] regular offerings for Sîn of the Egišnugal,[53] Sîn, the lord [. . .. Antioch]us, the prince, in the temple of Sîn in the Egišnugal [. . .] the [. . .] prostrated themselves. The prince [presented] a sheep as an of[fering . . .] the Egišnugal, the temple of Sîn, the lord [. . .]. He went out of Babylon (?) in the direction of Bīt-Gūrā. In the month of [. . . , that very month, the . . . th day, Antiochus, the prince], the crown prince, [. . .] his troops at Seleucia [. . .]. The king [. . .]. Gold [. . .].

(. . .)

[In the month of . . . , that very month], the eighteenth day, the waters toward [. . .]. The twenty-eighth day, [. . .]uṭṭuda, the Greek, [. . .]. In the month of Šebat, that very month, [the . . . +] eigh[th day], Antiochus, the prince, [the crown prince, . . .] toward Bīt-Gūr[ā . . .]. Antiochus, the prin[ce,

9'... qar *ú-še-šib ú-*[...] 10'*ri-ik-su dan-nu ir-ki-*[...] 11'[I*An-ti*]-*'-uk-su* dumu lugal šá é.[uš*tu*$_4$ ...] a

---

12'[mu ...kám i]tiApin iti.bi u$_4$ 20.[kám ...] bi 10 udu.nitámeš [... 13'...] *ana* lúdumu Eki [...] bi 10 udu.nitá *ana* [...] kám [... 14'...]-*' ina lìb-*[*i* ... 15'...] ... [...]

16'lúun[meš iti...] iti.bi [...] 17'*ina* u$_4$ 18.kám *šá* ... [...] *šú* ... [...] 18' itiZíz iti.bi *u$_4$-mu* nu zu [...] ... [...] 19'*ana* uru*Si-lu-uk-a-a i-*[...]

33. CHRONICLE OF SELEUCUS I (311 OR 305–281/280)

Sources: two small unconnected fragments from a large tablet.
Bibliography: Grayson 1975a: no. 12.
Language: Babylonian.
Date: Seleucid period.
Place: Babylon.
Contents: history of the years 283/282 to 281/280, or the end of the reign of Seleucus I. He having become king in 305, Babylonian sources attribute to Seleucus a reign of twenty-five years. Other later sources credit him with a reign of thirty-three years, probably deciding that he had been on the throne of Babylon since 311, on the day after his conquest of the city.

The campaign alluded to here was the last act of his reign. Departing from Sardis, Seleucus defeated Lysimachus at Corupedion and continued his military campaign in Europe, where he must have faced the revolt of his army. His assassination was alluded to in the Hellenistic Royal Chronicle (no 4).

The fragment perhaps ended with the return of Antiochus from the upper satrapies and his accession.

(Obv.) (...) [mu 29(?).kám ...] ... 2'*ina ma-la-ku šá É-sag-*[*íl*...]

3'[m]u 30.kám itiSig it[i.bi I*Si-lu-ku* lugal lúérinmeš-*šú* 4'i]*d-ke-e-ma ana* kur[... gin] 5' [l]ú*Ia-a-ma-na-a-a* [...] 6'è-*ma* ... [...] 7' lúgar ta [...] 8'*É-sag-*[*íl* ...] (...)

(Rev.) 1'mu 3[1.k]ám it[i ... iti.bi I*Si-lu-ku* lugal lúérin[meš]-*šú* ta kur*Sa-pa*[*r-du*] 2'*id-ke-e-ma* a.a[b.ba ...] ki-*šú ú-še-bi*[*r-ma*] 3'*ana* kur*Ma-ak-ka-du-nu* kur-*šú* [...]meš ta lúérinmeš [...] 4'*si-ḫi ana muḫ-ḫi-šú is-ḫu-u* [... iti]Sig iti.bi ta u$_4$ [...kám 5'e]n u$_4$ 11.kám lúérinmeš kur[...]-gim šu/ku è*i-*[*ma* 6'...] ... lú*Ia-a-ma-*[*na-a-a* i]$_7$Buranun dù [(?) 7'k]lúḫá *ina lìb-bi* kú'[... *l*]*ìb-bi* èmeš-*ni* 8' [i]tiŠu(?) iti.bi u$_4$ 12(?).[kám ...] *šá* kur*Ba-aḫ-tar* 9'[...] lugal

the crown prince, . . . d]aniachos, who in Babylon [. . .] he made remain [. . .] strong bond [. . . Anti]ochus, the prince, the crown prince, [. . .].

[The . . . th year, in the m]onth of Araḫsamnu, that very month, the twentie[th] day, [. . .], ten sheep [. . .] for the Babylonian [. . .] ten sheep for [. . .] in [. . . In the month of . . .], that very month, [. . .].

The inhabitants, [in the month of . . .], that very month, [. . .]. The eighteenth day of [. . .]. In the month of Šebat, that very month, on an unknown day, [. . .] he [*went* (?)] to Seleucia.

[The twenty-ninth (?) year, . . .] in the procession from the Esagila [. . .].

The thirtieth ye[ar], in the month of Siwan, [that] very month, [Seleucus (I), the king], mustered [his troops] and [marched (?)] on [. . .]. The Greeks [. . .]. He went out and [. . .]. The town official,[54] [. . .] from [. . .]. The Esag[ila . . .].

(. . .)

The thirty-[fir]st year, in the month of [. . . , that very month, Seleucus, the king], mustered his [army] from Sar[dis]; he had it cross the sea [. . .] with him, and in Macedonia, in his own country, the [. . .] of the troops [. . .] rebelled against him. In the month of Siwan, that very month, from the [. . .th] to the eleventh day, the troops of [. . .]. He left and [. . .] the Greeks constructed [. . .] the Euphrates. There was feasting [. . .] they left there. [In

ú [... i]ti.bi u_4 14(?).kám (...)

34. FROM ANTIOCHUS I (281–260) TO SELEUCUS II (245–226)

Sources: small fragment of a tablet.
Bibliography: Grayson 1975a: no. 13.
Language: Babylonian.
Date: Seleucid period.
Place: Babylon.
Contents: undoubtedly allusions to the assassination of Seleucus, crown prince, in 266/265,[55] and to the accession of Seleucus II in 245/244. The name of Minisu (perhaps Menneas, Menes, Minnis, or Minnas[56]), unfortunately, is not otherwise known.

(Obv.) (...) [mu 45(?).kám ... $^{2'}$...] *maš-šú-*$\textit{tu}_4$ [... $^{3'}$...] *ina tam-*$\textit{tu}_4$ uṣ tu_4 [... $^{4'}$...] ... *šá* kur *šá ina* ^{uru}... [... $^{5'}$...] ^{I}*Si-lu-ku* ^{lú}*pa-ḫat* [E^{ki}(?) $^{6'}$... $^{\text{i}_7}$Idig]na *u* i_7 lugal *mi-ṣir-šú* ki $^{7'}$[...]-*i* ki-*šú iš-kun-ma* ^{I}*Mi-ni-su* $^{8'}$[...]^{meš}-šú ^{I}*An-ti-'-uk<-su>* a *šá* [^{I}*An-ti-'-uk-su* lugal $^{9'\text{I}}$*Si-lu*]-*ku* gaz ^{lú}un^{meš} maḫ^{meš} $^{10'}$[... *ina É-s*]*ag-gíl ana* ^{lú}gala$^{\textit{ta}}$ $^{11'}$[...]-*a-a-am* záḫ-*ma* $^{12'}$[...] ^{iti}Kin iti.bi (...) (Rev.) (...) $^{2'}$[...] ki sar' $^{3'}$[...] dan ra bi *ina* ki-*šú* $^{4'}$[...] *ana lìb-bi É-sag-gíl* gar'

$^{5'}$[mu 66.kám ^{iti}Ne iti.bi] *al-te-me um-ma* ^{I}*Si-lu-ku* a *šá* $^{6'}$[^{I}*An-ti-'-uk-su*] ... a gu ... *u ina* ^{giš}gu.za lug[al]$^{\textit{ú}}$-[$^{\textit{ti}}$ dúr$^{\textit{a}}$]$^{\textit{b}}$

$^{7'}$mu 67(?).kám ^{I}*Si-lu-ku* l]ugal a *šá* ^{I}*An-ti-'-uk-su* [...] gar$^{\textit{at}}$
$^{8'}$[...^{I}*Si-lu-k*]*u* a *šá* ^{I}*Si-lu-ku* [lugal(?) ... $^{9'}$...] ab ^{iti}Ab (...)

35. CHRONICLE OF SELEUCUS III (225/224–223/222)

Sources: tablet fragment.
Bibliography: Grayson 1975a: no. 13b.
Language: Babylonian.
Date: Seleucid peiod.
Place: Babylon.
Contents: memorandum of the New Year's festival in Babylon, more precisely the food offerings presented to the gods the eighth day of the

the m]onth of Dumuzi (?), that very month, the twelf(?)[th] day, [. . .] from Bactria [. . .] the king [. . . T]he same month, the fourteen(?)th day, [. . .].

(. . .)

(. . .)

[The forty-fifth (?) year, . . .] the command (?) [. . .] the sea [. . .] of the country that, in the city of [. . .] Seleucus, the governor [of Babylon (?)[57] . . . the Ti]gris and the Royal Canal, its boundary [. . .] made [a treaty (?)] with him and Minisu [. . .] its [. . .]. Antiochus, son of [Antiochus (I?), the king], put [Seleu]cus (?) to death. Many people [. . . in the Es]agila, for the office of lamenter [. . .] escaped and [. . .] In the month of Elul, that very month, [. . .].

(. . .)

[. . .] they plundered [. . .] in its place [. . .] they placed in the Esagila.

[The sixty-sixth year, in the month of Ab, that very month], I heard:[58] "Seleucus (II?), son of [Antiochus (II?)], . . . and [as]cends the ro[ya]l throne."

[The sixty-seventh (?) year, Seleucus (II?), the k]ing, son of Antiochus (II?), [. . .] is placed [. . .] [Seleu]cus, son of Seleu[cus (II), the king (?), . . .]. In the month of Ṭebeth [. . .].

(. . .)

celebration. Besides a few peculiar notes on the connections the Seleucid king maintained with the Babylonian authorities, the document also pointed out that there was a special type of royal offering (in the year 88 of the Seleucid era, Seleucus still being without children, it therefore alludes to an earlier practice). This should not be confused with a royal cult unknown elsewhere.[59]

The end of the fragment perhaps concerned the arrival of Antiochus, the future Antiochus III, into Babylon from Syria.

(...) $^{2'}$[...] ...-*di-šú*

$^{3'}$[m]u 88.kám ^{I}*Si-lu-ku* lugal ^{iti}Bar iti.bi u$_4$ 8.kám 1^{en} dumu E^{ki} ^{lú}šà.tam *É-sag-gíl* $^{4'}$[...] *šá É-sag-gíl ina* ka lugal *lìb-bu-ú* ^{kuš}*ši-piš-tu*$_4$ *šá* lugal *šá ina* igi-*ma iš-šá-a* $^{5'}$[... g]ín kù.babbar ta é lugal ta é *ram-ni-šú* 11 gu$_4^{\text{ḫá}}$ *ma-ru-tu* 1 me u$_8$ $^{6'}$[*m*]*a-ru-tu* 11 ^{mušen}uz.tur *ma-ru-tu a-na* nidba *ina lìb-bi É-sag-gíl* $^{7'}$*a-na* ^{d}En *u* ^{d}Gašan^{ia} *u* dingir^{meš} gal^{meš} *ù a-na dul-lu šá* ^{I}*Si*-[*lu*]-*ku* lugal $^{8'}$*u* a^{meš}-*šú il-ta-kan* ḫa.la^{meš} *šá* gu$_4^{\text{meš}}$ *u* siskur^{meš} mu$^{a\text{-}t\grave{\imath}}$ *a*-[*na*] $^{9'}$ ^{lú}gala^{meš} *ù* ^{lú}šà.tam *iq-bi a-na* ^{lú}di.ku$_5^{\text{meš}}$ *šá* lugal *u* dumu dù^{i} [... $^{10'}$...] ... -*a-am ul-te-bil* $^{11'}$[^{iti}... iti].bi u$_4$ 14.kám ^{I}lagab mu-*šú* ^{lú}šeš *šá* ^{I}*Si-lu-ku* lugal ta [... $^{12'}$...] ... *a-di muḫ-ḫi* $^{\text{i}}{}_7$*Ma-rat-ta ma-dak-tu*$_4$ lugal ta *e-bir* I$_7$ $^{13'}$[...] lugal$^{\acute{u}\text{-}tu}$ *šá ana muḫ-ḫi* $^{\text{i}}{}_7$Idigna *u* i$_7$ lugal $^{14'}$[... ^{lú}gal].unkin kur *u* ^{lú}un^{meš} kur *a-na* igi-*šú* è$^{\acute{u}}$ *ni-gu-tú* $^{15'}$[*il-tak-nu*]

(...)

36. CHRONICLE FROM THE SELEUCID PERIOD

Sources: contiguous fragments from a large tablet.
Bibliography: Grayson 1975a: no. 13a; unpublished fragments in the British Museum.
Language: Babylonian.
Date: Seleucid period.
Place: Babylon.
Contents: these fragments are difficult to understand. Perhaps they concerned the death of Antiochus III in 187/186, year 125 of the Seleucid era, on the road to Bactria (Hellenistic Royal Chronicle no. 4 specified that he was killed in Elam). Unfortunately, the name of Mi[...], which might contribute to the understanding of the passage, remains unknown. If it was

(. . .)
[. . .] his [. . .].

The eighty-eighth year, Seleucus (III), the king. In the month of Nisan, that very month, the eighth day, a resident of Babylon, the administrator of the Esagila, [on the subject (?)] of the Esagila, on the order of the king (and) according to (the terms of the) royal parchment that the latter had previously sent, set up as offerings in the Esagila, for Bēl and Bēltiya and for the ritual of Seleucus, the king, and his children: [. . . sh]ekels of silver coming from the house of the king and his own house, eleven fat oxen, a hundred fat sheep, eleven fat ducks. He selected a portion of those oxen and sacrifices reserved for lamenters and the administrator. To the royal judges[60] and the nobles he sent [. . . The month of . . .], that [very month], the fourteenth day, "So-and-so is his name,"[61] brother of Seleucus, the king, from [. . .] to the Salt Sea, the king's camp, from beyond the Euphrates [. . .] kingship that [. . .] over the Tigris and the Royal Canal [. . . The sa]trap of the country and the people of the country went out to meet him [playing] music.

(. . .)

from the reign of Antiochus III, it might be Menippos or Minnion, two of that king's negotiators. But other names could be restored, such as Megasthenes, Menen, or Menneon.[62]

(Obv.) (...) $^{3'}$[...]^{meš} *šá É-sag-gíl* [... $^{4'}$...] ^{lú}gal.unkin ^{kur}Uri^{ki} [... $^{5'}$...] lú *ri-du-tu šá* [... $^{6'}$...] *šá É-zi-da ina* [... $^{7'}$...] ... sal in du *šá* ^{lú}*E*(?)-[*man-na*]-*a-a* ^{I}*Mi*-[... $^{8'}$...]^{meš} Uri^{ki} *ku-šá-tu*$_4$ ^{lú}dumu^{meš} E^{ki} [... $^{9'}$...]^{meš} *e-peš* nid[ba] si bu [... $^{10'}$...] ... na [...] u$_4$ 20.kám [... $^{11'}$...]^{meš} *ina* E^{ki} *ana* 1^{en} ^{lú}*Ḫa-ni-i* [... $^{12'}$...]-*si* lugal *šá ina e-bir* i$_7$ sa [... $^{13'}$...] *ana* ^{kur}*Ba-aḫ-tar u* ^{kur}*In*-[... $^{14'}$...] gaz *u i*-[...] (...)

(Rev.) $^{2'}$[...] mu$^{a\text{-}tì}$ [... $^{3'}$... n]idba *šá* [... $^{4'}$...] lugal ^{lú}érin[^{meš} ... $^{5'}$...]-*a* ^{lú}*E-man-na-a-a* ... [... $^{6'}$...] egir lugal *ana ma-dak-tu*$_4$ *ul-t*[*e-rib* ... $^{7'}$...]^{meš} *iš-ru-ut* 23 guškin [... $^{8'}$...]$^{\text{meš}\ ni}$ *ina* ki-*šú ina* ^{giš}kiri$_6$ ^{šim}li [... $^{9'}$...] ti^{qí} [... $^{10'}$...] u$_4$ ^{lú}érin^{meš}-*šú šá* ^{I}*An-ti-'*-[*uk-su* lugal ... $^{11'}$...] ... ^{lú}érin^{meš}-*šú* [... $^{12'}$...]-*ú-kin-nu-' ina* ^{giš}tukul g[az ...]

(...)

37. JUDICIAL CHRONICLE

Sources: fragment of a tablet.
Bibliography: Joannès 2000: 193–211.
Language: Babylonian.
Date: Seleucid period.
Place: Babylon.
Contents: in a chronographic style and inspired by the diaries, a presentation of judicial proceedings. The chronological order is not yet certain. The document seems to be a judicial chronicle written in the manner of the political ones.

^{1}mu.34.kam ^{I}*An u* ^{I}*Se* lugal^{meš} ^{iti}apin [iti.bi u$_4$.x.kam ...] ^{2}lú E$^{\text{ki.meš}}$ munus E$^{\text{ki.meš}}$ *ù* ^{lú}erín^{meš} [... ^{lú}*šar-ra-qu*] ^{3}*šá ina sar-tú ana* ^{giš}kiri$_6$ ^{šim}li ku$_4$^{ú} [...] ^{4} ^{d}gašan^{ia} ^{d}inanna tin.tir^{ki} *ù* dingir^{me}[^{š} ...] ^{5}*iš-šu-ú ina* izi *qa-lu-ú*

---

^{6}mu.90.kam ^{iti}kin iti.bi u$_4$.17.[kam ...] 7*ù* 1^{en} lú šeš-*šú ana muḫ-ḫi* x [... *šá*] ^{8}dù$^{'u}$ *ina a-šá-bi šá* ^{Id}U.gur.sùh.š[ur ^{lú}šà.tam É.sag.gíl] ^{9}lú E$^{\text{ki.meš}}$ lú unkin *šá* É.sag.gíl *ù* [...]^{10}*šá* di.ku$_5$^{meš} *šá* é.dingir^{meš} *ina ku-tal* k[á ...] ^{11}*ina* ^{giš}*sim-mil-tu*$_4$ *šá maš-a-a-al-tu*$_4$ š[*u-ú-lu-'u-ma šá-a-li-'u*] ^{12}*uk-tin-nu-ú u*$_4$-*mu* bi *ina* izi *qa-lu-ú*

(. . .)

The [. . .] of the Esagila [. . .] the satrap of Akkad [. . .]. The continuation of [. . .] from the Ezida into [. . .] of the Greek (?), Mi[. . .]. The [. . .] of Akkad [. . .] the inhabitants of Babylon [. . .] the [. . .] for the presentation of the offer[ings . . .]. The twentieth day, the [. . .] who, in Babylon, for the Ḫanean [. . .] the king who [. . .] beyond the Euphrates [. . .] toward Bactria and In[. . .] was killed (?) and [. . .].

(. . .)

[. . .] these [. . . off]erings of [. . .] the king, the troop[s . . .]a, the Greek, [. . .] the king made [enter] into the camp, [. . .], he tore the [. . .]. Twenty-three [. . .] of gold [. . .] in its place, in the garden of junipers [. . .] he took [. . .] day (?), the troops of Anti[ochus, the king, . . .] his troops [. . .] he executed [. . .]-ukīn (?) [. . .].

(. . .)

The thirty-fourth year, Antiochus (I) and Seleucus (II), the kings. In the month of Araḫsamnu, that very month, [the . . . day, . . .], men from Babylon and women from Babylon and soldiers [. . . thieves] who had entered the juniper garden and stolen [. . .] of the goddesses Bēltiya, Ištar of Babylon and the gods [. . .] were burned to death.

The ninetieth year. In the month of Elul, that very month, the seventeenth day, in the presence of Nergal-(ina)-têši-ēṭir, the administrator of the Esagila, Babylonians, members of the assembly of the Esagila and [. . .], judges of sanctuaries, [. . . (*So-and-so*)] and one of his brothers, concerning [a theft] they had committed, were put on a rack standing back of the door

---

^{13}mu.90.kam ^{iti}gu$_4$ iti.bi ^{lú}šà.tam É.[sag.gíl ...] ^{14}lú E$^{\text{ki.meš}}$ ^{lú}unkin *šá* É.sag.gíl *áš-šú* [... *šá*] ^{15}*ana* é *bu-še-e* [*a*]-*šar* dingir^{meš} gal^{meš} [...] ^{16}ku$_4$$^{\text{'}u}$ kù.babbar [kù.g]i na$_4$ *ga-la-la-nu* [...] ^{17}[*š*]*á* 2 x-*ti*-[*t*]*ú* maḫ^{meš} *ina lìb-bi* [...] ^{18}iti.bi *ina* [...] ^{19}*šá ina lìb-bi* x [...] ^{20}*ṣab-tu*-['*u*] *ina* [é *ṣib-te-e-ti šá* ...] ^{21}dab$_5$ iti.bi u$_4$.2+[x.kam ^{Id}en.numun].giš ^{lú}[kù.dim *u* ^{Id}en. ...] ^{22} ^{lú}kab.sar ^{lú}*paq-d*[*u šá*] é.dingir[^{meš} ...] ^{23}*ù* ^{Id}en-*šá-ra-a* ^{lú}*ma-ṣar* k[á ...] ^{24}*ina* ^{giš}*sim-mil-tu$_4$* *šá maš-a-a-al*-[*tu$_4$* *ina a-š*]*á-bi šá* ^{lú}di.ku$_5$^{meš}] ^{25}*šá* é.dingir^{meš} ^{lú}šà.tam É.sag.gíl [*ù* lú E$^{\text{ki.meš}}$] lú unkin] ^{26}*šá* É.sag.gíl ^{lú}un^{meš} kur ki.ta [...] ^{27}*ina* ki$^{\text{ti!}}$ *ki-da-nu šá-lu-ú* ^{Id}en.numun.[giš ^{lú}kù.dim] ^{28}*šá* kù.babbar *u* kù.gi *iš-šu-ú u* ^{Id}en.[... ^{lú}kab.sar] ^{29}*u* ^{lú}*ma-ṣar* ká *ul ú-kin-nu-ú ana* é [*ṣib-te-e-ti ṣab-tu-ú*] ^{30}u$_4$ 7 ^{Id}en.numun.giš ^{lú}kù.dim *ina* é *ṣib-te-e*-[*ti* ug$_7$] ^{31} ^{lú}bad-*su šu-ṣa-tú ina* izi *qa-la-at u$_4$-m*[*u* bi ^{Id}en. ...] ^{32} ^{lú}kab.sar 2 ^{lú}dumu^{meš}-*šú* $^{<\text{lú}>}$*ma-ṣar* ká *ù* [...] ^{33}*lìb-bu-ú* igi^{ú} *šá-lu-ú uk-tin-nu-ú ina* [izi *qa-lu-ú* ...] ^{34}dam ^{Id}en-*šá-ra-a ma-ṣar* ká *ina* [... *ḫi-ṭu*] ^{35}*šá šad-da-at ana* egir *u$_4$-mu* <E>^{ki} ^{iti}bar m[u ...]

[. . .] and tortured. They were convicted (of theft) and burned to death that very day.

The ninetieth year. In the month of Iyyar, that very month, the administrator of the Esagila [. . .], the Babylonian members of the assembly of the Esagila, concerning [. . . who] had entered the treasury, the place of the great gods [. . . (and) had stolen] silver, gold, and precious stones [. . .] of which two [. . .], holy [. . .]. That very month, in [. . .] who inside [. . .] were captured and put in [the jail of . . .]. That very month, the twenty+[xth day, Bēl-zēr]-līšir, the goldsmith, Bēl-. . .], the jeweler, in charge of the temples, and Bēl-šarâ, the doorkeeper, were interrogated outside, (put) on a ra[ck, in the presence of the judges] of the sanctuaries, the administrator of the Esagila, the Babylonian members of the assembly of the Esagila, the inhabitants of the Lower Country [. . .]. Bēl-zēr-lišir, the goldsmith, was not convicted of having stolen silver and gold, nor Bēl-[. . . , the jeweler], nor the doorkeeper, but [they were kept in jail]. The seventh day, Bēl-zēr-lis-ˇir, the goldsmith, died in ja[il]. His corpse was carried out and burned. That day, [. . . , Bēl-. . .], the jeweler, his two sons, the doorkeeper and [. . .], after having been interrogated as previously, were convicted (of theft) and [burned to] de[ath. (*So-and-so*)], the wife of Bēl-šarâ, the doorkeeper [. . . received the punishment] she incurred the rest of her life.

Babylon, month of Nisan, year [. . .].

Notes

1. That is to say, "he died."

2. An economic document (Clay 1912b: 22) was dated in the fourth year of this reign. In spite of this, was the chronicle correct? Such errors recording posthumous years were rather frequent in business texts; see, e.g., Brinkman and Kennedy 1983: 13 and n. 1, 16 and n. 5.

3. Not knowing the length of the reign, the scribe left a blank. On the reason for this omission, see the points of view of Grayson 1975a: 72 n. i 25; Weissert 1992: 275 n. 18.

4. This month was the first of the following year, or 721. Did the chronicler want to emphasize that Sargon and Merodach-baladan ascended to the throne the same year? We do not know. The author of no. 24 also had it that the year of Nebuchadnezzar's accession ended in Nisan with the celebration of the New Year.

5. That is to say, Bīt-Yakin.

6. In this section, as shown by the surviving elements, the narrative of the chronicle follows the pattern of the Annals of Sennacherib; restorations are based on the testimony of the Annals; see Luckenbill 1924: 51–55, lines 25–62.

7. Some of Sennacherib's inscriptions associated the massacre of the inhabitants of Ḫirimmu and the surrender of Ḫararātum, whose governor paid tribute to Assyria in this campaign; others see it as an episode in a campaign against the Medes.

8. Error for ^{kur}*Aš-šur.*

9. For this person, see chronicle 18.

10. The precise meaning of this expression is not clear; see Brinkman 1984a: 77 n. 375; Frame 1992: 243–44.

11. On these individuals, see Frame 1992: 85 and passim.

12. See above n. 10.

13. This refers to King Sanduarri: Röllig 1983: 341. The king of Sidon was Abdi-Milkutti; see Borger 1956: Ash 50 iii 34.

14. This occurrence appears out of place during Esarhaddon's reign. It may have been an error by the chronicler. Since the same incident had already happened, also in the sixth year of Aššur-nādin-šumi's reign, perhaps there was confusion between the two royal names, the writing of which was very similar: AN.ŠÁR.MU.MU and AN.ŠÁR.ŠEŠ.MU.

15. Chronicler's error, he reigned six years; compare chronicle 18.

16. On these individuals, see Frame 1992: 83–84.

17. Confronted with a broken original document, apparently a fragment detached from a tablet, the copyist valiantly attempted to restore what seemed possible to him. A certain chronological disorder resulted from this. If it is admitted that Šubria was taken in Ṭebeth, the booty could only have entered Uruk in Kislev of the following year, Kislev preceding Ṭebeth in the calendar. Compare with chronicle 18, which presented the events in a different order. This may also be a telescoping of two different events, the taking of Šubria and, later, the return of the gods of Uruk from exile.

18. C differed slightly; it seems that A's source had a break: (C iv) $^{1'}$[*3-šú d*]*i-ik-tu*$_{4}$ *šá Mi-ṣir di-kât* $^{2'}$[*šal-lat*]*-su šal-lat* dingir^{meš} *i-tab-ku* $^{3'}$[u$_{4}$ 2]2.kám *Me-em-pi* ^{uru} lugal^{tú} $^{4'}$[*ṣa-bi*]*t* lugal-*šú ul-te-zib* $^{5'}$[dumu^{m}]^{eš} šeš-*šú ina* šu$_{ii}$ *ṣa-ab-tu* $^{6'}$[*šal-lat*]*-su šal-lat* un^{meš} *ḫab-tu* nì.šu-*šú* $^{7'}$[*iš*]*-tal-lu-ni,* [three times], there was massacre in Miṣir. (The land) was pillaged and the gods deported. The [twenty-]second [day], Memphis, the royal city, [was tak]en, abandoned by its king, (whose) [children] and brother were captured. (The city) was pl]undered, the inhabitants pillaged, its possessions [plun]dered.

19. In fact, the king of Babylon was enthroned at the beginning of the following year.

20. On this person, see the discussion of Frame 1992: 117–18.

21. The computation is curious, to say the least. Was it the thirteenth year of the reign of Merodach-baladan, who, though a fugitive, was still considered king? This seems unlikely, the chronicler himself having noted previously the accession of Sargon. Chronicle 16 mentioned the simultaneous accession to power of Sargon and Merodach-baladan, linking to the earlier year an event that occurred the following year. The explanation most consistent with the facts is that the chronicler referred to Sargon's years of reign as king of Assyria, or the thirteenth year of this reign, and not as king of Babylon, in which case it would have been only the first.

22. Compare with the Assyrian Eponym Chronicle (no. 9) in the year 705.

23. There is nothing in it to reveal any pro-Assyrian bias.

24. See above n. 10.

25. Nabû-zēr-kitti-līšir, a son of Merodach-baladan, involved in the revolt against Esarhaddon, attacked Ur, then fled, anticipating the Assyrian attack. His more pru-

dent brother Nā'id-Marduk, having accompanied him at first, changed his mind and rejoined the Assyrian party.

26. See above n. 10.

27. See above n. 10.

28. Reading "eighth" is not impossible.

29. One of Babylon's rare acts of sedition under Esarhaddon.

30. Reading "ninth" is also possible.

31. See above n. 10.

32. On this point, see the hypothesis of Beaulieu 1997: 379.

33. A Babylonian placed on the throne of Babylon by Aššurbanipal. Such a date, "after Kandalānu," existed in practice documents; see Na'aman 1991: 246, 251; it corresponded to the year 626 or the year of Nabopolassar's enthronement.

34. This was not a deportation; their change of location undoubtedly anticipated the taking of the city by the Assyrians.

35. According to Beaulieu 1997: 377, "the first year in which. . . . "

36. The sequence of the months in this paragraph makes one think that the events described were spread over two years. In fact, the chronicler may have indulged in a flashback for the best arrangement of his narrative, which ended with Nabopolassar's victory on the eve of his enthronement.

37. See n. 33.

38. Probably a Babylonian general.

39. On this date, see Zawadzki 1990a.

40. Curiously, the chronicler placed the celebration of the New Year's festival at the end of the previous year. See above n. 4.

41. The brother of Nebuchadnezzar II.

42. Compare chronicle 28.

43. This was the taking of Jerusalem in 598 and the defeat of Jehoiakim; the city was later sacked in 587.

44. See von Soden 1989: 285–92.

45. This was an interruption looking ahead, the month of Sivan following Nisan and Iyyar. The scribe then returned to normal chronological order.

46. Reading <kur>*Lú*-[*ú-di il-li*]*k*.

47. Apparently there was great disorder in the chronology of events in this seventeenth year. In fact, the king must have returned to Babylon in the month of Ṭebeth of the sixteenth year; the celebration of the New Year's festival then followed, and, until the month of Elul, the entrance of the gods of Babylonia into the capital took place. Babylon fell in the month of Tešrit, and Nabonidus was taken prisoner. The following month, Araḫsamnu, Cyrus made his entrance into the city. The same month, Ugbaru died. From Kislev to Adar the displaced gods returned to their respective cities. In the interval, the queen died, and a mourning period was ordered that went on until the first days of the following year. The episode concerning Cambyses took place the fourth day of Nisan of the following year.

48. Compare chronicle 25.

49. On the complex matter of chronological computations, see Joannès 1979–80: 99–115.

50. Restoration prompted by the chronological consistency of the document, but the reported events go back to the third year of this reign.

51. This was Antigonus's title according to some economic documents: Kennedy 1968: 33–34.

52. On these matters, see Sherwin-White 1983a.

53. There were two Egišnugal temples devoted to the cult of Sîn, one at Ur, the other in Babylon; undoubtedly this was the second.

54. On *šaknu,* see Stolper 1988: 127–55.

55. On this episode, see Bouché-Leclerc 1963: 1:73–74, 2:542–43.

56. Robert 1972: 56, 345; 58, 270; 64, 462; 1965: 26; 1963: 226 and nn. 6 and 7.

57. Suggestion taken from Sherwin-White 1983a: 268.

58. Year 67 of the Seleucid era according to the Hellenistic Royal Chronicle (no 4). For the date, see Sachs and Hunger 1988–2001: 2, no. -245 = S.E. 66, B' Obv.3' and B l.s. 1.

59. On these matters, see Sherwin-White 1983b: 156–59; Kuhrt and Sherwin-White 1991: 71–86.

60. Royal judges were a Neo-Babylonian institution (see no. 18); they received part of the royal sacrifice at the time of the New Year's festival (Dandamayev 1979: 590–91).

61. LAGAB MU-*šu*.

62. On these names, see Bickerman 1938: 5 n. 9; Bouché-Leclerc 1963: 1:187; Robert 1972: 53, 224; 54, 197.

X

Babylonian Chronicles of Ancient Kings

38. CHRONICLE OF THE ESAGILA

Sources: tablets, more or less fragmentary; in total, seven exemplars of the work.
Bibliography: Grayson 1975a: no. 19; Finkel 1980: 72–74, 78; Al-Rawi 1990; unpublished exemplar in the British Museum. Some signs are still preserved at the ends of lines 30 to 40 in the examplar of the British Museum; because it is unpublished, this document has not been examined.
Language: Babylonian.
Date: Neo-Assyrian or Neo-Babylonian copies.
Place: Aššur, Uruk, Sippar.
Contents: this chronicle, the date of composition of which cannot be earlier than 1100, was in an unusual style, in the form of a fictitious royal letter. The classification criteria of the ancients were less rigorous than ours (see Charpin 1986: 453–59; Glassner 2001b: 216–21). Given the bad condition of the text, one hesitates on how to read the royal names and places at the beginning; in fact, another proposal is still possible:

Say to [Rīm-Sî]n, ki[ng of Lars]a, thus says Enlil-bāni (?), king of Isin.

The work, which claimed to draw lessons from earliest history, from the beginnings to the end of the third millennium, focused on the greatness of Babylon and Marduk, at the price of some anachronisms. Here and there the name of Enlil instead of Marduk gives evidence of recourse to more ancient sources.

Its philosophy is transparent: any king who neglected the cult of Marduk had no power.

(Sippar and duplicates) ^{1}*a-na* [*A-pil*-^{d}E]N.ZU *š*[*àr* Tin.ti]r$^{ki(?)}$ *qí-bi-ma um-mu Da-mi-iq-ili-šú šàr* PA.ŠE^{ki}.MA ^{2}[. . .]-*ú ki-ma* . . . [. . .] . . . *šu-ma* . . . ti . . . bala-*šu* ^{3}[*a-n*]*a-ku a-mat ši-tul-li a*-[*mat* . . .] . . . *áš-pur-kúm-ma at-ta* . . . *a-na lìb-bi-ka ul*(?) *taš-du-ud* ^{4}*a-na ur-ti ad-di-nu-k*[*úm* (?) *u*]*l ta*-[*aš-m*]*e-e-ma ú-zu-un-ka ul taš-ku-un* ^{5}*a-na ṭè-mi na-as-qí* šá ú . . . *ul ta-qul-ma šá-na-ti-ma téš-te-né-e'-e* ^{6}*gi-mil dum-qí e-li-ka a-na šá-ka-n*[*i* . . .-*kúm*]-*ma ina lìb-bi-ka ul i-ba-áš-ši* ^{7}*šá*(?) *ra-ma*(?)-*a*[*n*(?)-*ka*(?)] *šul-lu-me iš-di um*-[*ma-ni*]-*ka ku-un-ni a-na u*$_4$*-mi ru-qu-ti am*(!)-*li-ka-ma ina* šu$_{ii}$-*ka ul*(?) *tu-kin*(?) ^{8}*áš*-[*ra-ti*]-*šu*(?) *ki áš-te-'e-e ṭè-ma* . . . *na*(?)-*as*(?)-*qá-at ù ba-aṭ-la-at* ^{9}*i*-[*na*]-*an-na a-lak-ti lu-uq-bi-k*[*úm* . . .] ar(?) [. . .] . . . *ma-ti-ma šu*-[*a*]-*tu ar-ḫi-iš*(!) *li-mad* ^{10}*a-na* ^{d}*Nin-kar-ra-ak-a* gašan-*ia b*[*é-le*]-*et É-gal-maḫ ni-qa-a aq-qí-ši-ma* ^{11}*ut-nen-ši su-pe-e-šá aṣ-bat-ma* [*a*]-*ma-a-ti* <*šá*(?)> *ina lìb-bi* [*eš*]-*te-né-ú šá-a-šú* [*aq-bi*]-*šim um-ma lu-ú a-na-ku-ma* ^{12}*nam-maš-še-e* ^{kur}*Šu-me-ri u* Uri *a-na* šu$_{ii}$-*ia*$_5$ *mul-li*-[*i*] . . . *i-na ṣi*-[*i*]-*ri kiš-šat* kur.kur lu šá bu ^{13}un^{meš} kur *e-li-tì u šap-li-tì bi*-[*lat*]-*si-na ka-bit-tu*$_4$ *a-na qé-reb É-gal-maḫ li-še-ri-bu* . . . ^{14}kù^{tu_4} ^{d}*Gu-la be-el-ti ṣir-tú i-na šat mu-ši iz-zi-za-nim-ma* inim^{meš}-*ia* [*iš-me*]-*ma ki-niš i-ta-ma it-ti-ia* ^{15}*ik*(?)-*ru-ba-an*<-*ni*> *ina a-sur-rak-ki-i ma-an-za-za tu-ka-an ina an-za-nun*(?)-*ze-e ta*-. . .-*ri-nim* ak(?) la ^{16}[*a-na*] an^{e} *ru-qu-tu re-ši-ka ta-na-áš-ši ina ma-ri* . . . *e-li-iš ki-di-in-nu-tú* ^{17}[*ar*]-*ku*(?)-*ú* ^{d}Amar.utu *šàr* dingir^{meš} *šá kiš-šat* an^{e} *u* ki^{ti} ru . . . [. . .] . . . mu *ina muḫ-ḫi* ak(?) la(?) ^{18}[*nam-ma*]*š-še-e* ^{kur}*Šu-me-ri u* Uri^{ki} *a-na* kur uru-*šú* Tin.tir^{ki} . . . ig ki(?) ^{19}[*ana*] *a-bi-šu* ^{d}*É-a mu-um-me ma-lik* an^{e} *u* ki^{ti} *ana* é *ap-s*[*i-i i*]-*ḫi-iš-ma* ^{20}[. . . Tin].tir^{ki} uru *i-tu-ut ku-un lìb-bi-ia ina*(?) *kul-lat da-ád-me* [*lu-ú*] *šá-qat* ^{21}[*É-sa*]*g-íl* bára *ṣi-i-ri a-na pa-aṭ kiš-šat* an^{e} *u* ki^{ti} . . . mu . . . ^{22}en en.en *a-šib* bára *iš-tu ṣi-it* ^{d}Utu^{ši} *a-di e-reb* ^{d}Utu^{ši} . . . ṣa(?) bit(?) ti liš . . . ^{23}*ṣal-mat qaq-qa-du ki-ma ṣe-e-nu li-ir-te-e'*-[*i/ú* . . .] ^{24}uru *lu-ú na-šá-a re-e-ši šá* kur.kur šu ma an [. . .] ^{25}*a-ma-a*(!)-*ti ma-la iq-bu-ú-šú be-lu* ^{d}*Nu-dím-mu*[*d* . . .] ^{26}*iš-tu i-šid* an^{e} *a-di e-lat* an^{e} *ú-kan-ni-šu uš-b*[*al*(?) . . .] ^{27}*ina šá-ni-i* ^{d}*A-nu-um u* ^{d}En-líl dingir^{meš} gal^{meš} *ki-niš ip-pal-su-šu-ma* [. . .]-*nu-ma an*(!)-*ni-šu-nu ki-ni* . . . am [. . .] ^{28}*šá* kur *e-li-tu*$_4$ *u šap-li-ti lu-ú* ùz.sag^{gu}-*šú-nu* [. . .] ^{29}*a-na a-šìr-ti-šú* gal^{ti} *li-tar-ra-ru* dingir^{meš} gal^{meš} *šá* an^{e} *u* ki^{ti} . . . [. . .] ^{30}*šá É-sag-íl É*-KU-*a* é.gal an^{e} *u* ki^{ti} *re-ši-šú ki-ma* an^{e} *ul*-[*li* . . .] *lìb-bi-šu-nu* ig(?) . . . tu(?) ^{31}*te-me-en-šú ki-ma* an^{e} *u* ki^{ti} *ana* u$_4^{meš}$ *ṣa-a-ti ka-a-nam* [. . .] ^{32}*ina* udu.sískur-*ka a-mat taq-ba-a i-de-ma ba-la-ṭu* u$_4^{meš}$ *ru-qu-ti a-na* . . .[. . .] ^{33}*e-zib šá ina*(?) máš.gi$_6$ eš.bar *iq-qa-ba-a mil-ki dam-qu ka-a*-[. . .] . . . [. . . ^{34}*a-na*] dingir^{meš} uru *šá-a-šú* dingir^{meš} gal^{meš} *šá* an^{e} *u* ki^{ti} *ú-sa-aḫ* . . . im(?) . . . ^{35}*ana ba-laṭ te-líl*(?)-*tu*$_4$ *u*$_4$*-mu ár-ḫi u šat-ti-šam* ta pa ra [. . .] . . . *a-na* . . . ki-*šu* . . . *la* dingir *ma-am-ma ul i'-a-ri-šu* ma(?) *šá lìb-bi* . . . [. . .] ^{36}*ep-šú pi-i-šú ik-kam-mu-ú* dingir^{meš} *nak-ru-tu*$_4$ *lab-šu ár-šu-tu* . . . [. . .] .. meš

Say to [Apil-S]în (?), ki[ng of Babylo]n (?), thus says Damiq-ilišu, king of Isin:

[. . .] as [. . .] his reign. [I mys]elf have written propitious words for you to think about, words of [. . .], but you, you have never paid any attention to them! You have neither listened nor lent an ear to the instructions that I sent you. The valuable advice that I have [. . .] you, you have not heeded, and you have not ceased to pursue other ideas. In order to do you a good turn, [I have . . . you], but that was not in your heart. For your own well-being I have advised you to increase discipline in your army for the future, but you have not taken things in hand. Its sacred places (?) where I sought counsel [. . .] has ceased. Now I want to tell you about my experience [. . .] and take that rapidly to heart! I offered a sacrifice to my lady Ninkarak, mistress of the Egalmaḫ. I said prayers and beseeched her. I told her the thoughts that are always in my mind (and) said to her: "Deliver the people of Sumer and Akkad into my hands! May [. . .] in all lands (and) may the people of the Upper and Lower Countries carry their heavy tribute into the Egalmaḫ [. . .]" In the silence of the night, holy Gula, exalted mistress, stood before me; she [heard] my pleas, spoke with sincerity, and blessed me:

"You will define the limits of a place within subterranean waters, you [. . .] in the waters of the deep, you will raise your head toward the distant heavens, [. . .], on high, a privileged status. [The]n Marduk, king of the gods who [. . .] all heaven and earth, [*will put* (?) the peop]le of Sumer and Akkad under the authority (?) of his city, Babylon. [. . .]. Hurrying toward the dwelling-place in the Aps[û], toward his father Ea, the creator, the counselor of heaven and earth: 'May Babylon, the city that in the loyalty of my heart I have chosen, be exalted throughout the inhabited world! May Esagila, the exalted sanctuary, be [. . .] within the limits of all heaven and earth! May the lord of lords, who resides in the sanctuary, [be . . .] from the East to the West! May he lea[d] the black-headed folk like sheep and goats [. . .]! May the city be exalted! From every country [. . .]' Lord Nudimmud [. . .] all the words that he had said to him. From the base of the sky to its top, [. . .] will bow [. . .]. Then Anu and Enlil, the great lords, looked upon him steadfastly and [. . .]: 'May he be the guide of the Upper and Lower Countries [. . .]! May the great gods of heaven and earth tremble before his great sanctuary [. . .]! May the pinnacle of the Esagila, the EKUa, the palace of heaven and earth, be [. . .] as the sky! May its foundations, like heaven and earth forever be continually [. . .]!' I understood the words you expressed through your sacrifices, and I [. . . you] a long life."

Besides the judgment set forth in the dream, I want [to *favor you* (?) with] a sound piece of advice. [To the] gods of this city, the great gods of heaven and earth, you [. . .] a daily, monthly, and annual cleansing [. . .]. On his advice [. . .] (and?) nobody will march against him whose heart [. . .]. On his order, the hostile gods are captured, dressed in dirty garments, [. . .].

^{37}*šá*] *a-na* dingir^{meš} uru *šá-a-šú ú-gal-la-lu* mul-*šú ina* an^{e} *ul iz-za-zi* . . . ^{38}lugal$^{tu(?)}$ *i-qat-ta ḫaṭ-ṭa-šu in-na-ṭir i-šit-ta-šu i-ta-ar a-na ti-li u* [*kar-mi* ^{39}. . .] . . . me-*šú-ma šàr kiš-šat* an^{e} *ù* ki^{tì} *um*(?)-*ma*(?) dingir^{meš} *šá* an^{e} *u* ki^{tì} . . . [. . .] ^{40}*ù a-lak-ti* lugal *maḫ-ri šá áš-te-nem-mu-ú a-na* . . . a *šá* ib . . . b[al(?) . . .] ^{41} ^{I}*Ak-ka* dumu ^{I}*En-me-bára-a-ge-si* . . . ka ib ru ti(?) ma . . . [. . .] ^{42} ^{I}*En-me-kár šàr* Unu^{ki} *nam-maš-*[*še-e*] *ú-šal-pit* . . . *man-da šá* a . . . šu [. . .] ^{43}abgal *A-da-pà* dumu(?) ^{I}. . . la(?) . . . nun(?) . . . [. . . ^{44}. . . *i-na k*]*i-iṣ-ṣi-šu el-li iš-me-ma* ^{I}*En-me-kár i-ru-ur* [. . . ^{45}*ù* ^{d}Amar].utu lugal^{tu} *kiš-šat* kur.kur *id-din-šum-ma*[1] *par-si-šú* šu [. . . ^{46}. . .] . . . [. . . a]n na *ki-ma ši-ṭir šá-ma-mi ú-ban-ni-ma ina É-sag-íl* . . . [^{d}Amar.utu] ^{47}lugal *pa-qid kiš-šat* an^{e} *u* ki^{tì} dumu *reš-tu-ú* <*šá É-sag-íl*> *ana* 3,020(?) . . . tu mu^{meš}-*šú* [. . .] ^{48}*i-na* bala^{e} *Puzur-*^{d}Meš$^{(sic)}$ *šàr* Úḫ^{ki} ^{lú}*šu-ku*$_{6}$*-dak-*[*ka*] *šá É-sag-íl* [. . .] ^{49}*ina ki-du-de-e* . . .*-na a-na nap-tan* en gal^{i} ^{d}Amar.utu ku$_{6}^{meš}$ *i-ba-ru-ma* ^{lú}nu.bànda^{meš} *šàr nu-na e-ki-mu šu-ku*$_{6}$*-da-ku* . . . [. . .] ^{50}7(?)[2] u$_{4}^{meš}$ *ina na-sa-ḫu* ^{lú}*šu-ku*$_{6}$*-dak-*<*ka*> 1(?).kam ku$_{6}^{meš}$ *i-ba-ru* [. . .] ^{51}*ina* é ^{munus}*Kù-*^{d}*Ba-ba*$_{6}$ ^{munus}kurun.na *a*(!)*-na* ^{dug}*am-ma-am um-taš-*[. . . *É-sag-í*]*l uṭ-ṭaḫ-*[*ḫu*] ^{52}*i-nu-šú ti-mi-*<*in-šú*(?)> *ḫi-pí ud-diš a-na É-sag-íl* ul ir(?) ru bi *nu-nu* bala [. . .] ^{53} ^{munus}*Kù-*^{d}*Ba-ba*$_{6}$ *a-na* ^{lú}*šu-ku*$_{6}$*-dak-ka* ninda^{ḫá} *id-din me-e id-din* ku$_{6}^{meš}$ . . . [. . .] *a-na É-sag-íl uš-*. . .[. . .] ^{54} ^{d}Amar.utu[3] lugal <dumu> *ru-bé-e šá Ap-si-i ḫa-diš ip-pa-lis-si-ma um-ma ši-i lu ki-a-a*[*m*] ^{55}*a-na* ^{munus}*Kù-*^{d}*Ba-ba*$_{6}$ ^{munus}kurun nam.lugal$^{ú-tú}$ *kiš-šat* kur.kur *ug-dam-mir-*[*šim*][4] ^{56} ^{I}*Ur-*^{d}*Za-ba*$_{4}$*-ba*$_{4}$ *k*[*a-ra-ni*] *ma-aq-qa-a-ti šá É-sag-gíl a-na* Lugal.gi.[na] ^{lú}sagi-*šú šu-pel-li i*[*q*(?)*-bi*] ^{57} ^{I}Lugal.gin *ka-ra-*[*na u*]*l uš-pi-il it-ta-id-m*[*a*] *ana É-sag-gíl uš-taḫ-miṭ* ^{58} ^{d}Amar.utu *šàr ki*[*š-šat*] an^{e} *u* ki^{tì} dumu nun *šá ap-si-i ḫa-diš ip-pa-lis-su-ma* lugal^{ut} *k*[*ib-ra-a*]*t a*[*r-ba*]*-'i id-din-šú* ^{59}*za-ni-nu-ut É-sag-íl e-pu-uš gi-mir a-šib* bára^{meš} *ana* Ká.dingir.ra^{ki} *bi-lat-su-nu* [íl^{meš}] ^{60}*šu-ú a-mat* ^{d}En *iq-bu-šú i-ma-*[. . .] *e-pir šat pi-šú is-su-uḫ-ma ina mi-iḫ-ra-at A-kà-dè*^{ki} uru *i-pu-uš-ma* Ká.dingir.ra^{ki} *a-na* mu-*šú i*[*m-bi*] ^{61} ^{d}*En-líl šá iq-bu-šu ik-kir-ma ul-tu ṣi-it* ^{d}Utu^{ši} *a-di e-reb* ^{d}Utu^{ši} *ik-ki-ru-šu-ma la ṣa-la-lu* gar-[*su*] ^{62} ^{I}*Na-ram-*^{d}30 *nam-maš-*[*še-e š*]*á* Ká.dingir.ra^{ki} *ú-šal-pit-ma* en 2-*šú* erín *Gu-ti-um id-kaš-šum-ma* ^{63}un^{meš}-*šú ma-ak-ka-ra-niš it-ta-di*[5] lugal^{ut}-*su a-na* erín *Gu-ti-um it-ta-din* ^{64}*Qu-tu*(!)*-u šá ta-zi-im-te* dingir *pa-la-ḫa la kul-lu-mu par-ṣi u* ^{giš}ḫur^{meš} *šuk-lu-lu la i-du-*[*ú*] ^{65} ^{d}*Utu-ḫé-gál* ^{lú}*šu-ku*$_{6}$*-dak-ka ina pa-aṭ i-rat tam-tu*$_{4}$ ku$_{6}^{meš}$ *ta-mar-tu*$_{4}$ *i-bar-ma* ^{66}*i-nu-šú nu-un šu-a-tu a-di a-na be-lí* gal ^{d}Amar.utu *ṭè-ḫu-ú ana* dingir *šá-nim-ma ul uṭ-ṭaḫ-ḫu* ^{67}*Gu-ti-um nu-nu*

Whosoever offends the gods of this city, his star will not stand in the sky. [. . .], his (?) kingship will be no more, his scepter will be taken away, his treasure will become a heap of [rubble . . .], and the king of all heaven and earth [. . .] the gods of heaven and earth [. . .. . . .] and the behavior of the kings of yesteryear of whom I have heard about, I want [to tell (?)] you:

Aka, son of Enme(n)-baragesi, [. . .]. Enmekar, king of Uruk, destroyed the liv[ing] creatures and [. . .]. The wise Adapa heard [. . .] in his holy sanctuary and cursed Enmekar, [. . . and Mard]uk gave[6] him rule over all the lands and [. . .] his rites [. . .] he embellished like celestial writing[7] and exalted [. . .] in the Esagila. [Marduk], the king who administers all heaven and earth, the eminent son <of the Esagila>, for 3,020 (?) years [put his benevolent gaze on him (?)].

During the reign of King Puzur-Niraḫ of Akšak, fishermen from the Esagila caught fish on the banks of [. . .], they caught fish for the meal of the great lord Marduk, but the king's officers seized them. The fishermen [. . .]. Seven[8] days having gone by, the fishermen (again) caught fish, [. . . it] into the home of Ku-Baba, the innkeeper, [. . .] for the large beer vat. They carried [. . .] to the Esagila as an offering. At this time, its foun<dation> (?) BREAK, newly, for the Esagila, [. . .]. Ku-Baba offered bread to the fishermen and offered water to them, (but) she hurried to [deliver] the fish to the Esagila. Marduk, the king, the <son> of the prince of Apsû, looked benevolently upon her and she said: "Let it be so!" Ku-Baba was entrusted with the whole kingship over all the lands.

Concerning wine for the libation cups of the Esagila, Ur-Zababa ordered Sargon, his cupbearer: "Change (it)." Sargon did not change the wine; on the contrary, he took great care to deliver it promptly at the Esagila. Marduk, the king of all heaven and earth, the son of the prince of the Apsû, looked upon him benevolently and entrusted the kingship over the "four corners (of the earth)"[9] to him. He took care of the Esagila. All those who lived in palaces [carried] their tribute to Babylon. But he [forgot] the word that Bēl had said to him. He took earth out of the ground and, facing Akkade, made a city and named it Babylon.[10] Because of the [sacrilege] he had committed, Enlil changed the word he had said and, from the East to the West, there was a revolt against him, and he was afflicted with restlessness.

Narām-Sîn destroyed the living creatures of Babylon and twice (Marduk) raised the army of Guti against him; (the latter) goaded on his people. He entrusted his kingship to the army of the Gutians.

The Gutians, (being people given to arouse) cries of woe, did not know how to honor the gods nor how to perform divine rites and ceremonies correctly. Utu-ḫegal, the fisherman, caught a fish at the seashore (in order to make) an offering. This fish, to be offered to the great lord Marduk, was not presented as an offering to any other god. But the

ba-áš-lu la ṭuḫ-ḫa-a ina qá-ti-šú i-ki-im-ma ^{68}*ina qí-bi-ti-šú ṣir-ti* érin^{an} *Qu-ti-i a-na* lugal$^{ú-tu}$ kur-*šú i-ki-im-ma a-na* ^{d}*Utu-ḫé-gál it-ta-din* ^{69} ^{d}*Utu-ḫé-gál* ^{lú}*šu-ku*$_6$*-dak-ka* šu-*su a-na* uru-*šú ana* ḫul^{ti} *ú-bil-ma mi-iḫ-rit* i$_7$ ad$_6$-*šú it-bal* ^{70}*a-na* ^{d}*Šul-gi* dumu ^{I}*Ur-*^{d}*Namma* lugal$^{ú-tu}$ *kiš-šat* kur.kur *id-di-in-ma* ^{71}*par-ṣi-šú ul ú-šak-lil šu-luḫ-ḫi-šú ú-la-a'-i-ma an-na* šà *šú* ... *zu*(?)*-um-ri* ...*-tak-kan* ^{72} ^{I}*Amar-*^{d}EN.ZU^{na} dumu-*šu* gu$_4$^{meš} gal^{meš} *u* udu.sískur *zag-muk šá É-sag-íl uš-te*(?)*-pe*(?)*-el-ma* ^{73}*ni-kip* gu$_4$ *iq-qa-bi-šum-ma ina ni-šik* ^{kuš}e.sír^{e}-*šú im-<tu-ut>* ^{74} ^{I}*Šu-*^{d}EN.ZU^{na} *a-na* tin zi^{meš}-*šú É-sag-íl ki-ma ši-ṭir šá-ma-mi ú-* ^{75}*ḫi-pí* ^{d}*Šul-gi i-pu-šu a-ra-an-šú* ^{I}*Im-bi-*^{d}30 dumu-*šú i-<...>* ^{76}*ḫi-pí -ti* lugal *maḫ-ri a*(!)*-lik pa-ni* ... ta mu ka *šá lìb-bi-ka-ma* ^{77}*e-li* ad-*šú* ^{d}*É-a* an^{e} *u* ki^{ti} ... am(?) *ul ib-ni* An *u* ^{d}*Iš-tar ma-am*(?)-<...> ^{78}ibila-*šú ṣi-i-ri* en gal^{ú} ^{d}Amar.utu [lugal(?)] dingir^{meš} *šá* dingir^{meš} *ru-bu-<...>* ^{79}*li-ip-li-pi-šú* ^{d}Nà *šá* e ni i ka áš *šu-ú* lugal *i-nam*(!)*-bu-ú* ^{80}*a-na Su-mu-la-Èl* lugal *li-it-ti-šú šá* ^{d}*A-nu*$_4$ mu-*šú im-<bu-ú>* ^{81}*šá ra-man-ka šul-lu-mu ù* ... *ka-la-šú šub-ti* ni ^{82}*a-di* u$_4$^{meš} bala *da-<rí>-a-ti ina qa-ti-ka*

---

^{83}*ṭup-pi* ^{Id}Amar.utu.sur a-*šú šá* ^{I}Kar-^{d}...[...]...*-ḫa-a-a pa-liḫ* ^{d}Nà *ḫal-qa* gur

39. CHRONICLE OF ANCIENT KINGS

Sources: tablet.
Bibliography: Grayson 1975a: no. 20A.
Language: Babylonian.
Date: Late Babylonian period.
Place: unknown.
Contents: account of history from Sargon of Akkade to Enlil-bāni of Isin.

^{1} ^{I}Lugal.gin *šàr A-kà-dè*^{ki} *ina* bala ^{d}*Iš-tar i-lam-ma* ^{2}*šá-ni-na u ma-ḫi-ri ul i-ši šá-lum-mat-su* ugu kur^{meš} ^{3}*it-bu-uk* a.ab.ba *ina* ^{d}Utu.è *i-bi-ir-ma* ^{4}mu 11.kám kur ^{d}Utu.šú.a *a-di qí-ti-šú* šu-*su* kur^{ud} ^{5}*pi-i-šú a-na iš-ten ú-kin* nu^{meš}-*šú ina* ^{d}Utu.šú.a *uš-zi-iz* ^{6}*šal-lat-su-nu ina a-ma-a-ti ú-še-bi-ra* ^{7}dumu^{me} é.gal-*šú a-na* 5 danna$^{ta-àm}$ *ú-še-šib-ma* ^{8}*um-mat* kur^{meš} *mit-ḫa-riš i-be-el* ^{9}*a-na* ^{kur}*Ka-zal-la il-lik-ma* ^{kur}*Ka-zal-la ana* du$_6$ *u kar-me ú-tir* ^{10}*ina lìb-bi-šú man-za-az iṣ-ṣur ú-ḫal-liq* ^{11}*ar-ka-niš ina ši-bu-ti-šú* kur^{meš}

Gutians pulled the cooked fish out of his hands before it was offered. By his exalted command, (Marduk) removed the Gutian army from the kingship of his country and entrusted it to Utu-ḫegal. (Later), Utu-ḫegal, the fisherman, raised the hand of evil against his city, and the river carr[ied away] his corpse.

(Then Marduk) entrusted the kingship over all their lands to Šulgi, son of Ur-Namma, but he did not perform his rites in their totality, contaminated his cleansing ceremonies, and his mind [*was deranged* (?)]. Amar-Su'en, his son, changed the sacrifices of the large ox[en] and sheep and goats at the New Year's festival in the Esagila; it is said (that he died) from being gored by an ox, (but) he died from a "bite" of his shoe. Šū-Sîn, for his well-being (and) his life, <restored> the Esagila <similar> to the celestial writing. BREAK that Šulgi had committed. His fault, his son Ibbi-Sîn <...>.

BREAK an ancient king, (your?) predecessor, [...] according to your desire and <...>. More than his father Ea, heaven and earth, he did not create [...]. Anu and Ištar <...>. His exalted successor, the great lord Marduk, [king (?)] of the gods, prince (?) among the gods <...>. His grandson Nabû who [...] will name the king.

To King Sumu-lā-El, his descendant, whose name Anu has pron<ounced>, for your personal well-being and all [... will be] in your hands forever.

Colophon of the edition from Sippar:

Tablet of Marduk-ēṭir, son of Ēṭir-[...]ḫaya, devotee of Nabû. To be returned in case of loss.

King Sargon of Akkade arose during the reign of Ištar. He had neither rival nor opponent, his fame spread over all the lands, (and) he crossed the sea in the East. The eleventh year, he conquered the country of the West up to its farthest boundary (and) placed (it) under (his) sole authority, had his statues erected there (and) booty ferried across on barges. He made his courtiers live every five double hours and governed the community of the countries as one. He marched on Kazallu and reduced it to a

ka-la-ši-na ib-ba-al-ki-ta-ši-ma ^{12}*ina A-kà-dè*^{ki} *il-mu-šú-ma* ^{I}Lugal.gin *a-na* ^{giš}tukul è-*ma* ŠI.ŠI-*šú-nu im-ḫaṣ* ^{13}*ka-mar-šú-nu iš-kun um-man-šú-nu* dagal^{tì} *ú-šam-qí-it* ^{14}egir <<diš>> ^{kur}Su.bir$_4$^{ki} *ina gi-ip-ši-šú* zi-*ma ana* ^{giš}tukul *ik-mi-is-su-ma* ^{15}Lugal.gin *šu-šu-ba-a-tú ú-še-šib-ma* ŠI.ŠI-*šú-nu im-ḫaṣ* ^{16}*ka-mar-šú-nu iš-kun um-man-šú-nu* dagal^{tì} *ú-šam-qí-it* ^{17}nì.ga-*šú-nu a-na A-kà-dè*^{ki} *ú-še-ri-ba* ^{18}*e-pe-er e-se-e šá* Ká.dingir.ra^{ki} *is-suḫ-ma* ^{19}*i-te-e A-kà-dè*^{ki} gaba.ri Ká.dingir.ra^{ki} *i-pu-uš* ^{20}*a-na* nì.gig *i-pu-šu* en gal^{ú} ^{d}Amar.utu *i-gu-ug-ma* ^{21}*ina ḫu-šaḫ-ḫu* un^{me}-*šú ig-mu-ur* ^{22}*ul-tu ṣi-it* ^{d}Utu^{ši} *a-di e-reb* ^{d}Utu^{ši} ^{23}*ik-ki-ru-šú-ma la ṣa-la-la i-mi-id-*[*su*]

---

^{24} ^{I}*Na-ra-am-*^{d}EN.ZU dumu ^{I}Lugal.gin *a-na* ^{uru}*A-pi-šal*[^{ki} *il-lik*] ^{25}*pi-il-šú ip-lu-uš-ma* ^{I}*Ri-iš-*^{d}Is[kur] ^{26}*šàr* ^{uru}*A-pi-šal*^{ki} *u* ^{lú}sukkal *A-pi-šal*^{ki} šu-*su* kur$^{[ud]}$ ^{27}*ana Má-gan-na*^{ki} *il-lik-ma* ^{I}*Man-nu-da-an-nu šàr Má-gan*^{ki} [šu-*su* kur^{ud}]

---

^{28} ^{Id}*Šul-gi* dumu ^{I}*Ur-Namma* Eridu^{ki} *šá* gú *tam-tì ra-biš iz-nun* ^{29} ^{mí}ḫul *iš-te-'-e-ma* nì.ga *É-sag-íl u* Tin.tir^{ki} ^{30}*ina šál-lat* è ^{d}En … ma ad$_6$-*šú u-šá-kil* dù ud til-*šú*

---

^{31} ^{Id}*Èr-ra-*zà.dib lugal ^{Id}*En-líl-*dù ^{lú}nu.kiri$_6$ ^{32}*a-na* nu nì.sag.gil^{e} *ina* ^{giš}gu.za-*šú ú-še-šib* ^{33}aga lugal$^{ti-šú}$ *ina* sag.du-*šú iš-ta-kan* ^{34} ^{Id}*Èr-ra-i-mit-ti ina* é.gal-*šú pap-pa-su im-me-tú ina sa-ra-pi-šú im-tu-ut* ^{35} ^{Id}*En-líl-*dù *šá ina* ^{giš}gu.za *ú-ši-bi ul it-bi* ^{36}*a-na* lugal$^{ú-ti}$ *it-taš-kan*

---

^{37} ^{Id}*Ilu-šum-ma šàr* ^{kur}*Aš-šur a-na tar-ṣi* ^{I}*Su-a-bu*
^{38}gigam.didli

40. CHRONICLE OF ANCIENT KINGS

Sources: tablet in a bad state of preservation.
Bibliography: Grayson 1975a: no. 20B.
Language: Babylonian.
Date: Late Babylonian period.
Place: unknown.
Contents: history from Enlil-bāni of Isin to the Kassite Agum III. Iluma-ilu took Nippur during Samsu-ilūna's twenty-ninth year, that is, 1721. We call attention to the reference to the taking of Babylon by the Hittites, which brought an end to the dynasty of Ḫammurabi and opened access to the city for the Kassites.

pile of rubble, destroying it so that not even a bird could alight. Later, in his old age, all the countries revolted against him and besieged him in Akkade. Sargon went out, defeated his (adversaries), annihilated them, and slew their very large army.

Later yet, Subartu rose in all its power and forced him to take up arms. Sargon took it by surprise, inflicted a defeat on it, annihilated it, slew its very large army, and brought its wealth into Akkade. He took earth away from the clay pit of Babylon and built, near Akkade, a replica of Babylon. Because of (this) fault that he had committed, the great lord Marduk, overcome with rage, diminished his people by famine. From the East to the West there was a revolt against him, and he was afflicted with restlessness.

Narām-Sîn, son[11] of Sargon, [marched] on Apišal. He made a breach, seized King Rīš-A[dad] of Apišal and his minister. He marched on Magan and [seized] King Mannu-dannu of Magan.

Šulgi, son of Ur-Namma, abundantly provided food for Eridu that is on the seashore. However, full of bad intentions, he carried away as booty the wealth of the Esagila and Babylon. Bēl ... and made to consume (?) his corpse, ... destroyed him.

King Erra-imittī ordered Enlil-bāni, the gardener, to sit on the throne as royal substitute (and) put the crown of kingship on his head. Erra-imittī died in his palace while swallowing hot soup in little sips. Enlil-bāni, who sat on the throne, did not resign and was elevated to the royal office.

Ilu-šūma was king of Assyria in the time of Su-abu.
Battles (?).

(Obv.)^{1}[^{Id}*Èr-ra*-zà.dib lugal ^{Id}]*En-líl*-dù ^{lú}nu.kiri$_{6}$ ^{2}[*a-na* nu nì.sag.gil]^{e} *ina* ^{giš}gu.za-*šú ú-še-šib* ^{3}[a]ga lugal$^{ú-ti}$-*šú ina* sag.du-*šú iš-ta-kan* ^{4} ^{Id}*Èr-ra-i-mit-ti ina* é.gal-*šú pap-pa-si im-me-tú* ^{5}*ina sa-ra-pi-šú im-tu-ut* ^{6} ^{Id}*En-líl*-dù *ina* ^{giš}gu.za *ú-ši-bi ul it-bi* ^{6}*a-na* lugal$^{ú-ti}$ *it-taš-kan*

---

^{8} ^{I}*Ḫa-am-mu-ra-bi šàr* Tin.tir^{ki} érin^{me}-*šú id-ke-e-ma* ^{9}*a-na* ugu ^{I}Am.^{d}30 *šàr* Urí^{ki} *il-lik* ^{10}Urí^{ki} *u* Ararma^{ki} *qa-at-su ik-šu-ud* ^{11}*bu-šá-šu-nu a-na* Tin.tir^{ki} *il-qa-a* ^{12}[*u* ^{I}Am.^{d}30] *ina ki-is*-KAP-*pu ana* Tin.tir^{ki} *ú-bil-la*

---

^{13} ^{I}[*Sa-am-su-i-l*]*u-na šàr* Tin.tir^{ki} dumu ^{I}*Ḫ*[*a-am-mu-ra-bi* lu]gal ^{14}[. . .-*b*]*u-ut* [*id-ke*]-*e-ma*(?) ^{15}[. . . e]n zu na a ^{I}Am.^{d}30 *ana* $^{[uru(?)]}$. . . gin^{ik} ^{16}[. . .] šu$_{ii}$-*su* kur^{ud}-[*ma* ^{17}. . .] *bal-ṭu-ut-su ina* é.gal-š[*ú* . . . ^{18}. . .] gin-*ma il-mi* . . . [. . . ^{19}. . .] un^{me}-*šú* [. . .]

(. . .) (Rev.)$^{1'}$[. . . $^{2'}$ ^{I}*Ilu*(?)-*ma*(?)]-*ilu* ma [. . . $^{3'}$. . .] . . . e *ib-na* [. . .] $^{5'}$*ṣal-tú a-na* šà-*šú* dù-*m*[*a* . . .] $^{5'}$ad$_{6}$^{me}-*šú-nu tam-tì* [. . .] $^{6'}$*iš-ni-ma* ^{I}*Sa-am-su-i-lu-na* [. . .] $^{7'}$ ^{I}*Ilu-ma-ilu* zi^{am}-*ma* ŠI.ŠI. érin[^{me}-*šú im-ḫaṣ*]

$^{8'}$ ^{I}*A-bi-ši* dumu ^{I}*Sa-am-su-i-lu-na ka-šad* ^{I}*Ilu-ma-ilu iš*-[*kun*]-*ma* $^{9'}$ ^{i}$_{7}$Idigna *a-na se-ke-ri lìb-ba-šú ub-lam-ma* $^{10'}$ ^{i}$_{7}$Idigna *is-kìr-ma* ^{I}*Ilu-ma-ilu ul* [dib^{bat}]

$^{11'}$*ana tar-ṣi* ^{I}Man-*di-ta-na* ^{kur}*Ḫat-tu-ú ana* ^{kur}Uri^{ki} gin-*ma*

$^{12'}$ ^{Id}*É-a-ga-mil šàr* Kur *Tam-tì a-na* ^{kur}Elam.ma^{ki} *i*[*ḫ-liq*]-*ma* $^{13'}$egir-*šú* ^{I}*Ú-lam-bur-áš* šeš ^{I}*Kaš-til-iá-àš*(!) ^{kur}*Kaš-šu-ú* $^{14'}$érin-*šú id-ke-e-ma* Kur *Tam-tì* kur^{ud} en^{ut} kur *i-pu-uš*

$^{15'}$ ^{I}*A-gu-um* dumu ^{I}*Kaš-til-iá-àš* érin-*šú id-ke-e-ma* $^{16'}$*a-na* Kur *tam-tì il-lik* $^{17'}$ ^{uru}Bàd.^{d}50 kur^{ud} $^{18'}$*É-galga-šeš-na* é ^{d}50 *šá* Bàd.50 *ú-šal-pit*

---

41. FRAGMENTS OF A CHRONICLE OF ANCIENT KINGS

Sources: two unconnected fragments of a tablet in four columns.
Bibliography: Grayson 1975a: fragment of Babylonian chronicle 1.
Language: Babylonian.
Date: copy from the seventh century.
Place: Nineveh, Aššurbanipal's library.
Contents: fragments of the history of Isin and Babylon, with reference to Enlil and his temple, the Ekur. Was there here, perhaps, a different version of the taking of power by Enlil-bāni?

[King Erra-imittī] ordered Enlil-bāni, the gardener, to sit on the throne as royal substitute (and) put the crown of kingship on his head. Erra-imittī died in his palace while swallowing hot soup in little sips. Enlil-bāni sat on the throne, did not resign, and was elevated to the royal office.

Ḫammurabi, king of Babylon, mustered his troops and marched on Rīm-Sîn, king of Ur. He conquered Ur and Larsa, took away their possessions to Babylon, (and) brought [Rīm-Sî]n there in a ....

[Samsu-il]ūna, king of Babylon, son of Ḫ[ammurabi, the k]ing, [... mustere]d (?) and [...] Rīm-Sîn, marched on ..., seized [... and ...] in good health [...] in his palace. He marched on [...] and encircled [...] its people [...].

(...)

[... Iluma]-ilu [...] he made [...] he joined battle with him [...] their corpses [...] in the sea [...] he repeated, and Samsu-ilūna [...]. Iluma-ilu rose up and [inflicted] a defeat on his troops.

Abī-ešuḫ, son of Samsu-ilūna, put himself in a position to seize Iluma-ilu and decided to obstruct the flow of the Tigris. He obstructed the flow of the Tigris but did not [catch] Iluma-ilu...

During the time of Samsu-ditāna, the Hittites marched on Akkad.

Ea-gāmil, king of the Sealand, fled into Elam. Later, Ulam-Buriaš, brother of Kaštiliaš (III), the Kassite, mustered his army, conquered the Sealand, (and) governed the country.

Agum (III), son of Kaštiliaš (III), mustered his army and marched on the Sealand. He conquered Dūr-Enlil (and) desecrated the Egalgašešna, Enlil's temple there.

Fragment A

(i)(. . .) 1'[. . .] . . .-*su*(?) . . . é ^{d}*Nin-urta* . . . [. . . 2'. . .] . . . ^{giš}tukul *ra-biš ib-* . . . 3'[. . .] *a-na tab-rat kiš-šat* un^{meš} *uš-ziz*

4'[. . . *š*]*àr Ì-ši-in*^{ki} sukkal.maḫ *Li-pit-*^{d}*Iš-tar* 5'[. . . sís]kur bala-*ma* ^{d}*En-líl-ma lu ki-a-am* 6'[. . .] sískur-*sú ṣi-ra* gun-*su* dugud^{tú} 7'[.?. *a-na*] *É-kur na-ši-ma il-lak* 8'[. . .]-*il-ma* máš.gi$_{6}$ *i-na-aṭ-ṭal* 9'[. . .] . . . ^{d}*En-líl im-ḫu-ru-ma* 10'[. . .] . . . dab^{at}-*ma ul ì-ṭe-eḫ-ḫe* (. . .)

(ii) (. . .) 1' ^{d}*E*[*n-líl*(?) . . .] 2'*ul* [. . .] 3'lugal [. . .] 4'*i-nu-šu* [. . .] 5'*ki-i* [. . .] 6'*ki-sur-ru* [. . .] 7'*ana pa-*[*an*(?) . . .]

(iii) (. . .) 1'*ana* [. . .] 2'*i-gàr-šu* [. . .] 3'*ma-kàs* [. . .] 4'diš mu . . . [. . .] (. . .)

(iv) 1[. . .] *na-ši-*[. . . 2. . .] *in-na-pi-iḫ-ma* 3[. . .] . . . é ḫur$^{ti(?)}$ izi *it-ta-di* 4[. . .^{d}]*En-líl i-lak-ma* 5[. . .] *e*(?)-*re-bi-im-ma* 6[. . .] . . . izi *ana bul-li-i* 7[. . . Ká.dingir].ra^{ki} ku$_{4}$^{ub}-*ma* 8[. . .] . . .-*tu-ut* 9[. . .]. . .[. . .] (. . .)

Fragment B

(Obv.?) (i)(. . .) 1'[. . . *k*]*i-a-am* dù-*su* 2'[. . .]-*ši-na-a-ti* 3'[. . .] *uš-tin-ni* 4'[. . . *n*]*i-ši-ma* 5'[. . . ^{d}*E*]*n*(?)-*líl* 6'[. . .] . . . be (. . .)

(ii) (. . .) 1'[. . .] *Ì-ši-i*[*n*^{ki}(?) . . . 2' ^{d}*E*]*n-líl-*dù ^{lú}nu.kiri$_{6}$ *ina* [. . .] 3' ^{d}*Èr-ra-i-mit-ti ana ka-šad* [^{giš}gu.za(?). . .] 4'*ḫa-as-su ù ka-*.. [. . .] 5'*it-bu-ma* [. . .] 6'*ina a-mat* ^{d}*En-líl* [. . .] 7'*di-k*[*a* . . .] 8' ^{d}[. . .] (. . .)

(Rev.?) (i) (. . .) 1' ^{i}$_{7}$Idigna *a-n*[*a se-ke-ri* . . .] 2'*Ilu-ma-ilu na-*[*ki-ru* . . .] 3'*ina a-mat* en gal ^{d}*En-líl* [. . .] 4'*a-na se-kèr* [^{i}$_{7}$Idigna . . . 5'*Ilu-m*]*a-ilu na-ki-r*[*u* . . . 6'. . .] . . . ri . . . [. . .] (. . .)

42. FRAGMENTS OF A CHRONICLE OF ANCIENT KINGS

Sources: tablet fragments.
Bibliography: Grayson 1975a: fragment of Babylonian chronicle 2.
Language: Babylonian.
Date: Hellenistic period.
Place: Babylon.
Contents: fragments of the history of the Sealand.

(. . .) 1'[. . .]-*uš* giš.ḫu[r . . . 2'. . .] . . . 30 Utu *u* ^{d}Iškur *aṭ-ma-an-š*[*u-nu* . . .].

Fragment A

(. . .)

[. . .] the temple of Ninurta [. . .] he [. . .], lavishly, the arm [. . .]. He erected [. . .] to the astonishment of all the people.

[. . . k]ing (?) of Isin, the *sukkalmaḫ*,[12] Lipit-Ištar, [. . .] offered sacrifices to Enlil and (himself saying?): "May it be so!" He came, bearing his official sacrifices to the Ekur, his heavy tribute. [Being in bed], he had a dream. Enlil having received [. . .] he took [. . .] not being able to approach.

(. . .)

E[nlil (?) . . .] did not [. . .] the king [. . .] when [. . .] before (?) [. . .] territory [. . .] in fr[ont (?) . . .].

(. . .)

[. . .] for [. . .] his wall [. . .].

(. . .)

[. . .] for [. . .] bearer [. . .] took fire and [. . .] he set fire to that house [. . .] Enlil went and [. . .] having entered and [. . .] the fire to the [. . .] he entered into [Babylo]n and [. . .].

(. . .)

Fragment B

[. . .] he thus made [. . .] them [. . .] was changed (?) and [. . . En]lil [. . .].

(. . .)

[. . .] Isi[n . . . En]lil-bāni, the gardener, in [the . . . of] Erra-imittī, in order to seize [the throne (?) . . .] clever and [. . .] rose up and [. . .] according to Enlil's order [. . .].

(. . .)

To [obstruct] the flow of the Tigris [. . .] Iluma-ilu, the en[emy, . . .] on the order of the great lord Enlil [. . .] for the obstruction of [the flow of the Tigris, . . . Ilum]a-ilu, the enemy [. . .].

(. . .)

(. . .)

[. . .] the decree [. . .] the chapels of Sîn, Šamaš, and Adad [. . .].

$^{3'}$[. *n*]*a-din* ^{giš}pa aš.te bala [. . . $^{4'}$. . . k]in-*šu mi-iḫ-rit* ka dingir^{meš} gal^{meš} [. . .]

$^{5'}$[. . . *in*]*a* bala Dumu.nita.^{d}Iškur Kur *Tam-tì i-be-el* [. . . $^{6'}$. . . *i*]-*lam-ma* bala Dumu.nita.^{d}Iškur [. . .] *ana* Kur *Tam-tì* [. . . $^{7'}$. . . ^{d}Amar].utu(?) en Kur *Tam-tì i-ru-ru ù ša* Kur *Ta*[*m-tì* . . . $^{8'}$. . . *du*]-*ul-la ana* Ká.dingir.ra^{ki} *ú-kin* mu aš.te . . . [. . . $^{9'}$. . .]-*te* en *ina É-kur* šub^{a} *iq-ba-am-ma* [. . . $^{10'}$. . .^{m}]^{eš} Ká.dingir.ra^{ki} *ina* edin *di/ki-rim-ma gi-mil-l*[*a*(?) . . .] (. . .)

43. FRAGMENT OF A CHRONICLE OF ANCIENT KINGS

Sources: tablet fragment.
Bibliography: Lambert 1990: 29–33, text 1.
Language: Babylonian.
Date: copy from the seventh century.
Place: Nineveh, Aššurbanipal's library.
Contents: fragment of the history of Babylon. The wine reminds one of chronicle 38.

$^{1'}$(. . .) [. . .] . . . *it-ta-a-ti* . . . [. . . $^{2'}$. . .] . . . *muš-ta-n*[*u*/*m*[*u-ú* . . . $^{3'}$. . .] *a-na* sag-*ia lit*-[*bu*(?)-*uk*(?) . . . $^{4'}$. . .]-*a ze-nu-tú* [. . . $^{5'}$. . .] . . . *ma-a-ti i-šab-bu-us-su* . . . [. . . $^{6'}$. . .]. . .-*a a-pu-ul-šu-nu-ti-ma* s[u . . . $^{7'}$(.?.)] . . . *ḫul-liq a-mat* ḫ[ul^{ti} (.?.) $^{8'}$(.?.)] . . . *ša-a-šú-nu ina ma-ḫar* ^{d}*Nuska u* ^{d}Giš.bar [. . . $^{9'}$*l*]*a-am* ^{d}*Nuska* sukkal.maḫ *Sa-am-si-i*-[*lu-na* . . . $^{10'}$*l*]*a il-pu-ut-ma* úš *la* i[b . . . $^{11'}$g]ír^{zabar}-*šú la* . . . [. . . $^{12'}$. . . *d*]*i*(?)-*na-ma at-ta* geštin *l*[*e-qé*(?) . . . $^{13'}$. . .] id *šú-nu* . . . tir [. . .] (. . .)

44. FRAGMENT OF A CHRONICLE OF ANCIENT KINGS

Sources: tablet fragment.
Bibliography: Lambert 1990: 32–34, text 2.
Language: Babylonian.
Date: copy of the seventh century.
Place: Nineveh, Aššurbanipal's library.
Contents: tiny fragment of the history of Babylon.

(column A) (. . .) $^{1'}$[. . .]. . . $^{2'}$ [. . .] gar $^{3'}$[. . .] kal $^{4'}$[. . .] . . . uru $^{5'}$[. . .]-*ú-ki* $^{6'}$[. . .] . . . lu ri $^{7'}$[. . .] . . . tur^{meš} $^{8'}$[. . .] . . .-*e-šu* $^{9'}$[. . .] *ú-tar* $^{10'}$[. . .] *a-šá-ba* [. . .] . . . (. . .)

(column B) (. . .) $^{1'}$*a*(?)-*n*[*a*(?) . . .] $^{2'}$*Sa-am-s*[*i-i-lu-na* . . .] $^{3'}$*na-ad-nak-k*[*a* . . .] $^{4'}$*šum-ma e-nin* . . . [. . .] $^{5'}$*it-tur* an . . . [. . .] $^{6'}$ugu uru *šá* . . . [. . .] $^{7'}$*ip-ti* . . .[. . .] $^{8'}$ag . . . [. . .]

$^{9'}$[. . .] (. . .)

[... who gi]ves the scepter, the throne, and the mantle [...] his work, according to the decision of the great gods [...].

[... dur]ing the reign of Apil-Adad he governed the Sealand [...] he lifted up and the reign of Apil-Adad [...] in the Sealand [... whom Mar]duk (?) cursed, up to the Sealand and [...] of the Sea[land ...] he assigned [forc]ed labor to Babylon, because of the throne [...] placed in the Ekur, he told [the inhabitant]s (?) of Babylon, in the plain ... [...]

(...)

(...)

[...] signs [...] an adversary [...] that he [poured (?)] on my head [...] in anger [...] will be furious at him [...] answered them and [...] made the unpleasant matter go away [...] them, before Nuska and Girra [...]. Before Nuska [...] the *sukkalmaḫ*,[13] Samsu-i[lūna (.?.)]. He did not attack nor [...] of blood [...]. His dagger did not [...] you, you t[ook (?)] wine [...].

(...)

(...)

[...] for [...] Sams[u-ilūna ...] was given you [...]. If a favor [was granted ...].

(...)

45. CHRONICLE OF THE KASSITE KINGS

Sources: large tablet in four columns; only a third of it is preserved.
Bibliography: Grayson 1975a: no. 22.
Language: Babylonian, with a few dialectal peculiarities.
Date: copy from the Late Babylonian period.
Place: unknown.
Contents: history of the Kassite wars, from Kadašman-Ḫarbe (I) to Adad-šuma-iddina. The chronicle may be a Babylonian copy of Assyrian chronicle 10. This version of the history is identical, narrating the tragic end of Tukultī-Ninurta I, who struck a blow against Babylon.

(i) (...) $^{1'}$[...] ... a ... [... $^{2'}$...] *šàr* ^{kur}*Kar-an-dun-ía-*[*àš*] *ù* ^{Id}[... $^{3'}$*šàr* ^{kur}*Aš-šur*^{ki} *rík-sa-a-ni*] *ú-rak-kis ina bi-ri-šú-nu mi-ṣir a-ḫa-meš ú-*[*k*]*in-nu* $^{4'}$[...] ...*-si*(?)*-ma* dù*-ma a-na áš-ri-šú ú-ter*

$^{5'}$[^{I}*Ka-dáš-man-Ḫa*]*r-be* dumu ^{I}*Kara-in-da-áš* dumu *šá* ^{munus}*Mu-bal-liṭ-at-*^{d}Edin^{u-a} $^{6'}$[dumu.munus-*šú*] *šá* ^{I}An.šár.tin^{iṭ} *šàr* ^{kur}*Aš-šur*^{ki} *ka-ma-ri Su-ti-i rab-ba-a-tú* $^{7'}$ta *ṣi-it* ^{d}Utu^{ši} en *e-reb* ^{d}Utu^{ši} *iš-pur-ma* en nu gál e.muq^{meš}-*šú-nu* <*ú-šá-lik*> $^{8'}$ ^{uru}*bi-ra-a-tú ina qí-rib* ^{kur}Šár.šár *ú-kaṣ-ṣir* ^{pú}*ku-up-pu ip-te-e-ma* $^{9'}$a-na en.nun^{tú} *du-un-nu-nu* un^{meš} *ina* šà-*ši-na a-bur-riš ú-še-šib ár-ka-nu* $^{10'}$un^{meš} *Kaš-ši-i* bala^{meš}-*šú* gaz^{meš}-*šu* ^{I}*Šu-zi-ga-áš* ^{kur}*Kaš-šá-a* $^{11'}$dumu *la ma-am-nu a-na* lugal$^{ú-tu}$ *a-na* ugu-*šú-nu iš-šu-ú* ^{I}An.šár.tin^{iṭ} $^{12'}$[*šàr* k[^{ur}*Aš-šur*^{ki} *a-na tu-ru gi-mir šá* ^{I}*Ka-dáš-man-Ḫar-be* dumu dumu.munus-*šú* $^{13'}$[*a-n*]*a* ^{kur}*Kar-an-dun-ía-*[*áš i*]*l-lik* ^{I}*Šu-zi-ga-áš* ^{kur}*Kaš-šá-a* $^{14'}$[*i-duk* ^{I}*Ku-ri-gal-zu* dumu ^{I}*Ka-dáš*]*-man-Ḫar-be ina* ^{giš}g[u.za ad-*šú ú-še-šib*]

(ii) (...) $^{1'}$mu [...] $^{2'}$gi id [...] $^{3'}$*e-li-šú-nu* [...]*-ma ri-ig-mu i-*...[...] $^{4'}$ ^{lú}kúr *i-ḫ*[*u-u*]*s-su a-ḫa-meš* ^{ú}u$_4$.nígi[n ... *ina* ^{giš}tukul] $^{5'}$*ú-šam-qi*[*t-m*]*a kul-lat-su-nu* zi^{tì} *ul e-zib ma-aq-t*[*u-ti*(?) ...] $^{6'}$*ú-si-*[*iq*]*-qu* zi^{tì} *tam-tì gal-la-tu*$_4$ *ina da-mi-šú-nu li-*[*ib-ba-ša*(?) dir(?)] $^{7'}$id ... *ú-še-ṣu-u* ^{lú}érin^{meš}-*šú-ni ik-pu-du ni-iz-mat-su-un* ... [...] $^{8'}$*u*(?) ^{lú}érin^{meš} ú-pa-áš-ši-ḫu bu-še-e ^{lú}kúr *šad-lu-tu*$_4$ *ú-pa-aḫ-*[*ḫi-ir* $^{9'}$*a*]*-na gu-ru-né-e ú-še-li i-tur-ru-nim-ma mun-da-*[*aḫ-ṣu*(?) ...] $^{10'}$*ul ni-de-e-ma* ^{I}*Ku-ri-gal-zu ki-i kul-lat* un^{meš} *ta-*...[...] $^{11'}$*ina* un^{meš} *šá-nin-ni ul ni-ši e-nin-na-ma ta-t*[*u-* ... kaskal(?)] $^{12'}$*ni-iṣ-bat a-šar-ka ni-iš-te-e-ma ir-ba a-ni-ni n*[*e-* ... $^{13'}$...]-...*-tu nu-šak-ši-du qa-tuk-ku i-tu-ur-ma iš-*...[... $^{14'}$...]*-šú-nu-ti-ma* ... tu ta ... [... (iii) ^{1}...] ... [...] ... ú ... [...] ^{2}... *lim* gu ú lu šú(?) ú(?) ... [...] ^{3}... *lim* ... da ṣi ... [...] ^{4}1 *lim* anše.kur.ra^{meš} *bar-mu-tú i-rib-šú-nu ú-*...[...] ^{5}*šá li-šá-nu iṣ-bat-tam-ma re-da-a ú-bi-li ur-*[...] ^{6}*ma-ṣa-ar ú-še-eṣ-bit a-dan-na ú-gam-mi-ir* [...] ^{7}*ta-a-a-ri ur-ḫu-ku-nu* kù.babbar guškin *ni-siq-tu*$_4$ n[a$_4$ ...] ^{8}*ub-lam* an^{e} guškin.kù^{meš} *a-na* ^{d}Amar.utu en-*ia lu* [*e-pu-uš*(?) ...] ^{9}Tin.tir^{ki} *u Bár-sipa*^{ki} ugu edin-*ia lu ú-šá-*AD.DIR [...] ^{10} ^{I}*Ḫu-ur-ba-ti-la šàr* ^{kur}*E-lam-mat a-na*

(. . .)

[. . .], king of Karanduniaš, and [. . ., king of Assyria], concluded a mutual [accord] and, together, fixed the boundary. [. . .] constructed and restored [. . . . Kadašman-Ḫar]be (I), son of Kara-indaš (and) son of Muballiṭat-Šerūa, [daughter of] King Aššur-uballiṭ (I) of Assyria, gave the order to reduce the Suteans from the East to the West and annihilated their large forces. He strengthened the fortifications of the citadels in Šaršar (= Djebel Bišrī), dug wells there, and settled people on fertile lands in order to help guard it. Later the Kassite people revolted against him and killed him. They put Šuzigaš, a Kassite, son of a nobody, in kingship over them. [King] Aššur-uballiṭ of Assyria [m]arched [o]n Karanduni[aš] to avenge Kadašman-Ḫarbe, his daughter's son. [He killed] Šuzigaš the Kassite [and made Kurigalzu (II), son of Kadaš]man-Ḫarbe, ascend the thr[one of his father].

(. . .)

[. . .] over them [. . .] and a cry [. . .]. The enemy seized him. Together . . . [. . . he] crushed [them and] left no one alive. Those who had fa[llen (?) . . .] were treated (?) harshly, (and) their blood [stained (?)] the rough sea. [. . .] were ordered out, the troops mutinied, [. . .] their requests (and?) the troops were appeased. He gathered the enemy's great wealth (and) heaped it up. Again the contending [forces declared]: "We did not know, Kurigalzu, that you [had triumphed (?)] over all the people, that we had no rival among the people! Now you [. . .]. We took the road, found the place where you were, and we ourselves [carried (?)] gifts! We contributed [to your victories (?)]!" Again he [. . .]: "[. . .] their [. . .] and [. . ." . . .] thousands [. . .] thousands [. . .], a thousand piebald horses, their gifts [. . .]. He caught a spy and brought a soldier [. . .], put guards in place (and) the term allotted (?) [. . . ". . .] just back from your journey. I brought silver, gold, selected [*precious stones*, and I made (?)] a dais in pure gold for Marduk my lord, [.?.]. Babylon and Borsippa were seething (?) concerning my [. . .]." King Ḫurba-tela[14]

^{I}*Ku-ri-gal-zu* [. . .] ^{11}*um-ma al-kam-ma* [*ana*]-*ku ù ka-a-šú* <<diš>> *ina* Bàd.^{d}*Šul-g*[*i ṣal-ta* (*ana* šà)] ^{12}*a-ḫa-meš ni-pu-uš* ^{I}*Ku-ri-gal-zu iš-me-e-e-ma* [. . .] . . . [. . .] ^{13}*a-na* ^{kur}Elam^{ki} *a-na ka-šá-du* gin^{ik}-*ma* ^{I}*Ḫ*[*u-ur-ba-ti-la*] ^{14}*šàr* ^{kur}*E-lam-mat ina* Bàd.^{d}*Š*[*ul.g*]*i ṣal-tú ana* šà-*šú* [*i-pu-uš*] ^{15}*ina* igi-*šú ib-bal-kit-ma* ^{I}*Ku-ri-gal-zu* ŠI.ŠI-*šú-nu iš-ku-un* (.?.)] ^{16}*šàr* ^{kur}*E-lam-mat* šu$_{ii}$-*su* kur^{ud} *kul-lat* $^{k[ur]}$*E-lam-mat* mi . . . [. . .] ^{17}*ke-mi-iṣ ina kin-ṣi-šú* ^{I}*Ḫu-ur-ba-ti-la šàr* ^{kur}*E-lam-m*[*at* . . .] ^{18}*lu-ú i-di* lugal ^{I}*Ku-ri-gal-zu ki-i a-ga-a an-na-a*(?) [. . .] ^{19}*it-ti* lugal^{meš} *šá nap-ḫar* kur^{meš} *man-da-at-tu*$_{4}$ *E-lam-*[*mat*(?) *lu ub-la*(?)] ^{20}*a-na* ugu ^{Id}Iškur.érin.táḫ *šàr* ^{kur}*Aš-šur*^{ki} *ana* kur^{du} [*il-lik-ma* . . .] ^{21}*ina* ^{uru}*Su-ga-ga šá* ugu ^{i}$_{7}$*Ì-diq-lat ṣal-tu ana* [šà-*šú i-pu-uš* (.?.)] ^{22}érin^{meš}-*šú i-duk* ^{lú}gal^{meš}-*šú ina* šu$_{i}$[$_{i}$-*šú iṣ-bat* . . .]

---

^{23} ^{I}*Na-zi-múru-taš* dumu ^{I}[. . .] ^{24}*šàr* ^{kur}*Aš-šur*^{ki} *ina*(?) ^{u}[^{ru}(?) . . .] (. . .)

(iv) ^{1}[. . .] . . . [. . .] ^{2}[. . .] ḫar an.bar *id-di-ma*(?) . . . [. . .] ^{3}[. . . ^{I}*Tukul-t*]*i*-^{d}Maš *a-na* Tin.tir^{ki} *i-tu-ra-am-ma* ^{4}[. . .] . . . [. . . *ú*]-*qar-ri-bu* bàd Tin.tir^{ki} *iq-qur* kur Tin.tir^{ki} *ina* ^{giš}tukul ^{5}[*ú-šam-q*]*it* nì.ga *É-sag-gíl u* Tin.tir^{ki} *ina šál-lat uš-te-ṣi* ^{d}En gal^{ú} ^{d}Amar.utu ^{6}[*ina šu*]*b-ti-šú id-ke-e-ma a-na* ^{kur}*Aš-šur*^{ki} *ú-šá*(!)-*aṣ-bit ḫar-ra-an* ^{lú}*šak-nu-ti-šú* ^{7}*ina* ^{kur}*Kar-an-dun-ía-àš iš-kun* 7 mu^{meš} ^{I}*Tukul-ti*-^{d}Maš *Kar-an-dun-ía-àš* ^{8}*ú-ma-'-ir* egir ^{lú}gal^{meš} *šá* ^{kur}Uri^{ki} *šá* ^{kur}*Kar-an-dun-ía-àš* bala^{meš}-*ma* ^{9} ^{Id}Iškur.mu.ùri *ina* ^{giš}gu.za *ad-šú ú-še-ši-bu* ^{I}*Tukul-ti*-^{d}Maš *šá ana* Tin.tir^{ki} *ana* ḫul^{tú} ^{10}[šu]$_{ii}$ *ú-bil-lu* ^{I}An.šár-*na-ṣir*-a dumu-*šú u* ^{lú}gal^{meš} *šá* ^{kur}*Aš-šur*^{ki} bala^{meš}-*šu-ma* ^{11}[*ina*] ^{giš}gu.za-*šú id-ku-šu-ma ina* ^{uru}*Kar-Tukul-ti*-^{d}Maš *ina* é *i-si-ru-šu-ma ina* ^{giš}tukul gaz^{meš}-*šú* ^{12}[7]6(?) mu^{meš} *a-di* ^{I}*Tukul-ti*-An.šár ^{d}En *ina* ^{kur}*Aš-šur*^{ki} *a-šib ana tar-ṣi* ^{I}*Tukul-ti*-An.šár ^{d}En *a-na* ^{13}[Tin].tir^{ki} *it-tal-kám*

---

^{14}[*ana tar-ṣi*] ^{Id}*En-líl-na-din*-mu lugal *it-ba-am-ma* ^{I}*Ki-den*-^{d}*Ḫu-ut-ru-diš šàr* ^{kur}Elam.ma^{ki} ^{15}[*ú-bi*]*l-la* šu-*su a-na* Nibru^{ki} un^{meš}-*šú is-pu-uḫ* Bàd.an^{ki} *u É-dim-gal-kalam-ma* ^{16}[*ú-ab*]-*bit*(?) un^{meš}-*šú iš-tal-lu iṭ-ru-ud-ma* ^{Id}*En-líl-na-din*-mu lugal *uk-kiš be-lut-su*

---

^{17}[*ana tar-ṣi* ^{Id}Išk]ur.mu.sum^{na} *is-saḫ-ram-ma* ^{I}*Ki-den*-^{d}*Ḫu-ut-ru-diš* ^{kur}Uri^{ki} *ina* 2^{i} zi-*šú* ^{18}[. . .] . . . *ú-ab-bit* ^{uru}*I-šin i-bir* ^{i}$_{7}$Idigna *gi-mir* ^{19}[. . .] *Marad-da*^{ki} ŠI.ŠI un^{meš} *rab-ba-a-tú lim-niš* ^{20}[. . .] . . . DU(?)-*uš-ma ina* gu$_{4}$^{meš} *pa-qa-ar* ^{21}[. . .] ud ma *ú-šá-as-si ḫar-ba-a-ti* ^{22}[. . .]-*šum*(?)-*ma*

---

^{23}[. . .] *ú-ma-'-ir* ^{24}[. . .] *ni*(?)-*šú* (. . .)

of Elam [appealed] to Kurigalzu: "Come! Join battle, you and me, at Dūr-Šulgi!" Kurigalzu, having heard and [. . .], marched on Elam to conquer it. King Ḫ[urba-tela] of Elam [joined] battle with him at Dūr-Š[ulg]i. He beat a retreat before him, and Kurigalzu infl[icted] a defeat on him. He laid hands on the king of Elam (and) Elam in its totality [. . .]. Falling on his knees, King Ḫurba-tela of Elam (declared): "Yes, I know, O King Kurigalzu, that this . . . [. . .] with the kings of all the countries [I bring (?)] Elam's tribute." With conquest in mind [he marched] on King Adad-nārārī (I) of Assyria and [joined] battle [with him] at Sugaga that is on the Tigris; he massacred his troops and [captured] his officers.

Nazi-Muruttaš, son of [. . .], king of Assyria, into [. . .].

(. . .)

[. . .] he cast off (?) the iron chains and [. . . Tukult]ī- Ninurta (I) returned to Babylon and [. . .] brought together [. . .]. He battered down Babylon's wall, cru[shed] the Babylonians. Among the booty, he carried away the riches of the Esagila and Babylon. He took the great lord Marduk [out of] his [dwel]ling-place and made him set out for Assyria. He installed his own governors in Karanduniaš. For seven years Tukultī-Ninurta dominated[15] Karanduniaš. After the rebellion of the officials of Akkad (and) Karanduniaš and the installation of Adad-šuma-uṣur on the throne of his father, Aššur-nāṣir-apli, his son, and the Assyrian officials revolted against Tukultī-Ninurta, who for evil had laid [hands] on Babylon, deposed him from his throne, locked him in a room in Kār-Tukultī-Ninurta, and put him to death.[16] [For seventy-]six (?) years, up to (Ninurta)-tukultī-Aššur, Bēl resided in Assyria. In the time of (Ninurta)-tukultī-Aššur, Bēl went to [Bab]ylon.

[In the time of] King Enlil-nādin-šumi, King Kiden-Ḫutrudiš (= Ḫutran) of Elam took the offensive. [He ca]rried out a raid against Nippur (and) scattered its inhabitants; [he destro]yed Dēr and the Edimgal-kalama, led away the people whom he had driven into captivity and drove King Enlil-nādin-šumi from power.

[In the time of Ad]ad-šuma-iddina, for the second time, Kiden-Ḫutran took the offensive against Akkad. [. . .], he destroyed Isin, crossed the Tigris, all [. . .] Marad, [inflicted] a formidable defeat on a very great people. [. . .] with oxen [. . .] he changed (?) into desert [. . .].

[. . .] he dominated[17] [. . .].

(. . .)

46. CHRONICLE OF THE LAST KASSITE KINGS AND THE KINGS OF ISIN

Sources: fragmentary tablet in the same format as a Neo-Babylonian administrative text.
Bibliography: Walker 1982.
Language: Babylonian.
Date: Neo-Babylonian period.
Place: Babylon.
Contents: history of Babylon from Adad-šuma-uṣur to Adad-apla-iddina.

^{1}[^{I}*Tukul-ti-*^{d}Maš *šàr* ^{kur}*Aš-šur*^{ki} Tin.tir^{ki} *u Sip*]-*par* dib-*ma* ^{kur}*Kár-an-dun-ía-àš ú-ma-a-a-er* ^{2}[^{Id}Iškur.mu.ùri ... *ú-t*]*ir* bàd Nibru^{ki} dù^{uš} ^{3}[...] *ú-kin* ^{Id}*En-líl*-nì.du.ùri *šàr* ^{kur}*Aš-šur*^{ki} ^{4}[... ^{Id}Iškur.mu.ùri érin^{me}-*šú id-ke*]-*e-ma* ^{giš}tukul *iš-ši-ma* ŠI.ŠI-*šú im-ḫaṣ* ^{5}[... ^{Id}*En-líl*-nì.d]u.ùri en-*šú-nu* dib^{me}-*ma ana* ^{Id}Iškur.mu.ùri sum^{nu} ^{6}[... un^{m}]^{e} *šá* ^{kur}*Kar-dun-ía-àš šá ana* ^{kur}*Aš-šur in-na-bi-tu* ^{7}[... *ana* ^{Id}Iškur.m]u.ùri *id-dan-nu* ^{Id}Iškur.mu.ùri *ana ka-šad* uru ^{8}[gin^{ik} ...] *a-a-um-ma* dumu *la mam-ma-na-ma šá šum-šú la za-kar* ^{9}[... ^{Id}Iškur.mu.ùr]i *ina bu-us-rat ú-bar-ma* gissu dingir *da-ru-ú* ugu-*šú* gar-*ma* ^{10}[... kur *i*]-*be-el-ma ina* ^{giš}gu.za lugal$^{ú-ti}$-*šú i-ku-un*

---

^{11}[...] gaz^{me}-*šú*

---

^{12}[...] gu$_4$.ud-*ma šàr* ^{kur}*Má-rí*^{ki} *ina* ḫi.gar *id-ke-e-ma* ^{13}[...] ^{kur}*Má-rí ú-ma-a-a-er*

---

^{14}[... *ḫa-a*]*t-tú* Elam.ma^{ki} *im-qut-su-ma* ^{15}[... *i*]*na* gú ^{i}$_7$Buranun uru dù-*ma* ^{16}[...] ... ^{kur}*Šu-me-ri u* Uri^{ki} *ana* šà-*šú* ku$_4$^{ib} ^{17}[... *ip*]-*pa-ri-is-ma* un^{me} *ina bat-qa u ḫu-šaḫ-ḫu il-pu-nu* ^{18}[...] *ina* ḫi.gar gaz^{me}-*šú*

---

^{19}[^{Id}*En-líl-na-din*-a dumu ^{Id}Nà.nì.d]u.ùri *ana Bal-til*^{ki} *ana* kur^{di} gin^{ik} ^{20}[^{Id}Amar.utu-*na-din*-šeš^{meš} šeš ^{Id}]Nà.nì.du.ùri *u* ^{lú}dù^{me} *ib-bal-ki-tu-u-šú-ma* ^{21}[^{Id}*En-líl-na-din*-a *ana* ku]r-*šú u* u[ru-*šú i*]-*tur ina* ^{giš}[tukul ga]z^{me}-*šú*

---

^{22}[^{Id}*En-líl-na-din*-a ^{Id}Amar.utu-*n*]*a-din*-šeš^{meš} [*u* ^{lú}dù^{me} ḫi].gar^{me}-*ma* ^{23}[...] ... [...] *i-tur* ^{24}[... -*m*]*a* ŠI.[ŠI-*šú im-ḫa*]-*aṣ* ^{25}[... gu$_4$].ud-*ma* ... [...] *ina* ^{giš}tukul gaz ^{26}[... ^{I}*Tukul-ti-a-é-š*]*ár-ra š*[*àr* ^{kur}*Aš-šu*]*r*^{ki} zi-*ma*

[King Tukultī-Ninurta (I) of Assyria] took [Babylon and Sip]par and dominated[18] Karanduniaš. [Adad-šuma-uṣur] restored [. . .] (and) (re)built Nippur's wall. He firmly established [. . .]. King Enlil-kudurrī-uṣur of Assyria [. . . Adad-šuma-uṣur muster]ed [his troops], attacked and defeated him. [The officers of Assyria (?)] seized [Enlil-kudur]rī-uṣur, their lord, and delivered (him) to Adad-šuma-uṣur. [. . . the inhabitant]s of Karduniaš who had fled into Assyria surrendered [. . . to] Adad-šuma-uṣur. Adad-šuma-uṣur [moved .(?).] in order to conquer the city (= Babylon). Somebody, son of a person whose name is forgotten, [*ascended the throne* (?)]. At the announcement of this unexpected news, [Adad-šuma-uṣu]r stirred up a revolt, and, enjoying unlimited divine protection, [*he entered Babylon* (?). He] governed [the land] and ascended the royal throne.

[. . .] they killed him.

[. . .] attacked and thrust aside the king of Mari during an uprising and [. . .] he dominated[19] Mari.

[. . . the ter]ror that absorbed Elam overtook him and [. . .], he built a city on the banks of the Euphrates and [. . .] made to enter there [. . .] of Sumer and Akkad. [. . .] was set apart and the deprived and starving people grew poorer [. . .] they killed him during an uprising.

[Enlil-nādin-apli, son of Nebuchadn]ezzar (I), advanced in order to conquer Baltil. [Marduk-nādin-aḫḫē, brother of N]ebuchadnezzar, and the nobles rebelled against him. [Enlil-nādin-apli] returned [to his cou]ntry and [his] city. They were executed.

[Marduk-nā]din-aḫḫē [and the nobles r]ose up [against Enlil-nādin-apli]; he returned [. . .] and [def]eated [him. . . . he at]tacked and [. . .] he had him executed. [Tiglath-piles]er (I), k[ing of Assyr]ia, went out on a campaign and <.?.>.

---

^{27}[^{Id}Amar.utu.dub.numun dumu ^{Id}A]mar.utu-*na-din*-šeš[^{meš} bàd T]in.tir^{ki} *eš-šiš i-pu-uš* ^{28}[... za lugal^{me} *šá* kur.kur *im-ḫa*]*ṣ ina* bala-*šú* un^{me} kur ḫé.nun *u ṭuḫ-du* igi^{meš}

---

^{29}[^{Id}Iškur.eduru.mu a ^{I}Ki.^{d}Amar.u]tu.tin *A-ra-mu u* lugal im.gi *is-ḫu-šú-ma* ^{30}[*ma-ḫa-zu ka-la šá* kur *ú-šal*]*-pi-tu A-kà-dè*^{ki} Bàd.an^{ki} *Dur-an-ki* ^{31}[... Zimb]ir^{ki} *u Pàr-sa-a*^{ki} šub^{meš} ^{32}[^{kur}*Su-tu-u* zi-*ma šál-lat* ^{kur}Š]*u-me-ri u* Uri^{ki} *ana* kur-*šú ú-še-ṣi* ^{33}[*áš-rat* ^{d}Amar.utu *iš-te-'e*]*-em lìb-bi* ^{d}En *u* dumu ^{d}En *ú-ṭi-ib* ^{34}[... *par*]*-ṣi-šú-nu ú-šak-lil*

47. CHRONICLE OF THE KINGS OF BABYLON FROM THE SECOND ISIN DYNASTY TO THE ASSYRIAN CONQUEST

Sources: fragmentary tablet.
Bibliography: Grayson 1975a: no. 24; Walker 1982: 416.
Language: Babylonian.
Date: Neo-Babylonian period.
Place: Babylon.
Contents: when it was complete, the chronicle probably covered a time span from the second Isin dynasty to the taking of Babylon by Sennacherib. Some passages duplicate the preceding chronicle. With its choppy style, incomplete phrases, abbreviated presentation, and the incongruous character of the information that it gives, this chronicle is quite different from the others. Could it have been a memorandum?

(...) $^{1'}$[... *šál-la-t*]*u* dugud^{tú} *iš-lul*

$^{2'}$ ^{Id}Amar.utu.dub.numun du[mu ^{Id}Amar.utu-na-din-šeš^{meš} bàd Tin.tir^{ki} *eš-ši*]*š* dù^{uš} $^{3'}$... za lugal^{me} *šá* kur.kur *i*[*m-ḫaṣ ina* bala-*šú* un^{me} kur ḫé.nun] *u* ḫé.gal igi^{meš} $^{4'}$du$_{10}$^{tú} *u su-lum-mu-ú* ki ^{Id}*Aš-šur*-en-*k*[*a-la šá*]*r* ^{kur}*Aš-šur iš-kun* $^{5'}$*ina u*$_{4}$*-mi-šú-ma* man ta ^{kur}*Aš-šur ana Sip-par* gin^{kám}

$^{6'}$ ^{Id}Iškur.eduru.mu a ^{I}Ki.^{d}Amar.utu.din ^{kur}*A-ra-mu u* lugal.im.gi $^{7'}$*is-ḫu-ma ma-ḫa-zu ka-la šá* kur [*ú-šal-pi-t*]*u De-ri Dur-an-ki* $^{8'}$*Si*[*p-par u Pà*]*r-sa-a id-du-ú* ^{kur}*Su-tu-u* zi-*ma šál-lat* ^{kur}*Šu-me-ri u* Uri$^{[ki]}$ $^{i\ 9'}$*ana* kur-*šú ú-še-ṣi áš-rat* ^{d}Amar.utu ki[n-*m*]*a lìb-bi-šú* [du$_{10}$] garza-[*šú ú*]*-šak-lil*

[Marduk-šāpik-zēri, son of Ma]rduk-nādin-aḫḫ[ē], rebuilt [the wall of Ba]bylon. [... the kings of the countries he had defea]ted (?). During his reign, the people of the country enjoyed abundance and prosperity.

The Arameans and a usurper rebelled against [Adad-apla-iddina, descendant of Itti-Mard]uk-balāṭu, and [prof]aned [the holy cities, as many as there were in the country]. They destroyed Akkade, Dēr, Nippur, [..., Sip]par, Dūr-Kurigalzu. [The Suteans took the offensive] and carried [the booty] of Sumer and Akkad into their country. [He made frequent] visits to the [temples of Marduk] and appeased the heart of Bēl and the son of Bēl. [.?.], he totally restored their cults.

(...)

[...] he took a large [boot]y.

Marduk-šāpik-zēri, so[n of Marduk-nādin-aḫḫē, re]built [the wall of Babylon]. He con[quered ...] the kings of the lands. [During his reign, the people of the country] enjoyed [abundance] and prosperity. He concluded a mutual accord and a peace with King Aššur-bēl-kala of Assyria. At that time, the king went from Assyria to Sippar.

The Arameans and a usurper rebelled against Adad-apla-iddina, descendant of Itti-Marduk-balāṭu, and [prof]aned the holy cities, as many as there were in the country. They destroyed Dēr, Nippur, Si[ppar, and Dūr]-Kurigalzu. The Suteans took the offensive and carried the booty of Sumer and Akkad into their country. He made frequent [visit]s to the temples of Marduk and [appeased] his heart. He totally restored [his] cult.

10' ^{I}*Sim-bar-ši-i-pak* a ^{I}Su.^{d}30 ^{lú}aga.ús *šá* k[ur(?) *tam*(?)-*t*]*ì*(?) 11' ^{giš}gu.za ^{d}*En-líl*(!) *šá* É.kur.igi.gál dù^{uš}

12' *ina* Bár mu 5 *É-ul-maš*-gar.mu lugal

13' mu 14

14' mu 4 ^{d}A.é.eduru.ùri

15' [... m]u 1 ^{d}Nà.gin.eduru lugal

16' [... mu ...]

17' [(.?.]

18' ... n]u me mu

19' [... mu ... ^{I}Dumu.é.p]ap^{me}.mu 20' [...] *šar*$_{4}$ ^{kur}*Aš-šur ana tar-ṣ*[*i* ^{Id}Utu.si]g$_{5}$^{iq}

21' [*ana tar-ṣi* ^{Id}Nà.m]u-*ú-kin* ^{I}*Tukul*-[*ti*-^{d}Maš *šar*$_{4}$ ^{ku}]^{r}*Aš-šur*

22' [^{Id}Nà.ibil]a.mu dumu ^{Id}Nà.mu-*ú*-[*kin* ^{Id}*A*]*š-šur*-pa[p].a [*šar*$_{4}$] ^{kur}*Aš-šur*

23' ^{Id}Amar.utu-*za-kir*-mu dumu ^{Id}[Nà.ibila.m]u 24' ^{Id}Amar.utu.en-*ú-sat* ^{Id}[*Šùl-ma-nu*-sag.kal *šar*$_{4}$ ^{kur}*Aš-šu*]*r*

25' *ana tar-ṣi* ^{Id}Amar.utu.tin-*su*-du$_{11}$ <dumu> ^{Id}Amar.utu-*za-kir*-mu

---

26' ... mu^{me} man *ina* kur nu gál

27' ^{I}*Eri-ba*-^{d}Šú dumu ^{Id}Šú.gar.mu 28' *ina* mu 2.kám šu$_{ii}$ ^{d}En *u* dumu ^{d}En *iṣ-bat* 29' ^{kur}*A-ra-mu šá ina ši-gil-tú u saḫ-maš-tú* a.šà^{me} a-šib Tin.tir^{ki} *u* Bar-sip^{ki} *i-ki-mu* 30' *ina* ^{giš}tukul *im-ḫas-su-nu-ti-ma* ŠI.ŠI-*šú-nu iš-kun* 31' a.šà^{me} *u* ^{giš}kiri$_{6}$^{me} *i-kim-šú-nu-ti-ma ana* dumu^{me} Tin.tir^{ki} *u* Bár-sìp^{ki} *id-din* 32' mu.bi *ina É-sag-íl u É-zi-da* ... [... ^{giš}gu].za ^{d}En *ú-kin* 33' [...] ... ^{I}*Eri-ba*-^{d}Amar.utu *ana* Tin.tir^{ki} ...

34' [... ^{I}*Eri-b*]*a*-^{d}Šú ta [... k]^{i} è

Simbar-Šipak, descendant of Erība-Sîn, a soldier of the S[ealan]d (?), made the throne of Enlil in the Ekura'igigala.

In the <month> of Nisan, year 5 (of the reign) of Eulmaš-šākin-šumi, the king.

The year 14.

The year 4 (of the reign) of Mār-bīti-apla-uṣur.

[The ye]ar 1 (of the reign) of Nabû-mukīn-apli, the king.

[.?. The year . . .].
(.?.)

[. . . The year . . . . . . (of the reign) of Mār-bīti-a]ḫḫē-iddina.

[Adad-nērārī (II)] (was) king of Assyria at the time [of Šamaš-mudam]miq.

[At the time of Nabû-šu]ma-ukīn, Tukul[tī-Ninurta (II) (was) king] of Assyria.

[(At the time of) Nabû-ap]la-iddina, son of Nabû-šuma-u[kīn, Aš]šur-naṣ[ir]pal (II) [(was) king] of Assyria.

(At the time of) Marduk-zākir-šumi, son of [Nabû-apla-iddi]na (and) Marduk-bēl-usāte, [Šalmaneser (III) (was) king of Assyr]ia.

At the time of Marduk-balāṭsu-iqbi, <son of> Marduk-zākir-šumi.

For . . . years there was no king in the country.

Erība-Marduk, son of Marduk-šākin-šumi, in the second year (of his reign), took the hand of Bēl and the son of Bēl. He joined battle and defeated the Arameans who, (benefiting from) the disorder (?) and anarchy, had appropriated the fields of the inhabitants of Babylon and Borsippa. Having retaken from them their fields and gardens, he gave them to the inhabitants of Babylon and Borsippa. The same year, in the Esagila and the Ezida [. . .], he installed the [thro]ne of Bēl. [. . .] Erība-Marduk [. . .] to Babylon.

[. . . Erīb]a-Marduk left [. . .].

35'[. . . ^{Id}Nà-*n*]*a-ṣir*

36'[. . .] . . .

37'[. . . ^{I}*Tukul-ti*-ibila.É.šar.r]a *šar*$_4$ ^{kur}*Aš-šur ina* ^{giš}gu.za dúr^{ab}

38'[. . . *ina* ^{giš}gu].za dúr^{ab}

(. . .)

48. URUK CHRONICLE CONCERNING THE KINGS OF UR

Sources: tablet.
Bibliography: Hunger 1976: no. 2; Wilcke 1982a: 144.
Language: Babylonian.
Date: copy from the Seleucid era (dated 14 August 251 B.C.E.).
Place: Uruk.
Contents: portrait of Šulgi as an ungodly king. The chronicle's philosophy was the same as that of the Babylonian chronicles, the only difference being that local deities and temples replaced Marduk and the Esagila. Elsewhere, in chronicles 38 and 39, this same Šulgi was accused of altering the cult of Marduk.

(Obv) 1[*ina* inim ^{d}An *u* ^{d}*An-tu*$_4$] *mim-ma ep-pu-uš ina* šu$_{ii}$-ia *liš-lim la-la-a-šu lu-uš-bu* 2[. . .] ^{I}*Ur-*^{d}*Namma* lugal mu 18 in.ak

---

3[^{I}Š]ul.gi *šàr* Urí^{ki} dumu ^{I}Ur.^{d}Namma 4[*šà*]*r-ru-tu* kur.kur *ka-la-ši-na i-pu-uš* 5[. . .] *Ban-ga-ár u* ^{I}*Rab-si-si* lugal^{meš} *šá* ^{kur}Su.bir^{ki} *i-be-el* 6[uru(?)^{m}]$^{\mathrm{eš(?)}}$ kur *nu-kúr-ti iš-lu-lu* 7[nì.ga] *É-sag-il u* Tin.tir^{ki} *ina šál-lat uš-te-ṣi* 8[*É*]-*giš-nu*$_x$-*gal* é ^{d}30 *šá qé-reb* Urí^{ki} dù^{uš}-*ma ú-šak-li*[*l*] 9[bà]d Urí^{ki} dù^{uš}-*ma* suḫuš Urí^{ki} *ú-ki*[*n*] 10 $^{\mathrm{[Id]}}$Šul.gi dumu dumu.munus *šá* ^{Id}Utu.ḫé.en.gál *šàr* Unu$^{\mathrm{[ki]}}$ 11*ù* ^{I}Lú.^{d}Nanna igi$_{ii}$.nu.tuk ^{lú}*um-ma-nu* [(?) 12*šá* ḫ]ul^{tì} *ina lìb-bi-šú-nu ib-ba-šú-ú* 13[gar]za ^{d}An$^{ú\text{-}tu}$ giš.ḫur^{meš} *šá* Unu$^{\mathrm{[ki]}}$ 14[*n*]*i-ṣir-ti* ^{lú}*um-ma-na šá la si-mat ú-nak-k*[*ir-ma* 15*ši*]-*pir* ^{d}30 *be-lu* Urí^{ki} *iš-ṭur* 16[*ina p*]*al-e-šú* na.rú.a *sur-ra-at tup-pi šál-lat*^{meš} 17[*ana* šu].luḫ.ḫa dingir.ra *iš-ṭur-ma e-zib* 18[^{d}An] lugal *šá ši-ma-tu-šú rab-ba-a' ik-kil-me-šú-ma* 19[. . .] a *še-ret-su ra-bi-tu*$_4$ 20[. . . g]i *zu-mur-šú ú-lab-biš* 21[. . .] . . . [. . .]

[. . . Nabon]assar.

[. . .]

[. . . Tiglath-piles]er (III), king of Assyria, ascended the throne.

[. . . Šalmaneser (V), king of Assyria], as[cended the thr]one.

(. . .)

[At the command of Anu and Antu] I hope I may succeed in everything that I undertake (and) enjoy it fully.[20]

[. . .] Ur-Namma reigned eighteen years.

The divine Šulgi, king of Ur, son of Ur-Namma, reigned over all lands, commanded [. . .]-bangar and Rabsisi,[21] kings of Subartu, (and) sacked [the citie]s (?) of the enemy's country. He took out as booty [the treasures] of the Esagila and Babylon. He laid out and comp[leted] the [E]gišnugal, Sîn's temple, in the middle of Ur. He built the [wal]l of Ur and strength[ened] the foundations of the city.

The divine Šulgi, son of a daughter[22] of King Utu-ḫegal of Uruk, with the blind Lu-Nanna,[23] the scholar, [.?.]—there was [spiteful]ness in their hearts!—improperly tampered with the rites of the cult of Anu, Uruk's regulations, [the] secret [know]ledge of the wise, [and] put down in writing the forced labor exacted by Sîn, lord of Ur. [During] his [rei]gn, he composed untruthful stelae, insolent writings, [(concerning) the rites of pur]ification for the gods, and left them to posterity. [(But) An]u, the king, whose decisions are venerable, regarded him with anger and [. . .] his grave faults [. . .] he covered his body [with . . . .].

(. . .)

(Rev.) $^{1'}$[. . .] $^{2'}$[. . . me]š eš ud ^{I}A ku [. . .] nu gál$^{\acute{u}}$ $^{3'}$[48] mu ^{d}Š[ul.gi lugal$^{\acute{u}-t]a}$ *i-pu-uš*

$^{4'}$[^{I}Amar].^{d}EN.ZU^{na} mu 10 lá 1 [. . .] *šàr-ru-tú i-pu-*[*uš*]

$^{5'}$[gin$_7$] til-*šú* sar-*ma ba-rù ù up-puš*$_4$ ga[ba.ri *le-'i*] nì.ga ^{d}[An *u An-tu*$_4$ $^{6'}$dub] ^{Id}An.šeš.gál^{ši} a *šá* ^{I}*Ki-din-*^{d}An ^{lú}šà.bal.ba[l ^{I}É.kur-*za-kir*] ^{lú}[maš.maš ^{d}An *u An-tu*$_4$ $^{7'}$ ^{lú}še]š.gal^{i} *šá* é *re-eš* Unu^{ki} $^{\acute{u}}$ *qa-at* [^{Id}An].tin-*su-*[*iq-bi* a-*šú* $^{8'}$*ana*] *a-ḫa-a-zi-šú* gíd.da u$_4$^{meš}-šú tin zi[^{meš}-*šú u* gin suḫuš-*šú* sar-*ma* $^{9'}$*ina* Unu]^{ki} *u* é *re-eš* é en$^{\acute{u}-ti}$-*šú ú-k*[*in* $^{10'}$Unu^{ki}] ^{iti}Ne u$_4$ 21.kam mu 1 šu 1.kam ^{I}*An-ti-'u-ku-su šàr* kur.kur

(. . .)

[. . .] predictions of(?) Aku-[batila . . .] have not [. . . . The divine Šulgi] rei[gned forty-eight] years.

[Amar]-Su'en reigned nine (?) years.

Written [according] to its original, checked, revised, and edited. Copy of a wooden tablet, property of [Anu and Antu. Tablet] of Anu-aḫa-ušabši, son of Kidin-Ani, descendant of [Ekur-zākir], the e[xorcist of Anu and Antu, the *šeš*]*gallû*-[priest] of the Bīt-rēši temple at Uruk. Hand of [Anu]-balāssu-[iqbi, his son. He wrote it] to fulfill his education, the long duration of his days, his l[ife, the perpetuity of his office and] placed (it) in the Bīt-rēši, the temple of his lord [in Uruk. Uruk], month of Ab, twenty-first day, sixty-first year, Antiochus (III), king of all lands.

Notes

1. Variant: *ad-din-šum-ma.*
2. May be 8.
3. Variant: *be-lu*$_4$ gal$^{\acute{u}}$ ^{d}Amar.utu.
4. Variant: *id-din-ši.*
5. With the unpublished manuscript from the British Museum.
6. One variant (a trace of a source consulted, probably a hymn) puts the verb in the first-person singular.
7. Those which map out the constellations.
8. Variant: 8 (?).
9. That is to say, all the earth.
10. Undoubtedly the two place names should be reversed.
11. This tradition made Narām-Sîn a son of Sargon, whereas in reality he was a grandson.
12. In this period this could not have been an Elamite royal title, unless it is an anachronism, because this title at that time indicated the prime minister of the king of Isin.
13. See preceding note.
14. See the study, but not convincing, by Gassan 1989.
15. I call attention to the use of the verb "to dominate" and not "to reign." The verb *wu'uru* indicates that the Babylonian scribe did not recognize the legitimacy of the new person governing, whom he considered a usurper or a foreigner.
16. On the death of Tukultī-Ninurta I, see Harrak 1987: 263.
17. See n. 15 above.
18. See n. 15 above.
19. See n. 15 above.
20. This introduction was standard among the scribes of this family. For similar formulas elsewhere, see Sachs and Hunger 1988–2001: 2:2, 92, 186, 420, 456; Wilcke 1977: 200. Also see the colophons of the scholastic tablets of the temple of Nabû ša Ḫarē at Babylon: Cavigneaux 1981: 37–77. In general, see Roth 1988.

21. Both names appear together in a historical omen: "Prediction of [. . .]-gangar and Rabsisi, king of Subartu, [. . .], brother will kill brother." See Walker 1972: 53, BM 122643 rev. 12–15.

22. Therefore Utu-ḫegal was said to be the father-in-law and not the brother of Ur-Namma.

23. A wise man, reputed to have lived in the time of Šulgi.

XI

Putative Chronicles

Included here are five documents for which there is no assurance that they were chronicles. Some were too badly damaged to allow definitive identification. Others stand apart from the chronicles because of their different focuses of interest, although they claim a chronological presentation of recalled facts.

49. FRAGMENTS OF A HISTORY OF ANCIENT KINGS

Sources: fragments of tablets; four fragmentary exemplars of the text and one commentary.
Bibliography: Picchioni 1981: 102–9; Foster 1996: 435–36.
Language: Babylonian.
Date: copies from the Neo-Assyrian period to the Seleucid era.
Place: Nineveh, Aššurbanipal's library; Sippar; Uruk.
Contents: not a chronicle (despite Hunger 1976: no. 4) but a fragment of a history; it concerned Adapa and Enmerkar.

(obv) 1...[...] 2*a* [...]...-*šu iš-kun* 3*A-da-p*[*à* ...] 4ad [... -*s*]*a ib*-... [...] 5*a-n*[*a* ...] *a-na* ^{d}en *i-ṣar-ra-aḫ* 6*ṣi*-[*ir* (?)-*ḫa*(?) ...]... *iš-mu-ma* 7*um-m*[*a* ...] 8*ina šu* [...] *iṣ-ṣab-tu*$_4$ 9*ri-ig-mu an-nu-ú* [...] *ki-i ṭà-ab* 10*ina qí-bi*[*t*(?) ...] ... *i-ṣar-ra-aḫ* 11*ù* dingir^{meš} ga[l^{meš} ...] ... šu-*su* min$^{tu}{}_4$ 12[...] ...-*tur-šum-ma* 13šu-*su šá-ni-t*[*i* ...] 14*šá* ^{d}60 ^{d}50 [*ù* ^{d}40... *i*(?)-*ṣar*(?)]-*ra-aḫ* 15*ša* ^{d}en gal ^{d}Amar.utu ... [...]-*ú*

16*A-da-pà* ... [...]-*me* 17*En-me-kír*1 *ina* Unu^{ki} lugal[$^{ú-ta}$ *ip-pu-u*]*š* 18*i-nu-šu kul-lat* ^{kur}Ur[i^{ki} ...] 19*pa-la-šú a-di-na* dingir^{meš} ... [...] 20*A-da-pà* 9 kùš ZU.[AB ...] ...-*ri* 21*En-me-kír*2 *aš-šum A-da-pà* [...] 22*iš-šu-ma ana maḫ-ri* [...] 23*En-me-kír ana la ta*-[...] 24*šá-lam-ta la-bir-ta šá ul-t*[*u*] *u*$_4$-*me*3 sud^{meš} [...] 25*ú-še-él-mìn rig-ma ina* é.ga[l/*šu* ...] 269 kùš *ú-šap-pa-l*[*u* ... 27... 9 kù]š *qaq-qa-ra ú-šap-pi-lu* ... [... 28k]á ki.maḫ *ú-ḫal-l*[*i-iq* ...*šá-la*]*m-ta la*(?) *na-ṭa-la* 29*A-da-pà a*-[*na*] *ma*-[... 30... 31...] ...-*šum-ma* 32*A-da-pà ul im-tal-lik-ma* ... [... 33... 34...] ...-*'a-zu* 35*a-ḫu a-ḫa ip-pal-s*[*u* ... 36... 37...] ...-*nu-ti* 38*aš-šum* ^{giš}gu.za *ú*-[... 39... 40... -*k*]*um*(?) [...] (...)

(rev.) 1[...] ... *a-ši-ru* 2*iš-pur-ma* [...] ... [... 3... m]a.na urudu^{ḫá} *ina lìb-bi it-me-ru* 4 ^{lú}simug *ša* ... [... k]á *i-na muḫ-ḫ*[*i*] *uš-zi-z*[*u*(?) 5...] ... *ina dan-na-ti še-ret-su ir-ku-su-ma* ... 6[... *A-da-p*]*à su-qa*4 *ina ba-'i-i-šú* 7 ^{lú}simug *e-mur-ma ki-a-am iq-bi-šu* 8[...] ...-*šu-ka ina dan-na-at še-ret-ka šal-mat* 9[... m]a.na urudu^{ḫá} ...-[*t*]*u'-ú šá muḫ-ḫi-ia* 10*A-da*-[*pà* ...] *ip-pal*-[... 11...] ...-*ta te-em-ru* ... [... 12... *l*]*u-pu-ul-ma i-tin-ga*[*l-la* ...]

13[...] *iš-pur-ma k*[*u* ... 14... 15...] ... pi ... [... 16...] ... [...] (...)

50. CHRONICLE OF MARKET PRICES

Sources: fragment of a tablet.
Bibliography: Grayson 1975a: no. 23.
Language: Babylonian.

(. . .)

[. . .] he set his [. . .]. Adapa [. . .] for [. . .] he lamented for the lord [. . .] he heard, thus (he spoke): "[. . .] in [. . .] that he has seized, this clamor [. . .] how good." By order of [. . .] he lamented and the gre[at] gods [. . .] his other hand [. . .] to him. His other hand [. . .] of Anu, Enlil, [and Ea . . . he lamen]ted (?), of the great lord Marduk.

Adapa [. . .]. Enmekir [exercis]ed king[ship] in Uruk. At that time [. . .] all the land of Akkad, [he . . .] his reign, thus far, the gods [. . .]. Adapa [*went down* (?)] nine cubits in the depth. Enmekir because of Adapa [. . .]. They carried [. . .] and before [. . .] Enmekir [. . .] in order not to [. . .]. An old corpse from remotest time [. . .]. He made a frightful clamor in the palace/his house (?) [. . .]. They went down nine cubits [. . . . . . . nine cub]its of earth they went down [. . .]. He des[troyed] the [do]or of the tomb [. . .] without seeing [the cor]pse. Adapa [. . . t]o [. . .]. Adapa did not use good judgment and [. . .] answered each other [. . .]. Because of the throne [. . .].

(. . .)

[. . .] . . . he sent [. . .] and [. . .] they buried [. . .] minas of copper inside [. . .], the blacksmith who [. . .] and set up (?) [the do]or above, [. . .] and fastened its latch (?) to the frame (?). As [. . . Adap]a was passing through the street, he saw the blacksmith and spoke to him thus: "[. . .] is your latch (?) securely on the frame (?)? [. . .] minas of copper [. . .] which, in front of me, Adapa [. . .] buried [. . .]." [. . .] let me answer and the chief builder (?) [. . .].

[. . .] he sent and [. . .].

(. . .)

Date: copy of the Seleucid era.
Place: Babylon.
Contents: brief notices about market prices from Ḫammurabi, or even before, until perhaps Nabû-šuma-iškun. No other chronicle known at present deals with this theme (except nos. 12 and 30 in an episodic fashion), which was, however, very much present in the astronomical diaries.

(Obv.) ^{1}[*a-na tar*]-*ṣi* ^{Id}[...] ^{2}[...] ... gur síg^{ḫá} [... ^{3}ki].lam kur(?)-*šú a-na* [...]

---

^{4}*a-na tar-ṣi* ^{Id}[...] ^{5}ki.lam *in-ni-ip-pú*-[*uš* ...] ^{6}... ma.na urudu ki.lam kur-[*šú*(?) ...]

---

^{7}*ana tar-ṣi Am-mu-ra-p*[*í* ...]

---

^{8}*ana tar-ṣi Ku-ri-gal-z*[*u* ...] ^{9}še.giš 3(?) PI síg 3 ma.[na ...]

---

^{10}mu 21 ^{d}Amar.utu.a.sum [...] ^{11}1 gur še 1 gur zú.[(lum.ma) ...]

---

^{12}mu 13 kur(?) ku(?) áš(?) ka [...]

---

^{13}mu 9 ^{d}Nà-nì.d[u].ù[ri ...]

---

^{14}mu 2 ^{d}Amar.[utu ...] ^{15} ^{giš}bán 3(?) sì[la ...]
(...) (Rev.) (.?.) $^{1'}$[...] ... [...] $^{2'}$ ^{giš}bán ... sì[la ...]

$^{3'}$mu 10 11 12 1[3(?) ...] $^{4'}$še 1 gur (erased) ... [...] $^{5'}$*a*(?)-*na* 4(?) gín(?) ... [...]

$^{6'}$mu 5 mu 6 ... [...] $^{7'}$ ^{giš}bán 4(?) sìla [...]

---

51. RELIGIOUS CHRONICLE

Sources: fragment of a small tablet in four columns.
Bibliography: Grayson 1975a: no. 17.
Language: Babylonian.
Date: copy of the Seleucid era.
Place: Babylon.
Contents: in the context of unstable conditions because of the presence of Arameans, a succession of strange phenomena were observed at Babylon. Political events were secondary. The facts alluded to go back to the

[In the tim]e of [. . .], . . . *kor* of [. . . , . . .] wool, the market price, in his country (?), for [. . .].

In the time of [. . . , . . .] was readily purch[ased . . .] ten minas of copper, the market price in [his (?)] country (?) [. . .].

In the time of Ḫammurabi, [. . .].

In the time of Kurigalzu, [. . .] three PI of sesame [. . .] three minas of wool.

Year 21 (of the reign) of Merodach-baladan (I), [. . .] one *kor* of barley [. . .] one *kor* of dates.

Year 13 . . . [. . .].

Year 9 (of the reign) of Nebuchadnezzar (I), [. . .].

Year 2 (?) (of the reign) of Mar[duk-. . .], one *sûtu* [. . .] three (?) *q*[*û* . . .].
(. . .)
[. . .] one *sûtu* [. . .] . . . *q*[*û* . . .].

Years 10, 11, 12, 1[3(?) . . .], one *kor* of barley [. . .] for four shekels [. . .].

Year 5, year 6 [. . .], one *sûtu* [. . .] four *qû* [. . .].

---

eleventh–tenth centuries. The sole connection with the chronicles does not reside, curiously, in its chronological presentation, for chronology was not always respected, but in the author's interest in the celebration of the New Year's festival or its interruption.

(i)^{1}[. . .] . . . ^{2}[. . .] ^{d}30 ^{3}[. . .] . . . ^{meš} ^{4}[. . .]^{meš}-*ni* ^{5}[. . .] . . . ^{6}[. . . ^{d}]Gašan-*Ni-ná-a* . . . ^{7}[. . .] gaz^{meš}-*šú* ^{8}[. . .]Tin.tir^{ki} *it-ta*-[. . . ^{9}. . .] . . . ^{d}Gašan . . . ^{10}[. . .] sig$_{4}$ gin$^{meš\text{-}ni}$ ^{11}[. . .] . . . $^{i}{}_{7}$Idigna ^{12}[. . .] *it-te-*. . . ^{13}[. . .] . . . *a-di* Ká.gal.ki.lam ^{14}[. . .]é ^{d}Ur.sag *šá* nam.en É^{ki} ^{15}[. . .] . . .*-it-ti šá i-mu-ru-šu* ^{16}[. . . ^{d}Nà].mu-*li-bur* lugal ^{17}[. . .] ur.maḫ ná-*ma* gaz^{meš}-*šú* ^{18}[. . .] . . . gin$^{meš\text{-}ni}$ ^{19}[. . .] li *id-de-ki*(?) ^{20}[. . .] . . .*-šú id-da-bu-ub* ^{21}[. . .] ^{d}*Taš-me-tu*$_{4}$ ^{22}[. . .] *it-tan-mar* ^{23}[. . .] *it-tan-mar* ^{24}[. . .]. .*-us-su-ma* ^{25}[. . .] . . . ki.ta^{i} (. . .)(ii)^{1}*ina* ^{iti}Gu$_{4}$ u$_{4}$ 11.kám lugal *ik-šu-dam-*[*ma*] ^{2}sila$_{4}$^{meš} *šá a-ṣe-e* ^{d}En *ú-*. . .*-ma ul* . . . [. . .] ^{3}siskur^{meš} *u* ^{giš}banšur dingir *šá a-di u*$_{4}$*-mi a-ki-tì* [*il*(?)]*-qu-ú* ^{4}4 *u*$_{4}$*-mi ina É-sag-gìl* ù é dingir^{meš} *ki-i šal-me iq-qu* ^{5}*a-di u*$_{4}$*-mi* siskur^{meš} lugal *ul is-ruq* šeš.gal *is-ruq-ma* é *ip-qid* ^{6}*ina* ^{iti}Šu *ina* bal.ri ^{d}Utu.šú.a ur.bar.ra ná-*ma* gaz^{meš}-*šú* ^{7}*ina* ^{iti}Ne ur.ki *ina* Ká.gal-^{d}Uraš *ina* ká é šà.tam ^{lú}a.zu^{meš} ^{8}*ú-*. . . *i-tam-ru-šu* ^{9}*ina* ^{iti}Du$_{6}$ u$_{4}$ 25.kám *nim-ru bal-ṭu* ^{10}i$_{7}$ *iq-qé-lep-pu-ma ina ku-tal É-*^{giš}*gidri-kalam-ma-*[*sum-ma*] ^{11}*i-du-ku-šu-ma ana ta-ba-li ú-še-lu-niš-šu* ^{12}*ina* ^{iti}Ne u$_{4}$ 16.kám *šá* mu 7.kám 2 dàra.bar^{meš} ^{13}*a-na* Ká.dingir.ra^{ki} *i-ru-bu-nim-ma i-du-ku-šu-nu-ti* ^{14}*ina* ^{iti}Sig$_{4}$ u$_{4}$ 26.kám *šá* mu 7.kám *u*$_{4}$*-mu ana* gi$_{6}$ gur-*ma* izi *ina* šà an^{e} . . . [. . .] . . . ^{15}*ina* ^{iti}Kin *šá* mu 11.kám a^{meš} *ina* muru$_{4}$ é.sig$_{4}$ *šá* kisal.ki.ta^{i} gin$^{meš\text{-}ni}$ ^{16}mu 13.kám mu 14.kám mu 15.kám 3 mu^{meš} *ar-ki a-*[*ḫa*]*-meš* ^{17} ^{giš}gigir-*su šá* ^{d}En ta u$_{4}$ 3.kám *šá* ^{iti}Še en ^{iti}Bár *ul* [*ú-ṣa*]*-a* ^{18}*ina* ^{iti}Bár *šá* mu 15.kám ^{d}En *ul ú-ṣa-a* ^{19}*ina* ^{iti}Gu$_{4}$ u$_{4}$ 14.kám *šá* mu 17.kám *šal-ḫu-ú šá* Ká.gal-^{d}Uraš ^{20}*ki i-du-lu i-tam-ru-šú ina* ^{iti}Sig$_{4}$ u$_{4}$ 15.kám *šá* mu 18(?).kám [. . .] ^{21}ta Ká.gal-^{d}15 *ana* i$_{7}$ *ki-i ú-ri-du* ^{22}*ana* Tin.tir^{ki} *ki i-ru-ba ina* bal.ri ^{d}Utu.šú.a [. . .] ^{23}. . . a^{me} 2 érin^{meš} *id-duk* bára *šá* ká é [. . .] ^{24} ^{giš}ig^{meš} *šá* ká.gal *su-uš-ši šap-li-i* . . . [. . .] ^{25}*ù* [*a-na šu*]*-ut-ta-tu*$_{4}$ *ki im-qu-tu* gaz-*šú-ma* . . . [. . .] ^{26}. . . [. . .] . . .*-tu-ru-ni ina* mu 14.kám . . . [. . . ^{27}. . .] . . . [. . .] ^{d}Ešdar^{meš} érin^{meš} . . . [. . . ^{28}. . .] . . . *id-di-nu* [. . .] (. . .) (iii) (. . .) $^{1'}$[. . .] . . . [. . .] . . . [. . .] $^{2'}$*ina* ^{iti}Gu$_{4}$ ur.bar.ra

[. . .] Sîn [. . . In the temple of] Bēlet-Nina [. . .] Babylon [. . .] they s[aw (?). . .] killed it. Bēlet-[. . . In the month of] Siwan, they came [. . .] the Tigris [. . .] he reached [. . .] up to the Abul-maḫīri section [. . .] the temple of Ursag in the district of Nippur [. . .] who lives [. . . Nabû]-šumu-lībur, the king, [. . .] a lion was lurking, and it was killed. [. . .] they came [. . .] was out of place (?) [. . .] he spoke [. . .] Tašmētum [. . .] they saw [. . .] they saw [. . .] inferior [. . .].

(. . .)

The king arrived in the month of Iyyar, the eleventh day, [and slaughtered (?)] without the [. . .] the lambs prepared for Bēl's procession. For four days they prepared as usual in the Esagila and the (other) temples the sacrifices and the (offering) table for the gods, which the latter [rec]eived until the day of the New Year's festival. Until the day of the sacrifices the king made no libation, (but) the *šešgallû*-priest offered libations and inspected the temple.

In the month of Dumuzi, a wolf was lurking in the west, and they killed it. In the month of Ab, physicians having [. . .], saw a badger at the Gate of Uraš, in front of the door of the administrator. In the month of Teš rit, the twenty-fifth day, they killed a live panther drifting down the river behind the Egidri-kalama-[suma] and pulled it up to dry land.

In the month of Ab of the seventh year, the sixteenth day, two deer that had come into Babylon were killed. In the month of Siwan of the seventh year, the twenty-sixth day, the day grew dark and in the sky fiery [. . .].

In the month of Elul of the eleventh year, water flowed out of the wall of the lower forecourt.

The thirteenth, fourteenth, and fifteenth years, for three conse[cu]tive years, from the third day of Iyyar to the month of Nisan, Bēl's chariot did not [go] out (for the procession). In the month of Nisan of the fifteenth year, Bēl did not go out (for the procession).

In the month of Iyyar of the seventeenth year, the fourteenth day, the outer wall of the Gate of Uraš was seen to have shifted.

In the month of Siwan of the eighteenth (?) year, the fifteenth day, [a . . .] of water coming down from the Gate of Ištar toward the river and entering into Babylon, on the west, killed two soldiers. The cultic pedestal near the door of the temple of [. . .], the panels of the door . . . below [. . .] they killed it when it fell into a pit and [. . .].

The fourteenth year, [. . .] the goddesses, the troops [. . .] they handed over [. . .].

(. . .)

. . . [. . .] . . .-*tu*$_4$ ná-*ma i-mu-ru-šu-ma* gaz^{meš}-*šú* 3'*ina* ^{iti}Gu$_4$ dàra.bar *šá* [ku$_4$-*š*]*ú ana* uru *mam-ma la i-mu-ru ina* Ká-En-*ia* 4'*i-mu-ru-šu-ma* gaz^{meš}-*šú ina* ^{iti}Bár *šá* mu 7.kám ^{lú}*A-ra-mu na-kir* 5'lugal *ana* Tin.tir^{ki} *la el-la-am-ma* ^{d}Nà *la il-li-ku* 6'*ù* [^{d}En *la ú-ṣa-a*] *ina* ^{iti}Bár *šá* mu 8.kám ^{d}Nà.gin.a lugal 7' ^{lú}*A-ra-mu na-kir-ma* ká *ni-bi-ri šá* ^{uru}*Kar*-en.kur.kur 8'*iṣ-bat-ma* lugal *la i-bi-ram-ma* ^{d}Nà *la il-li-ku* 9'*ù* ^{d}En *la ú-ṣa-a* siskur *ša A-ki-ti ina É-sag-gìl ki-i pi-i . . . iq-qí* 10'*ina* ^{iti}Bár *šá* mu 19.kám ^{d}Nà.gin.a lugal kimin 11'siskur(?) . . . na ig *ina* ^{iti}Šu *šá* mu 16.kám ur.maḫ *šá* ku$_4$-*šú ana* uru *mam-ma* 12'*la i-mu-ru i-na* bal.ri ^{d}Utu.šú.a *i-na* ^{giš}kiri$_6$ 8-*ni-tu*$_4$ 13'*i-mu-ru-šu-ma* gaz^{meš}-*šú i-na* mu 20.kám ^{d}Nà.gin.a lugal 14' ^{d}En *ul ú-ṣa-a ù* ^{d}Nà nu gin^{ku} 9 mu^{me} egir *a-ḫa-meš* 15' ^{d}En *ul ú-ṣa-a ù* ^{d}Nà *ul* gin^{ku} *ina* mu 26.kám ^{d}Nà.gin.a lugal 16' ^{d}*Ka-ri-bu šá* zà.dib *šá* ká *pa-pa-ḫi* [. . .] . . . [. . .] 17'*ki i-du-lu i-tam-ru* ^{d}Sag.ḫul.ḫa.za *ina* é.^{giš}ná^{meš} 18'*ša* ^{d}Nà *it-tan-mar* . . . *ina* ugu . . . *šá* ^{d}Nà *ina* šà uzu *i*[*t*(?)-*tan*(?)-*mar*(?)] 19'*ina* ^{iti}Zíz u$_4$ 21.kám *šá* mu 26.kám ^{d}Nà.gin.a lugal ^{d}Iškur ka-*šú* šub^{di}-*ma* izi-*šú* nu ḫar [. . .] (iv) (. . .) 1'[. . .] . . . [. . .] . . . pa na 2'[. . . *ina lìb*]*b-bi ú-še-šib* 3'[. . .] *su-uš-šú ia-'-nu* 4'[. . . ^{d}Nà.du].ibila lugal 5'[. . .] ^{d}Nà.du.ibila lugal *su-uš-šú* 6'[. . .] . . .-*bu-ti iš-kun* 7'[. . . *b*]*u-ub kak-ku*

8'[. . .] ḫar ri ri [. . .] (. . .)

52. CHRONOGRAPHIC DOCUMENT CONCERNING NABÛ-ŠUMA-IŠKUN

Sources: fragmentary tablet in four columns.
Bibliography: von Weiher 1988: no. 58; Cole 1994.
Language: Babylonian.
Date: Late Babylonian period.
Place: Uruk.
Contents: history of Babylonia in the eighth century. In the context of tension between Arameans and Chaldeans, emphasis was placed on the slow breakdown of King Nabû-šuma-iškun, a Chaldean on the throne of

In the month of Iyyar, a wolf was lurking [. . .]; they saw it and killed it. In the month of Iyyar, a deer that nobody had seen enter the city was seen and killed at the Gate of My Lord.

In the month of Nisan of the seventh year, the Arameans showing hostility, the king did not go up to Babylon. Nabû did not go nor [Bēl go out].

In the month of Nisan of the eighth year (of the reign) of Nabû-mūkin-apli, the king, the Arameans showing hostility took possession of the ford at Kār-bēl-mātāti (so that) the king could not cross. Nabû did not go nor Bēl go out. In the Esagila, he (= the king) did [not] offer the New Year's sacrifices according to custom.

In the month of Nisan of the nineteenth year (of the reign) of Nabû-mūkin-apli, the king, *ditto.* [. . .] the sacrifices [. . .].

In the month of Dumuzi of the sixteenth year, a lion that nobody had seen enter the city was seen lurking, and they killed it in the eighth (?) orchard.

The twentieth year (of the reign) of Nabû-mūkin-apli, the king, Bēl did not go out nor Nabû go.

For nine consecutive years Bēl did not go out nor Nabû go.

The twenty-fifth (?) year (of the reign) of Nabû-mūkin-apli, the king, it was observed that the spirit at the right of the door of the room [. . .] was seen to have shifted. They saw an "evil" demon in Nabû's bedroom. [They saw (?) . . .] on [. . .] of Nabû in the sacrificial chair.

In the month of Šebat of the twenty-sixth year (of the reign) of Nabû-mūkin-apli, the king, the twenty-first day, Adad growled, his thunder [. . .].

(. . .)

[. . .] he established there [. . .] there was no [. . .].

[The . . .th year (of the reign) of Nabû-mūkin]-apli, the king, [. . .] Nabû-mūkin-apli, the king, [. . .] put down. [. . .] a weapon (?).

(. . .)

Babylon, predecessor of Nabonassar. Notwithstanding the obscurity of some passages, the progression is clear: the king stopped making war, compelled the priests to break the laws, put the gods under his orders, went so far as to sell his own subjects, violated justice, profaned the holy places, seized the treasures of the Esagila, introduced foreign gods into Babylon, and, lastly, insulted his own family.

(i)^{1}[. . . ^{I}]^{d}[Am]ar.utu.ibila.ùri ^{2}[. . .] ^{lú}*Kal-di*

---

^{3}[. . .] $^{\text{i}_7}$*Ì-diq-lat* ^{4}[. . .]. . .*-ši-ma*

---

^{5}[. . .] ^{lú}dumu *šip-ri* ^{6}[. . .] *i-*[*du*]*-uk-ma*

---

^{7}[. . .] . . .*-b/pu*(?)*-uš* ^{8}[. . .] . . . gal(?)^{ti}

---

^{9}[. . .] *il*(?)*-ku*(?) *in-*[*nen*(?)]*-du -ma* ^{10}[. . .] . . . lú^{tú}

---

^{11}[. . .] *u*(?) ninda šuku u$_4$ 5(?).kám ^{12}[*šá*(?) *iṣ*(?)*-ba*(?)]*-tu ig-mur* (?)*-ma*

---

^{13}[. . .] . . . kám . . . a ^{giš}má.i$_7$.ḫé.du$_7$ ^{14}[. . .] *ana É-sag-íl*

---

^{15}[. . .] du [. . .]*-ul* ^{16}[. . .] . . .*-ib*

---

^{17}[. . .]*-di* ^{18}[. . .] . . .

(. . .)

(ii)^{1}*ina* u$_4$ *šal-me-ma* ^{Id}Nà.mu.gar^{un} ta *qé-reb* ^{2}Tin.tir^{ki} *a-na* kur-*šú pa-ni-šú iš-kun-ma*

---

^{3}*ina a-mat* ^{d}Nà *u* ^{d}Amar.utu en^{meš} *ḫe-pí* ^{4}*ina* [. . .]*-ri ana qé-reb* é-*šú i-ru-um-ma*

---

^{5}*la i-tur-ma a-na e-peš ta-ḫa-zi* ^{6}*ù a-lak* kaskal *qer-be-šú la ú-ṣi*

---

^{7}*iš-ni-ma ina* mu 3.kám ^{d}*Na-na-a É-zi-da* ^{8}*ra-'i-mu* ^{d}Nà *a-na* é *mu-um-mu ú-še-rib-ma*

---

^{9} ^{d}Nà *ina* Tin.tir^{ki} *ik-le-e-ma nu-bat-tu$_4$* ^{10}*ù* u$_4$.èš.èš *a-na* 1^{en} *u$_4$-me ú-tir*

---

^{11}*it-ti* ^{túg}sig$_5$ ^{d}En *šá* ^{iti}Zíz.àm ^{12} ^{túg}Sig$_5$ ^{d}Nà *uk-ta-ti-in*

[. . .] Marduk-apla-uṣur [. . .] the Chaldean.

[. . .] the Tigris [. . .].

[. . .] a messenger [. . .] he killed and [. . .].

[. . .].

[Forced labor (?) and] corvée were imposed and [. . .] slave.

[. . .] and bread, the food offering for the fifth day [that he had sei]zed, he used up and [. . .].

[. . .] the boat Idḫedu [. . .] for the Esagila.

(. . .)

On a propitious day, from Babylon, Nabû-šuma-iškun turned his attention toward his country, but,

---

on the order of the BREAK lords Nabû and Marduk, he went into the [. . .], inside his house and

---

no longer went into battle nor started into the field.

In the third year, again, he brought (the statue of) Nanaya, (the goddess) of the Ezida, the beloved of Nabû, into the *bīt mummi* but

---

kept Nabû in Babylon and had the ceremonies of the evening before and those of the day of the *eššešu*-festival celebrated in only one day.

He covered the fine garment of Nabû with the fine garment of Bēl of the month of Šebat.

---

^{13}*šá-nu-ú šá-ki*[*n*] *áš-šú-ta šá* ^{d}En ^{14}*a-na* ^{d}*Taš-me-tum ú-šat-ri-iṣ*

---

^{15}*pe-er-tú šá-kin* šab.tur^{e}-*šú ú-gaṣ-ṣiṣ ni-is-qa* guškin ^{16}*šá-kin ù pa-paḫ* ^{d}En *i-ru-um-ma* … *ú-qar-rab*

---

^{17}ga.raš^{sar} *ik-kib É-zi-da ana* é ^{d}Nà ^{18}*ú-qar-rib u* ku$_{4}$.é^{meš} *ul-ta-kil*

---

^{19} $^{[d]}$*É-a* en *né-me-qí šá šu-bat-su* ^{20}*it-ti* an^{ú} kù(?) *u* ki^{ti} *šur-šu-da-tu*

---

^{21}*ina šu-bat si-mat ilu-ti-šú* gal^{ti} ^{22}*ú-šat-bi-ma ina* ká.maḫ ^{d}En(?) *ú-šeš-šib*

---

^{23} ^{d}Di.ku$_{5}$ ^{d}En Tin.tir^{ki} dingir *bi-bil* ^{24}*lìb-bi-šú i-de-ek-ki-ma ú-šá-rid*

---

^{25}*šá*(?) *la*(?) *a-mat* x […] uru *an-ni-ma* ^{26}gin$_{7}$ *bi-bil lìb-bi-šú ip-pu-uš*

---

^{27}*šá* [$^{I(?)}$]…-*ri* dumu(?) ^{Id}[…] … ^{28}*šá* […] id …

---

^{29}[…] *ḫe-pí* ^{30}[…] su muš

---

^{31}[…] *a-ši-bat* ^{giš}gu.za ^{32}[…] 7 *la-ab-bi*

---

^{33}[… *i*]*p-tur-ma* ^{34}[…] *ú-šak-bi-is*

---

^{35}[… *ú*]-*šat*(!)-*mi-iḫ-ši* ^{36}[… *ú-š*]*á-aṣ-mi-is-si*

---

^{37}[…] ^{d}Inanna giš(?) [… ^{38}…] *ú-šap-ṭir*

---

^{39}*ana* é.ì.dub *šá* edin sig$_{7}$ … im.saḫar.ra ^{40}[…] *ú-šat-ri-iṣ*

---

^{41}[…] ^{d}Nin.bàd ^{42}[…] *uq-tar-rib*

---

^{43}[…] ^{d}Nà *ina* Tin.tir^{ki} *bu-ut-ma* ^{44}[…]-*ma ina la* nam^{meš} *ú-šib*

---

^{45}[…] Tin.tir^{ki} … za ^{46}[…] *ina* izi *iq-lu$_{4}$*

---

^{47}[…] a šú en gal ^{d}Amar.utu ^{48}[…]*ana* ^{d}Amar.utu *ku-mu* lugal du-*ma*

Dressed as the latter, he proposed Bēl's marriage to Tašmētu.

Unshaven, he mutilated (the fingers of) his apprentice scribe, and, wearing fine gold, he entered into Bēl's cella of offering [. . .].

A leek, a thing forbidden in the Ezida, he brought to the temple of Nabû and gave to eat to the one "entering the temple."[5]

Ea, the lord of wisdom, whose dwelling place was founded with pure heaven and earth,

---

he made him get up from this dwelling place, which befitted his great divinity, and made him sit in the exalted gateway of Bēl.

He removed Madānu, "Bēl of Babylon," his favorite god, from his [seat] and made him leave.

Without the authority of [. . .] this city, he did as he pleased,

---

of [. . .]ri son of [. . .], who . . .

He [. . .] BREAK [. . .].

[. . .] she who sits on the throne [. . .] seven lions.[6]

[. . .] he unleashed and [. . .] allowed to roam freely.

He had her grasp [. . .] he had her leashed.

He had [. . .] of Ištar [. . .] disconnected.

[. . .] to the granary of the verdant countryside he offered [. . .] a dust storm (?) [. . .].

He presented [. . .] Bēlet-dūri [. . .].

[. . .] Nabû, detained several nights in Babylon and [. . .] seated among [. . .] without destinies.

[. . .] Babylon [. . .] which he destroyed by fire.

[. . .] the great lord Marduk [. . .] he went to Marduk in place of the king and

---

^{49}[...] ḫi *iq-bi* ^{50}[...]*-ma* gar^{an}

---

^{51}[... *ú*]*-šal-lim-ma* ^{52}[...] maḫ

---

^{53}[...] en *kám-su* ^{54}[... *ú-š*]*a-az-mir*

(iii)(...) $^{3'}$[...] u$_4$ ^{d}Nin [...]

$^{4'}$*i-nu* en *šit-ra-ḫu za-kut* tin *ḫe-pí* $^{5'}$*Bár-sipa*^{ki} *ù ḫe-pí*

$^{6'}$*ù a-de-e šá* ^{Id}50.aš.kur dumu ^{I}*Ku- ḫe-pí* $^{7'}$ ^{lú}gar.kur ^{uru}*La-rak ina muḫ-ḫi-ši-na ú-šaṣ- ḫe-pí*

$^{8'}$*ina* Tin.tir^{ki} *Bár-sipa*^{ki} *ù* Gú.du$_8$.a^{ki} $^{9'}$*ina ma-ḫar* ^{d}En ^{d}Nà *u* ^{d}U.gur *ú-šat-ri-iṣ*

$^{10'}$*šat-ti-šam-ma da-ku ḫa-ba-lu šá-ga-šú* $^{11'}$*ṣa-ba-ti il-ki u tup-šik-ki* ugu*-šú-nu ú-šá-tir*

$^{12'}$*ina* 1(!)^{en} *u*$_4$*-mi* 16 *Ku-ta-a-a ina* ká.gal ^{d}*Za-ba*$_4$*-ba*$_4$ $^{13'}$*šá qé-reb* Tin.tir^{ki} *ina* izi *iq-lu*$_4$

$^{14'}$dumu^{meš} Tin.tir^{ki} *ana* ^{kur}*Ḫat-ti u* ^{kur}Elam.ma^{ki} $^{15'}$*a-na šul-ma-nu-ti ú-bil*

$^{16'}$dumu^{meš} Tin.tir^{ki} dam^{meš}*-šú-nu* dumu^{meš}*-šú-nu* $^{17'}$*ù áš-ta-pi-ri-šú-nu* è*-ma ina* edin *ú- ḫe-pí*

$^{18'}$ká dumu^{meš} Tin.tir^{ki} *ḫe-pí eš-šú* šú sag *ḫe-pí* $^{19'}$*ana* du$_6$ *u kar-mu iš-pu-uk-ma ana* ugu é.gal *ú-tir*

$^{20'}$sila.dagal.la *mu-taq* ^{d}*Šár-ur*$_4$ *na-ram* en*-šú* $^{21'}$*šá* ^{iti}*Ú-lul*(!?) sila uru*-šú i-ba-'u-ú*

$^{22'}$sila *mu-ta-qí-šú is-kir-ma ana* ugu é.gal*-šú* gur*-ma* $^{23'}$*su-qí la mu-ta-qí-šú ú-šá-bi-'i-šú*

$^{24'}$ ^{I}Sig$_5$^{iq}.^{d}Iškur dumu ^{Id}Iškur.mu.kám en di*-šú* $^{25'}$*ba-lu ḫi-ṭi u bar-tu*$_4$ *iṣ-bat-su-ma*

[. . .] he spoke [. . .] was placed (?).

[. . .] kept in order (?) [. . .]

[. . .] the kneeling lord (?) [. . . he] made sing.

(. . .)
[. . .] Nin. . . [. . .].

When the proud lord, the freedom of Bab BREAK,[7] Borsippa, and BREAK[8]

---

and the sworn agreements of Enlil-ina-māti, the son of Ku. . . BREAK, the governor of Larak, in their time, . . . BREAK[9]

(and when) he had offered sacrifices at Babylon, Borsippa, and Cutha before Bēl, Nabû, and Nergal.

Year after year, he made unbearable (their burden) of slaughter, robbery, murder, corvée, and forced labor.

In (only) one day, he burned alive sixteen Cutheans at Zababa's Gate in the heart of Babylon.

He delivered inhabitants of Babylon to Ḫatti and Elam as a token of respect.

He made the inhabitants of Babylon with women, children, and servants go out and BREAK[10] into the countryside.

He heaped up the houses of Babylon's inhabitants RECENT BREAK . . . BREAK into piles of rubble, and he turned them into royal property.

The main street, the avenue of Šarur, his lord's beloved, who passes through the streets of his city in the month of Elul (?),

---

its passage he blocked off and turned into royal property, making him pass into a cul-de-sac.

He seized Mudammiq-Adad, son of Adad-šuma-ēreš, his court opponent, without his having committed either a crime or a rebellion, and

---

26'un^{meš}-*šú ma-la ba-šu-ú a-na Kal-di* 27' *ù* ^{lú}*A-ra-mu a-na šul-ma-nu-ti ú-bil*

28'uru^{meš}-*šú* a.šà^{meš}-*šú* é^{meš}-*šú* ^{giš}kiri$_6$^{meš}-*šú* 29' *ù mim-ma-a-šú ma-la ba-šú-ú pa-ni-šú ú-šad-gil*

30' ^{I}*Il-ta-gab-ìl šá* ^{uru}Bàd *šá* ^{I}Kar.bi *šá* gú ^{i}$_7$*Pu-rat-ti* 31' *ina a-de-e u ma-mit ana pa-ni-šú ú-ṣa-am-ma*

32' *ik-kib ru-be-e pa-ru-ti pi-šat la qa-bé-e* 33'dù-*su ù* uru-*šú ana šá-la-ti im-ni*

34' *ina* mu 6.kám *a-na É-sag-íl* é.gal ^{d}50 dingir^{meš} 35' *a-na ud-du-ši* šu-*su iš-kun-ma*

36'nì<.ga> *É-sag-íl ma-la ba-šu-ú šá* lugal^{meš} 37' *a-lik maḫ-ri-šú ú-še-ri-bu qé-reb-šú*

38' *ú-še-ṣa-am-ma ina qé-reb* é.gal-*šú ik-mis-ma* 39' *a-na i-di rama-ni-šú ú-tir-ma*

40'kù.babbar guškin na$_4$^{meš} *ni-siq-ti šu-qu-ru-ti* 41' *ù mim-ma si-mat* din-gir$^{\textit{ú-ti}}$ *ma-la ba-šú-u*

42'dingir^{meš} Kur *Tam-tì* ^{lú}*Kal-du u* ^{lú}*A-ra-mu* 43'gin$_7$ *bi-bil lìb-bi-šú ú-šat-ri-ṣa ina lìb-bi*

44'munus.šà.é.gal-*šú ú-za-an-a-na šul-ma-nu-ti* 45' *a-na* ^{kur}*Ḫat-ti u* ^{kur}E-lam.ma^{ki} *i-šar-rak*

46'7$^{\textit{tu}}$$_4$ mu.an.na *i-na ka-šá-di a-na qé-reb* 47'É-^{I}*Da-ku-ri ana* ḫul$^{\textit{tì}}$ *il-lik-ma*

48' *ár-ka-nu* ^{Id}Muati.mu.gar$^{\textit{un}}$ dumu ^{I}*Da-ku-ri* 49' *a-de-e u ma-mit* din-gir^{meš} gal^{meš}

50'anše.kur.ra^{meš} érin^{meš} *u* ^{giš}gigir^{meš} é-*ma* 51' *a-na a-lak* kaskal *it-ti-šú iš-pur*

52'ninda^{ḫá} kaš.sag *ù* še.bal.la 53' *a-na kal ma-dak-ti-šú id-din*

54' *ina* ^{iti}Še u$_4$ 20.kám u$_4$ *me-líl-ti šá* ^{d}Utu *u* ^{d}Amar.utu 55' *a-na a-de-e u ma-mit la ip-làḫ-ma*

his people, as many as there were, he carried off to the Chaldeans and the Arameans as a sign of respect.

His towns, his fields, his houses, his gardens, and everything that (belonged to him), as many as there were, he appropriated for himself.

The man Iltagal-il of the town of Dūr-ša-Karbi, which is on the bank of the Euphrates, came into his presence and swore agreements and oaths, but

---

he committed insult and unspeakable slander, that are forbidden of princes, against him and counted his town as booty.

In the sixth year, he turned his attention toward the Esagila, the palace of Enlil of the gods, with a view to restoring it, but

---

the possessions of the Esagila, as much as was there, what earlier kings had brought (there),

---

he took out, gathered (them) into his (own) palace, and made them his own:

---

silver, gold, choice and priceless stones, and everything that befits the deity, as much as was there.

According to his good pleasure, he made offerings (of them) to the gods of the Sealand, of the Chaldeans, and of the Arameans.

He would adorn the women of his palace (with them) and would give (them) to Ḫatti and Elam as signs of respect.

At the beginning of the seventh year, he marched on the Bīt-Dakkūri for evil.

Afterward, Nabû-šuma-iškun, the Dakkurean, (in violation of) the sworn agreements and the oath taken by the great gods,

---

ordered out horses, troops, and chariots and sent them to go on campaign with him.

He distributed bread, beer of first quality, and flour to all his camp.

In the month of Adar, the twentieth day, the day of games in honor of Šamaš and Marduk, he felt no fear with regard to the sworn agreements

---

56'ùn^{meš} *ma-la ina* edin *par-ga-niš rab-ṣa* 57'*i-pu-šá ḫi-du-tú u i-sin-ni*

(iv)(. . .) 2'[. . .]. . . *-ti* 3'[. . .]*-ma*

4'[. . .] ^{d}En 5'[. . . *ú*]*-še-šib*

6'[. . .] ^{d}30 7'[. . . *id-k*]*e-ma*

8'[. . .] ni 9'[. . .]*-ma*

10'[. . .]*-ti-šá* 11'[. . .]*-ma*

12'[. . . Ti]n.tir^{ki} 13'[. . .]*-in-šu-nu-ti*

14'[. . .]*-lu-ti* 15'[. . .] Tin.tir^{ki}

16'[. . .]*-am-ma* 17'[. . .] *ik-mi-su*

18'[. . .] *ul-te-lu* 19'[. . .] *lu-uš-pur*

20'[. . .] en gal^{ú} ^{d}Amar.utu 21'[. . . *É*]*-zi-da ik-kil-mu-ma*

22'[. . .]*-nu ú-šat-bu-niš-šum-ma* 23'[. . .]*-ti-šú iš-lul*

24'[. . .] *mul-taḫ-ṭi-šú* 25'[. . .] *in-né-sír-ma*

26'[. . .] *mun-nab-tu* 27'[. . .] *i-tu-úr-ma*

28'[. . .] ^{kur}*Ak-ka-di-i* 29'[. . .*-m*]*a iq-li*

30'[. . .]^{ki} [. . .]^{ki} *Bár-sipa*^{ki} 31'[. . .]^{ki} *Dil-bat*^{ki} *ù* Gú.da^{ki}

32'[. . . *ul-t*]*u*(?) ugu-*šú ana a-lik pa-na* 33'[. . .]*-di-šu-un i-maš-šá-'a bu-šá-šú-un*

34'[. . . UD].UD$^{ak\ ki}$ *il-lik-ma* 35'[. . . ^{I}]^{d}Nà(?). . .dù ^{lú}gar.kur *La-rak*

36'[. . . *a-de*]*-e u ma-mit* igi dingir^{meš} gal^{meš} en 7-*šú* 37'[. . .]*-ma iṣ-ba-tu it-ti-šú*

and oaths.

The people, as many as were lying like cattle in a meadow, made merry and celebrated.

(. . .)
[. . .]

[. . .] Bēl [. . .] he made dwell.

[. . .] Sîn [. . .] he made get up.

[. . .] in the room (?) [. . .].

[. . .]

[. . . Ba]bylon [. . .] he [. . .] them.

[. . .] Babylon.

[. . .] he [. . .] and [. . .] they knelt.

[. . .] they made go up [. . .]. "I want to send [. . .]."

[. . .] the great lord Marduk [. . .] looked angrily at [. . .] Ezida and

---

[. . .] they made [. . .] attack him and he plundered its [. . .].

[. . .] his survivors [. . .] he confined and

[. . .] the fugitives [. . .] he returned and

[. . .] Akkad [. . .] he burned.

[. . .] Borsippa, [. . .], Dilbat, and Cutha.

[. . .] . . . , toward those who are in the vanguard, [. . .] he stole their goods.

[. . .] he marched [to] Larak and [. . .], governor of Larak

[. . .] sworn agreements and oaths before the great gods, seven times, [. . .] entered into with him.

$^{38'}$[. . .] *ana* lú^{meš} ur$_5$(?)^{meš} *ina ba-lu ḫi-ṭi* $^{39'}$[. . .]-*ri-ia ú-ṣa-bit-ma*

$^{40'}$[. . .] *ú-bil-šú-nu-ti-ma* $^{41'}$[. . .] ri *ú-še-šib-šú-nu-ti*

$^{42'}$[. . .] a . . . *a-na me-e mar-ru-ti* $^{43'}$[. . .]-*šu-nu-ti*

$^{44'}$[. . .] *ik-šu-dam-ma* ^{d}Nà *šá ana pa-an* $^{45'}$[. . .] *ina* Tin.tir^{ki} *ik-la*

$^{46'}$[. . . *ú*]-*ma-ir* É.kur *la* $^{47'}$[. . .] bu *ú-še-piš-ma*

$^{48'}$[. . .] *u* ^{d}Nà ibila *ṣi-ra* $^{49'}$[. . .] *sa-paḫ-šú iq-bu-ú*

$^{50'}$[. . . *ḫe-p*]*í* $^{51'}$[. . .]

$^{52'}$[. . .]-*ki-šú* $^{53'}$[. . .]

$^{54'}$[. . . $^{55'}$. . .] *ḫe-pí*

(upper edge) [. . .] mu^{meš} *ḫe*<-*pí*>

53. CHRONOGRAPHIC DOCUMENT CONCERNING NABONIDUS

Sources: contiguous fragments from a tablet in four columns.
Bibliography: Lambert 1969: 1–8; Schaudig 2001: 590–95.
Language: Babylonian.
Date: Seleucid or Parthian era.
Place: Babylon.
Contents: history of the reign of Nabonidus. The condition of the document makes it impossible to know whether or not it was a chronicle. The events were properly arranged in chronological order; the lengthy expansions in which the author indulged betray him as awkward with his sources. Yet we learn that, in the second year of his reign, En-nigaldi-Nanna, the king's daughter, was consecrated high priestess of the god Nanna at Ur and that the Ebabbar at Sippar was restored.

(. . .) (ii) (. . .)$^{2'}$[. . .-*k*]*a* $^{3'}$[. . .n]in.dingir.ra $^{4'}$[. . . an^{e}] *u* ki^{tì} $^{5'}$[. . .] *šá ia-a-tú i-riš*^{11} $^{6'}$[. . .] *i-na* munus^{meš} *šá ma-ti-ia an-na* $^{7'}$[. . .*šá*] *i-na* dingir *i'-al-la-du* $^{8'}$[*an-na/ul-li*. . .*šá*] *i-na* dingir *i'-al-la-du ul-li* $^{9'}$[. . . ^{d}Utu *u* ^{d}Iškur dingir^{meš}] gal^{meš} *an-na* $^{10'}$. . .] *iš-ṭur*^{12}-*ma* $^{11'}$[. . .] ^{d}30 $^{12'}$[. . . *i-p*]*u-lu-uš* (iii) (. . .) $^{1'}$[*i*]-*ri*-

---

[. . .] those people, without their having committed any crime [. . .] he seized and

---

[. . .] he took them away and [. . .] made them live [on (?)] the steppe (?).

[. . .] toward the Bitter Waters [. . .] them.

[. . .] he reached [. . .] and Nabû who, before [. . .] kept hold of Babylon.

[. . .] he caused to be done [. . .] Ekur not [. . .] he made him do but

---

[Marduk, the great lord (?), and] Nabû, the exalted crown-prince, commanded his scattering [. . .].

[. . .]

[. . .]

[. . . BREA]K [. . .]

(remains of a colophon)

(. . .)

"[. . .] an *ēntu*-priestess [. . . heaven] and earth [. . .] whom he asked me [. . .] among the women of my country?" "Yes." "Is she . . . , whom] a god will beget? ["Yes"/"No." "Is she . . . , whom] a god will beget?" "No". [. . .

qa pa-nu-uš-šú $^{2'}$[. . .] . . . *ṭup-pi*^{meš} éš.gàr u$_4$ An ^{d}En.líl.lá $^{3'gi}$*pi-sa-an ul-tu* Tin.tir^{ki} *a-na nap-lu-su* $^{4'lú}$dub.sar^{meš} *ú-bil-lu-nu ma-ḫar-šú la še-mu* $^{5'}$*la i-di lib-bu-uš ba-la qa-bé-e-šú* ^{na_4}na.rú.a $^{6'}$ [*š*]*á* ^{Id}Nà.nì.gub.ùri *šàr* Tin.tir^{ki} dumu ^{Id}Nin.urta.sum.mu $^{7'}$[*šá*] *ṣa-lam* nin.dingir.ra *par-ṣi-šú al-ka-ka-ti-šú* $^{8'}$[*u k*]*i-du-de-e-šú šaṭ-ru* ugu-*šú it-ti ṭup-pi*^{meš} $^{9'}$[*ú-bil*(*lu-nu*) *a-n*]*a* Tin.tir^{ki} *ina la e-de-e* $^{10'}$[*šá* ^{d}30 en lugal] *i-ra-am-mu qa-tuš-šú* $^{11'}$[. . .] . . . $^{12'}$[*ṭup-pi*^{meš} *i*]*t-ta-aṭ-ṭal-ma ip-l*[*àḫ šá* ^{d}30 $^{13'}$*qí-bi-it-s*]*u* gal^{tú} *it-ta-'-id-ma* . . . [. . . $^{14'}$En.nì.al.d]i.^{d}Nanna *mar-ti ṣi-it l*[*i-ib-bi-šú* $^{15'}$*a-na* ^{d}]30 en lugal *šá la ut-tak-ka-ru q*[*í-bi-it-su* $^{16'}$*a-na*] *e-nu-tu iš-ru-uk ina* ^{iti}Kin ḫi [. . . $^{17'}$*šá* mu *šá*]-*a-šú* É.babbar.ra é ^{d}Utu *šá qé-reb* Zim[bir^{ki} $^{18'}$*šá* lu]gal^{meš} *a-lik maḫ-ri-šú te-me-e*[*n-šú la-bi-ri*] $^{19'}$*ú-ba-'-ú la i-mu-ru aš-ra-te* [. . .] $^{20'}$lugal$^{u\text{-}ti}$-*šú a-na šu-bat ṭu-ub lìb-bi-šú reš*!-[*ti-ti*] $^{21'}$*te-me-*<*en*>*-na* ^{I}*Na-ram-*^{d}30 dumu ^{I}Lugal-*ú-kin* (erased) $^{22'}$*šá-a-šú* ìr *pa-liḫ-šú mu-uš-te-'-ú áš-ri-šú* $^{23'}$*ú-kal-lim-šu-ma ina* mu.an.na.bi *ina* iti *šal-me ina* u$_4$ še.ga $^{24'}$šu.si *la a-ṣe-e* šu.si *la e-re-bu e-li* $^{25'}$*te-me-en-na* ^{I}*Na-ram-*^{d}30 dumu ^{I}Lugal-*ú-kin* $^{26'}$*šá* É.bab-bar.ra é ^{d}Utu *ú-kin uš-šú-šú ši-ṭir* mu $^{27'}$*šá* ^{I}*Na-ram-*^{d}30 *ip-pal-lis-ma la* kúr^{ru} *aš-ru-uš-šú* $^{28'}$*ú-tir-ma it-ti ši-ṭir* mu-*šú iš-ku-un* $^{29'}$*ṣa-lam* ^{I}Lugal-*ú-kin* ad ^{I}*Na-ram-*^{d}30 *ina qé-reb* $^{30'}$*te-me-en-na šá-a-šú ip-pa-al-li-is-ma meš-li* $^{31'}$sag.du^{meš}-*šú né-si-ma il-li-ku la-ba-riš la ut-tu-ú*

(iv)$^{32'}$*bu-un-na-an-nu-šú áš-šú* dingir^{meš} *pi-it-lu-ḫu šu-qu-ri* $^{33'}$lugal$^{ú\text{-}tú}$ *ú-še-šib-ma* ^{lú}*um-man-nu mu-de-e šip-ri* $^{34'}$sag.du alam *šá-a-šú ú-di-iš-ma ú-šak-lil* $^{35'}$*bu-un-na-an-nu-šú* nu *šú-a-tì a-šar-šú* nu kúr^{ir} $^{36'}$*qé-reb* É.bab-bar.ra *ú-še-šib-šú ú-kin-šú tak-li-mu* $^{37'}$É.babbar.ra *šú-a-tì ina ḫi-da-a-tú u re-šá-a-tú* $^{38'}$*a-na* ^{d}Utu ^{d}En gal^{ú} en-*šú i-pu-uš* 6 *lim* $^{39'}$ ^{giš}eren *dan-nu-tú a-na ṣu-lu-li-šú ú-šat-ri-iṣ* $^{40'}$é *šu-a-tú u*$_4$*-mi-iš ú-nam-mir-ma* $^{41'}$gin$_7$ kur^{i} *za-qa-ar ul-la-a re-šá-a-šú* $^{42'}$ ^{giš}ig^{meš} ^{giš}eren *ṣi-ra-a-tú* kun$_4$ urudu $^{43'}$ ^{giš}*me-de-lu u* ^{giš}nu.kúš.ù^{meš} *e-ma* ká.ká^{me}-*šú* $^{44'}$[*ú*]-*šar-ši-id-ma* (erased) *ú-šak-lil ši-pi-ir-šú* $^{45'}$*ina* . . . [. . .] . . . ^{d}Utu en ga[l^{ú} . . .] $^{46'}$*ina* é [. . .]-*ni-ma* a m[a . . .] $^{47'}$*ina* ^{iti}[. . . u$_4$ . . .ka]m egir ^{udu}sís[kur . . .] $^{48'}$i . . . [. . . *t*]*ak-li-mu* garza dingir-*š*[*u* . . .] $^{49'}$*ú-šar-m*[*u*(?)]-*ú ina šu-bat* [*ṭu-ub lìb-bi-šú*] $^{50'}$ ^{lú}ra.ga[b] *ul-tu* ^{kur}*Ḫat-ta* [. . .] $^{51'}$*ú-šá-an-na-*[*a ṭ*]*è-e-me um-ma* [. . . $^{52'}$. . .] be(?) [. . .] . . .-*na-šá pa*(?)-*na*(?) [. . . $^{53'}$. . . dingir]^{meš} gal^{m}[^{eš} . . . $^{54'}$. . . *ku-u*]*n lìb-b*[*u* . . . $^{55'}$. . . *r*]*u-qé-e-ti ur-ḫi* kur^{ú} . . . [. . . $^{56'}$. . . *ú-r*]*u-uḫ mu-ú-tu*$_4$ ^{giš}tukul *in-na-d*[*i-iq* $^{57'}$. . . u]n^{meš} ^{kur}*Ḫat-tu*$_4$ *ina* ^{iti}Gu$_4$ mu 3.kam $^{58'}$[. . . Tin].tir^{ki} *pa-ni* érin^{me}-*šú iṣ-ba-tu* $^{59'}$[. . . *i*]*d-ke-e-ma ina* 13ta *u*$_4$*-mu a-na* $^{60'}$[. . .]-*i ik-šu-du šá* un^{meš} *a-ši-bi* ^{uru}*Am-ma-na-nu* $^{61'}$[. . . -*š*]*ú-nu* sag.du^{meš}-*šú-nu ú-bat-tíq-ma* $^{62'}$[. . .] . . . *a-na gu-ru-un-né-e-ti* $^{63'}$[lugal *ina g*]*a-ši-šú i-lu-ul-ma* $^{64'}$[. . .]-*at* kur^{i} *ú-za-az* u[ru $^{65'}$*Am-ma-na-nu*(?)[13]] *šá qé-reb* kur^{meš} gurun ^{giš}kiri$_6$^{m}[^{eš} dù.a.bi $^{66'}$. . .]-*ṣi-li-ši-nu it-*[. . . $^{67'}$. . .] *a-na gi-mi-ri-šú* ^{d}BIL.G[I $^{68'}$*ú-šaq-mi* . . .] . . .-*tú*/*na šá mé-la-šú-nu ru-ú-q*[*u* $^{69'}$. . .] *a-na u*$_4$*-mu ṣa-a-tú ú-šá-li*[*k* $^{70'}$*kar-mu-tú* . . .] . . . *šá-a-šú né-re-bé-e-ti* [. . . $^{71'}$. . .] . . . *u*$_4$*-mu i-zi-i*[*b*(?) . . . $^{72'}$. . .] . . .-*te-ed-d*[*i* . . .] (. . .) (v)^{1}[. . .] . . . ^{2}[. . .] ki ^{3}[. . .] . . . -*ti-šú* ^{4}[. . .]-*am-ma*

Šamaš and Adad, the] great [gods. . .]: "Yes." [. . .] he/they wrote and [. . .] . . . Sîn [. . . they res]ponded to him [. . .].

(. . .)

His face became pale. [. . .] The scribes brought in front of him from Babylon the basket (containing) the tablets of the series When Anu and Enlil in order to consult them, but no one whatsoever heeded nor understood their content without his explanation. A stela of Nebuchadnezzar, king of Babylon, son of Ninurta-nādin-šumi, on [which] appeared the representation of an *ēntu*-priestess (and) were described the rites, rules, [and] ceremonies (relating to) her (office), [was brought] with other tablets [(from Ur?) t]o Babylon, in ignorance [of what Sîn, lord of kings], wished in (giving them) to him. [. . .] He took a good look at the tablets and was af[raid]. He was attentive to [Sîn's] great [commandment] and . . . He dedicated [En-nigald]i-Nanna, his daughter, [his chi]ld, [to] Sîn, lord of the kings, [whose] w[ord] is unchangeable, in the office of *ēntu*-priestess.

In the month of Elul, . . . [. . . of] this same [year], in the Ebabbar, the temple of Šamaš, which is in Sip[par, (and) in which] kings among his predecessors had searched in vain for [the ancient] foundati[on]—the ancient dwelling place [. . .] of his kingship that would make his heart glad—he revealed to him, to his humble servant who worshiped him, who was constantly in search of his holy places, the sacred enclosure of Narām-Sîn, Sargon's son, and, in this same year, in a propitious month, on a favorable day, he laid the foundations of the Ebabbar, the temple of Šamaš, above the sacred enclosure of Narām-Sîn, Sargon's son, without exceeding or shrinking a finger's breadth. He saw Narām-Sîn's inscription and, without changing its place, restored it and appended his own inscription there. He saw in this sacred enclosure a statue of Sargon, the father of Narām-Sîn: half of its head was missing, and it had deteriorated so as to make its face hardly recognizable. Given his reverence for the gods and his respect for kingship, he summoned expert artisans, restored the head of this statue, and put back (its) face. He did not change its place but installed it in the Ebabbar (and) initiated an oblation for it. For Šamaš, the great lord, his lord, he constructed this Ebabbar in joy and gladness. He caused six thousand strong cedar beams to be laid out for its ceiling. He made this temple shine like the day and raised its topmost height like a high mountain. For the entrance, [he brought] outstanding cedar doors, bronze doorsteps, bolts, and sockets, (and) he finished his work. In [. . .] Šamaš, the great lord, [. . .] in the temple [. . .], in the month of [. . ., the . . .]th [day (?)], after the offer[ings, . . .] he initiated an oblation according to the rite of [his] lord. They let (him) dwell in the dwelling place [that makes his heart glad].

A messenger [arrived (?)] from Ḫatti [and] repeated the information: "[. . .]" the great gods [. . .] heart's content [. . . dis]tant, the road through the

^{5}[... -*t*]*i-šú iš-me-e-ma* ^{6}[...] ...*-šú im-ḫaṣ/qut-su* ^{7}[...] *i-ta-mi it-ti-šú* ^{8}[... š]u$_{ii}$ *um-mi-id-ma* ^{9}[... *p*]*ar-ṣi-šú* ^{10}[...] *it-ti-šú* ^{11}[...]-*ú* ^{12}[...] *si-dir-tú* ^{13}[...] ... šeš šu érin$^{ḫ[á}$-*š*]*ú* ^{14}[...] ... ^{giš}tukul *iš-ši-ma ana* še ... [(?) ^{15}...] danna *qaq-qa-ri ur-ḫi pa-áš-qu-tú* ^{16}[... *qaq-q*]*a-ri nam-ra-ṣa* ^{17}[*a-šar kib-su šu-up-ru*]*-su-ma* gìr$_{ii}$ *la i-ba-áš-šu-u* ^{18}[...] *a-na zi-kir šu-mi-i-šú* ^{19}[...] ... ^{gi}edin^{na-a} ^{20}[... ^{me}]^{š} lugal *šá da-da-na* ^{21}[... ^{me}]^{š} *né-su-tú in-né-riq* ^{22}[...] *ú*(?)-*kap-pir-m*[*a* ^{23}... geš]tu$_{ii}^{meš}$ *na-*...[...] (...)

mountain [. . . a ro]ad of death, he donn[ed] his weapons [against (?) the peo]ple of Ḫatti.

In the month of Iyyar, the third year, [he] took the head of his troops at [Baby]lon, [and, having mu]stered [them], in thirteen days he reached [. . .] . . . , (and) he cut off the heads of the people who lived in Ammanānum [and th]eir . . . [. . . , and piled them up] in a heap. He hung [the king] on a stake and [. . .] . . . , he allocated (?) the town [. . .] . . . of a mountain, [Ammanānum], which is situated in the middle of the mountains, orchards [. . .], their shadow (?) . . . [. . . he let] Girr[a burn] all of it [. . .] . . . , whose tops were distant [. . .] he turned into [ruins] for all time . . . entrance ways . . . day, he left [. . .]

(. . .)

[. . .] his [. . .] he listened and [. . .] and fell upon him [. . .], he spoke with him [. . .] stretched his hands and [. . .] his rites [. . .] with him [. . .] battle array [. . .] his troops [. . .] he bore arms and toward [. . .] double hours, difficult roads [. . . ter]ritory full of difficulty, [dwelling places, the crossing of which is impossi]ble and where no foot is set [. . .] at the mention of his name [. . .] plants [. . .] the king of Dadanu [. . .] distant [. . .] he wiped off and [. . .]

(. . .)

Notes

1. Variant: *En-me-ki-ir.*
2. Variant: *En-me-ki-ir.*
3. Variant: *ša* u_4*-me.*
4. Variant: sila.
5. Generally the priest. The leek was a frequent taboo; a specific text says, "If a man enters into the temple of his god having eaten a leek, cress, garlic, onion, beef, or pork, he is not pure." From this document we learn that leek was a taboo in the Ezida.
6. Allusion to the goddess Ištar.
7. Read: "Babylon."
8. Read: "Cutha."
9. Read: "had established."
10. Read: "settled them."
11. For *-rišu.* The omission of the grammatical inflection *-u* is a possible influence of alphabetic consonantal writing; see M. P. Streck 2001.
12. For *-ṭuru;* see n. 11 above.
13. Ammanānum was well known for its orchards; compare chronicle 26.

Bibliography

Abusch, Tzvi, John Huehnergard, and Piotr Steinkeller, eds. 1990. *Lingering over Words: Studies in Ancient Near Eastern Literature in Honor of William L. Moran*. HSS 37, Atlanta: Scholars Press.

Afanas'eva, Veronika K. 1987. "Das sumerische Sargon-Epos: Versuch einer Interpretation." *AoF* 14:237–46.

Albenda, Pauline. 1986. *Le Palais de Sargon d'Assyrie*. Paris: Editions Recherche sur les civilisations.

Ali, Fadhil A. 1964. "Sumerian Letters: Two Collections from the Old Babylonian Schools." PhD. diss. University of Pennsylvania.

Al-Jadir, Walid. 1991. "Le quartier de l'É.BABBAR de Sippar (Sommaire des fouilles de 1985–1989, 8–11èmes campagnes)." Pages 193–96 in *Mesopotamie et Elam: Actes de la XXXVIème Rencontre assyriologique internationale*. Edited by Leon de Meyer and Hermann Gasche. Ghent: University of Ghent Press.

Al-Rawi, Farouk N. H. 1990. "Tablets from the Sippar Library, I. The 'Weidner Chronicle': A Suppostitious Royal Letter concerning a Vision." *Iraq* 52:1–13.

———. 1994. "Texts from Tell Haddad and Elsewhere." *Iraq* 56:35–43.

Alster, Bendt. 1973. "An Aspect of 'Enmerkar and the Lord of Aratta.'" *RA* 67:101–9.

———. 1974. "The Paradigmatic Character of Mesopotamian Heroes." *RA* 68:49–60.

———, ed. 1980. *Death in Mesopotamia: Papers Read at the XXVIe Rencontre Assyriologique Internationale*. Copenhagen: Akademisk Forlag.

———. 1987. "A Note on the Uriah Letter in the Sumerian Sargon Legend." *ZA* 77:169–73.

———. 1990. "The Sumerian Poem of Early Rulers and Related Poems." *OLP* 21:5–25.

Alster, Bendt, and Ulla Jeyes. 1986. "A Sumerian Poem about Early Rulers." *ASJ* 8:1–11.

Anbar, Moshe. 1991. *Les tribus amurrites de Mari*. OBO 108. Freiburg: Universitätsverlag; Göttingen: Vandenhoeck & Ruprecht.

Aron, Raymond. 1938. *Introduction à la philosophie de l'historie: Essai sur les limites de l'objectivité historique*. Paris: Gallimard.

Archi, A. 1998. "History and Time." *NABU* 86.

Arnaud, Daniel. 1985. *Recherches au pays d'Aštata*. Emar 6/2. Paris: Editions Recherche sur les civilisations.

———. 1987. *Recherches au pays d'Aštata*. Emar 6/4. Paris: Editions Recherche sur les civilisations.

Attinger, Pascal. 1984. "Remarques à propos de la 'Malédiction d'Accad.'" *RA* 78:99–121.

———. 1994. "La duplicité de Sargon: SgLeg., 3 N–T 296: 14–45." *NABU* 99.

Balandier, Georges. 1982. *Sociologie actuelle de l'Afrique noire: Dynamique sociale en Afrique centrale*. 4th ed. Paris: Presses Universitaires de France.

———. 1985. *Anthropo-logiques*. Paris: Le Livre de Poche.

Barnett, Richard D. 1959. *Assyrian Palace Reliefs and Their Influence on the Sculptures of Babylonia and Persia*. Prague: Artia.

Beaulieu, Paul-Alain. 1997. "The Fourth Year of Hostilities in the Land." *BaM* 28:367–94.

———. 2002. "Eanna = Ayyakkum in the Basetki Inscription of Narām-Sîn." *NABU* 36.

Berlin, Adele. 1979. *Enmerkar and Enšuḫkešdanna*. Philadelphia: University Museum.

Bernard, Paul. 1990. "Nouvelle contribution de l'épigraphie cunéiforme à l'histoire hellénistique." *BCH* 114:513–41.

Berque, Jacques. 1974. *Langages arabes du présent*. Paris: Gallimard.

Bickerman, Elias J. 1938. *Les Institutions des Séleucides*. Paris: Geuthner.

Bidmead, Julye. 2002. *The Akītu Festival, Religious Continuity and Royal Legitimation in Mesopotamia*. Piscataway, N.J.: Gorgias.

Biggs, Robert D. 1967. "More Babylonian 'Prophecies.'" *Iraq* 29:117–32.

———. 1985. "The Babylonian Prophecies and the Astrological Traditions of Mesopotamia." *JCS* 37:86–90.

———. 1987. "Babylonian Prophecies, Astrology, and a New Source for 'Prophecy Text B.'" Pages 1–14 in Rochberg-Halton 1987.

———. 1992. "The Babylonian Prophecies." *BCSMS* 23:17–20.

Birot, Maurice. 1980. "Fragment de rituel de Mari relatif au kispum." Pages 139– 50 in Alster 1980.

———. 1985. "Les chroniques 'assyriennes' de Mari." Pages 219–42 in in vol. 4 of *Mari: Annales de recherches interdisciplinaires*. Paris: Editions Recherche sur les civilisations.

Black, Jeremy A. 1981. "The New Year Ceremonies in Ancient Babylon: 'Taking Bel by the Hand' and a Cultic Picnic." *Religion* 11:39–59.

Black, Jeremy A., and Anthony Green. 1992. *Gods, Demons and Symbols of Ancient Mesopotamia*. London: British Museum.

Bloch, Marc. 1949. *Apologie pour l'histoire, ou, Métier d'historien*. Cahiers des Annales. Paris: Armand.

Bonechi, Marco. 1990. "AN.BU = *a-nu-bu*$_x$." *NABU* 124.

Borger, Riekele. 1956, *Die Inschriften Asarhaddons Königs von Assyrien*. AfOB 9. Graz: self-published.

———. 1957/58. "Die Inschriften Asarhaddons (AfO Beiheft 9), Nachträge und Verbesserungen." *AfO* 18:113–118, pls. XXI–XXII.

———. 1964. "Zu den Asarhaddon-Texten aus Babel." *BO* 21:142–48.

———. 1971a. "Gott Marduk und Gott-König Šulgi als Propheten: Zwei prophetische Texte." *BO* 28:3–24.

———. 1971b. "Gottesbrief." *RlA* 3:575–76.

———. 1974. "Die Beschwörungsserie *bīt mēseri* und die Himmelfahrt Henochs." *JNES* 33:183–96.

Bottéro, Jean. 1985. *Mythes et rites de Babylone*. Paris: Champion.

———. 1992. *L'Épopée de Gilgameš*. Paris: Gallimard.

Bottéro, Jean, and Samuel Noah Kramer. 1989. *Lorsque les dieux faisaient l'homme: Mythologie mésopotamienne*. Bibliothèque des histoires. Paris: Gallimard.

Bouché-Leclerc, Auguste. 1963. *Histoire des Séleucides (323–64 avant J.-C.)*. Bruxelles, Culture et Civilisation.

Bourdieu, Pierre. 1980. *Practical Reason: On the Theory of Action*. Stanford, Calif.: Stanford University Press.

Brinkman, John A. 1969–70. "The Akītu Inscription of Bēl-ibni and Nabû-zēra-ušabši." *WO* 5:39–50.

———. 1973. "Comments on the Nassouhi Kinglist and the Assyrian Kinglist Tradition." *Or* 42:306–19.

———. 1984a. *Prelude to Empire: Babylonian Society and Politics, 747–626 B.C.* Philadelphia: University Museum.

———. 1984b. "Through a Glass Darkly: Esarhaddon's Retrospects on the Downfall of Babylon." Pages 35–42 in Sasson 1984.

———. 1990. "The Babylonian Chronicle Revisited." Pages 73–104 in Abusch, Huehnergard, and Steinkeller.

Brinkman, John A., and Douglas A. Kennedy. 1983. "Documentary Evidence for the Economic Base of Early Neo-Babylonian Society: A Survey of Dated Babylonian Economic Texts, 721–626 B.C." *JCS* 35:1–91.

Burstein, Stanley Mayer. 1978. *The Babyloniaca of Berossos*. SM 1/5. Malibu: Undena.

Cagni, Luigi. 1969. *L'Epopea di Erra*. Studi Semitici 34. Rome: Istituto di Studi del Vicino Oriente, Università di Roma.

Calmeyer, Peter. 1995. "Museum." *RlA* 8:453–455.
Cassin, Elena. 1969. "Cycles du temps et cadres de l'espace en Mésopotamie ancienne." *RS* 90:241–57.
———. 1987. *Le Semblable et le différent: Symbolismes du pouvoir dans le Proche-Orient ancien.* Paris: La Découverte.
Cavigneaux, Antoine. 1981. *Textes scolaires du Temple de Nabû ša Ḫarê.* Vol. 1. Baghdad: The State Organization of Antiquities & Heritage.
———. 1983. "Lexikalische Listen." *RlA* 6:609–41.
Cavigneaux, Antoine, and Farouk N. H. Al-Rawi. 2000. *Gilgameš et la mort: Textes de Tell Haddad VI.* CM 19. Groningen: Styx.
Charpin, Dominique. 1984. "Inscriptions votives d'époque assyrienne." Pages 41–81 in vol. 3 of *Mari: Annales de recherches interdisciplinaires.* Paris: Editions Recherche sur les civilisations.
———. 1985a. "Les Archives d'époque 'assyrienne' dans le palais de Mari." Pages 243–68 in vol. 4 of *Mari: Annales de recherches interdisciplinaires.* Paris: Editions Recherche sur les civilisations.
———. 1985b. "Les Archives du devin Asqudum dans la résidence du 'chantier A.'" Pages 257, 453–62 in vol. 4 of *Mari: Annales de recherches interdisciplinaires.* Paris: Editions Recherche sur les civilisations.
———. 1986. *Le clergé d'Ur au temps de Hammurabi.* Geneva: Droz.
———. 1994. "Une décollation mystérieuse." *NABU* 59.
———. 1997. "La version mariote de l''Insurrection générale contre Narâm-Sîn.'" Pages 9–18 in Charpin and Durand 1997b.
Charpin, Dominique, and Jean-Marie Durand. 1985. "La Prise du pouvoir par Zimri-Lim." Pages 293–353 in vol. 4 of *Mari: Annales de recherches interdisciplinaires.* Paris: Editions Recherche sur les civilisations.
———. 1986. "'Fils de Sim'al': Les origines tribales des rois de Mari." *RA* 80:141–83.
———. 1997a. "Aššur avant l'Assyrie." Pages 367–91 in vol. 8 of *Mari: Annales de recherches interdisciplinaires.* Paris: Editions Recherche sur les civilisations.
———, eds. 1997b. *Recueil d'études à la mémoire de Marie-Thérèse Barrelet.* Florilegium marianum 3. Mémoires de NABU 4. Paris: SEPOA.
Charpin, Dominique, and Nele Ziegler. 2003. *Mari et le Proche-Orient à l'époque amorrite.* Florilegium marianum 5. Mémoires de NABU. 6. Paris: SEPOA.
Civil, Miguel. 1961."Texts and Fragments." *JCS* 15:79–80.
———. 1967. "Šū-Sîn's Historical Inscriptions: Collection B." *JCS* 21:24–38.
———. 1969. "The Sumerian Flood Story." Pages 138–45 in Lambert and Millard.
———. 1972. "Supplement to the Introduction to *ISET* I." *Or* 41:83–90.
———. 1974. "Lexicography." Pages 123–57 in *Sumerological Studies in Honor of Thorkild Jacobsen.* AS 20. Chicago: University of Chicago Press.

———. 1980. "Les Limites de l'information textuelle." Pages 225–32 in *L'Archéologie de l'Iraq du début de l'époque néolithique à 333 avant notre ère*. Edited by M.-Th. Barrelet. Paris: Éditions du CNRS.

———. 1985. "On Some Texts Mentioning Ur-Namma." *Or* 54:27–45, pl. VI.

Clay, Albert T. 1912a. "An Ancient Antiquary." *MJ* 3:23–25.

———. 1912b. *Babylonian Business Transactions of the First Millennium B.C.* BRM 1. New York: Pierpont Morgan Library.

———. 1923. *Epics, Hymns, Omens, and Other Texts*. BRM 4. New Haven: Yale University Press.

Cogan, Mordechai. 1991. "A Plaidoyer on Behalf of the Royal Scribes." Pages 121–28 in Cogan and Eph'al 1991.

Cogan, Mordechai, and Israel Eph'al, eds. 1991. *Ah Assyria. . . : Studies in Assyrian History and Ancient Near Eastern Historiography Presented to Hayim Tadmor*. Jerusalem: Magnes.

Cole, Stephen W. 1994. "The Crimes and Sacrileges of Nabû-šuma-iškun." *ZA* 84: 220–52.

Cooper, Jerrold S. 1980. "Apodotic Death and the Historicity of 'Historical' Omens." Pages 99–105 in Alster 1980.

———. 1983. *The Curse of Agade*. Baltimore: Johns Hopkins University Press.

———. 1986. *Presargonic Inscriptions*. Sumerian and Akkadian Royal Inscriptions 1. New Haven: Yale University Press.

Cooper, Jerrold S., and Wolfgang Heimpel. 1984. "The Sumerian Sargon Legend." Pages 67–82 in Sasson 1984.

Cunnison, Ian. 1957. "History and Genealogies in a Conquest State." *AA* 59: 20–31.

Dalley, Stephanie. 1991. *Myths from Mesopotamia: Creation, the Flood, Gilgamesh, and Others*. Oxford: Oxford University Press.

Dandamayev, Muhammad A. 1979. "State and Temple in Babylonia in the First Millennium B.C." Pages 589–96 in vol. 2 of *State and Temple Economy in the Ancient Near East: Proceedings of the International Conference Organized by the Katholieke Universiteit Leuven from the 10th to the 14th of April, 1978*. Edited by Edward Lipiński. 2 vols. OLA 5–6. Leuven: Departement Oriëntalistiek.

De Certeau, Michel. 1975. *L'écriture de l'histoire*. Paris: Gallimard.

Deller, Karlheinz. 1994. "Der Eponym des Jahres 794 v. Chr." *NABU* 92.

Dijk, Jan J. A. van. 1962. "Die Inschriftenfunde." Pages 39–62, pls. 27–28 in *XVIII. vorläufiger Bericht über die . . . Ausgrabungen in Uruk/Warka*. Edited by Heinrich J. Lenzen. Berlin: Mann.

———. 1976. *Cuneiform Texts, Texts of Varying Content*. Vol. 9 of *Texts in the Iraq Museum*. Leiden: Brill.

———. 1986. "Die dynastischen Heiraten zwischen Kassiten und Elamern: Eine verhängnisvolle Politik." *Or* 55:159–170.

———. 1989. "Ein spätbabylonischer Katalog einer Sammlung sumerischer Briefe." *Or* 58:441–52.

Durand, Jean-Marie. 1985. "La situation historique des šakkanakku: Nouvelle approche." Pages 147–72 in vol. 4 of *Mari: Annales de recherches interdisciplinaires*. Paris: Editions Recherche sur les civilisations.

———. 1988. *Archives Épistolaires de Mari* I/1. ARM 26. Paris: Editions Recherche sur les civilisations.

———. 1990. "Documents pour l'histoire du royaume de Haute-Mésopotamie II." Pages 271–301 in vol. 6 of *Mari: Annales de recherches interdisciplinaires*. Paris: Editions Recherche sur les civilisations.

———. 1991. "L'emploi des toponymes dans l'onomastique d'époque amorrite (I): Les noms en Mut-." *SEL* 8:81–97.

———. 1992. "Espionnage et guerre froide: la fin de Mari." Pages 39–52 in *Florilegium Marianum: Recueil d'études en l'honneur de Michel Fleury*. Edited by J.-M. Durand. Mémoires de NABU 1. Paris: SEPOA.

———. 1998–2000. *Documents épistolaires de Mari*. 3 vols. Paris: Cerf.

Durand, Jean-Marie, and Michaël Guichard. 1997. "Les rituels de Mari." Pages 19–78 in Charpin and Durand.

Eckhardt, Karl August. 1937. *Irdische Unsterblichkeit germanischer Glaube an die Wiederverkörperung in der Sippe*. Weimar: Böhlaus.

Edzard, Dietz Otto. 1960. "Neue Inschriften zur Geschichte von Ur III unter Šūsuen." *AfO* 19:1–32, pls. I–IV.

———. 1974. "Deux lettres royales d'Ur III en sumérien 'syllabique' et pourvu d'une traduction accadienne." Pages 9–34 in *Textes littéraires de Suse*. Edited by R. Labat. MDAI 57. Paris: Geuthner.

———. 1980. "Königslisten und Chroniken, Sumerisch." *RlA* 6:77–86.

———. 1981. "Neue Erwägungen zum Brief des Enna-Dagan von Mari (TM.75.G.2367)." *Studi Eblaiti* 4:89–97.

———. 1989. "La vision du passé et de l'avenir en Mésopotamie." Pages 157–66 in *Histoire et conscience historique dans les civilisations du Proche-Orient ancien, Actes du Colloque de Cartigny*. Leuven: Peeters.

———. 1997. *Gudea and His Dynasty*. RIME 3/1. Toronto: University of Toronto Press.

Eichler, Barry L. 1993. "mar-URU_5: Tempest in a Deluge." Pages 90–94 in *The Tablet and the Scroll: Near Eastern Studies in Honor of William W. Hallo*. Edited by Mark E. Cohen, Daniel C. Snell, and David B. Weisberg. Bethesda, Md.: CDL.

Eidem, Jesper. 1991. "The Tell Leilan Archives 1987." *RA* 85:109–35.

Ellis, Maria deJong, ed. 1977. *Essays on the Ancient Near East in Memory of Jacob Joel Finkelstein*. Hamden, Ct.: Archon.

———. 1987. "The Goddess Kititum Speaks to King Ibalpiel: Oracle Texts from Ischchali." Pages 235–66 in vol. 5 of *Mari: Annales de recherches interdisciplinaires*. Paris: Editions Recherche sur les civilisations.

Evans-Pritchard, Edward Evan. 1940. *The Nuer.* Oxford: Clarendon.

El Faïz, Mohammed. 1995. *L'Agronomie de la Mésopotamie antique: Analyse du "Livre de l'agriculture nabatéenne" de Qûṯâmä.* Studies in the History of the Ancient Near East 5. Leiden: Brill.

Fales, Frederick Mario, ed. 1981. *Assyrian Royal Inscriptions: New Horizons in Literary, Ideological, and Historical Analysis.* Orientis antiqui collectio 17. Rome: Istituto per l'Oriente.

Falkenstein, Adam. 1931. *Literarische Keilschrifttexte aus Uruk.* Berlin: Staatliche Museen.

Farber, Gertrud. 1997. "The Song of the Hoe." *COS* 1.157:511–13.

Finkel, Irving L. 1980. "Bilingual Chronicle Fragments." *JCS* 32:65–80.

Finkel, Irving L., and Julian E. Reade. 1995. "Lots of Eponyms." *Iraq* 57: 167–72.

———. 1998. "Assyrian Eponyms, 873–649 BC." *Or* 67:248–54.

Finkelstein, Jacob J. 1963a. "The Antediluvian Kings: A University of California Tablet." *JCS* 17:39–51.

———. 1963b. "Mesopotamian Historiography." *PAPS* 107: 461–72.

———. 1966. "The Genealogy of the Hammurapi Dynasty." *JCS* 20:95–118.

Foster, Benjamin R. 1990. "Naram-Sin in Martu and Magan." *ARRIM* 8:25–44.

———. 1991. "On Authorship in Akkadian Literature." *AION* 51:17–32.

———. 1996. *Before the Muses.* 2nd ed. Bethesda: CDL Press.

———. 2001. *The Epic of Gilgamesh.* New York: Norton.

Frahm, Eckart. 1998. "704 v. Chr." *NABU* 116.

———. 1999. "Nabû-zuqup-kēnu, das Gilgameš-Epos und der Tod Sargons II." *JCS* 51:73–90.

Frame, Grant. 1992. *Babylonia 689–627 B.C.: A Political History.* Leiden: Nederlands Instituut voor het Nabije Oosten.

Frankfort, Henri. 1988. *The Art and Architecture of the Ancient Orient.* Harmondsworth, Eng.: Penguin.

Frayne, Douglas R. 1993. *Sargonic and Gutian Periods (2334–2113 BC).* RIME 2. Toronto: University of Toronto Press.

Frayne, Douglas R., and Lynne George. 1990. "The 'Rake's' Progress: A Phantom King of Kish." *NABU* 30.

Freydank, Helmut. 1975. "Zur Assyrischen Königsliste." *AoF* 3:173–75.

Frymer-Kensky, Tikvah. 1984. "The Tribulations of Marduk: The So-Called 'Marduk Ordeal Text.'" Pages 131–41 in Sasson 1984.

Funck, Bernd. 1971. "Die babylonische Chronik Smith (BM 34660 & BM 36313) als Quelle des Diadochenkampfes (321–306 v. Chr.)." Pages 217–40 in *Beiträge zu Geschichte, Kultur und Religion des alten Orients: In Memoriam Eckhard Unger.* Edited by Manfred Lurker. Baden-Baden: Koerner.

Gadd, Cyril J. 1953. "Inscribed Barrel Cylinder of Marduk-apla-iddina II." *Iraq* 15:123–34.

Gadd, Cyril J., Léon Legrain, and Sidney Smith. 1928. *Royal Inscriptions.* UrET 1. London: British Museum; Philadelphia: University Museum.

Garelli, Paul. 1974. *Le Proche-Orient Asiatique.* Nouvelle Clio. Paris: Presses Universitaires de France. 2nd edition (1997) unchanged.

———. 1985. “Réflexions sur les listes royales assyriennes.” Pages 91–95 in *Miscellanea Babylonica: Mélanges offerts à Maurice Birot.* Edited by Jean-Marie Durand and Jean-Robert Kupper. Paris: Editions Recherche sur les civilisations.

Gassan, Marcel. 1989. “Hurpatila, roi d’Elammat.” *AION* 49:223–29.

Gelb, Ignace J. 1952. *Sargonic Texts from the Diyala Region: Materials for the Assyrian Dictionary I.* Chicago: University of Chicago Press.

Gelb, Ignace J., and Burkhart Kienast. 1990. *Die altakkadischen Königsinschriften des dritten Jahrtausends v. Chr.* FAOS 7. Stuttgart: Steiner.

Geller, Markham J. 1990. “Babylonian Astronomical Diaries and Corrections of Diodorus.” *BSOAS* 53:1–7.

———. 1991. “New Information on Antiochus IV from Babylonian Astronomical Diaries.” *BSOAS* 54:1–4.

George, Andrew R. 1999. *The Epic of Gilgamesh: A New Translation.* New York: Barnes & Noble.

Gerber, Manuel. 1998. “Die Inschrift H(arran) 1.A/B und die neubabylonische Chronologie.” *ZA* 88:72–93.

Gibert, Pierre. 1979. *Une théorie de la légende.* Paris: Flammarion.

Glassner, Jean-Jacques. 1983, Narām-Sîn poliorcète: Les avatars d’une sentence divinatoire.” *RA* 77:3–10.

———. 1984a. “La division quinaire de la terre.” *Akkadica* 40:17–34.

———. 1984b. “Pour un lexique des termes et figures analogiques en usage dans la divination mésopotamienne.” *JA* 272:15–46.

———. 1985a. “Aspects du don, de l’échange et formes d’appropriation du sol dans la Mésopotamie du IIIe millénaire avant la fondation de l’Empire d’Ur.” *JA* 273:11–59.

———. 1985b. “Sargon ‘roi du combat.’” *RA* 79:115–26.

———. 1986. *La Chute d’Akkadé, l’événement et sa mémoire.* BBVO 5. Berlin: Reimer.

———. 1988. “Le récit autobiographique de Sargon.” *RA* 82:1–11.

———. 1989. “Women, Hospitality and the Honor of the Family.” Pages 71–90 in *Women’s Earliest Records: From Ancient Egypt and Western Asia.* Edited by B. S. Lesko. Atlanta: Scholars Press.

———. 1991. “Les dieux et les hommes, le vin et la bière en Mésopotamie ancienne.” Pages 127–46 in Le Ferment divin. Edited by D. Fournier and S. D’onofrio. Paris: Éditions de la Maison des Sciences de l’Homme.

———. 1992. “Inanna et les me.” Pages 55–86 in *Nippur at the Centennial: Papers Read at the 35e Rencontre Assyriologique Internationale,*

Philadelphia, 1988. Edited by Maria deJong Ellis. Philadelphia: University Museum.

———. 1993. "Le roi prêtre en Mésopotamie, au milieu du 3e millénaire: Mythe ou réalité?" Pages 9–19 in *L'ancien Proche-Orient et les Indes: Parallélismes interculturels religieux: Colloque franco-finlandais les 10 et 11 novembre 1990 à l'Institut finlandais, Paris.* StudOr 70. Helsinki: Finnish Oriental Society.

———. 1994. "Ruḫušak-mār aḫatim: La transmission du pouvoir en Élam." *JA* 282:219–36.

———. 1995a. "La gestion de la terre en Mésopotamie selon le témoignage des kudurrus anciens." *BO* 52:5–24.

———. 1995b. "The Use of Knowledge in Ancient Mesopotamia." *CANE* 3:1815–23.

———. 1996a. "From Sumer to Babylon: Families as Landowners and Families as Rulers." Pages 92–127 in *Distant Worlds, Ancient Worlds.* Vol. 1 of *A History of the Family.* Edited by André Burguière et al. Translated by Sarah Hanbury Tenison, Rosemary Morris, and Andrew Wilson. Cambridge: Harvard University Press.

———. 1996b. "Les dynasties d'Awan et de Simaški." *NABU* 34.

———. 1997. "L'historien mésopotamien et l'événement." *Mètis* 12:97–117.

———. 1999. "Histoire babylonienne et sa réflexion dans les chroniques de l'époque babylonienne récente." Pages 157–66 in *Babylon: Focus mesopotamischer Geschichte, Wiege früher Gelehrsamkeit, Mythos in der Moderne.* Edited by Johannes Renger. Colloquien der Deutschen Orient-Gesellschaft 2. Saarbrücken: Saarbrücker, Druckerei und Verlag.

———. 2000a. *Écrire à Sumer: L'invention du cunéiforme.* Paris: Éditions du Seuil.

———. 2000b. "Historical Times in Mesopotamia." Pages 189–211 in *Israel Constructs Its History: Deuteronomistic Historiography in Recent Research.* Edited by Albert de Pury, Thomas Römer, and Jean-Daniel Macchi. JSOTSup 306. Sheffield: Sheffield Academic Press.

———. 2000c. "Les petits Etats mésopotamiens à la fin du 4e et au cours du 3e millénaire." Pages 35–53 in *A Comparative Study of Thirty City-State Cultures.* Edited by M. H. Hansen. Copenhagen: Royal Danish Academy of Sciences and Letters.

———. 2001a. "Le devin historien en Mésopotamie." Pages 181–93 in *Proceedings of the XLVe Rencontre Assyriologique Internationale: Historiography in the Cuneiform World.* Edited by Tzvi Abusch et al. Bethesda, Md.: CDL.

———. 2001b. "Scribes, érudits et bibliothèques en Mésopotamie." Pages 213–26 in *Du livre au texte.* Vol. 1 of *Des Alexandries.* Edited by Luce Giard and Christian Jacob. Paris: Bibliothèque nationale de France.

———. 2002. "Who Were the Authors before Homer in Mesopotamia." *Diogenes* 49:86–92.

———. 2003. "Entre le discours politique et la science divinatoire: Le récit historiographique en Mésopotamie." Pages 63–86 in *Événement, récit, histoire officielle: L'écriture de l'histoire dans les monarchies antiques.* Edited by Nicolas Grimal and Nichel Baud. Etudes d'égyptologie 3. Paris: Cybèle.

———. Forthcoming. "La date de la composition de la chronique de la monarchie une." In Jacob Klein Festschrift. Tel Aviv.

Goetze, Albrecht. 1947a. "Historical Allusions in Old Babylonian Omen Texts." *JCS* 1:253–65, 358.

———. 1947b. *Old Babylonian Omen Texts.* YOS 10. New Haven: Yale University Press.

———. 1968. "Akkad Dynasty Inscriptions from Nippur." *JAOS* 88:54–59.

Goodnick-Westenholz, Joan. 1984. "Heroes of Akkad." Pages 327–36 in Sasson 1984.

———. 1997. *Legends of the Kings of Akkade.* MC 7. Winona Lake, Ind.: Eisenbrauns.

Goody, Jack. 1977. *The Domestication of the Savage Mind.* Cambridge: Cambridge University Press.

Grayson, Andrew Kirk. 1965. "Problematical Battles in Mesopotamian History." Pages 337–342 in *Studies in Honor of Benno Landsberger on His Seventy-Fifth Birthday.* AS 16. Chicago: University of Chicago Press.

———. 1966. "Divination and the Babylonian Chronicles: A Study of the Rôle Which Divination Plays in Ancient Mesopotamian Chronography." Pages 69–76 in *La Divination en Mésopotamie ancienne et dans les régions voisines: XIVe Recontre assyriologique internationale, Strasbourg, 2–6 Juillet 1965.* Paris: Presses Universitaires de France.

———. 1972. *From the Beginning to Ashur-resha-ishi I.* Vol. 1 of *Assyrian Royal Inscriptions.* RANE 1. Wiesbaden: Harrassowitz.

———. 1975a. *Assyrian and Babylonian Chronicles.* TCS 5. Locust Valley, N.Y.: Augustin.

———. 1975b. *Babylonian Historical-Literary Texts.* Toronto: University of Toronto Press.

———. 1976. *From Tiglath-pileser I to Ashur-nasir-apli II.* Vol. 2 of *Assyrian Royal Inscriptions.* RANE 2. Wiesbaden: Harrassowitz.

———. 1977. "The Empire of Sargon of Akkad." *AfO* 25:56–64, pls. I–II.

———. 1980a. "Assyria and Babylonia." *Or* 49:140–94.

———. 1980b. "Königslisten, Akkadisch." *RlA* 6:86–135.

———. 1984. "Literary Letters from Deities and Diviners: More Fragments." Pages 143–48 in Sasson 1984.

———. 1985. "Rivalry over Rulership at Aššur: The Puzur-Sîn Inscription." *ARRIM* 3:9–14.

Grayson, Andrew Kirk, and Wilfred G. Lambert. 1964. "Akkadian Prophecies." *JCS* 18:7–30.

Günbattı, Cahit. 1997. "Kültepe'den Akadlı Sargon'a Âit Bir Tablet." *Archivum Anatolicum* 3:131–55.

Gurney, Oliver R., and Jacob J. Finkelstein. 1957. *The Sultantepe Tablets.* Vol. 1. London: British Institute of Archaeology at Ankara.

Gurney, Oliver R., and Peter Hulin. 1964. *The Sultantepe Tablets.* Vol. 2. London: British Institute of Archaeology at Ankara.

Güterbock, Hans Gustav. 1934. "Die historische Tradition und ihre literarische Gestaltung bei Babyloniern und Hethitern bis 1200" (part 1). *ZA* 42:1–91.

———. 1938. "Die historische Tradition und ihre literarische Gestaltung bei Babyloniern und Hethitern bis 1200" (part 2). *ZA* 44:45–145.

———. 1939/41. "Bruchstück eines altbabylonischen Naram-Sin-Epos." *AfO* 13:46–49.

Hallo, William W. 1963. "Beginning and End of the Sumerian King List in the Nippur Recension." *JCS* 17:52–57.

———. 1966. "Akkadian Prophecies." *IEJ* 16:231–242.

———. 1978. "Assyrian Historiography Revisited." *ErIsr* 14:1–7.

———. 1984. "Sumerian Historiography." Pages 9–20 in *History, Historiography and Interpretation: Studies in Biblical and Cuneiform Literatures.* Edited by Hayyim Tadmor and Moshe Weinfeld. Jerusalem: Magnes; Leiden: Brill.

———. 1988. "The Nabonassar Era and Other Epochs in Mesopotamian Chronology and Chronography." Pages 175–90 in *A Scientific Humanist: Studies in Memory of Abraham Sachs.* Edited by Erle Leichty, Maria deJong Ellis, and Pamela Gerardi. Philadelphia: University Museum.

———. 1991a. "The Death of Kings: Traditional Historiography in Contextual Perspective." Pages 148–65 in Cogan and Eph'al.

———. 1991b. "The Royal Correspondance of Larsa: III. The Princess and the Plea." Pages 377–88 in *Marchands, diplomates et empereurs: Études sur les civilisations mésopotamiennes offertes à Paul Garelli.* Edited by Dominique Charpin and Francis Joannès. Paris: Editions Recherche sur les civilisations.

Hanoun, Na'il. 1979. "Himrin Basin-Tell Al-Seib." *Sumer* 35:437–38.

Harrak, Amir. 1987. *Assyria and Hanigalbat: A Historical Reconstruction of Bilateral Relations from the Middle of the Fourteenth to the End of the Twelfth Centuries B.C.* Hildesheim: Olms.

Haul, Michael. 2000. *Das Etana-Epos: Ein Mythos von der Himmelfahrt des Königs von Kiš.* Göttingen: Seminar für Keilschriftforschung.

Hecker, Karl. 2001. "Ein Selbstpreis Sargons." *TUAT Ergänzungslieferung*, 58–60.

Hilprecht, Hermann V., et al. 1903. *Explorations in Bible Lands during the Nineteenth Century*. Philadelphia: University Museum.

Hirsch, Hans. 1963. "Die Inschriften der Könige von Agade." *AfO* 20:1–82.

Horowitz, Wayne. 1988. "The Babylonian Map of the World." *Iraq* 50:147–65, pl. X.

———. 1998. *Mesopotamian Cosmic Geography*. Winona Lake, Ind.: Eisenbrauns.

Hruška, Blahoslav. 1979. "Das Verhältnis zur Vergangenheit im alten Mesopotamien." *ArOr* 47:4–14.

Hulin, Peter. 1963. "The Inscriptions on the Carved Throne-Base of Shalmaneser III." *Iraq* 25:48–69.

Hunger, Hermann. 1968. *Babylonische und assyrische Kolophone*. AOAT 2. Neukirchen-Vluyn: Neukirchener.

———. 1972. "Ein 'neues' historisches Omen." *RA* 66:180–81.

———. 1976. *Spätbabylonische Texte aus Uruk*. Vol. 1. Berlin: Mann.

———. 1992. *Astrological Reports to Assyrian Kings*. SAA 8. Helsinki: Helsinki University Press.

Hunger, Hermann, and Erica Reiner. 1975. "A Scheme for Intercalary Months from Babylonia." *WZKM* 67:21–28.

Hurowitz, V., and J. Westenholz. 1990. "LKA 63: A Heroic Poem in Celebration of Tiglath-pileser I's Muṣru-Qumanu Campaign." *JCS* 42:1–49.

Jacobsen, Thorkild. 1939. *The Sumerian King List*. AS 11. Chicago: University of Chicago Press.

———. 1987. *The Harps That Once. . . : Sumerian Poetry in Translation*. New Haven: Yale University Press.

Jacoby, Felix. 1958. *Geschichte von Städten und Völkern*. Vol. 3 of *Die Fragmente der griechischen Historiker*. Part C. Leiden: Brill.

Jeyes, Ulla. 1980. "Death and Divination in the Old Babylonian Period." Pages 107–21 in Alster 1980.

Joannès, Francis. 1979–80. "Les successeurs d'Alexandre le Grand en Babylonie." *Anatolica* 7:99–115.

———. 1988. "Un lettré néo-babylonien." *NABU* 55.

———. 2000. "Une chronique judiciaire d'époque hellénistique." Pages 193–211 in *Assyriologica et Semitica: Festschrift für Joachim Oelsner anlässlich seines 65. Geburtstages am 18. Februar 1997*. Edited by Joachim Marzahn and Hans Neumann. AOAT 252. Münster: Ugarit-Verlag.

Johns, Claude H. W. 1898. *Assyrian Deeds and Documents Recording the Transfer of Property, Including the So-Called Private Contracts, Legal Decisions and Proclamations Preserved in the Kouyunjik Collections of the British Museum*. Cambridge: Bell.

Kennedy, Douglas A. 1968. *Late-Babylonian Economic Texts*. CT 49. London: British Museum.

Kienast, Burckhardt. 1990. "Naramsîn mut [d]INANNA." *Or* 59:196–202.

King, Leonard William. 1898. *Cuneiform Texts from Babylonian Tablets, &c., in the British Museum*. Part 5. London: British Museum.

———. 1900. *Cuneiform Texts from Babylonian Tablets, &c., in the British Museum*. Part 9. London: British Museum.

———. 1901. *Cuneiform Texts from Babylonian Tablets, &c., in the British Museum*. Part 13. London: British Museum.

———. 1905. *Cuneiform Texts from Babylonian Tablets, &c., in the British Museum*. Part 21. London: British Museum.

———, ed. 1907. *Chronicles concerning Early Babylonian Kings: Including Records of the Early History of the Kassites and the Country of the Sea*. London: Luzac.

Kinnier-Wilson, J. V. 1985. *The Legend of Etana*. Warminster: Aris & Phillips.

Kitchen, Kenneth A. 1977. "The King-List of Ugarit." *UF* 9:131–42.

Klein, Jacob. 1991. "A New Nippur Duplicate of the Sumerian King List in the Brockmon Collection, University of Haifa." Pages 123–29 in *Velles Paraules: Ancient Near Eastern Studies in Honor of Miguel Civil on the Occasion of His Sixty-Fifth Birthday*. Edited by Piotr Michalowski, Piotr Steinkeller, Elizabeth C. Stone, and Richard L. Zettler (= *AuOr* 9).

Komoróczy, Géza. 1973. "Berossos and the Mesopotamian Literature." *AAASH* 21:125–52.

———. 1977. "Ummān-manda." *AAASH* 25:43–67.

Koppen, Frans van 1997. "L'expédition à Tilmun et la révolte des Bédouins." Pages 417–29 in vol. 8 of *Mari: Annales de recherches interdisciplinaires*. Paris: Editions Recherche sur les civilisations.

Kramer, Samuel Noah. 1952. "A Fulbright in Turkey." *UMB* 17.

———. 1961. "New Literary Catalogue from Ur." *RA* 55:169–76.

Kraus, Fritz Rudolf. 1952. "Zur Liste des älteren Könige von Babylon." *ZA* 50:29–60.

———. 1955. "Provinzen des neusumerischen Reiches von Ur." *ZA* 51: 45–75.

———. 1965. *Könige, die in Zelten wohnten: Betrachtungen über den Kern der assyrischen Königsliste*. Mededelingen der Koninklijke Nederlandse Akademie van Wetenschappen, Afd Letterkunde, Nieuwe reeks, 28/2. Amsterdam: Noord-Hollandsche Uitg. Mij.

———. 1973. *Vom mesopotamischen Menschen der altbabylonischen Zeit und seiner Welt*. Amsterdam: North-Holland Publishing.

Krebernik, Manfred. 1984. *Die Beschwörungen aus Fara und Ebla*. Hildesheim: Olms.

Krecher, Joachim. 1974. "Neue sumerische Rechtsurkunden des 3. Jahrtausends." *ZA* 63:145–271.

———. 1975. "Vergangenheitsinteresse in Mesopotamien und Israel." *Saeculum* 26:14–30.

———. 1980. "Kataloge, literarische." *RlA* 5:478–85.

Kugler, Franz X. 1924. *Sternkunde und Chronologie der älteren Zeit.* Part 2 of *Sternkunde und Sterndienst in Babel, assyriologische, astronomische und astralmythologische Untersuchungen.* Münster: Aschendorff.

Kuhrt, Amelie, and Susan M. Sherwin-White. 1991. "Aspects of Seleucid Royal Ideology: The Cylinder of Antiochus I from Borsippa." *JHS* 111:71–86.

Kupper, Jean-Robert. 1957. *Les Nomades en Mésopotamie au temps des rois de Mari.* Paris: Les Belles Lettres.

Kupper, Jean-Robert, and Edmond Sollberger. 1971. *Inscriptions royales sumériennes et akkadiennes.* Paris: Cerf.

Kutscher, Raphael. 1989. *Royal Inscriptions: The Brockmon Tablets at the University of Haifa.* Haifa: Haifa Univversity Press.

Labat, René. 1949. "La mort du roi d'Elam Ḫumban-Ḫaltaš I, dans la chronique babylonienne." *ArOr* 17:1–6.

———. 1960. "Ordonnances médicales ou magiques." *RA* 54:169–76.

Lafont, Bertrand. 1988. "La correspondance d'Iddiyatum." Pages 461–541 in part 2 of vol. 1 of *Archives Épistolaires de Mari.* Edited by Dominique Charpin. ARM 26/2. Paris: Editions Recherche sur les civilisations.

Lambert, Wilfred G. 1957. "Ancestors, Authors, Canonicity." *JCS* 11:1–14, 112.

———. 1960a. *Babylonian Wisdom Literature.* Oxford: Clarendon.

———. 1960b. Gilgameš in Religious, Historical and Omen Texts and the Historicity of Gilgameš." Pages 39–56 in *Gilgameš et sa légende: Études recueilles par Paul Garelli à l'occasion de la VIIe Rencontre assyriologique internationale (Paris, 1958).* Edited by Paul Garelli. Paris: Klincksieck.

———. 1962. "A Catalogue of Texts and Authors." *JCS* 16:59–77.

———. 1968. "Literary Style in First Millennium Mesopotamia." *JAOS* 88: 123–32.

———. 1969. "A New Source for the Reign of Nabonidus." *AfO* 22:1–8.

———. 1973. "A New Fragment from a List of Antediluvian Kings and Marduk's Chariot." Pages 271–78 in *Symbolae biblicae et Mesopotamicae Francisco Mario Theodoro de Liagre Böhl dedicatae.* Edited by Martinus A. Beek et al. Leiden: Brill.

———. 1974a. "The Home of the First Sealand Dynasty." *JCS* 26:208–10.

———. 1974b. "The Seed of Kingship." Pages 427–40 in *Le Palais et la royauté, archéologie et civilisation: Compte rendu.* Edited by Paul Garelli. Paris: Geuthner.

———. 1976. "Berossus and Babylonian Eschatology." *Iraq* 38:171–73.

———. 1978. *The Background of Jewish Apocalyptic*. London: Athlone.

———. 1990. "Samsu-iluna in Later Tradition." Pages 27–34 in *De la Babylonie à la Syrie, en passant par Mari: Mélanges offerts à Monsieur J.-R. Kupper à l'occasion de son 70e anniversaire*. Edited by Ö. Tünca. Liège: Université de Liège.

———. 1998. "Literary Royal Cassite Correspondence as Historiography." Paper presented at the 45th Rencontre assyriologique internationale, Cambridge, Mass.

Lambert, Wilfred G., and Alan R. Millard. 1969. *Atra-ḫasīs: The Babylonian Story of the Flood*. Oxford: Clarendon.

Lambert, Wilfred G., and Simon B. Parker. 1966. *Enūma eliš*. Oxford: Clarendon.

Landsberger, Benno. 1937. *Die Serie ana ittišu*. MSL 1. Rome: Pontifical Biblical Institute.

———. 1954. "Assyrische Königsliste und 'dunkles Zeitalter.'" *JCS* 8: 31–133.

Langdon, Stephen. 1912. *Die neubabylonischen Königsinschriften*. VAB 4. Leipzig: Hinrichs.

———. 1923. *Historical Inscriptions, Containing Principally the Chronological Prism*. Vol. 2 of *The Weld-Blundell Collection*. OECT 2. Oxford: Clarendon.

Laroche, Emmanuel. 1966. *Les noms des Hittites*. Etudes linguistiques 4. Paris: Klincksieck.

Larsen, Mogens Trolle. 1976. *The Old Assyrian City-State and Its Colonies*. Copenhagen: Akademisk Forlag.

Lefort, Claude. 1978. *Les Formes de l'histoire: Essai d'anthropologie politique*. Paris: Gallimard.

Le Goff, Jacques. 1988. *Histoire et mémoire*. Paris: Gallimard.

Lerberghe, Karel van, and Gabriele Voet. 1991. *Transliterations, Translations, Comments*. Vol. 1, part 1 of *Sippar-Amnānum: The Ur-Utu Archive*. Ghent: Ghent University Press.

Lévi-Strauss, Claude. 1960. "L'anthropologie sociale devant l'histoire." *Annales ESC* 15:625–37.

———. 1966. *The Savage Mind*. Chicago: University of Chicago Press.

Lewis, Brian. 1980. *The Sargon Legend: A Study of the Akkadian Text and the Tale of the Hero Who Was Exposed at Birth*. ASOR Dissertation Series 4. Cambridge: American Schools of Oriental Research.

Lie, A. G. 1929. *The Annals*. Part 1 of *The Inscriptions of Sargon II, King of Assyria*. Paris: Geuthner.

Limet, H. 1968. *L'Anthroponymie sumérienne dans les documents de la 3e dynastie d'Ur*. Paris: Les Belles Lettres.

———. 1994. "La maîtrise du temps en droit mésopotamien." Pages 197–208 in *Cinquante-deux réflexions sur le Proche-Orient ancien offertes en hommage à Léon de Meyer*. Edited by Hermann Gasche et al.

Mesopotamian History and Environment, Occasional Publications 2. Leuven: Peeters.

Liverani, Mario. 1990. *Prestige and Interest: International Relations in the Near East ca. 1600–1100 B.C.* Padova: Sargon.

Livingstone, Alasdair. 1989. *Court Poetry and Literary Miscellanea*. SAA 3. Helsinki: Helsinki University Press.

Longman, Tremper, III. 1991. *Fictional Akkadian Autobiography: A Generic and Comparative Study*. Winona Lake, Ind.: Eisenbrauns.

Luckenbill, Daniel David. 1924. *The Annals of Sennacherib*. OIP 2. Chicago: University of Chicago Press.

Lukács, Béla, and L. Végsö. 1974. "The Chronology of the 'Sumerian King List.'" *AoF* 2:25–45.

Machinist, Peter. 1976. "Literature as Politics: The Tukulti-Ninurta Epic and the Bible." *CBQ* 38:455–82.

———. 1978. "The Epic of Tukultī-Ninurta I: A Study in Middle Assyrian Literature." Ph.D. diss. Yale University.

———. 1983. "Assyria and Its Image in the First Isaiah." *JAOS* 103:719–37.

———. 1984. "Rest and Violence in the Poem of Erra." Pages 221–26 in Sasson 1984.

Malbran-Labat, Florence. 1980. "Éléments pour une recherche sur le nomadisme en Mésopotamie au premier millénaire av. J.-C. I: 'L'image du nomade.'" *JA* 268:11–33.

Marello, P. 1992. Vie nomade." Pages 115–25 in *Florilegium Marianum: Recueil d'études en l'honneur de Michel Fleury*. Edited by Jean-Marie Durand. Mémoires de NABU 1. Paris: SEPOA.

Marzahn, Joachim. 1981. *Babylon und das Neujahrfest*. Kleine Schriften 1. Berlin: Vorderasiatisches Museum.

Mauss, Marcel. 1966. *Sociologie et Anthropologie*. Paris: Presses Universitaires de France.

McEwan, Gilbert J. P. 1980. "The Sargon Geography." *RA* 74:171–73.

Meyer, Leon de. 1982. Deux prières *ikribu* du temps d'Ammī-ṣaduqa." Pages 271–78 in *Zikir Šumim: Assyriological Studies Presented to F. R. Kraus on the Occasion of His Seventieth Birthday*. Edited by G. van Driel et al. Leiden: Brill.

Michalowski, Piotr. 1976. "The Royal Correspondence of Ur." Ph.D. diss. Yale University.

———. 1977. "Amar-Su'ena and the Historical Tradition." Pages 155–57 in Ellis 1977.

———. 1980a. "Königsbriefe." *RlA* 6:51–59.

———. 1980b. "New Sources concerning the Reign of Naram-Sin." *JCS* 32: 233–46.

———. 1984. "History as a Charter: Some Observations on the Sumerian King List." Pages 237–48 in Sasson 1984.

———. 1989. *The Lamentation over the Destruction of Sumer and Ur.* Winona Lake, Ind.: Eisenbrauns.

———. 1990. "Presence at the Creation." Pages 381–96 in Abusch, Huehnergard, and Steinkeller.

———. 2003. "A Man Called Enmebaragesi." Pages 195–208 in Sallaberger, Volk, and Zgoll.

Millard, Alan R. 1994. *The Eponyms of the Assyrian Empire, 910–612 B.C.* SAAS 2. Helsinki: Helsinki University Press.

Moran, William L. 1987. Some Considerations of Form and Interpretation in Atra-ḫasīs." Pages 245–55 in Rochberg-Halton 1987.

Na'aman, Nadav. 1991. "Chronology and History in the Late Assyrian Empire (631–619)." *ZA* 81:243–67.

———. 1994. "Assyrian Chronicle Fragment 4 and the Location of Idu." *RA* 88:33–35

Nemet-Nejat, Karen Rhea. 1982. *Late Babylonian Field-Plans in the British Museum.* Studia Pohl, Series Maior 11. Rome: Biblical Institute Press.

Neugebauer, Otto. 1948. "Solstices and Equinoxes in Babylonian Astronomy during the Seleucid Period." *JCS* 2:209–22.

———. 1957. *The Exact Sciences in Antiquity.* New York: Dover.

———. 1975. *A History of Ancient Mathematical Astronomy.* 3 vols. Studies in the History of Mathematics and Physical Sciences 1. Berlin: Springer.

Nougayrol, Jean. 1941. "Textes hépatoscopiques d'époque ancienne conservés au Musée du Louvre." *RA* 38:67–87.

———. 1945. "Note sur la place des 'présages historiques' dans l'extispicine babylonienne." *Annuaire de l'École Pratique des Hautes Études,* 5e section:5–41.

———. 1950. Review of Albrecht Goetze, *Old Babylonian Omen Texts. JAOS* 70:110–13.

———. 1969. "Note sur *bārūtu,* chapitre X, tablette 15." *Iraq* 31:59–63.

Novotny, Jamie R. 2001. *The Standard Babylonian Etana Epic: Cuneiform Text, Transliteration, Score, Glossary, Indices and Sign List.* SAACT 2. Helsinki: Helsinki University Press.

Oelsner, Joachim. 1974. "Keilschriftliche Beiträge zur politischen Geschichte Babyloniens in den ersten Jahrzehnten der griechischen Herrschaft (331–305 v. u. Z.)." *AoF* 1:129–51.

———. 2003. "Aus den sumerischen literarischen Texten der Hilprecht-Sammlung Jena: Der Text der Tummal-Chronik." Pages 209–24 in Sallaberger, Volk, and Zgoll.

Oppenheim, A. Leo. 1936. "Zur Keilschriftlichen Omenliteratur." *Or* 5: 199–228.

———. 1960. "The City of Assur in 714 B.C." *JNES* 19:133–47.

Parpola, Simo. 1980. "The Murderer of Sennacherib." Pages 171–182 in Alster 1980.

———. 1981. "Assyrian Royal Inscriptions and Neo-Assyrian Letters." Pages 117–42 in Fales.
———. 1983a. "Assyrian Library Records." *JNES* 42:1–30.
———. 1983b. *Letters from Assyrian Scholars to the Kings Esarhaddon and Assurbanipal*. AOAT 5/2. Neukirchen-Vluyn: Neukirchener Verlag.
———. 1993. *Letters from Assyrian and Babylonian Scholars*. SAA 10. Helsinki: Helsinki University Press.
———. 1997. *Assyrian Prophecies*. SAA 9. Helsinki: Helsinki University Press.
Parrot, André. 1961. *Assur*. Paris: Gallimard.
Pedersén, Olaf. 1986. *Archives and Libraries in the City of Assur: A Survey of the Material from the German Excavations*. Uppsala: Uppsala University.
———. 1998. *Archives and Libraries in the Ancient Near East, 1500–300 B.C.* Bethesda, Md.: CDL.
Pettinato, Giovanni. 1971. *Das altorientalische Menschenbild und die sumerischen und akkadischen Schöpfungsmythen*. Heidelberg: Winter.
———. 1980. "Bollettino militare della campagna di Ebla contro la città di Mari." *OrAnt* 19:231–45, pls. XIV–XV.
Picchioni, S. A. 1981. *Il poemetto di Adapa*. Budapest: Eötvös Loránd Tudományegyetem.
Pinches, Theophilus G. 1870. *The Cuneiform Inscriptions of Western Asia*. Vol. 5/2. London: Bowler.
———. 1963. *Cuneiform Texts from Babylonian Tablets, &c., in the British Museum*. Part 44. London: British Museum.
Pinches, Theophilus G., and Abraham J. Sachs. 1955. *Late Babylonian Astronomical and Related Texts*. Providence, R.I.: Brown University Press.
Pingree, David, and Erica Reiner. 1977. "A Neo-Babylonian Report on Seasonal Hours." *AfO* 25:50–55.
Postgate, John Nicholas. 1982. "A Plea for the Abolition of *šeššimur*!" *RA* 76:188.
Préaux, Claire. 1978. *Le Monde hellénistique: La Grèce et l'Orient de la mort d'Alexandre à la conquête romaine de la Grèce (323–146 av. J.-C.)*. Nouvelle Clio 6. Paris: Presses Universitaires de France.
Reade, Julian. 1981. "Neo-Assyrian Monuments in Their Historical Context." Pages 143–67, pls. I–X in Fales.
Reiner, Erica. 1960. "Plague Amulets and House Blessings." *JNES* 19:148–55.
———. 1961. "The Etiological Myth of the 'Seven Sages.'" *Or* 30:1–11.
———. 1974. "New Light on Some Historical Omens." Pages 257–61 in *Anatolian Studies Presented to Hans Gustav Güterbock on the Occasion of His Sixty-Fifth Birthday*. Edited by Kurt Bittel, Philo Hendrik Jan Houwink ten Cate, and Erica Reiner. Istanbul: Nederlands Historisch-Archaeologisch Instituut in het Nabije Oosten.
Reiner, Erica, and Miguel Civil. 1974. *The Series ḪAR-ra = ḫubullu: Tablets XX–XXIV*. MSL 11. Rome: Pontifical Biblical Institute.

Ricoeur, Paul. 1985. *Temps et récit*. Paris: Éditions du Seuil.

Robert, Louis. 1963. *Noms indigènes dans l'Asie Mineure gréco-romaine*. Paris: Adrien Maisonneuve.

———. 1965. *D'Aphrodisias à la Lycaonie: Compte Rendu volume VIII des Monumenta Asiae Minoris antiqua*. Vol. 13 of *Hellenica*. Paris: Adrien Maisonneuve.

———. 1972. *Let mots grecs*. Vol. 1 of *Index du Bulletin Epigraphique*. Paris: Les Belles Lettres.

Rochberg-Halton, Francesca, ed. 1987. *Language, Literature, and History: Philological and Historical Studies Presented to Erica Reiner*. AOS 67. New Haven: American Oriental Society

———. 1988. *Aspects of Babylonian Celestial Divination: The Lunar Eclipse Tablets of Enūma Anu Enlil*. AfOB 22. Horn: Berger.

Röllig, Wolfgang. 1969. "Zur Typologie und Entstehung der Babylonischen und Assyrischen Königslisten." Pages 265–77 in *Lišān mitḫurti: Festschrift Wolfram Freiherr von Soden zum 19.VI.1968 gewidmet von Schülern und Mitarbeitern*. Edited by Manfried Dietrich and Wolfgang Röllig. AOAT 1. Neukirchen-Vluyn: Neukirchener Verlag.

———. 1983. "Kundu." *RlA* 6:341.

Römer, Willem H. Ph. 1965. *Sumerische "Königshymnen" der Isin-Zeit*. Documenta et monumenta Orientis antiqui 13. Leiden: Brill.

———. 1985. "Zur Siegesinschrift des Königs Utuḫeĝal von Unug (± 2116–2110 v. Chr.)." *Or* 54:274–88.

Roth, Martha T. 1988. "Ina amat DN_1 u DN_2 lišlim." *JSS* 33:1–9.

———. *Law Collections from Mesopotamia and Asia Minor*. 2nd ed. SBLWAW 6. Atlanta: Society of Biblical Literature.

Rowton, Michael B. 1960. "The Date of the Sumerian King List." *JNES* 19: 156–62.

Russell, John Malcolm. 1999. *The Writing on the Wall: Studies in the Architectural Context of Late Assyrian Palace Inscriptions*. Mesopotamian Civilizations 9. Winona Lake, Ind.: Eisenbrauns.

Rutten, Marguerite. 1938. "Trente-deux modèles de foies en argile provenant de Tell-Hariri (Mari)." *RA* 35:36–70.

Sachs, Abraham J. 1948. "A Classification of the Babylonian Astronomical Tablets of the Seleucid Period." *JCS* 2:271–90.

———. 1952. "Sirius Dates in Babylonian Astronomical Texts of the Seleucid Period." *JCS* 6:105–14.

———. 1977. "Achaemenid Royal Names in Babylonian Astronomical Texts; Appendix: A New Fragment Referring to Arses and Alexander." *American Journal of Ancient History* 2:129–47.

Sachs, Abraham J., and Hermann Hunger. 1988–2001. *Astronomical Diaries and Related Texts from Babylonia*. Vols. 1–3 and 5. Vienna: Verlag der Österreichischen Akademie der Wissenschaften.

Sallaberger, Walther, Konrad Volk, and Annette Zgoll, eds. 2003. *Literatur, Politik und Recht in Mesopotamien: Festschrift für Claus Wilcke*. Wiesbaden: Harrassowitz.

Sasson, Jack M., ed. 1984. *Studies in Literature from the Ancient Near East: Dedicated to Samuel Noah Kramer*. AOS 65. New Haven: American Oriental Society.

———. 1987. "Yasmah-Addu's letter to God (ARM 1:3)." *NABU* 109.

Schaudig, Hanspeter. 2001. *Die Inschriften Nabonids von Babylon und Kyros' des Grossen*. AOAT 256. Münster: Ugarit-Verlag.

Schaumberger, Johann. 1935. *Ergänzungsheft zum ersten und zweiten Buch*. Part 3 of Franz X. Kugler, *Sternkunde und Sterndienst in Babel, assyriologische, astronomische und astralmythologische Untersuchungen*. Münster: Aschendorff.

Scheil, Vincent. 1931. "Dynasties élamites d'Awan et de Simaš." *RA* 28: 1–8.

Shaffer, Aaron. 1984. "Gilgamesh, the Cedar Forest and Mesopotamian History." Pages 307–13 in Sasson 1984.

Shehata, Dahlia. 2001. *Annotierte Bibliographie zum altbabylonischen Atramhasis-Mythos Inūma ilū awīlum*. Göttingen: Seminar für Keilschriftforschung.

Sherwin-White, Susan M. 1983a. "Babylonian Chronicle Fragments as a Source for Seleucid History." *JNES* 42:265–70.

———. 1983b. "Ritual for a Seleucid king at Babylon." *JHS* 103:156–59.

Sigrist, Marcel. 1984. *Les* sattukku *dans l'Ešumeša durant la période d'Isin et Larsa*. BM 11. Malibu, Calif.: Undena.

Sjöberg, Åke W. 1972a. "A Commemorative Inscription of King Šūsîn." *JCS* 24: 70–73.

———. 1972b. "Die göttliche Abstammung der sumerisch-babylonischen Herrscher." *OS* 21:87–112.

Slotsky, Alice Louise. 1997. *The Bourse of Babylon: Market Quotations in the Astronomical Diaries of Babylonia*. Bethesda, Md.: CDL.

Smith, Jonathan Z. 1976. "A Pearl of Great Price and a Cargo of Yams: A Study in Situational Incongruity." *HR* 16:1–19.

Smith, Sidney. 1924. *Babylonian Historical Texts Relating to the Capture and Downfall of Babylon*. London: Methuen.

Soden, Wolfram von. 1989. "Kyros und Nabonid: Propaganda und Gegenpropaganda." Pages 285–92 in *Aus Sprache, Geschichte und Religion Babyloniens*. Edited by Luigi L. Cagni and Hans-Peter Müller. Naples: Istituto Universitario Orientale.

Sollberger, Edmond. 1962. "The Tummal Inscription." *JCS* 16:40–47.

———, ed. 1965. *Royal Inscriptions*. Part 2. UrET 8. London: British Museum.

———. 1967. "The Rulers of Lagaš." *JCS* 21:279–91.

———. 1967–68. "The Cruciform Monument." *JEOL* 20:50–70.

———. 1982. "A New Inscription of Šar-kali-šarrī." Pages 344–46 in *Societies and Languages of the Ancient Near East: Studies in Honour of I. M. Diakonoff.* Edited by Muhammad A. Dandamaev et al. Warminster: Aris & Phillips.

Sommerfeld, W. 2000. "Nāram-Sîn, die 'Grosse Revolte' und MAR.TU^{ki}." Pages 419–36 in *Assyriologica et Semitica: Festschrift für Joachim Oelsner anlässlich seines 65. Geburtstages am 18. Februar 1997.* Edited by Joachim Marzahn and Hans Neumann. AOAT 252. Münster: Ugarit-Verlag.

Speiser, Ephraim A. 1955. "Ancient Mesopotamia." Pages 35–77 in *The Idea of History in the Ancient Near East.* Edited by Robert C. Dentan. New Haven: Yale University Press. Repr., 1983.

Spek, Robartus Johannes van der. 1992. "Nippur, Sippar, and Larsa in the Hellenistic Period." Pages 235–60 in *Nippur at the Centennial: Papers Read at the 35e Rencontre Assyriologique Internationale, Philadelphia, 1988.* Edited by Maria deJong Ellis. Philadelphia: University Museum.

———. 2003. "Darius III, Alexander the Great and Babylonian Scholarship." Pages 289–346 in *A Persian Perspective: Essays in Memory of Helen Sancisi-Weerdenburg.* Edited by W. Henkelman and Amelie Kuhrt. Achaemenid History 13. Leiden: Nederlands Instituut voor het Nabije Oosten.

Starr, Ivan. 1977. "Notes on Some Published and Unpublished Historical Omens." *JCS* 29:157–66.

———. 1985. "Historical Omens concerning Ashurbanipal's War against Elam." *AfO* 32:60–67.

———. 1986. "The Place of the Historical Omens in the System of Apodoses." *BO* 43:628–42.

Steible, Horst. 1982. *Die altsumerischen Bau- und Weihinschriften.* FAOS 5. Wiesbaden: Steiner.

———. 1991. *Die neusumerischen Bau- und Weihinschriften.* 2 vols. FAOS 9. Stuttgart: Steiner.

Steiner, G. 1979. "Altorientalische 'Reichs'-Vorstellungen im 3. Jahrtausend v. Chr." Pages 125–43 in *Power and Propaganda: A Symposium on Ancient Empires.* Edited by Mogens Trolle Larsen. Copenhagen: Akademisk Forlag.

———. 1988. "Der 'reale' Kern in den 'legendären' Zahlen von Regierungsjahren der ältesten Herrscher Mesopotamiens." *ASJ* 10:129–52.

———. 1989. "Die Dauer einer 'Generation' nach den Vorstellungen des Alten Orients." Pages 170–95 in vol. 3 of *High, Middle or Low? Acts of an International Colloquium on Absolute Chronology Held at the University of Gothenburg, 20th–22nd August, 1987.* Edited by Paul Åström. Gothenburg: Paul Åströms Förlag.

Steinkeller, Piotr. 1982. "The Question of Marḫaši: A Contribution to the Historical Geography of Iran in the Third Millennium B.C." *ZA* 72:237–65.
———. 1987. "On the Meaning of zabar-šu." *ASJ* 9:347–49.
———. 1992. Išbi-Erra's *Himmelfahrt;* Corrigendum to NABU 1992/4." *NABU* 4 and 56.
———. 2003. "An Ur III Manuscript of the Sumerian King List." Pages 267–92 in Sallaberger, Volk, and Zgoll.
Stephens, Ferris J. 1937. *Votive and Historical Texts from Babylonia and Assyria*. YOS 9. New Haven: Yale University Press.
Stol, M. 1997. "Muškēnu." *RlA* 8:492–93.
Stolper, Matthew W. 1988. "The *šaknu* of Nippur." *JCS* 40:127–55.
———. 1990. "In the Chronicle of the Diadochi r.3f." *NABU* 7.
Strassmaier, Johann Nepomuk. 1892. "Einige chronologische Daten aus astronomischen Rechnungen." *ZA* 7:197–205.
———. 1893. "Zur Chronologie der Seleukiden." *ZA* 8:106–13.
Streck, Maximilian. 1916. *Assurbanipal und die letzten assyrischen Könige bis zum Untergang Nineveh's*. VAB 7. Leipzig: Hinrichs.
Streck, Michael P. 2001. Keilschrift und Alphabet." Pages 77–97 in *Hieroglyphen, Alphabete, Schriftreformen: Studien zu Multiliteralismus, Schriftwechsel und Orthographieneuregelungen*. Edited by Dörte Borchers, Frank Kammerzell, and Stefan Weninger. Göttingen: Seminar für Ägyptologie und Koptologie.
Tadmor, Hayim. 1977. "Observations on Assyrian Historiography." Pages 209–13 in Ellis 1977.
———. 1994. *The Inscriptions of Tiglath-pileser III, King of Assyria*. Jerusalem: Israel Academy of Sciences and Humanities.
Tadmor, Hayim, Benno Landsberger, and Simo Parpola. 1989. "The Sin of Sargon and Sennacherib's Last Will." *SAAB* 3:3–51.
Thompson, R. Campbell. 1904. *Cuneiform Texts from Babylonian Tablets, &c., in the British Museum*. Part 20. London: British Museum.
———. 1930. *The Epic of Gilgamish*. Oxford: Oxford University Press.
Thureau-Dangin, François. 1912. *Une Relation de la huitième campagne de Sargon*. TCL 3. Paris: Geuthner.
———. 1918. "La chronologie de la dynastie de Larsa." *RA* 15:1–57.
———. 1921. *Rituels accadiens*. Paris: Ernest Leroux.
———. 1925. *Les Cylindres de Goudéa découverts par Ernest de Sarzec à Tello*. TCL 8. Paris: Geuthner.
———. 1937. "Une tablette en or provenant d'Umma." *RA* 34:177–78.
Toomer, G. J., trans. 1984. *Ptolemy's Almagest*. London: Duckworth.
Tyborowski, Witold. 1996. "The Third Year of Nebuchadnezzar II (602 B.C.) according to the Babylonian Chronicle BM 21946: An Attempt at an Interpretation." *ZA* 86:211–16.
Uehlinger, Christoph. 1995. "Nisroch." *DDD,* 1185–90.

Unger, Eckhard. 1931. *Babylon, die heilige Stadt nach der Beschreibung der Babylonier.* Berlin: de Gruyter.

Ungnad, Arthur. 1938a. "Datenlisten." *RlA* 2:131–95.

———. 1938b. "Eponymen." *RlA* 2:412–57.

Van Seters, John. 1983. *In Search of History.* New Haven: Yale University Press.

Vansina, Jan. 1965. *Oral Tradition: A Study in Historical Methodology.* Translated by H. M. Wright. Chicago: Aldine.

Vanstiphout, Herman. 2003. *Epics of Sumerian Kings: The Matter of Aratta.* SBLWAW 20. Atlanta: Society of Biblical Literature.

Veenhof, Klaas R. 1972. *Aspects of Old Assyrian Trade and Its Terminology.* Leiden: Brill.

———. 1985. "Eponyms of the 'Later Old Assyrian Period' and Mari Chronology." Pages 191–218 in vol. 4 of *Mari: Annales de recherches interdisciplinaires.* Paris: Editions Recherche sur les civilisations.

———, ed. 1986. *Cuneiform Archives and Libraries: Papers Read at the 30e Rencontre Assyriologique Internationale, Leiden, 4–8 July, 1983.* Publications de l'Institut historique-archéologique néerlandais de Stamboul 57. Istanbul: Nederlands Historisch-Archaeologisch Instituut te Istanbul.

———. 2003. *The Old Assyrian List of Year Eponyms from Karum Kanish and Its Chronological Implications.* Türk Tarih Kurumu 6/64. Ankara: Publications of the Turkish Historical Society.

Veldhuis, Niek. 2001. "The Solution of the Dream: A New Interpretation of Bilgames' Death." *JCS* 53:133–48.

Verbrugghe, Gerald P., and John M. Wickersham. 1996. *Berossos and Manetho, Introduced and Translated: Native Traditions in Ancient Mesopotamia and Egypt.* Ann Arbor: University of Michigan Press.

Vincente, Claudine-Adrienne. 1990. "Tell Leilan Recension of the Sumerian King List." *NABU* 11.

———. 1995. "The Tall Leilān Recension of the Sumerian King List." *ZA* 85: 234–70.

Visicato, Giuseppe. 1995. *The Bureaucracy of Šuruppak: Administrative Centres, Central Offices, Intermediate Structures and Hierarchies in the Economic Documentation of Fara.* ALASP 10. Münster: Ugarit-Verlag.

Wacholder, Ben Zion, and David B. Weisberg. 1971. "Visibility of the New Moon in Cuneiform and Rabbinic Sources." *HUCA* 42:227–42.

Waetzoldt, Hartmut. 1980. "Kleidung." *RlA* 6:18–31.

Walker, C. B. F. 1972. *Miscellaneous Texts.* Vol. 51 of *Cuneiform Texts from Babylonian Tablets in the British Museum.* London: British Museum.

———. 1982. "Babylonian Chronicle 25: A Chronicle of the Kassite and Isin II dynasties." Pages 398–417 in *Zikir Šumim: Assyriological Studies Presented to F. R. Kraus on the Occasion of His Seventieth Birthday.* Edited by G. van Driel et al. Leiden: Brill.

Weidner, Ernst F. 1928–29. "Historisches Material in der babylonischen Omina-Literatur." *MAOG* 4:226–40.
———. 1932–33. "Assyrische Beschreibungen der Kriegs-Reliefs Aššurbânaplis." *AfO* 8:175–203.
———. 1963. "Assyrische Epen über die Kassiten-Kämpfe." *AfO* 20:113–16, pl. V.
Weiher, Egbert von. 1988. *Spätbabylonische Texte aus Uruk*. Vol. 3. Berlin: Mann.
Weissert, E. 1992. "Interrelated Chronographic Patterns in the Assyrian Eponym Chronicle and the 'Babylonian Chronicle': A Comparative Study." Pages 273–82 in *La Circulation des biens, des personnes et des idées dans le Proche-Orient ancien: Actes de la XXXVIIIe Rencontre assyriologique internationale (Paris, 8–10 juillet 1991)*. Edited by Dominique Charpin and Francis Joannès. Paris: Editions Recherche sur les civilisations.
Westenholz, Alster B. 1977. "Old Akkadian School Texts: Some Goals of Sargonic Scribal Education." *AfO* 25:95–110.
Wiggerman, F. A. M. 1992. *Mesopotamian Protective Spirits: The Ritual Texts*. CM 1. Groningen: Styx.
Wilcke, Claus. 1974. "Zum Königtum in der Ur III-Zeit." Pages 177–232 in *Le Palais et la royauté, archéologie et civilisation: Compte rendu*. Edited by Paul Garelli. Paris: Geuthner.
———. 1977. "Die Anfänge der akkadischen Epen." *ZA* 67:153–216.
———. 1982a. Review of Hermann Hunger, *Spätbabylonische Texte aus Uruk*, I. *BO* 39:141–45.
———. 1982b. "Zum Geschichtsbewusstsein im alten Mesopotamien." Pages 31–52 in *Archäologie und Geschichtsbewusstsein*. Edited by Hermann Müller-Karpe. Kolloquien zur Allgemeinen und Vergleichenden Archäologie 3. Munich: Beck.
———. 1987a. "Familiengründung im alten Babylonien." Pages 213–317 in *Geschlechtsreife und Legitimation zur Zeugung*. Edited by Ernst Wilhelm Müller and Paul Drechsel. Freiburg: Alber.
———. 1987b. "Die Inschriftenfunde der 7. und 8. Kampagnen." Pages 83–120, pls. 33–44 in *Isin-Išān-Bahrīyāt III: Die Ergebnisse der Ausgrabungen 1983–1984*. Edited by Barthel Hrouda. Munich: Verlag der Bayerischen Akademie der Wissenschaften.
———. 1988a. "König Šulgis Himmelfahrt." Pages 245–55 in *Festschrift László Vajda*. Edited by Claudius Müller and Hans-Joachim Paproth. Münchner Beiträge zur Völkerkunde 1. Munich: Hirmer.
———. 1988b. "Die Sumerische Königsliste und erzählte Vergangenheit." Pages 113–40 in *Vergangenheit in mündlicher Überlieferung*. Edited by Jürgen von Ungern-Sternberg and Jansjörg Reinau. Stuttgart: Teubner.

———. 1989a. “Die Emar-Version von ‘Dattelpalme und Tamariske’: Ein Rekonstruktionsversuch.” *ZA* 79:161–90.

———. 1989b. “Genealogical and Geographical Thought in the Sumerian King List.” Pages 557–71 in *Dumu-e$_2$-dub-ba-a: Studies in Honor of Åke W. Sjöberg*. Edited by Hermann Behrens, Darlene Loding, and Martha T. Roth. Philadelphia: University Museum.

———. 1997. “Amar-girids Revolte gegen Narām-Su’en.” *ZA* 87:11–32.

Will, Edouard. 1979–82. *Histoire politique du monde hellénistique*. 2nd ed. 2 vols. Nancy: Presses Universitaires de Nancy.

Wiseman, Donald J. 1956. *Chronicles of Chaldaean Kings*. London: British Museum.

Wiseman, Donald J., and J. A. Black. 1996. *Literary Texts from the Temple of Nabû*. CTN 4. London: British School of Archaeology in Iraq.

Woolley, Leonard. 1925. “The Excavations at Ur, 1924–1925.” *AJ* 5:347–402.

Yamada, Shiego. 1994. “The Editorial History of the Assyrian King List.” *ZA* 84:11–37.

Yoshikawa, M. 1989. “An-šè. . . a (= è/e$_{11}$) ‘to die.’” *ASJ* 11:353.

Yuhong, Wu. 1994. *A Political History of Eshnunna, Mari and Assyria during the Early Old-Babylonian Period (from the End of Ur III to the Death of Šamši-Adad)*. Changchun: Institute for the History of Ancient Civilizations.

Zawadzki, Stefan. 1988. *The Fall of Assyria and the Median-Babylonian Relations in Light of the Nabopolassar Chronicle*. Poznan-Delft: Adam Mickiewicz University Press-Eburon.

———. 1990a. “Oriental and Greek Tradition about the Death of Sennacherib.” *SAAB* 4:69–72.

———. 1990b. “Ein wichtiger Fehler in der neubabylonischen Chronik BM 21946 und seine Folgen: das Krönungsdatum Nebukadnezars II.” *AoF* 17:100–106.

Indexes

1. Proper Names

2. Theonyms

3. Place Names and Names of Peoples